The Anthropolo

Blackwell Anthologies in Social and Cultural Anthropology
Series Editor: Parker Shipton, Boston University

Drawing from some of the most significant scholarly work of the nineteenth and twentieth centuries, the *Blackwell Anthologies in Social and Cultural Anthropology* series offers a comprehensive and unique perspective on the ever-changing field of anthropology. It represents both a collection of classic readers and an exciting challenge to the norms that have shaped this discipline over the past century.

Each edited volume is devoted to a traditional subdiscipline of the field such as the anthropology of religion, linguistic anthropology, or medical anthropology; and provides a foundation in the canonical readings of the selected area. Aware that such subdisciplinary definitions are still widely recognized and useful – but increasingly problematic – these volumes are crafted to include a rare and invaluable perspective on social and cultural anthropology at the onset of the twenty-first century. Each text provides a selection of classic readings together with contemporary works that underscore the artificiality of subdisciplinary definitions and point students, researchers, and general readers in the new directions in which anthropology is moving.

1   *Linguistic Anthropology: A Reader*
    Edited by Alessandro Duranti

2   *A Reader in the Anthropology of Religion*
    Edited by Michael Lambek

3   *The Anthropology of Politics: A Reader in Ethnography, Theory, and Critique*
    Edited by Joan Vincent

4   *Kinship and Family: An Anthropological Reader*
    Edited by Robert Parkin and Linda Stone

5   *Law and Anthropology: A Reader*
    Edited by Sally Falk Moore

6   *The Anthropology of Development and Globalization: From Classical Political Economy to Contemporary Neoliberalism*
    Edited by Marc Edelman and Angelique Haugerud

The Anthropology of Art

A Reader

Edited by

Howard Morphy and Morgan Perkins

Blackwell
Publishing

BLACKWELL PUBLISHING
350 Main Street, Malden, MA 02148-5020, USA
9600 Garsington Road, Oxford OX4 2DQ, UK
550 Swanston Street, Carlton, Victoria 3053, Australia

The right of Howard Morphy and Morgan Perkins to be identified as the Authors of the Editorial Material in this Work has been asserted in accordance with the UK Copyright, Designs, and Patents Act 1988.

First published 2006 by Blackwell Publishing Ltd

1   2006

Library of Congress Cataloging-in-Publication Data

The anthropology of art: a reader/edited by Howard Morphy and Morgan Perkins.
    p.cm.—(Blackwell anthologies in social and cultural anthropology)
Includes bibliographical references and index.
ISBN-13: 978-1-4051-0561-3 (hardcover: alk. paper)
ISBN-10: 1-4051-0561-5 (hardcover: alk. paper)
ISBN-13: 978-1-4051-0562-0 (pbk.: alk. paper)
ISBN-10: 1-4051-0562-3 (pbk.: alk. paper)
1. Art and anthropology. 2. Art and society. I. Perkins, Morgan. II. Morphy, Howard. III. Series.

N72.A56A67 2005
—dc22

2005013067

A catalogue record for this title is available from the British Library.

Set in 9/11pt Sabon
by SPI Publisher Services, Pondicherry, India
Printed and bound in the United Kingdom
by TJ International Ltd, Padstow, Cornwall

The publisher's policy is to use permanent paper from mills that operate a sustainable forestry policy, and which has been manufactured from pulp processed using acid-free and elementary chlorine-free practices. Furthermore, the publisher ensures that the text paper and cover board used have met acceptable environmental accreditation standards.

For further information on
Blackwell Publishing, visit our website:
www.blackwellpublishing.com

Contents

Acknowledgments   viii

About the Editors   x

The Anthropology of Art: A Reflection on its History and
Contemporary Practice   1
Howard Morphy and Morgan Perkins

Part I Foundations and Framing the Discipline   **33**

1 Primitive Art   39
Franz Boas

2 Split Representation in the Art of Asia and America   56
Claude Lévi-Strauss

3 Introduction to *Tribes and Forms in African Art*   74
William Fagg

4 Style, Grace, and Information in Primitive Art   78
Gregory Bateson

5 Tikopia Art and Society   91
Raymond Firth

6 The Abelam Artist   109
Anthony Forge

Part II Primitivism, Art, and Artifacts   **123**

7 Modernist Primitivism: An Introduction   129
William Rubin

8 Defective Affinities: "Primitivism" in 20th Century Art   147
Arthur C. Danto

9   Histories of the Tribal and the Modern   150
    James Clifford

10 A Case in Point and Afterwords to *Primitive Art in Civilized Places*   167
    Sally Price

11 Oriental Antiquities/Far Eastern Art   186
    Craig Clunas

12 Introduction to *Art/Artifact: African Art in Anthropology Collections*   209
    Susan Vogel

13 Vogel's Net: Traps as Artworks and Artworks as Traps   219
    Alfred Gell

Part III Aesthetics across Cultures   **237**

14 Yoruba Artistic Criticism   242
    Robert Farris Thompson

15 Style in Technology: Some Early Thoughts   270
    Heather Lechtman

16 "Marvels of Everyday Vision": The Anthropology of Aesthetics
    and the Cattle-keeping Nilotes   281
    Jeremy Coote

17 From Dull to Brilliant: The Aesthetics of Spiritual Power Among
    the Yolngu   302
    Howard Morphy

Part IV Form, Style, and Meaning   **321**

18 Visual Categories: An Approach to the Study of Representational
    Systems   326
    Nancy D. Munn

19 Structural Patterning in Kwakiutl Art and Ritual   339
    Abraham Rosman and Paula G. Rubel

20 Sacred Art and Spiritual Power: An Analysis of Tlingit Shamans' Masks   358
    Aldona Jonaitis

21 All Things Made   374
    David M. Guss

22 Modernity and the "Graphicalization" of Meaning: New Guinea
    Highland Shield Design in Historical Perspective   387
    Michael O'Hanlon

Part V Marketing Culture   407

23   Arts of the Fourth World   412
     Nelson H. H. Graburn

24   The Collecting and Display of Souvenir Arts: Authenticity and the
     "Strictly Commercial"   431
     Ruth B. Phillips

25   The Art of the Trade: On the Creation of Value and Authenticity in the
     African Art Market   454
     Christopher B. Steiner

Part VI Contemporary Artists   467

26   A Second Reflection: Presence and Opposition in Contemporary
     Maori Art   472
     Nicholas Thomas

27   Representing Culture: The Production of Discourse(s) for Aboriginal
     Acrylic Paintings   495
     Fred Myers

28   Aesthetics and Iconography: An Artist's Approach   513
     Gordon Bennett

29   Kinds of Knowing   520
     Charlotte Townsend-Gault

30   Cew Ete Haw I Tih: The Bird That Carries Language Back to Another   544
     Jolene Rickard

Index   549

Acknowledgments

First and foremost, much gratitude must go to our editor Jane Huber for her always affable and patient enthusiasm from the very beginning when the project was just a gleam in several pairs of eyes. The series editor Parker Shipton has provided much encouragement and commentary along the way. Emily Martin, Angela Cohen, Graeme Leonard, Lisa Eaton, and many Blackwell staff members have helped to guide the manuscript through its various stages and lent advice when most needed. Thanks to Loreen Murphy and Robert Nicholl for their help in negotiating the labyrinth of permission acquisition, and Elizabeth Wood-Ellem for producing the index at short notice. Karen Westmacott has made an invaluable contribution in facilitating communication, editorial assistance, and employing her eye for detail. Frances Morphy's critical reading of drafts of the introduction is greatly appreciated. Special thanks to all the authors of the articles who have been able to lend assistance with the often surprisingly complex details of republishing their work.

The editors and publisher gratefully acknowledge the permission granted to reproduce the copyright material in this book:

1 Franz Boas, pp. 183–188, 218–219, 222–230, 239–240, 251–255, 279–281 from *Primitive Art*. New York: Dover, 1955.
2 Claude Lévi-Strauss, "Split Representation in the Art of Asia and America," pp. 245–268, 385–398 from *Structural Anthropology*. New York: Basic Books, 1963.
3 William Fagg, pp. 11–18 from *Tribes and Forms in African Art*. New York: Tudor, 1965.
4 Gregory Bateson, "Style, Grace, and Information in Primitive Art," pp. 235–255 from Anthony Forge (ed.), *Primitive Art and Society*. Oxford: Oxford University Press, 1973. Reprinted by permission of the Wenner-Gren Foundation for Anthropological Research, Inc., New York.
5 Raymond Firth, "Tikopia Art and Society," pp. 25–48 from Anthony Forge (ed.), *Primitive Art and Society*. Oxford: Oxford University Press, 1973. Reprinted by permission of the Wenner-Gren Foundation for Anthropological Research, Inc., New York.
6 Anthony Forge, "The Abelam Artist," pp. 65–84, 291–294 from Maurice Freedman (ed.), *Social Organisation: Essays Presented to Raymond Firth*. London: Cass, 1967.
7 William Rubin, "Introduction," pp. 1–79 from *"Primitivism" in 20th Century Art: Affinity of the Tribal and the Modern*. New York: Museum of Modern Art, [1985] 1999. Reprinted by permission of the Museum of Modern Art, New York
8 Arthur Danto, "Defective Affinities," from *The Nation* 37226. New York, 1984. Reprinted by permission of *The Nation*.

9   James Clifford, "Histories of the Tribal and the Modern," pp. 189–214, 349–369 from *The Predicament of Culture: Twentieth-Century Ethnography, Literature, and Art*. Cambridge, MA: Harvard University Press, 1988. Originally published in *Art in America*, Brant Publications Inc., April 1985.

10 Sally Price, "A Case in Point, Afterword, Afterword to the Second Edition," pp. 108–136 (1st edition), 134–145 (2nd edition) from *Primitive Art in Civilized Places*, 2. Chicago: University of Chicago Press, [1989] 2001. Reprinted by permission of Chicago University Press.

11 Craig Clunas, "Oriental Antiquities/Far Eastern Art," pp. 413–446 from Tani Barlow (ed.), *Formations of Colonial Modernity in East Asia*. Durham and London: Duke University Press, 1997. © 1997 Duke University Press. All rights reserved. Used by permission of the publisher.

12 Susan Vogel, "Introduction," pp. 11–17 from Susan Vogel, *ART/Artifact: African Art in Anthropology Collections*. New York: Museum for African Art, 1988. Reprinted by permission of the Museum for African Art.

13 Alfred Gell, "Vogel's Net: Traps as Artworks and Artworks as Traps," pp. 15–38 from *Journal of Material Culture* 1 (1). Sage Publications, 1996. © Sage Publications 1996. Reprinted by permission of Sage Publications Ltd.

14 Robert Farris Thompson, "Yoruba Artistic Criticism," pp. 19–61, 435–454 from Warren D'Azevedo (ed.), *The Traditional Artist in African Societies*, 2. Bloomington: Indiana University Press, 1973. Reprinted by permission of Indiana University Press Ltd.

15 Heather Lechtman, "Style in Technology: Some Early Thoughts," pp. 3–20 from Heather Lechtman and Robert S. Merrill (eds.), *Material Culture: Styles, Organization and Dynamics of Technology. Proceedings of the American Ethnological Society for 1975*. St. Paul: West Publishing Company, 1975.

16 Jeremy Coote, "Marvels of Everyday Vision: The Anthropology of Aesthetics and the Cattle-Keeping Nilotes," pp. 245–273 from Jeremy Coote and Anthony Shelton (eds.), *Anthropology, Art and Aesthetics*. Oxford: Clarendon Press, [1992] 1995. Reprinted by permission of Oxford University Press.

17 Howard Morphy, "From Dull to Brilliant: The Aesthetics of Spiritual Power Among the Yolngu," pp. 181–208 from Jeremy Coote and Anthony Shelton (eds.), *Anthropology, Art and Aesthetics*. Oxford: Clarendon Press, 1992. Reprinted by permission of the University of California Press.

18 Nancy Munn, "Visual Categories: An Approach to the Study of Representational Systems," pp. 936–950 from *American Anthropologist* 68. Berkeley: University of California Press, 1966. Reprinted by permission from the American Anthropological Association.

19 Abraham Rosman and Paula Rubel, "Structural Patterning in Kwakiutl Art and Ritual," pp. 620–639 from *Man* 25 (4), 1990. Reprinted by permission of Blackwell Publishing.

20 Aldona Jonaitis, "Sacred Art and Spiritual Power: An Analysis of Tlingit Shamans' Masks," pp. 119–136 from Zena Mathews and Aldona Jonaitis (eds.), *Native North American Art History: Selected Readings*. Palo Alto, CA: Peek Publications, 1982.

21 David Guss, "All Things Made," pp. 69–85, 90–91, 231–232, 247–262 from *To Weave and to Sing: Art, Symbol and Narrative in the South American Rain Forest*. Berkeley: University of California Press, 1989. Reprinted by permission of the University of California Press.

22 Michael O'Hanlon, "Modernity and the 'Graphicalization' of Meaning: New Guinea Highland Shield Design in Historical Perspective," pp. 469–492 from *Journal of the Royal Anthropological Institute* 1, 1995. Reprinted by permission of Blackwell Publishing.

23 Nelson H. H. Graburn, "Introduction: Arts of the Fourth World," pp. 1–30, 372–393 from *Ethnic and Tourist Arts: Cultural Expressions from the Fourth World*. Berkeley: University of California Press, 1976. Reprinted by permission of the University of California Press.

24 Ruth Phillips, "The Collecting and Display of Souvenir Arts: Authenticity and the Strictly Commercial," pp. 49–71, 287–289, 311–325 from *Trading Identities: The Souvenir in*

Native North American Art from the Northeast, 1700–1900. Seattle: University of Washington Press, 1998. Reprinted by permission of the University of Washington Press.

25 Christopher B. Steiner, "The Art of the Trade: On the Creation of Value and Authenticity in the African Art Market," pp. 151–165 from George E. Marcus and Fred R. Myers (eds.), *The Traffic in Culture: Refiguring Art and Anthropology.* Berkeley: University of California Press, 1995. Reprinted by permission of the University of California Press.

26 Nicholas Thomas, "A Second Reflection: Presence and Opposition in Contemporary Maori Art," pp. 23–46 from *Journal of the Royal Anthropological Institute* 1, 1995. Reprinted by permission of Blackwell Publishing.

27 Fred Myers, "Representing Culture: The Production of Discourse(s) for Aboriginal Acrylic Paintings," pp. 26–62 from *Cultural Anthropology* 6 (1), 1991. Berkeley: University of California Press, 1991. Reprinted by the permission of the American Anthropological Association and the author.

28 Gordon Bennett, "Aesthetics and Iconography: An Artist's Approach," pp. 85–91 from *Aratjara, Art of the First Australians.* Cologne: DuMont Buchverlag, 1993.

29 Charlotte Townsend-Gault, "Kinds of Knowing," pp. 76–101 from Diana Nemiroff, Robert Houle, and Charlotte Townsend-Gault, *Land, Spirit, Power: First Nations at the National Gallery of Canada.* Ottawa: National Gallery of Canada, 1992. Reprinted by permission of the National Gallery of Canada.

30 Jolene Rickard, "CEW ETE HAW I TIH: The Bird That Carries Language Back to Another," pp. 105–111 from Lucy Lippard (ed.), *Partial Recall.* New York: New Press, 1992. Reprinted by permission of the New Press.

Every effort has been made to trace copyright holders and to obtain their permission for the use of copyright material. The publisher apologizes for any errors or omissions in the above list and would be grateful if notified of any corrections that should be incorporated in future reprints or editions of this book.

About the Editors

Howard Morphy is Director of the Centre for Cross-Cultural Research at the Australian National University and Honorary Curator of the Pitt Rivers Museum in Oxford. He has written and edited a number of books on the anthropology of art and Aboriginal Australian art, including *Ancestral Connections: Art and an Aboriginal System of Knowledge* (1991) and *Aboriginal Art* (1998). He has curated many exhibitions including (with Pip Deveson) *Yingapungapu* for the opening of the National Museum of Australia in 2001, and has collaborated for many years with Ian Dunlop of Film Australia on the *Yirrkala Film Project.*

Morgan Perkins is Assistant Professor of Anthropology and of Art, Director of the Weaver Museum of Anthropology, and of the Museum Studies Program, at SUNY, Potsdam. He has written on contemporary Native American and Chinese art and curated a number of exhibitions, including *What Are We Leaving for the Seventh Generation? Seven Haudenosaunee Voices* (2002), and *Icons and Innovations: The Cross-Cultural Art of Zhang Hongtu* (2003), both at the Roland Gibson Art Gallery, SUNY, Potsdam.

The Anthropology of Art: A Reflection on its History and Contemporary Practice

Howard Morphy and Morgan Perkins

The anthropology of art has entered an exciting stage in its history. It is in the process of moving from its place as a minority interest that most anthropologists could neglect towards a more central role in the discipline. In the past, disengagement from art as a subject of study reflected attitudes of anthropologists to material culture in general. It also sprang from a particular, overly narrow, Euro-American conception of art that made it, for some anthropologists, an uncomfortable field of study. The reasons why the narrowness of this definition inhibited anthropological analysis are both interesting and problematic, since historically anthropologists have adopted a critical stance to the presuppositions of their own cultures. For over a century, they have been at the forefront of debates over the definitions of religion, magic, kinship, gender, law and the economy, but art has, until recently, remained outside these definitional debates in anthropology at least. Yet in the context of Euro-American art practice the definition of art has been every bit as much contested as these other definitions, and indeed anthropological ways of thinking have often been influential in the debate about art while practitioners of anthropology have remained largely disengaged.

The discomfort that anthropologists have displayed over the inclusion of art among their data is shared with related disciplines such as archaeology, in which rock art remained for long divorced from other data, relegated to the concerns of a subdiscipline of committed, passionate and sometimes obsessive believers. Indeed it is only recently that it has begun to be accepted as a normal part of the archaeological record.[1] Being located on the margins has positive aspects. Studies of art have been interdisciplinary in their nature, engaging with ideas that come from outside the narrow confines of the core discipline, and often from outside the academy.

Art is associated almost equally with the two senses of the word "culture" – culture as a way of life or body of ideas and knowledge, and culture as the metaphysical essence of society, incorporating standards by which the finest products of society are judged. This may have been a factor in the discomfort that some

anthropologists felt about the term. Art in the first sense is associated with bodies of
knowledge, technologies, and representational practices that provide insights into
the whole lifeworld of a society. Art in the second sense has been seen as the product
of a particular stage of Euro-American history. In this sense, art is seen as disconnected from society as a whole and overdetermined by its role in the class structure
of Western capitalist society (e.g. Bourdieu 1984).[2] In this view art objects have
become tokens or repositories of symbolic capital in which the ruling class invests its
money to create value, and by which it reinforces its elite status; it is an interesting
topic in the study of class based Western societies, but not necessarily as relevant in
the rest of the world.

It is fundamentally important to separate out this aspect of art from more general
features that make it a relevant category for cross-cultural analysis – including
analysis of the phenomenon in its Western context. Its entanglement with recent
European history and its articulation with Western value creation processes is an
important dimension of art in the Euro-American social context, and worth investigating in its own right. Moreover, the role of art in contemporary Western society
has an effect on global processes and so is a factor in cross-cultural investigations
(see Myers 2002). Art as a category in Western society is more contested than is
allowed for by the view that sees it simply as a commodity or an object of aesthetic
contemplation. As Marcus and Myers write:

> By virtue of cross-cultural training and experience, most anthropologists encounter the category
> of "art" internal to our own culture, with suspicion and a sense of strangeness. Yet in this
> suspicion, anthropologists have also tried to reify the category and to simplify the complex
> internal dynamics of conflict within art worlds over issues of autonomy. Thus anthropologists'
> critical sensibilities of relativism, have largely failed to recognize modern art's own internal
> assault on "tradition" and challenge to boundaries. (Marcus and Myers 1995:6)

The synoptic view that emphasizes the unique characteristics of the Western
category of art, with its Eurocentric biases, is thus itself often both a simplification
and something of a stereotype, even though it is possible to find plenty of evidence
for this view from art world discourse. This idea of art is really the conjunction of a
number of themes: an emphasis on the autonomy of the aesthetic experience, where
art consists of a set of objects set aside for aesthetic contemplation, with no other
overt purpose; the development of a progressive evolutionary view of Western art
history associated with an established canon that stretches forward from classical
Greece to the present by way of the Renaissance; and the placing of an emphasis on
individual creativity – if not genius – and a premium on innovation.[3] These achieve
their most extreme and condensed form in the connoisseurship of the elite and the
rhetoric of the auction market with its emphasis on uniqueness. The emphasis on
individual creativity and the premium placed on originality – "the shock of the new"
– resulted in the ascendancy of the avant-garde.

Many of these themes are shared by other systems. However, the Western themes
co-exist in a particular way that has come to dominate the international art world.
Contemporary artists from a wide range of cultural backgrounds have increased
their engagement with the international art world and developed their own forms of
avant-garde art. These may coincide with the historical Western concept, yet may
also derive from indigenous concepts of innovation and rebellion. In its reaction
against the Maost conception of politically controlled art (Mao 1967), the Chinese
avant-garde art movement, for example, has engaged with contemporary Western

forms and concepts while also drawing upon the tradition of some literati painters who were noted for their rejection of prescribed styles and practices (Perkins 2001).[4] To create a more holistic view of cross-cultural art practices it has become important for the anthropology of art to move beyond its predominant focus on small-scale societies and address practices in art systems where there has been a long tradition of art historical practice and a culturally specific recognition of certain materials as art objects and certain individuals as artists.[5]

While certain characteristics of the contemporary Western art object provide a basis for differentiating contemporary Western art practice from that of many other societies, they must not be allowed to define the general category "art object." Nor need they do so: in themselves they connect with important general themes in anthropology which can provide cross-cultural insights and comparisons that overturn the essentialized uniqueness of the Western category. The making of collections, the accumulation of display goods, the integration of aesthetics within value creation processes, the articulation of cultural performance with political process and many other anthropological themes provide a basis for making comparisons between the "exotic" of the contemporary Euro-American art world and the art of other places and times.[6]

However distancing some anthropologists find the contemporary Euro-American concept of art or the art world(s) associated with it, that sense of distance cannot be the only explanation for the neglect of art by anthropologists for much of the recent history of the discipline. Some other reasons are discussed below.

From Inclusion to Exclusion: Anthropology and Art in the late 19th and early 20th Centuries

The idea of art in European culture has itself been subject to a continuous process of change. The conception of art in the mid-nineteenth century was very different to what it subsequently became under the influence of modernism. Art and material culture were an integral part of nineteenth-century anthropology. As a discipline, anthropology developed hand in hand with the cabinets of curiosity, with antiquarianism, and with the widening of European horizons following the Enlightenment. It was caught up with a more general interest in the exoticism of Otherness, and found itself in a constant state of tension between a comparative perspective that acknowledged a common humanity in all places and times and a teleological evolutionary tendency that saw European civilization as developing out of a progressive transformation of earlier societies. The classificatory projects of institutions like the Pitt Rivers Museum in Oxford captured this tension – recognizing common categories while ordering things and societies in evolutionary sequences. The typological method in British anthropology involved the identification of traits associated with particular cultures and levels of civilization, and artifacts and customary practices were equally components of those typological sets.[7] Art was included with other material culture objects in the evolutionary schema developed by anthropologists such as Pitt Rivers (1906), Tylor (1871, 1878),[8] and Frazer (1925). The most perfect simplification of this argument is Pitt Rivers's diagrammatic representation of the origin of artifacts of different types from the form of a simple stick (figure I.1).[9] He represents artifacts almost as if they reproduced biologically, with successions of minor mutations eventually resulting in differentiation and the production of more complex objects. It is significant that he chose Australian Aboriginal artifacts as the

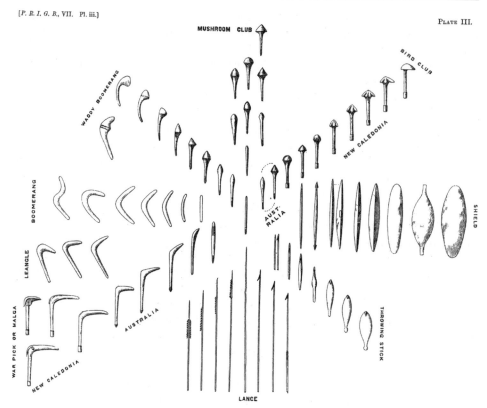

Figure I. 1 This diagram by General Lane-Fox Pitt Rivers 1875, was first produced as plate iii in his article "On the Evolution of culture," *Proceedings of the Royal Institute of Great Britain* VII:20–44. The figure was titled "Clubs, boomerangs, shields and lances" and illustrates the evolution of weapons of these types from a simple throwing stick shown in the center of the diagram. The diagram captures the essence of Pitt Rivers's theory of the development of material culture objects from the simple to the complex as the result of a cumulative process – analogous to Darwinian evolution

basis for his model since Aborigines for long remained the exemplar of "primitive" societies – those that could be taken to represent earlier stages of human cultural evolution. While today Pitt Rivers' model appears simplistic in the extreme, the questions posed by observable patterns in the data remain interesting.

To understand the problematic that drove evolutionary writers on art it is necessary to enter a mind set in which innovation is seen to be a rare component of human cultures, in which most motifs and styles of art are regarded as typically of long duration, in which copying was seen as integral to art practice, in which there were thought to be objective criteria for assessing representations either as decorative forms or as realistic representations of a world out there. The problems that needed to be tackled were: where did the idea or form of particular designs come from, and, on the other hand, how did techniques of realistic representation evolve?

Interestingly, the premises underlying those questions were challenged by modernism, which in turn gained much of its energy from reflecting on the very same set of artifacts that the anthropologists were analyzing. Ironically, modernism saw the diversity of cultural forms as a license for innovation. This was often associated with a rhetoric of "freeing" the artists from the constraints of tradition. Modernism viewed the inspirational works of "primitive art" as exemplars of a universal aesthetic yet simultaneously built in its own assumptions to explain the liberating nature of their forms: primitive art expressed the fundamental, primeval psychic energy of man, unconstrained by the academic tradition – it could be connected to the art of children and the insane. This tension between the modernist avant-garde approach to the arts of other cultures and the anthropological approach remains a continuing theme of debates over the interpretation and exhibition of art. While the emphasis of anthropology has long moved away from evolutionism, the tension remains between the avant-garde view that art speaks for itself and is open to universalistic interpretation, and an anthropological perspective, which requires an indigenous interpretative context.

The formal analyses of British anthropologists such as Haddon (1894; Haddon and Start 1936) and Balfour (1888, 1893a) articulated with the concerns of evolutionary theorists, but it could be argued that their method of analyzing sequences over time was relatively independent of the evolutionary hypotheses that the sequences were sometimes used to support. Their concern to trace the development of decorative motifs over time was connected to the general problematics of art history and antiquarian archaeology. In the archaeological record, motifs were seen to succeed each other over time and to have spread across boundaries, reflecting the relationships between groups.[10] The problem with the method was that the sequences themselves became proof of the evolutionary theory that lay behind them, giving temporal direction to the sequences, from simple to complex, or from figurative to abstract.[11]

In the USA, the pioneering anthropologist of art Franz Boas was equally interested in problems of form in his analyses of non-European art. He certainly saw studies of form in art as having the potential to reveal historical patterns and relationships between groups, but was fundamentally opposed to simple evolutionary theories. He begins his book on *Primitive Art* (1927) by noting that "the treatment given to the subject is based on two principles that, I believe, should guide all investigations of life among primitive people: one the fundamental sameness of mental processes in all races and in all cultural forms of the present day; the other the consideration of every cultural phenomenon as the result of historical happenings" (Boas 1927:1).

There was a close association between anthropology and museums in the late nineteenth and early twentieth century, and many anthropologists were also among the builders of the great ethnographic collections of institutions such as the Smithsonian, the Peabody, the British Museum, the Pitt Rivers Museum, and the Berlin Museum.[12] Anthropologists working under the auspices of the American Bureau of Ethnology and the parallel Boasian tradition made documented collections that have subsequently become a major resource in the anthropology of art, and produce rich ethnographies of art. The Australian ethnographies of Spencer and Gillen (1904, 1927) were rich in their coverage of the material culture and ceremonial performance of Australian Aboriginal societies. Spencer who, under the influence of Frazer, could never allow himself to refer to Aboriginal religion, nevertheless wrote in very positive terms about their "art."[13] Detailed accounts and recordings of art and material culture were also made by European anthropologists such as Nordenskiöld (1973 [1893], 1930), von den Steinen (1969 [1925]), and others.

However, as anthropology moved into the twentieth century a breach began to develop between academic anthropology and museum anthropology in both Britain and the USA. In Britain, evolutionary theory began to come in for strong criticism. The characterization of societies in terms of traits, and their ranking according to typologies based on the movement from simple to complex forms were seen as an impoverished theory based on inadequate method. Evolutionary theory, it was argued, failed to place cultural traits in the context of societies taken as a whole. It failed to show the interrelationship between components in the present, and failed to demonstrate the truth of its hypotheses on the basis of the data available.

There was simultaneously a methodological shift away from museum based studies and inventories of customs produced by missionaries, traders and government officials, towards studies based on long-term field research. Longer-term fieldwork revealed the relationship between different elements of a society as it was at a particular point in time and opened richer veins of sociological data.

There was no reason, a priori, why the study of art and material culture could not benefit from fieldwork based studies. However, in Britain the fieldwork "revolution" became associated with a particular theoretical shift in anthropology towards the structural functionalism of Radcliffe-Brown (1952, 1977) and Malinowski (1922, 1979). Radcliffe-Brown's "comparative science of society"[14] had a profound effect on developments in British social anthropology. In his concern to create a space for anthropology that differentiated it from surrounding disciplines he created an anthropology that centered on synchronic studies of social organization and the comparative study of social structures. He distanced anthropology from history, from psychology, and, in part as a reaction to developing trends in American anthropology, from culture. In emphasizing a synchronic study of human society he effectively buried the data of the evolutionists and their problematic. The opposition to psychology reinforced the social over the individual and behavior over emotions, excluding areas where the study of art has the potential to make a major contribution. In the minds of the new theorists the study of material culture was too closely associated with the more simplistic aspects of evolutionary theory and not central to the shifting concerns of the discipline.[15] Thus material culture – and art – became separated from the mainstream of British social anthropology. Objects were confined in the museum basements and little studied. This situation remained true of British anthropology until the 1960s – indeed the neglect of art and material culture was at its most profound just before the tables turned and art again became an important subject of anthropological writing. In Europe anthropology underwent a similar process of separation from the museum in those countries, such as Holland and France, that developed parallel fieldwork traditions.

In American anthropology the history has been a little different, though characterized by similar periods of neglect. Long-term fieldwork was associated with the development of the Bureau of American Ethnology and Boasian anthropology, which though it included a critique of evolutionism was certainly not a precursor to functionalism. Anthropology developed a little more holistically in the USA than in Britain. The four-field approach to anthropology (socio-cultural anthropology, biological anthropology, archaeology, and linguistics) allowed material culture studies to continue as a subject wedged between archaeology and socio-cultural anthropology. It is even possible to see in American anthropology a long-term influence from culture historical approaches to art. Marcus and Myers argue for recognition of the long-term impact of those approaches on American anthropology. For example, they note the influence of European art theories on the anthropology of

Boas and his students Kroeber, Sapir, and Benedict, in particular through the concepts of pattern and style in culture (Marcus and Myers 1995:11 ff.).[16] Nonetheless, relatively few studies of art were produced by American anthropologists in the first half of the twentieth century. And archaeology, concerned with its own disciplinary independence, tended to distance itself from the museum based study of material culture objects and the analysis of artifacts in living societies.

The distancing of material culture studies and art from the mainstream of anthropology created a self-fulfilling prophecy. Social anthropologists failed to take advantage of a major potential source of data, and museum anthropologists failed to connect the objects in their collections with the societies that produced them. Museum anthropology became disconnected from the main concerns of the discipline and no longer made a significant contribution to contemporary debates. Museum collections continued to be built through short-term field expeditions or through connections with government officials and missionaries. Ironically, museum anthropologists were at least as suspicious of the term "art" as were social anthropologists. Museum anthropology, quite correctly, was concerned to develop classifications of material culture that were as culturally neutral as possible. The typological classifications of the Pitt Rivers Museum, for example, further developed by Henry Balfour (1893b, 1904), Penniman (1953, 1965: 153 ff.), and Beatrice Blackwood (1970), had no place for art. Art was de-emphasized in museum exhibitions in favor of more general exhibitions of material culture and dioramas of daily life.

Many museum anthropologists viewed the category of art with as much suspicion as did other anthropologists. The reasons are complex, and they have not been fully researched. Factors include internal relations within museums, anthropological assumptions and the entanglement of indigenous art with the art market. In the museum world the term "art" tended to be associated with the more highly valued collections from classical civilizations whose objects were part of European heritage. The arts of classical civilizations were positioned in a trajectory that led to European fine art and were associated with the connoisseurship and value creation processes of the art market. The emphasis on the dating, appreciating, appraising and authenticating of classical antiquities created a category of objects removed from the primary concerns of ethnographic collections, whose curators emphasized more the cultural significance of objects. While many individual researchers transcended this divide, the opposition between art and ethnography and its entanglement with the categorization of collections as markers of civilization had a major impact on museum anthropology.

Those objects designated as "art" were often distanced from their cultural context and evaluated according to Western criteria and in relation to Western categories. Ethnographic objects were considered prior, in an evolutionary sense, to the great "art" traditions of Western civilization. If they were art, they were "primitive art." As material culture objects they were viewed as having functional roles in their producing societies that had nothing to do with the categories established by Western art history. Thus art came to be viewed as a Western category with no equivalence in most societies. Where it encompassed the works of other cultures it appropriated them and subordinated them to the history of Euro-American art. The art market appeared to be a party to the presuppositions of Western art history, categorizing certain objects as primitive art. Yet it was also engaged in a value creation process that shifted some objects from the artifact to art category (these issues are well covered by Price 2001 and Errington 1998).

Some ethnographic museum curators were offended by the activities of the art market. In their view it ripped objects out of their indigenous category as types of functioning artifact and placed them on the pedestal of art. They found themselves in competition with private collectors through the auction houses. Art moved objects beyond the acquisition budgets of the ethnographic museums and placed them in the hands of private collectors, or edged them towards the galleries of the art museums, who in turn viewed them in an ambivalent light.

In this period, which lasted until the 1960s, anthropologists in general saw art as an artificial category. It took the objects they studied as ritual objects, functional artifacts, prestige items or markers of status and placed them on a pedestal for aesthetic contemplation. The art dimension of the object seemed to be epiphenomenal – at worst the projection of European aesthetic values onto objects produced in quite different contexts for quite different purposes. This view became deeply embedded in the discipline. For example, it may in part explain the influence of Bourdieu's approach to art which does not require detailed attention to artistic process, form or creativity.[17] One might argue that a professional philistinism, a lack of belief in art as an area of significant human activity influenced anthropologists to neglect it. The ideology of "art for art's sake" that so restricted interpretations of Paleolithic art may well have reflected the general opinions of a particular class in Western society to which most anthropologists belonged. The concept of high art was so internalized by anthropologists, as part of their own cultural experience, that they could not adopt a more culturally neutral way of viewing it. On the one hand, they were socialized into the same aesthetic discourse as other members of their professional class while, on the other hand, they were sceptical about the applicability of the concept of art cross-culturally. It is ironic that Radcliffe-Brown's (1927) only essay on art concerned the art of the Australian modernist Margaret Preston, who used Indigenous Australian motifs in her paintings and was inspired by Aboriginal aesthetics – a topic that Radcliffe-Brown the anthropologist wrote nothing about!

The Exceptions

While the neglect of art was general among anthropologists there were a number of exceptional studies. Some social anthropologists such as Raymond Firth (1979) Melville Herskovits (1934, 1938, 1959 and 1966) and Robert Redfield (1959) maintained a holistic vision of anthropology in which art was an integral component. Firth characteristically managed to appreciate the liberating force of modernism in Western art while drawing lessons from modernism for the analysis of non-European art, without forgoing his anthropological relativism. It is always difficult to enter particular historical moments – especially moments of significant change – and capture the way in which the world appeared to people living through those times. The impact of modernism and the challenge of primitive art are almost unrecoverable experiences. Firth provides a glimpse of the excitement, of exposure to exotic forms when he writes: "the admission into the graphic and plastic arts of distortion, of change of form from the proportions given by ordinary vision, came as a liberating influence." And then the anthropologist takes over as he continues:

> It was significant not only for an appreciation of the contemporary Western art, but also for a clearer understanding of much medieval and exotic art. Like Romanesque painting and sculpture which have long captured my interest, the painting and sculpture which anthropologists encountered in exotic societies could be regarded, not as a product of imperfect vision, technical crudity,

or blind adherence to tradition, but as works of art in their own right, to be judged as expressions of artists' original conceptions in the light of their cultural endowment. (Firth 1992:19)

In the USA, Melville Herskovits, a student of Boas, led the study of African and African American art. In Britain colonial anthropologists such as Mills (1926, 1937) and Rattray (1954) produced important regional ethnographies of art. The school of French anthropologists who emerged around Marcel Griaule and later Germaine Dieterlen made a major contribution to the study of African art and were pioneers of visual anthropology.[18] In Belgium there were Luc de Heusch (1958, 1972, 1982) and Daniel Biebuyck (1969, 1973). In Australia Ronald Berndt was a passionate advocate for an anthropology of art, and the amateur anthropologist Charles Mountford made important documented collections.[19] And some museum based anthropologists such a William Fagg (1968, 1970, 1981, 1982) of the British Museum were unafraid to make art the central theme of their research.

However, more often than not, studies of art were absent where they might have been expected. Malinowski's (1922) study of the Kula played down the richness of the performances and the pageantry of the voyages and the exchanges that surrounded them, produced limited insights into the abundant art of the Kula voyages and overlooked the spectacle of the women's skirts.[20] Ironically it was the material dimension of the Kula that stimulated theoretical discourse from the beginning, in Mauss's (1950) analysis of the gift and the subsequent discourse in anthropology over exchange. But it was not until the late 1960s, beginning with Weiner's (1977) studies in the Massim that aesthetics, performance and material culture became integral to the research process and a broader understanding of the role of material culture in the processes of exchange and value creation began to emerge.[21] And it was not until the latter part of the twentieth century that the first major studies of Trobriand Island art were undertaken (Scoditti 1990; Campbell 2002).

A Revival of Interest

The 1960s saw a strong renewal of interest in art among anthropologists. It sprang from two sources – from changes in the research agenda of anthropology and from the fact that the current of Western art and art theory began to flow more in the direction of anthropological thinking. In neither case were these movements general but they helped to create an environment in which the anthropology of art could begin to grow and find new niches, both within the discipline itself and in the wider art world.

Anthropology as a discipline grew rapidly after World War II and this allowed or even encouraged new specializations. In Britain there was a move away from the focus on social relations and the analysis of social structure to an increased concern with myth, religion, and ritual. The anthropology of art received support from the renewed interest in symbolism, which in turn articulated with structuralist, semiotic and linguistic approaches to culture viewed as a system of meaning. Similar changes occurred in American anthropology, which already had an advantage in its diversity and the number of its practitioners.

The 1960s also saw the growth of interest in visual anthropology, a renewed interest in material culture and the development of an anthropological archaeology. These were synergistic with developments in the anthropology of art if relatively independent of it. Often there were crossovers in theory and method in these disciplines which were concerned with the cultural dimensions of things (Kubler 1962, 1979).

The anthropology of art benefited particularly from the development of theoretical interest in two areas – symbolism and exchange. Symbolic anthropology was concerned equally with the semantic aspects of symbolism and with the effectiveness of those symbols in ritual contexts – with linking the intentional aspects of ritual with the performative. Since "art" objects – body paintings, sacred objects, masks – were often integral to ritual performances they entered into the study of ritual and symbolism (see e.g. Forge 1973, 1979; Fernandez 1982, 1986; Turner 1973, 1986; Witherspoon 1977; and Munn 1973, 1986).

Exchange theory was closely connected to studies of symbolism. Exchange is one of the ways in which value is created, and material objects are both expressions of value and objects which in themselves gain in value through processes of exchange. Objects such as Kula valuables are integral to exchange systems and in many societies sacred objects, body paintings and designs add to the prestige and power of the groups or individuals controlling them. The role that objects played in these processes became a topic of increasing interest (see e.g. Gregory 1982; Munn 1986). Exchange theory and symbolic anthropology influenced the discourse over the nature of persons and things, in the context of their interrelationships. This became a central theme of anthropology in the 1980s and 1990s.

From the 1970s on there was also an increasing emphasis on topics such as the emotions, gender, the body, space and time. Art, broadly defined, often provided a major source of information. Sculptures and paintings offer insights into systems of representation (Morphy 1991; Taylor 1996), the aesthetics of the body (Boone 1986), value creating processes (Munn 1986; Gell 1992), social memory (Küchler 2002), the demarcation of space (Blier 1987) and so on. Song and drama provide rich sources of information on the poetics of culture (Feld 1982), the world of feeling, and reflective and introspective dimensions of culture as well as exemplifying performativity (Kratz 1994).[22]

Material culture objects were no longer regarded as passive; they began to be seen as integral to the processes of reproducing social relations and of developing affective relations with the world – "art as a way of doing, a way of behaving as a member of society, having as its primary goal the creation of a product or effect of a particular kind" (D'Azevedo 1973:7). Through their material possessions people produce an image of themselves in the world, and these material possessions also operate to create the stage on which people lead their daily lives – they are markers of status, gender relations and so on. We would argue that many studies of the era concerned failed to explore sufficiently the material dimensions of objects and missed the opportunity to use them as a truly independent source of data. Nevertheless, they created an environment in which the anthropology of art could develop.

Modernism and the Anthropology of Art

Changes in the Western art world also resulted in a more serious engagement with anthropology. The concept of art that developed at the turn of the nineteenth and twentieth centuries centered on the aestheticized object separated from the rest of life. As far as anthropology was concerned, this was an alien view. However, modernism also created the groundwork for a more positive and dynamic relationship between anthropology and art.

The rise of anthropology and the development of modernism in art were related, even though anthropologists neglected to study art either in their own society or in the non-European societies that were the primary focus of their research. For the practitioners of modern art in the early years of the twentieth century, the encounter with the arts of Africa and Oceania was a liberating experience. Although the critique of primitivism has rightly emphasized the appropriative nature of this aspect of modernism, the aesthetic shifts associated with the widening of the European tradition played an important role in awakening an appreciation of non-European art and in creating spaces for its exhibition. As Firth's statement (above) suggests, the advent of modernism had the potential to disturb the anthropologists' preconceptions about what art was, so that they could begin to see the analytic potential of the art of the societies they studied.

Anthropology's articulation with modernism has been long-term, and it is only recently that anthropologists have become fully aware of the complexities of that relationship. The challenge of anthropology to the contemporary Euro-American art world, only now being explicitly articulated, is twofold: it gives agency to the artist and asserts that cultural context plays an important part in the appreciation of art. Thus it problematizes the universalistic assumption behind the modernist enterprise. In turn the challenge for anthropology has been to open up its own interpretative practice to the aesthetic and affective dimension of objects.

Marcus and Myers (1995) draw attention to the fact both contemporary art and anthropology have "culture as [their] object." This is an interesting idea. Certainly one of the main trends in late twentieth-century modernism has been the emphasis on different forms of conceptual art in which the idea is the object. Art has increasingly become part of cultural commentary and of political discourse, involving a reflexive critique of the artist's own society. This synergy with anthropology's reflexive aspect and its focus on culture may be the reason why anthropology and ethnography have recently begun to figure in Euro-American art discourse and practice;[23] museums and their ethnographic collections have become installation sites and a springboard for cross-cultural dialogue among artists.

The present conversation between art and anthropology[24] reveals the dynamic, changing and complex nature of the Western art category as well as saying something about the increasing engagement of anthropology in popular discourse, and cautions against long-term generalizations about the relationship between the two.

An Anthropological Definition of Art

So far, we have skirted around two issues that are central to an anthropology of art – the definition of art and what characterizes an anthropological approach to art. The two are related – an anthropological definition of art is going to be influenced by the nature of anthropology itself. As a cross-cultural discipline, its definition of categories is affected by the desire to reduce cultural bias; the objective is to make categories as broadly applicable as possible without becoming meaningless. Those categories form part of an evolving and often implicit disciplinary metalanguage. Yet we would also argue that the definition of an artwork cannot come solely from within the discipline. Anthropology is the study of human societies and hence anthropological categories must be based in the real worlds in which people – including anthropologists – exist. Historically, anthropology's metalanguage has always been biased by its Western origins and our definition of art is no exception. That bias needs to be acknowledged and taken into account in the construction of the definition. In turn this process of revision may challenge and influence the categorical definitions of the anthropologists' own societies. In this regard we take a very different approach from Gell who eschews a definition of art.[25]

We will use a working definition of art that one of us developed previously: "art objects are ones with aesthetic and/or semantic attributes (but in most cases both), that are used for representational or presentational purposes" (Morphy 1994:655). The definition is not intended to be exclusive; rather, it indicates the kind of objects that anthropologists are usually referring to when they focus on "art objects." Components of the definition are likely to be found in most anthropologists' writing about art. To Boas "the very existence of song, dance, painting and sculpture among all the tribes known to us is proof of the craving to produce things that are felt as satisfying through their form, and [of the] capability of man to enjoy them" (1927:9). Boas also connected the form of art to meaning and saw the interaction between the two as contributing to the aesthetic effect:

> The emotions may not be stimulated by the form alone but by the close associations that exist between form and ideas held by the people. When forms convey meaning, because they recall past experiences or because they act as symbols, a new element is added to enjoyment. The form and its meaning combine to elevate the mind above the indifferent emotional state of everyday life. (Boas 1927:12)

Our position is that the anthropology of art is not simply the study of those objects that have been classified as art objects by Western art history or by the international art market. Nor is art an arbitrary category of objects defined by a particular anthropological theory; rather, art making is a particular kind of human activity that involves both the creativity of the producer and the capacity of others to respond to and use art objects, or to use objects as art.[26] We acknowledge that there are good arguments for deconstructing the art category and replacing it with more specific concepts such as depiction, representation, aesthetics, and so on, all of which are relevant to some or all of the objects we include under the rubric of art. We also acknowledge that the study of art can be nested within an anthropology of material culture (see Miller 2005 for a recent approach to materiality) and that the dividing lines between art and non-art within that category are often fine and not always relevant. Our response is to recognize that the category of art is fuzzy, involving a series of overlapping polythetic sets, which contain objects that differ widely in their form and effects. However, the narrower terms that are used to replace art as a general concept are often complementary to one another and they all seem to be drawn together in discourse that surrounds the objects that are usually designated art objects. And clearly we think that the more general concept of art is relevant to understanding the role of such objects in human social life. Otherwise we would not produce a reader on the anthropology of art!

It could be argued that we have narrowed the topic down too much by focusing on material objects, and that our separation of the visual arts from dance and music follows a categorization from Western art history that is inappropriate for cross-cultural analysis. But we suggest that our definition of art applies with little modification across different media of communication. Indeed we would argue that art making as a concept can be applied across media and that this strengthens our argument for its existence as a particular kind of human action. The justification for focusing primarily on the visual arts in this collection is that visual arts have properties of affect and performance that distinguish them from song, music, dance and other modes of performance and that require different skills and techniques and involve different senses.[27] But visual art is often produced as part of a performance that equally involves other media, or if it occurs separately it cross-refers to artistic practice in other media. Anthropological analysis must involve an understanding of how the parts contribute to the whole, and what makes an object an art object may only be determined by analysis across media and across contexts. Anthropology must also be open to classifications of the phenomenal world that do not correspond to Western categories.

The sets of objects that fall within the category of art object have to be determined in each particular case in the context of the society concerned. While there may be an overlap in the classifications employed by different cultures, it cannot be presumed. The anthropological category is an analytic one and will not necessarily conform to any category explicitly recognized by a particular society.[28] The point so often raised, that there is "no word for art" in the society concerned, is not an argument against an analytic category of art (see, for example, Perkins 2005).[29]

It is, however, relevant to ask what sets of terms are applied within the society to the sets of objects that might be encompassed within the category art. The analysis of the vocabulary employed may be relevant to determining whether the label art can be appropriately applied. If these objects are thought of first in their functional sense (such as fish hooks used in physical or magical ways), it does not follow that they lack qualities that overlap with and are considerably relevant to the category "art," anthropologically defined. The lack of a specific word is often an indication of the production and reception of imagery, performances, and so on, as integrally connected to other aspects of life (e.g. catching fish). The rationale for continuing to pursue the anthropology of "art" is threefold. First, art is a term that, for better or worse, has been either adopted or recognized on a nearly global scale. Second, art describes a range of thoughts and practices that employ creativity in the production of expressive culture, regardless of whether that production adheres to prescribed forms or embodies individual innovation. Third, the anthropology of art encompasses the history of this concept in cross-cultural encounters and the contemporary conditions that are the inheritance of this history. The application of expressive, aesthetic, evaluative terms to the objects concerned would on a priori grounds be good evidence that they fit into the cross-cultural category as we have defined it. However, the use of aesthetic criteria is not a necessary and sufficient condition.

The classification of works as art by the Western art world is not a relevant criterion for defining the category of non-Western arts, even if there is an overlap in the works that might be included. The criteria used to include works from non-Western societies under the European rubric of art are of more relevance to the history of Western art than they are to understanding the significance of those objects in their own cultural contexts. The Western category of art has been expanding, selectively swallowing up the arts of other cultures. For much of the twentieth century the categorization of non-European art as "primitive art" predominated. The recognition of the qualitative aspects of African and Oceanic objects reflected in part the engagement of European artists with these objects at the end of the nineteenth and turn of the twentieth centuries.

The dominant paradigm for exhibiting primitive art, until recently, subordinated it to the influence of the works on Euro-American artists and viewed the works as objects of aesthetic contemplation independent of their cultural context. In the 1935 exhibition at the Museum of Modern Art in New York, *African Negro Art*, the curator James Johnson Sweeney "felt that if African art was displayed in the same manner as European and American sculpture, viewers would evaluate it using the same aesthetic criteria" (cited in Webb 1995:32–3). First Nations art in Canada had received similar treatment in a 1927 exhibition at the National Gallery. As with a later exhibition at the Museum of Modern Art in New York – the subject of many of the articles in the Primitivism section of this volume – this exhibition presented West Coast Native works primarily as objects that had inspired non-Native Canadian artists. The purpose of this exhibition was, according to then Director, Eric Brown, "to mingle for the first time the art works of the Canadian West Coast tribes with that of our more sophisticated artists in an endeavour to analyse their relationships to one another, if such exist, and particularly to enable this primitive and interesting art to take a definite place as one of the most valuable of Canada's artistic productions."[30]

The European art world selected out objects that fitted within its own broad categories of sculpture and painting. These were portable and transportable works that could be exhibited in similar ways to their European equivalents. The set of objects relevant for analyzing art in Africa, Native America, or Aboriginal Australia is unlikely to be the same as the set selected out for inclusion in the Western category of art. It must be borne in mind, however, that if the objective of anthropology is partly to alter Western ways of thinking about different cultures, an anthropologically informed Western category of Aboriginal or African art (Yoruba art, San art and so on) is potentially realizable.

We agree with Gell (1992) that a degree of aesthetic agnosticism is required when analyzing aesthetics cross-culturally; however we do not go as far as he does in ruling aesthetics to be outside the province of an anthropology of art. It is vital not to presume how a particular object is interpreted on the basis of our own aesthetic judgements. An aesthetic response involves a physical, emotional and/or cognitive response to qualitative attributes of the form of an object. We would argue that there is a cross-cultural dimension to aesthetics and that some perceptions and even interpretations may be shared widely, but that this is a matter to be demonstrated in the particular case on the basis of relevant ethnography. In a sense there is a double problem of interpretation. We have to establish the quality of the aesthetic effect and then place it within an interpretative context to determine its meaning – how it is felt – in the context of the producing society. None of these qualifications suggests that we cannot explore the aesthetic dimension of these objects, and indeed in many parts of his analysis Gell does precisely this. He tends to equate the aesthetic with beauty and pleasure. Both of these are important components of aesthetic discourse, but the aesthetic dimension must also encompass their opposites – feelings of discomfort, the idea of ugliness and the potential for pain.

Works of art must first be defined in relation to particular traditions and in their social and cultural context. It may be that the concept of art is not useful in the analysis of the objects of some societies. It is certainly the case that an anthropological study of a particular topic, for example ritual, is likely to include objects that are non-art objects as well as those that can be usefully defined as art. Indeed there is no reason why the category art should be used at all in analyzing ritual objects, so long as the aesthetic attributes of the objects are considered when relevant, that is, when their aesthetic effect is part of the reason why the event in which they partake is thought to be ritually powerful. One might conclude from this, indeed, that rather than developing an anthropology of art anthropologists should simply be aware of the semantic and aesthetic dimensions of objects.

We are partly in agreement with this notion. There is no doubt that, as anthropologists from Boas to Coote (1992) have noted, the aesthetic dimension applies to the natural world as well as to cultural products.[31] One might argue that the concept of art is useful simply as a flag to remind anthropologists not to neglect this dimension of an object in their analysis. However art does not inhere simply in the aesthetic dimension of objects. It categorizes certain kinds of object and a certain way of acting in the world that shows common elements cross-culturally. The category differentiates art objects from other objects, even if the boundaries of the category are fuzzy around the edges.

Anthropological Approaches to Art or Anthropological Theories of Art

What is distinctive about an anthropological approach or rather anthropological approaches to art, apart from the cross-cultural definition of art itself? The easy answer is that the anthropological approach to art is as diverse as the discipline itself. There is no anthropological theory of art that is not also part of more general theory (see Layton 1991 for one approach to the discipline and Van Damme for a survey of "anthropologies" of art). However it is possible to make certain generalizations about an anthropological approach that most anthropologists would find uncontroversial. An anthropological approach to art is one that places it in the context of its producing society. The art of a particular society has to be understood initially in relation its place in the society where it was produced, rather than in relation to how members of another society might understand it. Subsequently it might be interpreted further in relation to some general propositions about the human condition or according to a comparative model of human societies. But initially it needs to be placed in its ethnographic context.

Once it is placed in its context we have to discover what kind of thing art is before we can begin to analyze it and see how it in turn contributes to the context in which it occurs. Anthropology is a dialogic discipline precisely because of its holistic approach. Analyzing what kind of object a work of art is may be a prerequisite to understanding its role or effect in a ritual performance. It is possible that its semantic density may be an important factor, or its aesthetic effect, or its historic significance to participants; there may be any number of factors acting separately or in conjunction. Analysis of the object contributes to an understanding and definition of context, and this in turn provides relevant information about the object itself.

For these reasons we do not think that there is any single anthropological theory of art. Since art is an encompassing category, it includes objects of very many different types that are incorporated in contexts in different ways. In some cases the semantic aspects of the object may be of central relevance to the way it functions. In other cases its expressive or aesthetic properties may be central. While some art systems encode meanings in almost language-like ways, in other cases meaning operates at a more general level. In most cases the same artworks in context can be approached from a variety of different perspectives, all of which are relevant to understanding some aspect of their form or significance. As O'Hanlon (1995:832) points out it is important "to recognise the multidimensionality of art" where the semantic, aesthetic, affective and purposive dimensions all apply to the same object or event.

Throughout its history anthropology has returned to the debate about whether the central focus of the subject is social relations or culture. This debate or chasm has affected the anthropology of art at various times and, as we suggested in the first section of this introduction, discomfort with a particular conception of culture may have contributed to the neglect of art by structural functionalists. Our simple – perhaps even simplistic – counter to this divide is to argue that it is equally important to study the social and the cultural aspects of art. Art is often integral to social relationships as Gell (1998) emphasizes, and no anthropological study of art would be complete if its social, political, and economic dimensions were neglected. However art is also closely associated with the ideational aspects of society and with the bodies of knowledge associated with those ideas. Here it enters the realm of culture. Its study requires attention to formal aspects of the art in order to answer certain questions: how does art convey meaning, how does it affect its audience, how does it represent subject matter, is it viewed as a manifestation of a God or spirit or as the genius of a creative individual? These questions link form to content. Too often, purely sociological theories of art neglect details of the form of objects. They consider them to be irrelevant or epiphenomenal to the way art works – to its place in the market or its value as a symbol of power. These can be termed "black box" theories of art in which every object – in formal terms – may as well consist of an empty and featureless black box. While the neglect of form may be adequate for certain analyses, it is likely to provide only a partial understanding of the role of art objects in social life.

The study of art encourages anthropologists to deal with the temporality of cultural processes, to connect the experiential dimension of culture, the immediacy of performance with longer-term and more general processes. Works of art have different durations. Some, such as a spectacular revelatory event in a performance, may be over in a matter of seconds, even if the impact on participants endures for a lifetime. Others – a mask or a body painting for example – may be present for a few hours until they are removed or wear away. Others may be part of a permanent structure – such as a temple icon, added to or modified, at times dressed, but ever present in place. Consider, for example, the case of the Zuni *Ahayu:da* (War God) that must be allowed to decay in order to release its dangerous power back into the environment. This stands in direct opposition to museums' efforts at preservation and has thus been used as a central argument in repatriation claims (Clifford ch. 9; Tedlock 1995). The different durations of presence will affect how such works are seen, how people relate to them over time, how they can be used in knowledge transmission, how they can be learned, and so on. The analysis of their form must take these factors into account – the work of art is not simply the object itself but the whole context in which it is produced, seen and used.

There is an added complication. The experience of an artwork is not necessarily confined to a single event or context. Different dimensions of the work may come into play over time as a result of multiple exposure or evocations of the memory of form. Yolngu paintings, for example, are inscribed on the bodies of initiates prior to their circumcision; they seldom last unmodified for more than a day after they are finished, and the boys receive little instruction as to the meaning of the designs. The immediate impact of the painting is intense; its painting on the body is part of a life changing experience. A boy lies still for hours while the fine cross-hatched lines are painted across his chest with a brush of human hair, and he will remember the event for the rest of his life. For his adult relatives the fine painting marks his change of status from boy to man; it is a symbol of pride and a sign of his connection to the ancestral world. Paintings are experienced as spiritually powerful objects, and the shimmering brilliance of the design as it appears on the boy's chest as he is carried on the shoulders of his mother's brothers to the place of circumcision is a sign of this ancestral presence. The paintings are semantically dense objects which refer to the actions of the ancestral beings in creating the land. They are also maps of the created land and they encode the structure of Yolngu clan organization. Each painting could be the subject of a book but it is only glimpsed at a distance by most participants in the ceremony and is not present to be examined in detail. Its semantic and cognitive significance is not located in the moment or instance of its physical expression, but in its existence within a mental archive of possible images, connected through the Yolngu system of knowledge to other instances of ancestral power in the form of songs, landscape, designs belonging to different places and associated with different ancestral beings. To attempt to understand its significance without reference to this wider context is as meaningful as trying to learn the meaning of a word from its occurrence in a single sentence (for a detailed analysis of Yolngu art see Morphy 1991).

In China by comparison, paintings in the literati tradition that have been produced by an individual artist at a specific moment in time may be altered by the addition of seals or later inscriptions made by the artist or subsequent collectors. The evolution of the painting itself, reactions of viewers, and the painting's provenance thus become marked on the object itself. A single painting can also become part of an ongoing system of inspiration and commentary involving calligraphy, poetry and subsequent paintings produced by the original artist or another. Artists use these multiple art forms to complement and comment upon one another's work over time (see Sullivan 1974 and Vinograd 1991). Even direct copies of a painting produced by another artist are often held in very high regard and this practice continues to be central to the current system of education. This practice is sometimes viewed as a form of competition with the master painters of the past that allows the tradition to evolve and remain vital (Fu 1991).

We have used specific examples, but we are making a general point that must be a central proposition of the anthropology of art: understanding the significance of the work requires placing it in the widest possible context. It is not sufficient – or perhaps possible – to understand its immediate effect or significance without first understanding the historical, social, and cultural backgrounds to its production. One of the advantages of studying art works is that they provide a means to access the processual dimension of culture. They connect events with processes and they connect experiences separated in time.

The Anthropology of Art and Interdisciplinary Discourse

Ironically the future anthropology of art must re-engage with those methods and problems that led a different generation of anthropologists to reject the study of art in the first place. It must engage with the study of form at the micro level, seeing in the production of art objects a form of agency that arises from bodies of knowledge.

At the macro level it must engage in the study of form for the purpose of comparative and historical analysis. Attention to form and the relative autonomy of form forces attention away from any single interpretative framework and encourages the researcher to look for the widest possible range of explanations for the existence of objects themselves and the contribution they make to an event. Different objects contribute in different ways. The study of form opens up a full range of avenues to explore the psychological impact of objects, their cognitive significance, the creative processes that underlie them and their contribution to systems of knowledge and meaning.

A revitalized study of form can also help reforge the links between the research of anthropologists and of scholars working in related disciplines such as social history, art history, and archaeology. Analyses of form can be central to the analysis of historical process and the dynamics of relationships between groups over time. Studies of dress, for example, can provide information about changes in the expression of religious ideology, in concepts of gender and in gender relations (e.g. Hendrickson 1995; Banerjee and Miller 2003). While not every anthropologist will be interested in historical processes, it is important to create a dialogue across disciplines that involves shared methodologies and problematics. The input of anthropology into archaeology has often been in the form of lessons in social theory, but in the absence of methodologies that enable those theories to be applied in concrete archaeological situations.

The analysis of the distribution of art styles can provide relevant data for social and historical studies aimed at establishing the nature, permeability and fluidity of social and cultural boundaries. The use of art in cultural mapping has a long history in studies of African art (see Fagg 1964 and Kasfir's, 1984, critique). While simple correlations between artistic styles and other components of culture – such as linguistic boundaries or kinship systems – are seldom going to be found, style in art nonetheless provides a relevant source of data for interrogating boundaries and the nature of movements across them in the context of long-term social and cultural processes (see Dietler and Herbich 1998 for a relevant discussion). Attempts to establish relationships between art styles and cognitive structures (Fisher 1961) or social systems (Berndt 1971) have been controversial, but may none the less provide interesting directions for research if the complexity of the relationships is sufficiently taken into account.

The anthropological study of art has recently had an important impact on anthropological studies of social change and processes of globalization. The impact has been in two main areas: in the study of processes of trade and exchange, and in the discourse on the process of globalization, including the conceptualization of cultural boundaries. The two issues are closely related since the "traffic in culture" has always been an area that problematizes an over-rigid and prescriptive model of cultures as bounded entities. The sale of art objects and craft has been one of the main entry points for small-scale societies into the global economy; it is also one of the main ways in which the image of such societies is created in the imagination of outsiders. While ethnographic museums were an integral component of the global trade in indigenous craft from the mid-nineteenth century onwards, anthropologists in general neglected to study – or perhaps even see – the trade, for a number of reasons. In part, anthropologists were interested in small-scale societies as they were before European colonization, and trade with Europeans shattered the illusion of the "uncontaminated savage." The primary aim of anthropology, for a long time, was to reconstruct societies as they were before colonization. Hence the influence of outsiders was something to be factored out or overlooked. For a long time anthropologists, on the whole, neglected social change. They saw it as something exogenous to the societies that they studied, rather than as a process in which such societies were fully engaged – albeit often from a position of disadvantage. In recent years understanding of these issues has been transformed. The pioneering work of Nelson Graburn (ch. 23) and his co-authors established that trade in art and artifacts was very much a component of contemporary relations between indigenous and non-indigenous societies. Nicholas Thomas's (1991, 1999) later work showed that the exchange of goods and mutual influence was integral to the colonial process from the very beginning. The writings of Appadurai (1986), Kopytoff (1986) and Steiner (ch. 25) explored the journeys of objects across boundaries and the implications of these journeys for our conceptions of the producing and consuming cultures.[32]

It is now understood that the value creation processes in which objects partake are not restricted to the place and time of their production, but inhere in all of the interactions in which they are involved. The nature of the value creation processes will depend on the role that art has in the producing society, and in particular historical circumstances. Trade in art objects that have a central role in a society's religious or ritual system can be a sign of the loss of value of those works in their indigenous context; a marker of religious transformation or the effect of missionary zeal. On the other hand, trade in highly valued religious art can be quite compatible with the role that the object has in its original context (as has been suggested for New Ireland Malangans (Gell 1998: 224–225)) and may contribute to increasing understanding in the consuming society of the religion and the values that underpin it (as is the case with much contemporary Australian Aboriginal art).

Art can be one of the means by which the image of a culture is conveyed across time and space. But the images that are created in this way often involve cultural stereotypes that belong to the consuming culture rather than to the producing culture. The processes of selection and interpretation can create a simplified, essentialized, atemporal image of a particular society which bears little relation to its recent history or contemporary existence. These processes have been well explored in the writings of Price (ch.10), Errington (1998) and Karp et al. (1991, 1992). However the critique of the appropriation of art to create representations of "other" cultures must not in itself be essentialized to cover all places and times. It has been recognized recently that such essentialization denies the agency of indigenous peoples in both the past and the present. Indigenous people have often used art as a means to economic survival, as a demonstration of skills and cultural values, and as a means to assert cultural identity in a changing world (Dussart 1997). Art production has also been integral to dynamic processes in the producing societies: changes in the relations between men and women, in religious ideology, in employment and occupation. Art is nearly always produced in contested environments and the study of art in colonial and post-colonial contexts provides a means to access those dynamic processes.

The denial of agency to indigenous artists takes us back to the very beginnings of this introduction; to the modernist myth that saw the Western artist as the person who recognized the value in the work of primitive art or folk music. However it is often the case that indigenous artists and craftspeople have been active in the process of manufacturing and marketing their art for new audiences, and creating new musical forms. We may now label such things as "world music" or "world art," which again tends to deny agency to the indigenous peoples. It is appropriation in modern dress. In cultural studies and some areas of anthropology a judgmental element has come into the analysis – this mixing of cultures has been celebrated as the production of a hybrid post-colonial world, in opposition to previous models that focussed on difference. The agency of individuals who contribute to local trajectories and identity formation processes as well as being participants in more global processes, is de-emphasized. The problem of scale is important here. We prefer instead to see people acting in several frames, which do not in any simple sense include each other. The local is not nested in the global (or displaced by it), but rather articulates with it. We would expect a future anthropology of art to contribute to a more subtle and nuanced understanding of the relationship between the local and the global, and to situate the social and cultural production of art in space and time in a way that reveals the reasons for its irrepressible diversity and inventiveness. This requires a sophisticated understanding of local contexts of production – not frozen in some precolonial time/space, but dynamic and productive.

Exhibiting Art Today

Changing anthropological ideas have had an impact on the role of museums and art galleries as repositories of cultural artifacts. Two almost unrelated processes have made museums exciting places again. First, they have been properly recognized as valued repositories of cultural and historical archives providing a resource that allows for the reanalysis of contact history, colonial processes, changes in material culture and so on. Second, indigenous peoples have rediscovered their pasts in the collections. They are using museums as means to come to terms with loss. In some cases they see the preservation of past histories as a source of strength, giving them unique identities within the nation states that have incorporated them. Museums and art galleries have become spaces for contesting the stereotyped images of the past and challenging the assumptions of the present. Indeed in some settler colonial societies such as Australia, Canada and New Zealand a more anthropologically informed understanding of history has led to the rise of a competing indigenous identity which is replacing some of the myths of nationhood associated with the colonial process.

In a contemporary context the notion of the museum has, like art, been exported and differentially adopted or rejected, based upon its relevance to a particular nation or range of cultures. Collection, preservation, and display are now no longer the province of museums as Western institutions. They have entered a cross-cultural space where their value is reappraised. The potlatch, for example, was and continues to be a forum for the collection and display of material objects in a social and cultural context that has been represented in museums in both local and urban settings. The repatriation of a potlatch collection to Cape Mudge and Alert Bay, British Columbia (Clifford 1991) highlights the way that Western standards of museum practice have, in some cases, been imposed (the criteria for this return stipulated that the objects must be housed in a museum) even as local communities alter those practices to become locally relevant. The current policy of the National Museum of the American Indian at the Smithsonian – where Native and non-

Native staff consult the relevant tribal communities on most aspects of the storage and display of cultural objects – is only the largest and most recent example of the adaptation of museum practice to indigenous systems of knowledge that has been occurring in countless tribal museums throughout North America. In the USA, the Native American Graves Protection and Repatriation Act (NAGPRA) has forced museums to adapt to the concerns of Native Americans over the handling of objects and human remains. Whether forced or voluntary, international debates over repatriation and the general control of material cultural property (and intangible cultural property according to a new UNESCO convention) have created a dialogue that both enhances the cross-cultural understanding of art and allows for increasing collaboration.

Significant yet invigorating challenges to art institutions are presented by the participation of artists with different cultural backgrounds – in contrast to the long history of including objects without the participation of their producers. Contemporary artists producing work in styles that range from historical to experimental have increasingly engaged with art institutions and, in so doing, presented alternative conceptions of art as cultural knowledge. The analysis of systems of art education is a useful method for understanding the role of art in different cultures. The pedagogical process sets the foundations for knowledge and determines how individuals learn – and sometimes learn to critique – the conventions of the different art worlds in which they may circulate.[33] Related cross-cultural studies of children's art also offer a particularly rich avenue for anthropological analysis in this respect. Artistic skills and accompanying cultural knowledge may be acquired through a range of methods that include independent study, family and community gatherings, apprenticeships, and training in art schools. Whether individual or institutional, a Western influence on art education has often impacted the evolution of contemporary art forms and practices in different cultures. The many pedagogical examples found throughout the world include the Western influence on Inuit (Houston 1952), Native American (Gritton and Cajete 2000), and Aboriginal Australian art (Bardon 1979), as well as art in Ghana (Svašek 1997) and China (Perkins 2001).[34] Although the centripetal forces of international art institutions draw artists from every culture into their sphere, these individuals may choose not to participate or, if they do, they may challenge the rules of those institutions. Since many contemporary artists now have training in a number of settings they can draw upon different cultural forms to address themes that are both cultural and personal to question the definitions of "indigenous," "traditional" and "modern" (see, for example, the contributions by Bennett and Rickard in this volume).

Conclusion

In this survey of the history of the anthropology of art we have been equally concerned with two questions: what anthropology can contribute to the study of art and what the study of art can contribute to anthropology. The first is easy to answer, in particular in relation to the recent European tradition of art history. An anthropological approach places art in its social context. The relativism of anthropological theory broadens the definition and conception of art by elucidating its contexts – whether they be local or global. This relativism is in harmony with trends in contemporary Western art practice that have seen a challenge to the presuppositions that underpin the definition of the Western canon. Anthropology has a role in this Western art world discourse, but it is also concerned with developing an ethnography of Western art practice and of the complex, multi-sited art world itself, through research into the passage of works from artist's studio, to commercial gallery, to art museum or private collection and into the lives of those involved in that world and the journey. An anthropological approach to art is not opposed to exhibiting works of art in art galleries. While the way objects are presented reflects and influences the way they are viewed by members of a particular society, it should not limit they way they are analyzed. An anthropological perspective may problematize the exclusivity of the art gallery as a venue but does not prescribe a particular way of viewing objects (see Morphy 2001). As Vogel (1991) demonstrated, there are many ways of exhibiting the same object, each of which may contribute in different ways to understanding and appreciation.

Finally, what can the study of art contribute to anthropology? It is our view that art is an integral part of most, if not all, human societies and that by failing to study it anthropologists deny themselves access to a significant body of information. An anthropology of art opens the way to understanding the processes of creativity and creative action. It can provide insights into human cognitive systems – how people conceptualize components of their everyday life and how they construct representations of their world. Art is often, indeed, employed in the creation of context – of the frame within which ritual action occurs, or of the stage and the accompanying regalia for political performance.

The neglect of art, and of the aesthetic dimension of human action in general has resulted in a failure of anthropology to understand or convincingly demonstrate the effect of participation in certain events on members of a society. The analysis of art or of the substance of ritual performance – the paintings, sculptures, songs and sequences of action – has often been the missing ingredient in the anthropological study of ritual, which has centered instead on debates between structural and symbolic analyses of the content of ritual action. It has focussed on performitivity in an Austinean[35] sense of what ritual does, and has neglected to study how ritual achieves its effects. The analysis of ritual forms opens avenues to understanding the effect of ritual action on the minds and bodies of the participants. More generally, the failure to acknowledge and investigate the place of the aesthetic in human life has resulted in the neglect of data that can enrich studies of embodiment, of dispositions, of "habitus" – of factors that are now acknowledged to play a crucial role in socio-cultural process and identity formation. One of the most unfortunate consequences of the acceptance of an essentialized definition of art was that it removed art from everyday life, making it epiphenomenal, a mere decorative or aesthetic veneer that social scientists did not have to take seriously into account. Yet for most of human history art has been an essential component of human action. Even in the West, art carried on as a normal part of life in its multiple interventions – as style, as design, as craft, as architecture, as decor, as dress, as bodily adornment, as advertisement and so on. These areas have also tended to be neglected until recently by social scientists perhaps as a consequence of their family resemblance to art, partly because they were simply taken for granted. Now that the significance of this dimension of human action has been realized, an immensely rich field of research has been opened up. Anthropologists are only now beginning to learn how to deal with it analytically. The study of art is essentially an interdisciplinary field that brings together anthropologists, artists, art historians, and social historians in an exciting venture.

NOTES

1 For example, see the essays in Heyd and Clegg (2005) or Morphy 1989 and the number of recent books on Australian Aboriginal rock art (e.g. Layton 1992, and Morwood 2002).

2 We are using "Western" here in a loose sense to refer to Euro-American class based capitalist societies while acknowledging that there is a danger both in essentializing the category of the West and creating an artificially bounded entity in the context of increasing globalization of economies.

3 Marcus and Myers' definition of the modern art world fits our purpose well: "a very specific historically situated art world: namely the contemporary, Western-centered tradition of fine arts that began with the birth of modernism and a transformed art market out of the previously dominant Academy system in nineteenth-century France. This is a world still defined, even with its post-modern attempts at transformation, by the creation of aesthetic experience through the disinterested contemplation of objects as *art* objects removed from their instrumental associations" (1995:3). This system of education has been exported widely, in Africa and Asia, for example, where contemporary artists are trained and often inherit the values of this system.

4 Literati painting refers to both the style and social system in which Chinese ink painting has been produced for more than a thousand years. Central to this system is a distinction between the perceived superiority in technique and intellectual sophistication of paintings done by scholarly amateurs (the literati) as opposed to the paintings produced by professionals for sale (see Cahill 1994 for a nuanced analysis of this system). While the changes in Chinese society during the 20th century have fundamentally altered the social system that produced literati painting, the style is still practiced extensively and has evolved over time. Some contemporary artists and intellectuals, however, have strongly rejected the efforts of those who continue in this style because they consider it to be hopelessly stagnant and irrelevant to contemporary China (see Andrews and Gao 1995).

5 Among the many relevant areas for study are practices in Japan (Moeran 1997), China (Yen 2005), India (Bundgaard 2005; Hart 1995; Pinney 2004), and in Islamic art (George 1998, 1999), as well as anthropological analysis of different Western systems (Marcus 1995, Herzfeld 1990).

6 It is not only in the West that objects are exhibited. This is well illustrated by Daniel Biebuyck in his analysis of Lega sculpture when he writes: "The final initiation takes place when a man is older, wiser, and familiar with all of Bwami visual culture. Therefore, the object combinations hold fewer surprises. The final performance strips away all metaphorical layers. The teacher escorts the initiate into an area where initiation objects are carefully laid out. No explanations are given: the initiate is left to understand the meaning through contemplation of the exhibition" (Biebuyck 1994:42).

7 The scrutiny of indigenous peoples has challenged many museum practices including systems of classification. In the National Museum of the American Indian at the Smithsonian Institution, for example, consultation with the affiliated tribes has resulted in indigenous categories of classification being implemented in the storage and display of objects.

8 For Tylor the development of the arts, whether weapons, pottery, textiles, or architecture, could be "traced along lines of gradual improvement," as in the development of stone age implements: "Beginning with the natural sharp stone, the transition to the rudest artificially shaped stone implement is imperceptibly gradual; and onward from this crude stage...till the manufacture at last arrives at admirable artistic perfection" (1929

[1871]:66–68). The movement from old to new materials and techniques is also anevolu-tionary process: "The keeping up in stone architecture of designs belonging to wooden buildings, furnishes conclusive proofs of growth, in several countries, of the art of building in stone from the art of building in wood" (1964 [1878]:141–142).

9   Pitt Rivers, 1906: plate III, between pages 44–45; accompanying discussion pp. 37–39.

10   Haddon and Start compare the occurrence of particular motifs in Iban textiles with other textile traditions (e.g. Malay), concluding that the distinctiveness of the Iban designs suggests indigenous development "since the Iban became separated from other peoples" (1982 [1936]:137–141).

11   For example, Balfour's analysis of face designs on South American pottery offers a developmental sequence moving from realism to increased decorative effect (1893a: 36–39).

12   See, for example, O'Hanlon and Welsch (2000) on the process and impact of ethno-graphic collection in Melanesia during this time.

13   Spencer's and Gillen's studies of the Arunta and other Aboriginal groups of central and northern Australia included chapters dedicated to "decorative art" and gave attention to designs across forms – on implements and weapons, rock drawings, decoration of cere-monial objects, and ground drawings (Spencer and Gillen, 1904:696–743; 1927:551–578). Other forms of art, such as body decoration, were covered within the analysis of ceremony (e.g. Spencer and Gillen, 1904:177–225).

14   See Radcliffe-Brown, 1968, ch. 10, and 1977, ch. 6.

15   As d'Azevedo puts it "The study of art and other aspects of culture that did not readily fit into the rigors of scientific method were swept out of favor along with Social Darwinism. The reaction against the excesses of nineteenth-century evolutionism, along with the rapid accumulation of new data from comparative ethnology, engen-dered a legitimate distrust of generalizations derived from anticipations of our own culture" (d'Azevedo 1973:2).

16   See Kroeber (1948, ch. 8, 1968 [1952] ch. 36, and 1957); see also Benedict (1934) and Sapir (1951).

17   Rather than focus on the artistic process, Bourdieu saw both the artist and the socially knowledgeable appreciator of art as more or less passive products of "the social norms which combine to define the always uncertain and historically changing frontier between simple technical objects and objets d'art" (1984:29).

18   Including Roger Caillois, Michel Leiris, and the filmmaker Jean Rouch. Marcel Griaule founded the collective French research project on the Dogon people of Mali, Germaine Dieterlen was his main collaborator; see Griaule (1938, 1947, 1970 [1948]); Griaule and Dieterlen (1951); Dieterlen (1941); also Leiris and Delange (1968); Caillois (1962, 1970).

19   See Berndt (1964, 1981; Berndt and Stanton 1980). Mountford collected widely in Australia from the 1930s to the 1950s, including during the 1948 American/Australian scientific expedition to Arnhem Land, see Mountford (1956–64, 1958, 1961).

20   As Michael Young (2004:398) writes of Malinowski: "His interest in arts and crafts ('primitive technology') was principally in their economic and social aspects, and he railed against the 'museum moles' who studied disembodied objects torn from the cultural contexts that gave them life and meaning. Such views were integral to Mal-inowski's temperament. and they are reflected in his earliest thinking about the kind of anthropology that most interested him: 'primitive sociology' rather than 'ethnology' ".

21   e.g. Munn 1986 [1976]; Weiner 1977; Leach and Leach 1982; see also Newton 1975; Norick 1976; Shack 1985; and Macintyre's (1983) bibliography on the Kula.

22   In this book we have largely restricted ourselves to the visual arts both because we argue that they have their own distinctive sets of properties but also because the scope of the book would otherwise be too large. In doing so we hope to have left the space for another set of readings that centers on the musical and performative arts. In leaving this space we

acknowledge that it is one that needs to crossed, redefined and even transgressed, according the categories of particular cultures and the nature of particular genres and media.

23 As exemplified in recent conferences and publications, art historians and artists have been especially active in their efforts to draw upon anthropological knowledge and methodologies (see Perkins 2004 and Westermann 2005).

24 This conversation is exemplified by the range of articles produced by those working across disciplines as featured in journals such as *Res* and *African Arts*.

25 Gell proposes that "the anthropological theory of art does not need to provide a criterion for art object status which is independent of the theory itself. The anthropologist is not obliged to define the art object, in advance, in a way satisfactory to aestheticians, or philosophers, or art historians . . . the theory is premised on the idea that the nature of the art object is a function of the social-relational matrix in which it is embedded. It has no 'intrinsic' nature, independent of the relational context" (Gell 1998: 7).

26 A good discussion of these definitional issues in sympathy with our own approach is provided by d'Azevedo (1973).

27 See Goodman (1969) for an important philosophical approach to the distinctions and relationships between different art forms. In its various forms, an anthropology of the senses (Howes 2003; Taussig 1993) also addresses the relationships between the visual arts and other forms of expressive culture.

28 As d'Azevedo rightly points out "A normative, non-analytic concept of art or the artist, derived from a particular tradition of our own culture, cannot be expected to comprehend either the manifold expressions of artistry in our society or in others any more than the formal tenets and social structure of Protestantism would comprehend the varieties of religious expressions among human groups" (d'Azevedo 1973:9).

29 In Mohawk, for example, there is still no indigenous word for art although the English term is used both for convenience and, to be gracious, as a courtesy to non-Mohawk speakers. There are, however, many terms describing both objects and the processes for making them such as basketry, beadwork and painting. In contrast, there are many words for art in Chinese reflecting the long and nuanced history of indigenous practice in which paintings and other objects, although embedded within complex social systems, have come to be regarded as distinct art objects.

30 The National Gallery has recently unveiled a new approach to Aboriginal art that consists of the entire reconfiguration of the permanent Canadian art galleries to integrate Aboriginal works under the exhibition title, "Art of this Land." For the 1927 exhibition see the catalogue (National Gallery of Canada 1927). For comparative purposes on the reception of Chinese art in Great Britain, see Clunas (ch. 11).

31 Boas (1955[1927]:349) writes: Artistic enjoyment . . . is based essentially on the reaction of our minds to form. The same kind of enjoyment may be released by impressions received from forms that are not the handiwork of man, but they may not be considered art, although the esthetic reaction is not different from the one we receive from the contemplation or the hearing of a work of art. When speaking of artistic production they must be excluded. When considering only esthetic reactions they must be included. See also Coote (ch. 16, this volume); Firth 1992:17–18 and Maquet 1986.

32 Appadurai suggests that, as a category of the intercultural flow of commodities, "ethnic and tourist arts" provide the best example of "the diversities in taste, understanding, and use between producers and consumers . . . tourist art constitutes a special commodity traffic, in which the group identities of producers are tokens for the status politics of consumers" (1986:47).

33 The psychologist Howard Gardner (1988, 1990) has explored the role of art education and the art of children at length. See Becker (1994) and Cahan and Kucor (1996) for inquiries into the relationship between contemporary art and art education. See Herzfeld (2004) for a relevant anthropological analysis of the pedagogical process among artisans and their apprentices in Crete.

34   The role of training is often central to the process of becoming acknowledged as an "artist" in various cultural contexts. Distinctions between skill and training are also related to debates over the term "primitive" and the perceived divisions between fine art and popular forms such as graffiti (see Jarman 1996 for a study that touches on mural art). "Outsider art" has been a term used to describe both the art of the untrained and art produced by the mentally ill (the latter usage being related though distinct from the well-established field of art therapy).

35   The philosopher of language John Austin moved away from an analytical emphasis on meaning in language toward a focus on the performative nature of certain utterances; see Austin 1962.

REFERENCES

Andrews, Julia and Gao Minglu, 1995 The Avant-garde's Challenge to Official Art. In *Urban Spaces: Autonomy and Community in Contemporary China*. Deborah Davis et al., eds. Cambridge: Cambridge University Press.

Appadurai, Arjun, 1986 Introduction: Commodities and the Politics of Value. In *The Social Life of Things: Commodities in Cultural Perspective*. Arjun Appadurai, ed. Cambridge: Cambridge University Press.

Austin, John, 1962 *How to Do Things with Words* (The William James Lectures delivered at Harvard University in 1955), edited by J. O. Urmson. Oxford: Clarendon Press.

Balfour, Henry, 1888 *On the Evolution of a Characteristic Pattern on the Shafts of Arrows from the Solomon Islands*. London: Harrison and Sons.

Balfour, Henry, 1893a *The Evolution of Decorative Art: An Essay upon Its Origin and Development as Illustrated by the Art of Modern Races of Mankind*. London: Rivington, Percival & Co.

Balfour, H., 1897 Notes on the Arrangement of the Pitt Rivers Museum. In Museums Association: Report of Proceedings with the Papers Read at the Eighth Annual General Meeting Held in Oxford – July 6 to 9, 1897. James Paton, ed. Pp. 51–54. London: Dulau and Co.

Balfour, H., 1904 Presidential Address: The Relationship of Museums to the Study of Anthropology. *JAI* 34: 10–19; *Museums Journal* vol. 3, June 1904:396–440.

Banerjee, Mukulika and Daniel Miller, 2003 *The Sari*. Oxford: Berg Publishers.

Bardon, Geoffrey, 1979 *Aboriginal Art of the Western Desert*. Sydney: Rigby.

Becker, Carol, 1994 The Education of Young Artists and the Issue of Audience. In *Between Borders: Pedagogy and the Politics of Cultural Studies*. Henry Giroux and Peter McLaren, eds. London: Routledge.

Benedict, Ruth, 1949[1934] *Patterns of Culture*. London: Routledge.

Berndt, Ronald and J. E. Stanton, 1980 *Australian Aboriginal Art in the Anthropology Museum of the University of Western Australia*. Perth: University of Western Australia Press.

Berndt, Ronald, 1964 *Australian Aboriginal Art*. Sydney: Ure Smith.

Berndt, Ronald 1971 Some Methodological Considerations in the Study of Australian Aboriginal Art. *Oceania* 29:26–43.

Berndt, Ronald, and Catherine H. Berndt with John E. Stanton 1981 *Aboriginal Australian Art: A Visual Perspective* Sydney: Methuen Australia.

Biebuyck, Daniel P. 1994 *La sculpture des Lega*. Paris; New York: Galerie Helene & Philippe Leloup.

Biebuyck, Daniel, 1973 *Lega Culture: Art Initiation, and Moral Philosophy among a Central African People*. Berkeley: University of California Press.

Biebuyck, Daniel, ed. 1969 *Tradition and Creativity in Tribal Art*. Berkeley: University of California Press.

Blackwood, Beatrice, 1970 *The Classification of Artefacts in the Pitt Rivers Museum Oxford.* Oxford: Oxford University Press.

Blier, Suzanne Preston, 1987, The Anatomy of Architecture: Ontology and Metaphor. In *Batammaliba Architectural Expression.* Cambridge: Cambridge University Press.

Boas, Franz, 1955[1927] *Primitive Art.* New York: Dover Publications Inc.

Boone, Sylvia Ardyn, 1986 *The Radiance from the Waters.* New Haven: Yale University Publications in the History of Art.

Bouquet, Mary, 1999 Academic Anthropology and the Museum: Back to the Future. *Focaal* 34:7–20.

Bourdieu, Pierre, 1984 *Distinction: A Social Critique of the Judgement of Taste*, Richard Nice, trans. London: Routledge & Kegan Paul.

Bundgaard, Helle, 2005 Contending Indian Art-Worlds: Patta Chitra Paintings in Orissa. In *Exploring World Art.* Eric Venbrux, Pamela Sheffield Rosi and Robert J. Welsch, eds. Longgrove, IL: Waveland Press.

Bürger, Peter, 1984 *Theory of the Avant-Garde.* Michael Shaw, trans. Minneapolis: University of Minnesota Press.

Cahan, Susan and Zoya Kucor, 1996 *Contemporary Art and Multicultural Education.* New York and London: New Museum of Contemporary Art and Routledge.

Cahill, James, 1994 *The Painter's Practice: How Artists Lived and Worked in Traditional China.* New York: Columbia University Press.

Caillois, Roger, 1962 *Esthétique generalisée.* Paris: Gallimard.

Caillois, Roger, 1970 *L'ecriture des pierres.* Genève: Skira.

Campbell, Shirley F., 2002 *The Art of Kula*, Oxford; New York: Berg.

Clifford, James, 1991 Four North West Coast Museums: Travel Reflections. In *Exhibiting Cultures: The Poetics and Politics of Museum Displays.* Ivan Karp and Steven Levine, eds. Pp. 212–254. Washington: Smithsonian Institution Press.

Coote Jeremy, 1992 Marvels of Everyday Vision. In *Anthropology, Art, and Aesthetics.* Jeremy Coote and Anthony Shelton, eds. Pp. 245–273. Oxford: Clarendon Press.

Coote, Jeremy and Anthony Shelton, eds. 1992 *Anthropology, Art, and Aesthetics.* Oxford: Oxford University Press.

D'Azevedo, Warren, 1973 *The Traditional Artist in African Societies.* Bloomington: University of Indiana Press.

Dieterlen, Germaine, 1941 *Les Ames des Dogons.* Paris: Institut d'Ethnologie (Travaux et mémoires de l'Institut d'ethnologie; no. 40).

Dietler, Michael and Ingrid Herbich, 1998 Habitus, Techniques and Style: An Integrated Approach to the Social Understanding of Material Culture and Boundaries. In *The Archaeology of Social Boundaries.* Miriam T. Stark, ed. Pp. 233–269. Washington: Smithsonian Institution Press.

Dussart, Francoise, 1997 A Body Painting in Translation. In *Rethinking Visual Anthropology.* Marcus Banks and Howard Morphy, eds. Pp. 186–202. New Haven : Yale University Press.

Errington, Shelly, 1998 *The Death of Authentic Primitive Art and Other Tales of Progress.* Berkeley: University of California Press.

Fagg, William, 1964 *Tribes and Forms in African Art.* New York: Tudor.

Fagg, William, 1968 *African Tribal Images: the Katherine White Reswick Collection*, Cleveland: Cleveland Museum of Art.

Fagg, William, 1970 *The Tribal Image: Wooden Figure Sculpture of the World.* London: British Museum Dept of Ethnography.

Fagg, William, 1981 *Yoruba Beadwork: Art of Nigeria*, edited and with a foreword by Bryce Holcombe; descriptive catalogue by John Pemberton, London: Lund Humphries [originally published to accompany an exhibition held at the Pace Gallery, New York].

Fagg, William, 1982 *Yoruba: Sculpture of West Africa*, text by William Fagg; descriptive catalogue by John Pemberton, edited by Bryce Holcombe, London: Collins.

Fardon, Richard 2005 *Fusions: Masquerades and Thought Style East of the Niger Benue Confluence, West Africa*. London: Saffron Books

Feld, Stephen 1982 *Sound and Sentiment: Birds, Weeping, Poetics and Song among the Kaluli*. Philadelphia: University of Philadelphia Press.

Fernandez, James W. 1982 *Bwiti: An Ethnography of the Religious Imagination in Africa*, drawings by Renate Lellep Fernandez. Princeton: Princeton University Press [esp. chapter 15, The Bwiti Chapel: Architectonics, pp. 371–412.]

Fernandez, James W. 1986 *Persuasions and Performances: The Play of Tropes in Culture*. Bloomington: Indiana University Press.

Firth, Raymond, 1979[1936] *Art and Life in New Guinea*. New York: AMS Press.

Firth, Raymond, 1992 Art and Anthropology. In *Anthropology, Art, and Aesthetics*. Jeremy Coote and Anthony Shelton, eds. Pp. 15–39. Oxford: Clarendon Press.

Fischer, J. L., 1961 Art Styles as Cultural Cognitive Maps. *American Anthropologist* 63(1): 79–93.

Forge, Anthony, 1973 Style and Meaning in Sepik Art. In *Primitive Art and Society*. A. Forge, ed. London: Wenner-Gren Foundation and Oxford University Press.

Forge, Anthony, 1979 The Problem of Meaning in Art. In *Exploring the Visual Art of Oceania*. Sidney M. Mead, ed. Honolulu: University Press of Hawaii.

Frazer, James George, 1925 *The Golden Bough: A Study in Magic and Religion*, abridged edition. London: Macmillan.

Fu, Shen C. Y., 1991 *Challenging the Past: The Paintings of Chang Dai-chien*. Washington: Smithsonian Institution Press.

Gardner, Howard, 1988 *To Open Minds: Chinese Clues to the Dilemma of Contemporary Education*. New York: Basic Books.

Gardner, Howard, 1990 *Art Education and Human Development*. Los Angeles: Getty Center for Education in the Arts.

Gell, Alfred, 1992 The Technology of Enchantment and the Enchantment of Technology. In *Anthropology, Art, and Aesthetics*. Jeremy Coote and Anthony Shelton, eds. Pp. 40–63. Oxford: Clarendon Press.

Gell, Alfred, 1998 *Art and Agency: An Anthropological Theory*. Oxford: Clarendon Press.

George, Kenneth M., 1998 Designs on Indonesia's Muslim Communities. *Journal of Asian Studies* 57(3):693–713.

George, Kenneth M., 1999 Signature Work: Bandung, 1994. *Ethnos* 64(2):212–231.

Goodman, Nelson, 1969 *Languages of Art: An Approach to a Theory of Symbols*. London: Oxford University Press

Graburn, Nelson, ed. 1976 *Ethnic and Tourist Arts: Cultural Expressions from the Fourth World*. Berkeley: University of California Press.

Gregory, C. A., 1982 *Gifts and Commodities*. London: Academic Press.

Griaule, Marcel, 1938 Masques Dogon. *Travaux et Mémoires de l'Institut D'Ethnologie*, vol. 33.

Griaule, Marcel, 1947 *Arts de l'Afrique Noire*. Paris: Editions du Chene.

Griaule, Marcel, 1970[1948], *Conversations with Ogotemmêli: An Introduction to Dogon Religious Ideas*, with an introduction by Germaine Dieterlin. London: Oxford University Press for the International African Institute.

Griaule, Marcel and Germaine Dieterlen, 1951 *Signes Graphiques Soudanias*. Paris: Hermann.

Gritton, Joy and Gregory Cajete, 2000 *The Institute of American Indian Arts: Modernism and U.S. Indian Policy*. Santa Fe: University of New Mexico Press.

Haddon, Alfred C. and Laura E. Start, 1982[1936] *Iban or Sea Dayak Fabrics and their Patterns: A Descriptive Catalogue of the Iban Fabrics in the Museum of Archaeology and Ethnology, Cambridge*; with new preface and extended bibliography by D. A. Swallow. Carlton: Ruth Bean.

Haddon, Alfred C., 1894 *The Decorative Art of British New Guinea: A Study in Papuan Ethnography*. Dublin: Royal Irish Academy.

Hart, Lynn M., 1995 Three Walls: Regional Aesthetics and the International Art World. In *The Traffic in Culture: Refiguring Art and Anthropology*. George Marcus and Fred Myers, eds. Pp. 127–150. Berkeley: University of California Press.

Hendrickson, Carol, 1995 *Weaving Identities: Construction of Dress and Self in a Highland Guatemala Town*. Austin: University of Texas Press.

Herskovits, Melville Jean, and Frances S. Herskovits 1934 *The Art of Dahomey*. Washington: American Federation of Arts.

Herskovits, Melville Jean, 1938 Art. In *Dahomey: An Ancient West African Kingdom*. Pp. 311–372. New York: Augustin.

Herskovits, Melville Jean, 1959 Art and Value. In *Aspects of Primitive Art*. R. Redfield, M. J. Herskovits and G. F. Ekholm, eds. Pp. 42–68. New York: Museum of Primitive Art.

Herskovits, Melville Jean, 1966 The Arts. In *The New World Negro: Selected Papers in Afroamerican Studies*. F. S. Herskovits, ed. Pp. 157–197. Bloomington: Indiana University Press.

Herzfeld, Michael, 1990, Icons and Identity: Religious Orthodoxy and Social Practice in Rural Crete. *Anthropological Quarterly* 63(3): 109–121.

Herzfeld, Michael, 2004, *The Body Impolitic: Artisans and Artifice in the Global Hierarchy of Value*. Chicago: University of Chicago Press.

Heusch, Luc de, 1958 *Essais sur le Symbolisme de L'inceste Royal en Afrique*. Bruxelles: Université libre de Bruxwell Institut de Sociologie Solvay.

Heusch, Luc de, c. 1972–c. 1982, *Mythes et Rites Bantous*. Paris: Gallimard.

Heusch, Luc de, c. 1982, *The Drunken King, or, The Origin of the State*, trans. and annotated by Roy Willis. Bloomington: Indiana University Press.

Heyd, Thomas and John Clegg 2005 *The Aesthetics of Rock Art*. Aldershot: Ashgate

Houston, James, 1952 In Search of Eskimo Art. *Canadian Art* 9:5.

Howes, David, 2003 *Sensual Relations: Engaging the Senses in Culture and Social Theory*. Ann Arbor: University of Michigan Press.

Jarman, Neil, 1996 Violent Men, Violent Land: Dramatizing the Troubles and the Landscape of Ulster. *Journal of Material Culture* 1(1):39–61.

Karp, Ivan and Steven D. Levine, eds. 1991 *Exhibiting Cultures: The Poetics and Politics of Museum Display*. Washington: Smithsonian Institution Press.

Karp, Ivan, Steven D. Levine and Christine Mullen Kreamer, eds., 1992 *Museums and Communities: The Politics of Public Culture*. Washington: Smithsonian Institution Press.

Kasfir, S. L., 1984 One Tribe One Style? Paradigms in the Historiography of African Art. *History in Africa* 9:163–193.

Kopytoff, Igor, 1986 The Cultural Biography of Things: Commoditization as Process. In *The Social Life of Things: Commodities in Cultural Perspective*. Arjun Appadurai, ed. Cambridge: Cambridge University Press.

Kratz, Corrine, 1994 *Affecting Performance: Meaning Movement and Experience in Okiek Women's Initiation*. Washington: Smithsonian Institution Press

Kroeber, Alfred Louis, 1948 *Anthropology: Race, Language, Culture, Psychology, Prehistory*. New York: Harcourt, Brace.

Kroeber, Alfred Louis, 1957 *Style and Civilizations*. Ithaca, New York: Cornell University Press.

Kroeber, Alfred Louis, 1968[1952] *The Nature of Culture*. Chicago: University of Chicago Press.

Kubler, George, 1962 *The Shape of Time: Remarks on the History of Things*. New Haven and London: Yale University Press.

Kubler, George, 1979 Towards a Reductive Theory of Visual Style. In *The Concept of Style* B. Lang, ed. Pp. 119–127 Philadelphia: University of Pennsylvania Press.

Küchler, Susanne, 2002 *Malanggan: Art, Memory and Sacrifice*. Oxford: Berg.

Layton, Robert, 1991 *The Anthropology of Art*. Cambridge: Cambridge University Press.

Layton, Robert, 1992 *Australian Rock Art: A New Synthesis*. Cambridge: Cambridge University Press.

Leach, E. R and J. W. Leach, eds. 1982 *The Kula: New Perspectives on Massim Exchange*. Cambridge: Cambridge University Press.

Leiris, Michel and J. Delange, 1968, *African Art*. M. Ross, trans. London: Thames and Hudson.

Macintyre, Martha, 1983 *The Kula: A Bibliography*. Cambridge and New York: Cambridge University Press.

Malinowski, Bronislaw, 1972[1922] *Argonauts of the Western Pacific: An Account of Native Enterprise and Adventure in the Archipelagoes of Melanesian New Guinea*, with a preface by James G. Frazer. London: Routledge & Kegan Paul.

Malinowski, Bronislaw, 1979 *The Ethnography of Malinowski: The Trobriand Islands 1915–18*. Michael W. Young, ed. London: Routledge & Kegan Paul.

Mao Tse-tung, 1967 *Mao Tse-tung on Literature and Art*. Peking: Foreign Language Press.

Maquet, Jacques, 1986 *The Aesthetic Experience: An Anthropologist Looks at the Visual Arts*. New Haven: Yale University Press.

Marcus, George, 1995, The Power of Contemporary Work in an American Art Tradition to Illuminate its Own Power Relations. In *The Traffic in Culture: Refiguring Art and Anthropology*. George Marcus and Fred Myers, eds. Pp. 201–223. Berkeley: University of California Press.

Marcus, George and Fred Myers, eds. 1995 *The Traffic in Culture: Refiguring Art and Anthropology*. Berkeley: University of California Press.

Mauss, Marcel, 1970[1950] *The Gift: Forms and Functions of Exchange in Archaic Societies*. Ian Cunnison, trans. London: Cohen & West.

Miller, Daniel, ed. 2005 *Materiality*. Durham: Duke University Press.

Mills, James Phillip, 1926 *The Ao Nagas*, with a foreword by H. Balfour and supplementary notes and bibliography by J.H. Hutton. London: Macmillan.

Mills, James Phillip, 1937 *The Rengma Nagas*. London: Macmillan.

Moeran, Brian, 1997 *Folk Art Potters of Japan: Beyond an Anthropology of Aesthetics*. London: Routledge.

Morphy, Howard, 1989 *Animals into Art*. London: Routledge.

Morphy, Howard, 1991 *Ancestral Connections: Art and an Aboriginal System of Knowledge*. Chicago: University of Chicago Press.

Morphy, Howard, 1994 The Anthropology of Art. In *Companion Encyclopedia of Anthropology*. Tim Ingold, ed. Pp. 648–685, London: Routledge.

Morphy, Howard, 2001 Seeing Aboriginal Art in the Gallery. *Humanities Research* 8(1):37–50.

Morwood, Michael, 2002 *Visions from the Past: The Archaeology of Australian Aboriginal Art*. Sydney: Allen and Unwin.

Mountford, Charles, 1958 *The Tiwi: Their Art, Myth and Ceremony*. London: Phoenix; Melbourne: Georgian House.

Mountford, Charles, 1961 *Aboriginal Art*. London: Longmans.

Mountford, Charles, ed. 1956–64 *Records of the American-Australian Scientific Expedition to Arnhem Land*. Melbourne: Melbourne University Press.

Munn, Nancy D., 1986[1976] *The Fame of Gawa: A Symbolic Study of Value Transformation in a Massim (Papua New Guinea) Society*. Cambridge and New York: Cambridge University Press.

Munn, Nancy, 1973 *Walbiri Iconography: Graphic Representation and Cultural Symbolism in a Central Australian Society*. Ithaca: Cornell University Press.

Myers, Fred, 2002 *Painting Culture: The Making of an Aboriginal High Art*. Durham: Duke University Press.

National Gallery of Canada, 1927 *Exhibition of Canadian West Coast Art*. Ottawa: National Gallery of Canada.

Newton, Douglas, 1975 *Massim: Art of the Massim Area, New Guinea*. New York: Museum of Primitive Art.

Nordenskiöld, Gustaf, 1973[1893] *The Cliff Dwellers of the Mesa Verde, South Western Colorado: Their Pottery and Implements*, translated by D. Lloyd Morgan, with a new introduction by Watson Smith. New York: AMS Press for Peabody Museum of Archaeology and Ethnology, Harvard University, Cambridge.

Norick, Frank Albert, 1976 An Analysis of the Material Culture of the Trobriand Islands Based upon the Collection of Bronislaw Malinowski, PhD thesis. University of California, Ann Arbor.

O'Hanlon, M., 1995 Communication and Affect in New Guinea Art. *Journal of the Royal Anthropological Institute* 1(4):832–833.

O'Hanlon, Michael and Robert Welsch, eds. 2000 *Hunting the Gatherers: Ethnographic Collectors and Agency in Melanesia, 1870s–1930s*. New York: Berghahn Press.

Penniman, T. K., 1953 The Pitt Rivers Museum. *Museum Journal* 52:243–46.

Penniman, T. K., 1965 *A Hundred Years of Anthropology*, with contributions by B. Blackwood and J. S. Weiner. 3rd edition. London: Duckworth.

Perkins, Morgan, 2001 Re-viewing Traditions: An Anthropological Examination of Contemporary Chinese Art Worlds. Doctoral dissertation, University of Oxford.

Perkins, Morgan, 2004 Anthropologists and Artists Talk. *Anthropology News*, January: 26–28.

Perkins, Morgan, 2005, "Do We Still Have No Word for Art?": A Contemporary Mohawk Question. In *Exploring World Art*. Eric Verbrux, Pamela Sheffield Rosi and Robert L. Welsch., eds. Longgrove, IL: Waveland Press.

Pinney, Christopher, 2004 *"Photos of the Gods:" The Printed Image and Political Struggle in India*. London: Reaktion Books.

Pitt Rivers, Augustus Henry Lane-Fox, 1906 *Evolution of Culture and Other Essays*, J. L. Myres, ed., with an introduction by H. Balfour. Oxford: Clarendon Press.

Price, Sally, 2001[1989] *Primitive Art in Civilized Places*. Chicago: University of Chicago Press.

Radcliffe-Brown, Alfred Reginald, 1927 Margaret Preston and Transition. *Art in Australia*, third series, no. 22, December.

Radcliffe-Brown, Alfred Reginald, 1968[1952] *Structure and Function in Primitive Society: Essays and Addresses by A. R. Radcliffe-Brown*, with a foreword by E. E. Evans-Pritchard and F. Eggan. London: Cohen & West.

Radcliffe-Brown, Alfred Reginald, 1977, *The Social Anthropology of Radcliffe-Brown*. Adam Kuper, ed. London: Routledge & Kegan Paul.

Rattray, Robert Sutherland, 1954 *Religion and Art in Ashanti*, with chapters by G. T. Bennett. London: Oxford University Press.

Redfield, Robert, M. J. Herskovits and G. F. Ekholm, 1959 *Aspects of Primitive Art*. New York: Museum of Primitive Art.

Sapir, Edward, 1951 *Selected Writings of Edward Sapir in Language, Culture and Personality*. D. G. Mandelbaum, ed. Berkeley: University of California Press.

Scoditti, Giancarlo, 1990 *Kitawa: A Linguistic and Aesthetic Analysis of Visual Art in a Melanesian Society*. Berlin: Mouton de Gruyter.

Shack, William A., 1985 *The Kula: A Bronislaw Malinowski Centennial Exhibition*, Berkeley: Robert H. Lowie Museum of Anthropology.

Spencer, Baldwin and F. J. Gillen, 1904 *The Northern Tribes of Central Australia*. London: Macmillan.

Spencer, Baldwin and F. J. Gillen, 1927 *The Arunta: A Study of a Stone Age People*. London: Macmillan.

Steinen, Karl von den, 1969[1925–28], *Die Marquesaner und ihre Kunst: Studien über die Entwicklung primitiver Sudseeornamentik nach eigenen Reiseergebnissen und dem Material der Mussen*. Reprint of 1925–28 edition. New York: Hacker Art Books.

Steinen, Karl von den, c. 1988 *Von den Steinen's Marquesan Myths*. Marta Langridge, trans. Jennifer Terrell, ed. Canberra: Target Oceania/*The Journal of Pacific History*. [Available from *The Journal of Pacific History*, c/-Dept. of Pacific and South East Asian History, Australian National University, Canberra ACT 2600].

Steiner, Christopher, 1994 *African Art in Transit*. Cambridge: Cambridge University Press.

Sullivan, Michael, 1974 *The Three Perfections: Chinese Painting, Poetry and Calligraphy.* London: Thames and Hudson.

Svašek, Maruška, 1997 Identity and Style in Ghanaian Artistic Discourse. In *Contesting Art: Art, Politics and Identity in the Modern World.* Jeremy MacClancy, ed. Oxford: Berg.

Taussig, Michael, 1993 *Mimesis and Alterity: A Particular History of the Senses.* London: Routledge.

Taylor, Luke, 1996 *Seeing the Inside: Bark Painting in Western Arnhem Land.* Oxford: Clarendon Press.

Tedlock, Barbara, 1995 Aesthetics and Politics: Zuni War God Repatriation and Katchina Representation. In *Looking High and Low: Art and Cultural Identity.* Brenda Jo Bright and Liza Bakewell, eds. Pp. 151–172. Tucson: University of Arizona Press.

Thomas, Nicholas, 1991 *Entangled Objects: Exchange, Material Culture, and Colonialism in the Pacific.* Cambridge, MA: Harvard University Press.

Thomas, Nicholas, and Diane Losche, eds. 1999 *Double Vision: Art Histories and Colonial Histories in the Pacific.* Cambridge and Melbourne: Cambridge University Press.

Turner, Victor, 1973 *The Forest of Symbols: Aspects of Ndembu Ritual.* Ithaca: Cornell University Press.

Turner, Victor, 1986 *The Anthropology of Performance,* New York: PAJ Publications.

Tylor, Edward Burnett, 1929[1871] *Primitive Culture: Researches into the Development of Mythology, Philosophy, Religion, Language, Art and Custom.* 5th edition. London: J. Murray.

Tylor, Edward Burnett, 1964[1878] *Researches into the Early History of Mankind and the Development of Civilisation,* edited and abridged with an introduction by Paul Bohannan. Chicago: University of Chicago Press.

Van Damme, Wilfried, 2003 Anthropologies of Art. *International Journal of Anthropology* 18(4): 231–244.

Vinograd, Richard, 1991 Private Art and Public Knowledge in Later Chinese Painting. In *Images of Memory: On Remembering and Representation.* Susanne Küchler and Walter Melion, eds. Pp. 176–204. Washington and London: Smithsonian Institution Press.

Vogel, Susan 1991 Always True to the Object in Our Fashion. In *Exhibiting Cultures: The Poetics and Politics of Museum Display.* Ivan Karp and Steven D. Levine, eds. Washington: Smithsonian Institution Press.

Webb, Virginia-Lee, 1995 Modern Times: Early Tribal Art Exhibitions at the Museum of Modern Art in New York, 1935–1946 *Tribal Arts* spring:30–40.

Westermann, Mariët, ed. 2005 *Anthropologies of Art.* Williamstown, MA: Sterling and Francine Clark Art Institute.

Weiner, Annette B., 1977 *Women of Value, Men of Renown: New Perspectives in Trobriand Exchange.* St. Lucia: University of Queensland Press.

Witherspoon, Gary, 1977 *Language and Art in the Navaho Universe.* Ann Arbor: University of Michigan Press.

Yen, Yuehping, 2005 *Calligraphy and Power in Contemporary Chinese Society.* London: Routledge.

Young, Michael, 2004 *Malinowski: Odyssey of an Anthropologist.* New Haven: Yale University Press.

Part I

Foundations and Framing the Discipline

Introduction

The texts we have included in this part are the relatively recent foundations of a recognizable contemporary anthropology of art. We make no attempt to cover the early history of writings about non-European art, to examine the place of art in evolutionist theories, to summarize the debates between the diffusionists and the evolutionists, or probe the relationship between the anthropology of art and the culture history school or the technique and form theories of Semper (1989). A number of these issues have indeed been addressed in our general introduction. The essays in this part are foundational in the sense that many of the current themes and debates in the anthropology of art are foreshadowed in them. From the dates of the essays in this section the part could almost be titled the late foundations.

The earliest essays are excerpts from Franz Boas's *Primitive Art*. This book was first published in 1927, but was based on earlier research and writings. It is often credited as being the most synthetic of his writings (Wax 1956). As often with his work, the detailed exemplification obscures the coherent development of his argument. *Primitive Art* is interlaced with critical asides that challenge the presuppositions of evolutionary theorists. Boas engaged with the core arguments of art historians of the time concerning such issues as the relationship between designs and technical processes and the relationship between geometric and figurative representations. He examined "the theory that all artistic representation is by origin naturalistic and that geometricization grows up only when the artist tries to introduce ideas that are not inherent in the object itself." He concluded that this "cannot be maintained, because realistic representation and geometric representation spring from distinctive sources" (Boas 1927:351). Boas's writing on art emphasized the formal, technical and aesthetic dimensions, and his work is frustrating for those who want to explore the meaning of Northwest Coast art in context (but see the Rosman and Rubel chapter and Jonaitis chapter).

Boas's approach (ch. 1) provided a firm link with the art discourse of the 19th century but at the same time made art relevant to the anthropologists who followed him by freeing it from simple deterministic theories. He inspired students such as Herskovits, Mead and Kroeber to include art and aesthetics as an integral part of their data and yet also enabled anthropology to remain relevant to art-historical discourse though his emphasis on style. Boas was attuned to the role of individual creativity in art and at the same time sensitive to the role that technique and skill play in habituating artists to a particular form of bodily practice. But it is not so much that contemporary theories are latent in Boas's work – it is more accurate to say that the range of his research topics and the questions that were left open by his open ended and somewhat atheoretical empiricism were a stimulus to the development of contemporary theories.

The readings selected for this part illustrate the wide range of approaches adopted by anthropologists interested in art. Raymond Firth maintained a strong interest in indigenous art throughout his long life, writing on Maori and New Guinea (Firth 1936) art early on in his career and later producing more synthetic analyses (e.g. Firth 1992). In Tikopia, Firth, an anthropologist with a great personal interest in art, found himself – ironically – working in a society with very limited plastic arts though a rich heritage of music, song, poetry, and dance. However, in his analysis of headrests Firth shows how aesthetic values extend beyond works of art to material culture objects in general (c.f. Coote's chapter (16)). Firth has something in common with Boas in his meticulous analysis of form and his attention to technique and stylistic detail. Firth's is a study of quality both in terms of skill and craftsmanship but also in the sense later developed by Munn (Munn 1986) using Peirce's concept of the qualisign. Firth connects the energy invested in the production of headrests to the structure of Tikopean society. There is almost a dialogic relationship between the form and composition of the headrests and structural features of Tikopean gender relations and social hierarchy.

Lévi-Strauss's important analysis (ch. 2) of split representation also concerns the relationship between the form of art and structural features of society. The chapter is an exemplar of his structuralist method and from that perspective is highly theoretical. Yet it also has Boasian associations. Not only does Lévi-Strauss base his analysis partly on Boas's Kwakiutl (Kwakwaka'wakw) data, he takes up a problem of interpretation highlighted by Boas and he too pays close attention to the relationship between technique, surface and form. But in analyzing the data he does precisely what Boas avoids: he attempts to explain the representations by seeking relationships between apparently disparate kinds of data and drawing connections between different levels of analysis, between the form of art objects and structural features of society.

Bateson's chapter (4) is equally bold and fundamentally comparative in intent though he exemplifies his argument with an analysis of a Balinese painting. Bateson applies to art a model drawn from communication theory, a model connected to structuralism through its emphasis on underlying structures and transformation. He presents a theory of art that locates it as a mode of communication separate to that of everyday language, allowing artists and their audiences to engage, often unconsciously, with important themes that connect human beings together and with the deep and fundamental issues of their lives. Bateson's approach to art is multilayered, focussing equally on the relationship between skill and pattern in the creation of aesthetic effect and on the domain of meaning. Bateson's chapter is inspirational rather than being a totally convincing analysis of Balinese painting: it poses fundamental questions about the kind of objects art objects are, and the possibility of cross-cultural communication through art, and opens up avenues for research. Bateson would almost certainly have appreciated Lévi-Strauss's heartfelt cry "These [comparative] studies have been jeopardized even more by intellectual pharisees who prefer to deny obvious relationships because science does not yet provide an adequate method for their interpretation" (ch. 4, p. 57). Forge's writings, though much more grounded in detailed ethnography than Bateson's analysis, cover very much the same terrain. Forge was the first British anthropologist to focus primarily on art. At the center of Forge's analysis of Abelam art is the relationship between style and meaning, concepts that link his work both to interests of art history and the symbolic anthropology of the 1960s (see e.g. Forge 1973). In contrast to societies such as the Northwest Coast (see chapters by Rosman and Rubel (19) and Jonaitis (20)) or the Yolngu of northern Australia (see Morphy chapter (17)) the Abelam lack a tradition of exegesis. Forge sought the underlying meanings of Abelam art through analyzing relationships between the formal elements and by placing the art in its social and religious context (see also Losche 2001 for a complementary analysis). In his chapter (6) Forge provides a rich ethnography of the Abelam artist at work and engages with issues of individuality, stylistic continuity, and change.

William Fagg's chapter (3) is also concerned as much with individuality as it is with definition of stylistic areas, even though, ostensibly, the aim of the book it introduces is to depict the typical styles of different African tribes by selecting representative art objects. The one tribe–one style approach to African art has been justly criticized by Kasfir (1984). However, in reading Fagg it is important to bear in mind who his audience was. Fagg's chapter is directed against the ethnocentrism of European art history and the status given to the European canon. His aim was to show the diversity of African art by representing each tribe as a potential nation with Africa having a heritage of artistic expression every bit as complex and diverse as that of Europe. The works selected were tokens for difference. In much of his work Fagg was indeed concerned to emphasize the individual nature of artistic creativity. Towards the end of his life the identification of the individual hand that distinguished one set of Yoruba carvings from another became a major focus of his research. However there is unquestionably a contradiction between the roles given to tribal style and to individual creativity that remains unresolved in Fagg's writing. While he emphasizes that the tribes have fuzzy boundaries, change over time, and mix together at the edges, they are still there as an important framework to explain difference. The problem is to see the patterns in art history, regional aspects to the distribution of styles, the relationships between art forms and society, the relationships between forms of art and temporality, without looking for a single explanatory framework and trying to contain all variation within little typological boxes. Style and identity, traditions of practice, forms of social organisation, religious systems, and regimes of meaning and value, are all structuring components of human action and it is essential that the explanation of form in art be approached from a diversity of perspectives. Fagg is unlikely to have disagreed.

Many of the topics of the anthropology of art reflect wider debates within the discipline and are subject to the same cumulative processes of understanding. These include the issue of group definition, the relationship between cultural process and individual agency, the nature of language, and the concept of structure, and so on. Art has been a productive arena for debating these core themes but the anthropology of art has also created its own discourse. Anthropologists writing about art have had two quite different audiences in mind. On the one hand, they have been concerned to challenge the presuppositions of the Western art audience for Indigenous art and to use art as a means of extending cross-cultural discourse. On the other, they have been concerned to demonstrate to their fellow anthropologists the validity of the concept of art for cross-cultural analysis and the contribution its analysis can make to anthropological research and understanding. The anthropology of art has maintained a broadly comparative perspective, perhaps in part because the issue of relativism versus universalism is deeply embedded in discourse over aesthetics. All the authors in this part are concerned with the relationship between pattern, style, structure and individual creativity; all are attuned to the analysis of form. All are people who are passionately interested in art and are attuned to the possibility of universals perhaps because they sense that aesthetic values are widely shared across cultures.

REFERENCES

Boas, Franz, 1927 *Primitive Art*. Oslo: Instituttet for Sammenlignende Kulturforskning.

Kasfir, Sydney, 1984 One Tribe One Style? Paradigms in the Historiography of African Art. *History in Africa* 9:163–193.

Losche, Diane, 2001 Anthony's Feast: the Gift in Abelam Aesthetics. *Australian Journal of Anthropology* 12(2): 155–165.

Firth, Raymond, 1936 *Art and Life in New Guinea*. London: Studio.

Firth, Raymond, 1992 Art and Anthropology. In *Anthropology, Art and Aesthetics*. Jeremy Coote and Anthony Shelton, eds. Pp. 15–39. Oxford: Clarendon Press.

Forge, Anthony, 1973 Style and Meaning in Sepik Art. In *Primitive Art and Society*. Anthony Forge ed. Pp. 169–192. London: Wenner-Gren Foundation and Oxford University Press.

Munn, Nancy, 1986 *The Fame of Gawa*. Cambridge: Cambridge University Press.

Semper, Gottfried 1989 *The Four Elements of Architecture & Other Essays*. Harry Mallgrave and Wolfgang Herrmann, trans. Cambridge: Cambridge University Press.

Wax, Murray, 1956 The Limitations of Boas' Anthropology, *American Anthropologist*, 58: 63–74.

1

Primitive Art

Franz Boas

The general principles discussed in the preceding chapters, may now be elucidated by a discussion of the style of the decorative art of the Indians of the North Pacific Coast of North America.

Two styles may be distinguished: the man's style expressed in the art of wood carving and painting and their derivatives; and the woman's style which finds expression in weaving, basketry, and embroidery.

The two styles are fundamentally distinct. The former is symbolic, the latter formal. The symbolic art has a certain degree of realism and is full of meaning. The formal art has, at most, pattern names and no especially marked significance.

We shall discuss the symbolic art first. Its essential characteristics are an almost absolute disregard of the principles of perspective, emphasis of significant symbols and an arrangement dictated by the form of the decorative field.

While the Eskimo of Arctic America, the Chukchee and Koryak of Siberia, the Negroes and many other people use carvings in the round which serve no practical ends, but are made for the sake of representing a figure, – man, animal, or supernatural being, – almost all the work of the Indian artist of the region that we are considering serves at the same time a useful end. When making simple totemic figures, the artist is free to shape his subjects without adapting them to the forms of utensils, but owing to their large size, he is limited by the cylindrical form of the trunk of the tree from which they are carved. The native artist is almost always restrained by the shape of the object to which the decoration is applied.

The technical perfection of carvings and paintings, the exactness and daring of composition and lines prove that realistic representations are not beyond the powers of the artist. This may also be demonstrated by a few exquisite examples of realistic carvings. The helmet shown in figure 1.1 is decorated with the head of an old man affected with partial paralysis. Undoubtedly this specimen must be considered a portrait head. Nose, eyes, mouth and the general expression, are highly characteristic. In a mask (figure 1.2) representing a dying warrior, the artist has shown faithfully the wide lower jaw, the pentagonal face, and the strong nose of the Indian. The relaxing muscles of mouth and tongue, the drooping eyelids, and the motionless eyeballs, mark the agonies of death. Figure 1.3 represents a recent carving, a human figure of rare excellence. Posture and drapery are free of all the formal characteristics of North West coast style. Only the treatment of the eye and the facial painting betray its ethnic origin. Here belongs also the realistic head previously referred to, made by the Kwakiutl Indians of Vancouver Island

From *Primitive Art* (New York: Dover, 1955), pp. 183–188, 218–219, 222–230, 239–240, 251–255, 279–281.

Figure 1.1 Tlingit helmet

Figure 1.2 Mask representing dying warrior, Tlingit

Figure 1.3 Carved figure, British Columbia

(figure 1.4), which is used in a ceremony and intended to deceive the spectators who are made to believe that it is the head of a decapitated dancer.

When the artist desires realistic truth he is quite able to attain it. This is not often the case; generally the object of artistic work is decorative and the representation follows the principles developed in decorative art.

When the form of the decorative field permits, the outline of the animal form is retained. The size of the head is generally stressed as against that of the body and of the limbs. Eyes and eyebrows, mouth and nose are given great prominence. In almost all cases the eyebrows have a standardized form, analogous to that in which the Indian likes to trim his own eyebrows, – with a sharp edge on the rim of the orbits, and a sharp angle in the upper border, the brows being widest at a point a little outward from the center, tapering to the outer and inner angles and ending quite abruptly at both ends. The eye is also standardized. In many cases it consists of two outer curves which indicate the borders of the upper and lower eyelids. A large inner circle represents the eyeball. The lip lines are always distinct and border a mouth which is given an extraordinary width. Generally the lips are opened wide

Figure 1.5 Carvings representing the beaver, from models of Haida totem poles carved in slate

Figure 1.4 Carved head used in ceremonial, Kwakiutl Indians

enough to show the teeth or the tongue. Cheeks and forehead are much restricted in size. The trunk is not elaborated. The ears of animals rise over the forehead (Figure 1.5). These are almost always applied in reproductions of mammals and birds, while they are generally missing in those of the whale, killer-whale, shark and often also of the sculpin. The human ear is represented in its characteristic form, on a level with the eye (figure 1.6). Whales and fish often have round eyes, but exceptions occur (figure 1.26).

For clear presentation of the principles of this art it seems advantageous to treat the symbolism and the adjustment of the animal form to the decorative field before taking up the purely formal elements.

Figure 1.5a is a figure from the model of a totem pole, which represents the beaver. Its face is treated somewhat like a human face, particularly the region around eyes and nose. The position of the ears, however, indicates an animal head. The two large incisors serve to identify the rodent par excellence, – the

Figure 1.6 Mask with eyebrows symbolizing the squid, Tlingit

beaver. The tail is turned up in front of the body. It is ornamented by cross-hatchings which represent the scales on the beaver's tail. In its forepaws it holds a stick. The nose is short and forms a sharp angle with the forehead. The nostrils are large and indicated by spirals. The large incisors, the tail with cross-hatchings, the stick, and the form of the nose are symbols of the beaver and the first two of these are sufficient characteristics of the animal.

Figure 1.5b is another representation of a beaver from the model of a totem pole. It resembles the former one in all details, except that the stick is missing. The beaver is merely holding its three-toed forepaws raised to the chin. In other carvings the beaver is shown with four or five toes, but the symbols described here never vary.

On the handle of a spoon (figure 1.7), the head and forepaws of the beaver are shown; and in its mouth are indicated an upper pair of incisors, all the other teeth being omitted. The scaly tail is shown on the back of the spoon. The nose differs from the one previously described only in the absence of the spiral development of the nostril. Its form and size agree with the preceding specimens.

In the centre of the front of a dancing headdress (figure 1.8), a beaver is represented in squatting position. The symbols mentioned before will be recognized here. The face is human, but the ears, which rise over the forehead, indicate that an animal is meant. Two large pairs of incisors occupy the center of the open mouth. The tail, with cross-hatchings, is turned up in front of the body, and appears between the two hind legs. The forepaws are raised to the height of the mouth, but they do not hold a stick (for additional representations of the beaver see figures 1.26, 1.29, 1.30,

Figure 1.8 Headdress representing beaver; a dragonfly is shown on the chest of the beaver, Haida

1.31). The nose is short, with large round nostrils and turns abruptly into the forehead. On the chest of the beaver another head is represented over which a number of small rings stretch upward. This animal represents the dragon-fly, which is symbolized by a large head and a slender segmented body. Its feet extend from the corners of its mouth towards the haunches of the beaver. Its face resembles a human face; but the two ears, which rise over the eyebrows, indicate that an animal is meant. In many representations of the dragon-fly there are two pairs of wings attached to the head. Combinations of two animals similar to the present one are found frequently, as in figures 1.14 and 1.19.

In a painting from a Kwakiutl housefront (figure 1.9), which was made for me by an Indian from Fort Rupert, the large head with the incisors will be recognized. The scaly tail appears under the mouth. The broken lines (1) around the eyes, indicate the hair of the beaver. The design on each cheek (3) the bones of the face, the high point of the nose (2) its sudden turn. The nostrils are large and round as in the specimens described before. Under the corners of the mouth are the feet. The meaning of the two ornaments over the head is doubtful.

[...]

Having thus become acquainted with a few of the symbols of animals, we will next investigate in what manner the native artist adapts the animal form to the object he intends to decorate. First of all, we will direct our attention to a series of specimens which show that

Figure 1.7 Carving from handle of spoon representing beaver, Tlingit

Figure 1.9 Painting for a house-front placed over the door, representing the beaver, Kwakiutl Indians

he endeavors, whenever possible, to represent the whole animal on the object that he desires to decorate.

[...]

Figure 1.10 represents a dish in the shape of a seal. The whole dish is carved in the form of the animal; but the bottom, which corresponds to the belly, is flattened, and the back is hollowed out so as to form the bowl of the dish. In order to gain a wider rim the whole back has been distended so that the animal becomes inordinately wide as compared to its length. The flippers are carved in their proper positions at the sides of the dish. The hind flippers are turned back, and join the tail closely. A similar method of representation is used in decorating small boxes. The whole box is considered as representing an animal. The front of the body is painted or carved on the box front; its sides, on the sides of the box; the hind side of the body, on the back of the box (see figure 1.11). The bottom of the box is the animal's stomach; the top, or the open upper side, its back. These boxes are bent of a single piece of wood and are represented here unbent.

In the decoration of silver bracelets a similar principle is followed, but the problem differs somewhat from that offered in the decoration of square boxes. While in the latter case the four edges make a natural division between the four views of the animal, – front and right profile, back and left profile, – there is no such sharp line of division in the round bracelet, and there would be great difficulty in joining the four aspects artistically, while profiles offer no such difficulty. This is the method of representation adopted by the native artists (figure 1.12). The animal is imagined cut in two from head to tail, so that the two halves cohere only at the tip of the nose and at the tip of the tail. The hand is put through this hole, and the animal now surrounds the wrist. In this position it is represented on the bracelet. The method adopted is

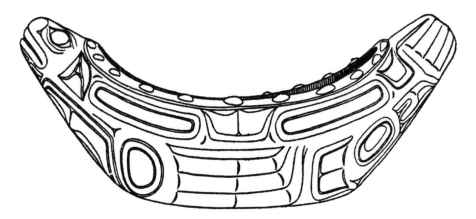

Figure 1.10 Grease dish representing seal

Figure 1.11 Carved trays

Figure 1.12 Design on a bracelet representing a bear, Nass River Indians

therefore identical with the one applied in the hat (figure 1.13), except that the central opening is much larger, and that the animal has been represented on a cylindrical surface, not on a conical one.

An examination of the head of the bear shown on the bracelet (figure 1.12), makes it clear that this idea has been carried out rigidly. It will be noticed that there is a deep depression between the eyes, extending down to the nose. This shows that the head itself must not be considered a front view, but as consisting of two profiles which adjoin at mouth and nose, while they are not in contact with each other on a level with the eyes and forehead. The peculiar ornament rising over the nose of the bear, decorated with three rings, represents a hat with three rings which designate the rank of the bearer.

We have thus recognized that the representations of animals on dishes and bracelets (and we may include the design on the hat, figure 1.13) must not be considered as perspective views, but as representing complete animals more or less distorted and split.

The transition from the bracelet to the painting or carving of animals on a flat surface is

Figure 1.13 Wooden hat with carving representing sculpin

not a difficult one. The same principle is adhered to; and either the animals are represented as split in two so that the profiles are joined in the middle, or a front view of the head is shown with two adjoining profiles of the body. In the cases considered heretofore the animal was cut through and through from the mouth to the tip of the tail. These points were allowed to cohere, and the animal was stretched over a ring, a cone, or the sides of a prism. If we imagine the bracelet opened, and flattened in the manner in which it is shown in figure 1.12, we have a section of the animal from mouth to tail, cohering only at the mouth, and the two halves spread over a flat surface. This is the natural development of the method here described when applied to the decoration of flat surfaces.

It is clear that on flat surfaces this method allows of modifications by changing the method of cutting. When the body of a long animal, such as that of a fish or of a standing quadruped, is cut in this manner, a design results which forms a long narrow strip. This mode of cutting is therefore mostly applied in the decoration of long bands. When the field that is to be decorated is more nearly square, this form is not favorable. In such cases a square design is obtained by cutting quadrupeds sitting on their haunches in the same manner as before, and unfolding the animal so that the two halves remain in contact at the nose and mouth, while the median line at the back is to the extreme right and to the extreme left.

Figure 1.14 (a Haida painting) shows a design which has been obtained in this manner. It represents a bear. The enormous breadth of mouth observed in these cases is brought about by the junction of the two profiles of which the head consists.

This cutting of the head is brought out most clearly in the painting, figure 1.15, which also represents the bear. It is the painting on the front of a Tsimshian house, the circular hole in the middle of the design being the door of the house. The animal is cut from back to front, so that only the front part of the head coheres. The two halves of the lower jaw do not touch each other. The back is represented by the black outline on which the hair is indicated by fine lines. The Tsimshian call such a design "bears meeting", as though two bears had been represented.

In a number of cases the designs painted on hats must also be explained as formed by the junction of two profiles. This is the case in the painted wooden hat (figure 1.16), on which the design of a sculpin is shown. It will be noticed that only the mouth of the animal

Figure 1.14 Painting representing bear, Haida

Figure 1.15 Painting from a house-front representing a bear, Tsimshian

coheres, while the eyes are widely separated. The spines rise immediately over the mouth. The flippers are attached to the corners of the face, while the dorsal fin is split into halves, each half being joined to an eye.

Figure 1.16 Wooden hat with the design of a sculpin, Haida

The beaver (figure 1.17) has been treated in the same manner. The head is split down to the mouth, over which rises the hat with four rings. The split has been carried back to the tail, which, however, is left intact, and turned up towards the centre of the hat. The importance of the symbols becomes very clear in this specimen. If the two large black teeth which are seen under the four rings, and the tail with the cross-hatchings, were omitted, the figure would represent the frog.

In other designs the cut is made in the opposite direction from the one described heretofore. It passes from the chest to the back, and the animal is unfolded so that the two halves cohere along the middle line of the back. This has been done in the Haida tattooings, figures 1.18 and 1.19, the former representing the duck, the latter the raven. In both the tail is left intact. The duck has been split along the back so that the two halves of the body do not cohere except in their lowest portions, while the two halves of the raven are left in contact up to the head.

Figure 1.20 is a dancing-apron woven from mountain-goat wool, and fastened to a large piece of leather, the fringes of which are set with puffin beaks. The woven design represents the beaver. Its symbols, the two pairs of incisors and the scaly tail, are clearly represented. While in most carvings and paintings the tail is turned upward in front of the body, it is hanging down here between the two feet. The meaning of the ornaments in the upper part of the apron to the right and to the left of the head is not quite clear to me, but, if they are significant at all, I believe they must be considered as the back of the body split and folded along the upper margin of the blanket. If this explanation is correct, we have to

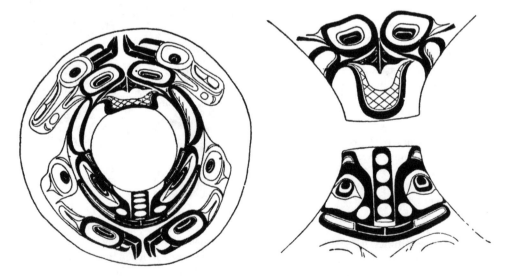

Figure 1.17 Hat made of spruce roots painted with design of a beaver, Haida or Tsimshian

Figure 1.18 Tattooing representing a duck, Haida

Figure 1.19 Tattooing representing a raven, Haida

consider the animal cut into three pieces, one cut running along the sides of the body, the other one along the back.

Figure 1.21 shows the design on a leather legging, a beaver squatting on a human head. In this specimen we observe that the proportions of the body have been much distorted owing to the greater width of the legging at its upper part. The head has been much enlarged in order to fill the wider portion of the decorative field.

The gambling-leather (figure 1.22) is treated in a similar manner. It represents the

beaver, and must probably be explained as the animal cut in two. The symbols, – the large incisors and a scaly tail, – appear here as in all other representations of the beaver, but the lower extremities have been omitted. It might seem that this design could be explained as well as a front view of the animal, but the deep depression between the two eyes is not in favor of this assumption. The head consists undoubtedly of two profiles, which join at the nose and mouth; but the cut has not been continued to the tail, which remains intact.

Figure 1.23 is one of a pair of leggings embroidered with quills on a piece of leather. The design, which represents the sea-monster, must also be explained as a representation of the animal split along its lower side, and flattened. In the lower portion of the legging the two profiles are seen, which are joined on a level with the eyes, while the two mouths are separated. The nostrils are shown in the small triangle below the line connecting the two eyes. Owing to the shape of the legging, the arms are not attached to the body, but to the upper part of the head. They appear at the right and left borders of the legging, and are turned inward along the lower jaws, the three-toed paws touching the lower border. The fins, which are supposed to grow out of the upper part of the arms, adjoin the elbows, and are turned upward. Another pair of fins, which do not appear in most representations of this monster, are attached to the upper part of the back, and form the two flaps to the right and left of the upper margin. On the back we see a series of circles, which probably represent the dorsal fin. The tail occupies the centre of the upper margin. The smaller ornaments in the outside corners of the head, adjoining the mouth, probably represent the gills.

In the following figures we find a new cut applied. Figures 1.24 and 1.25 represent the shark. I explained, when discussing the symbols of the shark, that in the front view of the animal the symbols are shown to best advantage. For this reason side views of the face of the shark are avoided, and in representing the whole animal a cut is made from the back to the lower side, and the two sides are unfolded, leaving the head in front view.

The painting (figure 1.24) has been made in this manner, the two halves of the body being

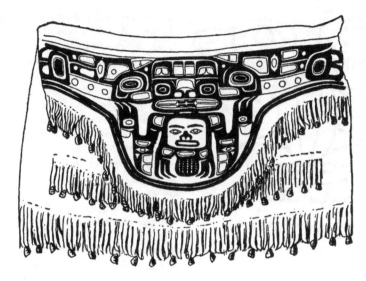

Figure 1.20 Dancing-apron woven of mountain-goat wool, design representing a beaver, Tsimshian

Figure 1.21 Painted legging with design representing a beaver sitting on a man's head, Haida

Figure 1.22 Gambling-leather with engraved design representing a beaver, Tlingit

entirely separated from each other, and folded to the right and to the left. The heterocerc tail is cut in halves, and is shown at each end turned downward. The pectoral fins are unduly enlarged, in order to fill the vacant space under the head.

The shark which is shown in figure 1.25 is treated in a slightly different manner. Again the head is left intact. The cut is made from back to chest, but the two halves of the animal are not separated. They cohere at the chest, and are unfolded in this manner, so that the pectoral fins and dorsal fins appear to the right and left of the body. The heterocerc tail is not clearly indicated in this specimen.

The method of section applied in figure 1.26 is still different. The figure represents a painting on the border of a large skin blanket. The

Figure 1.23 Embroidered legging representing a sea-monster with a bear's head and body of a killer-whale, Haida

animal here represented is the killer-whale. The upper painting clearly represents the profile of the animal. The lower painting represents the other profile, so that both the right and the left halves are visible. Since there was no room for showing the dorsal fin on the lower painting, it is indicated by a curved line on one of the series of wider fringes at the lower border. It is remarkable that the tails in the two halves of the animal are not drawn symmetrically; but it is possible that this is due to a mistake on the part of the painter, because the design is repeated on the opposite border of the blanket in the same manner, but with symmetrical tails. The two halves of the body differ in details, but their main features are identical. The flipper is shown on a very large scale. It is attached immediately behind the head, and extends to a point near the tail. Its principal part is occupied by a face, in front of which an eye is shown. [...]

Figure 1.27 is a copy of a painting on the front of a box, made on paper with colored crayons by a Haida Indian named Wiha. It represents a frog. By far the greater portion of the box-front is occupied by the head of the animal, which, according to what was said before, must be considered as consisting of two adjoining profiles. The symbol of the frog's head is its toothless mouth. The two black portions extending downward from the lower corners of the face are two halves of the body. To these are joined the fore paws, which occupy the space below the mouth; the upper arm and fore arm being turned inward, the fore feet being turned outward under the arm. The hind legs occupy the lateral field on both sides of the head. They are not connected in any way with the body of the animal.

In figure 1.28 we find a novel representation of the killer-whale, which was given to me as illustrating the painting on a house of the Kwa-

Figure 1.24 Painting representing a dog-fish, Haida

Figure 1.25 Slate dish design representing a shark, Haida

kiutl Indians. The sections that have been used here are quite complicated. First of all, the animal has been split along its whole back towards the front. The two profiles of the head have been joined, as described before. The painting on each side of the mouth represent gills, thus indicating that a water-animal is meant. The dorsal fin, which according to the methods described heretofore would appear on both sides of the body, has been cut off from the back before the animal was split, and appears now placed over the junction of the two profiles of the head. The flippers are laid along the two sides of the body with which they cohere only at one point each. The two halves of the tail have been twisted outward so that the lower part of the figure forms a straight line. This is done in order to fit it over the square door of the house.

Figure 1.26 Painting on edge of a blanket representing a killer-whale, Tlingit

Figure 1.27 Painting for a box front, design representing a frog, Haida

Figure 1.28 Painting for a house-front, design representing a killer-whale, Kwakiutl

In figure 1.29 the same animal has been treated in still a different manner. The figure illustrates also the painting from a house-front of the Kwakiutl Indians. The central parts of the painting are the two profiles of the head of the killer-whale. The notch in the lower jaw indicates that it also has been cut, and joined in its central part. The cut on the upper part of the face has been carried down to the upper lip. The body has disappeared entirely. The cut

of the head has, however, been carried along backward the whole length of the body as far as the root of the tail, which latter has been cut off, and appears over the junction of the two profiles of the head. The dorsal fin has been split, and the two halves are joined to the upper part of the head, from which they extend upward and outward. Immediately below them the two halves of the blow-hole are indicated by two small faces, the upper parts of which bear a semicircle each. The flippers are attached to the lower corners of the face. The painting on the face next to the mouth represents gills.

[...]

We will turn now to the purely formal side of the treatment of the decorative field. There is a tendency to cover the entire surface with design elements. Vacant places are avoided. When the surface of the object represented has no features that lend themselves to decorative development, the artist resorts to devices that enable him to fill the surface with patterns. On totem poles the bodies of the animals represented occupy considerable space. The monotony of the surface is broken by placing the forelegs and hindlegs across the front of the body, by turning up the tail in front, and by adding small animal figures.

Far more important is the application of a great variety of decorative elements, all of which consist of curved lines. The Indians have a decided disinclination to apply equidistant curves. In all work of the better class the

Figure 1.29 Painting for a house-front with design representing a killer-whale, Kwakiutl

lines are so arranged that more or less crescent shaped surfaces result, or that narrow, curved areas, wide in the middle, narrower at the ends, are formed.

The most striking decorative form which is used almost everywhere, consists of a round or oval field, the "eye design". This pattern is commonly so placed that it corresponds to the location of a joint. In the present stage of the art, the oval is used particularly as shoulder, hip, wrist, and ankle joint, and as a joint at the base of the tail and of the dorsal fin of the whale. It is considered as a cross section of the ball and socket joint; the outer circle the socket, the inner the ball. Often the oval is developed in the form of a face: either as a full face or a profile.

The general disposition of this design demonstrates that the explanation is not by any means always tenable. Thus in the blanket,

figure 1.30, the eye pattern in the two lower corners has no connection with a joint. In this position, in the mouth of an animal, it is sometimes described as food. The two profile faces higher up on the side of the same blanket, are obviously fillers. They might be replaced by "eye designs".

[...]

The most characteristic filler, next to the eye, is a double curve, which is used to fill angular and round fields that rise over a strongly or gently curved line. Many fillers of this type have a dark colored band at the upper end, generally rounded in paintings or carvings, square in blankets (see figure 1.31, lower lateral design on central panel; the tail patterns, figure 1.32). In the blankets the angular form is perhaps due to the technique in weaving, although the frequent eye designs prove that round forms are not impossible. On blankets

Figure 1.30 Chilkat blanket

Figure 1.31 Chilkat blanket

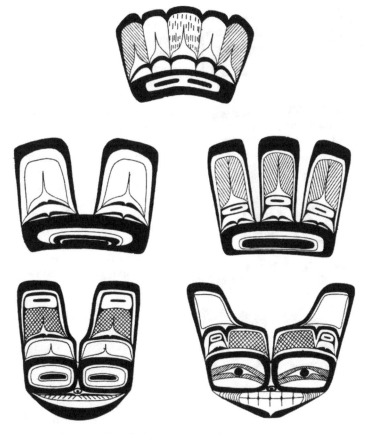

Figure 1.32 Styles of tails: above bird; below sea mammals

the heavy upper line is often drawn out into a tip (figure 1.33, over the "goggle" design on the side of the central panel). Examples of these forms have been collected by Lieutenant Emmons who states that the Tlingit call them "the wing-feather of red-winged flicker" (figure 1.34). The use of the pointed form of this design for a bird feather agrees with the theoretical claim of the Kwakiutl but obviously the explanation does not always fit the meaning of the

Figure 1.33 Chilkat blanket

Figure 1.34 Design elements from Tlingit blankets

pattern as a whole, as is shown by the killer-whale design figure 1.30 or the whale design figure 1.33.

[...]

Our consideration of the fixed formal elements found in this art prove that the principles of geometric ornamental form may be recognized even in this highly developed symbolic art; and that it is not possible to assign to each and every element that is derived from animal motives a significant function, but that many of them are employed regardless of meaning, and used for purely ornamental purposes.

The symbolic decoration is governed by rigorous formal principles. It appears that what we have called for the sake of convenience dissection and distortion of animal forms, is, in many cases, a fitting of animal motives into fixed ornamental patterns. We infer from a study of form and interpretation that there are certain purely geometric elements that have been utilized in the symbolic representation. Most important among these are the

double curve which appears always as a filler in an oval field with flat base, and the slit which serves to separate distinct curves. The typical eye design is presumably related to the circle and dot and may have developed from the double tendency of associating geometrical motives with animal forms and of the other, of standardizing forms derived from animal motives as ornamental elements.

This art style can be fully understood only as an integral part of the structure of Northwest coast culture. The fundamental idea underlying the thoughts, feelings, and activities of these tribes is the value of rank which gives title to the use of privileges, most of which find expression in artistic activities or in the use of art forms. Rank and social position bestow the privilege to use certain animal figures as paintings or carvings on the house front, on totem poles, on masks and on the utensils of every day life. Rank and social position give the right to tell certain tales referring to ancestral exploits; they determine the songs which may be sung. There are other obligations and privileges related to rank and social position, but the most outstanding feature is the intimate association between social standing and art forms. A similar relation, although not quite so intimate, prevails in the relation of religious activities and manifestations of art. It is as though the heraldic idea had taken hold of the whole life and had permeated it with the feeling that social standing must be expressed at every step by heraldry which, however, is not confined to space forms alone but extends over literary, musical and dramatic expression. Who can tell whether the association between social standing and the use of certain animal forms, – that is the totemic aspect of social life, – has given the prime impetus to the art development or whether the art impetus has developed and enriched totemic life? Our observations make it seem plausible that the particular symbolic development of art would not have occurred, if the totemic ideas had been absent and that we are dealing with the gradual intrusion of ever fuller animal motives into a well established conventionalized art. On the other hand it seems quite certain that the exuberance of totemic form has been stimulated by the value given to the art form. We may observe among all the tribes that high chiefs claim highly specialized art forms that are built up on the general background of totemic representation. In the south, there is clear evidence of the late exuberant development of the totemic, or perhaps better, crest idea, owing to the strong endeavor to raise by the possession of art forms the standing of the social units to which the individual belongs. The multiplicity of forms among the numerous small divisions of the Kwakiutl and the sporadic appearance of animal forms among the adjoining Salish are ample proof of these relations.

2

Split Representation in the Art of Asia and America

Claude Lévi-Strauss

CONTEMPORARY ANTHROPOLOGISTS seem to be somewhat reluctant to undertake comparative studies of primitive art. We can easily understand their reasons. Until now, studies of this nature have tended almost exclusively to demonstrate cultural contacts, diffusion phenomena, and borrowings. The discovery of a decorative detail or an unusual pattern in two different parts of the world, regardless of the geographical distance between them and an often considerable historical gap, brought enthusiastic proclamations about common origin and the unquestionable existence of prehistoric relationships between cultures which could not be compared in other respects. Leaving aside some fruitful discoveries, we know to what abuses this hurried search for analogies "at any cost" has led. To save us from these errors, experts in material culture even now need to define the specific characteristics which distinguish a trait, trait complex, or style that may be subject to multiple independent recurrences from one whose nature and characteristics exclude the possibility of repetition without borrowing.

It is, therefore, with some hesitation that I propose to contribute several documents to a hotly and legitimately debated body of materials. This voluminous collection involves the Northwest Coast of America, China, Siberia, New Zealand, and perhaps even India and Per-

sia. What is more, the documents belong to entirely different periods: the eighteenth and nineteenth centuries for Alaska; the first to second millennia B.C. for China; the prehistoric era for the Amur region; and a period stretching from the fourteenth to the eighteenth century for New Zealand. A more difficult case could hardly be conceived. I have mentioned elsewhere[1] the almost insuperable obstacles generated by the hypothesis of pre-Columbian contacts between Alaska and New Zealand. The problem is perhaps simpler when one compares Siberia and China with North America: Distances are more reasonable and one need overcome only the obstacle of one or two millennia. Even in this case, however, and whatever the intuitive convictions which irresistibly sway the mind, what an immense marshalling of facts becomes necessary! For his ingenious and brilliant work, C. Hentze can be called the "scrap-collector" of Americanism, pulling his evidence together from fragments gathered from the most diverse cultures and often mounting insignificant details[2] for exhibition. Instead of justifying the intuitive feeling of connectedness, his analysis dissolves it; nothing among these *membra disjecta poetae* appears to justify the deep sense of affinity which familiarity with both arts had so strongly elicited.

And yet, it is impossible not to be struck by the analogies presented by Northwest Coast

From *Structural Anthropology* (New York: Basic Books, 1963), pp. 245–268, 385–398.

and ancient Chinese art. These analogies derive not so much from the external aspect of the objects as from the fundamental principles which an analysis of both arts yields. This work was undertaken by Leonhard Adam, whose conclusions I shall summarize here.[3] The two arts proceed by means of: (1) intense stylization; (2) schematization or symbolism, expressed by emphasizing characteristic features or adding significant attributes (thus, in Northwest Coast art, the beaver is portrayed by the small log which it holds between its paws); (3) depiction of the body by "split representation"; (4) dislocation of details, which are arbitrarily isolated from the whole; (5) representation of *one* individual shown in front view with *two* profiles; (6) highly elaborate symmetry, which often involves asymmetric details; (7) illogical transformation of details into new elements (thus, a paw becomes a beak, an eye motif is used to represent a joint, or vice-versa); (8) finally, intellectual rather than intuitive representation, where the skeleton or internal organs take precedence over the representation of the body (a technique which is equally striking in northern Australia).[4] These techniques are not characteristic solely of Northwest Coast art. As Leonhard Adam writes, "The various technological and artistic principles displayed in both China and North West America are almost entirely identical."[5]

Once these similarities have been noted, it is curious to observe that, for entirely different reasons, ancient Chinese and Northwest Coast art have been independently compared with Maori art in New Zealand.[6] This fact is the more remarkable when we note that Neolithic art of the Amur – some of whose themes (such as the bird, with wings unfolded, whose abdomen is formed by a solar face) are almost identical with themes of the Northwest Coast – exhibits, according to some scholars, "an unexpectedly rich, curvilinear ornamentation related to that of the Ainu and Maori on one side and to the Neolithic cultures of China (Yangshao) and Japan (Jomon) on the other; consisting particularly of that type of ribbon ornamentation characterized by complex motifs such as the weave, spiral and meander in contradistinction to the rectangular geometric decoration of the Baikalian culture."[7] Thus art forms from very different regions

and periods which exhibit obvious analogies suggest, each of them and for independent reasons, relationships which are, however, incompatible with geographical and historical requirements.

Do we rest, then, on the horns of a dilemma which condemns us either to deny history or to remain blind to similarities so often confirmed? Anthropologists of the diffusionist school did not hesitate to force the hand of historical criticism. I do not intend to defend their adventurous hypotheses, but it must be admitted that the negative attitude of their cautious opponents is no more satisfactory than the fabulous pretensions which the latter merely reject. Comparative studies of primitive art have probably been jeopardized by the zeal of investigators of cultural contacts and borrowings. But let us state in no uncertain terms that these studies have been jeopardized even more by intellectual pharisees who prefer to deny obvious relationships because science does not yet provide an adequate method for their interpretation. The rejection of facts because they appear to be unintelligible is surely more sterile from the viewpoint of scientific progress than the formulation of hypotheses. Even if these should prove to be unacceptable, they will elicit, precisely because of their inadequacy, the criticism and research that will one day enable us to progress beyond them.[8]

We reserve, therefore, the right to compare American Indian art with that of China or New Zealand, even if it has been proved a thousand times over that the Maori could not have brought their weapons and ornaments to the Pacific Coast. Cultural contact doubtless constitutes the one hypothesis which most easily accounts for complex similarities that chance cannot explain. But if historians maintain that contact is impossible, this does not prove that the similarities are illusory, but only that one must look elsewhere for the explanation. The fruitfulness of the diffusionist approach derives precisely from its systematic exploration of the possibilities of history. If history, when it is called upon unremittingly (and it must be called upon *first*), cannot yield an answer, then let us appeal to psychology, or the structural analysis of forms; let us ask ourselves if internal connections, whether of a psychological or logical nature, will allow us to understand parallel recurrences whose frequency and cohesion cannot possibly be the result of chance. It is in this spirit that I shall now present my contribution to the debate.

Split representation in Northwest Coast art has been described by Franz Boas as follows: "The animal is imagined cut in two from head to tail...there is a deep depression between the eyes, extending down the nose. This shows that the head itself must not have been considered a front view, but as consisting of two profiles which adjoin at mouth and nose, while they are not in contact with each other on a level with the eyes and forehead...either the animals are represented as split in two so that the profiles are joined in the middle, or a front view of the head is shown with two adjoining profiles of the body."[9] Boas analyzes the two paintings in the following terms:

> Figure 1.14 (a Haida painting) shows a design which has been obtained in this manner. It represents a bear. The enormous breadth of mouth observed in these cases is brought about by the junction of the two profiles of which the head consists. This cutting of the head is brought out most clearly in the painting figure 1.15 which also represents the bear. It is the painting on the front of a Tsimshian house, the circular hole in the middle of the design being the door of the house. The animal is cut from back to front, so that ony the front part of the head coheres. The two halves of the lower jaw do not touch each other. The back is represented by the black outlines on which the hair is indicated by fine lines. The Tsimshian call such a design "bears meeting", as though two bears had been represented.[10]

Let us now compare this analysis with that given by H. G. Creel of a similar technique in the art of ancient China (figure 2.1): "One of the most distinctive characteristics of Shang decorative art is a peculiar method by which animals were represented in flat or in rounded surfaces. It is as if one took the animal and split it lengthwise, starting at the tip of the tail and carrying the operation almost, not quite, to the tip of the nose, then the two halves are pulled apart and the bisected animal is laid out flat on the surface, the two halves joined only at the tip of the nose."[11] The same author, who apparently does not know Boas' work, after having employed almost exactly the same terminology as the latter, adds: "In

Figure 2.1 Bronze discovered near An-Yang (China). In the middle panel a split *t'ao t'ieh* mask without a lower jaw. The ears make up a second mask above the first. The eyes in the second mask may also be seen as belonging to two small dragons represented by the ears of the first mask. The two small dragons are shown in profile and face to face, like those in the upper panel. The latter may in turn be seen as a ram mask shown in front view, the horns being represented by the bodies of the dragons. The design on the lid can be similarly interpreted. After W. P. Yetts, *An-Yang: A Retrospect*

studying Shang design I have constantly been aware of the feeling that this art has great resemblance, certainly in spirit and possibly in detail, to that of...the Northwest Coast Indians."[12]

This distinctive technique, which is found in ancient Chinese art, among the Siberian primitives, and in New Zealand, also appears at the other extremity of the American continent, among the Caduveo Indians. A drawing, which we reproduce here in figure 2.6, represents a face painted according to the traditional custom of the women of this small tribe of southern Brazil, one of the last remnants of the once flourishing Guaicuru nation. I have described elsewhere how these paintings are executed and what their function is in the native culture.[13] For present purposes it is, therefore, sufficient to recall that these paintings have been known since the first contacts with the Guaicuru in the seventeenth century and that they do not seem to have evolved since that time. They are not tattooings, but cosmetic facial paintings, which must be renewed after a few days and which are executed with a wooden spatula dipped in the juices of wild fruit and leaves. The women, who paint one another's faces (and who formerly also painted men), do not work from a model but improvise within the limits of a complex, traditionally defined range of themes. Among four hundred original drawings gathered in the field in 1935, I did not find two alike. The differences, however, stem more from the ever-varied arrangement of fundamental elements than from a renewal of these elements – whether simple and double spirals, hatching, volutes, frets, tendrils, or crosses and whorls. The possibility of Spanish influence should be excluded, given the remote date when this refined art was described for the first time. At present, only a few old women possess the ancient skill, and it is not difficult to foresee the time when it will have disappeared altogether.

Figure 2.2 presents a good example of these paintings. The design is built symmetrically in relation to two linear axes, one of them vertical, following the median plane of the face, the other horizontal, dividing the face at eye level. The eyes are schematically represented on a reduced scale. They are used as starting points for two inverted spirals, one of which covers the right cheek and the other the left side of the forehead. A motif in the shape of a compound bow, which is located in the lower part of the painting, represents the upper lip and is applied on it. We find this motif, more or less elaborated and more or less transformed, in all the facial paintings, where it seems to constitute a constant element. It is not easy to analyze the design, because of its apparent asymmetry – which, nonetheless masks a real, though complex, symmetry. The two axes intersect at the root of the nose, thus dividing the face into four triangular sections: left side of the forehead, right side of the forehead, right wing of the nose and right cheek, and left wing of the nose and left cheek. Opposite triangles have a symmetrical design, but the design within each triangle itself is a double design, which is repeated in inverted form in the opposite triangle. Thus, the right side of the forehead and the left cheek are covered, first by a triangle of frets, and, after a separation in the form of an empty oblique strip, by two double spirals in alignment, which are decorated with tendrils. The left side of the forehead and the right cheek are decorated with a simple large spiral adorned with tendrils; it is topped by another motif in the shape of a bird or flame, which contains an element reminiscent of the empty oblique stripe in the opposite design. We thus have two pairs of themes, each of which is repeated twice in

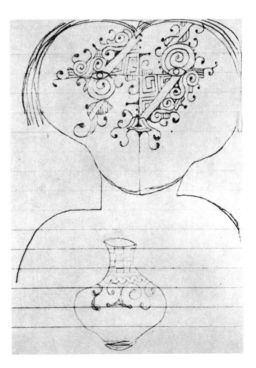

Figure 2.2 Caduveo woman's drawing representing a figure with a painted face. Author's collection

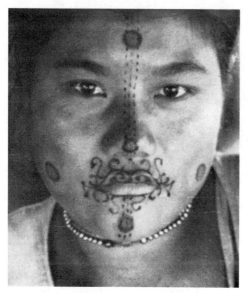

Figure 2.3 Caduveo woman with painted face. Photographed by the author, 1935

Figure 2.5 Caduveo woman with painted face. Drawing by Boggiani, an Italian painter who visited the Caduveo in 1892. After G. Boggiani, *Viaggi d'un artista nell' America Meridionale*

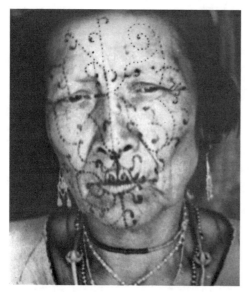

Figure 2.4 Caduveo woman with painted face. Photographed by the author, 1935

symmetrical fashion. But this symmetry is expressed either in relation to one of the two horizontal and vertical axes, or in relation to the triangles defined by the bisection of these axes. While far more complex, this pattern recalls that of playing cards. Figures 2.3, 2.4 and 2.5 are other examples which illustrate variations on what is fundamentally the same pattern.

In figure 2.2, however, it is not only the painted design which draws the attention. The artist, a woman approximately thirty years old, intended also to represent the face and even the hair. Now she obviously accomplished this by split representation: The face is not really seen in a frontal view; it consists of two joined profiles. This explains its extraordinary width and its heart-shaped outline. The depression dividing the forehead into two halves is a part of the representation of the profiles, which merge only from the root of the nose down to the chin. A comparison of figures 1.14, 1.15 and 2.2 shows that this technique is identical with that used by artists of the Northwest Coast of America.

Other important traits are also characteristic of both North and South American art. We have already stressed the dislocation of the subject into elements which are recombined according to conventional rules having nothing to do with nature. Dislocation is just as striking in Caduveo art, where it takes, however, an indirect form. Boas minutely described the dislocation of bodies and faces in Northwest Coast art: The organs and limbs themselves are split and used to reconstitute an arbitrary individual. Thus, in a Haida totem pole, "the figure must be ... explained in such a way that the animal is twisted twice, the tail being turned up over the back, and the head being first turned down under the stomach, then split and extended outward."[14] In a Kwakiutl representation of a killer whale (*Orca sp.*), "the animal has been split along its whole back towards the front. The two profiles of the head have been joined ... The dorsal fin, which according to the methods described heretofore [split representation] would appear on both sides of the body, has been cut off from the back before the animal was split, and appears now placed over the junction of the two profiles of the head. The flippers are laid along the two sides of the body, with which they cohere only at one point each. The two halves of the tail have been twisted outward so that the lower part of the figure forms a straight line."[15] See figure 1.28. These examples could easily be multiplied.

Caduveo art carries the dislocation process both further than, yet not as far as, Northwest Coast art. It does not carry it as far, because the face or body on which the artist works is a flesh-and-bone face and body, which cannot be taken apart and put together again. The integrity of the real face is thus respected, but it is dislocated just the same by the systematic asymmetry by means of which its natural harmony is denied on behalf of the artificial harmony of the painting. But since this painting, instead of representing the image of a deformed face, actually deforms a real face, the dislocation goes further than in the case previously described. The dislocation here involves, besides the decorative value, a subtle element of sadism, which at least partly explains why the erotic appeal of Caduveo women (expressed in the paintings) formerly attracted outlaws and adventurers toward the shores of the Paraguay River. Several of these now aging men, who intermarried with

Figure 2.6 Caduveo: facial design reproduced by a native woman on a sheet of paper. Author's collection

the natives, described to me with quivering emotion the nude bodies of adolescent girls completely covered with interlacings and arabesques of a perverse subtlety. The tattooings and body paintings of the Northwest Coast, where this sexual element was probably lacking and whose symbolism, often abstract, presents a less decorative character, also disregarded symmetry in the human face.[16]

In addition, we observe that the arrangement of Caduveo paintings around a double axis, horizontal and vertical, divides the face according to a process of double splitting, so to speak – that is, the painting recombines the face not into two profiles but into four quarters (see figure 2.6). Asymmetry serves the formal function of insuring the distinction between quarters, which would merge into two profiles if the fields were to be symmetrically repeated to the right and left instead of being joined by their tips. Dislocation and splitting are thus functionally related.

If we pursue this comparison between Northwest Coast and Caduveo art, several other points are worthy of consideration. In each case, sculpture and drawing provide the two fundamental means of expression; in each case, sculpture presents a realistic character, while drawing is more symbolic and decorative. Caduveo sculpture is probably limited, at least during the historical period, to fetishes and representations of gods, which are always of small size, in contrast to the monumental art of Canada and Alaska. But the realistic character and the tendency toward both portrait and stylization are the same, as well as the essentially symbolic meaning of drawn or painted motifs. In both cases, masculine art, centered on sculpture, expresses its representational intention, while feminine art – limited to weaving and plaiting on the Northwest Coast, but also including drawing among these natives of southern Brazil and Paraguay – is a non-representational art. This is true, in both cases, for textile motifs; as regards the Guaicuru facial paintings, we know nothing about their archaic character. It is possible that the themes of these paintings, whose import has become lost today, formerly had a realistic or at any rate symbolical meaning. Northwest Coast and Caduveo art both carry out decoration by means of stencils, and create ever-new combinations through the varied arrangement of basic motifs. Finally, in both cases, art is intimately related to social organization: Motifs and themes express rank differences, nobility privileges, and degrees of prestige. The two societies were organized along similar hierarchical lines and their decorative art functioned to interpret and validate the ranks in the hierarchy.[17]

I should now like to make a brief comparison between Caduveo art and another art which also used split representation – that of the Maori of New Zealand. Let us first recall that Northwest Coast art has been frequently compared, for other reasons, to the art of New Zealand. Some of these reasons turned out to be specious – for instance, the apparently identical character of woven blankets used in the two areas. Others seem more valid – for example, those deriving from the similarity between Alaskan clubs and the Maori *patu mere*. I have mentioned this enigma elsewhere.[18]

The comparison of Maori with Guaicuru art is based on other convergences. In no other region of the world has facial and corporal decoration attained such high levels of development and refinement. Maori tattooings are well known. I reproduce our of them (figures 2.7 and 2.8), which may be fruitfully compared with the photographs of Caduveo faces.

The analogies between them are striking: complexity of design, involving hatching, meanders, and spirals (the spirals are often replaced in Caduveo art by frets, which suggest Andean influences); the same tendency to fill the entire surface of the face; and the same localization of the design around the lips in the simpler types. The differences between the two arts must also be considered. The difference due to the fact that Maori design is tattooed whereas Caduveo design is painted may be dismissed, since there is hardly any doubt that in South America, too, tattooing was the primitive technique. Tattooing explains why the Abipone women of Paraguay, as late as the eighteenth century, had "their face, breast, and arms covered with black figures of various shapes, so that they present the appearance of a Turkish carpet."[19] This made them, according to their own words as recorded by the old missionary "more beautiful than beauty it-

Figure 2.7 Maori chief's drawing representing his own tattooed face. After H. G. Robley, *Moko, or Maori Tattooing*

Figure 2.8 Three Maori tattooing designs carved in wood, late nineteenth century: top row, men's faces; bottom row, woman's face. After A. Hamilton, *The Art Workmanship of the Maori in New Zealand*

self."[20] On the other hand, one is struck by the rigorous symmetry of Maori tattooings, in contrast with the almost licentious asymmetry of some Caduveo paintings. But this asymmetry does not always exist; and I have shown that it resulted from a logical development of the splitting principle. It is thus more apparent than real. It is clear, nevertheless, that as regards typological classification, Caduveo facial designs occupy an intermediary position between those of the Maori and those of the Northwest Coast. Like the latter, they have an asymmetrical appearance, while they present the essentially decorative character of the former.

This continuity is also apparent when one considers the psychological and social implications. Among the Maori, as among the natives of the Paraguayan border, facial and corporal decoration is executed in a semi-religious atmosphere. Tattooings are not only ornaments. As we already noted with respect to the Northwest Coast (and the same thing may be said of New Zealand), they are not only emblems of nobility and symbols of rank in the social hierarchy; they are also messages fraught with spiritual and moral significance. The purpose of Maori tattooings is not only to imprint a drawing onto the flesh but also to stamp onto the mind all the traditions and philosophy of the group. Similarly, the Jesuit missionary Sanchez Labrador has described the passionate seriousness with which the natives devoted whole days to letting themselves be painted. He who is not painted, they said, is "dumb."[21] And, like the Caduveo, the Maori use split representation. In figures 2.7, 2.9, 2.10 and 2.11, we note the same division of the forehead into two lobes; the same representation of the mouth where the two halves meet; the same representation of the body, as though it had been split in the back from top to bottom and the two halves brought forward on the same plane. We note, in other words, all the techniques which are now familiar to us.

How shall we explain the recurrence of a far from natural method of representation among cultures so widely separated in time and space? The simplest hypothesis is that of historical contact or independent development from a common civilization. But even if this hypothesis is refuted by facts, or if, as seems more likely, it should lack adequate evidence, at-

Figure 2.9 Jade figure (tiki), New Zealand, characterized by the three-lobed division of the face. Courtesy of the American Museum of Natural History

tempts at interpretation are not necessarily doomed to failure. I shall go further: Even if the most ambitious reconstructions of the diffusionist school were to be confirmed, we should still be faced with an essential problem which has nothing to do with history. Why should a cultural trait that has been borrowed or diffused through a long historical period remain intact? Stability is no less mysterious than change. The discovery of a unique origin for split representation would leave unanswered the question of why this means of expression was preserved by cultures which, in other respects, evolved along very different lines. External connections can explain transmission, but

Figure 2.10 Maori wood carving, New Zealand, eighteenth century (?). After A. Hamilton, *The Art Workmanship of the Maori in New Zealand*

only internal connections can account for persistence. Two entirely different kinds of problems are involved here, and the attempt to explain one in no way prejudges the solution that must be given to the other.

One observation immediately follows from the comparison between Maori and Guaicuru art. In both cases, split representation appears as a consequence of the importance that both cultures ascribe to tattooing. Let us consider figure 2.2 again and ask ourselves why the outline of the face is represented by two joined profiles. It is clear that the artist intended to draw, not a face, but a facial painting; it is upon doing the latter that she concentrated all her attention. Even the eyes, which are sketchily indicated, exist only as points of reference for starting the two great inverted spirals into whose structure they merge. The artist drew the facial design in a realistic manner; she respected its true proportions as if she had painted on a face and not on a flat surface.

She painted on a sheet of paper exactly as she was accustomed to paint on a face. And because the paper *is* for her a face, she finds it impossible to *represent* a face on paper, at any rate without distortion. It was necessary either to draw the face exactly and distort the design in accordance with the laws of perspective, or to respect the integrity of the design and for this reason represent the face as split in two. It cannot even be said that the artist *chose* the second solution, since the alternative never occurred to her. In native thought, as we saw, the design *is* the face, or rather it creates it. It is the design which confers upon the face its social existence, its human dignity, its spiritual significance. Split representation of the face, considered as a graphic device, thus expresses a deeper and more fundamental splitting, namely that between the "dumb" biological individual and the social person whom he must embody. We already foresee that split representation can be explained as a function of a sociological theory of the splitting of the personality.

The same relationship between split image and tattooing may be observed in Maori art. If we compare figures 2.7, 2.9, 2.10 and 2.11, we will see that the splitting of the forehead into two lobes is only the projection, on a plastic level, of the symmetrical design tattooed on the skin.

In the light of these observations, the interpretation of split representation proposed by Boas in his study of Northwest Coast art should be elaborated and refined. For Boas, split representation in painting or drawing would consist only in the extension to flat surfaces of a technique which is naturally appropriate in the case of three-dimensional objects. When an animal is going to be represented on a square box, for instance, one must necessarily distort the shape of the animal so that it can be adapted to the angular contours of the box. According to Boas,

In the decoration of silver bracelets a similar principle is followed but the problem differs somewhat from that offered in the decoration of square boxes. While in the latter case the four edges make a natural division between the four views of the animal, – front and right profile, back and left profile, – there is no such sharp line of division in the round bracelet, and there would be great difficulty

Figure 2.11 Three Maori wood carvings, eighteenth or nineteenth century. After A. Hamilton, *The Art Workmanship of the Maori in New Zealand*

in joining the four aspects artistically, while two profiles offer no such difficulty...The animal is imagined cut in two from head to tail, so that the two halves cohere only at the tip of the nose and at the tip of the tail. The hand is put through this hole and the animal now surrounds the wrist. In this position it is represented on the bracelet...The transition from the bracelet to the painting or carving of animals on a flat surface is not a difficult one. The same principle is adhered to.[22]

Thus the principle of split representation would gradually emerge in the process of transition from angular to rounded objects and from rounded objects to flat surfaces. In the first case, there is occasional dislocation and splitting; in the second case, splitting is systematically applied, but the animal still remains intact at the level of the head and the tail; finally, in the third case, dislocation goes to the extreme of splitting the caudal tie, and the two halves of the body, now free, are folded forward to the right and left on the same plane as the face.

This treatment of the problem by the great master of modern anthropology is remarkable for its elegance and simplicity. However, this elegance and simplicity are mainly theoretical. If we consider the decoration of flat and rounded surfaces as special cases of the decoration of angular surfaces, then nothing has been demonstrated with respect to the latter. And, above all, no necessary relationship exists a priori, which implies that the artist must remain faithful to the same principle in moving from angular to rounded surfaces, and from rounded to flat surfaces. Many cultures have decorated boxes with human and animal figures without splitting or dislocating them. A bracelet may be adorned with friezes or in a hundred other ways. There must, then, be some fundamental element of Northwest Coast art (and of Guaicuru art, and Maori art, and the art of ancient China) which accounts for the continuity and rigidity with which the technique of split representation is applied in them.

We are tempted to perceive this fundamental element in the very special relationship which, in the four arts considered here, links the plastic and graphic components. These two elements are not independent; they have an ambivalent relationship, which is simultaneously one of opposition and one which is functional. It is a relationship of opposition because the requirements of decoration are imposed upon the structure and change it, hence the splitting and dislocation; but it is also a functional relationship, since the object is always conceived in both its plastic and graphic aspects. A vase, a box, a wall, are not independent, pre-existing objects which are subsequently decorated. They acquire their definitive existence only through the integration of the decoration with the utilitarian function. Thus, the chests of Northwest Coast art are not merely containers embellished with a painted or carved animal. They are the animal itself, keeping an active watch over the ceremonial ornaments which have been entrusted to its care. Structure modifies decoration, but decoration is the final cause of structure, which must also adapt itself to the requirements of the former. The final product is a whole: utensil-ornament, object-animal, box-that-speaks. The "living boats" of the Northwest Coast have their exact counterparts in the New Zealand correspondences between boat and woman, woman and spoon, utensils and organs.[23]

We have thus pushed to its most abstract expression the study of dualism, which has been commanding our attention with increasing persistence. We saw in the course of our analysis that the dualism between representational and non-representational art became transformed into other kinds of dualism: carving and drawing, face and decoration, person and impersonation, individual existence and social function, community and hierarchy. We are thus led to acknowledge a dualism, which is also a correlation, between plastic and graphic expression, which provides us with a true "common denominator" of the diverse manifestations of the principle of split representation.

In the end, our problem may be formulated as follows: Under what conditions are the plastic and graphic components necessarily correlated? Under what conditions are they inevitably functionally related, so that the modes of expression of the one always transform those of the other, and vice versa? The comparison between Maori and Guaicuru art already provided us with the answer to the latter question. We saw, indeed, that the relationship had to be functional when the plastic component consisted of the face or human body and the graphic component of the facial or corporal decoration (painting or tattooing), which is applied to them. Decoration is actually *created* for the face; but in another sense the face is predestined to be decorated, since it is only by means of decoration that the face receives its social dignity and mystical significance. Decoration is conceived for the face, but the face itself exists only through decoration. In the final analysis, the dualism is that of the actor and his role, and the concept of *mask* gives us the key to its interpretation.

All the cultures considered here are, in fact, mask cultures, whether the masking is achieved predominantly by tattooing (as is the case for the Guaicuru and Maori) or whether the stress is placed literally on the mask, as the Northwest Coast has done in a fashion unsurpassed elsewhere. In archaic China, there are many references to the ancient role of masks, which is reminiscent of their role in Alaskan societies. Thus, the "Impersonation of the Bear" described in the *Chou Li*, with its "four eyes of yellow metal,"[24] recalls the multiple masks of the Eskimo and Kwakiutl.

Those masks with louvers, which present alternately several aspects of the totemic ancestor – sometimes peaceful, sometimes angry, at one time human, at another time animal – strikingly illustrate the relationship between split representation and masquerade. Their function is to offer a series of intermediate forms which insure the transition from symbol to meaning, from magical to normal, from supernatural to social. They hold at the same time the function of masking and unmasking. But when it comes to unmasking, it is the mask which, by a kind of reverse splitting, opens up into two halves, while the actor himself is dissociated in the split representation, which aims, as we saw, at flattening out as well as displaying the mask at the expense of the individual wearing it.

Our analysis thus converges with that of Boas, once we have explored its substructure. It is true that split representation on a flat surface is a special case of its appearance on a rounded surface, just as the latter is itself a special case on three-dimensional surfaces. But not on *any* three-dimensional surface; only on the three-dimensional surface *par excellence*, where the decoration and form cannot be dissociated either physically or socially, namely, the *human face*. At the same time, other curious analogies between the various art forms considered here are illuminated in a similar way.

In the four arts, we discover not one but two decorative styles. One of these styles tends toward a representational, or at least symbolic, expression, and its most common feature is the predominance of motifs. This is Karlgren's Style A for archaic China,[25] painting and low relief for the Northwest Coast and New Zealand, and facial painting for the Guaicuru. But another style exists, of a more strictly formal

and decorative character, with geometric tendencies. It consists of Karlgren's Style B, the rafter decoration of New Zealand, the woven or plaited designs of New Zealand and the Northwest Coast, and, for the Guaicuru, a style easily identifiable, ordinarily found in decorated pottery, corporal paintings (different from facial paintings), and painted leatherwork. How can we explain this dualism, and especially its recurrence? The first style is decorative only in appearance; it does not have a plastic function in any of the four arts. On the contrary, its function is social, magical, and religious. The decoration is the graphic or plastic projection of a reality of another order, in the same way that split representation results from the projection of a three-dimensional mask onto a two-dimensional surface (or onto a three-dimensional one which nevertheless does not conform to the human archetype) and in the same way that, finally, the biological individual himself is also projected onto the social scene by his dress. There is thus room for the birth and development of a true decorative art, although one would actually expect its contamination by the symbolism which permeates all social life.

Another characteristic, shared at least by New Zealand and the Northwest Coast, appears in the treatment of tree trunks, which are carved in the form of superimposed figures, each of which occupies a whole section of the trunk. The last vestiges of Caduveo carving are so sparse that we can hardly formulate hypotheses about the archaic manifestations of it; and we are still poorly informed about the treatment of wood by Shang carvers, several examples of which came to light in the excavations at An-Yang.[26]

I would like to draw attention, nevertheless, to a bronze of the Loo collection reproduced by Hentze.[27] It looks as though it could be the reduction of a carved pole, comparable to the slate reductions of totem poles in Alaska and British Columbia. In any case, the cylindrical section of the trunk plays the same role of archetype or "absolute limit" which we ascribed to the human face and body; but it plays this role only because the trunk is interpreted as a living being, a kind of "speaking pole." Here again, the plastic and stylistic expression serves only as a concrete embodiment of *impersonations*.

However, our analysis would be inadequate if it permitted us only to define split representation as a trait common to mask cultures. From a purely formal point of view there has never been any hesitation in considering the *t'ao t'ieh* of archaic Chinese bronzes as a mask. On his part, Boas interpreted the split representation of the shark in Northwest Coast art as a consequence of the fact that the characteristic symbols of this animal are better perceived in a front view[28] (see figure 2.12). But we have gone further: We discovered in the splitting technique, not only the graphic representation of the mask, but the functional expression of a specific type of civilization. Not all mask cultures employ split representation. We do not find it (at least in as developed a form) in the art of the Pueblo of the American Southwest nor in that of New Guinea.[29] In both these cultures, however, masks play a considerable role. Masks also represent ancestors, and by wearing the mask the actor incarnates the ancestor. What, therefore, is the difference? The difference is that, in contrast to the civilizations we have been considering here, there is no chain of privileges, emblems, and degrees of prestige which, by means of masks, validate social hierarchy through the primacy of genealogies. The supernatural does not have as its chief function the creation of castes and classes. The world of masks constitutes a *pantheon* rather than an *ancestrality*. Thus, the actor incarnates the god only on the intermittent occasions of feasts and ceremonies. He does not acquire from the god, by a continuous process of creation at each moment of social life, his titles, his rank, his position in the status hierarchy. The parallelism which we established is thus confirmed, rather than invalidated, by these examples. The mutual independence of the plastic and graphic components corresponds to the more flexible interplay between the social and supernatural orders in the same way that split representation expresses the strict conformity of the actor to his role and of social rank to myths, ritual, and pedigrees. This conformity is so rigorous that, in order for the individual to be dissociated from his social role, he must be torn asunder.

Even if we knew nothing about archaic Chinese society, an inspection of its art would be sufficient to enable us to recognize prestige struggles, rivalry between hierarchies, and competition between social and economic privileges – showing through the function of masks and the veneration of lineages. Fortunately, however, there are additional data at our disposal. Analyzing the psychological background of bronze art, Perceval Yetts writes: "The impulse seems almost invariably to have been self-glorification, even when show is made of solacing ancestors or of enhancing the family prestige."[30] And elsewhere he remarks: "There is the familiar history of certain *ting* being treasured as emblems of sovereignty down to the end of the feudal period in the third century B.C."[31] In the An-Yang tombs, bronzes were found which commemorate successive members of the same lineage.[32] And the differences in quality between the specimens excavated can be explained, according to Creel, in terms of the fact that "the exquisite and the crude were produced side by side at Anyang, for people of various economic status or prestige."[33] Comparative anthropological analysis, therefore, is in agreement with the conclusions of Sinologists. It also confirms the theories of Karlgren, who, unlike Leroi-Gourhan[34] and others, states, on the basis of a statistical and chronological study of themes, that the representational mask existed before the mask's dissolution into decorative elements and therefore could not have grown out of the experimentation of the artist who discovers resemblances in the fortuitous arrangement of abstract themes.[35] In another work Karlgren showed how the animal decorations of archaic objects became transformed in the later bronzes into flamboyant arabesques, and he related phenomena of stylistic evolution to the collapse of feudal society.[36] We are tempted to perceive in the arabesques of Guaicuru art, which are so strongly suggestive of birds and flames, the final stage of a parallel transformation. The baroque and affected quality of the style would thus represent the formal survival of a decadent or terminated social order. It constitutes, on the esthetic level, its dying echo.

The conclusions of our work do not preclude in any respect the always-possible discovery of hitherto unsuspected historical connections.[37] We are still faced with the question of finding out whether these hierarchical societies based on prestige appeared independently in different parts of the world, or whether some of them do not share a common

Figure 2.12 Haida painting representing a shark. The head is shown in front view to bring out the features characteristic of the shark, but the body is split lengthwise, with the two halves laid out flat on the surface to the right and left of the head. After Bureau of American Ethnology, *Tenth Annual Report*, plate XXV

cradle. With Creel,[38] I think that the similarities between the art of archaic China and that of the Northwest Coast, perhaps even with the arts of other American areas, are too marked for us not to keep this possibility in mind. But even if there were ground for invoking diffusion, it would not be a diffusion of details – that is, independent traits traveling each on its own and disconnected freely from any one culture in order to be linked to another – but a diffusion of organic wholes wherein style, esthetic conventions, social organization, and religion are structurally related. Drawing a particularly striking analogy between archaic Chinese and Northwest Coast art, Creel writes: "The many isolated eyes used by the Northwest Coast designers recall most forcibly their similar use in Shang art and cause me to wonder if there was some magical reason for this which was possessed by both peoples."[39] Perhaps; but magical connections, like optical illusions, exist only in men's minds, and we must resort to scientific investigation to explain their causes.

NOTES

1 "The Art of the North West Coast," *Gazette des Beaux-Arts* (1943).

2 Carl Hentze, *Objets rituels, Croyances et Dieux de la Chine antique et de l'Amérique* (Antwerp: 1936).

3 Leonhard Adam, "Das Problem der asiatisch-altamerikanischen Kulturbeziehungen mit besonderer Berücksichtigung der Kunst," *Wiener Beiträge zur Kunst und Kulturgeschichte Asiens*, V (1931); "Northwest American Indian Art and Its Early Chinese Parallels," *Man* XXXVI, no. 3 (1936).

4 See, for example, F. D. McCarthy, *Australian Aboriginal Decorative Art* (Sydney: 1938), fig. 21, p. 38.

5 Review of Carl Hentze, *Frühchinesische bronzen und Kultdarstellungen* (Antwerp: 1937), in *Man*, XXXIX, no. 60 (1939).

6 For China and New Zealand, see R. Heine-Geldern in *Zeitschrift für Rassenkunde*, vol. 2 (Stuttgart: 1935).

7 Henry Field and Eugene Prostov, "Results of Soviet Investigation in Siberia, 1940–1941," *American Anthropologist*, XLIV (1942), p. 396.

8 In his book, *Medieval American Art* (New York: 1943), Pal Kelemen regards the resemblances between American art and some of the arts of the highest civilizations of the Eastern hemisphere as only "optical illusions" (vol. I, p. 377). He justifies this opinion by writing that "Pre-Columbian art was created and developed by a mentality totally alien to ours" (p. 378). I doubt that in the whole work of the diffusionist school one could find a single statement so completely unwarranted, superficial, and meaningless.

9 Franz Boas, *Primitive Art*, Instituttet for Sammenlignende Kulturforskning, series B, vol. VIII (Oslo: 1927), pp. 223–24 [pp. 43–44 in this vol.].

10 Ibid. pp. 224–25 [p. 45 in this vol.].

11 H. G. Creel, "On the Origins of the Manufacture and Decoration of Bronze in the Shang Period," *Monumenta Serica*, vol. I (1935), p. 64.

12 *Loc. cit.*

13 "Indian Cosmetics," *VVV*, no. 1 (New York: 1942). *Tristes Tropiques* (Paris: 1955).

14 Franz Boas, p. 238.

15 Ibid., p. 239 [p.50 in this vol.] and fig. 247 [figure 1.28 in this vol.].

16 See, for example, the Tlingit tattooings reproduced by J. R. Swanton in *Bureau of American Ethnology, 26th Annual Report*, plates XLVIII to LVI; and Franz Boas, *op. cit.*, pp. 250–1 (body paintings).

17 I have developed this analysis further in *Tristes Tropiques*, chapter XX (Paris: 1955).

18 "The Art of the North West Coast."

19 M. Dobrizhoffer, *An Account of the Abipones*, trans. from the Latin, vol. II (London: 1822), p. 20.

20 Ibid., p. 21.

21 See also H. G. Creel: "The fine Shang pieces are executed with a care, extending to the most minute detail, which is truly religious. And we know, through the study of the oracle bone inscriptions, that almost all the motifs found on Shang bronzes can be linked with the life and religion of the Shang people. They had meaning and the production of the bronzes was probably in some degree a sacred task." "Notes on Shang Bronzes in the Burlington House Exhibition," *Revue des Arts asiatiques*, X (1936), p. 21.

22 Boas, pp. 222–24 [pp. 43–44 in this vol.].

23 John R. Swanton, *Tlingit Myths and Texts*, Bureau of American Ethnology, Bulletin 59 (1909), pp. 254–255; E. A. Rout, *Maori Symbolism* (London: 1926), p. 280.

24 Florance Waterbury, *Early Chinese Symbols and Literature: Vestiges and Speculations* (New York: 1942).

25 Bernhard Karlgren, "New Studies on Chinese Bronzes," *The Museum of Far Eastern Antiquities*, Bulletin 9 (Stockholm: 1937).

26 H. G. Creel, *Monumenta Serica*, vol. I (1935), p. 40.

27 Carl Hentze, *Frühchinesische bronzen und Kultdarstellungen* (Antwerp: 1937), table 5.

28 Boas, p. 229 [p.47 in this vol.]. One should distinguish, however, between two forms of split representation – namely, split representation proper, where a face and sometimes a whole individual are represented by two joined profiles, and split representation as shown in figure 2.12, where *one* face is shown with *two* bodies. We cannot be certain that the two types derive from the same principle, and in the passage which we summarized at the beginning of this chapter, Leonhard Adam wisely distinguishes between them. The split representation so well illustrated in figure 2.12 reminds us, indeed, of a similar technique well known in European and Oriental archaeology This is the *beast with two bodies*, whose history E. Pottier attempted to reconstruct ("Histoire d'une bête," in *Recueil E. Pottier*, Bibliothèque des Ecoles d'Athènes et de Rome, section 142). Pottier traces the beast with two bodies to the Chaldean representation of an animal whose head appears in a front view and the body in profile. A second body, also seen in profile, is assumed to have been subsequently attached to the head. If this hypothesis is correct, the representation of the shark analyzed by Boas should be considered either as an independent invention or as the easternmost evidence of the diffusion of an Asiatic theme. This last interpretation would be based on evidence which is far from negligible, namely the recurrence of another theme, the "whirl of animals" (see Anna Roes, "Tierwirbel," *Ipek* [1936–37]) in the art of the Eurasian Steppes and in that of certain areas of America (especially in Moundville). It is also possible that the beast with two bodies derives independently, in Asia and America, from a technique of split representation which has not survived in the archaeological sites of the Near East, but which left traces in China and may still be observed in certain areas of the Pacific and in America.

29 The art of Melanesia presents rudimentary forms of split representation and dislocation. See, for example, the wooden containers of the Admiralty Islands reproduced by Gladys A. Reichard, "Melanesian Design: A Study of Style in Wood and Tortoise Shell Carving," *Columbia University Contributions to Anthropology*, II, no. 18 (1933), and the following comment by the same author: "Among the Tami, joints are represented by an eye motif. In the face of the fact that tattooing is exceedingly important to the Maori and that it is represented on the carvings, it seems to me more than possible that the spiral often used on the human figures may emphasize the joints" (p. 151).

30 W. Perceval Yetts, *The Cull Chinese Bronzes*, London, 1939, p. 75.

31 W. Perceval Yetts, *The George Eumorphopoulos Collection Catalogue*, Vol. I (London: 1929), p. 43.

32 W. Perceval Yetts, "An-Yang: A Retrospect," *China Society Occasional Papers*, n.s., no. 2 (1942).

33 H. C. Creel, p. 46.

34 A. Leroi-Gourhan, "L'Art animalier dans les Bronzes chinois," *Revue des Arts asiatiques* (Paris: 1935).

35 B. Karlgren, pp. 76–78.

36 B. Karlgren, "Huai and Han," *The Museum of Far Eastern Antiquities*, Bulletin 13 (Stockholm: 1941).

37 The problem of ancient relations across the Pacific Ocean has recently come to the fore again, owing to the surprising discovery, in a provincial museum of southeastern Formosa, of a low-relief in wood which could be of local origin. It represents three persons standing. Those located at the extremities are in the purest Maori style, while the person in the middle offers a kind of transition between Maori art and that of the Northwest Coast. See Ling Shun Sheng, "Human Figures with Protruding Tongue," *Bulletin of*

the Institute of Ethnology, Academia Sinica, no. 2 (September 1956), Nankang, Taipei, Taiwan.

38 H. C. Creel, pp. 65–66.
39 Ibid., p. 65.

REFERENCES

Adam, L. Das Problem der Asiatisch-Altamerikanischen Kulturbeziehungen mit besonderer Berücksichtigung der Kunst, *Wiener Beiträge zur Kunst und Kultur Geschichte Asiens*, V, 1931.

——. Northwest American Indian Art and Its Early Chinese Parallels, *Man*, XXXVI, no. 3, 1936.

Boas, F. *Primitive Art*. Oslo: 1927; New York: 1955.

Boggiani, G. *Viaggi d'un artista nell' America Meridionale*. Rome: 1895.

Creel, H. G. On the Origins of the Manufacture and Decoration of Bronze in the Shang Period, *Monumenta Serica*, I, Section 1, 1935.

——. Notes on Shang Bronzes in the Burlington House Exhibition, *Revue des Arts Asiatiques*, X, 1936.

Dobrizhoffer, M. *An Account of the Abipones*. 3 vols. Trans. from the Latin. London: 1822.

Field, H., and E. Prostov. Results of Soviet Investigation in Siberia, 1940–1941, *American Anthropologist*, n.s., XLIV, 1942.

Hamilton, A. *The Art Workmanship of the Maori Race in New Zealand*. Dunedin: 1896–1900.

Hentze, C. *Objets rituels, croyances et dieux de la Chine antique et de l'Amérique*. Antwerp: 1936.

——. *Frühchinesische Bronzen*. Antwerp: 1937.

Karlgren, B. *New Studies on Chinese Bronzes*. The Museum of Far Eastern Antiquities Bulletin no. 9. Stockholm: 1937.

——. *Huai and Han*. The Museum of Far Eastern Antiquities Bulletin No. 13. Stockholm: 1941.

Kelemen, P. *Medieval American Art*. 2 vols. New York: 1943.

Leroi-Gourhan, A. L'Art animalier dans les bronzes chinois, *Revue des Arts Asiatiques*, Paris, 1935.

Lévi-Strauss, C. Indian Cosmetics, *VVV*, No. 1, New York, 1942.

——. The Art of the Northwest Coast, *Gazette des Beaux-Arts*, New York, 1943.

——. *Tristes Tropiques*. Paris: 1955. Trans. John Russell. New York: 1961.

Ling Shun Sheng. Human Figures with Protruding Tongue Found in the Taitung Prefecture, Formosa, and Their Affinities Found in Other Pacific Areas, *Bulletin of the Institute of Ethnology, Academia Sinica*, no. 2, Nankang, Taipei, Taiwan, 1956.

McCarthy, F. D. *Australian Aboriginal Decorative Art*. Sydney: 1938.

Pottier, E. Histoire d'une bête. In *Recueil E. Pottier*. Bibliothèque des Ecoles d'Athènes et de Rome, Section 142, 1937.

Reichard, G. A. *Melanesian Design: A Study of Style in Wood and Tortoise Shell Carving*. 2 vols. Columbia University Contributions to Anthropology, no. 18. New York: 1933.

Robley, H. G. *Moko, or Maori Tattooing*. London: 1896.

Roes, A. Tierwirbel, *Ipek*, 1936–1937.

Rout, E. A. *Maori Symbolism*. London: 1926.

Swanton, J. R. *Social Condition, Beliefs and Linguistic Relationship of the Tlingit Indians*. Bureau of American Ethnology, 26th Annual Report. Washington, D.C.: 1908.

——. *Tlingit Myths and Texts*. Bureau of American Ethnology, Bulletin 59. Washington, D.C.: 1909.

Waterbury, F. *Early Chinese Symbols and Literature: Vestiges and Speculations*. New York: 1942.

Yetts, W. P. *The George Eumorphopoulos Collection Catalogue*. 3 vols. London: 1929.

——. *The Cull Chinese Bronzes*. London: 1939.

——. An-Yang: A Retrospect, *China Society Occasional Papers*, n.s., no. 2, London, 1942.

3

Introduction to *Tribes and Forms in African Art*

William Fagg

Among the most striking and (for better or for worse) fruitful results of the vast development (I had almost said the hypertrophy) of world communications in this century is the present condition of art in the "civilized" world, a state of virtually complete eclecticism, of freedom from the blinkers formerly imposed by the Western tradition upon the vision of artists and of the patrons of art. Hence has arisen the International Style, which may look anywhere for its inspiration, subject only to the trammels of fashion and commerce.

It is possible for M. Malraux to speak of the Universe of Forms – and to exclude from it no art known to mankind – precisely because we have now adopted into our own artistic universe the last of the exotic arts which used to be beyond the pale, in the exterior darkness. Yet here there arises a question of relativity. All these arts form a single universe *for us*; but they do not form a single universe absolutely. On the contrary, when we examine the tribal arts in themselves, we find that every tribe is, from the point of view of art, a universe to itself; and this great paradox is the central fact about African art (and all other tribal art) – a fact which is hardly yet appreciated by the Western world, and which it is the prime purpose of this book to illustrate.

If the idea of a multitude of universes of art – rather than provinces of one universe – seems at first strange and hardly acceptable to us, this is because, following the logic of civilization, we have enlarged our horizons until they are all-embracing. The use of the plural is justified only if the universes of which we speak are indeed mutually exclusive, with artistic horizons limited to the frontiers of each universe. Broadly, this appears to be a characteristic feature of tribal society: the tribe is an exclusive "in-group", which uses art among many other means to express its internal solidarity and self-sufficiency, and conversely its difference from all others.

In a tribal art there is no problem of communication, such as is typical of the malaise of European art. Such an art is of the people, by the people and for the people; it expresses values, religious and philosophical, which the artist shares not only with his patron but with the whole community. He is using a "language" of form which all can "understand", even though it is never put into words; their comprehension and his composition are intuitive to an extent rarely known in Europe for several centuries past. It is the unity of art and belief which makes understanding and acceptance of the forms of art easy for members of the tribe, but correspondingly difficult for non-members, since they do not share the belief. Tribal art, then, is "functional" within the tribe, but not outside it. And since the concept of "art for art's sake" is a modern

From *Tribes and Forms in African Art* (New York: Tudor, 1965), pp. 11–18.

invention of the European decadence, and is not present in tribal Africa, it follows that the sculpture of one tribe will be meaningless and unintelligible to people of another tribe, because it is art divorced from its content of belief. Indeed, the tribal African will normally show less appreciation of the art of another tribe than does a European; this is because the European, indoctrinated, however slightly, with the eclectic attitude to art, may well be able to appreciate in it some of the universal values which are found in all good art, whereas the tribal African is likely to be biased by his own matrix of belief against responding to these universalities. (Any such inhibition is, of course, likely to leave him as and when his attachment to his tribal belief and culture falls away, though his "detribalisation" would only rarely be accompanied by the development of a positive appreciation of universal values in art.)

Thus far, we have for the sake of simplicity spoken of the tribe as though it were a static and clearly defined entity, a kind of fixed datum to which we could attach each style of African art. In fact, the case is far more complicated: the tribe is essentially a dynamic phenomenon, constantly changing under gradual or violent pressures, and often very difficult to pin down in terms of the categories of Western science. Social anthropologists, political scientists and others concerned chiefly with the immaterial aspects of culture sometimes find it so difficult to apply the concept (especially in current conditions of accelerated change) that they often prefer to minimize or discard it. (In some countries of Africa, the hostility of the régime to "tribalism" – by which are meant the abuses of tribalism – creates strong pressures upon social scientists to adopt an obscurantist attitude towards the tribe and its works.) The two surest guides in the identification of tribes appear to be linguistics and material culture, and it is upon these that we have especially relied in this book. Material culture studies are especially valuable for the purpose because the data with which the student works are facts of the most concrete and incontrovertible kind (however vague their documentation may be), rather than observations, abstractions and opinions derived from human behaviour such as are the stuff of social anthropology and sociology.

Art therefore provides one of the principal criteria for the identification and delimitation of tribes. It is theoretically possible (though it would call for a vast amount of fieldwork by the rather small group of anthropologists who are both qualified and interested in these studies) to compile a tribal map of Africa on which the frontiers enclosing tribal styles of art are shown as a continuous line wherever the distinction between one style and the next is clear-cut and indisputable, and as a broken line where the artistic frontier is "open", permitting stylistic influences to pass in one direction or both, or where, for reasons which may now be obscure, it is difficult to draw a clear line. Such a map – which would need to be drawn as at a date such as 1900 or 1918, so heavy has been the erosion of African art since then by the processes of social and material decay and of commerce – would certainly include many lengths of broken line, but its main effect would be to exhibit a high degree of firm correlation between tribal styles and language frontiers, and the proportion of continuous line might well exceed 90 per cent. In the body of this book will be found many observations which would be relevant in the planning of such an enterprise, and although it is the main purpose of the book to draw attention to the extent of "tribality" in African sculptural form, every care has been taken not to weight the evidence in favour of the thesis but rather to define its nature by giving full emphasis to exceptions and qualifications.

In a continent such as Africa, no tribe can be completely an island, for all must have relations with others. Such relations may or may not have visible effects upon a tribe's art. The Balega have an art which is absolutely characteristic of them and, it seems, of no one else; their artistic universe, then, is completely circumscribed. The same would seem to be true of the Bakwele and the Kuyu, of the Tiv and probably of the Kisi. Many tribes have an effectively self-contained art which nevertheless forms a compromise or local fusion with one or other of the surrounding styles. The Yoruba provide an excellent example: it is astonishing that the art of this most prolific of all the art-producing tribes should retain its immediately identifiable Yoruba character so consistently while permitting a remarkable degree of local and individual variation; yet there is one direction, to the south-east, in which this consistency lapses, the Yoruba style being displaced by an almost pure version of western Ijo style, owing, we may surmise, to a failure of the inland-based Yoruba gods to cope so successfully with the watery environment of Okitipupa as the water spirits of the Ijo fishermen. The Basonge, again, have one of the "strongest" and, as one might think, most inflexible of African styles, with its severely cubistic abstractions of the human figure; yet in one small area a remarkably successful fusion has been achieved between this style and that of the Baluba, which in many ways is of an almost opposite character, favouring undulating, almost fleshy, surfaces.

Another and more complicated kind of contact between styles is seen in the style clusters such as the Dan-Ngere complex, the Cameroons Grasslands complex, the Balumbo and other tribes using the white-faced mask style, and the great Lunda-Bajokwe complex. A similar case involving two tribes only is the Bayaka-Basuku grouping. In all these cases some degree of stylistic symbiosis exists between two or more tribes, although further research may reveal more definite regularities in the component styles which would lead us to modify our present assumption that these tribes inhabit multilaterally shared universes of art. In one sense, for example, the Grassland tribes may be said to accept and perhaps even appreciate each other's styles, since Babanki carvings are frequently found in use among the Bamileke peoples, and Bamileke carvings among other tribes of the complex; yet each of these small tribes continued at least until recently to practise its own clearly identifiable style, and so may be regarded as having an artistic universe of its own, even though several of these universes may be said to be compatible with each other.

Another complicated situation is found in tribes such as the Fang, the Bakota and the Bena Lulua, who, so far as their most characteristic forms are concerned, occupy their own exclusive universes, yet among their minor art forms have one or more which are shared with surrounding tribes. The Fang and the Bakota are famous for their reliquary figures in contrasting styles, and the Bena Lulua for their beautifully scarified standing figures, yet all

three have yielded (though much more rarely) a type of mask shared with one or more of their neighbours; for example, the Bakota have been found to use whitefaced masks typical of the Balumbo complex, while the Bena Lulua mask seems to be shared with, and more characteristic of, the southern Bakuba. It may well be significant that in all these three cases it is a mask which seems to have breached the exclusive universes of these tribes; for it appears that dance societies whose activities have a largely recreational purpose may provide a favourable mechanism for the transfer of cultural traits from one tribe to another. A remarkable example of this phenomenon has occurred in Eastern Nigeria, where the skin-covered heads used as dance headdresses by the *Ekkpe* society in the Ekoi cluster of tribes on the Cameroons border became so popular that they spread to the Ibibio, displacing the indigenous forms, and from the Ibibio spread to some Ibo groups notably in the Bende and Aba districts. This is no doubt because, when a masquerade is being played, almost everybody (including Christians) will turn out for it and the people of the next village, even if of another tribe and language group, may want to set up their own lodge for the same masquerade cult. These masquerades may have a very definite therapeutic value for the community if they are well performed, and there may be strong competition between rival cults. In this case the diffusion of the Ekoi type of headdress represented the progressive supplanting of more abstract by more naturalistic forms, and this change of fashion may have been influenced by the infiltration of European ideas into Eastern Nigeria during the past century.

Some of the examples that we have been considering may be regarded as cases of cultural fission, a portion of a tribe becoming detached and modified under the influence of a neighbouring tribe, while others seem rather to represent incipient fusion of one style with another. But all are demonstrations of the dynamic character of the tribe and of tribal styles. Such phenomena are sometimes quoted as evidence in refutation of the view that African art is essentially tribal; in fact, of course, given that a tribe is to be regarded as a dynamic and not a static entity, they provide the best possible proof of tribality, for in each case we are able to analyse the modified styles into their component elements and assign tribal origins to them. Clearly it is through such processes – of fission probably more often than of fusion – that African art has differentiated itself through the ages into so rich a variety of sculptural forms. Such a development in art must have been more or less parallel to the proliferation of African languages during the last few millennia.

What is the relevance for modern Africa of the facts presented in this book? Many Africans may regret that the evolutionary process has worked in the direction of the development of thousands of languages rather than of a few or of one, with the unavoidable result that they must speak and think in English or French; yet the oral literature of Africa is immeasurably richer as a result of this proliferation. How much more valuable to the world has been the proliferation of sculptural forms! For it is in this field surely that Africa has made her greatest and finest contribution to world civilization – a contribution far more fundamental and profound than the influence indirectly exerted by Africa on Western popular music.

It is true that modern artists have not yet taken sufficient account of the fact that African art was an art of belief – nor should this surprise us, since for the most part their art is not an art of belief. Too often they have treated African sculptures as though they were *objets trouvés*, a kind of compendium of artistic possibilities, to be drawn upon like a commonplace book. Yet even without the penetration of content (which may still be achieved in the future), western art, and especially sculpture, has greatly benefited from its encounter with the immense range of the exploration of form by the tribal artists of Africa. The processes of evolution, working along the diverging lines of development of Africa's innumerable tribes – and greatly assisted and accelerated by the destructive processes of nature – have produced for our time this great corpus of forms, in which few possibilities have remained unexplored; and the real importance of this for modern art lies in the freeing of artists from formal preconceptions. Freedom from preconceptions will not produce great art, which needs great artists, yet this process may be an essential one if the new kind of art – international art – is in the future to achieve anything comparable to the great periods of human art of the past.

But perhaps the greatest contribution which Africa could make to world art would be to redress the balance of the intellect and the intuition. For whereas the dominance of the intellect in European art, established in the Renaissance, has become excessive in recent times, African art is a field in which intuitive judgment has had full expression. This is indeed only another aspect of the "directness" which has been so much admired by modern artists in tribal art, and it is of course natural enough that non-literate peoples should be free of that literariness in art which is equally present in the academic and the modern art of Europe and America. If Africa is to be able to act as a leaven in the art of the world, it is of the utmost importance that African intellectuals – who have an acquired bias towards the dominance of the intellect – should come to know and admire the qualities of the dying tribal arts of their past and if possible preserve them for the world.

4

Style, Grace, and Information in Primitive Art

Gregory Bateson

Introduction

This paper consists of several still separate attempts to map a theory associated with culture and the non-verbal arts. Since no one of these attempts is completely successful, and since the attempts do not as yet meet in the middle of the territory to be mapped, it may be useful to state, in non-technical language, what it is I am after.

Aldous Huxley used to say that the central problem for humanity is the quest for *grace*. This word he used in what he thought was the sense in which it is used in the New Testament. He explained the word, however, in his own terms. He argued – like Walt Whitman – that the communication and behaviour of animals has a naïveté, a simplicity, which man has lost. Man's behaviour is corrupted by deceit – even self-deceit – by purpose, and by self-consciousness. As Aldous saw the matter, man has lost the 'grace' which animals still have. In terms of this contrast, Aldous argued that God resembles the animals rather than man: ideally he is unable to deceive and incapable of internal confusions. In the total scale of beings, therefore, man is as if displaced sideways and lacks that grace which the animals have and which God has.

I argue that art is a part of man's quest for grace; sometimes his ecstasy in partial success, sometimes his rage and agony at failure. I argue also that there are many species of grace within the major genus; and also that there are many kinds of failure and frustration and departure from grace. No doubt each culture has its characteristic species of grace towards which its artists strive, and its own species of failure. Some cultures may foster a negative approach to this difficult integration, an avoidance of complexity by crass preference either for total consciousness or total unconsciousness. Their art is unlikely to be 'great'.

I shall argue that the problem of grace is fundamentally a problem of integration and that what is to be integrated is the diverse parts of the mind – especially those multiple levels of which one extreme is called 'consciousness' and the other the 'unconscious'. For the attainment of grace, the reasons of the heart must be integrated with the reasons of the reason.

In the previous chapter Edmund Leach (1973) presents in a compelling form the question: how is it that the art of one culture can have meaning or validity for critics raised in a different culture? My answer would be that, if art is somehow expressive of something like grace or

From Anthony Forge (ed.), *Primitive Art and Society* (Oxford: Oxford University Press, 1973), pp. 235–255. Reprinted by permission of the Wenner-Gren Foundation for Anthropological Research, Inc., New York.

psychic integration, then the *success* of this expression might well be recognizable across cultural barriers. The physical grace of cats is profoundly different from the physical grace of horses, and yet a man who has the physical grace of neither can evaluate that of both. And even when the subject-matter of art is the frustration of integration, cross-cultural recognition of the products of this frustration is not too surprising.

The central question is: in what form is information about psychic integration contained or coded in the work of art?

Style and Meaning

They say that 'every picture tells a story' and this generalization holds for most of art if we exclude 'mere' geometric ornamentation. But I want precisely to avoid analysing the 'story'. That aspect of the work of art which can most easily be reduced to words – the *mythology* connected with the subject-matter – is not what I want to discuss. I shall not even mention the unconscious mythology of phallic symbolism, except at the end.

I am concerned with what important psychic information is in the art object quite apart from what it may 'represent'. '*Le style est l'homme même*' (Buffon). What is implicit in style, materials, composition, rhythm, skill, and so on? Clearly this subject-matter will include geometrical ornamentation along with the composition and stylistic aspects of more representational works. The lions in Trafalgar Square could have been eagles or bulldogs and still have carried the same (or similar) messages about empire and about the cultural premises of nineteenth-century England. And yet, how different might their message have been, had they been made of wood! But representationa*lism* as such is relevant. The extremely realistic horses and stags of Altamira are surely not about the same cultural premisses as the highly conventionalized black outlines of a later period. The *code* whereby perceived objects or persons (or supernaturals) are transformed into wood or paint is a source of information about the artist and his culture. It is the very rules of transformation that are of interest to me – not the message but the code.

My goal is not instrumental. I do not want to use the transformation rules when discov-

ered, to undo the transformation or to 'decode' the message. To translate the art object into mythology and then examine the mythology would be only a neat way of dodging or negating the problem of 'what is art?'. I ask, then, not about the meaning of the encoded message but rather about the meaning of the code chosen. But still that most slippery word 'meaning' must be defined. It will be convenient to define meaning in the most general possible way in the first instance. 'Meaning' may be regarded as an approximate synonym of pattern, redundancy, information, and 'restraint', within a paradigm of the following sort:

Any aggregate of events or objects (e.g. a sequence of phonemes, a painting or a frog or a culture) shall be said to contain 'redundancy' or 'pattern' if the aggregate can be divided in any way by a 'slash mark', such that an observer perceiving only what is on one side of the slash mark can *guess*, with better than random success, what is on the other side of the slash mark. We may say that what is on one side of the slash contains *information* or has *meaning* about what is on the other side. Or, in engineer's language, the aggregate contains 'redundancy'. Or, again, from the point of view of a cybernetic observer, the information available on one side of the slash will restrain (i.e. reduce the probability of) wrong guessing. Examples:

The letter T in a given location in a piece of written English prose proposes that the next letter is likely to be an H or an R or a vowel. It is possible to make a better than random guess across a slash which immediately follows the T. English spelling contains redundancy.

From a part of an English sentence, delimited by a slash, it is possible to guess at the syntactic structure of the remainder of the sentence. From a tree visible above ground, it is possible to guess at the existence of roots below ground. The top provides information about the bottom. From an arc of a *drawn* circle, it is possible to guess at the position of other parts of the circumference. (From the diameter of an *ideal* circle, it is possible to assert the length of the circumference. But this is a matter of truth within a tautological system.) From how the boss acted yesterday, it may be possible to guess how he will act today. From what I say, it may be possible to make predictions about how you will answer. My words contain meaning or information about your reply.

Telegraphist A has a written message on his pad and sends this message over wire to B, so that B now gets the same sequence of letters on his message pad. This transaction (or 'language game' in Wittgenstein's phrase) has created a redundant universe for an observer O. If O knows what was on A's pad, he can make a better than random guess at what is on B's pad.

The essence and *raison d'être* of communication is the creation of redundancy, meaning, pattern, predictability, information, and/or the reduction of the random by 'restraint'. It is, I believe, of prime importance to have a conceptual system which will force us to see the 'message' (e.g. the art object) as *both* itself internally patterned *and* itself a part of a larger patterned universe – the culture or some part of it.

The characteristics of objects of art are believed to be *about,* or to be partly derived from, or determined by, other characteristics of cultural and psychological systems. Our problem might therefore be oversimply represented by the diagram:

[Characteristics of art object/Characteristics of rest of culture]

where square brackets enclose the universe of relevance, and where the oblique stroke represents a slash across which some guessing is possible, in one direction or in both. The problem, then, is to spell out what sorts of relationships, correspondences, etc., cross or transcend this oblique stroke.

Consider the case in which I say to you 'it's raining' and you guess that if you look out the window you will see raindrops. A similar diagram will serve:

[Characteristics of 'It's raining'/Perception of raindrops]

Notice, however, that this case is by no means simple. Only if you know the *language* and have some trust in my veracity will you be able to make a guess about the raindrops. In fact, few people in this situation restrain themselves from seemingly duplicating their information by looking out of the window. We like to prove that our guesses are right, and that

our friends are honest. Still more important, *we like to test or verify the correctness of our view of our relationship to others.*

This last point is non-trivial. It illustrates the necessarily hierarchic structure of all communicational systems: the fact of conformity or non-conformity (or indeed any other relationship) between parts of a patterned whole may itself be informative as part of some still larger whole. The matter may be diagrammed thus:

[('It's raining'/raindrops)/you–me relationship]

where redundancy across the slash mark within the smaller universe enclosed in round brackets proposes (is a message about) a redundancy in the larger universe enclosed in square brackets. But the message 'It's raining' is itself conventionally coded and internally patterned, so that several slash marks could be drawn across the message indicating patterning within the message itself. And the same is true of the rain. It too is patterned and structured. From the direction of one drop, I could predict the direction of others, and so on.

But the slash marks across the verbal message 'It's raining' will not correspond in any simple way to the slash marks across the raindrops. If, instead of a verbal message, I had given you a picture of the rain, some of the slashes on the picture would have corresponded with slashes on the perceived rain. This difference provides a neat formal criterion to separate the 'arbitrary' and digital coding characteristic of the verbal part of language from the *iconic* coding of depiction. But verbal description is often iconic in its larger structure. A scientist describing an earthworm might start at the head end and work down its length – thus producing a description iconic in its sequence and elongation. Here again we observe a hierarchic structuring, digital or verbal at one level and iconic at another.

Levels and Logical Types

'Levels' have been mentioned. It was noted: a. that the *combination* of the message 'It's raining' with the perception of raindrops can itself constitute a message about a universe of personal relations; and b. that when we change our focus of attention from smaller to larger units of message material, we may discover that a larger unit contains iconic coding though the smaller parts of which it was made are verbal: the verbal description of an earthworm may, as a whole be elongated.

The matter of levels now crops up in another form which is crucial for any epistemology of art:

The word 'know' is not merely ambiguous in covering both *connaître* (to know through the senses, to recognize, or perceive) and *savoir* (to know in the mind), but varies – actively shifts – in meaning for basic systemic reasons. Something of what we know through the senses can be re-coded to become knowledge in the mind.

'I know the way to Cambridge' might mean that I have studied the map and can give you directions. It might mean that I can recall details all along the route. It might mean that when driving that route I *recognize* many details even though I could recall only a few. It might mean that when driving to Cambridge I can trust to 'habit' to make me turn at the right points, without having to *think* where I am going, and so on.

In all cases, we deal with a redundancy or patterning of a quite complex sort:

[('I know...'/my mind)//the road]

and the difficulty is to determine the nature of the patterning within the round brackets or – to put the matter another way: what *parts* of the mind are redundant with the particular message about 'knowing'.

Last, there is a special form of 'knowing' which is usually regarded as adaptation rather than information. A shark is beautifully shaped for locomotion in water but the genome of the shark surely does not contain direct information about hydrodynamics. Rather the genome must be supposed to contain information or instructions which are the *complement* of hydrodynamics. Not hydrodynamics, but what hydrodynamics requires, has been built up in the shark's genome. Similarly a migratory bird perhaps does not know the way to its destination in any of the senses outlined above but the bird may contain the complementary instructions necessary to cause it to fly right.

Le coeur a ses raisons que la raison ne connaît point. It is this – the complex layering

of consciousness and unconsciousness – that creates difficulty when we try to discuss art or ritual or mythology. The matter of *levels* of the mind has been discussed from many points of view at least four of which must be mentioned and woven into any scientific approach to art:

1. Samuel Butler's insistence that the better an organism 'knows' something, the less conscious it becomes of its knowledge, i.e. there is a process whereby knowledge (or 'habit' – whether of action, perception, or thought) sinks to deeper and deeper levels of the mind. This phenomenon which is central to Zen discipline (cf. Herrigel, *Zen in the Art of Archery*, London, 1953), is also relevant to all art and all skill.

2. Adalbert Ames' demonstrations that the conscious, three-dimensional visual images, which we make of that which we see, are made by processes involving mathematical premises of perspective, etc. of the use of which we are totally unconscious. Over these processes, we have no voluntary control. A drawing of a chair with the perspective of Van Gogh affronts the conscious expectations and, dimly, reminds the consciousness of what had been (unconsciously) taken for granted.

3. The Freudian (especially Fenichel's) theory of dreams as metaphors coded according to *primary process*. I shall consider style – neatness, boldness of contrast, etc. – as metaphoric and therefore as linked to those levels of the mind where primary process holds sway.

4. The Freudian view of the unconscious as the cellar or cupboard to which fearful and painful memories are consigned by a process of repression.

Classical Freudian theory assumed that dreams were a *secondary* product, created by 'dream work'. Material, unacceptable to conscious thought, was supposedly translated into the metaphoric idiom of primary process to avoid waking the dreamer. And this may be true of those items of information which are held in the unconscious by the process of repression. As we have seen, however, many other sorts of information are inaccessible to conscious inspection including most of the premisses of mammalian interaction. It would seem to me sensible to think of these items as existing *primarily* in the idiom of primary process, only with difficulty to be translated into 'rational' terms. In other words, I believe that much of early Freudian theory was upside down. At that time many thinkers regarded conscious reason as normal and self-explanatory while the unconscious was regarded as mysterious, needing proof, and needing explanation. Repression was the explanation, and the unconscious was filled with thoughts which could have been conscious but which repression and dream work had distorted. Today we think of consciousness as the mysterious, and of the computational methods of the unconscious, e.g. primary process, as continually active, necessary, and all-embracing.

These considerations are especially relevant in any attempt to derive a theory of art or poetry. Poetry is not a sort of distorted and decorated prose but rather prose is poetry which has been stripped down and pinned to a Procrustean bed of logic. The computer men who would programme the translation of languages sometimes forget this fact about the primary nature of language. To try to construct a machine to translate the art of one culture into the art of another would be equally silly.

Allegory, at best a distasteful sort of art, is an inversion of the normal creative process. Typically an abstract relation, e.g. between truth and justice, is first conceived in rational terms. The relationship is then metaphorized and dolled up to look like a product of primary process. The abstractions are personified and made to participate in a pseudo-myth, and so on. Much advertising art is allegorical in this sense, that the creative process is inverted.

In the cliché system of Anglo-Saxons, it is commonly assumed that it would be somehow better if what is unconscious were made conscious. Freud, even, is said to have said, 'Where id was, there ego shall be,' as though such an increase in conscious knowledge and control would be both possible and, of course, an improvement. This view is the product of an almost totally distorted epistemology and a totally distorted view of what sort of thing a man, or any other organism, is.

Of the four sorts of unconsciousness listed above, it is very clear that the first three are necessary. Consciousness, for obvious mechanical reasons,[1] must always be limited to a rather small fraction of mental process. If useful at all, it must therefore be husbanded. The unconsciousness associated with habit is an economy both of thought and of consciousness; and the same is true of the inaccessibility of the processes of perception. The conscious organism does not require (for pragmatic purposes) to know *how* it perceives – only to know *what* it perceives. (To suggest that we might operate without a foundation in primary process would be to suggest that the human brain ought to be differently structured.) Of the four types, only the Freudian cupboard for skeletons is perhaps undesirable and could be obviated. But there may still be advantages in keeping the skeleton off the dining-room table.

In truth, our life is such that its unconscious components are continuously present in all their multiple forms. It follows that in our relationships we continuously exchange messages about these unconscious materials, and it becomes important also to exchange meta-messages by which we tell each other what order and species of unconsciousness (or consciousness) attaches to our messages.

In a merely pragmatic way, this is important because the orders of truth are different for different sorts of messages. In so far as a message is conscious and voluntary, it could be deceitful. I can tell you the cat is on the mat when in fact she is not there. I can tell you 'I love you' when in fact I do not. But discourse about relationship is commonly accompanied by a mass of semi-voluntary kinesic and autonomic signals which provide a more trustworthy comment on the verbal message. Similarly, with skill, the fact of skill indicates the presence of large unconscious components in the performance.

It thus becomes relevant to look at any work of art with the question: What components of this message material had what orders of unconsciousness (or consciousness) for the artist? And this question, I believe, the sensitive critic usually asks, though perhaps not consciously. Art becomes, in this sense, an exercise in communicating about the species of unconsciousness. Or, if you prefer it, a sort of play behaviour whose function is, amongst other things, to practise and make more perfect communication of this kind.

I am indebted to Anthony Forge for a quotation from Isadora Duncan: 'If I could tell you what it meant, there would be no point in dancing it.' Her statement is ambiguous. In terms of the rather vulgar premises of our culture, we would translate the statement to mean: 'There would then be no point in dancing it, because I could tell it to you, quicker and with less ambiguity, in words.' This interpretation goes along with the silly idea that it would be a good thing to be conscious of everything of which we are unconscious.

But there is another possible meaning of Isadora Duncan's remark: if the message were the sort of message that could be communicated in words, there would be no point in dancing it, but it is not that sort of message. It is, in fact, precisely the sort of message which would be falsified if communicated in words, because the use of words (other than poetry) would imply that this is a fully conscious and voluntary message, and this would be simply untrue.

I believe that what Isadora Duncan or any artist is trying to communicate is more like: 'This is a particular sort of partly unconscious message. Let us engage in this particular sort of partly unconscious communication.' Or perhaps: 'This is a message about the interface between conscious and unconscious.' The message of *skill* of any kind must always be of this kind. The sensations and qualities of skill can never be put in words and yet the fact of skill is conscious.

The artist's dilemma is of a peculiar sort. He must practise in order to perform the craft components of his job. But to practise has always a double effect. It makes him, on the one hand, more able to do whatever it is he is attempting; and, on the other hand, by the phenomenon of habit formation, it makes him less aware of how he does it. If his attempt is to communicate about the unconscious components of his performance, then it follows that he is on a sort of moving stairway about whose position he is trying to communicate but whose movement is itself a function of his efforts to communicate. Clearly, his task is impossible but, as has been remarked, some people do it very prettily.

Primary Process

'The heart has its *reasons* which the reason does not perceive at all.' Among Anglo-Saxons, it is rather usual to think of the 'reasons' of the heart or of the unconscious as inchoate forces or pushes or heavings – what Freud called 'Trieben'. To Pascal, a Frenchman, the matter was rather different, and he no doubt thought of the reasons of the heart as a body of logic or computation as precise and complex as the reasons of consciousness.

(I have noticed that Anglo-Saxon anthropologists sometimes mis-understand the writings of Claude Lévi-Strauss for precisely this reason. They say he emphasizes too much the intellect and ignores the 'feelings'. The truth is that he assumes that the heart has precise algorithms.)

These algorithms of the heart, or as they say, of the unconscious, are, however, coded and organized in a manner totally different from the algorithms of language. And since a great deal of conscious thought is structured in terms of the logics of language, the algorithms of the unconscious are doubly inaccessible. It is not only that the conscious mind has poor access to this material, but also the fact that when such access is achieved, e.g. in dreams, art, poetry, religion, intoxication, and the like, there is still a formidable problem of translation. This is usually expressed in Freudian language by saying that the operations of the unconscious are structured in terms of *primary process*, while the thoughts of consciousness (especially verbalized thoughts) are expressed in *secondary process*. Nobody, to my knowledge, knows anything about secondary process. But it is ordinarily assumed that everybody knows all about it, so I shall not attempt to describe secondary process in any detail, assuming that you know as much about it as I.

Primary process is characterized (e.g. by Fenichel) as lacking negatives, lacking tense, lacking in any identification of linguistic mood (i.e. no identification of indicative, subjunctive, optative, etc.) and metaphorical. These characterizations are based upon the experience of psycho-analysts, who must interpret dreams and the patterns of free association.

It is also true that the subject-matter of primary process discourse is different from the subject-matter of language and consciousness. Consciousness talks about things or persons, and attaches predicates to the specific things or persons which have been mentioned. In primary process the things or persons are usually not identified and the focus of the discourse is upon the *relationships* which are asserted to obtain between them. This is really only another way of saying that the discourse of primary process is metaphoric. A metaphor retains unchanged the relationship which it illustrates, while substituting other things or persons for the relata. In a simile, the fact that a metaphor is being used is marked by the insertion of the words 'as if' or 'like'. In primary process (as in art) there are no markers to indicate to the conscious mind that the message material is metaphoric. (For a schizophrenic, it is a major step towards a more conventional sanity when he can frame his schizophrenic utterances or the comments of his voices in an 'as if' terminology.)

The focus of 'relationship' is, however, somewhat more narrow than would be indicated merely by saying that primary process material is metaphoric and does not identify the specific relata. The subject-matter of dream and other primary process material is, in fact, relationship in the more narrow sense of relationship between self and other persons or between self and the environment.

Anglo-Saxons who are uncomfortable with the idea that feelings and emotions are the outward signs of precise and complex algorithms, usually have to be told that these matters, the relationship between self and others, and the relationship between self and environment are, in fact, the subject-matter of what are called 'feelings' – love, hate, fear, confidence, anxiety, hostility, etc. It is unfortunate that these abstractions referring to *patterns* of relationship have received names, which are usually handled in ways that assume that the 'feelings' are mainly characterized by quantity rather than by precise pattern. This is one of the nonsensical contributions of psychology to a distorted epistemology.

Be all that as it may, for our present purposes it is important to note that the characteristics of primary process as described above are the inevitable characteristics of any communicational system between organisms who must use only iconic communication. This same limitation is characteristic of the artist and of the dreamer and of the pre-human mammal or bird. (The communication of insects is, perhaps, another matter.) In iconic communication, there is no tense, no simple negative, no modal marker. The absence of simple negatives is of especial interest because it often forces organisms *into saying the opposite of what they mean in order to get across the proposition that they mean the opposite of what they say.*

Two dogs approach each other and need to exchange the message: 'We are *not* going to fight.' But the only way in which fight can be mentioned in iconic communication is by the showing of fangs. It is then necessary for the dogs to discover that this mention of fight was, in fact, only exploratory. They must, therefore, explore what the showing of fangs means. They therefore engage in a brawl; discover that neither ultimately intends to kill the other; and, after that, they can be friends. (Consider the peace-making ceremonials of the Andaman islanders. Consider also the functions of inverted statement or sarcasm, and other sorts of humour in dream, art, and mythology.)

In general, the discourse of animals is concerned with relationship either between self and other or self and environment. In neither case is it necessary to identify the relata. Animal A tells B about his relationship with B and he tells C about his relationship with C. Animal A does not have to tell animal C about his relationship with B. Always the relata are perceptibly present to illustrate the discourse, and always the discourse is iconic in the sense of being composed of part actions ('intention movements') which mention the whole action which is being mentioned. Even when the cat asks you for milk, she cannot mention the object which she wants (unless it be perceptibly present). She says, 'Mama, Mama', and you are supposed from this invocation of dependency to guess that it is milk that she requires.

All this indicates that primary process thoughts and the communication of such thoughts to others are, in an evolutionary sense, more archaic than the more conscious operations of language, etc. This has implications for the whole economics and dynamic structure of the mind. Samuel Butler was perhaps first to point out that that which we know best is that of which we are least conscious, i.e. that the process of habit formation is a sinking of knowledge down to less conscious and more archaic levels. The unconscious contains not only the painful matters which consciousness prefers not to inspect but also many matters which are so familiar that we do not need to inspect them. Habit, therefore, is a major economy of conscious thought. We can do things without consciously thinking about them. The skill of an artist or rather his demonstration of a skill becomes a message *about* these parts of his unconsciousness. (But not perhaps a message *from* the unconscious.)

But the matter is not quite so simple. Some types of knowledge can conveniently be sunk to unconscious levels but other types must be kept on the surface. Broadly, we can afford to sink those sorts of knowledge which continue to be true regardless of changes in the environment, but we must maintain in an accessible place all those controls of behaviour which must be modified for every instance. The lion can sink into his unconscious the proposition that zebras are his natural prey but in dealing with any particular zebra he must be able to modify the movements of his attack to fit with the particular terrain and the particular evasive tactics of the particular zebra.

The economics of the system, in fact, pushes organisms towards sinking into the unconscious those generalities of relationship which remain permanently true and towards keeping within the conscious the pragmatics of particular instances.

The premises may, economically, be sunk but particular conclusions must be conscious. But the 'sinking', though economical, is still done at a price – the price of inaccessibility. Since the level to which things are sunk is characterized by iconic algorithms and metaphor, it becomes difficult for the organism to examine the matrix out of which his conscious conclusions spring. Conversely, we may note that what is *common* to a particular statement and a corresponding metaphor is of a generality appropriate for sinking.

Quantitative Limits of Consciousness

A very brief consideration of the problem shows that it is not conceivably possible for any system to be totally conscious. Suppose that on the screen of consciousness there are reports from many parts of the total mind, and consider the addition to consciousness of those reports necessary to cover what is, at a given stage of evolution, not already covered. This addition will involve a very great increase in the circuit structure of the brain but still will not achieve total coverage. The next step will be to cover the processes and events occurring in the circuit structure which we have just added, and so on. Clearly, the problem is insoluble and every next step in the approach to total consciousness will involve a great increase in the circuitry required.

It follows that all organisms must be content with rather little consciousness and that if consciousness has any useful functions whatever (which has never been demonstrated but is probably true), then *economy* in consciousness will be of the first importance. No organism can afford to be conscious of matters with which it could deal at unconscious levels. This is the economy achieved by habit formation.

Qualitative Limits of Consciousness

It is, of course, true for the TV set that a satisfactory picture on the screen is an indication that many parts of the machine are working as they should; and similar considerations apply to the 'screen' of consciousness. But what is provided is only a very indirect report of the working of all those parts. If the TV suffers from a blown tube, or the man from a stroke, *effects* of this pathology may be evident enough on the screen or to consciousness, but diagnosis must still be done by an expert.

This matter has bearings upon the nature of art. The TV which gives a distorted or otherwise imperfect picture is, in a sense, communicating about its unconscious pathologies – exhibiting its symptoms and one may ask whether some artists are not doing something similar. But this still won't do.

It is sometimes said that the distortions of art (say Van Gogh's 'Chair') are directly representative of what the artist '*sees*'. If such statements refer to 'seeing' in the simplest physical sense (e.g. remediable with spectacles), I presume that they are nonsense. If Van Gogh could only see the chair in that wild way, his eyes would not serve properly to guide him in the very accurate placing of paint on canvas. And, conversely, a photographically accurate representation of the chair on the canvas would also be seen by Van Gogh in the wild way. He would see no need to distort the painting.

But suppose we say that the artist is painting today what he saw yesterday – or that he is painting what he somehow knows that he *might* see. 'I see as well as you do – but do you realize that this other way of seeing a chair exists as a human potentiality? And that that potentiality is always in you and in me?' Is he exhibiting symptoms which he *might* have, because the whole spectrum of psychopathology is possible for us all?

Intoxication by alcohol or drugs may help us to see a distorted world, and these distortions may be fascinating in that we recognize the distortions as *ours. In vino pars veritatis.* We can be humbled or aggrandized by realizing that this too is a *part* of the human self, a *part* of Truth. But intoxication does not increase skill – at best it may release skill previously acquired.

Without skill is no art.

Consider the case of the man who goes to the blackboard – or to the side of his cave – and draws, freehand, a perfect reindeer in its posture of threat. He cannot *tell* you about the drawing of the reindeer ('If he could, there would be no point in drawing it'). 'Do you know that this perfect way of seeing – and drawing – a reindeer exists as a human potentiality?' The consummate skill of the draftsman validates the artist's message about his relationship to the animal – his empathy.

(They say the Altamira things were made for sympathetic hunting magic. But magic only needs the crudest sort of representations. The scrawled arrows which deface the beautiful reindeer may have been magical – perhaps a vulgar attempt to murder the artist, like moustaches scrawled on the Mona Lisa.)

The Corrective Nature of Art

It was noted above that consciousness is necessarily selective and partial, i.e. that the content of consciousness is, at best, a small part of truth about the self. But if this part be *selected* in any systematic manner, it is certain that the partial truths of consciousness will be, in aggregate, a distortion of the truth of some larger whole.

In the case of an iceberg we may guess, from what is above surface, what sort of stuff is below; but we cannot make the same sort of extrapolation from the content of consciousness. It is not merely the selectivity of preference, whereby the skeletons accumulate in the Freudian unconscious, that makes such extrapolation unsound. Such a selection by preference would only promote optimism.

What is serious is the cross-cutting of the circuitry of the mind. If, as we must believe, the total mind is an integrated network (of propositions, images, processes, neural pathology, or what have you – according to what scientific language you prefer to use), and if the content of consciousness is only a sampling of different parts and localities in this network; then, inevitably, the conscious view of the network as a whole is a monstrous denial of the *integration* of that whole. From the cutting of consciousness, what appears above the surface is *arcs* of circuits instead of either the complete circuits or the larger complete circuits of circuits. What the unaided consciousness (unaided by art, dreams, and the like) can never appreciate is the *systemic* nature of mind.

This notion can conveniently be illustrated by an analogy: the living human body is a complex, cybernetically integrated system. This system has been studied by scientists – mostly medical men – for many years. What they now know about the body may aptly be compared with what the unaided consciousness knows about the mind. Being doctors, they had purposes: to cure this and that. Their research efforts were therefore focused (as attention focuses the consciousness) upon those short trains of causality which they could manipulate, by means of drugs or other intervention, to correct more or less specific and identifiable states or symptoms. Whenever they discovered an effective 'cure' for something, research in that area ceased and attention was directed elsewhere. We can now prevent polio but nobody knows much more about the systemic aspects of that fascinating disease. Research on it has ceased or is, at best, confined to improving the vaccines.

But a bag of tricks for curing or preventing a list of specified diseases provides no overall *wisdom.* The ecology and population dynamics of the species has been disrupted; parasites have been made immune to antibiotics; the relationship between mother and neonate has been almost destroyed; and so on. Characteristically, errors occur wherever the altered causal chain is part of some large or small circuit structure or system. And the remainder of our technology (of which medical science is only a part) bids fair to disrupt the rest of our ecology.

The point, however, which I am trying to make in this paper is not an attack on medical science, but a demonstration of an inevitable fact: that mere purposive rationality unaided by such phenomena as art, religion, dream, and the like is necessarily pathogenic and destructive of life; and that its virulence springs specifically from the circumstance that life depends upon interlocking *circuits* of contingency, while consciousness can see only such short arcs of such circuits as human purpose may direct. In a word, the unaided consciousness must always involve man in the sort of stupidity of which evolution was guilty when she urged upon the dinosaurs the common-sense values of an armaments race. She, inevitably, realized her mistake a few million years later and wiped them out.

Unaided consciousness must always tend towards hate; not only because it is good common-sense to exterminate the other fellow, but for the more profound reason that, seeing only arcs of circuits, the individual is continually surprised and necessarily angered when his hard-headed policies return to plague the inventor.

If you use D.D.T. to kill insects, you may succeed in reducing the insect population so far that the insectivores will starve. You will then have to use more D.D.T. than before to kill the insects which the birds no longer eat. More probably, you will kill off the birds in the first round when they eat the poisoned insects. If the D.D.T. kills off the dogs, you will have to have more police to keep down the burglars. The burglars will become better armed and more cunning...and so on. That is the sort of world we live in – a world of circuit structures – and love can survive only if wisdom (i.e. a sense or recognition of the fact of circuitry) has an effective voice.

What has been said so far proposes questions about any particular work of art somewhat different from those which have been conventionally asked by anthropologists. The

'culture and personality' school, for example, has traditionally used pieces of art or ritual as samples or probes to reveal particular psychological themes or states.

The question has been: Does the art tell us about what sort of person made it? But if art, as suggested above, has a positive function in maintaining what I called 'wisdom', i.e. in correcting a too purposive view of life and making the view more systemic, then the question to be asked of the given work of art becomes: What sorts of correction in the direction of wisdom would be achieved by creating or viewing this work of art? The question becomes dynamic rather than static.

Analysis of a Balinese Painting

Turning now from the consideration of epistemology to a specific work of art, we note first what is most general and most obvious. With almost no exceptions, the behaviours called art or their products (also called art) have two characteristics: they require or exhibit *skill* and they contain redundancy or pattern. But those two characteristics are not separate: the skill is first in maintaining and then in modulating the redundancies.

The matter is perhaps most clear where the skill is that of the journeyman and the redundancy is of comparatively low order. For example, in the Balinese painting (figure 4.1, by Ida Bagus Djati Sura of the village of Batuan, 1937[2]), skill of a certain elementary but highly disciplined sort was exercised or practised in the background of foliage. The redundancies to be achieved involve rather uniform and rhythmical repetition of leaf forms, but this redundancy is, so to speak, fragile. It would be broken or interrupted by smudges or irregularities of size or tone in the painting of the successive leaves.

When a Batuan artist looks at the work of another, one of the first things he examines is the technique of the leafy background. The leaves are first drawn, in free outline in pencil; then each outline is tightly redefined with pen and china ink. When this has been done for all the leaves, the artist begins to paint with brush and brick ink. Each leaf is covered with a pale wash. When these washes are dry, each leaf receives a smaller concentric wash and after this another still smaller and so on. The final

Figure 4.1 The start of a cremation procession, Bali. By Ida Bagus Djati Sura of Batuan, Bali, 1937. Reproduced by Permission of Lois Bateson.

result is a leaf with an almost white rim inside the inked outline, and successive steps of darker and darker colour towards the centre of the leaf. A 'good' picture has up to five or six such successive washes on every leaf. (This particular painting is not very 'good' in this sense. The leaves are done in only three or four steps.) The skill and the patterning so far discussed depend upon muscular rote and muscular accuracy – achieving the perhaps not negligible artistic level of a well laid-out field of turnips.

I was watching a very gifted American carpenter-architect at work on the woodwork of a house he had designed. I commented on the sureness and accuracy of each step. He said:

'Oh, that. That's only like using a typewriter. You have to be able to do that without thinking.' But on top of this level of redundancy is another. The uniformity of the lower level redundancy must be modulated to give higher orders of redundancy. The leaves in one area must be *different* from the leaves in another area and these *differences* must be, in some way, mutually redundant: they must be part of a larger pattern. Indeed, the function and necessity of the first level control is precisely to make the second level possible. The perceiver of the work of art must receive information that the artist *can* paint a uniform area of leaves because without this information, he will not be able to accept, as significant, the variations in that uniformity. Only the violinist who can control the quality of his notes can use variations of that quality for musical purposes.

This principle is basic and accounts, I suggest, for the almost universal linkage in aesthetics between skill and pattern. The exceptions – e.g. the cult of natural landscapes, 'found objects', ink blots, scattergrams, and the works of Jackson Pollock – seem to exemplify the same rule in reverse. In these cases, a larger patterning seems to propose the illusion that the details must have been controlled. Intermediate cases also occur: e.g. in Balinese carving, the natural grain of the wood is rather frequently used to suggest details of the form or surface of the subject. In these cases, the skill lies not in the draftsmanship of the details, but in the artist's placement of his design within the three-dimensional structure of the wood. A special 'effect' is achieved, not by the mere representationalism, but by the perceiver's partial awareness that a physical system *other* than that of draftsmanship has contributed to determine his perception.

We now turn to more complex matters, still concentrating attention upon the most obvious and elementary.

Composition

1. The delineation of leaves and other forms does not reach to the edge of the picture but shades off into darkness so that almost all around the rectangle there is a band of undifferentiated dark pigment. In other words, the picture is framed within its own fade-out. We are allowed to feel that the matter is in some sense 'out of this world'; and this in spite of the fact that the scene depicted is familiar – the starting out of a cremation procession.

2. The picture is *filled*. The composition leaves no open spaces. Not only is none of the paper left unpainted but no considerable area is left in uniform wash. The largest such areas are the very dark patches at the bottom between the legs of the men.

To occidental eyes this gives an effect of 'fussiness'. To psychiatric eyes, the effect is of 'anxiety' or 'compulsivity'. We are all familiar with the strange look of those letters from cranks, who feel that they must fill the page.

3. But before trying too fast to diagnose or evaluate, we have to note that the composition of the lower half of the picture, apart from this filling of background space, is turbulent. Not merely a depiction of active figures, but a swirling composition mounting upwards and closed off by the contrasting direction of the gestures of the men at the top of the pyramid.

The upper half of the picture, in contrast, is serene. Indeed, the effect of the perfectly balanced women with offerings on their heads is so serene that, at first glance, it appears that the men with musical instruments must surely be sitting. (They are supposed to be moving in procession.)

But this compositional structure is the reverse of the usual occidental. We expect the lower part of a picture to be the more stable and expect to see action and movement in the upper part – if anywhere.

4. At this point, it is appropriate to examine the picture as a sexual pun and, in this connection, the internal evidence for sexual reference is at least as strong as it is in the case of the Tangaroa figure discussed by Leach (1973) All you have to do is to set your mind in the correct posture and you will see an enormous phallic object (the cremation tower) with two elephants' heads at the base. This object must pass through a narrow entrance into a serene courtyard and thence onward and upward through a still more narrow passageway. Around the base of the phallic object you see a turbulent mass of homunculi, a crowd in which

> Was none who would be foremost
> To lead such dire attack;
> But those behind cried 'Forward!'
> And those before cried 'Back!'

And if you are so minded, you will find that Macaulay's poem about how Horatius kept the bridge is no less sexual than the present picture. The game of sexual interpretation is easy if you want to play it. No doubt the snake in the tree to the left of the picture could also be woven into the sexual story.

It is still possible, however, that something is added to our understanding of a work of art by the hypothesis that the subject-matter is double: that the picture represents both the start of a cremation procession and a phallus with vagina. With a little imagination, we could also see the picture as a symbolic representation of Balinese social organization in which the smooth relations of etiquette and gaiety metaphorically cover the turbulence of passion. And, of course, 'Horatius' is very evidently an idealized myth of nineteenth-century imperial England.

It is probably an error to think of dream, myth, and art as being about any one matter other than relationship. As was mentioned earlier, dream is metaphoric and is not particularly about the relata mentioned in the dream. In the conventional interpretation of dream, another set of relata, often sexual, is substituted for the set in the dream. But perhaps by doing this we only create another dream. There indeed is no *a priori* reason for supposing that the sexual relata are any more primary or basic than any other set.[3]

In general, artists are very unwilling to accept interpretations of this sort, and it is not clear that their objection is to the sexual nature of the interpretation. Rather, it seems that rigid focusing upon any single set of relata destroys for the artist the more profound significance of the work. If the picture were *only* about sex or *only* about social organization, it would be trivial. It is non-trivial or profound precisely because it is about sex *and* social organization *and* cremation, *and* other things. In a word, it is only about relationship and not about *any* identifiable relata.

5. It is appropriate then to ask how the artist has handled the identification of his subject-matter within the picture. We note first that the cremation tower which occupies almost one third of the area of the picture is almost invisible. It does not stand out against its background as it should if the artist wanted to assert unequivocally 'this is a cremation'. Notably also, the coffin, which might be expected to be a focal point, is appropriately placed just below the centre but, even so, does not catch the eye. In fact, the artist has inserted details which label the picture as a cremation scene but these details become almost whimsical asides, like the snake and the little birds in the trees. The women are carrying the ritually correct offerings on their heads, and two men appropriately bring bamboo containers of palm toddy, but these details, too, are only whimsically added. The artist plays down the subject identification and thereby gives major

stress to the contrast between the turbulent and the serene mentioned in section 3 above.

6. In sum, it is my opinion that the crux of the picture is the interwoven contrast between the serene and the turbulent. And a similar contrast or combination was also present, as we have seen, in the painting of the leaves. There too, an exuberant freedom was overlaid by precision.

In terms of this conclusion, I can now attempt an answer to the question posed above: What sorts of correction, in the direction of systemic wisdom, could be achieved by creating or viewing this work of art? In final analysis, the picture can be seen as an affirmation that to choose either turbulence or serenity as a human purpose would be a vulgar error. The conceiving and creating of the picture must have provided an experience which exposed this error. The unity and integration of the picture assert that neither of these contrasting poles can be chosen to the exclusion of the other, because the poles are mutually dependent. This profound and general truth is simultaneously asserted for the fields of sex, social organization, and death.

NOTES

1   Consider the impossibility of constructing a television set which would report upon its screen *all* the workings of its component parts, including especially those parts concerned in this reporting.

2   Three photographs of this artist at work have been published in G. Bateson and M. Mead, *Balinese Character*, New York, 1942, Pl. 23.

3   Cf. Gregory Bateson, 'Sex and Culture', *Annals of the New York Academy of Sciences*, vol. XLVII, 9 May 1947, art. 5, pp. 647–60.

REFERENCE

Leach, Edmund, 1973. 'Levels of Communication and problems of Taboo in the Appreciation of Primtive Art.' In Anthony Forge (ed.), *Primitive Art and Society*. Oxford: Oxford University Press.

5

Tikopia Art and Society

Raymond Firth

Most studies of primitive art heretofore have concentrated on cultures and aesthetic spheres in which the art could be described as 'rich' in character. The Tikopia offer a contrast to such studies. Generalizations about art in the broadest sense have often stressed its expressive function, its role as a material sign of ideas and emotions held collectively or manifested individually by different members of a particular society. For Lethaby 'art is man's thought expressed in his handwork' (1949, p. 1). For Hinks and others it is the 'concrete expression of abstract ideas' (1935, p. 2), and so on. Art crystallizes aspirations and indicates consciousness of a particular era of national life. Different eras have their own particular method of aesthetic expression, a product of the traditions of art workmanship and the 'national equation of the moment' (Lethaby, p. 2). So the recognition of periods of art can be coincident with the recognition of periods of general development. Among the complex set of forces which becomes manifest in the art of a particular society at a particular period not only the aesthetic structure but also the social structure is held to be involved. Arnold Hauser (1952, pp. 35–9) connects a geometric style of neolithic peasantry, for example, with a uniformity of organization, stable institutions, an autocratic form of government, and a very largely religiously

oriented outlook on life. Such art, he thinks, is conventional, solid, stable, and inflexible, even invariable, in its form.

These are merely samples of well-known views, some of them clearly exaggerated, which try to give some kind of explanation in social terms to the variation which appears in the character of art in different societies and at different periods. Sometimes a further factor is added, the degree to which the society itself is subject to change and development. Lethaby holds that periods of art have coincided with crests of general development, and emphasizes that the most important characteristic of art, apart from individual artistic genius, is its continuity and response to change (1949, p. 2).

The Poverty of Tikopia Graphic Art

In the light of such views the Tikopia pose a problem. Evidence from their tradition and from observations on the state of their society over more than a century indicates that despite conflict and occasional violence the form of their society may be regarded as relatively stable. Again, their institution of chieftainship and the great respect shown to their chiefs, whose orders on critical occasions have until recent times been carried out without question, allow their form of government to be

From Anthony Forge (ed.), *Primitive Art and Society* (Oxford: Oxford University Press, 1973), pp. 25–48. Reprinted by permission of the Wenner-Gren Foundation for Anthropological Research, Inc., New York.

categorized as relatively autocratic. In the pagan conditions which obtained until recently their outlook on life, with their elaborate ritual cycles and complex pantheon of spirits to whom prayers, offering, and libations were made, was religiously oriented to a high degree. Yet fascinating as all this has been, to an anthropologist interested in primitive art their culture has been disconcertingly barren. Their plastic arts traditionally and in recent times have been relatively undeveloped, simple in form and often poor in quality of workmanship. Their chiefs were not a leisured class but they did command some patronage; they and some other senior men in the community have been able to employ craftsmen of skill to make sea-going canoes, wooden bowls, clubs, dance bats of a reasonable degree of efficiency. Such things were ornamented, but very simply. The craftsmen responsible were recompensed for their effort and skill. But the emphasis has been upon securing effective working implements rather than objects of particular aesthetic interest. Plastic art as such in Tikopia has had no commercial value, that is, artist as distinct from craftsman has had no material reward and no special social status. In Tikopia fine craftsmanship has had some social approval but this has been primarily related to the technical workmanship and utilitarian elements of the product rather than to its aesthetic effect. Yet all this in itself would not necessarily inhibit the production of art objects of high quality. In some primitive societies men have produced 'high art' apparently irrespective of material recognition or perhaps even of status recognition of their aesthetic efforts. More important, perhaps, is the lack of any great degree of competitiveness in the craft sphere, of that emulative striving for excellence which might lead to a search for more effective, more striking, modes of presentation.

Is one to conclude, however, that the Tikopia, lacking any developed plastic art, have lacked also any degree of sophistication in thought, feeling, or abstract ideas? My answer is decidedly in the negative.

In many primitive societies art appears to be selective. In Tikopia, while plastic art has been relatively undeveloped, upon music and associated arts of poetry and dance the Tikopia have focused a great deal of attention. It is true that in the field of poetry and dance in particular their aesthetic expression may be described as robust rather than refined, but in these fields they cannot be said to lack either sensibility or abstract ideas. In music, poetry, and dance Tikopia seem to have developed a very considerable range of variation and elaborate articulation, with many nuances of form and expression. They also seem to have associated these aesthetic products much more closely with the organization of their society, with the expression of social bonds and status differences, than their creations in the field of the plastic arts.

What I am arguing is not novel, but perhaps needs restating – that a community which has been remote and very isolated for a long period may develop its aesthetic tradition differentially. It may lack certain kinds of aesthetic creation, or concentrate on one sphere to the neglect of others, without necessarily lacking a general vitality, capacity for abstract thought, aesthetic sensibility, and interest in new ideas and experiences.

But a second question – is the lack of Tikopia plastic art due to a deficiency in the conceptual handling of solid form, to an absence of a specifically sculptural art tradition, or to some repressive influences in the society (comparable to the Muslim ban on religious iconography)? – is more difficult, perhaps impossible, to answer.

In the sphere of plastic and graphic expression Tikopia offers a case of almost minimal art. Painting and drawing generally and their analogues in bodily decoration have had very limited scope. Bark-cloth is sometimes dyed orange with turmeric, though never painted; pandanus mats may be given a border of chevrons and allied design; tattooing has traditionally been applied in a limited range of naturalistic and geometric designs to the human body (Firth, 1936; 1947); white flowers are worn in ears and round the neck; beads, traditionally black or white, and later coloured from European sources, were strung round necks and wrists. But all these decorative elements, though very important to Tikopia as social indexes, were relatively minor as contributions to aesthetic production in any comparative sense. Minor also, though of potential interest to students of comparative design, are the elaborate systematic 'geometrical' variations in Tikopia string figures (Firth and Maude, 1968).

Tikopia sculpture has been confined almost entirely to woodwork. On a small scale, neck pendants and wrist ornaments were constructed of clam shell, pearl shell, or horn (turtle shell). Pleasant in their simple shape, these too showed little aesthetic development. The greatest range of variation has been in the production of objects from wood. But almost none of these can be regarded as objects of primarily aesthetic interest in their manufacture. Possible exceptions were figures, conventionally described as birds (figure 5.1), set as decoration on temple ridgepole or canoe of the Fangarere chief. But even these had a strong ritual connotation and might be regarded as essentially symbolic presentations with religious orientation rather than primarily art objects (Firth, 1960). Only the decorative elements such as the rows of notches (*fakatara*) on many wooden objects, or the incised outline drawings of fish on houseposts, have had a non-utilitarian, elaborative, putatively aesthetic role (figures 5.2 and 5.3). The only painting applied to woodwork was a white clayey kind of stone sometimes roughly smeared on for general effect of contrast (Firth 1967, Pl. la).

In woodwork the Tikopia have had a strong craft tradition. There has been no very specific system of instruction or apprenticeship in woodworking, but a fair amount of empirical information has been passed on, particularly from father to son or grandfather to grandson. But by no means every Tikopia is a woodcarver; this is certainly one society where *not* every man is a 'natural artist'. Woodcarvers have tended to be professional specialists – not devoting all their time to the work but making it a definite occupation, sometimes

Figure 5.2 Coconut grating stool. Courtesy of the Museum of Primitive Art, New York

Figure 5.3 Fish ornament on house-post, Raniniu temple, 1966. Monberg Photo

on commissioned jobs. There has been some tendency to role aggregation – men skilled in woodworking have often been expert fishermen and dancers too. (One lineage in particular in recent times, that of Avakofe, has had a special reputation in these fields.)

The work of the woodcarvers has been pragmatic and technically effective. Manual

Figure 5.1 'Bird' carving on canoe

dexterity has been admired but traditional forms have been given high value and scope for invention has been relatively limited. In canoes, bowls, dance bats, and most other objects of wood, experiment either in form or in ornament seems to have been extremely restricted. In myths and other traditional tales the author is unknown. But, as with songs and string figure designs, many wooden objects are labelled as items of named personal authorship. All the major items of recent workmanship, such as canoes and bowls, can have their maker identified not only by those who commissioned the work, but also by other people at large. This is not basically a matter of style recognition. The construction of such important objects is a matter of social interest and consequently the maker is borne in memory. Again, the Tikopia prize things which remind them of their ancestors, and often identify wooden objects as formerly the property of ancestors. In such a case they also may attribute the object to the workmanship of the ancestor concerned, crediting him with the reputation of a noted craftsman. This personalization of the manufacture of wooden objects, though possibly apocryphal, does mean that some elements of status are involved in the construction. But the status factor does not seem to have been strong enough and pointed enough to have resulted in stimulating any very specific aesthetic achievement.

The form of Tikopia wooden objects has been fairly closely determined by their function. In general shape, line, and proportion Tikopia bowls, turmeric ovens, netting needles, or clubs offer few surprises. Many of their forms can be considered tasteful by western critics. Their simple notched-row ornament diversifies but does not radically modify their functional outline.

Traditionally the Tikopia had nothing in the field of anthropomorphic figure sculpture. Unlike some other Polynesian peoples, they seem to have found it quite simple to symbolize their gods by stones of natural shape or structural members of buildings such as house-posts and rafters, whose primary purpose was to serve an architectural need. In Tikopia temples, house-posts were traditionally symbolic. But they were adorned with very little ornamentation – occasionally a fish design or a series of rough notches – and the aesthetic handling of

a post was almost irrelevant to its symbolic role. This does not entitle one to say that the Tikopia lack abstract ideas or powers of conceptualization. On the contrary, it may be argued that their power of conceptualization has been such that it has needed no stimulus of any quasi-representational kind. As with some 'higher' religions, they needed no graven images to assist them in the worship of their gods. Distressing though this lack of anthropomorphic iconography may seem from the aesthetic point of view, the Tikopia were able to invest their crude, functional items with strong symbolic value.

It is difficult to give reasons for this lack of Tikopia aesthetic achievement in sculpture and lack of interest in aesthetic possibility of working in wood when they had canoes, bowls, and other objects with which to demonstrate their skill. It may perhaps reflect the absence of an artistic tradition dating back to the colonization of their island. It is feasible (if tradition has any relevance here) that their ancestors arrived in driblets, perhaps mainly as castaways, and may have carried with them no memory and technique of fine craftsmanship and artistic invention. But if tradition is to be believed (and it is supported by a little other evidence – Firth, 1961), there has been ample time for individual artistic impulses to develop and express themselves in some overt cultural form. Such indeed seems to have taken place in the musical and allied fields. The lack of tradition then is not a sufficient explanation. I cannot point to any simple set of factors which seems to be involved here. Tikopia preoccupation with ritual and social institutions in a non-iconographic milieu may have tended to militate against the devotion of elaborate time to aesthetic achievement. Relevant also perhaps is an attitude of acceptance of convention, of a notion of standardized shapes for objects of major cultural interest, and an unwillingness to incur criticism by departing from recognized standards.

Tikopia Headrests

But some aesthetic interest, if only embryonic, emerges in a domestic context. In the production of headrests the Tikopia seem to have shown much less inhibition than in other fields of sculpture, much more freedom of individual expression. One may speculate that in this field, where the objects are of a highly personal character, traditional form is on the whole less important, and initiative and aesthetic interest can find play. This hypothesis is the reverse of a common view, that whereas religion provides a stimulus to 'high' art, the domestic field is one of convention and lack of experiment.

I do not wish here to magnify the idea of variation in a small sector of Tikopia woodwork into the notion of a very serious field of personal artistic expression. But the problem of such individual expression is of interest – if only because of Hauser's generalization that the geometric style of the autocratic, stable type of society is relatively invariant. Evidence from Tikopia shows that such a statement needs clarification and modification.

During my first visit to Tikopia in 1928–9 I was struck by the wide range of variation to be seen in Tikopia wooden headrests. I collected about two dozen examples of these headrests, and on my second visit to Tikopia decided to investigate more closely this matter of variation. Further examples collected in 1952, and again in 1966,[1] demonstrated still more the range of variation in style of these relatively simple articles of furniture. Moreover, I was able to obtain, though not easily, some Tikopia opinions on the significance of this variation.

Technical and Social Background

The Tikopia have two major types of headrests, differentiated as part of what may be termed the 'cultural signatures' which marked sex division in that society. One type is a soft bundle of bark-cloth resembling a European pillow, but rolled and not stuffed. It is used by women and small children of both sexes. The other type, cut out of wood and the subject of discussion here, is used by men and adolescent males. In methods of dress, carrying loads and seating, conformity to the recognized sex pattern is very high, even from the earliest years. But whereas children follow these sex patterns from the time they begin to wear clothing, in the use of headrests small male children are assimilated to the resting pattern of the women who tend them. In this connection it is probably relevant that the use of the bark-cloth pillow is a pattern which makes no demands on bodily skill,

whereas use of a male type headrest normally requires some little care to keep it upright. A wooden headrest is less comfortable than a bark-cloth pillow, and Tikopia sometimes attribute bumps or indentations in the head to the use of such headrests from an early age. But until recent years male status required the use of such a headrest. (In modern times some men have been ready to use more ordinary types of pillow.) But though traditionally a male Tikopia would not use a bark-cloth pillow, the use of a properly constructed headrest was optional, not mandatory. An upturned bowl or a billet of wood was equally appropriate and was commonly used in huts in the orchards where often no ordinary headrest was available. (In 1952 I noted that a rectangular block of wood which had drifted ashore, apparently from some Japanese war vessel, had been used as a headrest by a Tikopia family.)

Headrests of any kind are termed *urunga*, and wooden headrests are commonly known as *urunga nga tangata* (headrests of men). They are often made from fairly hard wood such as *fetau* (*Calophyllum inophyllum*), but softer timbers such as those of breadfruit, *Plumeria*, *poumuri*, and *afatea* may also be used. An average headrest weighs about two lb. The tool ordinarily used in cutting out a headrest, as for other woodwork, is a small adze with a European plane iron as a blade; a piece of coral rock is used as a rasp to rub down the rough edges of the wood. Making a headrest is not highly restricted but may be done by any man of ordinary skill. The opinion was expressed to me that to make a headrest is not difficult. 'Any man picks up a piece of wood and hews out his headrest.' Some men, however, tend to specialize in this work and turn out headrests in their spare time – one woodworker I knew had made thirteen over about twenty years. But any man who wishes may try his hand, and many headrests are clearly amateur jobs. One I saw (of ordinary single-foot type) had been made by a boy. Though not specifically encouraged to work in wood, male children are allowed to exercise initiative in this field, and may be helped by a father or other kinsman. One exception to all this is the most delicate type of headrest with high 'wings' and lashed legs (figure 5.24). This is usually made by a professional woodcarver, who constructs also canoes, bowls, etc. as commissioned items.

Headrest Styles

I do not find the classification of styles in these Tikopia headrests at all easy. Tikopia themselves, including the woodcarvers, used simple descriptive categories such as 'solid block' type (*urunga potu rakau*), 'holed' type (*urunga fakafotu*), 'legged' type (*urunga fai vae*), etc., and I have broadly followed their divisions. But these are very rough. Three main criteria may be identified – general shape, principle of construction, and supporting or ancillary details. From a sample of forty headrests I examined, about a dozen styles may be recognized, though some are subdivided by the Tikopia themselves. These are illustrated in simplified form by the accompanying sketches. The simplest, figure 5.4, is a wooden block, usually hollowed slightly to take the neck and back of the head. Developing from this are various shapes, retaining the form of the block but removing some material to provide a neck platform and/or feet. Figure 5.5 illustrates one of these. A further development, figure 5.6, is to cut a hole from side to side through the middle of the block. This hole may be of varying size. If it is comparatively large, then the amount of material remaining at the base of the block as the foot platform is thin and the side pieces assume almost the form of legs (figure 5. 17). Instead of cutting the hole through the centre of the block, material may be cut away through the base so as to alter the particular style though not the general form.

Figure 5.5

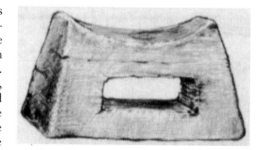

Figure 5.6

An instance of this is cutting a large groove longitudinally at the base of the block and shaping the remainder so that the result is rather like a wooden shoe with a V-shaped hole underneath (figure 5.7). Another style is not to cut through the base of the block but to cut around the sides in such a way that a solid central pillar remains with a base platform or

Figure 5.4

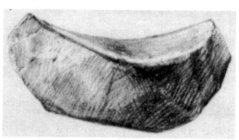

Figure 5.7

foot. Stylistically, three types may be recognized here: one, figure 5.8, deeply cut into the central column at the base to form a Y-shaped headrest; another leaving the central column in a bulbous shape, figure 5.9; and still another, in which the central column is

Figure 5.10

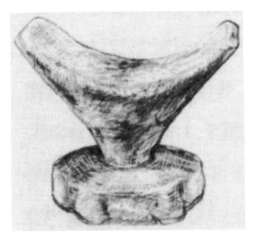

Figure 5.8

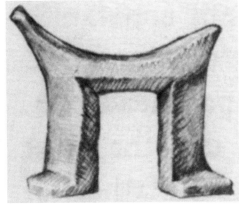

Figure 5.11

Figure 5.9

Figure 5.12

rectangular, figure 5.10 (said by one informant in 1952 to be a modern style) (see figures 5.21 and 5.22). The major alternative to the single column support is to provide the headrest with two legs. Here again there are several different styles. In one, the most common, the base of the block is cut out in approximately rectangular form so that the legs form two relatively straight columns (figures 5.11–5.15

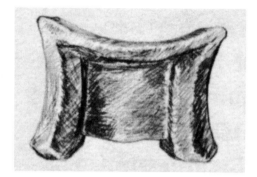

Figure 5.13

in various forms). Another style is similar except that the central space is triangular, not rectangular, and thus gives a different shape to the legs (figure 5.16). (Examples of both of these, as also of a couple of other two-legged varieties, were identified in 1952 as of traditional style.) Still another style, figure 5.17, may be classified as either a much extended version of figure 5.6 or as a variety with two legs joined together at the base by a platform. (This latter was the classification into which it was put by Tikopia themselves.) Another associated type (figures 5.18 and 5.23), has a bar hewn out of the solid adjoining the two legs. In all the types described so far the headrest has been cut completely out of the solid. But in one further type, figure 5.24, the headrest is composite. It is made up of three sections, the top section where the head lies

Figure 5.14

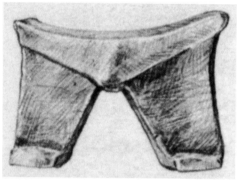

Figure 5.16

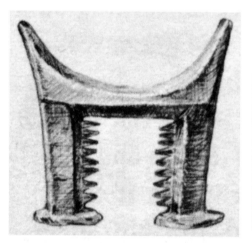

Figure 5.15

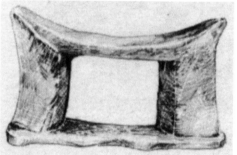

Figure 5.17

Figure 5.18

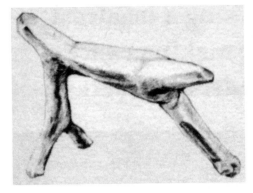

Figure 5.19

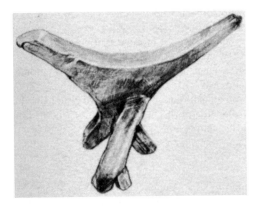

Figure 5.20

and two legs attached by coconut sinnet lashings to this. A normal distinguishing mark of this type of headrest is that one leg is straight and the other is forked with two feet, but a stylistic variant in one example I saw had both legs forked. (Naturalistic prototypes are shown in figures 5.19 and 5.20).

What can be said about the origination and relationships of these styles, with particular reference to the relation between individual and social factors involved? It must be said at once that at the ordinary anthropological level of inquiry, granted the imperfections of field technique, I could obtain little direct information from the Tikopia themselves on this question. For any systematic answer to this question we must rely primarily on indirect evidence, even speculation. But one thing is clear – that this range of styles in Tikopia headrests is not primarily of overt symbolic significance. How far is it due to variations in taste among headrest makers or users?

The Demand for Headrests

The most general element in the Tikopia demand for headrests has been the wish for a pillow of the kind prescribed by custom for men. Yet despite the permissive attitude towards wooden headrest style, and the relative ease with which any man can cut one out for himself in rough form, there has been a strong differentiation in demand between individual pieces.

One component of this demand has been interest in workmanship as such. But this has often been commingled with interest in a particular design. A man might wish to have something of greater comfort or utility than the ordinary. Pa Panapa, a well-known maker of headrests, made one of a solid block, hollowed out at top and sides and about five inches broad at the flat base. He was very proud of this. He said it was his own design and that his idea was that there should be three ways in which it could be used, each giving a different height to the head: upright, sideways, and upside down – when the straight base would give rather more height. This headrest was much praised by one of his friends, he said, who wanted him to make one like it. I doubt if he did.

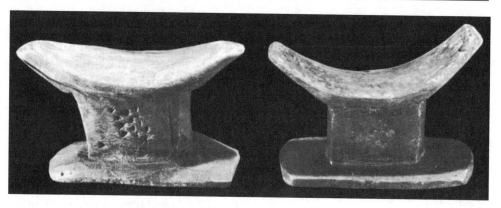

Figure 5.21 Pillared type of headrest

Figure 5.22 Pillared type of headrest

Figure 5.23 Headrest with bar

I was told in 1952 that sometimes a well-known carver was commissioned to make a specified kind of headrest. The client would go along with a basket of food to proffer his request, and then when the headrest was ready he would go to collect it bearing a gift of food, with three or four pieces of bark-cloth in payment. (No pandanus mat was given; this was a reciprocation for more weighty objects.) Alternatively, a man might wish for a certain headrest which he had seen in the carver's home, and bear it off – with or without reciprocation. Pa Panapa told me how a man of rank from the other side of the island came over to visit him one evening with a basket of food, slept in his house and then said to him, 'Uncle [mother's brother], I am going with this headrest,' and took it, unchallenged. Another headrest was in use by Pa Panapa in his house when an adopted son of his came and slept there one night. As he left the next day he took the headrest with him, saying nothing to anyone. A search was made and it was finally located. The man stoutly objected to giving it back, saying that he wanted to keep it, as a memorial of his 'father', the maker; so he was allowed to retain it. Altogether eight of Pa Panapa's headrests were borne off by kinsmen, in each case by someone whose relation to him was such that he could carry off such property with impunity.

A component in the demand, then, has often been not so much an interest in workmanship or design of a headrest as in an object associated with the personality of the maker or the user. A rather subtle balance may be involved here. When a kinsman bears off a headrest from the house of the maker, alleging that he wishes a personal memento, is this because he is moved primarily by affection, or is using kinship sentiment to cover his acquisitive spirit? After all, it can be argued, the woodworker can always make himself another one.

But the non-utilitarian interpretation is supported by the general Tikopia evaluation of the place of headrests in their cultural scheme. A headrest (whether made by the owner or not) is 'the valuable property of man'. It can be used as a weapon on occasion – if a thief is heard at night in the house the householder may take the headrest from under his neck and hurl it at him. But principally it has a peculiar association with its owner's personality since it pillows his head, the most important part of the body, which it is forbidden to a man's children to touch. Though not taboo, the headrest of a householder ordinarily is handled by others with discretion, as a piece of his private property. As a consequence of this, a man's headrest tends to be one of the items of his property most commonly buried with him. A headrest is 'the death property of this land; when a man dies, he is pillowed upon it. After a man has slept constantly upon it, when he is put into the ground, his head is laid upon it, then he is wrapped up and buried.' One of Pa Panapa's headrests, for example, was taken by Pae Avakofe, in his day the most respected senior man of rank in Tikopia, and a 'grandfather' of his; this headrest was buried with the old man when he died.

But since the headrest has been so closely associated with the personality of the user, it can serve as a very convenient memorial to

him, if it is preserved by his kin after his death. Hence sometimes a conflict of sentiment occurs. Some relatives argue for interring the dead man's headrest with him, with the idea that he should not be separated from what he was so intimately linked with in life. Others argue for keeping it in the house as a visible reminder of him. I was shown one valued headrest, made by my informant's brother, a noted craftsman of the Avakofe lineage, with the words, 'This headrest is a token of sentiment (tau arofa); the headrest of our father the chief' (long deceased). Another headrest, of type 3, was said to have been made by a great-grandfather of the Ariki Taumako and his kinsman Pa Fatumaru, and to have been used in turn by the chief's grandfather and father. The latter left it as an heirloom to his 'son' Pa Fatumaru with the words, 'This is our headrest. It shall remain for you as your headrest.' It was a token of affection between 'father' and 'son' said Pa Fatumaru to me; he obviously prized it greatly. A man's eldest son usually decides at his burial whether the headrest is to be interred with the corpse or not.

So, there is a distinct non-utilitarian element in the appraisal of Tikopia headrests. But this has a sentimental, rather than an aesthetic, base. That headrests preserved as memorials or buried as intimate property seem usually to have been examples of relatively fine workmanship does not invalidate this stress upon the sentimental aspect.

One further element in the demand for headrests has been the association of a special style with men of rank. The headrests with high wings, though not restricted to chiefs, have been regarded as being particularly appropriate for use by chiefs or by other men of high rank.[2] The construction of such a headrest is a job of considerable skill and delicacy, and examples of this style seem always to have been relatively rare in Tikopia. According to one informant, himself a skilled carpenter, in 1952 only one man, Pa Nukutapu of Avakofe lineage, then knew how to make such headrests, though every man knew how to make ordinary headrests. I think this was an exaggeration, but it illustrates the particular value attached to this design.

There are then several distinct elements recognizable in the Tikopia appraisal of their headrests: design; quality of craftsmanship;

personal association with elder kinsman, or with men of rank. Aesthetic elements seem to have been present in the construction and evaluation, but in any individual case I found these almost impossible to separate out from the other factors in the situation.

Tikopia recognition of differences in the value of headrests was exemplified by differences in the rates at which they were willing to exchange headrests with me. For most of the two dozen headrests which I collected on my first expedition I paid a standard rate of nine fishhooks each. But for a few older examples, heirlooms, the owners refused to accept such a price (or knowing this in advance I offered more); I paid ten fishhooks, a pipe, a belt, and even in one case a plane iron which the Tikopia regarded as extremely valuable. By 1952 the exchange rate had become about three times as great in fishhooks.[3] In 1966, at the request of the people themselves, fishhooks and other trade goods were abandoned altogether, and exchange was conducted in money. Here the price range for a headrest was between about six shillings and ten shillings dependent upon the quality. In no case was any price differential asked for on account of the headrest being of better *design* than others.

The Maker's Attitude to Design

Having considered the consumer's view of headrests, we now look at the maker's view. When a Tikopia who is not a woodcarver by vocation makes himself a headrest, it is usually either a roughly shaped block of wood or a simple, single-footed design. But when a woodcarver of experience makes such an object his attitude is rather different. He may be guided by the interest of a client in having a headrest of a particular type, in which case his aim is primarily to produce a headrest of good workmanship in accordance with the request. A craftsman who is in the habit of making headrests for other men in this way tends to work in a recognized style. Other men later may identify headrests as his workmanship by such style, and I observed some cases of such identification.[4] But the craftsman may also be motivated by experimental interest, as Pa Panapa described, seeking a design which is novel or a variant which seems more satisfac-

tory to him. It was said, too, that a craftsman hopes to make something by which he will be remembered and so tries to invent a new style which people can point to and link with his name: 'This is the headrest of So-and-so.'

I could obtain from craftsmen no detailed reasons why they chose to work with one design rather than another. I did not actually sit down with a carver while he was making a headrest, though I did talk with craftsmen while they were making canoes, wooden bowls, and ritual objects, and with headrest makers at other times. In answer to a question as to why he chose to make a headrest with one foot rather than with two, one craftsman said:

> It is there in my desire. It carves according to the thought. Like you Europeans, one seeks skill. A man who has found his thought is a man of firm mind. Like you [he continued, referring to me], we say you are of firm mind because you are skilled in writing. Because thought is confused one seeks that one may be firm.

He was describing by this the process of a craftsman debating with himself, considering alternatives and rejecting them until he has found the design which suits his fancy. I could get from few Tikopia any overt expression that one kind of design was regarded as being better than any others, or even that they themselves had any definite preferences. But craftsmen did say that amateurs, men simply making headrests for themselves, would keep to the styles known as 'billet of wood' – that is, a simple wooden block – or 'single-footed', which are not difficult to carve. When asked about differences in style, craftsmen were apt to reply always, 'It is the thought of the man. The styles are all equally good.' Pa Motuata, a man of taste and judgement in most affairs, but not a craftsman in wood, described figure 5.5 as 'bad' – but added that some men liked it. I found that while craftsmen were usually ready to differentiate good and bad workmanship, they did not stand out more than ordinary men as judges of design.

I got the most detailed description of the craftsman's attitude from Pa Panapa, in speaking of the headrest he adapted from a solid block (see above). Of the originality of this he was proud. He said, 'I sought an idea and as

I went on and on it parted and turned round [crystallized] to cut out a single platform.' He also had the idea that if he wished he could cut away part of the body of the block and round it off into a foot. But he decided to keep it as it was, partly to serve the needs of different men on different occasions. But he also gave another reason for not carving out this headrest further – that his good headrests were carried off by kinsmen or friends, and he thought that if he made this one as a mere 'billet of wood' no one would be tempted. He said also that by this time his working adze had become very worn!

Speculative Interpretation

This is about as far as I could go in the time available in direct consultation with wood-carvers in the assignment of reasons why different types of headrests were made. Indirectly, however, at a more speculative level one may examine further the problem of headrest styles.

The first point to make is that the description of parts of a headrest involves no special terms peculiar to woodcarving. The terms used are ordinary words from other fields of experience, utilizing in particular names for parts of the human body. (This is a convention which Europeans also commonly follow.) So the 'foot' of a headrest and its 'body' are known by the Tikopia equivalent of these terms, as they are applied also to animals and human beings. The platform on which the head is laid is known as the *marae*, a term used ordinarily for an open space for assembly – it conveys the notion of breadth and flatness. The ends of the platform, what we might call the 'ears' of the headrest, are known by the Tikopia as 'ends' or 'noses'. (The term which when applied to a human face is translated as nose is used by the Tikopia to indicate a much wider range of protuberances, as with ourselves in English, e.g. the nose of a boat.) There is then a vague analogy between the headrest and the human body or, more accurately, headrest and human body are regarded as showing certain characteristics of shape in common.

With this anthropomorphic analogy in mind, attention can be drawn to the fact that fairly clearcut distinctions exist between Tikopia domestic wooden objects according to the number of legs or feet which they display. At one end of the scale are ordinary food bowls

and nearly all bowls of other kinds, e.g. for turmeric or coconut cream manufacture, which have no separate legs at all, but rest upon a single solid base. In more abstract classification this type might be said to be supported by one leg or foot, especially if the base is shaped. Most headrests have one leg or two legs. At the other end of the scale, four legs constitute the support of a special kind of bowl, the kava bowl, which was used for religious occasions alone; the heavy, low, flat stool used primarily as a seat by an expert engaged in turmeric filtration or occasionally by a chief or other man of rank on a more casual occasion was supported likewise. So, four legs were reserved for bowls and stools of ritual or semi-ritual use, while two legs and one leg – or no legs at all – were most characteristic of headrests and objects of personal, non-ritual association. Intermediate between these two classes of objects were certain others of more complex character. The coconut grating stool (figure 5.2) had one leg together with the seat and projection for attaching the grater carved out of the solid, while another leg was lashed on. This second leg, however, was forked so that the stool had two legs but three feet.

To some extent the differences in type of support can be linked with different requirements for stability. The low seat used by the expert in turmeric filtration required to be absolutely steady. Hence four legs gave it the required stability. The coconut cream stool needed to be firm but could to some extent be supported by the legs of the person seated upon it – since when at work he faced forward with one leg on either side, his feet being in line with the two feet of the stool. Stability enough for the work was thus assured by three wooden and two human feet. With headrests, provided that the base platform was reasonably steady, one or two feet were adequate – and two feet seems to have been a traditional style.

But stability was not the sole requirement – the four inward-sloping legs of the kava bowl were no more efficient, possibly rather less stable, than the solid, legless, flat base of an ordinary bowl for coconut cream. Differentiation for ritual emphasis would seem to be the reason for this special style; so also in the case of headrests with three feet (figures 5.19, 5.20, 5.24 and 5.25). These may be slightly more stable than the headrests with two feet or one

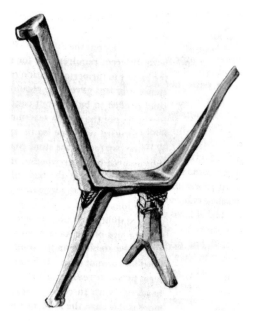

Figure 5.24

foot, but the difference cannot be great. This design of headrest is clearly structurally closely related to the coconut cream stool. In its principle of support it is thus aligned with an object which raises a man more than does any other seat in Tikopia. Associated with this particular design of headrest, then, is the notion of *elevation*, a notion which is carried through further by the very high slender 'wings'. It is thus no surprise to find that this type of head-

rest is regarded as particularly appropriate to chiefs and men of rank, who in many contexts are more elevated than ordinary men. In terms of legs then one can see a rough scale: four legs, ritual; three legs, social status; two legs, one leg, or no legs, ordinary domestic affairs. The scale is not perfect because three legs includes the coconut grating stool which serves a domestic purpose – but such stools are also commonly used by chiefs in general assembly and so have a kind of associated status.

I have said that there is no overt symbolism in the design of Tikopia headrests. One type of headrest (figure 5.22), which was specifically said to be a recent style invented by a well-known woodcarver, seems to me to have a distinct resemblance in form to the design of the 'sacred bird' carving which used to be set upon the canoes of the Ariki Fangarere (figure 5.1). But this resemblance was not recognized by my informants.

In reviewing the material on Tikopia headrests the following points can be made:

(a) The ornamentation on these headrests is simple and crude compared with the elaborate carving on many examples of New Guinea headrests. But the variety of styles is considerable, even surprising, for such a small community, and apparently much greater than for other Polynesian small island communities of analogous cultural development (cf. Burrows, 1937, pp. 121–2; MacGregor, 1937, p. 124).

(b) Although the styles illustrated by these headrests apparently combined both traditional and modern features, all the examples quoted were contemporary, i.e. of recent manufacture. Even in 1966 none was regarded as of an archaic type not normally to be reproduced nowadays. In other words, the manufacture of these headrests represented a living tradition not an archaic survival.

(c) The objects illustrated can be placed in a design sequence which might indicate a logical scheme of development. From the simplest wood block type there could develop either the pillared support with its variations or the pierced type with its free legs. From this latter a further development could be the composite type of refined headrest platform with attenuated side

Figure 5.25

'wings', necessitating for symmetry delicate legs which could not be safely cut from the solid but had to be separately made and attached.

(d) But such a sequence is quite hypothetical as regards any of the examples here illustrated. The block type may have been, and probably was, due to the inertia of the carver in not wishing to go to the trouble of cutting a more delicate support. The pierced type may have been initially purposeful or may have been due to the omission of the last stage of cutting out legs. Some headrests with three legs are not composite but have clearly taken advantage of the natural shape of the timber (figures 5.19 and 5.20).

What we are dealing with in the range of Tikopia headrests, then, seems to be a field for the exercise of relatively free design interest. Some social factors do give certain designs a special appeal, but the influence of these factors is not overt. The result is that from a field of design untrammelled by many ritual or overtly symbolic rules, the Tikopia craftsman has produced a series of headrest styles in which a combination of cultural pattern and individual fantasy has been at work. Alternate stylistic principles of removal of the solid from the sides of a block to leave a central pillar, or removal of the centre of a block to leave supports at the sides, are regarded as equally good solutions to a problem of production of a pattern from a wooden block, and even retention of the solid block shape in itself is regarded as permissible. What is striking is the versatility of invention in this 'free market' for design of such a simple, mundane instrument.

Some General Conclusions

Are these Tikopia headrests to be considered as art, if only as 'minimal art'? I think so. In essence, aesthetic experience is the recognition, with affect, of relationship between elements of form. Art is that product which, in expressing formal relationships either directly or symbolically, communicates or evokes such aesthetic experience. Whether art can be solely in the private experience of creator or observer is arguable – for an anthropologist it would

seem that relevant data should embody some element of public recognition.

But for anthropologists, art has historically been considered primarily as a conventional field involving objects or actions in which the formal elements were a matter of strong public attention. Moreover, anthropological interest has focused mainly on 'primitive' cultural objects of striking design, often elaborated with ornament and often of ritual use and highly symbolic. Masks have probably been the high point of interest in this field. But art can also imply the scrutiny of relations of form in a broader sense. Meaning is regarded as obtainable in a more general, less culture-bound way by the observer's perceptive construction and the affect related to this.

Here I have been distinguishing in effect between art as an observer's relation to material, as a producer's relation, and as a consumer's relation. These all cannot be assumed necessarily to coincide, and I would argue that the definition of art is not necessarily to be found in any one of them alone. Part of the problem in anthropological studies of art, which particularly involve an analytical culture-comparative standpoint, is to examine the relationship between these aspects of art definition. The difficulty is that for much of the field surveyed by the anthropologist only the observer is apt to be highly articulate. For producer and immediate consumer there may be non-explicit relations of form which the observer can hope to elucidate only inferentially.

Sometimes all three standpoints may be combined. In my view the surrealists, however defective their theory of art in some directions, were right about classifying their 'found objects' as art. Here an observer discovers for himself in his environment an object with a set of elements so disposed that for him they constitute a pattern with symbolic or emotional content. From the apparent irrelevance of such external objects the observer has constituted himself a producer of relationships and a primary consumer of art. In a way this is a return to Clive Bell's notion of 'significant form', but at another level.

In line with modern conceptions, art may be regarded as a kind of communication, but from the everyday common sense point of view a communication in a code which may be difficult to comprehend.

At first sight Tikopia headrests have a minimal element of communication. Superficially the meaning of their design is non-symbolic. They seem to involve no 'other order of cultural fact' (Forge, 1965, p. 23) such as ritual or myth; and they imply status factors only to a very limited degree. What they seem to indicate is, in Herbert Read's words, an innate drive to pattern, superficial aesthetic values so simple that they can be reduced to skill (Read, 1961, pp. 17–19). But the variation in their design is expressive for the maker. As Tikopia craftsmen themselves have indicated, the forms in which they couch their craftsmanship are not irrelevant to them and it is not their skill alone which matters to them. Apart from the technical relevance of the different designs – the degree of physical comfort they offer, the social status they indicate – the maker shows his preference on a basis of what is plausibly recognizable as taste, with aesthetic components, however concealed. Also at a low level, but recognizable, there is differential interest on the part of consumers. The men who command or take away the maker's headrests prefer one style to another, though the reasons they may state for this are often obscure.

In an attempt to understand the communication implicit in the variety of forms of Tikopia headrests one becomes concerned with the categories in which Tikopia arrange the objects of their natural and social universe. Our anthropological techniques are still so relatively unsubtle that one can do little more than speculate here. But among the categories which appear to be of concern for the Tikopia in this field are those which relate body parts and posture to social status. Physical positions seen in contrast between standing, sitting, kneeling, lying are relevant for the interpretation of social positions.[5] Relevant also is the interposition of an object between body and ground according to one's position. If a Tikopia is standing or walking, traditionally he wears no foot covering. If he kneels it may be also on bare ground. But if he sits in any situation of social significance politeness demands that he be given a mat or some coconut frond or a block of wood, upturned bowl or a stool to sit upon. If he lies down his head should not only be supported but also kept off the ground by a headrest. Differentiated social values are also involved in these different types of contact

and the part of the body concerned. The sole of the foot, commonly in direct contact with the ground, is that part of the body to which the most abject apology can be directed. The knee may be also the site of a gesture of apology. But not so the fundament or the head.

The form which the headrest may bear is not very finely oriented towards bodily features and social differences, but there is a broad relationship. In the headrest code recumbency demands head support. A simple block of wood may stand for firewood, or hewing into a betel mortar or other manufactured object. It may serve as a headrest, but it is of neutral or low status. A guest is not offered a rough block of wood for his head if a shaped headrest is available. The shaping of a headrest has then some social significance. It has little or no technical function in relation to coiffure, although in former times male Tikopia wore their hair long, except in mourning. More broadly, wooden headrests in general stand for men in domestic roles. Taboo as to head, when prone they may be objects of sympathy to others of the household and kin group. Headrests represent then 'tokens of affection' of a high order. In the very considerable latitude in headrest shaping, no significant value attaches very precisely to the different shapes. But, broadly, refinement of technique and elaboration of base-support convey association with higher status.

Briefly my argument here is: Tikopia craftsmen have some aesthetic interest in sculpture, if only at a low level of development. This did not emerge in the field of their religious art, possibly because of the competing demands of ritual for time and energy and perhaps also because the Tikopia conceptual apparatus did not demand iconographic material. In some sculptural fields, e.g. production of wooden bowls, functional requirements tended to dictate considerable variation. In the field of headrests the functional demands were simple. But the domestic situation was relatively free for experiment, and the peculiar associations of headrest with the head as personality symbol, with bodily posture, and with social status promoted an awareness of individuality which stimulated the inventive potentialities of the craftsmen.

Much may be made of the relation of art to ambiguities in experience. But the element of art in Tikopia headrests seems to be related not so much to expression of *ambiguities* in social status as to a statement in very generalized allusive terms of formally recognized *differences* in social status. One of the major expressions involved is the special position of men as distinguished from women – the latter have only rough packages of bark-cloth as headrests and by convention never use the shaped man's headrest. Male headrests are always of wood, the material associated in canoes, bowls, house construction, and other fields especially with male activity. Moreover, the range of forms within which headrests are conceived is one in which attention may be focused to a considerable degree upon 'feet' or 'legs' as means of support. This in turn is linked with the social differentiation of male position on formal occasions.

Tikopia headrests are a form of minimal art. They are made for use rather than aesthetic enjoyment. Experiment in their form or ornamentation is extremely restricted. The shapes they employ are hardly capable of generating any very subtle affect in the observer. Yet the variations in these shapes are an expression of personal creative activity, and they seem to be generated by diverse individual reactions to the significance of bodily features and positions in domestic situations. As such they seem to display a code for communication of generalized diffuse social values.

The influence of society on art can vary greatly in its degree of organization. Tikopia headrests are an example of the relatively unorganized influence of society in a field of creative achievement in which there are almost no formal training patterns and very few rewards for the craftsman. Society provides the craftsman with traditional patterns and some guidelines of popular choice, but leaves him to develop his experimental interest in design. The result is art on a very low level. But elementary as the variations in Tikopia headrest design may be, they do suggest that Tikopia craftsmen have aesthetic interests, and that these are primarily in the field of geometric design. Moreover these variations convey, albeit in non-explicit fashion, statements about the structure of Tikopia society. Signs of a critical attitude by Tikopia artists to their own society or to the novel forces by which it is confronted in modern

times appear as yet only in their songs and not in their graphic art.

What can be the role of an anthropologist in studying such minimal art? His systematic exploration and classification can uncover information about the objects from their makers and their consumers in the society, which while not necessarily altering his aesthetic experience as an observer, does amplify the communication received from the art material. From his general experience of the social behaviour of members of the society, too, the anthropologist can suggest clues to interpretation which are not explicit at the verbal level.

NOTES

1   In this I was helped by my colleagues James Spillius in 1952 and Torben Monberg in 1966. The specimens from 1928–9 were added to the Australian National Research Council collections in the University of Sydney; those from 1952 went to the Australian National University collection in Canberra, now housed in the Institute of Anatomy, to which the earlier material has now been joined. Monberg's collections have gone to the Royal Danish Ethnographical Museum, in Copenhagen. I am grateful to Professor Monberg for Plate 1. The drawings have been done from photographs by Tass Hesom.

2   I saw one huge example of this type, attributed to Pu Kafika Lasi, a chief of the early nineteenth century. I was told by several informants that formerly such large headrests were provided with a bar across the high wings, to ward off a blow from the sleeper's head in the troublous time when prominent men sought to seize power by killing one another (Firth, 1961). But this may be apocryphal.

3   For these and other rates, see Firth, 1959, p. 144.

4   Sometimes, however, the identification goes wrong. In 1952 a man of rank identified from a photograph a headrest which I had collected twenty-three years before as the work of the craftsman Pa Panapa who was with us. Pa Panapa did not deny this at the time, but later explained that the other man had been mistaken. He himself did

pick out from the photographs other examples which he said quite categorically that he had actually made earlier.

5 I discuss this in some detail in an article on posture and gesture (Firth, 1970).

REFERENCES

Burrows, Edwin G., 'Ethnology of Uvea (Wallis Island)', *Bernice P. Bishop Museum Bulletin 145*, Honolulu, 1937.

Firth, Raymond, 'Tattooing in Tikopia', *Man*, no. 236, London, 1936.

——, 'Bark-Cloth in Tikopia, Solomon Islands', *Man*, no. 74, London, 1947.

——, *Social Change in Tikopia*, London, 1959.

——, 'Tikopia Woodworking Ornament', *Man*, no. 27, London, 1960.

——, *History and Traditions of Tikopia*, Wellington, N.Z., 1961.

——, *Work of the Gods in Tikopia*, 2nd edn. London School of Economics Monographs on Social Anthropology nos. 1 and 2, London, 1967.

——, 'Postures and Gestures of Respect' in J. Pouillon and P. Maranda (eds.), '*Échanges et communications; mélanges offerts à Claude Lévi-Strauss à l'occasion de son 60ème anniversaire*, vol. I, The Hague, 1970.

Firth, Raymond, and Honor C. Maude, *Tikopia String Figures*, Royal Anthropological Institute Occasional Paper no. 29, London, 1968.

Forge, Anthony, 'Art and Environment in the Sepik', *Proceedings of the Royal Anthropological Institute for 1965*, London, 1966, pp. 23–31.

Hauser, Arnold, *The Social History of Art*, 2 vols., New York, 1952.

Hinks, Roger, *Carolingian Art*, London, 1935.

Lethaby, W. R., *Medieval Art: From the Peace of the Church to the Eve of the Renaissance 312–1350* (rev. edn. by D. Talbot Rice), London, 1949.

MacGregor, Gordon H., 'Ethnology of Tokelau Islands', *Bernice P. Bishop Museum Bulletin 146*, Honolulu, 1937.

Read, Herbert, 'Art in an Aboriginal Society: A Comment', *The Artist in Tribal Society*. Proceedings of a Symposium held at the Royal Anthropological Institute (ed. Marian W. Smith), London, 1961.

6

The Abelam Artist

Anthony Forge

One of Raymond Firth's earliest articles, 'The Maori Carver', published in 1925, testifies to the early formation of that interest in art which has remained with him ever since. It is an enthusiastic piece, establishing the right of the Maori artist to be judged by his own standards and not merely as a primitive whose attempts to reach the style and vision of the Greek artist are vitiated by his dull and brutish nature. That such arguments do not have to be repeated today is due to the change in attitude which Raymond Firth has had a part in shaping. Although he would hardly have called himself a social anthropologist in those days, his approach to the problem of the artist in society was basically sociological, and that it was also ahead of its time is amply demonstrated by the several officious and carping footnotes inserted by the editors of *The Journal of the Polynesian Society*. A quotation shows his approach well and might be taken as a text for the present essay in his honour. 'It is important to know what kind of a person the carver was, what position he and his work occupied in the social scheme, and the seriousness with which both he and his labour were regarded.' This attitude, which was elaborated and refined in his later publications (Firth, 1936a, and 'The social framework of primitive art' in Firth, 1951), has always distinguished him from his contemporaries and immediate successors in

social anthropology. He has always made it clear that to him art is not only a fit subject of study by social anthropologists but also a field of human activity which they ignore at their peril. Always opposed as he has been to any narrowing of the field of social anthropology, this attitude stems both from his interest in and appreciation of art, and from his view that it is in such highly regarded and deeply felt activities as art that human societies and their members express their values.

This essay is rather heavily ethnographic. I wish it could be more analytical, but despite Firth's advocacy we have still not developed the necessary concepts to be able to handle the relation of art and its creators to their society at anything above the descriptive level. However, it is at least now realized that such concepts are necessary, not only for plastic art, but for music, dance, architecture, and poetry as well as ritual and myth.

The truism of art history, that art reflects the society that produced it, is usually expounded with reference to some period of history in which known artists expressed their view of their culture and times in terms of the acceptance or rejection, and subsequent modification, of the art of the period immediately before their own. The artist is envisaged, as is the poet or musician, as expressing himself and his times in two main ways: first, by developing and perfecting forms and

From Maurice Freedman (ed.), *Social Organisation: Essays Presented to Raymond Firth* (London: Cass, 1967), pp. 65–84, 291–294.

techniques used by his predecessors; second, by expressing in his art different conceptions and values, either by modification of the available styles and forms, or by the introduction of new ones. In short, the artist is seen as an individual receptive to his social environment and capable of mirroring his view of it in his art. The artist also codifies change; he starts with the conception of beauty common to the society of his childhood, and if he is great, he leaves the society with a modified conception of beauty, with new standards – a changed aesthetic. This view of the artist in his social setting presupposes change both in the society and the art; not just actual change, but also a conception of change, frequently, but not always, of progress. What the artist really expresses is not the values of his culture in any direct way, but the change in those values. A study of the art can therefore tell us nothing about the artist or even his values unless we also know something of the society and culture in which he operated, as the reflections of aestheticians on prehistoric and ethnographic art have frequently demonstrated. Just as it is impossible to have history without some concept of change, so art history and its techniques, being concerned primarily with change, cannot be used in any simple way on the sort of material presented by New Guinea societies. These societies have no concept of history or indeed of change, although since the advent of various European administrations they have become aware of the effects of change. In the view of members of these societies, they had always been the same since they came into existence and should ideally remain the same for ever. Similarly, the art of these societies had magico-religious value for them precisely because it re-created the art of the ancestors; its whole social function consisted in being unchanging. What then becomes of the artist as the supersensitive receiver and distiller of the essence of his culture and times? Does he become merely a craftsman skilfully reproducing traditional objects in the traditional style to satisfy social demands whose springs are in concepts of magico-religious efficiency rather than any ideal of beauty? Someone must have created the art, and to judge from the favour many, though by no means all, of the highly prized objects have found with European artists and

critics, the creator or creators were artists rather that craftsmen.

I shall not be able to give final answers to the problems outlined above, but hope at least to clarify some of them. In this essay I shall be examining the artist in his society with reference to the Abelam tribe of New Guinea.[1] The Abelam number about 30,000 and live in the southern foothills of the Prince Alexander mountains to the north of the Sepik River. They live in large villages from 300 to 800 in population, and have a vigorous art. They are also distinguished for a cult of long yams; single yams of up to twelve feet long have been recorded.

The Context of Abelam Art

As in most New Guinea societies, all art among the Abelam is basically cult art and can only be displayed in the context of the ceremonials of the tambaran cult.[2] Decorative art, of course, exists, but its *motifs* are entirely drawn from the art of the tambaran cult; and it carries with it overtones of status from that cult. Half coconut shells, polished black and beautifully engraved with designs filled with white, are among the finest small objects produced by the Abelam; they are used for drinking soup, but may be carried only by big-men or men fully initiated in the tambaran cult and successful in the yam cult; young men can and do inherit them but cannot use them until they have the full ceremonial status of organizers of ceremonies. Similarly the engraved pottery bowls, holding anything from one to four gallons of white soup, made by women but decorated by men, can be used for serving soup only when ceremonial exchanges are taking place. Such examples could be multiplied to cover the whole field of decorative art, showing that not only is it stylistically derived from the cult art, but that the use and display of decorated objects are limited, by virtue of their decoration, to prescribed contexts and statuses also stemming from the cult. There are therefore no artists who produce decorated objects who are not also cult artists, and it is in the context of the cult that they acquire and perfect their skills. There is one exception to this statement: the women who make netted string bags (*wut*) using red, yellow, white, and a sort of dark purple string, in various excellent designs. The use of the bags by the men is determined by their ceremonial status, one design being reserved for fully initiated men, another for those who have only one ceremony to go, and so on. The small bags used by young men gradually increase in size with the age and status of their users. The production of the bags, however, is regarded simply as a skill which a woman learns from her mother or mother's or father's sister, and the ability to produce any design, although highly prized, is no indicator of status.

The tambaran cult shares its basic features with such cults throughout New Guinea. In essence it is a series of ceremonies at each of which the initiates are shown art objects of one sort or another and are told that these are the sacred spirits, tambaran. At the next ceremony they are told that the last one was just pretence but that this time they are going to see the real tambaran, and so on until the last of the ceremonies when they are in fact shown the most sacred objects; and as fully initiated men they may go through the cycle again, this time as stagers of the ceremonies and themselves initiators. Each ceremony is performed by one half of a dual organization, called *ara*, who initiate the sons of their exchange partners in the other *ara*; the initiators are fed by their partners while they prepare the ceremony, and after the initiation are presented with pigs. *Ara* perform ceremonies alternately: one will perform ceremonies 1, 3, 5, and 7, the other 2, 4, 6, and 8, going on then to 1, 3, 5, and 7, so that two full cycles have to be performed before an individual has been initiated into all the eight ceremonies.

All ceremonial activity is regarded as balanced exchange between *ara* and the individual partners who compose them. There is three-way reciprocity with increasing exactness of return at each level. First the food and the live pig are regarded as a return for ceremonial services in preparing the ceremony, acting as initiators, and providing decorations for the initiate (the son of the donor). A man will reproach his partner if the decorations are not up to standard, asking whether he has been eating all the food provided just to produce this. Second, the next ceremony of the cycle will be performed by the other *ara* and the donor will now be recipient. Rough

equivalence is expected in size of pig between each pair of ceremonies, 1 and 2, 3 and 4, etc.; the scale increases until 7 and 8, which may require three months each to prepare, a very large drain on the resources of the *ara* responsible for feeding the initiators, and demanding the most enormous pigs for presentation at the end. The third and final form of reciprocity, at which exact equivalence in the girth of the pig presented is essential, comes with the next cycle, when the *ara* who initiated at ceremony 1 last time are now paying for their sons to be initiated into the same ceremony. The lapse of time involved in the completion of a cycle can never have been less than ten years, and is nowadays, and probably always was, considerably longer. Although this is not the place for an analysis of the social structure, it is worth noting that these inescapable reciprocal obligations, stretching over the decades covered by two full cycles, are a potent factor in maintaining the stability of the component groups of the ceremonial organization, since to default imperils the ceremony and exposes the culprit to sanctions from the whole village and not just from his own clan or ceremonial partner.

The preparation of tambaran ceremonies provides the context in which all Abelam artists work, and the ceremonies themselves the only opportunity for them to display their work to any large group of people. It is also during the preparations that the training, if it can be called that, of future artists takes place. All the ceremonies have as central features the display of some series of objects which stand for the *nggwalndu*, that is, the major clan spirits. The earliest of the sequence are said to be very simple, but I have never seen either of the first two in any part of the Abelam area, and it would seem that they have been dropped from the repertoire, at least since the war. To go by the descriptions of older informants, the tambaran consisted of patterns on the floor of the ceremonial house made with the four earth paints (red, yellow, white, and black) with the addition of flowers, particularly the scarlet single hibiscus, and certain leaves, those with a silvery grey back being present in all tambaran ceremonies. While these patterns are the focus of the initiation and the representation of the *nggwalndu*, and give little scope for artistic expression, they are surrounded by painted panels of sago spathe which line and provide the ceiling for the initiation chamber constructed inside the ceremonial house – the painting and arrangement of which provide ample opportunity for the artists to display their skill, and which are the basis on which visitors from other villages evaluate the success of the ceremony. These paintings on the flat are sacred in that they are associated with the *nggwalndu* and the ceremonial house, whose façade is decorated with similar paintings, but the designs are not tambarans, being open and visible on the façade to women and uninitiated males. When used inside the house the designs and the panels on which they are painted are called *wut*, and referred to as the beautiful string bags of the *nggwalndu*. *Wut* has, however, many other meanings and is one of the most emotionally loaded words in Abelam. In this instance the most obvious symbolic referent is *nyan wut* – womb (*nyan* meaning child) – the initiation chamber being a small dark room built inside the large female house with its low entrance through which the initiates crawl when entering and leaving. The women are not supposed to know that *wut* is used for the painted panels which they, of course, never see in place, and I have heard artists, as they paint, laughing at the women's illusion that only they can make beautiful *wut*.[3]

Wut panels are to be found at all eight stages of initiation into the tambaran cult, but in later ceremonies the tambaran itself has a larger and more elaborate structure. There is a great deal of variation within the Abelam area in what is displayed at each stage, although there is far less variation in the names of the ceremonies, the same name being used for very different displays in different parts of the area. Much more is involved than simple wood-carving and painting on the flat in all parts of the area. For example, there is the setting up of 50 ft. poles with great masses of dry and thorny yam vines, and leaves of the spiny lawyer cane fastened on them to represent *nggwalndu* (see pl. III, Forge, 1966); bamboo roots are made into bird heads; and larger than life-size seated figures with extended arms and legs, covered with brightly painted patterned matting and stuffed with fibre, have to be constructed on armatures of wood and palm,

themselves difficult to construct, with only split cane lashings to fasten the pieces together. Of such a figure all that is saved after the break-up of the display is the carved wooden head. The fact that much of the work of the artist for such ceremonies is ephemeral does not mean that the demands of the public are less, or that a high degree of both technical skill and aesthetic sense is not essential in the artist.

Each ceremony of the tambaran cycle has as its core a specified tambaran with a definite name and a prescribed form. The form is traditional and highly valued because it is believed to be that used by the ancestors and therefore the most powerful in a supernatural sense. Abelam tambaran ceremonies appear to the casual attender to be secular occasions; the emphasis is all on the magnificence of the decorations, both of the objects and of the initiators, and the desire to create an impression on the visitors. The fathers of the initiates are watchful that all should be correct, but when they do complain it is on the grounds of value for the food and pigs they are providing rather than out of concern for the proper instruction of their children. In general, the initiates, the ostensible purpose of the ceremony, get scant attention, the parts of the ceremony that concern them are often rushed, and they are hustled off and told to wait until wanted again. In most ceremonies a few initiates get lost at some stage, either because they have run away or have simply wandered off; their fathers may protest, but the rituals continue without them and they are considered fully initiated, whether they were there or not, as long as the father has fulfilled his exchange obligations. Nor is there any sort of instruction of the initiates; they are told what to do but never why to do it. There are puberty initiations which involve seclusion and a certain amount of instruction of youths, but these are usually separate from the tambaran ceremonies and the instruction is not about these ceremonies.

The initiates have to observe some minor food taboos and a period of sexual abstinence before and after the ceremony, but it is on the initiators that the burden of the ritual restrictions falls. It is only during the preparations for a ceremony that the observer becomes aware of the magico-religious elements of the whole:

elements that are represented during the ceremony by a brief invocation almost drowned by the noise of the audience, or the fumbling of the bewildered initiates as they try to perform some ritual actions of which they understand nothing. The supernatural benefit of the ceremony to the community, the other communities that assist, and the individuals concerned, accrues during the long and careful preparations, and the observance of a whole series of taboos and ritual performances by the initiators, some continuing for three months before and six months after the ceremony. All the artistic and other work of preparation is performed in the name of the *nggwalndu*, and their benevolence is assured, first by the performance of ritual and the observance of taboos, and second by the skill of the artists in creating the objects to which the *nggwalndu* names are given, and the magnificence of the ancillary *wut* and other decorations both of humans and objects. The magico-religious benefits of the ceremony may be released during the noisy and crowded public climax, but they are created by artists and organizers working in small groups during the preceding months behind sago palm frond fences which may not be passed by women, uninitiated men, or even initiated men of the other *ara*.

There is a clear necessity for artists in Abelam society. Every ritual group has to be able to draw on artists with the varied skills necessary to produce displays adequate to please the *nggwalndu* and other spirits, maintain the prestige of the group vis-à-vis other ritual groups and villages, and keep up the ceremonial exchange system within the group. The *ara* dual organization and the exchanges between partners which provide the social framework for ceremony also act to restrict the availability of artists from within the group. Each ceremony is prepared by one *ara* for the other, and members of the initiates' *ara*, whether fully initiated or not, may not take any part in the preparations, or even see the raw materials used, until all is ready and displayed at the ceremony itself. Thus any artist, no matter how skilled, may only work on alternate ceremonies within his own ritual group. It is very rare for one *ara* of any ritual group to be able to supply all the necessary talent from its own ranks, and recruitment from outside is the rule.

Peace is anyhow necessary for the performance of a ceremony, but neutrality is not enough; active co-operation is necessary between enemy villages for any of the more elaborate ceremonies. Peace ceremonies involve the exchange of men of equal age and social status between villages; each pair so exchanged become *waunindu* and call each other brother, and it is through these relationships that help is mobilized. Usually the work is sub-contracted, that is, so many painted panels of specified sizes and so much patterned matting are prepared in the enemy village and ceremonially carried in when the whole job has been done. The party bringing such contributions appears as a war party in full war paint, preceded by a screen of spearmen. They cut down young trees and lop branches off bigger ones, destroy banana plants, and generally leave a trail of licensed destruction in their wake. As they approach the ceremonial ground the spearmen advance and throw spears at warriors from the recipient group. These warriors are especially selected for their ability to dodge; no reciprocation is allowed and casualties are said to occur – certainly on the occasions when I have been present, great skill in dodging was very necessary. The rest of the party throw armfuls of rubbish and the remains of the ruined breadfruit and banana trees into the doorways of the dwelling houses. The demands of hostility are then superseded by the demands of hospitality, and the visitors are stuffed with the finest soup and yams, and laden with yams and pork to take away with them; but uneasiness prevails on both sides until the visitors are safely on the way home, having promised to attend the final ceremony and a further and major food distribution after it.

Aid from friendly and allied villages is obtained in more informal ways, but again only by the activation of specific pre-existing interpersonal relationships. Help, whether for general labour or from a specific artist, can only be solicited through established relationships, and for a big ceremony every possible link, through kinship, clanship, and the various forms of quasi-brotherhood and exchange relationship, is utilized. From the point of view of the artist, the *ara* system means that although he may be debarred from half the ceremonies of his own ritual group, if he has any sort of reputation he will be in demand for the ceremonies of others, and his rewards are not only in the immediate return for his work in food, honour, and prestige, but in the activation of remote and otherwise dormant ties with men in other villages. Wide-spreading ties are of benefit to him in everyday life and enhance his prestige within his group. In short, a successful artist is sought after both within his ritual group and outside it, and if he can speak well in debate and grow reasonably long yams for presentation to his partner, he is assured of high prestige. An artist of considerable experience will often be called a big-man, but very rarely are artists big-men in the aggressive entrepreneurial sense – they are not leaders in secular affairs and manipulators of public opinion as are the real big-men. Although I am neither competent nor possessed of adequate systematic material to make any generalizations about the temperament of Abelam artists and big-men, my entirely subjective impression from acquaintance or friendship with several dozens of each is that the artists are nearly always comparatively modest men (no Abelam could be called modest *tout court*!), not given to violent expressions of emotion; their debating style tends to be quiet and authoritative but not excessively controversial, and they can usually expect a respectful and attentive hearing; the practice of their skills gives them general prestige and particularly a reputation for understanding and knowledge of the supernatural which invests their opinions with something of wisdom. These differences have some social concomitants; successful carving and painting are believed to be incompatible with the practice of sorcery, whereas the entrepreneur big-man is usually believed to be an adept at sorcery. Furthermore, the artist's reputation may be expected to grow until he is literally too weak to hold an adze or a paint brush, while the big-man is in constant danger of being displaced by more energetic rivals from the moment he achieves his position, and is virtually certain to have lost his position by late middle age. Whether it is due to an increased sense of security or a manifestation of the artistic genius, artists, in my experience, claim fewer homicides, their adulteries are more discreet, and they quarrel less flamboyantly with their wives and clansmen. In fact, the Abelam expect their artists

to be good men (*yigen ndu*), and by and large the artists conform to those expectations.

The Materials and Techniques of Abelam Art

Although the tambaran cult demands the use of many materials for its ceremonies, an artist's reputation is based primarily on his ability as a wood-carver and painter; skill in engraving on coconut shell, bone, and pottery is also highly valued, but is considered to go with ability as a carver, while the making of basketry masks, and shell decorated mannikins from string by a sort of crochet technique, are important, but much more widely distributed, skills. The traditional equipment for carving was thoroughly neolithic: polished stone adzes, pig, dog, and flying fox teeth mounted as awls, gravers, and chisels, certain lizard skins and even a rough-surfaced leaf for smoothing. Fire was used for hollowing out drums or the backs of large figures. Softwoods were used green and the splits that tended to occur were deplored but disregarded unless they seriously distorted the figure. Current tools, although vastly improved by the use of steel, have hardly changed; the steel plane blades are mounted in exactly the same way, with the same angle between blade and handle as before. Indeed, some of the handles, beautifully carved, were originally made for stone blades and have been inherited from the preceding generation of artists. Cheap trade knives or large nails replace the teeth, but the method of mounting and use is traditional; sides of tins full of nail holes make a sort of rasp, but finishing work, now less necessary because of the superior edge of steel tools, is often done with the old materials. European adzes may be used for roughing out, but never for carving. The adze is always used with short rapid strokes towards the carver, removing only very small amounts of wood at each stroke. Modern carvers using four or five graded adzes often carve so finely that no further smoothing is needed. The backs of figures and masks are usually left rough, or hollowed out to reduce the weight, but in the case of pierced plaques and wood head-dresses both sides are carved and engraved with equal care.

All Abelam carvings are painted in polychrome and engraving is often added round the eyes, penis, and navel so that the effect of the paint is enhanced by low relief.

Paint itself is highly valued by the Abelam, and almost all magic involves some form of coloured mineral substance that is classified as paint; a form of paint is also the active principle of sorcery and long yam magic. The paint used for tambaran ceremonies is not, unlike the other types, inherently powerful; it is obtained locally or in open trade, and large quantities are assembled, whereas the powerful paints are always obtained in small quantities in secrecy from distant villages. Red and yellow ochres and white and black are the only colours used, the first three being stored in the form of powders; the black, however, has to be made as required by chewing scrapings from the bottoms of cooking pots, sap from a species of shrub, and leaves from a tree, and spitting the result into a paintpot as needed. This rather unpleasant task is delegated to young assistants, and forms a part of the apprenticeship of the would-be artist.[4]

Although the paint itself is not intrinsically powerful, painting is a sacred activity, and after the paint has been used on tambaran carvings, or *wut*, or on the initiators themselves, it becomes the principal vehicle by which the benefit of the ceremony is transmitted to the participants. Carving, although carried on in seclusion either in the bush or in an enclosure near the ceremonial house, is hardly a ritual activity; some artists have their own spells to stop the unseasoned wood splitting, but carving has no communal ritual connected with it. It is only when the artist has finished the carving and put in the eyes and pubic hair with a piece of charcoal that the figure becomes an object of concern to the whole ritual group. If the charcoaling is done in the village, the log gongs are beaten to announce the arrival of the tambaran. This call also serves to warn everybody that the final phase of preparations is about to begin. Stocks of paint are checked and augmented, and the final food distribution before the ceremony takes place. The work of painting is carried out under taboos similar to and almost as stringent as those of the long yam cult; men who are going to participate in the painting bleed their penes and must abstain from all sexual contact until after the ceremony; meat and certain vegetable foods are forbidden, but they can and do eat large quantities of the yam soup and finest steamed yams provided by their exchange partners. Painting is done at great speed – usually all the workers sleep within the ceremonial enclosure and work from dawn till dusk with frequent but short breaks for food and betel nut. To begin with, any old figures that are being re-used have to be washed, and this is done in running water, the standard Abelam way of disposing of potentially dangerous material. Then both wood and the sago spathe *wut* have to be coated with the mud base on which the painting is done. A good deal of technical expertise is needed to get just the right sort of mud mixed to the right consistency, so that it will provide a smooth absorbent surface and adhere to the material. Sago spathe, which has a very shiny surface, is particularly difficult and is usually rubbed down before the mud is applied with stinging nettles and the bulb of a species of wild ginger (?), both substances which, in the Abelam view, bite and therefore improve the adhesion. The mud base used is black throughout the southern and eastern Abelam but grey in the north. On the grey mud, black has to be applied as a separate colour, but with the black mud those portions of the design calling for black are usually left unpainted, simply being glazed with tree sap when the painting is finished.

Abelam painting technique is extraordinary because it combines great speed with firm control by the artist. All the preparers of the ceremony join in the painting and all are found employment regardless of their lack of talent. The artist outlines the design to be painted in thin white lines. He may use lengths of split cane to help him work out the proportions of the design relative to the panel, or cane tied in rings to give him a guide for a smooth curve or circle; but he usually just starts from one edge and builds up the design as a series of elements as he works across the panel. With carved figures, artists usually start with the head, which is the most intricate part; the proportions are of course given by the form of the carving, but otherwise the techniques for figures and panels are identical. As soon as the artist has painted a few white lines for one part of the design, he instructs an assistant to paint a red or yellow line just beside it. Abelam art rarely uses a single line – multiple lines of varied colour, often further emphasized by white dots on one of the colours, are the rule. The artist now moves on to the next part of the design but keeps an eye on his first assistant. When the white lines have been satisfactorily doubled or trebled by the assistant or assistants, a second grade of assistant is employed to fill in solid areas of a single colour: subordinate grades of assistant are employed to put on the lines of white dots and glaze the black mud with tree sap or chew up black paint if the painting is on grey. Other men will be employed powdering and mixing paints and coating objects and panels with mud. An artist at work on painting usually keeps from eight to ten men more or less busy while still maintaining complete control over the design and its execution.

The paints are mixed with water in which certain very bitter species of wild lime have been steeped; again the idea of bite is produced as an explanation. The containers are usually half coconut shells, but they must be lined with a portion of wild taro leaf; wild taro is an important plant in all Abelam ceremonial – intimately connected with the ancestors, it is also a symbol of the *ara* and their rivalry, and is much used in tambaran ceremonies. Brushes are made from fibres tied to the end of a splinter of wood; small feathers or the chewed end of a fibrous twig are similarly used. For the drawing of white lines a long narrow single chicken feather, made pliable by bending, is drawn along with about two inches of the feather flat on the surface. This technique, which properly used produces a narrow line but manages to keep a reasonable charge of paint on the brush, is employed with great boldness by experienced artists and enables them to draw the sweeping curves characteristic of Abelam design with speed and accuracy.[5]

Although supplies of mud base are kept handy in case of mistakes, artists rarely need it; they refer to no model or sketch and appear to lay out the whole design in their heads. When several artists are painting together, as happens during the painting of a ceremonial house façade, they share out the available width between them and each paints his own section of the bands of identical motifs that stretch across the façade. In such a case they agree in advance on the proportions and number each is going to paint; while working they watch one another's progress to ensure that the styles are reasonably matched and that the meeting of their respective zones will be harmonious, but there is nothing like copying involved; no artist who is not known to be capable of producing the required designs in isolation would be employed on a façade.

At the conclusion of the painting stage, when the display has been completed, the log gongs are beaten to announce the fact to the entire area, and the artists are honoured by having the log gong calls of their totems beaten immediately after the announcement. The initiation chamber is now sealed and final arrangements are made about facepaint, feathers, head-dresses, and other decorations by the initiators, and about pigs by their exchange partners. The ceremony follows in three or four days.

The Artist in Society

Every initiated Abelam man aspires to be an artist in some way or other. All, in the context of the tambaran ceremonies, have a place in the process of artistic production. The amount of time they spend helping with the actual painting and carving, as opposed to the many other activities necessary in the preparation of ceremony, is largely a matter of choice. A rebuff to a middle-aged man for bad work from one of the directing artists can be expected to disillusion him with artistic activity for the rest of that ceremony, but younger men are less conscious of their dignity and stay and learn.[6] The training and selection of artists are completely informal. A youth who shows aptitude will be encouraged and allowed to perform increasingly difficult tasks under supervision until he is allowed to try the painting of a minor figure and later a small *wut* panel for himself. The artist will correct and guide him, taking over now and then when difficulties occur. A young man will have to do all stages of the painting himself, unless a friend will help him, since the various grades of assistant are attracted only to artists of established prestige. A young man with interest in becoming an artist is not restricted to his own village for tuition, nor does he attach himself to one artist as an apprentice; he can of course attend all the ceremonial preparations in his own village for which he is qualified as an initiator, and assist and learn from all the artists who are at work there. He can also, through ties of kinship or clanship, help in ceremonies at allied villages or with contracted-out work which his own or allied villages are performing for enemy villages, always provided he has been initiated into the ceremony concerned. In this way a young man may well be able to work every year on some preparations or other, and come into contact with artists from villages five or more miles apart. Since considerable variation in style and type of production is to be found even in such short distances among the densely packed Abelam, a would-be artist will acquire a wider range and understanding of tambarans and their production than would be possible if he were confined to the set traditional to his natal village.

What has been said about training applies to the painting and constructional phases of ceremonial preparation; to obtain instruction in carving is more difficult, while a reputation as a carver is essential if an artist is to have prestige. Every Abelam male claims to be able to paint, and painting is a semi-sacred activity, the responsibility of personnel laid down by the social structure (particularly the system of initiation grades and the dual organization), performed at a prescribed time during the ceremonial preparations, preceded and closed by essential ritual, and governed by a series of taboos which apply to all the initiators whether in fact they paint or not. Carving, on the other hand, is a much more personal activity and not subject to the formal prescriptions of painting. All carving is undertaken either for the clan of the carver or as a commission from another clan or village, and except for the head board that goes across the base of the painted façade of a ceremonial house, a carving is the responsibility of a single artist. 'Commission' does not imply a contract with a stated reward. Carvings are occasionally produced in return for a stipulated payment in shell rings and pigs, but usually only under exceptional circumstances for a major undertaking such as the carving of new *nggwalndu* when the village and its immediate allies lack sufficient talent, or in the introduction of new types of figure or tambaran where what is being bought is not just the carvings but also the right to display them and to reproduce them in the future. In general, however, carvers are recruited with the promise of no more than good food, as much betel and tobacco as they need, and, of course, the prestige that will accrue to them. All the work of preparation is divided up among the initiators according to their clans and sub-clans; each sub-clan owns its own figures and assumes responsibility for them as well as its share of the *wut* panels and other decorations. Large clans have one *nggwalndu* and are split into sub-clans divided between the *ara* so that there is always a group among the initiators to care for the *nggwalndu*; clans too small to have sub-clans have to form pairs, one in each *ara*, and look after two *nggwalndu* at any ceremony. It is the responsibility of the clan to provide the necessary artistic talent, and it is through the social relationships of individual clan members that the artists are recruited. In addition to the panels or figures necessary for the particular ceremony, each clan has minor figures, often unnamed, which it also includes in the display. Their number and beauty reflect the prestige of the clan, although in many cases they are so numerous that they have to be placed on top of one another and sometimes even obscure the tambarans that are the focus of the ceremony. A big-man would usually commission at least one minor figure at an important ceremony as a mark of his prestige. Such a new carving would become the property of his exchange partner at the end of the ceremony and exchanges; the exchange partner of course would provide all the food for the artist, and reciprocation would be expected at the next suitable opportunity.

A carver selects his timber on the land of the commissioning clan, and they cut it and drag it to his studio, also doing the cutting to size and other unskilled tasks. The studio may be on the ceremonial ground. If so, it will be away from other activities; more frequently it is in a secluded patch of bush near the artist's house; it will always be in the shade to minimize the risks of splitting. The artist does not welcome company or conversation, and spends a good deal of time sitting in silence and looking at his work – this is in great contrast to normal Abelam activity, and especially to painting, where speed, movement, and noise are predominant. An assistant is usually present, but some artists carve entirely alone; anyone else, such as the curious ethnographer, is regarded as a pest. Young men who cheerfully help in the painting do not always care to spend days in silence and inactivity doing occasional minor tasks, and it is only the minority who persist and start to acquire carving skills. These gradually undertake more and more skilled parts of the work until they try some small simple object themselves, showing it to the artist at each stage and relying on him to give the finishing touches. When such a piece is accepted for inclusion in a display the apprenticeship phase is coming to an end. It is here, in the carving and the acceptance of their work for display, that the relationship between the artist and his society can be seen most clearly.

From the view of the Abelam as a whole the tambaran cult and the art associated with the long yam cult are means of creating and releasing magico-religious power and benefit; the art is essential for the performance of ceremonial, and the artist is a technician whose chief virtue is his power to reproduce exactly the powerful patterns and designs used by the ancestors. The tambarans and their benefit are traditional; to be effective they must be re-creations of the original tambarans, and, furthermore, the fathers of the initiates are anxious to ensure that the ceremony they are paying for is full and correct. These are both forces opposed to innovation, but at the same time the ceremonies are opportunities for display and the acquisition of prestige by the village, ritual group, *ara*, clan, and individuals concerned; magnificence is consciously sought; magical bundles are fastened to the newly painted figures and carvings, not connected with the ritual but solely so that the eyes of the beholders shall be dazzled by the brightness of the paint and the beauty of the workmanship. Obviously this aspect of the ceremonial allows an element of fashion into the art, but since the benefits of the ceremony extend beyond the village, innovation that has not some good magico-religious justification or precedent will be subject to wide disapproval.

The Abelam artist works within fairly narrow stylistic limits sanctioned by the total society in which he lives; any work he produces cannot be shown outside the tambaran cult, and will only be accepted for that if it satisfies the criteria of magico-religious effectiveness. A young man of Malmba village who had found a growth on a tree that resembled in general shape the human head, had taken it home and carved on it eyes, nose, and mouth and painted it in the traditional style. When he produced it during the preparations for a ceremony at which he was an initiator, the organizers refused to display it or allow it in the ceremonial house; although the painting was in correct style, the shape of the head was nothing like any of the head shapes of tambaran figures. His plea that it was the shape of a human head carried no weight and he was forced to wrap it up and hide it in his hut until he sold it to me in 1959. In 1962, at Yanuko village a mile or so to the south, two artists painting the façade of a new ceremonial house introduced a very narrow band of stylized leaf decoration similar to a traditional form but with important differences. There was some doubt about it, and some of the older men were against it; the two artists and their helpers were adamant – they were both of high reputation and no alternative artists were available; in the event this innovation was much admired in the surrounding villages. The artists were courted by people from other villages who wished to be able to call on them for houses in the future, while the ritual group whose house it was won more prestige than the other ritual group of Yanuko village whose new house, without any innovation, opened at much the same time.

A much more important example of innovation occurred at Wingei village in 1959. While a new house was under construction the organizers and the six artists involved decided to abandon the traditional style of façade-painting in favour of one that was used around Kalabu, a village about ten miles to the west; the reason for the change was the superior length of long yam grown in Kalabu. The experiment was not a great success – the bottom row of huge *nggwalndu* heads, which was the principal innovation, was badly painted, mainly because of the unaccustomed style. That Wingei changed the style of their ceremonial house façade to get longer yams, rather than change the planting season which is three months earlier in Kalabu, indicates the confidence the Abelam have in the power of art, and brings into focus the position of the artist who, if not exactly a mediator between man and the supernatural, is in contact with it and able to influence it through his skill as a carver and painter. The latter point is reinforced by the explanation offered for the bad painting: one of the artists died a week after the painting had been completed; the sorcery that killed him had obviously been working in him and prevented him and his fellows from correctly releasing the supernatural energy inherent in the design. Since this explanation was accepted even among traditional enemies of Wingei it was presumably sincerely believed and representative of Abelam thought on these matters.

The Abelam language has no vocabulary of aesthetics; there are two words of approbation used about art; one means 'good' and can be used about almost anything; the other appears to mean primarily 'correct', that is, traditional, powerful. Neither has any necessary connotations of beauty and I know of no word that has. The social demand for art is concerned with its magico-religious power. This is said to depend on the correct placing of the elements of any design with no prescription of a harmonious relation between them. Criticism of art is always in terms of correctness and effectiveness. Artists, particularly when carving, discuss among themselves such things as the shape and size of a limb and its relation to other parts of the figure, but these things are not appreciated by the non-artist. I have heard carvers reproached for holding up the beginning of the painting by fiddling about, taking a piece off here and there, when the figure already had all the necessary attributes, legs, penis, navel, arms, and head. The artists, although they lack any specific terms, do talk about such things as form and proportion, and derive considerable pleasure from carving and painting things satisfying to their aesthetic sense. They carefully examine and discuss works by other artists and rate one another as more or less talented by criteria that are primarily aesthetic. Although not capable of, or not interested in, discussing art in the same terms, most non-artists asked to rate a group of figures or paintings in order of effectiveness, both in ritual power and secular prestige, rank them in the same order as do the artists and the ethnographer. Since, with Raymond Firth, I believe in a universal human aesthetic, this is not surprising; what is important, I think, is that the skilful artist who satisfies his aesthetic sense and produces beauty is rewarded not for the beauty itself but because the beauty, although not recognized as such, is regarded by the rest as power.

Apart from conscious innovation seen as such by the whole community, there also occurs a gradual change in style which is much more difficult to document. Several villages possess very old *nggwalndu*, and at least two villages have a series of *nggwalndu* obviously made at various dates. How far back these specimens go it is difficult to say, but genealogical information about their carvers suggests that the oldest might be eighty to a hundred years old. These old figures invariably show a different style from that of the present; those in series show a consistent change in style, the development of the recent style from the antecedent one. The differences are much greater than could be attributable to a change from stone tools to steel – there are definitely changes in the way the human form has been conceived over the period. This situation leads to some difficulties, since the present style is the correct style, that is the ancestral style, yet it is different from the style in which the old *nggwalndu* were actually carved by the ancestors. When such *nggwalndu* are washed and repainted, as they are for the final ceremony of each tambaran cycle, the current style of painting does not fit happily on the old style of carving; the surfaces and their relationship to each other are different and the painted designs sit uncomfortably on forms intended for different designs. While the painting is going on such difficulties are recognized. Normally, however, the stylistic difference does not worry anyone; it is simply ignored; only when the impertinent ethnographer holding an artist firmly by the wrist has pointed out all the differences, will he admit their existence; otherwise, the insistence is firm on all sides that the present style is the ancestral style. In discussion with me, artists have speculated on the change in style, wondering whether their style or the old style is the right one, ending by saying that anyhow they know how to carve only in their present style and could not re-create the old style if they wanted to. It is interesting to note in passing that the older figures invariably have much more definite sculptural form – the features are boldly carved and in general they do not seem to be merely pleasant surfaces for painting as much of the present Abelam carving is. Their forms, though varied, are often more reminiscent of the Iatmül styles of the Middle

Sepik to the south. It seems possible that the very high development of polychrome painting so much admired among the Abelam may have resulted in the declining interest in sculptural form evident in the figure sequences. With its conscious desire for ostentation and display it has to be confessed that some Abelam sculpture tends to be rather vulgar by European standards.

This gradual stylistic change makes it obvious that whatever they believe, Abelam artists do not slavishly reproduce the work of their predecessors. It would be surprising if they did since, as already mentioned, they never copy one another or any model. A famous artist of Kalabu, asked by a village across a dialect boundary to produce a type of figure that was used in their ceremonies but not at Kalabu, was given a 2-foot-high carving to work from. This he studied but kept in his house, never taking it to his bush studio until the 10-foot carving was finished, when he satisfied himself that he had done it correctly. As everything an artist produces comes from his picture of what the object required should look like, every artist must to some extent impose his own vision of a 'good' piece on the work in hand.

The artist is free to express himself within the stylistic limits prevailing at the time, and by so doing may marginally change those limits. There is of course a feedback here; the society may impose stylistic limits on what is acceptable for a tambaran ceremony and so control the artist, but the artist creates all the art and therefore forms the society's conceptions of what is acceptable. In such a situation gradual change is probably inevitable. It offers the artist self-expression, and keeps the art vital and capable of expressing the changing values of the society, while at the same time ensuring that it can continue to fulfil its main function of being the traditional and powerful mode of access to the supernatural. I have argued elsewhere (Forge, 1966) that Abelam art is intimately connected with the values of Abelam society, and that it makes statements about Abelam society that are not made by other means. If this is so the artist must be the essential link. Up till now the contact with the Australian administration and the missions has not affected the art in style or content. The war and its aftermath virtually stopped artistic ac-

tivity, but it has been taken up again, at least in the north, with great vigour. This revival has coincided with, and been a symbol of, a withdrawal from excessive contact with European values and a reaffirmation of traditional values. In fact up to now, the art, far from changing, has been reinforced in its conservatism by taking on the additional value of acting as a symbol of Abelam culture in the face of colonial culture.

NOTES

1   I am grateful to the Emslie Horniman Scholarship Fund of the Royal Anthropological Institute and to the Bollingen Foundation, New York, for financing two trips to the Abelam, in 1958–9 and 1962–3 respectively. For a general description of Abelam society see Kaberry, 1941 and 1966.

2   The Pidgin English (Neo-Melanesian) words tambaran and big-man have become part of anthropological terminology, so I use them here without italics. Tambaran corresponds to the Abelam word *maira*, while *nemandu* is exactly translated as big-man.

3   In view of the anomalous position of *wut* as an artistic production of both sexes, it is worth noting that for a man to use the words *nyan wut* in the presence of a woman is a formidable insult, certain to result in a quarrel, and possibly leading to a hostile exchange relationship with her protector, or even to a complex village-wide ceremony of cross-sex hostility.

4   For a fuller discussion of the manufacture and use of paints and their magical character, see Forge, 1962.

5   In the Wosera area, S. W. Abelam, a further type of brush is used, made of a single short feather, found between the tail plumes of the lesser bird of paradise, mounted in a grass stem. This will produce exceptionally fine lines, which are used mainly in polychrome cross-hatching. Bands of such cross-hatching are typically used to replace the polychrome multiple lines of the northern Abelam, and as an embellishment to certain other patterns otherwise common to both styles. The technique is laborious

but aesthetically effective. Painting with these brushes cannot be delegated to the less skilled, and the number and size of the *wut* panels so painted were a sure index of prestige. Although painting with the fine line technique was visible on the façades of Wosera ceremonial houses, the means by which these results were produced was secret, the brushes themselves being regarded as a tambaran and very carefully concealed; they were called *vi* (spear) and were integrated into the spear/penis symbolic complex. Brushes elsewhere in the Abelam area are not specially regarded and are abandoned without concern.

6 Since the only two essential qualifications for initiation into a ceremony are that the initiate be alive and that the father or guardian be prepared to pay, babies are frequently initiated; it follows that youths of fifteen or so appear among the initiators.

REFERENCES

Firth, R., 1925. 'The Maori Carver', *Journal of the Polynesian Society*, vol. 34.

Firth, R., 1936. *We, The Tikopia, A Sociological Study of Kinship in Primitive Polynesia*, London.

Firth, R., 1951. *Elements of Social Organization*, London.

Forge, A., 1962. 'Paint – A Magical Substance', *Palette*, no. 9, Basle.

Forge, A., 1966. 'Art and Environment in the Sepik', *Proceedings of the Royal Anthropological Institute, 1965*, London.

Kaberry, P. M., 1941. 'The Abelam Tribe, Sepik District, New Guinea', *Oceania*, vol. 11, nos. 3, 4.

Kaberry, P. M., 1966. 'Political Organization among the Northern Abelam', *Anthropological Forum*, vol. 1, nos. 3, 4.

Part II

Primitivism, Art, and Artifacts

Introduction

Concerns regarding the "primitive" question have been central to the anthropological study of art ever since Boas used the term in his extensive cross-cultural study (ch. 1). Many anthropologists who study art have addressed the obvious negative connotations of this term. The concern is closely tied to the discipline's past theoretical evolutionism – approaching some contemporary indigenous cultures as if they represented earlier stages in the evolution of Western cultures. The term "primitive" implies a lack of development and sophistication that seems incongruous when paired with the term "art" – the achievement of which is often held up as an indicator of a culture's achievement of the highest levels of development. Yet the difficulty in defining a general rubric for a range of objects produced from cultures that have been defined at various times by terms such as indigenous, small-scale, tribal, or non-Western, alludes both to the seeming need to categorize objects from vastly disparate cultures into general frameworks, and to the hazards of that generalization beyond a case-by-case basis. Modern art in the West and anthropology both have complex relationships with the objects produced in different cultures (see Clifford 1988 for a related discussion of Lévi-Strauss, Surrealism, and the collection of culture) and most of the articles in this part explore those relationships with particular reference to a 1984 exhibition at the Museum of Modern Art (MOMA) and debates over the relationship between art and artifacts.

The MOMA exhibition, "'Primitivism' in 20th Century Art," was a catalyst for considerable debate among anthropologists due in part to issues that had been increasingly at the fore of the discipline – changes in the predominant concern with small-scale societies and the problems with the study of cultures as bounded entities in an increasingly globalized system. The relative merits of the exhibition were debated at length in the art press through a series of exchanges between Thomas McEvilley and the exhibition curators, William Rubin and Kirk Varnedoe (McEvilley 1984, 1985a, 1985b; see McEvilley 2002 for a later reflection on the exhibition). The excerpted text from Rubin's introduction to the exhibition catalogue included in this volume outlines the rationale behind the exhibition and the affinities that it explores between objects produced in different cultural contexts. The comparisons are primarily based upon visual similarities and, in some cases, these affinities are based on contact of a speculative nature – that a particular artist may have seen a certain variety of objects and then been influenced by that encounter. Not all of these contacts were hypothetical since Picasso's exposure to the works of various unknown Africans is well known. Indeed Picasso made the now notorious comment to Rubin: "Everything I need to know about Africa is in those objects" (Rubin, ch. 7, n. 5). The anonymity of those producers was secured, not by the fact that the person or persons who made an object were unknown to the community where and when they were made, but by the preference by Western collectors and artists to have those objects stand for a culture, or rather, the idea of a culture and its projected emotional qualities. The recognition of skill and quality became a fundamental consideration in the elevation of a vast range of unrelated objects to the category of "primitive art" (see Goldwater 1967 on this process in relation to the "Primitivist" style in Western art) and was often paired with the simultaneous disregard for their indigenous meanings.

The review of the exhibition by Arthur Danto gives a very concise appraisal of the exhibition's unmet potential as an important cross-cultural encounter that brought together such a wide range of materials for potential analysis. A primary criticism of the exhibition has been its focus on visual resemblance and its subsequent neglect of the many levels on which other, perhaps more significant, comparisons could be made based upon other qualities. James Clifford's essay provides the next layer of context by exploring some of these other comparisons based on a range of other affinities – such as appropriations and collections – that demonstrate the complex relationships underlying these cross-cultural encounters. The selections from the book by Price (2001) place these debates in the particular ethnographic context of Maroon art to demonstrate how Western categories of art contrast with and influence the understanding of objects produced in different cultural contexts. The article by Craig Clunas demonstrates how objects of Chinese material culture were initially categorized as primitive in museum collections before being separated into a distinct category. This highlights how the Western system of art has reinterpreted objects according to its own changing categories, even when those objects come from cultural systems with long art historical traditions of their own. In order to lay the "primitive" question to rest, the anthropological analysis of art must occur in the broadest cross-cultural context. Artists in different cultures have always been influenced by different cultural forms and contemporary artists working in a variety of cultural traditions often include the appropriation of Western art forms and categories (see, for example, the work of Gordon Bennett, ch. 28, figure 28.3).

The essays by Vogel and Gell address the debates that have circulated around the relevance of using either the terms "art" or "artifact" by exploring the relationship between form and function. The terminology reflects general differences between the art historical and the anthropological approach that are slowly changing – the former having generally been more interested in the formal or artistic qualities of an object and the latter being more concerned with function and context. The pairing of the two essays demonstrates that these two views are not mutually exclusive since many objects can be viewed or used in multiple ways without one necessarily negating the other. Vogel's introduction to an exhibition entitled "Art/artifact" presents this debate in the context of the display of objects from Africa. This exhibition and an accompanying catalogue essay by Arthur Danto (1988) form the basis for the critique by Alfred Gell who explores the relationship between traps (embodying forms that reflect their functional nature) and contemporary conceptual art (see Spring 1997 for a critique of Gell's approach and Gell 1997 for the reply). While the conceptual contrast between the formal qualities of art and the functional qualities of the artifact may be tempting in comparing Western art to that of other cultures it must be remembered that, even in the "art for art's sake" model, Western art serves a wide range of functions – as investment, political commentary, expression of emotion, status, taste, and so on.

The question of intention and the related argument that some objects cannot be viewed as "art" because the people who produce them do not have that specific word in their indigenous language, has become less relevant as an increasing number of producers define themselves as artists. In short they *intend* that the work they produce should be considered art. It could be argued that since in many cases there is no direct equivalent in the "art-makers" own language to the English word "art," the intentional production of a work to fit in with the category "art" is the result of the imposition of Western terms and values on another cultural system. However, in addition to failing to recognize the complexity of the English word itself, this would be to place too much of a load on the absence of a direct translation of the term in the languages concerned. There is often an extensive vocabulary that can be applied to objects in the artist's own language and which encompass much of the ground covered by the English term (see, for example, the terms used in Maroon design elements described by Price (ch. 10) and the complex language and system of Yoruba art criticism described by Thompson (ch. 14) in this volume). We do not, of course, deny the existence of a global discourse over art that can influence the categorization of objects cross-culturally. Certainly the market has created a forum where objects acquire a new function as commodities and the work of contemporary practitioners (whether or not they define themselves as artists) has encouraged the use of the term "art" to describe a level of quality and promote respect on a cross-cultural level. The increasingly self-conscious adoption of the category of art by those producing objects that may in the past have been used exclusively for ritual, political, or any combination of functional purposes thereof has made the question less relevant.

REFERENCES

Clifford, James, 1988 On Collecting Art and Culture. In *The Predicament of Culture: Twentieth-Century Ethnography, Literature, and Art*. Cambridge: Harvard University Press.

Danto, Arthur 1988 Artifact and Art. In *ART/Artifact*. Susan Vogel, ed. New York: Center for African Art and Prestel Verlag.

Gell, Alfred 1997 Reply to Spring (1997). *Journal of Material Culture* 2(1):129–131.

Goldwater, Robert 1967 *Primitivism in Modern Art*. New York: Random House.

McEvilley, Thomas 1984 Letters on "Doctor, Lawyer, Indian Chief: 'Primitivism' in 20th Century Art" at the Museum of Modern Art in 1984. *Artforum* 23(3):54–61.

McEvilley, Thomas 1985a Letters on "Doctor, Lawyer, Indian Chief: 'Primitivism' in 20th Century Art' at the Museum of Modern Art in 1984," *Artforum* 23(6):51–52.

McEvilley, Thomas 1985b Letters on "Doctor, Lawyer, Indian Chief: 'Primitivism' in 20th Century Art" at the Museum of Modern Art in 1984, II. *Artforum* 23(9):63–71.

McEvilley, Thomas 2002 Whose Day is This? Reflections on Multiculturalism as History and
    Theory. In *Under [De]construction: Perspectives on Cultural Diversity in Visual and
    Performing Arts*. Helsinki: Nordic Institute for Contemporary Art.
Price, Sally, 2001[1989] *Primitive Art in Civilized Places*. Chicago: University of Chicago
    Press.
Spring, Chris 1997 Slipping the Net: Comments on Gell (1996). *Journal of Material Culture*
    2(1):125–129.

7

Modernist Primitivism:
An Introduction

William Rubin

No pivotal topic in twentieth-century art has received less serious attention than primitivism – the interest of modern artists in tribal[1] art and culture, as revealed in their thought and work. The immense bibliography of modern art lists only two instructive books on the subject: the pioneering text by Robert Goldwater, first published almost half a century ago, and that of Jean Laude, written two decades ago, considerably more limited in scope, never translated from the French, and long out of print.[2] Neither author had access to certain important collections, that of Picasso among them, or to much significant documentation now available. The need for a scholarly literature consistent with the historical importance of the subject is reflected in the unusual scope of the present undertaking – though, at best, this book is but a beginning.

Upon reflection, it is perhaps not surprising that primitivism has received so little searching consideration, for intelligent discourse on the subject requires some familiarity with both of the arts whose intersection in modern Western culture accounts for the phenomenon. The studies of the two have traditionally remained separate. Until fairly recently, tribal objects were largely the preserve, at least in scholarly and museological terms, of ethnologists. Only since World War II has the discipline of art history turned its attention to this material; however, graduate-level programs in Primitive[3] art are still comparatively rare, and few of their students are also involved in modern studies. It should come as no surprise, therefore, that much of what historians of twentieth-century art have said about the intervention of tribal art in the unfolding of modernism is wrong. Not familiar with the chronology of the arrival and diffusion of Primitive objects in the West, they have characteristically made unwarranted assumptions of influence. As an example, I cite the fact that none of the four types of masks proposed by eminent scholars as possible sources for *Les Demoiselles d'Avignon* could have been seen by Picasso in Paris as early as 1907 when he painted the picture. On the other hand, few experts in the arts of the Primitive peoples have more than a glancing knowledge of modern art, and their occasional allusions to it sometimes betray a startling naiveté.[4]

The quite different kinds of illumination cast upon tribal objects by anthropologists and by art historians of African and Oceanic cultures are ultimately more complementary than contradictory. Both naturally focus on understanding tribal sculptures in the contexts

From *"Primitivism" in 20th Century Art: Affinity of the Tribal and the Modern* (New York: Museum of Modern Art, [1985] 1999), pp. 1–79. Reprinted by permission of the Museum of Modern Art, New York.

in which they were created. Engaged with the history of primitivism, I have quite different aims; I want to understand the Primitive sculptures in terms of the Western context in which modern artists "discovered" them. The ethnologists' primary concern – the specific function and significance of each of these objects – is irrelevant to my topic, except insofar as these facts might have been known to the modern artists in question. Prior to the 1920s, however, at which time some Surrealists became *amateurs* of ethnology, artists did not generally know – nor evidently much care – about such matters. This is not to imply that they were uninterested in "meanings," but rather that the meanings which concerned them were the ones that could be apprehended through the objects themselves.[5] If I therefore accept as given a modernist perspective on these sculptures (which like any other perspective is by definition a bias), I shall nevertheless try to make a virtue of it, hoping that despite the necessarily fragmentary character of our approach – whose primary purpose is the further illumination of modern art – it may nevertheless shed some new light even on the Primitive objects.

Discourse on our subject has suffered from some confusion as to the definition of primitivism. The word was first used in France in the nineteenth century, and formally entered French as a strictly art-historical term in the seven-volume *Nouveau Larousse illustré* published between 1897 and 1904: "*n.m. B.-arts. Imitation des primitifs.*"[6] Though the Larousse reference to "imitation" was both too extreme and too narrow, the sense of this definition as describing painting and sculpture influenced by earlier artists called "primitives" has since been accepted by art history; only the identity of the "primitives" has changed. The Larousse definition reflected a mid-nineteenth-century use of the term insofar as the "primitives" in question were primarily fourteenth- and fifteenth-century Italians and Flemings. But even before the appearance of the *Nouveau Larousse illustré*, artists had expanded the connotations of "primitive" to include not only the Romanesque and Byzantine, but a host of non-Western arts ranging from the Peruvian to the Javanese – with the sense of "primitivism" altering accordingly. Neither word, however, as yet evoked the tribal arts

of Africa or Oceania. They would enter the definitions in question only in the twentieth century.

While primitivism began its life as a specifically art-historical term, some American dictionaries subsequently broadened its definition. It appears for the first time in Webster in 1934 as a "belief in the superiority of primitive life," which implies a "return to nature." Within this expanded framework, Webster's art-related definition is simply "the adherence to or reaction to that which is primitive."[7] This sense of the word was evidently firmly entrenched by 1938 when Goldwater used it in the title of *Primitivism in Modern Painting*. The general consistency of all these definitions of primitivism has not, however, prevented certain writers from confusing primitivism (a Western phenomenon) with the arts of Primitive peoples.[8] In view of this, we have drawn attention to the former's very particular art-historical meaning by enclosing it within quotation marks in the title of our book.

Nineteenth-century primitivist painters had appreciated pre-Renaissance Western styles for their "simplicity" and "sincerity" – which they saw in the absence of complex devices of illusionist lighting and perspective – and for their vigor and expressive power, qualities these artists missed in the official art of their own day, which was based on Classical and academic models. The more that bourgeois society prized the virtuosity and finesse of the salon styles, the more certain painters began to value the simple and naive, and even the rude and the raw – to the point that by the end of the nineteenth century, some primitivist artists had come to vaunt those non-Western arts they called "savage." Using this word admiringly, they employed it to describe virtually any art alien to the Greco-Roman line of Western realism that had been reaffirmed and systematized in the Renaissance. Given the present-day connotations of "primitive" and "savage," we may be surprised to discover what art these adjectives identified for late nineteenth-century artists. Van Gogh, for example, referred to the high court and theocratic styles of the ancient Egyptians and the Aztecs of Mexico as "primitive," and characterized even the Japanese masters he revered as "savage" artists. Gauguin used the words "primitive" and "savage" for styles as different as those of Persia, Egypt, India, Java, Cambodia, and Peru. A self-proclaimed "savage" himself, Gauguin later annexed the Polynesians to his already long list of "primitives," but he was less drawn to their art than to their religion and what remained of their life-style. Decades before African or Oceanic sculpture would become an issue for artists, the exotic arts defined as "primitive" by Gauguin's generation were being admired for many qualities that twentieth-century artists would prize in tribal art – above all, an expressive force deemed missing from the final phases of Western realism, which late nineteenth-century vanguard artists considered overattenuated and bloodless. With the exception of Gauguin's interest in Marquesan and Easter Island sculpture, however, no nineteenth-century artist demonstrated any serious artistic interest in tribal art, either Oceanic or African.[9] Our contemporary sense of Primitive art, largely synonymous with tribal objects, is a strictly twentieth-century definition.

The first decades of the twentieth century saw both a change in meaning and a shrinkage in the scope of what was considered Primitive art. With the "discovery" of African and Oceanic masks and figure sculptures by Matisse, Derain, Vlaminck, and Picasso in the years 1906–07, a strictly modernist interpretation of the term began. As the fulcrum of meaning shifted toward tribal art, the older usages did not fall away immediately. "Primitive art" simply became increasingly identified, during the following quarter-century, with tribal objects. As far as vanguard artists of the beginning of the century were concerned, this meant largely African and Oceanic art, with a smattering (in Germany) of that of American Indians and Eskimos (which would become better known among Paris artists only in the twenties and thirties).

In Paris, the term "art nègre" (Negro art)[10] began to be used interchangeably with "primitive art." This seemingly narrowed the scope of meaning to something like tribal art.[11] But as a term that should have been reserved for African art alone, it was in fact so loosely employed that it universally identified Oceanic art as well. It was not until the 1920s that Japanese, Egyptian, Persian, Cambodian, and most other non-Western court styles ceased to be called Primitive, and the word came to be

applied primarily to tribal art, for which it became the standard generic term.[12] In Goldwater's book, written the following decade, the "primitive" is synonymous with African and Oceanic art. To be sure, pre-Columbian court styles such as the Aztec, Olmec, and Incan continued to be called Primitive (and artists did not always distinguish between them and tribal art). But this was an inconsistency, and should now be recognized as such. In their style, character, and implications, the pre-Columbian court and theocratic arts of Mesoamerica and South America should be grouped with the Egyptian, Javanese, Persian, and other styles that together with them had consituted the definition of the Primitive during the later nineteenth century.[13] The progressive change in the meaning of the word after 1906 was a function of a change in taste. Consistent with it, pre-Columbian court art enjoyed – except for Moore, the Mexican muralists, and, to a lesser extent, Giacometti – a relatively limited interest among early twentieth-century vanguard artists. Picasso was not unique in finding it too monumental, hieratic, and seemingly repetitious. The perceived inventiveness and variety of tribal art was much more in the spirit of the modernists' enterprise.[14]

The inventiveness just mentioned, which led in some African and Oceanic societies to an often astonishing artistic multiformity, constitutes one of the most important common denominators of tribal and modern art. Few remaining sculptures of the Dan people, to take perhaps the most startling example, are much more than a century old; yet the range of invention found in their work far outdistances that of court arts produced over much longer periods – even millennia of Ancient Egypt after the Old Kingdom.[15] And unlike Egyptian society, which placed a positive value upon the static as regards its imagery, the Dan not only explicitly appreciated diversity but recognized the value of a certain originality. As the fascinating study by the ethnologist P. J. L. Vandenhoute showed, the Dan were even willing "to recognize a superior social efficacity in [such originality]."[16] Although tribal sculptors were guided by established traditional types, the surviving works themselves attest that individual carvers had far more freedom in varying and developing these types than many commentators have assumed. This relative variety and flexibility, along with the concomitant incidence of change, distinguish their art from the more static, hieratic – and often monumental – styles of the court cultures in question (which for the sake of convenience I shall refer to generically as Archaic, in what amounts to but a slight broadening of that term's usual art-historical application).[17]

During the last two decades, [since the 1980s], the words Primitive and primitivism have been criticized by some commentators as ethnocentric and pejorative, but no other generic term proposed as a replacement for "primitive" has been found acceptable to such critics, none has even been proposed for "primitivism." That the derived term primitivism is ethnocentric is surely true – and logically so, for it refers not to the tribal arts in themselves, but to the Western interest in and reaction to them. Primitivism is thus an aspect of the history of modern art, not of tribal art. In this sense, the word is comparable to the French "japonisme," which refers not directly to the art and culture of Japan, but to the European fascination with it. The notion that "primitivism" is pejorative, however, can only result from a misunderstanding of the origin and use of the term, whose implications have been entirely affirmative.

Objections to the adjective "primitive," on the other hand, focus not unfairly on the pejorative implications of certain of its many meanings.[18] These have had no place, however, in its definition or use as an art-historical term. When Picasso, in the ultimate compliment, asserted that "primitive sculpture has never been surpassed,"[19] he saw nothing contradictory – and certainly nothing pejorative – in using the familiar if now-contested adjective "primitive" to identify the art. It is precisely the admiring sense with which he and his colleagues invested the word that has characterized its use in art writing. Employed in this restricted way, the word has a sense no less positive than that of any other aesthetic designations (including Gothic and Baroque, which were both coined as terms of opprobrium).[20] The "effective connotations" of "primitive" when "coupled with the word art," as Robert Goldwater concluded, are of "a term of praise."[21] As we are using the term Primitive essentially in an art-historical

spirit, we have decided to insist upon this sense of its meaning by capitalizing its initial letter (except within quotation marks). All this does not mean that one would not happily use another generic term if a satisfactory one could be found.[22] And, to be sure, William Fagg, dean of British ethnologists of Africa, proposed that "tribal" be universally substituted for "primitive."[23] But the critics who object to "primitive," object with equal if not greater vehemence to "tribal."[24]

It is clear that art history is not the only discipline that has sought and failed to find a generic term for the Primitive that would satisfy critics. After struggling with the problem for some time, Claude Lévi-Strauss noted that "despite all its imperfections, and the deserved criticism it has received, it seems that *primitive*, in the absence of a better term, has definitely taken hold in the contemporary anthropological and sociological vocabulary." "The term *primitive*," he continued, "now seems safe from the confusion inherent in its etymological meaning and reinforced by an obsolete evolutionism." Lévi-Strauss then added a reminder hardly necessary for those who admire tribal art. "A primitive people," he insisted, "is not a backward or retarded people; indeed, it may possess, in one realm or another, a genius for invention or action that leaves the achievements of other peoples far behind."[25] This last was recognized by modern artists at the beginning of this century, well before the attitudes summarized by Lévi-Strauss were to characterize anthropological or art-historical thinking.

For the bourgeois public of the nineteenth century, however, if not for the art lovers of the twentieth, the adjective "primitive" certainly had a pejorative meaning. Indeed, that public considered any culture outside Europe, or any art outside the parameters of Beaux-Arts and salon styles – which meant all non-Western and some Western art – inherently inferior. (Even Ruskin opined that there was "no art in the whole of Africa, Asia or America.") To the extent that the "fetishes" of the tribal peoples were known at all, they were considered the untutored extravagances of barbarians. In fact, tribal objects were not then considered art at all. Gathered first in *cabinets de curiosités*, the masks and figure sculptures (along with other material) were increasingly preserved during the later nineteenth century in ethnographic museums, where no distinctions were made between art and artifact. As artifacts were considered indices of cultural progress, the increasing hold of Darwinian theories could only reinforce prejudices about tribal creations, whose makers were assigned the bottom rung of the cultural evolutionary ladder.

We shall explore in depth in our chapter on Gauguin a quite opposite Western view of the Primitive that had already begun to form in the eighteenth century, especially in France. But this affirmative attitude, of which Jean-Jacques Rousseau's Noble Savage is the best-known embodiment, involved only a segment of the small educated public. It remained, moreover, literary and philosophical in character – never comprehending the plastic arts. Antipodal to the popular view, it tended to idealize Primitive life, building upon it the image of an earthly paradise, inspired primarily by visions of Polynesia, especially Tahiti. If we trace this attitude to its source in Montaigne's essay "On Cannibals," we see that from the start the writers in question were primarily interested in the Primitive as an instrument for criticizing their own societies, which they saw as deforming the innately admirable spirit of humankind that they assumed was still preserved in the island paradises.

Needless to say, most of these writers knew little of life in Polynesia or other distant lands, and the body of ideas they generated may be justly characterized as "the myth of the primitive." Indeed, even among those having firsthand contact with tribal peoples, the fantasy of the Primitive often overrode reality. The French explorer Bougainville, for example, one of the discoverers of Tahiti, saw evidence there of cannibalistic practices. But all of this is forgotten in this classic description of the island as "la Nouvelle Cythère," the New Cythera. By identifying Tahiti with the island of Greek mythology where, under the reign of Venus, humans lived in perpetual harmony, beauty, and love, Bougainville was equating the "myth of the primitive" with the already long-established but almost equally unreal "myth of the antique." It mattered little, however, that the affirmative view of the Primitive we have been describing had almost as little relation to reality as the negative one. The myth was from the start the operative factor, and until the third decade of the twentieth century, it had far more

influence on artists and writers than did any facts of tribal life, of which, in any case, the first social scientists themselves knew but little.

This interest in the Primitive as a critical instrument – as a countercultural battering ram, in effect – persisted in a different form when early twentieth-century vanguard artists engendered a shift of focus from Primitive life to Primitive art. Modernism is unique as compared to the artistic attitudes of past societies in its essentially critical posture, and its primitivism was to be consistent with this. Unlike earlier artists, whose work celebrated the collective, institutional values of their cultures, the pioneer modern artists criticized – at least implicitly – even when they celebrated. Renoir's *Boating Party*, for example, affirmed the importance of gaiety, pleasure, and informality, in short, the life of the senses. But by that very fact, it criticized the repressive and highly class-conscious conventions of contemporary Victorian morality. The Cubist artist's notion that there was something important to be learned from the sculpture of tribal peoples – an art whose appearance and assumptions were diametrically opposed to prevailing aesthetic canons – could only be taken by bourgeois culture as an attack upon its values.

That the modern artists' admiration for these tribal objects was widespread in the years 1907–14 is sufficiently (if not very well) documented in studio photographs, writings, reported remarks, and, of course, in their work itself. Artists such as Picasso, Matisse, Braque, and Brancusi were aware of the conceptual complexity and aesthetic subtlety of the best tribal art, which is only simple in the sense of its reductiveness – and not, as was popularly believed, in the sense of simple-mindedness.[26] That many today consider tribal sculpture to represent a major aspect of world art, that Fine Arts museums are increasingly devoting galleries, even entire wings to it, is a function of the triumph of vanguard art itself.[27] We owe to the voyagers, colonials, and ethnologists the arrival of these objects in the West. But we owe primarily to the convictions of the pioneer modern artists their promotion from the rank of curiosities and artifacts to that of major art, indeed, to the status of art at all.

[. . .]

That tribal art influenced Picasso and many of his colleagues in significant ways is

beyond question. But that it caused no fundamental change in the direction of modern art is
equally true. Picasso himself put it succinctly
when he said: "The African sculptures that
hang around ... my studios are *more witnesses
than models*."[28] That is, they more bore witness to his enterprise than served as starting
points for his imagery. Like the Japanese prints
that fascinated Manet and Degas, Primitive
objects had less to do with redirecting the
history of modern painting than with reinforcing and sanctioning developments already
under way. Nevertheless, Picasso – who had
an instinct for the *mot juste* – chose his words
carefully, and his "more ... than" construction
must be looked at with care. Though more
"witnesses" than "models," the sculptures
were admittedly thus models to some extent.
Hence, while first elected for their affinity
to the artist's aims, once in the studio, the
tribal objects took on a dual role, and exerted
some influence.

Just how much and what kind of influence
these objects exerted is, as noted, extremely
difficult to gauge. In his classic text, Goldwater
took a very conservative position on this question, to which Laude's book largely adhered.
While arguing a "very considerable influence
of the primitive on the modern"[29] in very general terms ("allusion and suggestion"), Goldwater insisted on the "extreme scarcity of the
direct influence of primitive art forms" on
twentieth-century art.[30] As our study will
show, Goldwater substantially underestimated
that aspect of the issue. Moreover, he considered most of the influence of tribal art to be
poetic, philosophical, and psychological,
granting it only a "very limited direct formal
influence."[31] It was his view that Brancusi, for
example, never adapted "specific forms of
Negro sculpture, and ... his work is never related to any particular tribal style." Yet the
attitude, shape, and convex-concave structure
of the head and the elongated form of the
neck (as well as the obliquely projecting
coiffure or "comb") of Brancusi's *Madame
L. R.* (1914–18) seem to me unquestionably
derived from Hongwe reliquary figures. Moreover, as Geist has shown, the peculiarly shaped
mouth in the head that remains from the otherwise destroyed *First Step*, 1913, was almost
certainly derived from a Bambara sculpture
in the Trocadéro Museum. Comparable ex-

amples can be adduced in the work of many
artists whose primitivism was discussed by
Goldwater only in general terms.

In the examples mentioned above, the juxtapositions of the modern and African works
speak for themselves. But I am firmly of the
opinion that there exists a whole body of other
influences, *no less dependent on particular
forms in individual tribal objects*, where a simple comparison of the modern and tribal works
involved would not signal the relationship between them. Indeed, I consider it axiomatic
that among modern artists who admired and
collected tribal works, many of the most important and profound influences of "art nègre"
on their work are those that we do not recognize and will never know about. While artists
of all periods have taken the shape of a head,
the position of a body, or a particular pattern
from the work of other artists, their assimilation of their colleagues' work often takes a
more complicated, less recognizable form –
all the more so in the twentieth century, given
the degree of metamorphosis of visual raw
materials in most modern styles.[32] By the
time the plastic idea – borrowed knowingly
or unconsciously – is fully digested and
reemerges in the context of the borrower's
very different style, it is often "invisible." The
influence of tribal art is no exception to this
principle.

Since *this* sort of direct influence is not recognizable through the juxtaposition of particular objects (at least without some guidance),
the reader might well ask on what basis
I postulate it. Apart from the testimony of a
few artists, the answer lies in my sense of how
the artistic mind operates, by what byways and
indirect paths it achieves its goals.

[...]

[Rubin develops a distinction between affinities and influences and illustrates this through
a discussion of some works by Max Ernst with
tribal objects to which they bear a striking
resemblance.] When we compare Ernst's *Bird-
Head* to an African mask of the Tusyan people,
for example, we find among their common
characteristics – apart from a general sense of
the apparitional – such particulars as a flat
rectangular head, straight horizontal mouth,
small round eyes, and a bird's head projecting
from the forehead. Let us also take Ernst's

engraved stone sculpture, *Oval Bird*, of that same year (1934), comparing it to the Bird-Man relief from Easter Island in the British Museum. Both *Oval Bird* and the Easter Island image are egglike in contour and depict a syncretistic birdman whose rounded forms echo the contour of the sculptural field.[33] The upper arm of both figures descends in a curve and the forearms project forward; both birdmen have a large round eye. Though the oversized hand of the Easter Island figure gives way in the Ernst stone to a second bird's head (birdmen with large hands are, however, found in other works by Ernst), and while the head of Ernst's *personnage* projects forward like that of the Easter Island relief, it is much less beaklike in form. Nevertheless, that form is almost exactly matched in another Ernst bird head, also in an oval field, in the painting *Inside the Sight: The Egg.*

One of the most celebrated of Polynesian objects, the Easter Island Bird-Man relief was collected in 1915 and acquired by the British Museum in 1920; it was reproduced in a number of publications beginning in 1919. Unlike his Cubist predecessors – and even more than most of his Surrealist colleagues – Ernst was a great *amateur* of ethnology and possessed a considerable library on the subject, probably including, both Maurer and Spies believe,[34] one or more of the early publications in which the Easter Island relief was reproduced. Hence we would be on reasonably solid ground in speaking here of an influence of the Bird-Man relief on his work. On the other hand, the resemblance between Ernst's *Bird-Head* and the Tusyan mask, striking as it is, is fortuitous, and must therefore be accounted a simple affinity. *Bird-Head* was sculpted in 1934, and no Tusyan masks appear to have arrived in Europe (nor were any reproduced) prior to World War II.

That such striking affinities can be found is partly accounted for by the fact that both modern and tribal artists work in a conceptual, ideographic manner, thus sharing certain problems and possibilities. In our own day it is easy to conceive of art-making in terms of problem-solving. But this was also substantially true for tribal artists, though their solutions were arrived at incrementally – as in much Western art – over a period of generations.[35] Ethnologists might argue that I am falsely attributing to

the tribal artists a sense of Western art-making, that the tribal sculptor creating ritual objects for a cult had no consciousness whatever of aesthetic solutions. (The latter is simply their assumption, of course, based on the fact that many tribal cultures had no word for "art.")[36] Even if this could be proven true, however, it would not contradict my contention insofar as the finding of artistic solutions is ultimately an intuitive rather than an intellectual activity. The art-making process everywhere has certain common denominators, and as the great ethnologist Robert Lowie quite rightly observed, "the aesthetic impulse is one of the irreducible components" of mankind.[37] The "art-ness" of the best tribal objects alone demonstrates that great artists were at work and that a variety of aesthetic solutions were arrived at, however little the artists themselves might have agreed with our description of the process. Now these solutions, insofar as they were to problems held in common – a sign for "nose," for example – were certainly likely to bear a resemblance to one another in ways that are independent of influences and traditions. Hence the similarity of tribal works from entirely unrelated regions, as in the head of a New Hebrides (Melanesia) fern sculpture and an African Lwalwa mask. Is it so surprising, then, that Picasso's solution for the head of the upper right maiden in the *Demoiselles* should resemble a mask from the Etoumbi region of Africa of a type he could not have seen at the time?[38]

To say that Picasso's solution and that of the Etoumbi artist resemble each other is not, of course, to equate them. Quite apart from the fact that the Picasso head is painted and the Etoumbi mask carved – so that a different set of artistic conventions apply – there are many aspects of the Picasso image that presuppose ontogenetically the whole phylogeny of Western art. Moreover, the aesthetic affinities between signifiers, such as they are, do not permit us to assume comparable relationships on the level of the signified. Thus Herbert Read was rightly criticized for attributing Expressionist anxiety (*angst*) – a peculiarly modern state of mind – to African sculpture.[39] And Picasso's reference to the exorcistic character of African art, which he said was created to make man "free," turned on a definition of freedom in terms of private psychological emancipation of a kind that would make no sense to a member of a tribal society.

[...]

The modernist tendency to interpret certain signs in tribal art in ways alien to Primitive cultures – to attribute to its signifiers twentieth-century signifieds – is only one of the many ways in which we respond to tribal art ethno-centrically. Underinterpretation is another. To the extent that certain modern artists (Matisse, for example) savored tribal objects purely for their plastic beauty, they detached them from the symbolic and thaumaturgic role central to their place in the matrix of Primitive culture. To be sure, some modern artists, beginning with Picasso and extending into our own day, have responded intuitively to the animistic aspects of most tribal art, though these artists soon abut the limits of their ethnological knowledge.[40]

Lack of familiarity with the cultural context of tribal objects is just one of many factors that condemn the modern artist to see them fragmentarily. More literal aspects of this fragmentariness include the fact that tribal objects often arrive in the West incomplete. A mask, for example, may be shorn of its fiber "beard" or headdress as well as other symbolic accouterments. Masks are seen, moreover, in isolation from the costumes of which they were a part. By the same token, costumes are "fragments" of the dance, which is in turn a "fragment" of a more extended rite. Thompson observes, moreover, that many of the forms of African art were conceived to be seen in motion.[41] And while this is probably not true of most ritual figures, it does necessarily further distance us from some of the art that has most influenced modern painters and sculptors.

This general situation is hardly unique, however. We experience the entire history of past art in varying degrees fragmentarily and largely shorn of context. Few artists who appreciated Egyptian or Japanese art knew any more about its purpose or its cultural context than they did about that of Africa or Oceania. This ethnocentrism is a function nevertheless of one of modernism's greatest virtues: its unique approbation of the arts of other cultures. Ours is the *only* society that has prized a whole spectrum of arts of distant and alien cultures.[42] Its consequent appropriation of these arts has invested modernism with a particular vitality that is a product of cultural cross-fertilization.

[...]

The Surrealists preferred Oceanic to African art in part for its seemingly greater closeness to nature and its more varied, more aleatory use of natural materials. It is sometimes said that African art is Classic and Oceanic art Romantic, and although such generalizations can obscure as much as clarify, one could certainly agree that Melanesian art is more Romantic than that of Africa in the character of its identification with the world of nature. While there are numerous hybrids of men and animals among African masks and figure sculptures, they tend conceptually to be further removed, further abstracted from nature than the more ubiquitous monsters of the Melanesian peoples. Relative to many Oceanic arts, African sculpture could almost be characterized in terms of a prevailing anthropomorphism and anthropocentrism, both qualities of the Classic.[43] The New Guinea artist, on the other hand, tends to find his monsters more nearly "ready-made" in the very substance of nature. Nowhere in African art, for example, do we find anything comparable to the malevolent hybrid Imunus of the Papuan Gulf region, which are largely made up of branches or roots of trees. The result of this "natural selection" is an accident-accommodating, meandering, linear object, the near formlessness of whose contours is antipodal to African aesthetic ideals.

But not to modern taste – especially that of the Surrealists, who particularly liked such objects. We see affinities to their structures, if not direct echoes of them, in the contouring of many works by Ernst and Miró, as well as later, in the work of Dubuffet. But it is in the art of Calder, who was close to the Surrealists in the thirties, that one discovers what appears to be a direct influence of an Imunu. Calder, whose interest in tribal art began early, had formed a fairly extensive collection of Primitive art by the later thirties. He was friendly with the dealer Pierre Loeb who, aside from exhibiting such Surrealists as Giacometti and Miró, did much to advance the cause of tribal art from the South Seas in general and Papua in particular.[44] Calder's *Apple Monster*, 1938 – largely formed from the branches of an apple tree – is an altogether unusual work in his oeuvre and responds directly, I believe, to the artist's fascination with an Imunu. Like the Imunus, whose "serendipitous" character was bound to appeal to vanguard taste, Calder's piece consists largely of found objects subjected to a minimum of alteration after their selection. Both Calder and the New Guinea artist divined the monster while it still lurked in the raw material of nature. Such seerlike prescience especially appealed to the Surrealists, who would have categorized both the Imunu and *Apple Monster* as "objets trouvés aidés."

The New Guinea object has, however, the mordant and truly hallucinatory quality of a work whose creator really believes in monsters. None of that malevolence is present in the Calder, which expresses rather a whimsical and decidedly unthreatening sense of the forces of nature. Like the monsters in Klee and Miró, Calder's does not frighten us because neither he nor we still believe in monsters – at least in nature. For us, the truly monstrous emanates from man's mind – as was expressed so forcefully by Picasso's 1930s Minotaur (the beast-in-the-head instead of in-the-body), which is now stamped so indelibly on the modern psyche.

[...]

The early twentieth-century emancipation from the restrictions of a perceptually based art encouraged a variety of aesthetic attributes that parallel those of tribal art. Not the least of these was the freedom to sacrifice the essentially naturalistic proportions to which European artists – however different their styles – had adhered from the Gothic period through Post-Impressionism (and even into the Fauvism of 1905–06). During those centuries, the proportion of the height to the width of the body, and the proportion of the head to the body's total height, varied only within distinct limits.[45] The change in favor of extreme ratios of proportion is anticipated in the latter part of 1906 in Picasso's "Iberian" style, in such pictures as *Two Women*. But it is in 1907 – in the *Demoiselles* (the lower right-hand figure particularly), and in Matisses such as *Le Luxe* – that freedom from the older conventions was definitively established. It was soon adapted by the German artists to a practice of "expressive disproportion." Their art tended, as Meyer Schapiro observed, to polarize into

two figure types, as represented by the work of Lehmbruck and Barlach: tall, attenuated "dolichocephalic" figures and squat, "brachycephalic" ones respectively.[46] We see a comparable contrast in Fang masks that flatten the oval proportions of the human face into perfect circles or elongate them in the extreme.

The modernist tendency toward such a polarization could only have been reinforced by familiarity with the astonishing proportions of some tribal objects. Giacometti probably saw the extraordinarily attenuated Nyamwezi figure, a sculpture owned for decades, beginning in the thirties, by André Lefebvre, one of the great collectors of modern art. However, tribal material constituted only one of many possible precedents for his elongated figures. Giacometti was thoroughly familiar, for example, with the attenuated Etruscan figures at the Villa Giulia in Rome. And I suspect that as compared to Picasso's "broomstick" sculptures of 1931, both Primitive and Etruscan models probably functioned more as a reinforcement than an inspiration for the unusual proportions of Giacometti's later work.[47]

That Picasso should have made the first modern construction sculpture in the same year he invented collage, and that these interdependent developments should have been launched at a time when he was deeply involved with tribal art, appear to me quite logical. The seeming simplicity and rawness of collage certainly constituted for Picasso a second primitivizing reaction, in this case against the hermeticism and *belle-peinture* of high Analytic Cubism. It paralleled that of six years earlier when he had overcome the late Symbolist refinement of his Blue and Rose Period paintings with the primitivism that culminated in the *Demoiselles*. In the spring of 1912, when Picasso glued a piece of oilcloth on his *Still Life with Chair Caning* and ordered an "endless" mariner's rope to go round it in place of a frame, he not only short-circuited the refined painterly language of high Analytic Cubism, but undercut its "classical" structure by introducing a mélange of materials previously considered incompatible with the Fine Arts. His subsequent application of the collage technique to constructed sculpture created the hybrid form known as "assemblage."

While Picasso's admixture of cloth and rope was unprecedented in the Western tradition, the principle of such mélanges was familiar to him in tribal sculptures whose makers often utilized cloth, raffia, string, bark, metal, mud, and found objects in conjunction with wood and other materials (as in fetishes and emblems . . .). Picasso's reliefs were constructed, moreover, to hang upon and project outward from the wall – which is precisely the way the European artists displayed their tribal masks. I do not want to imply this means that tribal objects were necessarily the primary inspiration of collage or assemblage, for the latter have other possible precedents, but given Picasso's deep involvement with tribal art in 1912, they had to have played an important role in his thinking.

Picasso's use of variegated materials did not lead to objects resembling tribal art. That was not his way. Picasso usually abstracted the principle involved, but used it to his own ends. However, the use of such materials in the hands of the Dadaists and Surrealists reflected a conscious desire to evoke Primitive prototypes. The same is certainly true with regard to many contemporary examples. Italo Scanga's *Potato Famine #1* recalls the Berlin Museum Dog Fetish in its cloth streamers, while its inclusion of an animal horn reminds one of Fon and Songye fetishes. Conner's *Cross*, which may be compared to an assemblage-like Ejagham emblem, turns the tables on Christianity by recasting it in the animist spirit of the tribal religions (while also recalling fetishistic aspects of Christian devotion in ex-votos and the cult of relics).

[. . .]

An undertaking such as this book, and the exhibition to which it is ancillary, must inevitably raise questions in the curator's mind as to its necessity – if for no other reason than its cost in time, effort, and money. Nor can the curator, though he has seen the works individually over the years in differing contexts, truly foresee the effect of bringing them together – the revelation, or lack thereof, that their confrontation may engender. Indeed, in a sense he organizes the exhibition to see what will happen. It would be disingenuous, nevertheless, to pretend that in proposing our exhibition I did not feel fairly certain that it would

result in a significant correction of the received history of modern art, and draw to the attention of that art's very large public some unfamiliar but particularly relevant masterpieces from other cultures. There was also the thought that some modern works we know quite well might seem all the richer for being seen from a new perspective. However presumptuous it may seem, all this lies within the realm of my expectations.

In the realm of my hopes, however, there is something less explicit, more difficult to verbalize. It is that the particular confrontation involved in our exhibition will not only help us better to understand our art, but in a very unique way, our humanity – if that is not saying the same thing. The vestiges of a discredited evolutionary myth still live in the recesses of our psyches. The vanguard modernists told us decades ago that the tribal peoples produced an art that often distilled great complexity into seemingly simple solutions. We should not therefore be surprised that anthropology has revealed a comparable complexity in their cultures.[48] I hope our effort will demonstrate that at least insofar as it pertains to works of the human spirit, the evolutionary prejudice is clearly absurd.

The various metamorphoses of Picasso's *Demoiselles d'Avignon* were but the visible symbols of the artist's search within his own psyche. This self-analysis, this peeling away of layers of consciousness, became associated with a search into the origins of man's way of picturing himself. Having retraced those steps through the Archaic in his Iberian studies, Picasso was prepared for the "revelation" of Primitive art at the Trocadéro Museum, which led him to the deeper, more primordial solution for which he was searching. At the Trocadéro, Picasso apprehended something of profound psychological significance that Gauguin had failed to discover in the South Seas.

That Picasso would call the *Demoiselles* his "first exorcism picture" suggests that he understood the very making of it as analogous to the kind of psycho-spiritual experiences or rites of passage for which he assumed the works in the Trocadéro were used. The particular kind of personal freedom he experienced in realizing the *Demoiselles,* a liberating power that he associated with the original function of the tribal objects he saw, would have been meaningless –

as the anthropologists would be the first to insist – to tribal man. Yet there *is* a link, for what Picasso recognized in those sculptures was ultimately a part of himself, of his own psyche, and therefore a witness to the humanity he shared with their carvers. He also realized that the Western artistic tradition had lost much of the power either to address or to change the inner man revealed in those sculptures.

Like all great art, the finest tribal sculptures show images of man that transcend the particular lives and times of their makers. Nevertheless, the head of the African figure has for us at first an almost shocking sense of psychological otherness, while the New Guinea carving has a comparable otherness in terms of the way we understand our bodies. Nothing in Western (or Eastern) art prepares us for them. Yet they move us precisely because we *do* see something of ourselves in them – a part of ourselves that Western culture had been unwilling to admit, not to say image, before the twentieth century. If the otherness of the tribal images can broaden our humanity, it is because we have learned to recognize that otherness in ourselves. "Je," as Rimbaud realized, "est un autre."

I spoke earlier about Picasso's notion of the affinity of modern and tribal art as paralleling, in certain respects, the relationship between the arts of the Renaissance and Classical Greece. The analogy does not, however, capture the furthest reaches of implication in the affinity ... For while the Italians of the fifteenth century were not in many significant ways, material or spiritual, advanced over the Greeks of the fifth century B.C., we, technologically speaking, are far beyond both, and with our consciousness of this we think of ourselves as having progressed light years beyond the tribal peoples. But insofar as art is a concrete index to the spiritual accomplishments of civilizations, the affinity of the tribal and the modern should give us pause.

NOTES

1 During the past twenty years, the word "tribal" has been frequently used in preference to "primitive" in characterizing a wide variety of arts of more or less noncentralized societies with simple technologies. Both words are profoundly problematic; we use them reluctantly (and interchangeably) ... to answer the need for a generalizing collective term for the art we are addressing. No adequate or generally agreed-upon substitutes for "tribal and "primitive" have been proposed. Among some specialists, "tribal" has been used in preference to "primitive" because the latter is felt to contain too many negative Darwinian connotations. Others prefer "primitive" to "tribal" because many of the cultures commonly referred to as tribal (in Africa especially) are not tribal in the ethnological sense of the term.

Our use of "tribal" is obviously not anthropological in spirit. It corresponds roughly to Webster's (*New International Dictionary*, 2nd edn.) third definition of "tribe" – as the word is used "more loosely": "Any aggregation of peoples, especially in a primitive or nomadic state, believed to be of common stock and acting under a more or less central authority, like that of a headman or chief." The word "tribal" should thus be understood as simply a conventional counter. The Africanist Leon Siroto observes:

"Tribal" in this connection would have to be no more than an arbitrary convention chosen to avoid the pitfalls of the term "primitive" as an expedient minimal designation in general discourse. It has been used so long and so widely that it seems to have gained significant acceptance.

Caution is indicated: many, if not most, of the peoples intended by the term do not form tribes in the stricter sense of the concept. They may speak the same languages and observe more or less the same customs, *but* they are not politically coordinated and have no pragmatic recognition or corporate identity. Moreover, a number of them, for these reasons, have disparate iconographies and practice markedly contrastive styles, tendencies that should caution against the notion that their art is *tribal* (i.e., ethnically unitary and distinctive) ... Anthropologists tend to agree that tribal groups are more of a European creation than a fact of life. (Letter to W. R. of November 1983.)

Until the 1960s, "tribal" was still widely used by anthropologists to fill the need for a general term cutting across cultures and continents. Hence, for example, the collection of essays edited by Daniel Biebuyck for the University of California Press in 1969 was called *Tradition and Creativity in Tribal Art*. Today it might be titled differently; but the problem of nomenclature has not been solved. William Fagg has been the most eloquent proponent of the concept of "tribality in African art." This art, he insists, "is a product and a function of the tribal system," though he observes that "tribal is not a static concept, but a dynamic one" and that "tribal styles are subject to constant change" ("The African Artist" in Biebuyck, ed., p. 45).

African scholars (among others) have criticized "tribal" as "Eurocentric" (Ekpo Eyo, cited in the *New York Times*, October 12, 1980, p. 70), and their point is well taken, although the anathema cast on the word in Africa (it has literally been banned by one African parliament) probably responds in part to the political problem of melding unified nations and a national consciousness from ethnically diverse populations. That the "Eurocentrism" in question still exists – despite efforts to overcome it – is hardly surprising considering that the disciplines of art history and anthropology are themselves European inventions.

When addressing individual cultures, art historians can easily avoid such problematic terms as "tribal." But the need for a general term arises from the wish to allude to characteristics that appear (to some Western eyes, at least) similar in a variety of cultures in different parts of the world. The most up-to-date histories of world art still employ, if somewhat gingerly, the words "tribal" and "primitive" (e.g., Hugh Honour and John Fleming, *The Visual Arts: A History* [Englewood Cliffs, N.J., 1982], p. 547). Some anthropologists would argue that any perceived common characteristics implied in such use of the word "tribal" are fictions – which explains why the word has largely disappeared from anthropological literature. Even if true, however, this does not mean that it is inappropriate in the study of modernist primitivism. On the contrary, precisely because we are *not* directly addressing the cultures in question, but investigating *the ideas formed of them in the West* over the last hundred years, the use of the word "tribal" – which

is a function of such ideas and the context in which they were formed – is not misleading. The word's ethnocentric drawbacks become, in effect, illuminating, for they characterize the nature of the primitivist perspective.

2   Goldwater's *Primitivism in Modern Painting* was first published in 1938; a revised and enlarged edition appeared in 1967 under the title *Primitivism in Modern Art* (New York: Random House, Vintage Books). Laude's *La Peinture française (1905–1914) et "l'art nègre"* (Paris: Editions Klincksieck) appeared in 1968. These are the only completely serious general treatments of the subject in anything like reasonable wholeness. Charles Wentinck's lay-oriented *Modern and Primitive Art* (Oxford: Phaidon Press, 1979 [originally published in the Netherlands 1974 as *Moderne und Primitive Kunst*]) is an inadequate account which fails to distinguish satisfactorily between actual (or possible) historical influences and chance resemblances. Failure to make this crucial distinction also dogs the chapters on modernism and African and Oceanic art in the catalog *World Cultures and Modern Art. The Encounter of 19th and 20th Century European Art and Music with Asia, Africa, Oceania, Afro- and Indo-America* (Exhibition on the occasion of the games of the Twentieth Olympiad, Munich 1972) (Munich: Haus der Kunst, June 16–September 30, 1972). More valuable is the treatment of our subject as limited to modern sculpture in the catalog *Gauguin to Moore: Primitivism in Modern Sculpture,* by Alan Wilkinson (Toronto: Art Gallery of Ontario, November 7, 1981–January 3, 1982). To these books one might add Werner Schmalenbach, *Die Kunst der Primitiven als Anregungsquelle für die europäische Kunst bis 1900* (Cologne: DuMont-Schauberg, 1961), and his "Grundsätzliches zur primitiven Kunst," *Acta tropica* 15, no. 4 (1958), pp. 289–323.

3   As explained, . . . we have retained the term "primitive" but have decided to capitalize it (except within quotation marks) in order to underline that aspect of its many meanings having to do with art-historical designation (as opposed to using it as a strictly descriptive term).

4   Symptomatic of this is the tendency of one of the leading authors on African art to characterize masks as "cubist" simply because they have rectilinear geometrical structures.

5   Anthropologists, especially those who consider the characterization of tribal objects *as art* irrelevant to their concerns, often write as if only the scientifically verifiable and verbalizable anthropological constituents of these objects have meaning. Art historians' interests naturally include the aesthetic and expressive potential of many of these objects. In general, artists usually consider only the direct apprehension of the latter as truly meaningful. This is exemplified in a remark made to me by Picasso to this effect: "Everything I need to know about Africa is in those objects."

6   *Nouveau Larousse illustré*, 7 vols. and 1 suppl. (Paris: Librairie Larousse, 1897–1904), vol. 7, p. 32.

7   *Webster's New International Dictionary*, 2nd edn., s.v. "primitivism."

8   Ekpo Eyo (*Two Thousand Years of Nigerian Art* [Lagos, 1977], p. 28) wrongly uses the word "primitivism" simply to characterize Europeans' use of the word "primitive" in relation to non-Western art. In regard to the same use, he stated (as quoted in the *New York Times*) that Western scholars "invented the notion of primitivism [*sic*] and spread it to wherever their influence reached."

9   This does not mean that they did not collect such art as "curiosités".
    Beyond Gauguin's limited interest in Polynesian art...he may also have owned two small African figures.

10 This took place in the years preceding World War I. The usual translation of "art nègre" as "Negro art," loses something of the pejorative flavor of the French "nègre" (as in "travail de nègre," for example). This connotation notwithstanding, many cultivated French still use the term "art nègre" although they might eschew the word "nègre" in other contexts.

11 It should be kept in mind that early in the century the term "art nègre" universally evoked the tribal art of Oceania as well as Africa. The same was true of the word "Negerkunst" and its variants. Both

editions (1915 and 1920) of Carl Einstein's *Negerplastik* contain some examples of Oceanic art. The designation "art nègre" was used for the court art of the kingdom of Benin as well as for tribal styles.

12 In the period between the two World Wars, and for some time afterward, "primitive" was used in the titles of books and university courses and for classification in fine-arts museums (the forerunner of the Michael C. Rockefeller wing at the Metropolitan Museum was known as the Museum of Primitive Art, and the relevant department of the Metropolitan is still called the Department of Primitive Art). Until fairly recently the word was widely if sometimes reluctantly used by anthropologists as well (see citation from Lévi-Strauss, p. 132). A collection of anthropological essays published by Oxford University Press in 1973 (Anthony Forge, ed.) was titled *Primitive Art and Society*.

13 Pre-Columbian civilization was (and still is) popularly identified by artists and others primarily with art from large-scale, complex, later-period theocratic societies of the Maya, Toltec, and Aztec in Mesoamerica and the Inca in Peru. These societies were characterized by a high degree of both specialization and social, economic, and political hierarchization, which are reflected in their monumental architecture and sculpture, which I would classify as more Archaic than Primitive in nature. Less known, but certainly not unknown to some artists, were many simpler pre-Columbian socio-cultural entities that did not have state-level government, monumental public works, written languages (which were, in any case, confined to the Maya), and other features of more complex societies. Notable among these were the Chrotega, Chiriqui, Chibcha, and many other chiefdoms that occupied the area between Mesoamerica and the northern Andes.
    If, in terms of their art, the Maya, Toltec, Aztec, and Inca should be grouped with such cultures as the Cambodian or Egyptian, they present an exception insofar as the social and religious fabric of all the pre-Columbian cultures was marked by certain characteristics otherwise generally associated with Primitive rather than court cultures. Since, however,

modern artists knew little or nothing of this, and approached pre-Columbian cultures entirely through works of art (or their reproductions), these works entered modernism in the late nineteenth century not in the company of the tribal arts of Africa and Oceania (which were overlooked by artists at that time) but as Archaic arts, like those of the other court cultures such as the Egyptian that had passed for "primitive" to Gauguin and van Gogh. The "primitive" aspects of pre-Columbian technology, sociology, and communications account for the cultures' still being sometimes classified as Primitive in terms of their art (which, at the Metropolitan Museum and most others, is in the same department as African and Oceanic art).

Monumental Mesoamerican architecture and sculpture were visible in museums and world's fairs (the 1889 Paris Exposition Universelle had a reconstruction of an "Aztec House") and were of interest to artists generations before "art nègre" was known. Museum collections also contained a certain amount of material from the more remote, less centralized pre-Columbian regions, which art had somewhat more in common with tribal art. Yet how much of the latter was seen by artists, at least before the 1920s and 1930s, is open to question.

Pre-Columbian art unquestionably had an influence on modern art, but most of that influence was from the Archaic sculpture of the Aztec, Maya, Toltec, and Olmec cultures. After Gauguin and van Gogh, interest in it is largely associated with the generation of the 1930s (although, on a conceptual more than an aesthetic level, pre-Columbian civilizations have been of interest to recent artists). The measure of how deep or widespread this influence was will require a study that can satisfactorily distinguish demonstrable influences from simple affinities. Barbara Braun, with whom I have consulted on the organization of *"Primitivism" in Twentieth Century Art*, is presently at work on a book about pre-Columbian sources of modern art.

In addition to pre-Columbian objects, most natural history museums also possessed some specimens of the tribal arts of Mesoamerica and South America. Examples of these more recent objects are

the Mundurucú trophy head that Nolde included in his painting *Masks*.

14 Picasso seems to have had conflicting emotions about what he called "l'art aztèque," by which he meant the whole of pre-Columbian art as he knew it. My notes of conversations with him contain a reference to this art which I set down from memory as "boring, inflexible, too big...figures without invention." However, he praised the beauty of an "Aztec head" in a conversation with Brassaï (*Picasso and Company*, trans. Francis Price from the French *Conversations avec Picasso* [Garden City, N.Y.: Doubleday, 1966], p. 242). As recorded by Brassaï (for May 18, 1960), Picasso and he were looking at an album of his photographs. The chapter in the album entitled "Primitive Images," an "Aztec head," Brassaï tells us, "makes Picasso pause abruptly, and then he cries: 'That is as rich as the façade of a cathedral.' "

Picasso's feeling for the inventiveness of tribal art was a response to a reality – African and Oceanic art *is* more variegated and inventive than pre-Columbian art – as is evident if one compares visits to Mexico City's Museo Nacional de Antropologia and the Oceanic wing of Berlin's Museum für Völkerkunde, the two most beautiful and elaborate presentations of these respective arts that I know. But Picasso's attitude was also partly a matter of his perspective, hence my phrase "perceived inventiveness." What Picasso saw in the Trocadéro and the curio shops as the art of "les nègres" was thought of by him as issuing, broadly speaking, from a single cultural entity, Africa, when in fact the variety of African styles is in part a function of an immense number of ethnic groups of different religions, languages, and traditions covering an area far more vast than Western Europe.

15 Note that I differentiate here between the Old Kingdom, on the one hand, and the Middle Kingdom and New Empire, on the other. Old Kingdom art strikes me as very rich in invention. Such "academicism" (as opposed to simple "Traditionalism") as one finds in Egyptian art becomes a factor only after that period. Invention, however,

is a quantitative aspect of a work of art and has no necessary relation to quality. To find more invention in the work of Old Kingdom artists than subsequent ones is not to deny the quality of the many masterpieces that come down to us from the Middle Kingdom and New Empire.

16   "Classification stylistique du masque dan et guéré de la Côte d'Ivoire Occidentale (A.O.F.)," *Medelingen van het Rijksmuseum voor Volkenkunde, Leiden,* no. 4. (Leiden: E. J. Brill, 1948). This impressive study, though published in 1948, was based upon research done prior to World War II.

17   Goldwater (*Primitivism in Modern Art,* as in note 2, p. 150) quite rightly used "Archaic" to characterize the Iberian sculpture that interested Picasso and that subsequently "leads into the 'Negro' paintings." Picasso's interest in that sculpture was continuous with his even earlier interest in Egyptian art. The latter shares sufficient common denominators with certain non-Western court arts – at least as perceived by artists in the late nineteenth and early twentieth centuries – to warrant a global term; "Archaic," I believe, serves this purpose better than does any other adjective.

18   In the 1897–1904 *Nouveau Larousse illustré* (in which the word "primitivisme" made its first appearance, see pp. 130–1 and note 6), "primitive" was given (as both adjective and noun) sixteen different definitions, ranging from the algebraic and geological to the historical and ecclesiastical. Two of the sixteen were pejorative in connotation, notably the one marked "ethnological": "Les peuples qui sont encore au degré le moins avancé de civilisation." The fine-arts definition, given as a noun, was simply: "Artistes, peintres ou sculpteurs qui ont précédé les maîtres de la grande époque."

19   In conversation with Sabartés in his studio at villa Les Voiliers, Royan, 1940. (See Jaime Sabartés, *Picasso, An Intimate Portrait,* trans. Angel Flores from the Spanish *Picasso, Retratos y Recuerdos* [New York, 1949], p. 213.)

20   "Gothic" was traditionally paired with "barbaric" in the classicist critique of Western art. Only in the nineteenth century did the word begin to attain respectability. The speed at which pejorative connotations can drop away from art-historical terms may be measured by the rapidity with which the designation "Impressionist" was accepted by the public and even the painters themselves, despite the fact, as Meyer Schapiro has observed, that it had pejorative connotations relating to artisanal house decoration ("peinture d'impression").

21   Robert Goldwater, "Judgments of Primitive Art, 1905–1965," in *Tradition and Creativity in Tribal Art,* ed. Biebuyck, p. 25.

22   Such candidates as "ethnic" and "indigenous" have been found to have so many art-historical and/or sociological drawbacks that no serious attempt has been made to substitute them for "primitive."

23   "The Dilemma Which Faces African Art," *The Listener,* September 13, 1951, pp. 413–15.

24   This is particularly true of African scholars, for the political reasons referred to in note 1.

25   *Structural Anthropology,* trans. C. Jacobsen and B. G. Schoepf (London, 1963), pp. 101–02.

26   "Simplicity" was an idea to which Picasso returned frequently in my discussions with him, sometimes in terms of his own work or (more often) that of other modern artists (e.g., Matisse) and on two occasions in connection with "art nègre." It was clear that what he meant by this was not just the absence of elaborate effects but an economy that implied the distillation of complexities. "Simplicity" was generally used in his conversation as an antonym for the type of complexity characteristic of nineteenth-century salon illusionism. Picasso's overall criticism of the received art of his youth was that artists had forgotten how to be simple. With Sabartés, as with me, he lauded Primitive artists for their simplicity. (See Sabartés, *Picasso, An Intimate Portrait,* e.g., note 20, p. 213.)

27   The Michael C. Rockefeller wing of the Metropolitan Museum is the classic instance of this. It depended directly upon

Nelson Rockefeller's passion for tribal art, which had led to his earlier founding of the Museum of Primitive Art. This in turn depended on and followed from his taste for and involvement with twentieth-century art and his knowledge of the importance of tribal art for many modern artists.

28 Statement made to Florent Fels, in the course of successive conversations that led to the "interview" published by Fels (in *Les Nouvelles littéraires, artistiques et scientifiques*, no. 42, August 4, 1923, p. 2): "Je vous ai déjà dit que je ne pouvais plus rien dire de 'l'art nègre'.... C'est qu'il m'est devenu trop familier, les statues africaines qui traînent un peu partout chez moi, sont plus des témoins que des exemples."

29 Goldwater, *Primitivism in Modern Art*, p. xvi.

30 Ibid., p. xxi.

31 Ibid., p. 254.

32 It is not by chance, as I will show, that the tribal form of modernist primitivism begins simultaneously with the inception of radical metamorphosis in modernist formal structures (in the *Demoiselles* of 1907). Thus it is that the very process of conceptualizing common to both Primitive and twentieth-century art made the latter's debt to the former more difficult to identify.

33 This would apply, in the case of the Easter Island stone, only to the surface that is relieved and painted...Unlike the stone engraved by Ernst, the Polynesian one is otherwise irregular in contour.

34 From Maurer and Spies in conversation with the author. The first association of the Easter Island stone and work of Max Ernst that I know is in Lucy Lippard's introductory essay "The Sculpture" for the exhibition catalog *Max Ernst: Sculpture and Recent Painting*, ed. Sam Hunter (New York: The Jewish Museum, March 3–April 17, 1966), pp. 38–39, where Ernst's untitled painted granite sculpture of 1934 and the Easter Island stone carving of a bird-headed man are reproduced across from each other without commentary in the text.

35 This is a universally shared assumption. We do not, however, possess enough tribal sculpture unquestionably predating colonial times – nor is that which we possess datable with sufficient accuracy – to know the extent to which tribal art altered over the centuries.

36 As noted above, there is – and no doubt was – discourse among tribal peoples regarding at least certain aesthetic aspects of cult objects. The proof, however, that tribal artists solved aesthetic problems is in the objects themselves. That the majority of artists merely imitated received ideas is true for all cultures, though this fact is ably "masked" by many recent Western artists. What certainly differs is the degree of consciousness of the artists that they are, in fact, solving aesthetic problems. But the solutions of genius in the plastic arts are all essentially instinctual, regardless of such intellectual superstructures as might be built around them after the fact by the artists themselves, other artists, or critics and art historians.

37 *Primitive Religion* (New York, 1924), p. 260.

38 For the history of this mask, see Leon Siroto, "A Mask from the Congo," *Man* 54, October 1954, pp. 149–50, and an unpublished memorandum on file in the collection of the Museum.

39 "Tribal Art and Modern Man" in *The Tenth Muse: Essays in Criticism* (London: Routledge and Kegan Paul, 1957). This essay originally appeared in *The New Republic*, September 1953.

40 Few modern artists have been readers of ethnological books. Nolde and Kirchner seem to have consulted some of the specialized literature of their day, but Carl Einstein's *Negerplastik* (1915), which approached tribal sculpture from a purely aesthetic point of view, was of far greater interest to them. Max Ernst was exceptional in having read very widely in ethnology. Picasso, on the other hand, gleaned his impressions of the function of tribal objects in the Musée d'Ethnographie du Trocadéro from his imagination and from labels. Although Lydia Gasman

suggests the contrary in her strongly argued dissertation "Mystery, Magic and Love in Picasso, 1925–1938" (Columbia University, 1981), pp. 476–82, Picasso surely did not read Mauss or other early twentieth-century French ethnologists. Indeed, scholarly literature, as he said to me with regard to art history, bored him. Moreover, his grasp of French in the crucial period (1907–08) was such that reading Mauss would have been beyond him. It is perfectly possible, nevertheless, that Picasso absorbed some much-generalized, watered-down versions of ethnological ideas through his passing contacts with Mécislas Golberg and J. Deniker, and to that extent Gasman has a point. The ideas of the French school of ethnologists could well have been "in the air" of some Paris vanguard studios in much the same way as what passed for "Existentialism" – a studio catchword in the New York of the late forties and fifties – was known to the Abstract Expressionists. Picasso's grasp of the nature of Primitive art was, however, unquestionably instinctive.

41 This is the underlying thesis of Robert Farris Thompson's *African Art in Motion: Icon and Art in the Collection of Katherine Coryton White*, exhibition catalog (Washington, D.C., National Gallery of Art, and Los Angeles, Frederick S. Wight Art Gallery, University of California, 1974). See esp. pp. xii–xiv, 1–5, 47–48, 111–12, 117, 152, 154.

42 The modern West is not the first society to prize the art of other cultures, but is the first to prize cultures which (unlike Antiquity in its relation to the Renaissance) are not consonant with its own received traditions, and the first simultaneously to value a large number of alien cultures whose value systems are mutually contradictory.

43 Susan Vogel carries the analogy between the sculpture of Africa and of classical antiquity even further than similar statements by Fagg ("The African Artist") and others. In "The Buli Master and Other Hands" (*Art in America,* no. 5, May 1980, pp. 132–42) she states: "Traditional African art...is in fact a classical art in its insistence upon order and con-

formity to tradition, and in its low regard for radical innovations and personal expression...African art's concern with controlled emotion, balance and proportion, and its general restraint, make it fundamentally classical." In *African Aesthetics* (Milan, forthcoming) she underlines the fact that African words for beauty used in connection with works of art have a moral connotation, as in the Greek *kalokagathia,* which means simultaneously the beautiful and the good. She also stresses "the cardinal value of moderation which underlies all African aesthetic systems," which is the counterpart of the Greek ideal of *sophrosyne.*

44 Loeb was responsible for financing important trips to Oceania, particularly Lake Sentani, by Jacques Viot.

45 The extreme of these limits was set by Mannerist art, notably El Greco. The special popularity of El Greco in the first years of the century – he was singled out by such writers as Salmon, and the angularities and distortions of his work influenced Picasso in the Gosol work of 1906 and in the *Demoiselles* – reflects his proximity to primitivist concerns.

46 Kirk Varnedoe has pointed out that the typological treatment of human proportions was virtually parodied in Nazi "science," where the squat proportions of modern sculpture were compared with those of victims of elephantiasis (cf. Helmut Lehmann-Haupt, *Art under a Dictatorship* [New York, 1954], pp. 38–41).

47 It is quite impossible – nor should one even try – to sort out the many different influences fused in the refining fire of creative work in such a way as to assign them specific degrees of importance. My own impression is that what I have called the "broomstick" sculptures – which Picasso actually whittled, according to Werner Spies, from the wood of picture stretchers – had an important meaning for Giacometti even though their influence would not be felt for many years. This type of Picasso carving (see William Rubin, ed., *Picasso: A Retrospective* [New York: The Museum of Modern Art, 1980], p. 284) – elliptically related to a motif in nature rather than devised

wholly from the imagination as was Giacometti's art in 1931 – subsequently provided, along with Cézanne, models for the
artist's attenuated figures. If the latter
were also as I believe – at least as regards
their proportions – influenced by Archaic
(Etruscan) and Primitive art, the same is
probably also indirectly true of the
Picasso figures, which were made at a

time when his larger sculptures reflected
his interest in Baga sculpture.

48 This is the burden of Lévi-Strauss's structuralist analysis of Primitive language,
kinship patterns, and myth (see *Structural
Anthropology*: the comparison of the
workings of the "primitive" and modern
mind on p. 230).

8

Defective Affinities
"Primitivism" in 20th Century Art

Arthur C. Danto

In one of its less felicitous efforts to instruct its readership in matters of high culture, *Life* once ran a photographic essay on Abstract Expressionism. It consisted of juxtapositions of paintings with objects in the world that resembled them, sometimes quite precisely: heavy black scaffolding silhouetted against a blank sky went with a painting by Franz Kline; tangles of waterweeds were put next to a Jackson Pollock; perhaps – my memory here grows vague – faded and peeling posters on a worn fence, a found collage, were placed beside a Willem de Kooning. All this was meant to reassure readers that these new and perplexing artists had not really abandoned the mimetic imperatives of Western art but had merely changed the subjects to be imitated, copying fragments of reality heretofore neglected. The implied rule of appreciation was to treat the paintings somewhat like the photographs of most-wanted criminals in the post office: carry the image around until you find something to match it, then collect your reward. It would be difficult to think of a more serious perversion of the art movement this essay set out to clarify. If the artists in question had not altogether forsaken what was referred to as The Image, they never used images in the manner of exact resemblance that the *Life* juxtapositions required.

I am reminded of that dim didactic effort by the publicity for "Primitivism" in 20th Century Art at the Museum of Modern Art, which sets beside one another examples of primitive and modern art: an elongated Nyamwezi effigy is yoked with Alberto Giacometti's "Tall Figure" of 1949; a Zuni war god is put alongside Paul Klee's "Mask of Fear" of 1932; a Mbuya mask from Zaire keeps company – both have concave noses! – with one of the heads from the right side of "Les Demoiselles d'Avignon," and so on. All this is placed under the teasing title "Which is primitive?" The difficulty of answering that question on the basis of visual data alone – there are, admittedly, the resemblances, making the title teasing in a different way from, say, placing a wigwam beside the Chateau de Versailles – is doubtless meant to make the observer rethink his or her concept of primitivism. If those dark exotic cultures could produce objects indistinguishable from artworks produced by some of the most celebrated artists of our culture, well, either they are not so primitive or we are not so advanced as we might have thought. Nothing, I believe, could more seriously impede the understanding

From *The Nation* 37226. New York: 1984. Reprinted by permission of *The Nation*.

either of primitive or of modern art than these inane pairings and the question they appear to raise.

If there is a single lesson to be learned from recent philosophical analyses of art, it is that it is possible to imagine objects that are visually indistinguishable though one is a work of art and the other not; or where both might be works of art with such different meanings, styles, structures, references and thematizations that their perfect resemblance is incidental to any point save the demonstration of its irrelevance. That lesson could be nowhere more usefully kept in mind than in approaching so stupendously misconceived an exhibition as the present one, which obligingly deconstructs itself by making that very point midway through. Next to an Ibibio mask from Nigeria is installed Edvard Munch's celebrated lithograph "The Shriek." The print provides the visual equivalent of an auditory phenomenon in that we not only see that the woman on the bridge is screaming, we in effect *see the scream*, since the artist has transduced the landscape into a pattern of soundwaves. The mask, like Munch's screamer, has an open mouth, and it is covered with a linear pattern which, if read like the one in the Munch, would yield the stunning interpretation that the mask bears a scream on its forehead. I heard a number of visitors express doubts about this pairing, but had they read the guide booklet, they would have seen it was made precisely to raise that doubt. "This association would be fortuitous on the formal level," the booklet reads, "and badly misguided with regard to meaning."

But where in this entire display are the pairings not, in this fashion, fortuitous and misguided? Picasso, who collected and admired primitive objects, certainly gave the heads of his crouching demoiselles the power of African masks, but the connotations of primitiveness available to him were scarcely available to the mask makers themselves, for whom masks meant whatever they did mean in the magical transactions of tribal existence, but certainly not whatever heart of darkness Picasso may have meant to paint in a harlot's corner. He was not painting pictures of masks in the way in which Max Weber painted a Congo figure in one of the still lifes shown, one of the few cases where there is a convincing but almost point-

less connection between a primitive and a modern work: the former is the subject of the latter, as if it were a plate of apples or a vase. Nor was he simply borrowing exotic forms, as Victor Brauner did in an awful 1934 canvas which takes over a frightening image of the God A'a from the Austral Islands. Mostly, as with the Picasso, we are told of "affinities," "prototypes," "influences," "reflections," "compelling resemblances," "uncanny similarities" and similar tenuous relationships conveyed with the thin and dreary lexicon of the art-appreciation course. One watches the visitors playing the imposed game of resemblances, pointing with excitement to the meaningless similarities the framers of the exhibition have assembled for their edification. It is an unhappy experience to observe these hopeful pilgrims coerced by as acute an example of museological manipulation as I can think of. The only outcome can be a confusion as deep as that which underlies the entire array.

I don't think we really know the first thing about primitive art, not even whether it is right to treat it as art, however handsome and strong its objects may be. We do not know whether there is sufficient parity of purpose and content among all cultures identified as "primitive" to justify bracketing them together under an overarching designation. Indeed, this habit of identification may be as vivid a transport of cultural imperialism as the concept of Orientalism is according to Edward Said's famous polemic. In one room of the show there is a case with figures from New Guinea, Zambia, Zaire, Nigeria. But what do they have in common, really, with one another, or with objects from Easter Island or the American Southwest or Papua or New Ireland or the Arctic?

One may speculate that whatever ends they serve will not be esthetic, or will rarely be that, and that they typically exist in a universe of forces, powers, gods and magic with which they may put their users in touch. There is in this respect a possible "affinity" with some Western works, Byzantine icons, for example, in which the saints were believed not so much to be depicted as to be actually and mysteriously present. Such a concept of presentness contrasts sharply with the distancing manner of representation that animates a good bit of Western art, including most of the modern works in the exhibition. Primitive art, if indeed primitive in this sense, was not meant for audiences, viewers, dealers and collectors, but for participants and celebrants. The objects are instruments of ritual existence to which the suitable response might be a dance or a howl, not the peering and pointing that goes on in museums. In saying they are not works of art I do not mean that they cannot be treated esthetically but that treating them so is at odds with their raison d'être. The cultures they came from almost certainly lacked a Western concept of art, and these things answered to something deeper and – well – more *primitive* than art as art can tap.

In a sense, their appropriate habitat in our culture is the glass case of the ethnographic museum, where they squat in a kind of quarantine that underscores their aboriginal dangerousness. The only primitive pieces that look at home in MOMA just now are some exhibited in a case brought over from the Musée d'Ethnographie de Trocadéro to show us where Picasso – "in all likelihood" – made his acquaintance with objects that expressed? influenced? stimulated? reinforced? his own use of primitive motifs. Liberated from their cases, allowed to be perceived as "art objects," they become decorative touches destined for tasteful interiors, as in the failed Rockefeller Wing of the Metropolitan Museum, which looks like a detached segment of Bloomingdale's. Because we only know how to treat these objects as artifacts or *bibelots*, they are crudely manhandled to suit our own concepts of art: as expressive objects or, more often, as objects which satisfy the ever-ready formalistic premises, enabling curators to do violence to things that have no real business with one another just because they may look enough alike to be perceived as exercises in good design. A section of this exhibition is called "Affinities," grouping objects together with reference to the shallowest criteria of similitude, like seeing faces in clouds. There is no other way to describe wrestling into contiguity a Miró and an Eskimo mask. Under formalist principles, all works are brothers and contemporaries, but at the cost of sacrificing whatever makes them interesting or vital or important.

The idea of such an exhibition is, of course, a splendid one. There is little doubt that primitivism plays the role in twentieth-century art that Orientalism did in the nineteenth century or that classical forms did in the Renaissance. But then what must be shown is not adventitious visual congruities but what these objects meant to artists and how, not especially caring to understand them, they made them their own. Sometimes the impact was moral and transformative, if the same impulses that drove Gauguin to employ aboriginal forms explain as well his going native in Tahiti. Sometimes the connection is more narrowly artistic. There is the fascinating question of why Picasso and not Braque, both shown here in wonderful old photographs with some of the things they collected, used primitive objects to recognizable artistic purpose. Here one must conjecture, but the way the primitive masks rearrange features of faces, leaving them all the while identifiable as faces, must have been a powerful stimulus to the art of rearrangement and reinvention that is the mark of Picasso. And perhaps the license furnished by the primitives must enter partially into the explanation of Cubism, even when direct citation of primitive orderings is absent, as from the still lifes and interiors of Braque, who may after all have responded to the same stimuli as Picasso. But to show such things requires something more than finding explicit counterparts for the eye to make out, especially because they may only conceal the vast distances that separate primitive from modern object. Giacometti, for example, did make totemic-looking objects. But the thin presence forced here to share space with the marvelous Nyamwezi figure surely derives from different formal impulses, even if Giacometti "probably saw this particular object." His attenuated figures are drawn up out of their heavy feet in an almost godlike gesture making man out of earth, and possess the verticality of cathedrals.

"Primitivism" in 20th Century Art is a failed product of misapplied ingenuity, a ransacking of the ethnographic collections to compose parallels which yield a triple misunderstanding, first of primitive art, then of modern art, then of the relationships between them. A three-way failure in a show meant to be educational raises serious doubts about how qualified MOMA is to use its exceptional resources to carry out its didactic aims.

9

Histories of the Tribal and the Modern

James Clifford

You do not stand in one place to watch a masquerade.

An Igbo Saying

During the winter of 1984–85 one could encounter tribal objects in an unusual number of locations around New York City. This chapter surveys a half-dozen, focusing on the most controversial: the major exhibition held at the Museum of Modern Art (MOMA), " 'Primitivism' in 20th Century Art: Affinity of the Tribal and the Modern." The chapter's "ethnographic present" is late December 1984.

The "tribal" objects gathered on West Fifty-third Street have been around. They are travelers – some arriving from folklore and ethnographic museums in Europe, others from art galleries and private collections. They have traveled first class to the Museum of Modern Art, elaborately crated and insured for important sums. Previous accommodations have been less luxurious: some were stolen, others "purchased" for a song by colonial administrators, travelers, anthropologists, missionaries, sailors in African ports. These non-Western objects have been by turns curiosities, ethnographic specimens, major art creations. After 1900 they began to turn up in European flea markets, thereafter moving between avant-garde studios and collectors' apart-

ments. Some came to rest in the unheated basements or "laboratories" of anthropology museums, surrounded by objects made in the same region of the world. Others encountered odd fellow travelers, lighted and labeled in strange display cases. Now on West Fifty-third Street they intermingle with works by European masters – Picasso, Giacometti, Brancusi, and others. A three-dimensional Eskimo mask with twelve arms and a number of holes hangs beside a canvas on which Joan Miró has painted colored shapes. The people in New York look at the two objects and see that they are alike.

Travelers tell different stories in different places, and on West Fifty-third Street an origin story of modernism is featured. Around 1910 Picasso and his cohort suddenly, intuitively recognize that "primitive" objects are in fact powerful "art." They collect, imitate, and are affected by these objects. Their own work, even when not directly influenced, seems oddly reminiscent of non-Western forms. The modern and the primitive converse across the centuries and continents. At the Museum of Modern Art an exact history is told featuring

From *The Predicament of Culture: Twentieth-Century Ethnography, Literature, and Art* (Cambridge, MA: Harvard University Press, 1988), pp. 189–214, 349–369.

individual artists and objects, their encounters in specific studios at precise moments. Photographs document the crucial influences of non-Western artifacts on the pioneer modernists. This focused story is surrounded and infused with another – a loose allegory of relationship centering on the word *affinity*. The word is a kinship term, suggesting a deeper or more natural relationship than mere resemblance or juxtaposition. It connotes a common quality or essence joining the tribal to the modern. A Family of Art is brought together, global, diverse, richly inventive, and miraculously unified, for every object displayed on West Fifty-third Street looks modern.

The exhibition at MOMA is historical and didactic. It is complemented by a comprehensive, scholarly catalogue, which includes divergent views of its topic and in which the show's organizers, William Rubin and Kirk Varnedoe, argue at length its underlying premises (Rubin 1984). One of the virtues of an exhibition that blatantly makes a case or tells a story is that it encourages debate and makes possible the suggestion of other stories. Thus in what follows different histories of the tribal and the modern will be proposed in response to the sharply focused history on display at the Museum of Modern Art. But before that history can be seen for what it is, however – a specific story that excludes other stories – the universalizing allegory of affinity must be cleared away.

This allegory, the story of the Modernist Family of Art, is not rigorously argued at MOMA. (That would require some explicit form of either an archetypal or structural analysis.) The allegory is, rather, built into the exhibition's form, featured suggestively in its publicity, left uncontradicted, repetitiously asserted – "Affinity of the Tribal and the Modern." The allegory has a hero, whose virtuoso work, an exhibit caption tells us, contains more affinities with the tribal than that of any other pioneer modernist. These affinities "measure the depth of Picasso's grasp of the informing principles of tribal sculpture, and reflect his profound identity of spirit with the tribal peoples." Modernism is thus presented as a search for "informing principles" that transcend culture, politics, and history. Beneath this generous umbrella the tribal is modern and the modern more richly, more diversely human.

The power of the affinity idea is such (it becomes almost self-evident in the MOMA juxtapositions) that it is worth reviewing the major objections to it. Anthropologists, long familiar with the issue of cultural diffusion versus independent invention, are not likely to find anything special in the similarities between selected tribal and modern objects. An established principle of anthropological comparative method asserts that the greater the range of cultures, the more likely one is to find similar traits. MOMA's sample is very large, embracing African, Oceanian, North American, and Arctic "tribal" groups.[1] A second principle, that of the "limitation of possibilities," recognizes that invention, while highly diverse, is not infinite. The human body, for example, with its two eyes, four limbs, bilateral arrangement of features, front and back, and so on, will be represented and stylized in a limited number of ways.[2] There is thus a priori no reason to claim evidence for affinity (rather than mere resemblance or coincidence) because an exhibition of tribal works that seem impressively "modern" in style can be gathered. An equally striking collection could be made demonstrating sharp dissimilarities between tribal and modern objects.

The qualities most often said to link these objects are their "conceptualism" and "abstraction" (but a very long and ultimately incoherent list of shared traits, including "magic," "ritualism," "environmentalism," use of "natural" materials, and so on, can be derived from the show and especially from its catalogue). Actually the tribal and modern artifacts are similar only in that they do *not* feature the pictorial illusionism or sculptural naturalism that came to dominate Western European art after the Renaissance. Abstraction and conceptualism are, of course, pervasive in the arts of the non-Western World. To say that they share with modernism a rejection of certain naturalist projects is not to show anything like an affinity.[3] Indeed the "tribalism" selected in the exhibition to resemble modernism is itself a construction designed to accomplish the task of resemblance. Ife and Benin sculptures, highly naturalistic in style, are excluded from the "tribal" and placed in a somewhat arbitrary category of "court" society (which does not, however, include large chieftanships). Moreover, pre-Columbian works, though they have a place in the catalogue, are largely omitted from the exhibition. One can question other selections and exclusions that result in a collection of only "modern"-looking tribal objects. Why, for-example, are there relatively few "impure" objects constructed from the debris of colonial culture contacts? And is there not an overall bias toward clean, abstract forms as against rough or crude work?

The "Affinities" room of the exhibition is an intriguing but entirely problematic exercise in formal mix-and-match. The short introductory text begins well: "AFFINITIES presents a group of tribal objects notable for their appeal to modern taste." Indeed this is all that can rigor-ously be said of the objects in this room. The text continues, however, "Selected pairings of modern and tribal objects demonstrate com-mon denominators of these arts that are inde-pendent of direct influence." The phrase *common denominators* implies something more systematic than intriguing resemblance. What can it possibly mean? This introductory text, cited in its entirety, is emblematic of the MOMA undertaking as a whole. Statements carefully limiting its purview (specifying a con-cern only with modernist primitivism and not with tribal life) coexist with frequent implica-tions of something more. The affinity idea it-self is wide-ranging and promiscuous, as are allusions to universal human capacities re-trieved in the encounter between modern and tribal or invocations of the expansive human mind – the healthy capacity of modernist con-sciousness to question its limits and engage otherness.[4]

Nowhere, however, does the exhibition or catalogue underline a more disquieting quality of modernism: its taste for appropriating or redeeming otherness, for constituting non-Western arts in its own image, for discovering universal, ahistorical "human" capacities. The search for similarity itself requires justifica-tion, for even if one accepts the limited task of exploring "modernist primitivism," why could one not learn as much about Picasso's or Ernst's creative processes by analyzing the *differences* separating their art from tribal models or by tracing the ways their art moved away from, gave new twists to, non-Western forms?[5] This side of the process is unexplored in the exhibition. The prevailing

viewpoint is made all too clear in one of the "affinities" featured on the catalogue's cover, a juxtaposition of Picasso's *Girl before a Mirror* (1932) with a Kwakiutl half-mask, a type quite rare among Northwest Coast creations (figure 9.1). Its task here is simply to produce an effect of resemblance (an effect actually created by the camera angle). In this exhibition a universal message, "Affinity of the Tribal and the Modern," is produced by careful selection and the maintenance of a specific angle of vision.

The notion of affinity, an allegory of kinship, has an expansive, celebratory task to perform. The affinities shown at MOMA are all on mod-ernist terms. The great modernist "pioneers" (and their museum) are shown promoting for-merly despised tribal "fetishes" or mere ethno-graphic "specimens" to the status of high art and in the process discovering new dimensions of their ("our") creative potential. The capacity of art to transcend its cultural and historical context is asserted repeatedly (Rubin 1984: 73; this vol., p. 139). In the catalogue Rubin tends to be more interested in a recovery of elemental expressive modes, whereas Varnedoe stresses the rational, forward-looking intellect (which he opposes to an unhealthy primitivism, irrational and escapist). Both celebrate the gen-erous spirit of modernism, pitched now at a global scale but excluding – as we shall see – Third World modernisms.

At West Fifty-third Street modernist primi-tivism is a going Western concern. It is, Varne-doe tells us, summing up in the last sentence of the catalogue's second volume, "a process of revolution that begins and ends in modern culture, and because of that – not in spite of it – can continually expand and deepen our contact with that which is remote and different from us, and continually threaten, challenge, and reform our sense of self" (Rubin 1984: 682). A skeptic may doubt the ability of the modernist primitivism exhibited at MOMA to threaten or challenge what is by now a thoroughly institutionalized system of aes-thetic (and market) value; but it is appropriate, and in a sense rigorous, that this massive collection spanning the globe should end with the word *self*.

Indeed an unintended effect of the exhib-ition's comprehensive catalogue is to show once and for all the incoherence of the modern

Figure 9.1 The making of an affinity. (a) Pablo Picasso, *Girl before a Mirror*, 1932 (detail), oil on canvas. Courtesy the Museum of Modern Art, New York, gift of Mrs Simon Guggenheim. (b) Kwakiutl mask, painted wood. Photograph by Gisela Oestreich. Courtesy Museum für Völkerkunde. (c) Picasso, *Girl before a Mirror* (detail). This detail from the Picasso painting and the Kwakiutl mask were juxtaposed on the cover of the exhibition catalog *Primitivism in 20th Century Art: Affinity of the Tribal and Modern*, vol. 1.

Rorschach of "the primitive." From Robert Goldwater's formalism to the transforming "magic" of Picasso (according to Rubin); from Lévy-Bruhl's mystical *mentalité primitive* (influencing a generation of modern artists and writers) to Lévi-Strauss's *pensée sauvage* (resonating with "systems art" and the cybernetic binarism of the minimalists); from Dubuffet's fascination with insanity and the childish to the enlightened rational sense of a Gauguin, the playful experimentalism of a Picasso or the new "scientific" spirit of a James Turrell (the last three approved by Varnedoe but challenged by Rosalind Krauss, who is more attached to Bataille's decapitation, *bassesse*, and bodily deformations[6]); from fetish to icon and back again; from aboriginal bark paintings (Klee) to massive pre-Columbian monuments (Henry Moore); from weightless Eskimo masks to Stonehenge – the catalogue succeeds in demonstrating not any essential affinity between tribal and modern or even a coherent modernist attitude toward the primitive but rather the restless desire and power of the modern West to collect the world.

Setting aside the allegory of affinity, we are left with a "factual," narrowly focused history – that of the "discovery" of primitive art by Picasso and his generation. It is tempting to say that the "History" section of the exhibition is, after all, the rigorous part and the rest merely suggestive association. Undeniably a great deal of scholarly research in the best *Kunstgeschichte* tradition has been brought to bear on this specific history. Numerous myths are usefully questioned; important facts are specified (what mask was in whose studio when); and the pervasiveness of tribal influences on early modernist art – European, English, and American – is shown more amply than ever before. The catalogue has the merit of including a number of articles that dampen the celebratory mood of the exhibition: notably the essay by Krauss and useful contributions by Christian Feest, Philippe Peltier, and Jean-Louis Paudrat detailing the arrival of non-Western artifacts in Europe. These historical articles illuminate the less edifying imperialist contexts that surrounded the "discovery" of tribal objects by modernist artists at the moment of high colonialism.

If we ignore the "Affinities" room at MOMA, however, and focus on the "serious" historical part of the exhibition, new critical questions emerge. What is excluded by the specific focus of the history? Isn't this factual narration still infused with the affinity allegory, since it is cast as a story of creative genius recognizing the greatness of tribal works, discovering common artistic "informing principles"? Could the story of this intercultural encounter be told differently? It is worth making the effort to extract another story from the materials in the exhibition – a history not of redemption or of discovery but of reclassification. This other history assumes that "art" is not universal but is a changing Western cultural category. The fact that rather abruptly, in the space of a few decades, a large class of non-Western artifacts came to be redefined as art is a taxonomic shift that requires critical historical discussion, not celebration. That this construction of a generous category of art pitched at a global scale occurred just as the planet's tribal peoples came massively under European political, economic, and evangelical dominion cannot be irrelevant. But there is no room for such complexities at the MOMA show. Obviously the modernist appropriation of tribal productions as art is not simply imperialist. The project involves too many strong critiques of colonialist, evolutionist assumptions. As we shall see, though, the scope and underlying logic of the "discovery" of tribal art reproduces hegemonic Western assumptions rooted in the colonial and neocolonial epoch.

Picasso, Léger, Apollinaire, and many others came to recognize the elemental, "magical" power of African sculptures in a period of growing *négrophilie*, a context that would see the irruption onto the European scene of other evocative black figures: the jazzman, the boxer (Al Brown), the *sauvage* Josephine Baker. To tell the history of modernism's recognition of African "art" in this broader context would raise ambiguous and disturbing questions about aesthetic appropriation of non-Western others, issues of race, gender, and power. This other story is largely invisible at MOMA, given the exhibition's narrow focus. It can be glimpsed only in the small section devoted to "La création du monde," the African cosmogony staged in 1923 by Léger, Cendrars, and Milhaud, and in the broadly pitched if still largely uncritical catalogue article by Laura Rosenstock devoted to it. Overall one would be hard pressed to deduce from the exhibition that all the enthusiasm for things *nègre*, for the "magic" of African art, had anything to do with race. Art in this focused history has no essential link with coded perceptions of black bodies – their vitalism, rhythm, magic, erotic power, etc. – as seen by whites. The modernism represented here is concerned only with artistic invention, a positive category separable from a negative primitivism of the irrational, the savage, the base, the flight from civilization.

A different historical focus might bring a photograph of Josephine Baker into the vicinity of the African statues that were exciting the Parisian avant-garde in the 1910s and 1920s; but such a juxtaposition would be unthinkable in the MOMA history, for it evokes different

affinities from those contributing to the category of great art (figure 9.2). The black body in Paris of the twenties was an ideological artifact. Archaic Africa (which came to Paris by way of the future – that is, America) was sexed, gendered, and invested with "magic" in specific ways. Standard poses adopted by "La Bakaire," like Léger's designs and costumes, evoked a recognizable "Africanity" – the naked form emphasizing pelvis and buttocks, a segmented stylization suggesting a strangely mechanical vitality. The inclusion of so ideologically loaded a form as the body of Josephine Baker among the figures classified as art on West Fifty-third Street would suggest a different account of modernist primitivism, a different analysis of the category *nègre* in *l'art nègre*, and an exploration of the "taste" that was something more than just a backdrop for

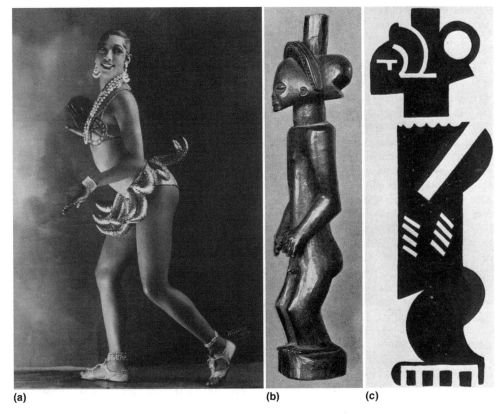

(a)   (b)   (c)

Figure 9.2 Affinities not included in the MOMA "Primitivism" show. 1. Bodies. (a) Josephine Baker in a famous pose, Paris ca. 1929. Courtesy the Granger Collection, New York. (b) Wooden figure (Chokwe, Angola). Published in Carl Einstein, *Negerplastik*, 1915; (c) Fernand Léger, costume design for *The Creation of the World*, 1922–23. Courtesy of the Kay Hillman Collection, New York

the discovery of tribal art in the opening decades of this century.[7]

Such a focus would treat art as a category defined and redefined in specific historical contexts and relations of power. Seen from this angle and read somewhat against the grain, the MOMA exhibition documents a *taxonomic* moment: the status of non-Western objects and "high" art are importantly redefined, but there is nothing permanent or transcendent about the categories at stake. The appreciation and interpretation of tribal objects takes place within a modern "system of objects" which confers value on certain things and withholds it from others (Baudrillard 1968). Modernist primitivism, with its claims to deeper humanist sympathies and a wider aesthetic sense, goes hand-in-hand with a developed market in tribal art and with definitions of artistic and cultural authenticity that are now widely contested.

Since 1900 non-Western objects have generally been classified as either primitive art *or* ethnographic specimens. Before the modernist revolution associated with Picasso and the simultaneous rise of cultural anthropology associated with Boas and Malinowski, these objects were differently sorted – as antiquities, exotic curiosities, orientalia, the remains of early man, and so on. With the emergence of twentieth-century modernism and anthropology figures formerly called "fetishes" (to take just one class of object) became works either of "sculpture" or of "material culture." The distinction between the aesthetic and the anthropological was soon institutionally reinforced. In art galleries non-Western objects were displayed for their formal and aesthetic qualities; in ethnographic museums they were represented in a "cultural" context. In the latter an African statue was a ritual object belonging to a distinct group; it was displayed in ways that elucidated its use, symbolism, and function. The institutionalized distinction between aesthetic and anthropological discourses took form during the years documented at MOMA, years that saw the complementary discovery of primitive "art" and of an anthropological concept of "culture" (Williams 1966).[8] Though there was from the start (and continues to be) a regular traffic between the two domains, this distinction is unchallenged in the exhibition. At MOMA treating tribal objects as art means excluding

the original cultural context. Consideration of context, we are firmly told at the exhibition's entrance, is the business of anthropologists. Cultural background is not essential to correct aesthetic appreciation and analysis: good art, the masterpiece, is universally recognizable.[9] The pioneer modernists themselves knew little or nothing of these objects' ethnographic meaning. What was good enough for Picasso is good enough for MOMA. Indeed an ignorance of cultural context seems almost a precondition for artistic appreciation. In this object system a tribal piece is detached from one milieu in order to circulate freely in another, a world of art – of museums, markets, and connoisseurship.

Since the early years of modernism and cultural anthropology non-Western objects have found a "home" either within the discourses and institutions of art or within those of anthropology. The two domains have excluded and confirmed each other, inventively disputing the right to contextualize, to represent these objects. As we shall see, the aesthetic-anthropological opposition is systematic, presupposing an underlying set of attitudes toward the "tribal." Both discourses assume a primitive world in need of preservation, redemption, and representation. The concrete, inventive existence of tribal cultures and artists is suppressed in the process of either constituting authentic, "traditional" worlds or appreciating their products in the timeless category of "art."

Nothing on West Fifty-third Street suggests that good tribal art is being produced in the 1980s. The non-Western artifacts on display are located either in a vague past (reminiscent of the label "nineteenth-twentieth century" that accompanies African and Oceanian pieces in the Metropolitan Museum's Rockefeller Wing) or in a purely conceptual space defined by "primitive" qualities: magic, ritualism, closeness to nature, mythic or cosmological aims (see Rubin 1984:10, 661–689). In this relegation of the tribal or primitive to either a vanishing past or an ahistorical, conceptual present, modernist appreciation reproduces common ethnographic categories.

The same structure can be seen in the Hall of Pacific Peoples, dedicated to Margaret Mead, at the American Museum of Natural History (figure 9.3 (b)). This new permanent hall is a

(a)

(b)

Figure 9.3 Affinities not included in the MOMA "Primitivism" show. 2. Collections. (a) Interior of Chief Shake's house, Wrangel, Alaska, 1909. Neg. no. 46123. Photograph by H. I. Smith. Courtesy Department Library Services, American Museum of Natural History, New York. (b) View of the Margaret Mead Hall of Pacific Peoples. Courtesy Department of Library Services, American Museum of Natural History

superbly refurbished anthropological stopping place for non-Western objects. In *Rotunda* (December 1984), the museum's publication, an article announcing the installation contains the following paragraph:

Margaret Mead once referred to the cultures of Pacific peoples as "a world that once was and now is no more." Prior to her death in 1978 she approved the basic plans for the new *Hall of Pacific Peoples.* (p. 1)

We are offered treasures saved from a destructive history, relics of a vanishing world. Visitors to the installation (and especially members of *present* Pacific cultures) may find a "world that is no more" more appropriately evoked in two charming display cases just outside the hall. It is the world of a dated anthropology. Here one finds a neatly typed page of notes from Mead's much-disputed Samoan research, a picture of the fieldworker interacting "closely" with Melanesians (she is carrying a child on her back), a box of brightly colored discs and triangles once used for psychological testing, a copy of Mead's column in *Redbook.* In the Hall of Pacific Peoples artifacts suggesting change and syncretism are set apart in a small display entitled "Culture Contact." It is noted that Western influence and indigenous response have been active in the Pacific since the eighteenth century. Yet few signs of this involvement appear anywhere else in the large hall, despite the fact that many of the objects were made in the past 150 years in situations of contact, and despite the fact that the museum's ethnographic explanations reflect quite recent research on the cultures of the Pacific. The historical contacts and impurities that are part of ethnographic work – and that may signal the life, not the death, of societies – are systematically excluded.

The tenses of the hall's explanatory captions are revealing. A recent color photograph of a Samoan *kava* ceremony is accompanied by the words: "STATUS and RANK were [sic] important features of Samoan society," a statement that will seem strange to anyone who knows how important they remain in Samoa today. Elsewhere in the hall a black-and-white photograph of an Australian Arunta woman and child, taken around 1900 by the pioneer ethnographers Spencer and Gillen, is captioned

in the *present* tense. Aboriginals apparently must always inhabit a mythic time. Many other examples of temporal incoherence could be cited – old Sepik objects described in the present, recent Trobriand photos labeled in the past, and so forth.

The point is not simply that the image of Samoan *kava* drinking and status society presented here is a distortion or that in most of the Hall of Pacific Peoples history has been airbrushed out. (No Samoan men at the *kava* ceremony are wearing wristwatches; Trobriand face painting is shown without noting that it is worn at cricket matches.) Beyond such questions of accuracy is an issue of systematic ideological coding. To locate "tribal" peoples in a nonhistorical time and ourselves in a different, historical time is clearly tendentious and no longer credible (Fabian 1983). This recognition throws doubt on the perception of a vanishing tribal world, rescued, made valuable and meaningful, either as ethnographic "culture" or as primitive/modern "art." For in this temporal ordering the real or genuine life of tribal works always precedes their collection, an act of salvage that repeats an all-too-familiar story of death and redemption. In this pervasive allegory the non-Western world is always vanishing and modernizing – as in Walter Benjamin's allegory of modernity, the tribal world is conceived as a ruin (Benjamin 1977). At the Hall of Pacific Peoples or the Rockefeller Wing the actual ongoing life and "impure" inventions of tribal peoples are erased in the name of cultural or artistic "authenticity." Similarly at MOMA the production of tribal "art" is entirely in the past. Turning up in the flea markets and museums of late nineteenth-century Europe, these objects are destined to be aesthetically redeemed, given new value in the object system of a generous modernism.

The story retold at MOMA, the struggle to gain recognition for tribal art, for its capacity "like all great art . . . to show images of man that transcend the particular lives and times of their creators" (Rubin 1984: 73; this vol.: p. 139), is taken for granted at another stopping place for tribal travelers in Manhattan, the Center for African Art on East Sixty-eighth Street. Susan Vogel, the executive director, proclaims in her introduction to the catalogue of its inaugural exhibition, "African Masterpieces from the Musée de l'Homme," that the "aesthetic-anthropological debate" has been resolved. It is now widely accepted that "ethnographic specimens" can be distinguished from "works of art" and that within the latter category a limited number of "masterpieces" are to be found. Vogel correctly notes that the aesthetic recognition of tribal objects depends on changes in Western taste. For example it took the work of Francis Bacon, Lucas Samaras, and others to make it possible to exhibit as art "rough and horrifying [African] works as well as refined and lyrical ones" (Vogel 1985:11). Once recognized, though, art is apparently art. Thus the selection at the Center is made on aesthetic criteria alone. A prominent placard affirms that the ability of these objects "to transcend the limitations of time and place, to speak to us across time and culture... places them among the highest points of human achievement. It is as works of art that we regard them here and as a testament to the greatness of their creators."

There could be no clearer statement of one side of the aesthetic anthropological "debate" (or better, *system*). On the other (anthropological) side, across town, the Hall of Pacific Peoples presents collective rather than individual productions – the work of "cultures." But within an institutionalized polarity interpenetration of discourses becomes possible. Science can be aestheticized, art made anthropological. At the American Museum of Natural History ethnographic exhibits have come increasingly to resemble art shows. Indeed the Hall of Pacific Peoples represents the latest in aestheticized scientism. Objects are displayed in ways that highlight their formal properties. They are suspended in light, held in space by the ingenious use of Plexiglas. (One is suddenly astonished by the sheer weirdness of a small Oceanic figurine perched atop a three-foot-tall transparent rod.) While these artistically displayed artifacts are scientifically explained, an older, functionalist attempt to present an integrated picture of specific societies or culture areas is no longer seriously pursued. There is an almost dadaist quality to the labels on eight cases devoted to Australian aboriginal society (I cite the complete series in order): "CEREMONY, SPIRIT FIGURE, MAGICIANS AND SORCERERS, SACRED ART, SPEAR THROWERS, STONE AXES

AND KNIVES, WOMEN, BOOMERANGS." Elsewhere the hall's pieces of culture have been recontextualized within a new cybernetic, anthropological discourse. For instance flutes and stringed instruments are captioned: "MUSIC is a system of organized sound in man's [sic] aural environment" or nearby: "COMMUNICATION is an important function of organized sound."

In the anthropological Hall of Pacific Peoples non-Western objects still have primarily scientific value. They are in addition beautiful.[10] Conversely, at the Center for African Art artifacts are essentially defined as "masterpieces," their makers as great artists. The discourse of connoisseurship reigns. Yet once the story of art told at MOMA becomes dogma, it is possible to reintroduce and co-opt the discourse of ethnography. At the Center tribal contexts and functions are described along with individual histories of the objects on display. Now firmly classified as masterpieces, African objects escape the vague, ahistorical location of the "tribal" or the "primitive." The catalogue, a sort of *catalogue raisonné*, discusses each work intensively. The category of the masterpiece individuates: the pieces on display are not typical; some are one of a kind. The famous Fon god of war or the Abomey shark-man lend themselves to precise histories of individual creation and appropriation in visible colonial situations. Captions specify *which* Griaule expedition to West Africa in the 1930s acquired each Dogon statue (see Leiris 1934 and Chapter 2 [in Clifford 1988]). We learn in the catalogue that a superb Bamileke mother and child was carved by an artist named Kwayep, that the statue was bought by the colonial administrator and anthropologist Henri Labouret from King N'Jike. While tribal names predominate at MOMA, the Rockefeller Wing, and the American Museum of Natural History, here personal names make their appearance.

In the "African Masterpieces" catalogue we learn of an ethnographer's excitement on finding a Dogon hermaphrodite figure that would later become famous. The letter recording this excitement, written by Denise Paulme in 1935, serves as evidence of the aesthetic concerns of many early ethnographic collectors (Vogel and N'diaye 1985:122). These individuals, we are told, could intuitively distinguish masterpieces from mere art or ethnographic specimens. (Actually many of the individual ethnographers behind the Musée de l'Homme collection, such as Paulme, Michel Leiris, Marcel Griaule, and André Schaeffner, were friends and collaborators of the same "pioneer modernist" artists who, in the story told at MOMA, constructed the category of primitive art. Thus the intuitive aesthetic sense in question is the product of a historically specific milieu. See Chapter 4 [in Clifford 1988].) The "African Masterpieces" catalogue insists that the founders of the Musée de l'Homme were art connoisseurs, that this great anthropological museum never treated all its contents as "ethnographic specimens." The Musée de l'Homme was and is secretly an art museum (Vogel 1985:11). The taxonomic split between art and artifact is thus healed, at least for self-evident "masterpieces," entirely in terms of the aesthetic code. Art is art in any museum.

In this exhibition, as opposed to the others in New York, information can be provided about each individual masterpiece's history. We learn that a Kiwarani antelope mask studded with mirrors was acquired at a dance given for the colonial administration in Mali on Bastille Day 1931. A rabbit mask was purchased from Dogon dancers at a gala soirée in Paris during the Colonial Exhibition of the same year. These are no longer the dateless "authentic" tribal forms seen at MOMA. At the Center for African Art a different history documents both the artwork's uniqueness and the achievement of the discerning collector. By featuring rarity, genius, and connoisseurship the Center confirms the existence of autonomous artworks able to circulate, to be bought and sold, in the same way as works by Picasso or Giacometti. The Center traces its lineage, appropriately, to the former Rockefeller Museum of Primitive Art, with its close ties to collectors and the art market.

In its inaugural exhibition the Center confirms the predominant aesthetic-ethnographic view of tribal art as something located in the past, good for being collected and given aesthetic value. Its second show (March 12–June 16, 1985) is devoted to "Igbo Arts: Community and Cosmos." It tells another story, locating art forms, ritual life, and cosmology in a specific, changing African society – a past *and* present heritage.

Photographs show "traditional" masks worn in danced masquerades around 1983. (These include satiric figures of white colonists.) A detailed history of cultural change, struggle, and revival is provided. In the catalogue Chike C. Aniakor, an Igbo scholar, writes along with co-editor Herbert M. Cole of "the continually evolving Igbo aesthetic": "It is illusory to think that which we comfortably label 'traditional' art was in an earlier time immune to changes in style and form; it is thus unproductive to lament changes that reflect current realities. Continuity with earlier forms will always be found; the present-day persistence of family and community values ensures that the arts will thrive. And as always, the Igbo will create new art forms out of their inventive spirit, reflecting their dynamic interactions with the environment and their neighbors and expressing cultural ideals" (Cole and Aniakor 1984: 14).

Cole and Aniakor provide a quite different history of "the tribal" and "the modern" from that told at the Museum of Modern Art – a story of invention, not of redemption. In his foreword to the catalogue Chinua Achebe offers a vision of culture and of objects that sharply challenges the ideology of the art collection and the masterpiece. Igbo, he tells us, do not like collections (figure 9.4).

The purposeful neglect of the painstakingly and devoutly accomplished *mbari* houses with all the art objects in them as soon as the primary mandate of their creation has been served, provides a significant insight into the Igbo aesthetic value as *process* rather than *product*. Process is motion while product is rest. When the product is preserved or venerated, the impulse to repeat the process is compromised. Therefore the Igbo choose to eliminate the product and retain the process so that every occasion and every generation will receive its own impulse and experience of creation. Interestingly this aesthetic disposition receives powerful endorsement from the tropical climate which provides an abundance of materials for making art, such as wood, as well as formidable agencies of dissolution, such as humidity and the termite. Visitors to Igboland are shocked to see that artifacts are rarely accorded any particular value on the basis of age alone. (Achebe 1984:ix)

Figure 9.4 The Earth Deity, Ala, with her "children" in her *mbari* house, Obube Ulakwo, southwest Nigeria, 1966. Photograph by Herbert M. Cole.

Achebe's image of a "ruin" suggests not the modernist allegory of redemption (a yearning to make things whole, to think archaeologically) but an acceptance of endless seriality, a desire to keep things apart, dynamic, and historical.

The aesthetic-anthropological object systems of the West are currently under challenge, and the politics of collecting and exhibiting occasionally become visible. Even at MOMA evidence of living tribal peoples has not been entirely excluded. One small text breaks the spell. A special label explains the absence of a Zuni war god figure currently housed in the Berlin Museum für Völkerunde. We learn that late in its preparations for the show MOMA "was informed by knowledgeable authorities that Zuni people consider any public exhibition of their war gods to be sacrilegious." Thus, the label continues, although such figures are routinely displayed elsewhere, the museum decided not to bring the war god (an influence on Paul Klee) from Berlin. The terse note raises more questions than it answers, but it does at least establish that the objects on display may in fact "belong" somewhere other than in an art or an ethnographic museum. Living traditions have claims on them, contesting (with a distant but increasingly

Figure 9.5 Affinities not included in the MOMA "Primitivism" show. 3. Appropriations. (a) Mrs. Pierre Loeb in her family apartment with modern and tribal works, rue Desbordes-Valmore, Paris, 1929. Courtesy Albert Loeb Gallery, Paris. (b) New Guinea girl with photographer's flash bulbs (included in the "Culture Contact" display at the Hall of Pacific Peoples). Neg. no. 336443. Photograph by E. T. Gilliard. Courtesy Department Library Services, American Museum of Natural History, New York

palpable power) their present home in the institutional systems of the modern West.[11]

Elsewhere in New York this power has been made even more visible. "Te Maori," a show visiting the Metropolitan, clearly establishes that the "art" on display is still sacred, on loan not merely from certain New Zealand museums but also from the Maori people. Indeed tribal art is political through and through. The Maori have allowed their tradition to be exploited as "art" by major Western cultural institutions and their corporate sponsors in order to enhance their own international prestige and thus contribute to their current resurgence in New Zealand society (Mead 1984).[12] Tribal authorities gave permission for the exhibition to travel, and they participated in its opening ceremonies in a visible, distinctive manner. So did Asante leaders at the exhibition of their art and culture at the Museum of Natural History (October 16, 1984–March 17, 1985). Although the Asante display centers on eighteenth- and nineteenth-century artifacts, evidence of the twentieth-century colonial suppression and recent renewal of Asante culture is included, along with color photos of modern ceremonies and newly made "traditional" objects brought to New York as gifts for the museum. In this exhibition the *location* of the art on display – the sense of where, to whom, and in what time(s) it belongs – is quite different from the location of the African objects at MOMA or in the Rockefeller Wing. The tribal is fully historical.

Still another representation of tribal life and art can be encountered at the Northwest Coast collection at the IBM Gallery (October 10–December 29, 1984), whose objects have traveled downtown from the Museum of the American Indian. They are displayed in pools of intense light (the beautifying "boutique" decor that seems to be modernism's gift to museum displays, both ethnographic and artistic). But this exhibition of traditional masterpieces ends with works by living Northwest Coast artists. Outside the gallery in the IBM atrium two large totem poles have been installed. One is a weathered specimen from the Museum of the American Indian, and the other has been carved for the show by the Kwakiutl Calvin Hunt. The artist put the finishing touches on his creation where it stands in the atrium; fresh wood chips are left scattered around the base. Nothing like this is possible or even thinkable at West Fifty-third Street.

The organizers of the MOMA exhibition have been clear about its limitations, and they have repeatedly specified what they do not claim to show. It is thus in a sense unfair to ask why they did not construct a differently focused history of relations between "the tribal" and "the modern." Yet the exclusions built into any collection or narration are legitimate objects of critique, and the insistent, didactic tone of the MOMA show only makes its focus more debatable. If the non-Western objects on West Fifty-third Street never really question but continually confirm established aesthetic values, this raises questions about "modernist primitivism's" purportedly revolutionary potential. The absence of any examples of Third World modernism or of recent tribal work reflects a pervasive "self-evident" allegory of redemption.

The final room of the MOMA exhibition, "Contemporary Explorations," which might have been used to refocus the historical story of modernism and the tribal, instead strains to find contemporary Western artists whose work has a "primitive feel."[13] Diverse criteria are asserted: a use of rough or "natural" materials, a ritualistic attitude, ecological concern, archaeological inspiration, certain techniques of assemblage, a conception of the artist as shaman, or some familiarity with "the mind of primitive man in his [sic] science and mythology" (derived perhaps from reading Lévi-Strauss). Such criteria, added to all the other "primitivist" qualities invoked in the exhibition and its catalogue, unravel for good the category of the primitive, exposing it as an incoherent cluster of qualities that at different times have been used to construct a source, origin, or alter ego confirming some new "discovery" within the territory of the Western self. The exhibition is at best a historical account of a certain moment in this relentless process. By the end the feeling created is one of claustrophobia.

The non-Western objects that excited Picasso, Derain, and Léger broke into the realm of official Western art from outside. They were quickly integrated, recognized as masterpieces, given homes within an anthropological-aesthetic object system. By now this process has been sufficiently celebrated. We need exhibitions that question the boundaries of art and of the art world, an influx of truly indigestible "outside" artifacts. The relations of power whereby one portion of humanity can select, value, and collect the pure products of others need to be criticized and transformed. This is no small task. In the meantime one can at least imagine shows that feature the impure, "inauthentic" productions of past and present tribal life; exhibitions radically heterogeneous in their global mix of styles; exhibitions that locate themselves in specific multicultural junctures; exhibitions in which nature remains "unnatural"; exhibitions whose principles of incorporation are openly questionable. The following would be my contribution to a different show on "affinities of the tribal and the postmodern." I offer just the first paragraph from Barbara Tedlock's superb description of the Zuni Shalako ceremony, a festival that is only part of a complex, living tradition (1984:246):

Imagine a small western New Mexican village, its snow-lit streets lined with white Mercedes, quarter-ton pickups and Dodge vans. Villagers wrapped in black blankets and flowered shawls are standing next to visitors in blue velveteen blouses with rows of dime buttons and voluminous satin skirts. Their men are in black Stetson silver-banded hats, pressed jeans, Tony Lama boots and multicolored Pendleton blankets. Strangers dressed in dayglo orange, pink and green ski jackets, stocking caps, hiking boots and mittens. All crowded together they are looking into newly constructed houses illuminated by bare light bulbs dangling from raw rafters edged with Woolworth's red fabric and flowered blue print calico. Cinderblock and plasterboard white walls are layered with striped serapes, Chimayó blankets, Navajo rugs, flowered fringed embroidered shawls, black silk from Mexico and purple, red and blue rayon from Czechoslovakia. Rows of Hopi cotton dance kilts and rain sashes; Isleta woven red and green belts; Navajo and Zuni silver concha belts and black mantas covered with silver brooches set with carved lapidary, rainbow mosaic, channel inlay, turquoise needlepoint, pink agate, alabaster, black cannel coal and bakelite from old '78s, coral, abalone shell, mother-of-pearl and horned oyster hang from poles suspended from the ceiling. Mule and white-tailed deer trophy-heads wear-

ing squash-blossom, coral and chunk-turquoise necklaces are hammered up around the room over rearing buckskins above Arabian tapestries of Martin Luther King and the Kennedy brothers, The Last Supper, a herd of sheep with a haloed herder, horses, peacocks.

NOTES

1   The term *tribal* is used here with considerable reluctance. It denotes a kind of society (and art) that cannot be coherently specified. A catchall, the concept of tribe has its source in Western projection and administrative necessity rather than in any essential quality or group of traits. The term is now commonly used instead of *primitive* in phrases such as *tribal art*. The category thus denoted, as this essay argues, is a product of historically limited Western taxonomies. While the term was originally an imposition, however, certain non-Western groups have embraced it. Tribal status is in many cases a crucial strategic ground for identity. In this essay my use of *tribe* and *tribal* reflects common usage while suggesting ways in which the concept is systematically distorting. See Fried 1975 and Sturtevant 1983.

2   These points were made by William Sturtevant at the symposium of anthropologists and art historians held at the Museum of Modern Art in New York on November 3, 1984.

3   A more rigorous formulation than that of affinity is suggested in Leiris 1953. How, Leiris asks, can we speak of African sculpture as a single category? He warns of "a danger that we may underestimate the variety of African sculpture; as we are less able to appreciate the respects in which cultures or things unfamiliar to us differ from one another than the respects in which they differ from those to which we are used, we tend to see a certain resemblance between them, which lies, in point of fact, merely in their common differentness" (p. 35). Thus, to speak of African sculpture one inevitably shuts one's eyes "to the rich diversity actually to be found in this sculpture in order to concentrate on the respects in which it is *not* what our own sculpture

generally is." The affinity of the tribal and the modern is, in this logic, an important optical illusion – the measure of a *common differentness* from artistic modes that dominated in the West from the Renaissance to the late nineteenth century.

4   See, for example, Rubin's discussion of the mythic universals shared by a Picasso painting and a Northwest Coast half-mask (Rubin 1984:328–330). See also Kirk Varnedoe's association of modernist primitivism with rational, scientific exploration (Rubin 1984:201–203, 652–653).

5   This point was made by Clifford Geertz at the November 3, 1984, symposium at the Museum of Modern Art (see n.2).

6   The clash between Krauss's and Varnedoe's dark and light versions of primitivism is the most striking incongruity within the catalogue. For Krauss the crucial task is to shatter predominant European forms of power and subjectivity; for Varnedoe the task is to expand their purview, to question, and to innovate.

7   On *négrophilie* see Laude 1968; for parallel trends in literature see Blachère 1981 and Levin 1984. The discovery of things "nègre" by the European avant-garde was mediated by an imaginary America, a land of noble savages simultaneously standing for the past and future of humanity – a perfect affinity of primitive and modern. For example, jazz was associated with primal sources (wild, erotic passions) and with technology (the mechanical rhythm of brushed drums, the gleaming saxophone). Le Corbusier's reaction was characteristic: "In a stupid variety show, Josephine Baker sang 'Baby' with such an intense and dramatic sensibility that I was moved to tears. There is in this American Negro music a lyrical 'contemporary' mass so invincible that I could see the foundation of a new sentiment of music capable of being the expression of the new epoch and also capable of classifying its European origins as stone age – just as has happened with the new architecture" (quoted in Jencks 1973:102). As a source of modernist inspiration for Le Corbusier, the figure of Josephine Baker was matched only by monumental, almost Egyptian, concrete grain elevators, rising from the American plains and built by nameless "primitive" engineers (Banham

1986: 16). The historical narrative implicit here has been a feature of twentieth-century literary and artistic innovation, as a redemptive modernism persistently "discovers" the primitive that can justify its own sense of emergence.

8   The twentieth-century developments traced here redeploy these ideas in an intercultural domain while preserving their older ethical and political charge ...

9   On the recognition of masterpieces see Rubin's confident claims (1984:20–21). He is given to statements such as the following on tribal and modern art: "The solutions of genius in the plastic arts are all essentially instinctual" (p. 78, n.80). A stubborn rejection of the supposed views of anthropologists (who believe in the collective production of works of tribal art) characterizes Rubin's attempts to clear out an autonomous space for aesthetic judgment. Suggestions that he may be projecting Western aesthetic categories onto traditions with different definitions of art are made to seem simplistic (for example p. 28).

10   At the November 3, 1984, symposium (see n.2) Christian Feest pointed out that the tendency to reclassify objects in ethnographic collections as "art" is in part a response to the much greater amount of funding available for art (rather than anthropological) exhibitions.

11   The shifting balance of power is evident in the case of the Zuni war gods, or Ahauuta. Zuni vehemently object to the display of these figures (terrifying and of great sacred force) as "art." They are the only traditional objects singled out for this objection. After passage of the Native American Freedom of Religion Act of 1978 Zuni initiated three formal legal actions claiming return of the Ahauuta (which as communal property are, in Zuni eyes, by definition stolen goods). A sale at Sotheby Parke-Bernet in 1978 was interrupted, and the figure was eventually returned to the Zuni. The Denver Art Museum was forced to repatriate its Ahauutas in 1981. A claim against the Smithsonian remains unresolved as of this writing. Other pressures have been

applied elsewhere in an ongoing campaign. In these new conditions Zuni Ahauuta can no longer be routinely displayed. Indeed the figure Paul Klee saw in Berlin would have run the risk of being seized as contraband had it been shipped to New York for the MOMA show. For general background see Talbot 1985.

12 An article on corporate funding of the arts in the *New York Times*, Feb. 5, 1985, p. 27, reported that Mobil Oil sponsored the Maori show in large part to please the New Zealand government, with which it was collaborating on the construction of a natural gas conversion plant.

13 In places the search becomes self-parodic, as in the caption for works by Jackie Winsor: "Winsor's work has a primitivist feel, not only in the raw physical presence of her materials, but also in the way she fabricates. Her labor – driving nails, binding twine – moves beyond simple systematic repetition to take on the expressive character of ritualized action." [See also ch. 13, p. 221 and figure 13.3.]

REFERENCES

Achebe, Chinua. 1984. "Foreword." *Igbo Arts: Community and Cosmos,* ed. H. M. Cole and C. C. Aniakor, pp. vii–xi. Los Angeles: Museum of Cultural History, UCLA.

Benjamin, Walter. 1977. *The Origin of German Tragic Drama.* London: New Left Books.

Clifford, James. 1988. *The Predicament of Culture: Twentieth-century Ethnography, Literature and Art.* Cambridge: Harvard University Press.

Cole, Herbert, and Chike Aniakor, eds. 1984. *Igbo Arts: Community and Cosmos.* Los Angeles: Museum of Cultural History, UCLA.

Einstein, Carl. 1915. *Negerplastik.* Trans. T. and R. Burgard as *La sculpture africaine.* Paris: Crès, 1922.

Fried, Morton. 1975. *The Notion of Tribe.* Menlo Park, Calif.: Cummings.

Jencks, Charles. 1973. *Le Corbusier and the Tragic View of Architecture.* London: Penguin.

Laude, Jean. 1968. *La peinture française (1905–1914) et "l'art nègre."* Paris: Editions Klincksieck.

Leiris, Michael. 1934. *L'Afrique fantôme.* Reprinted with new introduction. Paris: Gallimard, 1950.

—— 1953. "The African Negroes and the Arts of Carving and Sculpture." In *Interrelations of Cultures,* pp. 316–351. Westport, Conn.: UNESCO.

Mead, Sidney Moka, ed. 1984. *Te Maori: Maori Art from New Zealand Collections.* New York: Harry Abrams.

Rubin, William, ed. 1984. *"Primitivism" in Modern Art: Affinity of the Tribal and the Modern.* 2 vols. New York: Museum of Modern Art.

Sturtevant, William. 1983. "Tribe and State in the Sixteenth and Twentieth Centuries." In *The Development of Political Organization in Native North America,* ed. Elizabeth Tooker, pp. 3–15. Washington: The American Ethnological Society.

Talbot, Steven. 1985. "Desecration and American Indian Religious Freedom." *Journal of Ethnic Studies* 12(4):1–18.

Tedlock, Barbara. 1984. "The Beautiful and the Dangerous: Zuñi Ritual and Cosmology as an Aesthetic System." *Conjunctions* 6:246–265.

Vogel, Susan. 1985. Introduction. In *African Masterpieces from the Musée de l'Homme,* pp. 10–11. New York: Harry Abrams.

——, and Francine N'Diaye, eds. 1985. *African Masterpieces from the Musée de l'Homme.* New York: Harry Abrams.

Williams, Raymond. 1966. *Culture and Society, 1780–1950.* New York: Harper and Row.

10

A Case in Point and Afterwords to *Primitive Art in Civilized Places*

Sally Price

A Case in Point

The huts along the rivers of Surinam are like the huts beside the Congo, as they were in the days of Stanley and the early explorers. And in these huts, polygamously, the Bush Negroes live.

Morton C. Kahn[1]

As we near the end of this little book, it is time to explore more pointedly what the generalities and abstractions discussed up to this point mean in the actual lives of real people. Rather than continuing to build a patchwork of anecdotal secondhand evidence from around the world, it will be useful to lend some firsthand attention to a single case, looking at the ways in which Western notions about Primitive Art have operated. The Suriname Maroons, descendants of Africans imported to South America as slaves in the seventeenth and eighteenth centuries, will be the focus of this chapter, simply because I have, together with Richard Price, been studying their way of life since 1966 and have extended experience with their arts, both in their villages and in museological settings.

The Maroons are united by a heritage of rebellion from the oppression of plantation slavery but divide into six politically distinct groups; the Saramaka and Djuka each number some 22,000, while the Paramaka, Aluku, Matawai, and Kwinti together include roughly 6,000 people. Their ancestors' sustained wars of liberation ended with peace treaties in the eighteenth century which granted them independence from the Dutch colonial government, territorial rights in the interior, and periodic tribute in the form of manufactured goods from the coast such as soap, cooking pots, cloth, guns, and axes. The Djuka, Paramaka, and Aluku (in eastern Suriname) speak variants of one language, the Saramaka, Matawai, and Kwinti (in central Suriname) variants of another; and cultural differences (in dress, diet, rituals, and so on) tend to follow the same bipartite division. When Suriname became independent from the Netherlands in 1975, the bulk of the Maroon population still lived in small villages strung along the rivers of the tropical rain forest, though the men (like their fathers and grandfathers) spent a significant part of their adult lives engaged in wage labor outside of tribal territories, and even

From *Primitive Art in Civilized Places*, 2 (Chicago: University of Chicago Press, [1989] 2001) pp. 108–136 (1st edition), 134–145 (2nd edition). Reprinted by permission of Chicago Univerity Press.

women were participating in this pattern, as communities began allowing lineage daughters to accompany their husbands to the coast for periods of a year or more. In 1986, the peaceful expansion of Maroon involvements with the other population groups of Suriname was brutally arrested, as a new rebellion (a Djuka-led attack on the regime of Desi Bouterse) met with the military resources and tactics of the Modern World. The Maroon populations have been decimated by death squads, the bombing of villages, and "interrogation" sessions in the courtyard of the seventeenth-century fort that, as the Suriname National Museum, once housed the artistic treasures of Maroons and other inhabitants of this culturally diverse republic. As of this writing, the future of the Suriname Maroons – as individuals and as social-cultural groups – is very much in question.

The artistry of the Maroons is one of the better documented aspects of their cultural life. Their best-known medium is woodcarving, which Maroon men produce both for internal use and for sale to outsiders. In the villages, handsomely carved objects – from combs, food stirrers, winnowing trays, and peanut-grinding boards to paddles, canoes, doors, and whole housefronts – serve as gifts to wives and lovers. In return, women sew garments elaborately decorated with embroidery, patchwork, and appliqué, as well as crocheting colorful calfbands for the men to wear and carving elegant calabash utensils to serve at their meals. The art of cicatrization, too, is focused on sexual relations; women (and to a lesser extent men) adorn themselves with raised keloids designed to contribute to their erotic appeal through both visual and tactile means. In contrast, ritual objects – from funeral masks to ancestor shrines – are decorated crudely and do not, in the Maroon vision of things, belong to the realm of aesthetic concerns. In these societies, then, art is more part of social than religious life. Indeed, art objects are the primary currency in the ongoing exchanges between the sexes.[2]

Black, cicatrized, polygynous, nonliterate, snake- and ancestor-worshipping, and either naked, barebreasted or loincloth-clad (depending on age and sex), the Maroons (or "Bush Negroes") meet the most demanding criteria for primitive exoticism. That their communities were formed in response to European co-

lonialism only adds to the image, imbuing it with the proud defiance of rebel warriors against an imperialist society distant enough in time to pose no threat of association with Ourselves. Those aspects of their life that outside observers gloss as "the arts" – dancing and drumming, songs in both everyday and esoteric languages, a variety of decorative media, and carved "fetishes," ancestral shrines, and masks – contribute importantly to the fascination of Westerners with their way of life.

The Maroons' historical and cultural ties with Africa have been central to the image. One commentator suggested that they constituted a "little Africa in America" (Kahn 1954), another wrote a book called *Bush Negro Art: An African Art in the Americas* (Dark 1954), and a third labeled Maroon woodcarving "an original African art form" (Volders 1966: 141). The titles of articles written about Maroon life are sometimes quite explicit: "We Find an African Tribe in the South American Jungle" (Vandercook 1926b), "African Customs and Beliefs Preserved for Two Centuries in the Interior of Dutch Guiana" (van Panhuys 1934), and "Africa's Lost Tribes in South America: An On-the-spot Account of Blood-chilling African Rites of 200 Years Ago Preserved Intact in the Jungle of South America by a Tribe of Runaway Slaves" (Kahn 1939). The pioneer Afro-Americanist, Melville J. Herskovits, whose first foreign fieldwork was with the Saramaka, wrote an article called "Bush Negro Art," which characterized Maroons as "having remained faithful to their African traditions [thus presenting] the unique phenomenon of an autonomous civilization of one continent – Africa – transplanted to another – South America" (1930: 160). The recent assertion that twentieth-century Maroon communities are "more African than much of Africa" (Counter and Evans, n.d.) suggests how unbounded the enthusiasm for this idea can be.

In addition to the implication of primitivism in such depictions of the Maroons, the assertion that their customs have been "preserved intact" over the centuries is of central relevance for the problems we have been confronting in these pages. As one author expressed the vision,

The flush tides of imperialism have passed over these people, leaving them practically unaltered and unknown, unique among the

Negro peoples of the world. They still maintain the life of jungle dwellers of the immemorial past. Today they are hunting game with the long bow. Tonight their bodies will be contorted with the sinuous movements of African dances, to the dull thudding of the tomtom. (Kahn 1931: 3–4)

Or, as a more recent description put it,

We had never expected the people to be this classical, . . . this purely African and isolated from the outside world. . . . it seemed that for every mile we had traveled into the rain forest we had traveled back about a year in time, until we had gone back more than two centuries. (Counter and Evans 1981: 32–33)

Like other aspects of Maroon life, the arts are understood by many outsiders as static traditions, originally imported to Suriname in the seventeenth and eighteenth centuries by enslaved Africans whose descendants now faithfully carry them forward in time, intact and unaltered. The demonstration that this view has been created and nurtured by Western preconceptions at least as much as by valid historical or ethnographic documentation has been presented elsewhere (Price and Price 1980: chap. 8; R. Price 1970; S. Price 1984, 1986). Rather than rehearsing the full, and rather complex, argument here, I cite just a few of the findings that have persuaded me of the relevance, for the Maroon case, of the concept of "art history" – including the presence of stylistic and technical change, recognized individual creativity, and communal attention to chronological development.

It is important to note that the existence of a Maroon "art history" emerged from discussions in the field (between Maroons and us or, more frequently, among Maroons within range of our hearing), and was only later confirmed and enhanced by our consultation of museum collections and written documentation. Dealing mainly (but not exclusively) with Saramakas, we learned about the named styles and techniques that characterized different periods since the mid-nineteenth century, the individuals responsible for introducing them, the ways in which particular innovations were adopted and expanded, and the relationships among different media, with designs and styles often passing from one to the other. If Joseph Alsop had scrutinized traditional schol-

arly resources for evidence of a known art history in the villages of the Suriname interior, he surely would have concluded that such a notion did not exist. Maroons have no museums and no written documents, nor do they maintain a body of oral historical traditions, transmitted *formally* from generation to generation, of the sort one can find in many African kingdoms. There is, however, a great deal of knowledge of the past and, more important, interest in it.

Saramakas think about their art of woodcarving in terms of four named styles, which they can place quite precisely in time (not in terms of dates, but by association with individual personalities and contemporaneous events). Similarly, they are aware of important changes in their calabash art (e.g., the shift from external to internal decoration, and the associated transfer of the medium from men to women). And they show equal knowledge and articulateness about the periodization of their textile arts, which have gone from free-form embroidery to a mosaiclike style of patchwork, to narrow-strip compositions, and finally to an elaborate art of cross-stitch embroidery. Their discourse differs in its rhetoric from Western "art history" and the examples they cite are not preserved in local museum cases, but the level of analysis constitutes in every respect the kind of attention to artistic developments in time, as well as the aesthetic ideas that accompanied them, that we associate with our own notion of art history.

Images of timelessness, . . . are often reinforced by assumptions of anonymity, and the treatment of Maroon art is no exception. One literary device that has frequently served to bolster the anonymity of Maroon artists is the use of the masculine singular to refer to the roughly 50,000 men, women, boys, and girls who belong to the six Maroon groups. Many authors tell us about "the Maroon" (or "the Bush Negro") and "his" wives and children. "He" clears the forest for gardens, hunts and fishes, performs rites for spirits and ancestors, and fashions beautiful woodcarvings for "his" women. This practice not only helps perpetuate distortions in the depiction of Maroon women as artists (see, for discussion of this point, S. Price 1982/1988, 1984), but also contributes to the process of forgetting that the people under discussion are as varied in personality, temperament, and talents as, for example, Cézanne, Gauguin, and Matisse.

Maroons, however, do not generalize their fellows, past or present. Nor do they ignore or minimize the particular contributions of individual artists. Saramakas from the Upper River region recognize the work of Seketima, a carver of the early twentieth century, as readily as an habitué of the Museum of Modern Art recognizes a Jackson Pollock. Most women distinguish with confidence and accuracy calabashes carved in the 1960s by Keekete from the many imitations they inspired. And innovations in both design and technique in any medium are credited to the persons originally responsible for developing them. In short, the blurring of individuals to form a composite "Bush Negro artist" is one aspect of Maroon art history for which the Maroons themselves cannot properly be given credit.

The Universality Principle is also relevant to the representation of Maroon art. As we saw in chapter 3 [Price 1989], Primitives are often taken to represent human nature stripped to its essentials and are thus central figures within the Brotherhood of Man. In this context, Maroons, like other Primitives, are depicted as simpler, more childlike versions of ourselves, subject to the same "primal drives," but less encumbered by the "overlay of civilization" that blankets our own, more sophisticated, life experience. Linguistic support for this view is particularly pervasive. The *Guinness Book of World Records* memorializes the languages of "bush blacks" (misunderstood as a single language, mislabeled as "Taki Taki" [a pejorative term for the language of coastal Surinamers], and mislocated in French Guiana) by crowning it the "Least Complex" of the world's languages and asserting that its vocabulary, with an alleged total of only 340 words, is the smallest in the world (see R. Price 1976: 44).

The presence of English-derived words in the actual languages spoken by Maroons has encouraged many observers to conceptualize their speech as a kind of badly broken English or baby talk. This facilitates the citation of direct discourse in writing for English-speaking readers. Morton Kahn's report of an attempt to secure woodcarvings gives an idea of the style. He begins by offering some practical advice:

The only way to acquire these objects is to bargain for them in Dutch money or tobacco, or cheap knick-knacks. Among the more distant villages money is useless. Blue beads are very effective in bargaining, for blue is the Djuka's favourite colour. Ear-rings are also good, but not perfume; they prefer the acrid odour of insecticides.

Kahn then goes on to relate his own experience:

We say: "*Me wanny buy timbeh*" – "I want to buy wooden pieces."

The Negro's common reply is that he has none to part with: "*Me no habbe, massra.*" The word *massra* is a corruption of "master," a vestige of the slave days.

We point to a pierced and inlaid stool and say "*How many?*" meaning, how much does he want for it.

"*Me no wanny fu selly*" – "I don't want to sell it."

To show him we mean business, a concrete offer is made, "*Me gon gibbe sixa banknoto*" – "I'm going to give six banknoto."

The bargaining is in silver half-guilder pieces, called *banknoto*. The Dujkas do not understand large sums of money, except when counted in half-guilder pieces.

If he refuses six coins, we offer seven, eight, nine, and throw in the added temptation of some tobacco leaves. To each of these offers he shakes his head in negation, saying doggedly, "No, no."

Finally, in a tone of voice that indicates we are amazed at our own generosity, we say: "*Me gon gibbe tena banknoto, nanga twee weefee tabak.*" – "I'm going to give ten banknoto, as well as three leaves of tobacco."

The reply is short and spirited.

"*Gimme.*"

Which does not have to be translated. (1931: 48–50)

This utterance (and perhaps the entire dialogue) does not have to be translated for Kahn's readers, but it might well for the Maroons who are alleged to have participated in it. The exchange took place, according to Kahn's account, in Saramaka territory, where, even making generous allowances for orthographic liberties, the words reported have little overlap with the local language. If we were to adopt Kahn's spelling conventions, "I want" could be rendered *Me kay*, but not *Me wanny*; "I'm going to give you" would be *Me o da-ee,* not *Me gon gibbe;* and "three leaves" would be *dee u-wee,* not *twee weefee.* The Saramaka language *does* contain English cognates (e.g., the word for "tobacco" is – in Kahn's orthography – *tabaku* and "six" is *seekeessee*), and Saramaka men *do* employ the more anglicized coastal language for contact situations, but that does not mean that their speech is mutually intelligible with American baby talk.[3]

Kahn's linguistic fallacy is far from being simply a relic of early twentieth-century innocence. During a summer that I spent in Suriname in the late 1970s, I heard two Saramaka men reminiscing with considerable amusement about how an Afro-American visitor to their village from the United States had recently combined gesticulations with simple English utterances, appropriately simplified for a tropical context, to present his own vision of cross-cultural Brotherhood; with an index finger poking first at the forearm of the Saramaka listener and then at his own, the speaker is said to have insisted repeatedly, "You blackah. Me blackah. We bruddahs."

Morton Kahn's account of bargaining in the bush reflects, in addition to linguistic misunderstandings, the nature of the encounters which allow Maroon art to be transferred into non-Maroon hands. Beginning the bargaining with "cheap knick-knacks" and a claim that insecticides are preferred over perfume, the escalation of prices never threatens to exceed the White Man's admittedly amazing generosity. All that is then required is perseverance. Melville and Frances Herskovits gave another account of bargaining for woodcarvings in the same region of Saramaka.

When we suggested that we might care to acquire the board, the woman became apprehensive. She took up the board, and excusing herself, disappeared with it inside her hut.

"No, no," she called from the house, when her brother went to tell her of the offer we had made for it. "I don't want money for it. I like it. I will not sell it."

The sum we offered was modest enough, but not inconsiderable for this deep interior. We increased it, then doubled our original offer. There was still no wavering on the woman's part, but the offer began to interest her family. Such wealth should not be refused. Bassia Anaisi began to urge her in our behalf.

"With this money you can buy from the white man's city a hammock, and several fine cloths. You should not refuse this."

The old woman took up the discussion, then another sister, and a brother. At last the bassia took us aside, and asked us to leave his sister alone with them.

"We will have a krutu [meeting], and tomorrow you will hear. She is foolish not to sell. But she cares for the board. It is good, too, when a woman loves what her man has carved for her. We will krutu about it, and you shall hear."

Three days passed before the woman's permission was given to dispose of the piece.

"When they see this, your people will know our men can carve!" she exclaimed in a voice which held as much regret as pride. (1934: 281)

Interpretations of the meaning of this art have followed a similar pattern, with Maroons giving in to the determination and apparent power of outside visitors. Here, Western preconceptions about erotic symbolism pervading the life of Primitives have been reinforced by Maroon attitudes toward literacy, which has always been viewed as a powerful and somewhat mystical phenomenon. Although very few Maroons have had the opportunity to learn to read, they have always had contact with people who are literate (plantation bookkeepers, government officials, missionaries, store-owners, employers, etc.), and have great respect for the power it conveys. In principle, they view any marking as potentially communicative, but themselves as untrained in the art of deciphering. It is for this reason that Maroons use blank (undecorated) calabash bowls for ritual purposes. Any carved calabash, they reason, must carry some message, but since they are unable to "read," they do not know what it says; rather than risk offending the spirits for whom a particular ritual is being performed, then, they utilize special unmarked bowls.

Books and articles on Maroon art, however, give no hint that this is the case and present a unanimous vision of symbol-laden motifs. An urban Surinamer named F. H. J. Muntslag wrote a very popular book on Maroon art (1966, 1979), which is essentially a dictionary of motifs and their (alleged) iconographic meaning. One page, for example, illustrates a circular design element, identifying it as *koemba*, a word that in the language of eastern Maroons means "navel." The text explains that "the navel has a very mystical significance to the Bush Negro. Young women are frequently tattooed [sic; their decorations are cicatrizations, not tattooing] around the navel. It is the symbol of erotic love" (1979: 59). Another page presents a crescent-shaped design element with the label *liba,* a word that in the language of central Maroons means "moon"; the text is about fertility and love symbols, projecting onto a more poetic plane the Herskovitses' assertion that it represented "the male member" (1934: 280). How, we asked ourselves in the course of our fieldwork, do Maroons react to this sort of lexicon?

First, Maroons do, in fact, attach labels such as *koemba* and *liba* to design elements, as part of a larger practice of assigning names to everything in the physical environment, from particular cloth patterns and styles of hair-braiding to subtly differentiated varieties of rice and kinds of machetes. For them, however, these names are descriptive labels, not symbolic allusions. A design element known as *koemba* ("navel") is being identified in much the same way that we might use the term "navel" in talking about a kind of orange – that is, without implications of fertility, eroticism, or mystical associations. Claims that a crescent shape has sexual meaning are put in perspective by the reaction of a 60-year-old Maroon who had divided his adult residence between eastern and central Maroon villages. When we reported the Herskovitses' discourse on this motif, the man looked somewhat puzzled and declined to comment, but the next day he returned to ask the question that had been bothering him; with apologies for his ignorance on the matter, he wanted to know whether perhaps *white* men's penises took on a curved and pointed shape like that when erect.

Those writers who include descriptions of their encounters in the field give us some insight into the process by which the Maroons' reputation as symbolism-focused artists maintains its vigor in spite of its lack of fit with the Maroons' intentions and understandings. The Herskovitses, for example, described with frustration being "completely balked by the unwillingness of the Bush Negroes to discuss their carvings" during the first of their two visits (1934: 276), but they also made clear their own refusal to take no for an answer on the matter of symbolic interpretation. On their second trip they prodded Saramakas with explanations of their own invention which their hosts finally accepted, along with enough money to pay for the pieces under discussion (1934: 276–77).

This approach has been adopted by many subsequent visitors to the Suriname interior. Even when Maroons refuse to acquiesce to a proposed interpretation, it is always the person who writes up the report who has the last word. In an article on "folk art in general and that of Suriname in particular," the author's determination to establish a "pagan" meaning for an embroidered cloth hanging in the doorway of a Christian Maroon's house was pursued as follows:

> On inquiry concerning the meaning of [the central] motif, no one gave a direct answer. The women of the village...answered:...'a flower.' As this response was not very enlightening, a very old man was asked. His unsatisfactory answer was the same, 'a flower.' Obviously, people considered it inappropriate to clarify the meaning of this private decoration to foreign visitors, especially when it referred to religious beliefs that were no longer (openly) professed. (De Vries-Hamburger 1959: 109)

Sometimes native exegeses have been reported only as examples of faulty thinking; the prolific student of Maroon culture L. C. van Panhuys, for example, favored this method. One design, he wrote, depicted "a human form, even though the Bush Negroes explained to us...[etc.]." Another represented "what my informant thought to be perhaps... [etc.], but what is, in reality...[etc.]." Regarding a third, a Maroon informant "could give no other explanation than... [etc.]. But if we place the drawing upside down as is done in our illustration, we presume the whole represents...[etc.]" (1928, 1930).

The most recent attempt to establish a lexicon of symbols for Maroon art was carried out by Jean Hurault, who declared his aim as the pursuit of "a better understanding of *the intention of the artists* and of their principles of composition" (1970: 94, emphasis added). He described his method as follows:

We have enumerated and classified the entire body of symbolic and ornamental motifs on these [4000] objects by examining the way in which they are grouped and opposed [in this book's analysis]. This inventory has allowed us to establish with almost absolute certainty the meaning and value of a large number of motifs that have been forgotten by present-day Maroons. (1970: 94)

While Hurault's technique is ostensibly more systematic and scientific than those of van Panhuys or the Herskovitses, it still shares with them a disregard for what *Maroons* have to say about the meaning of their art. They all allow the tradition of interpreting Maroon art to be relatively unperturbed by the understandings and intentions of the Maroons themselves.

The consequences of such cavalier attitudes toward the interpretation of other people's art are varied. When Western authors write books for Western readers, the dissemination of ideas that would puzzle Maroons (such as a pointed crescent representing a penis) rarely creates a problem. But sometimes such misunderstandings make their way into contact situations, and when this happens it is usually members of the Primitive rather than the Civilized world who end up making concessions in order to maintain harmonious relations. An example may illustrate.

In the 1960s, a Saramaka man set up a stall next to the road leading to the Suriname airport, where he carved a variety of objects and offered them for sale to passing tourists. In response to his customers' repeated requests for the symbolic meaning of the pieces they were buying, the artist explained each time that his carvings were intended only to be decorative. Perceiving their dissatisfaction in one case after another, and sometimes being drawn into arguments with them on the subject, he finally gave up and adopted a different strategy. He purchased Muntslag's dictionary of Maroon motifs (the source of the "navel" and "crescent" examples discussed earlier in this chapter), even though he could not understand it because he had never learned to read. He then used its illustrations as models for the motifs in his carvings, and simply showed the book to his customers so they could look up the meaning of their purchases. Through this self-service technique, the man's life became

more tranquil, his profits picked up considerably, the tourists boarded their planes in better spirits, and the myth of a pervasive iconography in the arts of the Maroons circumvented a potentially troubling setback.[4]

The "collecting" of Primitive Art, whether by field anthropologists or by souvenir-buying tourists, often allows discrepancies between the views of artists and patrons to surface (at least momentarily) simply because both parties are involved in the encounter. Once an art object leaves its original setting, however, intercultural dialogue is transformed into intracultural discourse. The criteria for evaluating interpretive claims are then drawn from the realm of related knowledge, as preserved in written form and in Westerners' conceptual understandings. With the fit between native and outside exegesis unavailable for assessment, the fit between the general body of Western knowledge and a new candidate for inclusion in that body becomes the crucial factor.

The mode of presentation for a particular art form from an "exotic" setting is thus often selected on the basis of its compatibility with received ideas, on its lack of abrasion with what an audience already has in mind. Again, a specific example from my own experience will serve to illustrate the point.

As curators of an exhibition of Maroon art that traveled across the United States during 1980–82, Richard Price and I participated in numerous aspects of its organization and promotion. One of these involved the designing of a poster to publicize the exhibit in each of the four cities where it would appear (figure 10.1). We suggested featuring a textile that was both attractively colorful and stylistically representative of the little-known Maroon art of patchwork, and this proposal was greeted with enthusiasm by the designer of the catalog, who even adopted a piece of the same textile for the cover and dust jacket. Once the idea reached the public relations office of the sponsoring institution, however, objections were raised, and it was only after a certain amount of debate that our choice was reluctantly approved.

The problem, we were told, was that the cloth looked too much like a painting by Mondrian to be effective in publicizing an exhibit of Primitive Art. We were strongly urged to select instead a mask or a "fetish."

IF WE DIDN'T TELL YOU IT CAME FROM THE SURINAME RAIN FOREST, YOU'D THINK IT WAS MODERN ART.

It looks like a painting by Mondrian, but it isn't. It's a man's cape, designed and worn by the Suriname Maroons in the 1920's.

The Maroons live in the rain forest of South America, descendants of slaves who escaped from Dutch plantations in the 17th and 18th centuries. And in the rain forest, they created a distinctive art style, drawing upon their African heritage.

Now, the art of the Suriname Maroons is the subject of a special exhibition at the American Museum of Natural History. On view are 350 spectacular pieces: wood and calabash carvings, metalwork, a decorated canoe, carved stools and, of course, their intricately patterned textiles. Not to mention photographs of their daily life. So come see the art of the Maroons. For them, art is more than decoration. It's a way of life.

"AFRO-AMERICAN ARTS FROM THE SURINAME RAIN FOREST." NOW THROUGH JANUARY 24 AT THE AMERICAN MUSEUM OF NATURAL HISTORY, CENTRAL PARK WEST AT 79TH STREET.

Figure 10.1 Ad for American Museum of Natural History exhibit Afro-American Arts from the Suriname Rain Forest, *New York Times*, 6 November 1981, p. C30. Courtesy American Museum of Natural History

Indeed, nothing about this cloth makes the statement: "Primitive Art." The raw materials are not woven fibers stained with local dyes, but rather a cheap trade cotton imported to Suriname and sold to Maroon men during their wage-labor trips to the coastal region. Its colors are not the muted tones of earth, shells, and berries, but rather commercial hues ranging from yellow and blue to red and even shocking pink. Its design is not irregular and free-form, but rather symmetrical and rigidly geometric. And, unlike a mask or "fetish," this patchwork cape appears unlikely to lend itself to symbolic interpretation of motifs or to associations with exotic rituals. It should be no surprise, then, that a public relations officer – thinking about how best to promote a collection of art objects made by people with immodest clothing, scarified faces, pagan beliefs, "talking" drums, polygynous marriages, lineage-based kinship, menstrual taboos, and slash-and-burn tropical gardens – leaned toward a poster that would convey that ensemble of characteristics through a quickly absorbed, unambiguous visual image.

The debate about this cloth's appropriateness as an emblem of Primitive Art came up again over a year later, when a professional agency designed an ad for the exhibition that appeared, full-page, in the *New York Times*. Playing on the same apparent irony of primitive forest dwellers producing a design that resembled the work of one of the Western world's most famous modern painters, the ad writers counted on New Yorkers' familiarity with Mondrian's colorful geometric compositions and left the comparison implicit on the level of visual imagery.

In spite of its single-object focus, however, the ad was a direct forerunner of the riddle-ad that was used some three years later to promote the MOMA's "Primitivism" exhibit. Is it Primitive or is it Modern?

It would be possible to argue that while the first publicist shied away from correcting the stereotype of Primitive Art, the New York ad agency boldly challenged it. Yet it is worth keeping in mind that the primary goal of ads is to sell a product, not to educate; in this context, rather than being contradicted, the stereotype was being exploited to attract the attention of readers. Like the later "Primitivism" ads (and the MOMA show they promoted), the message here was clearly not that Maroon artists are like Mondrian in being individuals who engage in deliberate, dynamic creative expression; despite the detailed documentation available in the exhibition catalog, the man's cape illustrated in the ad is described, not as being designed by a particular Maroon woman, but rather as being "designed and worn by the Suriname Maroons." The point of the comparison, then, is that Maroon art, in spite of being "a way of life" for people living in the rain forest, has nonetheless come up with some objects that bear a bizarre and rather uncanny resemblance to paintings that represent their antithesis in terms of artistic creativity, independence, innovation, and self-awareness. The ad writers hoped New Yorkers would be jolted enough by this unexpected look-alike to want to see the rest of the exhibit. But, like their colleagues who juxtaposed the $80 imitation with the $800 designer top, they certainly did not expect the illustrated cape and the unillustrated Mondrian to be conceptualized by their audience as equivalent except in the sense of an intriguing trompe-l'oeil.

Another aspect of our experience with the Maroon exhibition that shed light on the Western conceptualization of Primitive Art involved reactions to our goal of presenting Maroon artistry in the context of Maroon aesthetic ideas. Descriptions of the exhibit, as well as the text of the accompanying catalog, made explicit our efforts to follow Maroon aesthetic concepts and criteria in the selection of pieces, the arrangement of displays, and the composition of interpretive label texts. That is, our intent was to eschew *both* apparently "pure," or "universal," principles of the sort that, for example, Nelson Rockefeller might have drawn on *and* the social, cultural, and technological criteria that might have structured a traditional anthropology-museum exhibit. We did our best to present Maroon art as Maroon *art* and as *Maroon* art, complete with its makers' well-articulated *aesthetic* principles and consciousness of art *history*, as these had been laid out to us during our several years' residence in the interior of Suriname.

Because the exhibition was mounted in four major museums (in Los Angeles, Dallas, Baltimore, and New York), it had excellent exposure within the United States. But we wanted to make it available also to people from the Caribbean, and especially to Surinamers. An installation in Suriname was ruled out because of the lack of climate controls and security measures adequate to meet the conditions of some of the lenders. The Netherlands, with its Suriname population of over 200,000, was the next logical choice, and we therefore tried very hard to find a Dutch museum that was interested in hosting the exhibit. All of the museums we approached (except one that was unable to raise the necessary funds) rejected the exhibit, but the reasons they gave divided into two very different kinds of discourse.

Art museums in the Netherlands responded that the material in the exhibit was too contextualized to be appropriate for their galleries. Here were objects presented in the midst of photographs, musical recordings, charts of style progressions, and commentary on native aesthetic principles. If we were willing to isolate the pieces from all the ethnographica, they suggested, they would be happy to reconsider their decision. But as the exhibit was currently envisioned, it was "anthropology," not "art."

Anthropology museums – operating in the context of a post-1968 social consciousness – also made a redefinition of the exhibit's aims a precondition for their acceptance of it. It would be necessary to add, they said, extensive information on the current political situation of this Third World republic, on the economic oppression of Maroons, and on the ecological threats to their environment. There would have to be a stronger political message.

Art museums categorized all anthropological contextualization as alien to the aesthetic character of objects; if the displays were intended to show "art," they would need to do so according to Western conventions, which kept aesthetic considerations purely implicit. Anthropology museums categorized the recognition of another society's art historical consciousness and aesthetic sophistication as being alien to the promotion of social liberalism; if the displays were intended to communicate a political message, they would need to do so according to the accepted canons. Both rejected our contention that to *recognize* Maroon objects as *art*, maintained in the context of a legitimate aesthetic system and possessing a history of its own, constituted a radical intellectual and political argument. Neither "art" nor "anthropology" according to then-current definitions, the exhibition never made it to Europe and was seen by no more than a few dozen Surinamers.[5]

The collective message of the Dutch museums is not unrelated to Joseph Alsop's stance that other people simply do not have a concept in any sense equivalent to the one that defines and vertebrates our own art world. What this implies is that objects can be presented either in terms of that concept (in which case they are "art," are best appreciated on the basis of an unmediated visual experience, and have no need of further explanation) or in terms of

their place within a sociocultural context (in which case someone viewing them as art would be guilty of "ethnocentrism"). If one subscribes to this division, the question then becomes, as an *African Arts* editorial put it, whether we respond to a particular set of objects as Art or merely from a sense of "social curiosity."

It may be, however, that a merger of the "art" and the "anthropology" of non-Western cultural expression, would require little more on our part than a less proprietorial attitude toward the idea of aesthetic sensitivity.

Afterword

In a discussion of Arthur Danto's concept of an "artworld," B. R. Tilghman considers the hypothetical possibility of a world in which art is isolated from all of the related activities that we expect to cluster about it.

> We can imagine a tribe that draws and paints, plays music, and recites poetry, but keeps its talk about it all to a minimum. Instruction is carried out mostly by example along with occasional comments such as "make this line thicker." "Play it like this," and so on. There are no schools of criticism, no reviews in the papers, and certainly no art history. People nevertheless take it all very seriously and are most attentive to what they see and hear; they react with gestures and facial expressions, and sometimes shift their preferences with their moods. (1984: 62–63)

In this nonartworld, not only are newspaper reviews and art schools unknown, but even evaluative language itself. In spite of their painting and music and poetry, Tilghman's hypothetical tribal beings call on gestures and facial expressions to convey their aesthetic reactions, which are, in any case, little more than the product of shifting moods. The tribal world in this example is explicitly fictional, purposefully created to advance a logical philosophical argument about the nature of art. But it has close cousins on other shelves of our libraries, where the same image sheds its philosophical function and assumes the appearance of descriptive prose. Tribal peoples *become*, in those pages, faceless producers of art who cannot appreciate or assess or review or document their work except through grunts and shrugs. Their world is imagined to be less hypothesized than "documented" as having neither history nor aesthetics, neither scholarship nor connoisseurship, neither humor nor irony.

A classical Western education offers little protection against the seductive attractions of this image, which casts such flattering light on our own higher sensibilities. E. H. Gombrich's elaboration of the attributes of Tribal Society adds yet another example to those already cited in earlier chapters, authenticating for current and future generations of readers stereotypic images of the Third World as a land of ignorance, confusion, and childishness. In a chapter that makes repeated use of the word "strange," the latest edition of Gombrich's *The Story of Art* explains that

> If most works of these civilizations look weird and unnatural to us, the reason lies probably in the ideas they are meant to convey. . . . Negroes in Africa are sometimes as vague as little children about what is a picture and what is real . . . they even believe that certain animals are related to them in some fairy-tale manner . . . [they] live in a kind of dream-world. . . . It is very much as if children played at pirates or detectives till they no longer knew where playacting ended and reality began. But with children there is always the grown-up world about them, the people who tell them, "Don't be so noisy", or "It is nearly bed-time". For the savage there is no such other world to spoil the illusion. (1966: ch.1, "Strange Beginnings")

Gombrich illustrates his point by the reactions that "we" and "they" would experience to a scrawled doodle of a face: "To us all this is a joke, but to the native it is not." He thus corroborates William Rubin's analysis of the difference between look-alike sculptures by Alexander Calder and his counterpart from New Guinea. From this perspective, the Primitive World is a sober place indeed, where doodled faces and sculpted branches are perceived as living monsters. No wonder, then, that its inhabitants have no time or inclination for such pleasurable pursuits as aesthetic discussion, intellectual history, or art-for-art's sake, preoccupied as they are with chasing spirits and demons from their midst, with no grown-ups to remind them that it is all just a game.

It is rarely necessary to mention explicitly the racial component of this other world. Like Leonard Bernstein, we can express warm pride in our Persian princes, conveying benevolence and admiration while maintaining our cultural boundary and the position of dominance that it protects.

At a time when revisionist art history is reassessing the traditional isolation of that discipline's subject matter from the fabric of social and cultural life, and at a time when anthropology is delving more and more insistently into the nature of culture in modern industrial societies, we are also at a time when our qualitative division of world art into "ours" and "theirs" stands ready for a serious reappraisal. A part of that change is already underway, as distinguished institutions such as the Metropolitan Museum of Art and the Museum of Modern Art invite into their galleries selected Primitive Masterpieces. But their doors have been opened more willingly to the objects themselves than to the aesthetic sensibilities that gave them birth. The final, and more meaningful, step will be to recognize that the vision of Western art lovers is neither more nor less conditioned by cultural ideas – both prejudices and insights – than that of their counterparts in other societies and to follow through on our newly invigorated appreciation of "exotic" art by acknowledging the cultural diversity, intellectual vitality, and aesthetic integrity of its creators.

Afterword to the Second Edition

First the good news. In the dozen or so years since this book was written, the discourse surrounding what, for purposes of discussion, we call "art" has opened up noticeably to perspectives outside of its traditional territory. A determinedly optimistic reading of these developments might run roughly as follows.

In the field of "fine" arts, the complex workings – social, cultural, economic, political – that give structure, texture, and (contested or uncontested) meaning to the more traditional matter of art objects and their collective history have been moving into greater prominence. Both scholarly and popular writings on art have been engaging in the scrutiny of museum ethics, curatorial strategies, auction politics, market dynamics, and collecting agendas.

Even the very sensitive possibility that ethno-centrism lurks in the foundations of the edifice of connoisseurship has become more widely recognized. Artworks once viewed as visual entities set into more or less elaborate wooden borders are now being framed in a completely different sense, as contextualized productions undergoing contextualized readings. Setting art objects, artists' biographies, and the evolution of stylistic sequences more forcefully in the context of perceptions conditioned by social and cultural factors brings them closer to long-standing anthropological concerns and interests, and acts to erode the lingering temptation (stronger in some commentators than others) to view art history as the pristine, apolitical study of aesthetic forms. And sacred territories of art historical scholarship, where original works authenticated by erudite connoisseurship once held pride of place, are being quietly invaded by a growing interest in copies, fakes, appropriations, and derivative forms.

Approaches to art from beyond the Euro-cultural orbit have also undergone significant changes over the past decade or two. Especially pivotal has been a diminished focus on cultural isolates, a by-product of the tendency for today's anthropologists to set the societies and cultures they study in broader fields of vision than did their predecessors of the mid-twentieth century. While scholars once strained to discern the stylistic essences of particular arts in particular cultures, they are now directing their gaze more frequently toward the doorways where artistic and aesthetic ideas jostle each other in their passage from one cultural setting to the next. While the site of artistic production was once located in lineages of convention within bounded communities, it now spreads into the global arena, pulling in players from every corner of the world, from every kind of society, and from every chamber of the artworld's vast honey-comb. And while the emphasis was once on abstracting back from an overlay of modernity to discover uncorrupted artistic traditions (think of Franz Boas holding up a blanket to block out the two-story houses behind the Kwakiutl natives he was filming for the anthropological record, as captured in the Odyssey series video devoted to this father of American anthropology), modernization is now seen as lying at the heart of the enterprise,

providing a springboard for explorations of cultural creativity and self-affirmation.

Not surprisingly, these shifts are being accompanied by a marked, if gradual, rapprochement among the various sectors of the popular and scholarly art world. In museums, the most visible evidence has been an explosion, over the past couple of decades, of exhibitions integrating anthropological and art historical issues and scholarship, juxtaposing arts from previously segregated categories, and calling attention to the defining (and redefining) power of display context.[6] Community museums, with vigorous local participation, have sprung up in unprecedented numbers, providing active loci for grassroots cultural creativity and self-representation. Rights of interpretation are under lively discussion; cultural authority is being renegotiated; the privileged status of long established canons is under attack; and museum acquisition policies designed to maximize the preservation of data and the growth of scientific knowledge are being contested by more ethically-focused debates aimed at responsible de-accessioning and repatriation. The legal definitions of both cultural property and artistic authorship in a video-and-computer age of sampling and photoshop have begun to be recognized as a thorny bundle deeply entangled in multicultural ideologies and highly inflated economic stakes.[7]

The social/cultural atmosphere created by these changes has, among other things, brought the specific critiques made in this book more frequently into mainstream art critical discourse. Associations that have long relegated "primitive art" to a world of irrationality, superstition, voodooesque rituals in flickering torchlight, and symbolic meanings linked to fertility and witchcraft still pop up in texts authored by variably informed commentators, but their frequency is diminishing significantly, giving way to a less generalizing gaze that recognizes the staggering diversity of art worlds in the non-Eurocultural universe. Exhibitions of works owned by particular collectors continue to be mounted, implicitly reinforcing the logic critiqued in chapter 7 [in Price 1989] that "pedigree" deserves to trump "signature" when aesthetic merit depends on the eye of the connoisseur rather than the sensitivities of the artist, but at the same time it is becoming increasingly common to run across arguments that, as Roslyn Adele Walker puts it, "Anonymous Has a Name" (1994), which confront head-on stereotypic notions of generic natives plodding mindlessly in the art-producing footsteps of their communal ancestors. We're also witnessing, across the board, a growing tendency for the hierarchies that assigned distinct roles (and value) to fine and folk, art and craft, primitive and modern, high and low to give way to an investigation of these categories' interpenetrations and a deconstruction of the categories themselves. Concern with the ethics of cultural ownership is also moving center-stage, thanks largely to the rising volume of voices coming from third- and fourth-world populations, cultural studies programs, and spectators of the postmodern scene from the fields of anthropology, literature, history, philosophy, economics, and political science.[8]

Although these changes are extremely multifaceted, they all operate in the direction of breaking down long-established barriers – barriers between disciplinary perspectives, between geographical focuses, between hierarchized settings, between elite and popular media, and more. While much of the initiative for the reorientation has taken place in North America (Canada at least as much as the United States), Europe has shown signs of shifting along similar lines. To cite just a few indications: Paris's global-art extravaganza, *Magiciens de la Terre*, constituted a magisterial (if flawed, according to many of its reviewers) effort to embrace the "arts of the world" as a single conceptual whole (Musée d'Art Contemporain 1989; see also Michaud 1989), and the more recent debates sparked by Jacques Chirac's agenda for establishing a museum of *"arts premiers"* have produced thoughtful reflections on the place of premier/primitive arts in the supremely civilized setting of central Paris (for example, Vaillant and Viatte 1999, Taffin 2000; see also Price 2001). In the Netherlands, an exhibition of "Art from Another World" in Rotterdam brought together "high" and "low" art from non-Western settings in 1988; scholars have been asking hard questions about the political and ethical dimensions of collecting practices and museum displays (for example, Bouquet 1999, Corbey 2000, Lavreysen 1998, Leyten

1995, Leyten and Damen 1993), and a museum of Aboriginal Art has just opened (March 2001) in the city of Utrecht. In Austria, a special issue of the *Archiv für Völkerkunde* published an important collection of 32 essays on "Museums of Ethnology on the Eve of the Third Millennium" that covered developments throughout the world, from Greenland, Rome, St. Petersburg, and New York to Australia, South Africa, Mexico, and Kuala Lumpur. In England, Routledge has been bringing out one volume after another devoted to the same series of issues (for example, Greenberg, Ferguson, and Nairne 1996, Barringer and Flynn 1998). In Germany, a collection of essays on "ethnographic and modern" art spans commentators from Boas to Clifford (Prussat and Till 2001). And in Switzerland, a recent exhibit-cum-book focused attention on contact zones, cultural strategies behind today's art critical discourse, the international traffic in art, the classificatory transfer of objects from "ethnography" to "art," and the overlaps in categories of art such as *contemporain, appliqué, populaire, classique, pompier, pauvre, transgressif* and *convenu* (Gonseth, Hainard, and Kaehr 1999). Around the globe, the art of Australian aborigines has been providing a testing ground for every legal and ethical dilemma in the book, supplying the media with a steady stream of news items involving issues of ethnic identity, cultural property, artistic authenticity, and market concerns.[9]

All this complicates the cultural geography of art, the hierarchy of traditional art scholarship, and the division between producers and commentators. It means, for example, that while the "affinities" between the "tribal" and the "modern" could be analyzed in terms of a comfortably agreed-upon definition of a "here" (homes, galleries, museums, and studios in Europe and North America) and a "there" (remote settlements and "exotic" cultures), with objects being imported to the former on the basis of the importers' criteria, artworld traffic is now recognized as running along a much busier thoroughfare. We're forced to notice that it's not a one-way route and that it's not just the objects that are traveling. While Picasso's exploitation of African masks as inspiration for the prostitutes in *Les Demoiselles d'Avignon* may have caused European art history to turn a corner in the early years of the twentieth century, today's appropriative possibilities are being defined in more multifaceted terms. Faith Ringgold's *The Picnic at Giverny* (an acrylic-and-fabric story quilt), for example, casts Picasso as the nude model in a gender-reversal of Manet's *Le Déjeuner sur l'Herbe*, set in the garden of Monet's *Nymphéas*, with ten (fully clothed) American women artists and writers having a picnic and discussing the role of women in art. And as bell hooks has noted, in the hands of Jean-Michel Basquiat, who took from Pollock, de Kooning, and Rauschenberg on the one end and "the guys painting on the trains" on the other, a depiction of "him and Andy Warhol duking it out in boxing attire is not as innocent and playful as it appears to be" (1995: 36, 42).[10]

As the "traffic in culture" continues to erode the distinctions once segregating first- and third- or fourth-artworlds, "high" and "low" genres, producers and critics, and even anthropologists and art historians, lanes are being opened up in many exciting directions. Anthropologists are reading art historical literature and art historians are reading anthropology, artists are increasingly demanding an interpretive role, and the influx of voices from previously underrepresented groups is gaining momentum.

And yet, if the goal is to liberate the study of art from its Eurocentric shell, much still remains to be done. My own reading of the situation suggests that the most underdeveloped aspect of artworld globalization lies less in the realm of art than in the realm of art criticism. Supplying the product is one thing, but having a say over what it represents (aesthetically, iconographically, referentially, historically) is quite another. Making the case for African American art, bell hooks cited a *Time* magazine cover story called "Black Renaissance: African American Artists Are Truly Free At Last." She lamented that the article

assessed the development and public reception of works by black artists without engaging, in any way, the ideas and perspectives of African American scholars who write about the visual arts. The blatant absence of this critical perspective serves to highlight the extent to which black scholars who write about art, specifically about work created by African American artists, are ignored by the mainstream. Ironically, the insistence in this essay that the "freedom" of black artists can be measured solely

by the degree to which the work of individual artists receives attention in the established white-dominated art world exposes the absence of such freedom. (1995: 110–11)

Carrying this observation further from home territory, and setting it in a more explicitly anthropological context, I would second Clifford Geertz's argument that "art talk" has been reported as rarely as it has for non-Western societies, not because people in such societies don't engage in it, but because they frequently do it through forms that are different from those of Western art criticism (1983: 94–120). If we wish to tune in to the aesthetic frameworks of other cultures, we need to make a special effort to push aside our everyday understandings of how art is talked or written about and open ourselves to different modes of discourse. Often this means softening the distinction between artist and critic and paying closer attention to what art producers themselves have to say. And once we begin to listen, the commentary is abundantly available, as an eye-opening complement to European traditions of art criticism, both academic and journalistic.

The rapid globalization of recent years – from migrations of work forces and the proliferation of tourism to the border-crashing forces of the Internet or CNN's soundbite coverage of what it calls "Hotspots" – brings the absurdity of a monovocal Eurocentric criticism into full view and presents exciting new challenges for intercultural conversations about the nature and meaning of art in all its varied settings. We are profoundly enriched by being able to read the interpretive texts bordering Faith Ringgold's acrylic and strip-cloth story quilts,... by being able to talk to inhabitants of the Amazonian rain forest about the meaning of the dances they are performing on the Washington Mall,... by being able to view Maori arts from New Zealand as presented by a tribal elder formally trained in traditional Western art history,... by being able to visit an exhibition of Malaysian, Nigerian, Filipino, and other "Black British" art from London conceptualized by Caribbean-born curators based in New York,... and by being able to study Romare Bearden's analysis of compositional principles, in which paintings of the Italian Renaissance are seen through the eyes of an artist equally familiar with the one in Harlem.[11]

The need to redefine the scaffolding of art critical discourse along more multicultural lines is being argued in countless outposts of the international art world. In a consistently insightful Jamaican journal called *Small Axe*, for example, Annie Paul has cited Gerardo Mosquera's distinction between "curating cultures" and "curated cultures," and pointed the finger at a curatoriat that invests in the construction of what it passes off as "universal values" on the basis of Eurocentric and even "Manhattan-centric" criteria (1999: 66). She writes:

> High modern avatars of art have gone through many transformations this century, always mirroring Europe's own response to the discovery of extra-European forms of life in the Universe. One such has been the idea of art as the release of messages from the unconscious, automatic art as it were, simple and immediate no matter whether the artist comes from the most technologically sophisticated society or the most primitive. In this particular narrative, the primitive artist represents the noble savage, a superior sensibility trapped in prehistoric circumstances. In opposition to this is the figure of the modern artist, the savage noble who can psychically tap into the collective unconscious by courting the irrational and systematically flouting convention. Both are based on a concept of the artist as a "primal" creature.... These two groups are locked in a strategic embrace by Jamaican art history. (1999: 62)

Paul's depiction of the artist (whether primitive or modern) as a primal creature with special gifts for tapping into the unconscious is very close to the one I found in the heads of many of the French and American art collectors I interviewed in the 1980s. The effect that this pervasive conception has had on art criticism (which is, as bell hooks understands so well, where the real power lies) has been to keep artists locked up in their studios, painting or sculpting like the silent natives of the stereotype critiqued by Clifford Geertz (1983: 97), or the Baule artist ventriloquized by Susan Vogel (see chapter 2 [in Price 1989]), rather than entering the discourse.

But we're clearly turning a corner, and there are promising indications that the History of Art, as a Western-authored metanarrative, is being challenged with growing success by a multiplicity of alternative frameworks. In place of the comprehensive texts familiar to anyone who's taken a course in introductory art history, where an impeccably credentialed Ph.D. narrates a unilinear evolution from cave paintings to Andy Warhol, we are now beginning to discern at least a Table of Contents for a multi-authored anthology of art histories that reflects and celebrates the variety of ways people around the world enrich their lives through artistic creativity – and, perhaps even more importantly, the variety of discourses they call on to think and talk about it.

NOTES

1   *Djuka: The Bush Negroes of Dutch Guiana* (New York: Viking, 1931), p. 4.
2   For discussion of art and exchange, see S. Price 1984; for further illustrations of Maroon art, see also Hurault 1970 and Price and Price 1980.
3   Kahn (1931) mentions in passing that "Djukas," as he calls Saramakas, also speak another language, but minimizes its importance by contrasting it with what he claims is their "ordinary tongue" and describing it as a device for the preservation of tribal lore, historical accounts of slave rebellions, and other carefully guarded secrets. His discussion of language, such as it is, also comes at the end of his book (chap. 10, Djuka Talk), long after the image of the baby-talking native has settled into the consciousness of his readers. (Given its popular reputation for simplicity, it is perhaps worth pointing out that the very real complexities of the Saramaka language have come to constitute a major focus of historical and theoretical linguistics, spawning numerous recent articles and books.)
4   Vladimir Nabokov captured the spirit of this aggressive faith in the sexual symbolism of human behavior, drawing his illustration from its child-psychology incarnation – an only lightly modified variant of its presence in Primitive Art studies.

> Victor was a problem child insofar as he refused to be one. From the Winds' [his psychiatrist-parents'] point of view, every male child had an ardent desire to castrate

his father and a nostalgic urge to re-enter his mother's body. But Victor did not reveal any behavior disorder, did not pick his nose, did not suck his thumb, was not even a nail biter. Dr. Wind, with the object of eliminating what he, a radiophile, termed "the static of personal relationship," had his impregnable child tested psychometrically at the Institute by a couple of outsiders, young Dr. Stern and his smiling wife (I am Louis and this is Christina). But the results were either monstrous or nil: the seven-year-old subject scored on the so-called Godunov Drawing-of-the-Animal Test a sensational mental age of seventeen, but on being given a Fairview Adult Test promptly sank to the mentality of a two-year-old. How much care, skill, inventiveness have gone to devise those marvelous techniques! What a shame that certain patients refuse to co-operate! There is, for instance, the Kent-Rosanoff Absolutely Free Association Test, in which little Joe or Jane is asked to respond to a Stimulus Word, such as table, duck, music, sickness, thickness, low, deep, long, happiness, fruit, mother, mushroom. There is the charming Bievre Interest-Attitude Game (a blessing on rainy afternoons), in which little Sam or Ruby is asked to put a little mark in front of the things about which he or she feels sort of fearful, such as dying, falling, dreaming, cyclones, funerals, father, night, operation, bedroom, bathroom, converge, and so forth; there is the Augusta Angst Abstract Test in which the little one (*das Kleine*) is made to express a list of terms ("groaning," "pleasure," "darkness") by means of unlifted lines. And there is, of course, the Doll Play, in which Patrick or Patricia is given two identical rubber dolls and a cute little bit of clay which Pat must fix on one of them before he or she starts playing, and oh the lovely doll house, with so many rooms and lots of quaint miniature objects, including a chamber pot no bigger than a cupule, and a medicine chest, and a poker, and a double bed, and even a pair of teeny-weeny rubber gloves in the kitchen, and you may be as mean as you like and do anything you want to Papa doll if you think he is beating Mama doll when they put out the lights in the bedroom. But bad

Victor would not play with Lou and Tina, ignored the dolls, struck out all the listed words (which was against the rules), and made drawings that had no subhuman significance whatever. (1957: 90–91)

In a sense, what distinguishes Saramaka artists from little Victor is nothing more than their perceptiveness of outsiders' expectations for their psyches, plus a rather cynical willingness to play along, upon occasion, with the game.

5   The resistance to presenting art in nonestablished niches is not limited to Primitive Art. According to a journalistic account, the National Museum of Women in the Arts, which opened in Washington in 1987, was originally opposed by feminists because it did not propose to cover women's social history and by other critics because it segregated women's art from that of men. This project, too, was inspired by a wish to recognize the achievements of artists who had been subjected to more than their fair share of anonymity (Conroy 1987).

6   Reactions to these exhibits have often been more stimulating than the exhibits themselves. Witness the tidal wave of discussion that came on the heels of the "Primitivism" show at New York's Museum of Modern Art in 1984, "Into the Heart of Africa" at Toronto's Royal Ontario Museum in 1989 (for an overview, see Butler 1999), and "Africa: The Art of a Continent" at London's Royal Academy in 1995. K. Anthony Appiah's reflections on Asante goldweights, inspired by this last exhibit but fueled by memories of his childhood in Ghana, represent to my mind the best of this rich literature (1997).

7   Appearing the same year as the present book's original publication, Jeanette Greenfield's *The Return of Cultural Treasures* and Phyllis Messenger's edited volume, *The Ethics of Collecting Cultural Property*, heralded an attention to cultural property rights that was to develop into a pervasive wave of soul-searching on the part of anthropologists, museum personnel, and others interested in Western practices for collecting artifacts in third- and fourth-world societies.

8 For an update of the specific example presented here, see S. and R. Price 1999.

9 The bibliography of works reflecting post-1990 perspectives on the representation of art and culture in "civilized places" is extensive enough to make any selection both partial and arbitrary, but a reasonable English-language starter list might include Clifford 1997, Coombes 1994, Coote and Shelton 1992, Dilworth 1996, Errington 1998, Henderson and Kaeppler 1996, Hilden 2000, Jonaitis 1991, Karp and Lavine 1991, Karp, Kreamer, and Lavine 1992, Kirshenblatt-Gimblett 1998, MacClancy 1997, Marcus and Myers 1995, Pearce 1993, Phillips and Steiner 1999, R. and S. Price 1992 and 1995, Root 1995, Schildkrout and Keim 1998, Sherman and Rogoff 1994, Simpson 1996, Thomas 1999, Tucker 1992, and Ziff and Rao 1997. (See also Price 1999.)

10 For more on such appropriations, see Tawadros 1996.

11 See Cameron et al. 1998, R. and S. Price 1994, Mead 1984, Beauchamp-Byrd et al. 1997, Bearden and Holty 1969; these references are but a sampling from a much larger reservoir.

REFERENCES

Appiah, K. Anthony. 1997. "The Arts of Africa." *New York Review of Books*, 24 April, pp. 46–51.

Barringer, Tim, and Tom Flynn (eds.) 1998. *Colonialism and the Object: Empire, Material Culture and the Museum*. New York and London: Routledge.

Bearden, Romare, and Carl Holty. 1969. *The Painter's Mind: A Study of the Relations of Structure and Space in Painting*. New York: Crown Publishers.

Beauchamp-Byrd, Mora J., and M. Franklin Sirmans (eds.) 1998. *Transforming the Crown: African, Asian & Caribbean Artists in Britain 1966–1996*. New York: Caribbean Cultural Center.

Bouquet, Mary (ed.) 1999. "Academic Anthropology and the Museum: Back to the Future." Special issue (#34) of *Focaal: Tijdscrift voor Antropologie* (Utrecht, Netherlands).

Butler, Shelley Ruth. 1999. *Contested Representations: Revisiting* Into the Heart of Africa. Amsterdam: Gordon and Breach.

Cameron, Dan, et al. 1998. *Dancing at the Louvre: Faith Ringgold's French Collection and Other Story Quilts*. Berkeley: University of California Press.

Clifford, James. 1997. *Routes: Travel and Translation in the Late Twentieth Century*. Cambridge: Harvard University Press.

Coombes, Annie E. 1994. *Reinventing Africa: Museums, Material Culture and Popular Imagination*. New Haven: Yale University Press.

Coote, Jeremy, and Anthony Shelton (eds.) 1992. *Anthropology, Art, and Aesthetics*. Oxford: Clarendon Press.

Corbey, Raymond. 2000. *Tribal Art Traffic: A Chronicle of Taste, Trade and Desire in Colonial and Post-Colonial Times*. Amsterdam: Royal Tropical Institute.

Counter, S. Allen, Jr., and David L. Evans. N.d. "The Bush Afro-Americans of Surinam and French Guiana: The Connecting Link." Pamphlet.

——. 1981. *I Sought My Brother: An Afro-American Reunion*. Cambridge, Mass.: MIT Press.

Dark, Philip, J. C. 1954. *Bush Negro Art: An African Art in the Americas*. London: Tiranti.

De Vries-Hamburger, L. 1959. "Over Volkskunst in het Algemeen en die van Suriname in het Bijzonder." *Kultuurpatronen* 1: 106–10.

Dilworth, Leah. 1996. *Imagining Indians in the Southwest: Persistent Visions of a Primitive Past*. Washington, DC: Smithsonian Institution Press.

Errington, Shelly. 1998. *The Death of Authentic Primitive Art and Other Tales of Progress*. Berkeley: University of California Press.

Geertz, Clifford. 1983. *Local Knowledge: Further Essays in Interpretive Anthropology*. New York: Basic Books.

Gombrich, E. H. 1966. *The Story of Art*. 11th ed., revised and enlarged. London: Phaidon Press.

Gonseth, Marc-Olivier, Jacques Hainard, and Roland Kaehr (eds.) 1999. *L'art c'est l'art*. Neuchâtel: Musée d'Ethnographie.

Greenberg, Reesa, Bruce W. Ferguson, and Sandy Nairne (eds.) 1996. *Thinking about Exhibitions*. London: Routledge.

Greenfield, Jeanette. 1989. *The Return of Cultural Treasures.* Cambridge: Cambridge University Press.

Henderson, Amy, and Adrienne L. Kaeppler (eds.) 1997. *Exhibiting Dilemmas: Issues of Representation at the Smithsonian.* Washington, DC: Smithsonian Institution Press.

Herskovits, Melville J. 1930. "Bush Negro Art." *Arts* 17(51): 25–37, 48–49.

Herskovits, Melville J., and Frances S. Herskovits. 1934. *Rebel Destiny: Among the Bush Negroes of Dutch Guiana.* New York: McGraw-Hill.

Hilden, Patricia Penn. 2000. "Race for Sale: Narratives of Possession in Two 'Ethnic' Museums." *The Drama Review* 44(3):11–36.

hooks, bell. 1995. *Art on My Mind: Visual Politics.* New York: The New Press.

Hurault, Jean. 1970. *Africains de Guyane: La vie matérielle et l'art des Noirs réfugiés de Guyane.* Paris and the Hague: Mouton.

Jonaitis, Aldona (ed.) 1991. *Chiefly Feasts: The Enduring Kwakiutl Potlatch.* New York: American Museum of Natural History; Seattle: University of Washington Press.

Kahn, Morton C. 1931. *Djuka: The Bush Negroes of Dutch Guiana.* New York: Viking Press.

——. 1939. "Africa's Lost Tribes in South America: An On-the-Spot Account of Blood-Chilling African Rites of 200 Years Ago Preserved Intact in the Jungles of South America by a Tribe of Runaway Slaves." *Natural History* 43: 209–15, 232.

——. 1954. "Little Africa in America: The Bush Negroes." *Americas* 6(10): 6–8, 41–43.

Karp, Ivan, and Steven D. Lavine (eds.) 1991. *Exhibiting Cultures: The Poetics and Politics of Museum Display.* Washington, DC: Smithsonian Institution Press.

Karp, Ivan, Christine Mullen Kreamer, and Steven D. Lavine (eds.) 1992. *Museums and Communities: The Politics of Public Culture.* Washington, DC: Smithsonian Institution Press.

Kirshenblatt-Gimblett, Barbara. 1998. *Destination Culture: Tourism, Museums, and Heritage.* Berkeley: University of California Press.

Lavreysen, Ria. 1998. *Global encounters in the world of art: Collisions of tradition and modernity.* Amsterdam: Royal Tropical Institute.

Leyten, Harrie (ed.) 1995. *Illicit traffic in cultural property: museums against pillage.* Amsterdam: Royal Tropical Institute; Bamako: Musée National du Mali.

Leyten, Harrie, and Bibi Damen (eds.) 1993. *Art, anthropology, and the modes of representation: Museums and contemporary non-Western art.* Amsterdam: Royal Tropical Institute.

MacClancy, Jeremy (ed.) 1997. *Contesting Art: Art, Politics and Identity in the Modern World.* Oxford: Berg.

Marcus, George E., and Fred R. Myers (eds.) 1995. *The Traffic in Culture: Refiguring Art and Anthropology.* Berkeley: University of California Press.

Mead, Sidney Moko (ed.) 1984. *Te Maori: Maori Art from New Zealand Collections.* New York: Harry N. Abrams.

Messenger, Phyllis Mauch (ed.) 1989. *The Ethics of Collecting Cultural Property: Whose Culture? Whose Property?* Albuquerque: University of New Mexico Press.

Michaud, Yves (ed.) 1989. *Magiciens de la Terre.* Special issue of *Les Cahiers du Musée National d'Art Moderne* no. 28.

Muntslag, F. H. J. 1966. *Tembe: Surinaamse Houtsnijkunst.* Amsterdam: Prins Bernhard Fonds.

——. 1979. *Paw a Paw Dindoe: Surinaamse Houtsnijkunst.* Paramaribo: VACO.

Musée National d'Art Moderne. 1989. *Magiciens de la Terre.* Paris: Centre Georges Pompidou.

Paul, Annie. 1999. "Uninstalling the Nation: The Dilemma of Contemporary Jamaican Art." *Small Axe* 6:57–78.

Pearce, Susan M. 1993. *Museums, Objects, and Collections: A Cultural Study.* Washington, DC: Smithsonian Institution Press.

Phillips, Ruth B., and Christopher B. Steiner (eds.) 1999. *Unpacking Culture: Art and Commodity in Colonial and Postcolonial Worlds.* Berkeley: University of California Press.

Price, Richard. 1970. "Saramaka Woodcarving: The Development of an Afroamerican Art. *Man* 5: 363–78.

——. 1976. *The Guiana Maroons: A Historical and Bibliographical Introduction.* Baltimore: Johns Hopkins University Press.

Price, Richard, and Sally Price. 1992. *Equatoria.* New York: Routledge.

—— 1994. *On The Mall.* Bloomington: University of Indiana Press.

—— 1995. *Enigma Variations*. Cambridge: Harvard University Press.

Price, Sally. 1982/1988. "Sexism and the Construction of Reality: An Afro-American Example." *American Ethnologist* 10: 460–76. Reprinted in Johnnetta B. Cole (ed.), *Anthropology for the Nineties*, pp. 126–48. New York: Free Press.

——. 1984. *Co-wives and Calabashes*. Ann Arbor: University of Michigan Press.

——. 1986. "L'esthétique et le temps: commentaire sur l'histoire orale de l'art." *Ethnologie* 82(98–99): 215–25.

——. 1989. *Primitive Art in Civilized Places*, 2. Chicago: Chicago University Press.

—— 1999. Representations of Art and Arts of Representation. *American Anthropologist* 101:841–44.

—— 2001. Museums of the World à la française. *American Anthropologist* 103.

Price, Sally, and Richard Price. 1980. *Afro-American Arts of the Suriname Rain Forest*. Berkeley: University of California Press.

——. 1999. *Maroon Arts: Cultural Vitality in the African Diaspora*. Boston: Beacon Press.

Prussat, Margrit, and Wolfgang Till (eds.) 2001. *"Neger im Louvre": Texte zu Kunstethnographie und moderner Kunst*. Dresden: Verlag der Kunst.

Root, Deborah. 1995. *Cannibal Culture: Art, Appropriation, and the Commodification of Difference*. Boulder, CO: Westview Press.

Schildkrout, Enid, and Curtis A. Keim (eds.) 1998. *The Scramble for Art in Central Africa*. Cambridge: Cambridge University Press.

Sherman, Daniel J., and Irit Rogoff (eds.) 1994. *Museum Culture: Histories, Discourses, Spectacles*. Minneapolis: University of Minnesota Press.

Simpson, Moira G. 1996. *Making Representations: Museums in the Post-Colonial Era*. London: Routledge.

Taffin, Dominique (ed.) 2000. *Du musée colonial au musée des cultures du monde*. Paris: Maisonneuve et Larose.

Tawadros, Gilane. 1996. "Beyond the Boundary: The Work of Three Black Women Artists in Britain." In Houston A. Baker, Jr., Manthia Diawara, and Ruth H. Lindeborg (eds.), *Black British Cultural Studies: A Reader*, pp. 240–277. Chicago: University of Chicago Press.

Thomas, Nicholas. 1999. *Possessions: Indigenous Art / Colonial Culture*. New York: Thames and Hudson.

Tilghman, B. R. 1984. *But Is It Art? The Value of Art and the Temptation of Theory*. Oxford: Basil Blackwell.

Tucker, Marcia (ed.) 1992. *Different Voices: A Social, Cultural, and Historical Framework for Change in the American Art Museum*. New York: Association of Art Museum Directors.

Vaillant, Émilia, and Germain Viatte (eds.) 1999. *Le musée et les cultures du monde*. Paris: École nationale du patrimoine.

Van Panhuys, L. C. 1928. "Quelques ornements des nègres des bois de la Guyane Néerlandaise." *Proceedings of the International Congress of Americanists* 22: 231–74.

——. 1934. "African Customs and Beliefs Preserved for Two Centuries in the Interior of Dutch Guiana." *Proceedings of the International Congress of Anthropological and Ethnological Sciences* 1: 247–48.

Tilghman, B. R. 1984. *But Is It Art? The Value of Art and the Temptation of Theory*. Oxford: Basil Blackwell.

Vandercook, John Womack. 1926. "We Find an African Tribe in the South American Jungle." *Mentor* 14(3): 19–22.

Volders, J. L. 1966. *Bouwkunst in Suriname: Driehonderd Jaren Nationale Architectuur*. Hilversum: G. van Saanen.

Walker, Roslyn Adele. 1994. "Anonymous Has a Name: Olowe of Ise." In Rowland Abiodun, Henry J. Drewal, and John Pemberton III (eds.), *The Yoruba Artist: New Theoretical Perspectives on African Arts*, pp. 90–106. Washington, DC: Smithsonian Institution Press.

Ziff, Bruce, and Pratima V. Rao (eds.) 1997. *Borrowed Power: Essays on Cultural Appropriation*. New Brunswick, NJ: Rutgers University Press.

11

Oriental Antiquities/Far Eastern Art

Craig Clunas

When I was fourteen I came to London with my father. We were on the way to Cambridge, where I was to investigate the possibility of studying Chinese. I visited the Victoria and Albert Museum for the first time, and there in a large room titled "Far Eastern Art" I was enthralled to see a great carved lacquer seat, labeled "Throne of the Emperor Ch'ien-lung." While the uniformed warder looked or pretended to look away, I knelt down and put my forehead to the black linoleum in homage.

These are not the tales curators tell. Their role in maintaining objects (in both senses of the word) demands that they suppress such embarrassing personal engagements and secret fetishisms, which threaten to reopen the space between the viewer and the artifact. The throne was there, and the Emperor of China sat on it. Now it is here, and you the visitor view it. Do not ask how it got here, or where it was from 1770 to now; that does not matter. You are here to engage with "China," not with "Britain," so do not ask what the presence of the throne of the emperor of China might tell you about Britain and its narratives about

China over the two centuries since the thing was made.

Admission of this bit of adolescent theatricality may undermine my professional identification as a member of the staff of that same museum, entrusted by the British state with the power to place that same "throne," write about it, and display it. Failure to admit to it, however, to accept the object's presence in South Kensington as being an untroubling and natural occurrence, which need not touch anyone's fantasy life today, can only in the end reproduce a stifling identity of self-regard. What follows is a step toward compilation of the inventory that Gramsci saw as necessary, if a consciousness of myself and my colleagues as a product of the historical process to date is to be produced. The dates, deeds, and institutional affiliations of past scholars that I write down here are presented not simply as what happened but rather as an essential part of any critical elaboration of present practice in the production of "Chinese Art" in Britain, in a context where the displays of the major public museums are the principal visible construc-

From Tani Barlow (ed.), *Formations of Colonial Modernity in East Asia* (Durham and London: Duke University Press, 1997), pp. 413–446. © 1997 Duke University Press. All rights reserved. Used by permission of the publisher.

tions from which a discourse of "Chinese culture" can be derived.

Possessions/Identities

C. B. Macpherson's work on the political theory of possessive individualism in eighteenth-century England has made familiar the notion that possessions are seen as constitutive of identity within the dominant discourses of political and moral economy in Britain.[1] More recently, the works of Susan Stewart and James Clifford have extended this notion to the position that possessing is also central to the generation and sustaining of the identities of collectivities.[2] This is particularly so in the case of the imagined community of the nation-state. The National Museum acts as a key site of promotion of the existence and validity of the state formation. It does so with particular force in that the discursive practices at the heart of the museum lay claim to scientific objectivity, to a transcendental mimesis of what is "out there." It thus can act with particular force to validate the claims to sovereignty and independence by proving through displays of archaeology and ethnography the inevitability of the existence of the actually contingent conditions that give it its very existence. This role of the museum as constitutive of national identity emerges very sharply in historical contexts such as post-Habsburg central Europe, but it is no less well developed in the museums of imperial and post-imperial Britain, where the refusal to privilege the presentation of distinctively "British" material (and if anything rather the reverse) within the collections is constitutive of an identity that eschews national definition in favor of a claim of universal hegemony, as a transcendent fixed point which observes all other "cultures."

The British Museum could never be restricted to British things, for to do so would set a limit to the reach of British power, as well as to the gaze of the all-comprehending and autonomous subject. British museums of the imperial era are a cultural technology of display that form part of what Carol Breckenridge has termed an "imagined ecumene":

This Victorian ecumene encompassed Great Britain, the United States and India (along with other places) in a discursive space that was global, while nurturing nation-states that

were culturally highly specific. One condition for the construction of cultural specificity... was a concept of the cultural other, for these new technologies, routines and rituals of rule were frequently developed in relation to this imperialized or imperializing other.[3]

The British colonial presence in China differed from that in India in duration and intensity, but many of the same practices in the field of culture can be observed, practices constitutive of a "British" identity differentiated not only from the other of Asia but from more immediate colonial rivals such as France and then the United States. However, this type of identity is in no sense a fixed one; it is subject to contestation both from within and without. The works of Arjun Appadurai and Igor Kopytoff on the social life of things, and the biography of the object, should have made us sensitive to the proposition that while social situations encode objects with fluctuating meanings, methodologically a close attention to the particulars of the objects will illuminate those very social contexts.[4] I would wish here to extend this idea to take in the social life of the collection. They too shift their meaning over time.

In what follows I want to look at some changes in the presentation of material from China in the British Museum and in the Victoria and Albert Museum in London, two institutions directly patronized and supported by the British state, conscious that the framing of Chinese objects in these institutions conditions their viewing as expressive of discourses of national and imperial identity. The interplay of private and public possession, between individual collectors and public museums that they patronized and supported, and which ultimately came to possess the objects they had amassed, is of particular importance in forming the collections of material out of which representations of "China" and "Chinese art" were manufactured in Britain. The number of men who made a full-time living out of explaining China to Britain at this period was very small but tightly integrated through personal and professional networks, even if formal structures, other than the national museums, were very few. No women formed part of this project before the 1970s. Having told one story that should not be told, I will write further, with intentional ambiguity, about

Figure 11.1 Throne, carved lacquer on a wood core. Made about 1775–80, taken from the *Nan yuan* hunting park in 1901. W.399-1922, Swift gift. Photo courtesy of the Trustees of the Victoria and Albert Museum

Britain's possession of the "throne" of China (figure 11.1), to which I bowed as a teenager.

Commodities and Works of Art

In eighteenth-century Britain, not only members of the aristocracy and gentry but also those whom Jonathan Swift called "the middling sort" encountered luxury goods from Asia in their daily lives. These included a broad range of goods from China: silk piece goods for clothing and furnishings, tea, and the porcelain vessels necessary for brewing and drinking it, lacquered and hardwood furniture, small-scale carving in a number of materials, and pictures.[5] These goods were available through a network of specialist retailers, called "Chinamen" in London, a considerable number of whom were women. They might employ other women, and a significant portion of their clientele was made up of women, too.[6] Certainly it was an article of faith among male

arbiters of taste that the fashion for Asian imported goods was concentrated in two groups rigorously marginalized in elite cultural discourse – namely, the nouveaux riches, grown wealthy on trade rather than by the more socially prestigious route of landholding, and women, whose irrational desire for the hideous products of the East Indies was seen as being matched only by the rapacity and frivolity with which they spent their husbands' money.

Despite the ease with which Chinese goods found customers, and despite the existence on continental Europe of intellectuals willing to speak with warmth of the supposed virtues of a Confucian empire of the rational, no British intellectual of the period had a good word to say for China, in particular for the aesthetic manifestations of its culture.[7] China was at this time becoming firmly fixed as the "other," the irrationality of its intellectual productions becoming set as the essential counterweight to the enduring canons of quality represented by the art of Greece and Rome. As such it was associated by men at some level with the equally problematic "other" of the female. There is the real possibility that this double marginalization, and the gendering of Asian artifacts in everyday life, was used by at least some women in the period to create a measure of cultural space for themselves that was beyond criticism. What else could the male social critic expect of women than that they would like Chinese things? Significantly, they could act freely as consumers, but were not allowed to go the further stage of creating a publicly visible discourse about "Chinese art." Like many women, Lady Dorothea Banks built up a large collection of Chinese ceramics, but it was her husband, not she herself, who categorized and ordered it in a handwritten catalog of 1807.[8] By the time of major museum formation in the middle nineteenth century, a masculinist gendered understanding of collecting separated the "scientific" activities of taxonomy and categorization from the realm of mere accumulation.

Such notice as was given in Britain to the concept of Chinese art was universally derogatory. To be more precise, the notion of Chinese art was an oxymoron, since the Western hierarchy of media put painting at the top, with representations of the human form at the highest point therein. The "fine arts" of painting and sculpture, as opposed to the "mechanical arts," were universally believed to be extinct among the Chinese. Almost no Chinese painting for the domestic, as opposed to export, market left for Europe or America before the end of the nineteenth century. John Barrow, writing in 1804, can be taken as indicative of widely held views:

> With regard to painting, they can be considered in no other light than as miserable daubers, being unable to pencil out a correct outline of many objects, to give body to the same by the application of proper lights and shadows, and to lay on the nice shades of colour, so as to resemble the tints of nature.[9]

In general the creation of goods for the export market was taken, by the nineteenth century, not as a sign of entrepreneurial flexibility but as a sign of a culture hopelessly decayed and static, one with a vaunted (though unsubstan-

tiated) aura of past greatness, but with no present and no future. This "inability to represent" on the part of Chinese artists swelled as a theme in the decades leading up to the first British imperial assault on the Chinese state in 1840.

The Institutional Framing of "Chinese Art" in Britain

This preamble may seem of doubtful relevance. However, it is impossible to discuss the creation of the broader category of Chinese art in Europe and America over the past hundred years without first accepting the existence of a discourse (and a gendered discourse) of China that has its primary locus in the context of domestic consumption, since it is against, or by contrast with, what is done in the home that so much of what happens in the institutional context of museums and of the academy is defined. This is particularly striking in the case of objects of luxury consumption for the Chinese domestic market redirected by the museum and put under the category "decorative arts": chairs, items of clothing, ceramic wine jars, and personal religious images, to take a few random examples. Chinese elite categorizations of art, as expressed in texts, as well as in the practices of the art and craft markets, excluded much of the Chinese material subsequently displayed in the museum context in Britain. (This is not to say that fissures on gender, class, and ethnic lines within the Qing polity did not exist over this issue of definition.)

Indeed "art" is not a category in the sense of a preexistent container filled with different contents as history progresses. Rather, it is a way of categorizing, a manner of making knowledge, that has been applied to a wider and wider set of manifestations of material culture, paralleling the constant expansion of an "art market" that is applied to a wider and wider range of commodities. It remains a site of conflicting interpretations, fissured on class and gender lines, among others, and the right to define something as "art" is typically seen as an important attribute of those dominant in society at a given moment.

Crucial to this way of categorizing in European museum and academic practice is the strategy whereby notions of *function* must largely be removed from the objects of the exercise. In order to be an object of "decorative art" a cup must no longer be drunk from, and questions of how it would be drunk from have to be occluded. Thrones must no longer be bowed down to. Michael Podro has shown how what he calls "the disregard of function" was consciously conceived by nineteenth-century German theorists such as Karl Schnaase as a programmatic part of the creation of "art history." Schnaase saw any concern with function as making for a lack of the *dis*engagement necessary to appreciate true artistic import, an import which is inextricably formed from the work of art's "modifying its antecedents and as carrying intimations of its successors" (or what we would more insidiously call just "stylistic change").[10] This privileges the diachronic over the synchronic, and leads naturally to the situation in which talk of "influences" and "trends" supplants a notion of links from given objects horizontally toward the total assemblage of objects present in a specific social and historical context. Objects transferred from the domain of "ethnography" to that of "art" typically find diachronic links privileged at the expense of connections with others that have failed to make the transition.[11]

But narrative art history, which from its origins in the German-speaking world was translated into the Anglo-Saxon one in the later nineteenth century, is only one interpretive framework into which the things made in China have been construed in Europe and America. Despite its role as the dominant paradigm in the United States today, it is arguable whether narrative art history has ever actually taken root in Britain at all. Another framework of representation has historically flourished here, one with an equal power of generating discourse, though this time originating in the study of the natural world – the framework of taxonomy. In the later nineteenth century, most particularly in Britain, taxonomy exercised a powerful hegemony over the ordering of manmade products as well as over those of nature.[12] It is the program of a universal taxonomy of the "industrial arts" that formed the explicit project of the South Kensington Museum, known after 1897 as the Victoria and Albert Museum. In 1863 (immediately after the Second Opium War against China) the Lords of the Committee of the Council on Education had stated "that the aim of the Museum is to make the historical and geographical series of all decorative art complete, and fully to illustrate human taste and ingenuity."[13] The aim of completeness was qualified by the exclusion from the South Kensington collections of the material culture of those peoples, dubbed "primitive," who had neither art nor history. They were consigned to the historic present of ethnography collections, represented in 1863 primarily by the British Museum but later in the century by collections such as those of the Horniman Museum in London and the Pitt Rivers Museum in Oxford.[14]

As the dominant institutions in defining not simply Chinese culture in Britain, but in defining to an extent what could be thought of as "culture" at all, it is necessary to talk in some more detail about the evolution of the Victoria and Albert Museum and the British Museum, and of the Chinese collections within them.[15] One problem immediately presents itself: What is the Victoria and Albert Museum a museum of? Its various historic titles singularly fail to announce its contents, though it has in my brief curatorial career been variously subtitled for marketing purposes as "the nation's attic," "Britain's national museum of art and design," and "the world's greatest museum of decorative arts."[16] The refusal to announce itself is surely indicative of the institution's totalizing claims for a taxonomic universality over which the monarch, symbol of the British imperial state, holds sway. What, then, is the British Museum a museum of? Again the title significantly gives us no clue, while transparently (even naively) telling us that it is a Museum *of* Britain, where Britain is displayed to itself and the world. Both institutions have since their inception (and in the case of the British Museum, that is well back in the eighteenth century) included Chinese objects in their collections, and the administrative arrangements they have made for them, as well as the contexts and combinations in which they have presented them to the public, have done much to form a current discourse of "Chinese art."

It is very hard to research the history of a museum. The point of a museum is that it has no history, but represents the objects it contains transparently, in an unmediated form. In

James Clifford's paraphrase of the idea of Susan Stewart, "the *making* of meaning in museum classification and display is mystified as adequate *representation*. The time and order of the collection erase the concrete social labour of its making."[17] It is even harder to create a history of the display of Chinese material in British museums, since very little descriptive or pictorial information exists as to what was shown where or when, what juxtapositions (almost the most powerful creators of meaning in display) were made, which objects were privileged by particularly prominent positioning, and what was said about them on labels.[18] This is more than an accident, or a piece of forgetfulness on the part of my predecessors. The museum cannot allow itself to document its own frequently changing display arrangements, since then it will have a history, and if it becomes a historical object in its own right, then it can be investigated, challenged, opposed, or contradicted.[19] Much of what we have (and that often only patchily and in no coherent form) in place of a history of representations through display is a history of representations through essentially administrative arrangements, which make extremely dry reading, but which at least give us some way of coming to grips with the rhetoric of stable, unchanging truth and getting a glimpse of the contingency and historical concreteness of the arrangements into which objects have been placed.[20] For there have in fact been many changes in the contexts and categories into which Chinese artifacts have been inserted in Britain. Only some of these contexts have involved a deployment of the notion of Chinese art, but all have operated with the notion of an integral Chinese culture, for which certain types of luxury artifact, mediated through the international art market and categorized by British individual and institutional collectors, were a satisfactory synecdoche.

Chinese objects came to the British Museum in the founding bequest of Sir Hans Sloane in 1753, and appear at first to have been included under the rubric of ethnography. That this was felt to be in some sense inadequate by the mid-nineteenth century is shown by the complaint in David Masson's *The British Museum, Historical and Descriptive* (1850) that works of China and Japan were crammed into "five paltry cases" among a "collection of articles illustrative of the manners and customs of nations lying at a distance from our own, as well as of rude ancient races."[21] Masson argued that there should be distinct rooms for the antiquities of China, India, and Japan, which should be separated from those of more primitive peoples.

In constructing the Chinese holdings of the British Museum as "antiquities," Masson is drawing on a venerable European tradition of the study of material objects as essentially historical evidence, supplementary to the written record, which had developed since the fourteenth century with regard to ancient Greek and Roman civilization. Since 1807 the British Museum had included a Department of Antiquities, restricted in scope to the products of the West. It could encompass objects deemed to be of high aesthetic value (like Roman portrait sculpture), as well as more humble objects, as, for example, simple pottery oil lamps, which might aid an understanding of an obscure joke in the writing of a Roman comedian. Aesthetics as such did not play the decisive role in the decision as to whether to include an item in the collections. It was rather as evidence of "culture" that objects were collected.[22]

In 1860 there were formed out of the Department of Antiquities three new departments:[23] Oriental Antiquities (including the prehistoric British, Western Medieval, and ethnographic/Asian collections), Coins and Medals, and Greek and Roman Antiquities. The year marked a new degree of advance for British imperialism in East Asia, being the one in which Britain invaded north China and sacked the Summer Palace, an action that was to have a major effect on the flow of high-quality artifacts to British private and public collections. In 1866 Oriental Antiquities became a department devoted to Egypt and Assyria, while the Chinese material (together with the bulk of the ethnographic collections) remained part of the new Department of British and Medieval Antiquities, headed by Sir Augustus Franks (1826–1897).[24]

In 1921 the ceramic and ethnographic collections (in which China by now bulked very large) were formed into a Department of Ceramics and Ethnography for Robert Lockhart Hobson (1872–1941).[25] In 1933 Hobson, "the world's leading authority on Chinese ceramics," who had joined the British Museum as far back as 1897, became head of a newly created Department of Oriental Antiquities and Ethnography, with "the Orient" now having moved decisively further east to include only the Islamic world, India, and East Asia. Hobson remained in post until 1938, and his department also included for the first time all Asian pictorial collections, transferred from the Subdepartment of Oriental Prints and Drawings, which had been founded in 1913 to support the personal interests of Laurence Binyon (1869–1943).[26] This ended the separate and privileged status of Chinese painting in the British Museum (discussed below), as Binyon's most famous acquisition in the field of Chinese painting, the Gu Kaizhi *Admonitions of the Court Instructress* scroll found itself recategorized as an "antiquity." Finally in 1946 ethnography was trimmed off to create the Department of Oriental Antiquities, which exists today (though Japan was hived off in 1986 into a separate Department of Japanese Antiquities).[27]

There was clear privileging of Chinese and Japanese pictorial works throughout the nineteenth century, though this owed more to Western notions of the hierarchy of the arts than it did to any recognition of their equal prominence in any scheme of things to be found in China. The fact that they were a "higher" art form is shown by their inclusion in the collections of the Department of Prints and Drawings (formed out of the Department of Antiquities as far back as 1836), where they were collected and curated on a par with European material.

This is a significant point. At a time when Chinese ceramics were still, at least administratively, the same thing as canoes and weapons, a Hiroshige print was the same as a Rembrandt print. A picture could not, by definition, be simply an antiquity, a piece of historical evidence, but it was of necessity part of the realm of (fine) art. A Chinese picture could be bad art, failed art, but it could not cease to be art at this point. Note however that there was no question of including Chinese painting with Western painting in the National Gallery, and it remained alongside items (prints) that occupied a subsidiary, if still honored, ranking in the Western canon. However, the relative privileging of pictures is also shown by the

fact that the Japanese and Chinese paintings were the first part of the British Museum collection other than books to have a published catalog.[28] This appeared in 1886, and was written not by a member of the museum's staff but by the Scottish surgeon William Anderson (1842–1900), who had sold to the museum the large collection of Japanese paintings he had amassed in Japan between 1873 and 1880.[29] The collection had been augmented by many gifts of Chinese painting from Augustus Franks, who though an official of the museum also functioned as a wealthy private collector, often buying objects for the collections with his own money (he was a major donor of the British Museum's Chinese ceramics). Thus we see a situation in which private initiative, as much as institutional policy, dictated what should be collected, and even (in the case of Anderson) how it should be cataloged and described. This private ethos remains a strand in the history of the creation of Chinese art in Britain, and it remained standard practice from before World War I to entrust museum publications to noninstitutional authors.

London's other major institutional collection, the South Kensington Museum, has also included Chinese material since its inception in the museum attached to the central design school of the Department of Practical Art in the decades immediately prior to the Great Exhibition of 1851.[30] The initial aim of the collection was stringently didactic, aimed at improving the quality of British manufactured goods in a situation of intense commercial rivalry, above all with the French. Consequently, the South Kensington Museum aimed to concentrate on "ornamental art," which meant excluding pictures and sculpture, though this program was modified shortly after its inception, and a considerable quantity of Chinese pictures were acquired. The institution was very closely linked to the British Museum through the person of Franks, who loaned it a large collection of Chinese and Japanese ceramics from his extensive private collection, and also acted officially as an art referee, responsible for the selection of acquisitions.[31]

In the historicist climate of the time, China was a perfectly acceptable source of design solutions, though one held in lower esteem by many. In 1856, in *The Grammar of Ornament*, the designer and theorist Owen Jones, who was closely associated with the whole South Kensington project, could write that Chinese art was totally familiar, through the medium of imported goods, and could condemn it thus: "The Chinese are totally unimaginative, and all their works are accordingly wanting in the highest grace of art – the ideal."[32] The complaint is really one about the "Chinese mind," to which an assemblage of designed objects will provide an infallible key. Nevertheless, large quantities of objects in a variety of media were accumulated at South Kensington, in an institution that became increasingly confused as the nineteenth century wore on as to whether it was there to educate British craftsmen by exposing them to a broad range of often contemporary practice, or to assemble a great historical corpus of material in which connoisseurly criteria of quality would be the deciding factor.

The struggles over this issue are no necessary part of this article; suffice it to say that in 1897 a new director, Caspar Purdon Clarke, moved to improve the scholarly standing of the Victoria and Albert Museum by dividing the Department of Art (which had endured since 1857) into Departments of Furniture, Textiles, Sculpture and Ivories, Ceramics, and Metalwork, as well as a Department of Prints and Drawings, and the Library. This division was spoken of at the time and later as being one "by materials," and was presented as this museum's distinctive and original contribution to museum organization. However, there were occasions when other criteria overrode this classificatory scheme. Most significantly, a well-orchestrated outcry by a cadre of colonial administrators, led by two former viceroys including Lord Curzon himself, prevented Purdon Clarke's proposal that the Indian collections be divided in this way.[33] Clearly it was felt necessary to retain the integrity of the holdings of objects from the greatest of imperial possessions, a symbolic model on British soil of the breadth and variety of the empire on the subcontinent, and a separate Indian Museum was maintained. China was a lesser concern within the imperial scheme. The Chinese collections were accordingly divided between these until 1970, when a Far Eastern Department was created.[34] Throughout those six and a half decades, the fragmentation of

the Chinese collections meant that "Chinese art" (as opposed to "Chinese woven textiles" or "Chinese porcelain") was rarely raised as an issue at a formal level within the museum and that the degree of interest shown in various aspects of it tended to fluctuate within the departments, depending on the interest of individual curators, hardly any of whom were specialists in material of East Asian origin. This had the effect of creating a hierarchy based not so much on explicit notions of "fine art" versus "decorative art," or of the relative positions of different art forms, as on the degree of interest and activity generated in different parts of the museum.[35]

Ceramics as the Flowering of Chinese Art

In the interwar years and after, the Department of Ceramics was broadly responsible for the sustenance and construction of Chinese art within the Victoria and Albert Museum. With what were, both numerically and in terms of prominence in display, the most important Chinese collections, and with internationally renowned scholars such as William Bowyer Honey (1891–1956) and Bernard Rackham (1877–1964) on its staff, the department exercised an unofficial hegemony, as guardian of the master narrative in which Chinese ceramics and Chinese art were collapsed into each other.[36] In one of several volumes published to coincide with the Royal Academy of Art exhibition of Chinese Art of 1935, the sections on Sculpture and Lacquer and Textiles were both provided by Leigh Ashton (1897–1983), then an assistant keeper in the Department of Ceramics.[37]

In this interwar period, however, there was a significant turn in all the departments to an engagement with the idea of "national heritage," and a redirection of publishing and acquisitory activity toward British (in fact largely English) things. Perceptions of national and imperial decline, particularly in competition with America, lent this a greater urgency. The Victoria and Albert Museum's Chinese collections, physically and administratively divided by their materials, remained, "scattered in various odd corners and obscure passages," until 1939, when for the first time "these priceless objects [were] permanently assembled in chronological sequence in the spacious and brightly lit North Court (incidentally one of the Museum's largest galleries). The arrangement is most effective, following the method so effectively adopted at the Chinese Exhibition at Burlington House a few years ago."[38] The display was to prove even less "permanent" than any other such presentation, being necessarily dismantled when the Museum's entire collections were shipped out of London at the beginning of World War II. Ceramics also played a dominant role in the British Museum, within the Department of Ceramics and Ethnography and its successor, Oriental Antiquities and Ethnography.

During this interwar period, the British Museum's Subdepartment of Oriental Prints and Drawings (established in 1913) employed the young Arthur Waley (1889–1968), nowadays better remembered as a translator of Chinese and Japanese literature.[39] Waley had been employed by Laurence Binyon (1899–1943), author in 1908 of *The Painting of the Far East*.[40] Both Waley and Binyon enjoyed wide literary reputations that gave them an authority not essentially derived from their museum offices. Although his championing of painting might make him seem a more faithful transmitter of "traditional" Chinese connoisseurly criteria, Binyon's views are those of the classic orientalist position as defined by Edward Said, where "the East" cannot represent itself but must be revealed to itself by the Western expert, who has penetrated its essential and unchanging characteristics.[41] They are summed up in a series of lectures delivered at Harvard in 1933–1934, dedicated to his great American contemporary, Langdon Warner, director of the Freer Gallery.[42]

These construct Chinese art as a reflection of essential and largely historically invariant characteristics of the "Chinese race," and are full of typically reductive aphorisms – "The Chinese have kept their eyes fresh"; "This race has always had a turn to the fabulous"; "It [Chinese art] has its roots deep in the earth." Binyon certainly shared the view described here that the touchstone of quality lay in the early achievements of Chinese culture and that these were in some sense unknown to the Chinese themselves; "for it is only in the present century that the real achievements of Chinese art have been revealed."[43] He also provided a theoretical underpinning for the prominent role given to ceramics in museum collections, in his typically florid panegyric in Bergsonian vein to a Tang dynasty ceramic jar:

> No less than a great picture or statue, this vase typifies what art is and art does: how it has its being in the world of the senses yet communicates through the senses so much more than we can express in words. You cannot tell the body from the spirit, the thing expressed from its expression. The complete work is filled with a mysterious life like a human personality.[44]

The anonymity of potters saved the connoisseur from even having to consider any named, individuated Chinese maker as a conscious social or political actor. No actual person had made the pot, it had been made by "the race."

Writing Chinese Art History at South Kensington

Prior to 1939, only one attempt had been made at South Kensington to address the entire field of Chinese Art and to improve the scholarly treatment of the Chinese collections in line with the European holdings, but this had been done right at the beginning of the century by recourse to knowledge held by a private collector, in this case Stephen Wooton Bushell (d. 1908).[45] The South Kensington Museum commissioned his *Chinese Art* (originally of 1904, but with numerous reprints), using the museum's pieces as illustrations almost exclusively. The use of private expertise was a standard practice at this time, but the book is still the first one in Europe to equate the holdings of a single institution with the total field of knowledge. Predecessors such as M. Paleologue's *L'art Chinois* (Paris, 1887) had drawn on the holdings of a large number of private collectors for its examples and illustrations. However, in Britain the move to bring definitions of the subject within the parameters of the "national collections" can be read as an affirmation of public, official powers of definition in the field of culture, the very purpose for which a museum like that at South Kensington was created.

The book never states, but assumes as self-evident, that the collection of the South Kensington Museum can stand practically for the totality of Chinese art. Only in the case of painting is significant recourse had to another collection, and not to any private holdings but to the British Museum. By visiting these two imperial institutions, "Chinese art" can be seen in its totality. The work is structured in a series of chapters that reveal something of how Bushell saw this essential category as breaking down, and which is idiosyncratic by both contemporary elite Chinese criteria of categorization of the arts and by the terms of the "rational" departmental organization recently erected at the South Kensington Museum. The chapters are (after an historical introduction) Sculpture, Architecture, Bronze, Carving in Wood, Ivory, Horn etc., Lacquer, Carving in Jade and Other Hard Stones, Pottery and Porcelain, Glass, Enamels (subdivided into Cloisonné, Champleve, and Painted), Jewellery, Textiles (Woven Silks, Embroidery, Carpets), and finally, Pictorial Art. To begin with sculpture and end with painting may look like both an inversion of traditional Chinese canons of high and low, as well as sundering the unity of the fine arts in the Western tradition; however, the author does refer to pictorial art as "the most important branch of our subject."[46] This was despite the fact that the collection included almost no Chinese painting, by this date the major focus of acquisition of American collections such as those of railroad-car magnate Charles Lang Freer and the Boston Museum of Fine Arts. A distinctively British official definition of Chinese art was being born.

Chinese Art and Imperial Decline

The years after World War I saw a major shift in the valuation of Chinese art in Britain, with a collapse in the status of the types of Qing (1644–1911) porcelain that had been the focus of interest for an early generation of collectors (including Bushell and those advised by him), and a new engagement with the art of early China.[47] It has been traditional to view this in rather mechanistic terms, as the simple reaction to the increased opportunity to see early Chinese things concomitant on the progress of excavation, legal and illegal, in China. Clearly there was a connection between railway building and the flood of tomb ceramics onto the market. But it is also the case that changed attitudes made for a greater receptivity to

early Chinese artifacts. (After all, plenty of bronzes were available aboveground in the Qing period, but there is no evidence that they moved Whistler or Oscar Wilde in the same way as did Kangxi blue-and-white ceramics.) Rachel Gotlieb has shown how the philosophy of Henri Bergson, and to a lesser extent that of Jung, was explicitly cited in advanced aesthetic circles promoting the shift of taste, and how in particular early Chinese art was seen as embodying a spontaneity and vitality that was invigoratingly different from (and superior to) the more highly finished porcelain that had attracted an earlier generation.[48] This notion of a tired Europe refreshing itself from the vital springs of more primitive cultures is clearly part of the larger picture of appropriation of the other seen in the art of the cubists and surrealists.[49] In the particular case of China, the otherness is seen as distance in time, not space. Chinese culture has a glorious past, a decayed and exhausted present and no future. As the French aesthete Georges Soulié de Morant put it in 1928, "Aucun signe n'apparait encore d'une renaissance des arts."[50] His views were echoed by many and created a simple device for structuring canons of quality and importance in Chinese art – older was better.

Running parallel to this development, expressed above all in critical writing like that of Roger Fry, was a deepening fetishization by the Victoria and Albert Museum of objects manufactured at what was deemed to be both the apogee and the end of "traditional China," the eighteenth century. The reign of the Qianlong emperor (1736–1795) was held to mark the last era of artistic excellence before the catastrophic nineteenth-century "decline" (the causes of which, if they are discussed at all in artistic literature, are usually put down to something like "exhaustion" on the part of the "tradition"). The role of imperialism in China's decline is not commented on. The Qing empire disappeared in 1911, closely followed by the emperors of Russia, Germany, and Austria. By 1920 only the emperors of Abyssinia and Japan and the King-Emperor George V kept their thrones. The latter ruled over territories that were expanded after World War I, reaching a physical extent from which they were so swiftly to shrink. It is in the light of this that we must examine the fascination with the Chinese imperial court that was to permeate writing about, collecting, and displaying Chinese artifacts in an institution like the Victoria and Albert Museum. The signs of rulership (crowns, thrones, and other regalia) had been prominent in the Indian courts of the Great Exhibition of 1851, the event from which the Victoria and Albert Museum rhetorically derived (and continues to derive) legitimacy.[51] The fascination with the imperial provenance of the loot from the 1862 sack of the Summer Palace was reflected in the museum's collecting in the decades after the event, but the supply of objects of high enough status and sufficient aesthetic quality was seen as necessarily limited before the ending of Qing rule.

In 1922 the museum was given what has remained one of its most famous and most re-produced treasures (figure 11.2). It is a late-eighteenth-century throne-chair, looted from an imperial hunting park to the south of Peking in the 1901 multinational invasion of China and sold on the London art market by Mikail Girs, a White Russian émigré who had been Tsarist ambassador there at that time. It cost £2,250 and earned the donor of those funds the thanks of Queen Mary, who was known to have "expressed a hope that, by some means, it might find a place" in the museum that bore her husband's grandparents' names.[52] The throne has remained on display ever since, labeled until recently "The [note the definite article] throne of the Emperor Ch'ien-lung."

The screen with which it once formed a pair remains unpublished in the Museum of Ethnography in Vienna, but then possession of the screen of China is not the same thing as possession of the throne of China. It would of course be recognized that Qing political discourse made no room for a throne of China, no ruler's seat symbolically equated with right of rule. The object's meaning is entirely a product of its context of display.

In Stewart's terms, the throne is more of a souvenir than an item in a collection:

We need and desire souvenirs of events that are reportable, events whose materiality has escaped us, events that thereby exist only through the invention of narrative. Through narrative the souvenir substitutes a context of perpetual consumption for its context of origin. It represents not the lived experience of its maker but the "secondhand" experience of its possessor/owner. Like the collection it always displays the romance of contraband, for its scandal is its removal from its "natural" location. Yet it is only by means of its material relation to that location that it acquires its value.[53]

As the British Empire became more and more remote, souvenirs of the emperor such as the throne of China played an ever-increasing role in the national imaginary, as nostalgia for one empire slid across into nostalgia for all, and souvenirs of empire became fetishes of consolation. British colonial power in China was *less* effective in 1922 than it had been two decades earlier, at the point of the looting of the throne, and it was to decline significantly over the next two decades, leading to a final collapse under Japanese assault. The throne thus comes to signify not the empire from which it was taken but the equally vanished empire that took it.

Private Collections/Public Institutions

In the interwar period immediately after the throne's acquisition, the pace in the study of Chinese art in London was being made to an equal, if not actually greater, extent by private individuals, of whom the most significant are perhaps George Eumorfopoulos (1863–1939) (figure 11.3) and Sir Percival David (1892–1964).[54] The former, a business magnate of Greek descent, was intimately involved in the founding of the Oriental Ceramic Society in 1921, of which he was the first president. This private organization, its membership initially limited to fifteen, had as its object "to widen appreciation and to acquire knowledge of Eastern Ceramic Art by periodic meetings for the purpose of discussion."[55] (Originally objects from the Middle East were also collected, but this strand of interest soon faded.)

Validation of "Eastern Ceramic Art" as a coherent and discrete field drew both on the Bergsonian interest in ceramics as an "immediate" and "vital" form of artistic creation and on the growing body of dealers in the London art market prepared to specialize in this type of goods. These included businesses such as Spinks, Sparks, Bluett and Sons, and Marchants, all of which survived until very recent years.[56] Dealers were initially excluded from

THE ILLUSTRATED LONDON NEWS, July 8, 1922.—59

AN EMPEROR OF CHINA'S THRONE: 18TH-CENTURY RED LACQUER.

By Courtesy of Messrs. Spink and Son, Ltd.

MADE FOR THE EMPEROR KIEN-LUNG (1736-1795): A SUPERB RED LACQUER THRONE; AND LACQUER BOXES.

The throne here illustrated was made for the Emperor Kien-Lung, in whose sixty years' reign Chinese art was at its height. It is one of the only two such thrones in existence, and is probably the largest single piece of eighteenth-century carved red lacquer in the world. At the time of the Boxer Rising it was in the Imperial Palace at Nan-Haidze, near Peking, and was bought by a distinguished foreign diplomat at that city. It is 4 ft. high and 4 ft. wide. The seat is still covered with the original pad of silk and gold brocade. It forms the *pièce de* *résistance* of a wonderful collection of old Chinese red lacquer and cloisonné enamel, of the sixteenth, seventeenth, and eighteenth centuries, on view at the galleries of Messrs. Spink and Son, in King Street, St. James's. Above are shown the lids of three lacquer boxes of the same Emperor's reign—in the same collection. That on the left (16½ in. diam.) is in three-colour lacquer, with waves of deep green. The centre box (27 in. across) has a dragon design. The right-hand one (16½ in.) has engraved metal panels round the sides.

Figure 11.2 The throne as it appeared in the *Illustrated London News*, 8 July 1922, prior to its purchase for the Victoria and Albert Museum. Reproduced by kind permission of the Illustrated London News Picture Library

membership of the Oriental Ceramic Society (OCS), but they were essential to its functioning, since most of the members' purchasing was done in London rather than in Asia. Questions of a Chinese provenance were by and large not of concern, in contrast to the nineteenth century when "from the Summer Palace" was extremely important in market terms.

From its inception the OCS was involved in setting the agenda for public institutional

Figure 11.3 Bronze bust of George Eumorfopoulos, by Dora Gordine, FRBS. A.12-1944, Scaramanga Gift. Photo courtesy of the Trustees of the Victoria and Albert Museum

display of Chinese art, with a program of exhibitions at the Victoria and Albert Museum of ceramic pieces drawn from the holdings of members (often, particularly with regard to early pieces, as fine as anything the museums had themselves). However, the fact that museum staff too (Hobson from the British Museum, and Honey from the Victoria and Albert Museum) were among its founding members reflects the social class from which such scholars were drawn in the interwar years, as well as the intimate relations they enjoyed with private collectors.

Eumorfopoulos and David were both prominently involved in organizing the famous 1935 Exhibition of Chinese Art held at Burlington House. David was described in 1985 by Basil Gray, the last survivor of the British organizing committee, as the person thanks to whom "above all ... this concept was brought to fruition."[57] The show was a massive one, with 3,080 exhibits (750 of them loans from the Chinese government), and was seen by 422,123 visitors. Judging by the volume of press coverage, it was certainly a popular success.[58] In reflecting on it fifty years after the event, however, Gray commented that, "I hold from the point of view of scholarship, the occasion was largely missed."[59] His point is that it did relatively little to reorder priorities of study in Britain, which were to remain dominated by the study of ceramics into the postwar period, supported by the same constellation of interests among private collectors, dealers, and museum curators.

Chinese Art in the Academy

David, while also building up a major collection of Chinese ceramics, provided in 1930 the funds for an experimental lectureship in Chinese Art and Archaeology, to be tenable at the School of Oriental and African Studies, London University.[60] This lectureship, the first formal teaching to be made available in Britain in the field, was given to Walter Perceval Yetts (1878–1957).[61] In 1932 the post was made into a chair attached to the Courtauld Institute of Art and funded by the Universities China Committee in London, a grant-giving body supported by the monies extorted from the Chinese government by Britain as part of the "Boxer indemnity" after 1901.

Although Yetts wrote about a wide variety of subjects, from architecture to Ming ceramics, he was principally renowned in his own day as a scholar of, first, archaic bronzes and, second, Buddhist sculpture. His major scholarly monuments are the catalogs not of any of the public collections of the day but of the bronzes and sculpture in the Eumorfopoulos collection, which was sold to the British government in 1935 and divided between the British Museum and the Victoria and Albert Museum. He came at both subjects squarely from an "antiquities" point of view – that is, with an interest as much in the epigraphy of the material as anything else. Yetts has therefore disappeared totally from the lineage of the study of the subject laid out by Wen Fong in his essay accompanying the catalog of the *Great Bronze Age of China*, and indeed in the sense of the rigorous formalism of a figure like Max Loehr (1903–1991) was not an art historian at all.[62] Yetts valued bronzes as historical evidence, and in doing so he was probably (like his Swedish contemporary Bernhard Karlgren) closer to the mainstream of Ming and Qing thinking and writing about this material than were those who sought (ultimately with success) to assimilate bronze vessels into the Western category "art." His anonymous obituarist in the *Times* was slightly apologetic about this

and felt constrained to point out that "approaching the subject of Chinese art from the archaeological and ethnographical sides, Yetts was by no means indifferent to aesthetic qualities."[63] His recreation, it is pointed out in defense of his aesthetic side, was watercolor painting.

Yetts was succeeded as a teacher of Chinese art and archaeology at London University by S. Howard Hansford (1899–1973), who initially also had no formal background in art history or academic sinology, having worked rather until his mid-thirties with the family firm of Wright and Hansford, China and Japan Merchants. He was a Universities China Committee (again the Boxer indemnity) scholar in China from 1938 to 1939, served as an intelligence officer from 1940 to 1945, then studied in China again (this time under Chinese government auspices) from 1945 to 1947. In that year he returned to London to teach, but significantly by this point the post remained attached to the Courtauld Institute, London University's specialist postgraduate *art history* unit, rather than to the School of Oriental and African Studies.

In 1950 David began negotiations with the University of London that culminated in the presentation of his collection of Chinese ceramics to the university, and its opening to the public in June 1952 as the Percival David Foundation of Chinese Art. The PDF, as it quickly became known, was administratively part of the School of Oriental and African Studies, and Hansford left the Courtauld to become its first head. What would have happened if the teaching of Chinese art in London had remained within the Courtauld Institute is a moot point, and exactly why the switch was made remains murky, even if the effect is clear. The effect was to consolidate the coherence of an orientalist discursive field.[64]

Hansford's lectureship at the School of Oriental and African Studies was made a chair in 1956, and he held the post through 1966, when he was succeeded by William Watson. In his inaugural lecture, Hansford took the opportunity to review the study of the subject in Britain, but he primarily stressed the long history of "archaeoloatry – the worship of antiquity" in China. In a further statement, very much in the manner of the orientalist concentration on "essences," he argues that "all Chinese" are conscious of the antiquity and unity of their civilization, and adds: "The Chinese, like the British, are quite sure that they are the salt of the earth, and do not feel the need of proving it by tedious argument."[65] His definition of the field is one that begins with bronzes, then Buddhist sculpture, then "glyptics," or the jade carving that was his own special field. For the study of these subjects, London, with its three major museum collections, its private collections, and above all its thriving art market, "offers conditions as near ideal as possible" and in particular better than those of China. He then remarks, "I have said nothing yet about two subjects which properly fall within the scope of our studies, though some might hesitate to admit them to the category of Chinese antiquities, because the bulk of their material dates only from the last thousand years or so. I refer to painting and ceramics."[66]

Binyon and Waley are given the credit for "the pioneer work of interpreting Chinese painting to the West and enunciating canons of judgement" (the existence of traditional Chinese canons of judgment is implicitly denied in this sweeping phrase). However, Hansford accepts that the torch of scholarship in this field has passed to Americans and Germans, while the major collections are all in Japan or the United States. He never mentions China, and we are left with the clear impression that oriental art is too important a subject to be left to Orientals.

By this post-World War II period, political hegemony in Asia had clearly passed from the British Empire to the United States. But Hansford's inaugural lecture, and the practices of the national museums, both clearly embody a claim to a continuing hegemony in the sphere of cultural definition, expressed in opposition to the claims of the United States. Hansford explicitly describes London as the best place to learn about Chinese art, much better in all respects than China itself, and better than the United States with regard to the early materials he places at the head of a hierarchy of types of materials. The PDF that Hansford headed is a Foundation of Chinese Art that contains only ceramics and concentrates on those of the last thousand years. Contrast this with the contents of Ludwig Bachhofer's *Short History of Chinese Art*, written in Chicago in 1944, where the only ceramics discussed are those of the Neolithic Age and "Chinese art" is seen as consisting of archaic bronzes, sculpture, and painting. Bachhofer was in his own day a controversial figure (like his British counterparts, he knew no Chinese), a main conduit, at the University of Chicago, for the transfer of German scholarly *Kunstgeschichte* to the United States.[67] However, the divergence between his project and that of the London museums is visible and dramatic. In Britain it was and has remained the norm to work on ceramics, metalwork, textiles, jade, furniture, and other manifestations that in the United States have received less attention than painting. There has been correspondingly little work done in Britain on Chinese painting and none at all on calligraphy. The language-based scholarship of Chinese art in America is clearly part of the broader "area studies" movement, answering demands from the American state for agents in Asia who could effectively operate a mode of hegemony different in its aims and agencies from the British imperialism it had superseded. The differences between British and American discourses of "Chinese art" show that there is no such thing out there, that those who present the essence of "China" present essentially themselves.

The End of Empire and the Art of Empire

Hansford's 1956 inaugural lecture was delivered in a context in which the study of Chinese art in Britain seemed to him to indeed be flourishing. A new generation of scholars at the national museums had become active. The Victoria and Albert Museum was now headed by a director who had worked extensively with the Chinese collections, Leigh Ashton (director in 1945–1955 and knighted in 1948). He undertook a major program of renovation of the museum's displays, creating what were known as the Primary Galleries, "illustrating a single theme, such as the art of a particular civilisation, country or age, by grouping together the finest things available in a single gallery."[68] The Primary Gallery of Far Eastern Art opened on 12 September 1952, dominated visually by a display of Qing dynasty robes and by Qing dynasty lacquered furniture (figures 11.4 and 11.5), the most prominent single

ART OF THE FAR EAST—IN THE V. AND A.'S NEW PRIMARY COLLECTION.

THE NEWLY-OPENED FAR EASTERN COURT IN THE V. AND A. MUSEUM: IN WHICH THE PRIMARY COLLECTION OF THE ARTS OF CHINA, JAPAN, KOREA AND SIAM ARE DISPLAYED.

A WOODEN STATUE OF A SEATED FIGURE OF KUAN-YIN, THE BUDDHIST DIVINITY OF MERCY. FROM THE EUMORPHOPOULOS COLLECTION.

IN THE FAR EASTERN COURT: THE RED LACQUER THRONE OF THE EMPEROR CHIEN LUNG, FROM THE PEKIN SUMMER PALACE, BEFORE A BLACK LACQUER COROMANDEL SCREEN.

A CHINESE EMPEROR'S ICE-CHEST (EIGHTEENTH CENTURY): OF GILT BRONZE AND CLOISONNÉ. THE PURPOSE OF THE CHEST WAS TO COOL THE AIR.

A SPLENDID GROUP OF CHINESE IMPERIAL ROBES OF THE 18TH AND EARLY 19TH CENTURIES—PERHAPS THE MOST STRIKING SINGLE GROUP IN THE NEW COURT.

Figure 11.4 The Victoria and Albert Museum's new "Primary Gallery" of Far Eastern Art, featured in *The Illustrated London News*, 20 September 1952. Of four objects chosen for special attention, three – the throne, ice chest, and group of robes – are given specifically "imperial" connections. Reproduced by kind permission of the Illustrated London News Picture Library

THE NEWLY-OPENED FAR EASTERN COURT IN THE V. AND A. MUSEUM: IN WHICH THE PRIMARY
COLLECTION OF THE ARTS OF CHINA, JAPAN, KOREA AND SIAM ARE DISPLAYED.

Figure 11.5 View of the Primary Gallery in 1952. The throne, robes, and ice chest are situated together at the far end of the gallery, to form a focus of imperial associations. Given the sources of the gallery's architecture in a Christian basilica, it is hard not to read this positioning as making this group of imperial objects functionally equivalent to the altar. Reproduced by kind permission of the Illustrated London News Picture Library

item being the "throne" now standing in display terms not for the apogee of Chinese woodwork but as the very focus of "Far Eastern Art." Nevertheless, for administrative purposes the gallery was a responsibility of the Department of Ceramics, which maintained its primacy within the museum as the center of Chinese studies.[69] The British Museum's galleries were also reinstalled after the war, the Department of Oriental Antiquities being headed there for over twenty of the postwar years (1946–1969) by Binyon's son-in-law, Basil Gray (1904–1988).[70]

What was happening in London at this period was the emergence of a more distinctive profile for Chinese art. Distinguished now from "ethnography" at the British Museum (in 1946) and recognized at the Victoria and Albert Museum as a distinct phenomenon by the creation of the Primary Gallery (1952), above all enshrined in the prestigious Percival David Foundation of Chinese Art (1952), as well as supported by a flourishing art market and the collectors grouped around an expanded Oriental Ceramic Society, the subject seemed to enjoy a new degree of discursive coherence, but one still centered on museums rather than on academic teaching. The Percival David Foundation remains at the time of writing the only teaching institution in Chinese art, and from 1966 to the present each head has been a scholar whose career began in a museum (William Watson, 1966–1983; Roderick Whitfield, 1983–).

This discursive coherence nevertheless operated in a political climate of massively reduced British colonial power in Asia. The decolonization of India, Pakistan, and Burma was swiftly followed by a collapse in the visibility of the art of those parts of the world, with the demolition in the mid-1950s of the Indian Museum (which Curzon's efforts had preserved in 1909) and the removal into storage of most of its collections.[71] The collapse of the market for Japanese art after Britain's series of defeats in the Pacific meant that the amount of display space allotted to it was also severely restricted in proportion to the size of the collections acquired in the nineteenth century. Colonial power in Asia, particularly after the end of the Malaysian emergency (fought as Britain's contribution to the global containment of communism in Asia) was now focused almost solely on China, through the retention of Hong Kong. Yet throughout this period, and down to the present, colonialism was displaced into culture. Hong Kong remained invisible to the public culture represented in museums like the Victoria and Albert and the British, and "China" remained, the two colliding only in the last decade with the reinstallation of the galleries at both the Victoria and Albert and the British Museums using funds donated by individuals from the Hong Kong business community.[72]

As government restrictions on museum budgets mirror national economic decline, and as the private sector of corporate and personal sponsorship becomes the major support for once-imperial institutions, the question of who gets to represent what to whom comes to the fore. To a sector of a museum's visitors, the loot of empire is what they expect to see – a literal "empire of things." In this world of insecure meanings and private fetishisms, major displays of Chinese art in the national museums, paid for with money from Hong Kong, come to seem in their entirety like souvenirs of that empire that is fast vanishing into the imaginary consolations of costume drama.

NOTES

1 Macpherson, *The Political Theory of Possessive Individualism: Hobbes to Locke* (Oxford: Oxford University Press, 1962).

2 Stewart, *On Longing: Narratives of the Miniature, the Gigantic, the Souvenir, the Collection* (rpt., Durham, N.C.: Duke University Press, 1993); James Clifford, *The Predicament of Culture: Twentieth-Century Ethnography, Literature, and Art* (Cambridge, Mass.: Harvard University Press, 1988).

3 Breckenridge, "The Aesthetics and Politics of Colonial Collecting: India at World Fairs," *Comparative Studies in Society and History* 31 (1989): 196.

4 Appadurai, ed., *The Social Life of Things: Commodities in Cultural Perspective* (Cambridge: Cambridge University Press, 1986).

5 Craig Clunas, ed., *Chinese Export Art and Design* (London: Victoria and Albert Museum, 1987).

6 Aubrey Toppin, "The China Trade and Some London Chinamen," *Transactions of the English Ceramic Circle* 3 (1934): 45.

7 This point is well made in Ch'ien Chung-shu, "China in the English Literature of the Eighteenth Century: Part 1," *Quarterly Bulletin of Chinese Bibliography*, n.s., 2 (1941): 7–48; "Part 2," ibid., 2 (1941): 113–152, a work of great erudition that, like its companion piece on the seventeenth century, deserves to be much better known. The interest in Chinese architectural forms, particularly in landscape architecture, by William Chambers is perhaps best seen as a way of positioning his own practice in the marketplace, and is accompanied by statements such as the following: "Though I am publishing a work of Chinese Architecture, let it not be suspected that my intention is to promote a taste so much inferiour to the antique, and so very unfit for our climate" (Chambers, "Preface," *Designs of Chinese Buildings, Furniture, Dresses, Machines and Utensils...* [London: 1757]).

8 Rose Kerr, "The Chinese Porcelain at Spring Grove Dairy," *Apollo* 129 (1989): 30–34.

9 Barrow, *Travels in China* (London: 1804), 327, quoted in Clunas, *Chinese Export Watercolours*, Victoria and Albert Museum Far Eastern Series (London: Victoria and Albert Museum, 1984), 96.

10 Michael Podro, *The Critical Historians of Art* (New Haven, Conn.: Yale University Press, 1982), 40.

11 Clifford, *Predicament of Culture*, 224–225.

12 For a study of natural history collecting that parallels the activity of antiquities museums see Robert A. Stafford, "Annexing the Landscapes of the Past: British Imperial Geology in the Nineteenth Century," in *Imperialism and the Natural World*, ed. John M. Mackenzie, Studies in Imperialism (Manchester: Manchester University Press, 1990), 67–89.

13 Cited in Joe Earle, "The Taxonomic Obsession: British Collectors and Japanese Objects, 1852–1986," *Burlington Magazine* 128 (1986): 866.

14 Annie E. Coombes, "Museums and the Formation of National and Cultural Identity," *Oxford Art Journal* 11 (1988): 57–68.

15 What happened in America, without a single metropolitan center exercising hegemony over the whole cultural sphere, is not only more complex, and outside the competence of the present author, but has been broadly mapped out in Warren I. Cohen, *East Asian Art and American Culture: A Study in International Relations* (New York: Columbia University Press, 1992), which contains much valuable material in a convenient form but would be even more valuable with a less narrow focus on the United States and a greater awareness of at least some of the controversy surrounding the notion of "orientalism" in recent decades.

16 I joined the museum in 1979, after training in the Faculty of Oriental Studies, Cambridge University, at Peking Languages Institute and the School of Oriental and African Studies, London University. The presumption of China's unshakable alterity underwrote every stage of that training and was unchallenged by me until very recently.

17 Clifford, *Predicament of Culture*, 220.

18 In the course of the last year, the staff of the National Art Library at the Victoria and Albert Museum have for the first time pulled together in one sequence all of the guide-books to the collections published since the mid-nineteenth century, making it possible for such research to begin. A pathbreaking endeavor in this vein is Rupert Faulkner and Anna Jackson, "The Meiji Period in South Kensington: The Representation of Japan in the Victoria and Albert Museum, 1852–1912," in *Japanese Art in the Khalili Collection*, ed. O. R. Impey (forthcoming). However, my point holds: each guidebook presents itself as a transcendent present, with no sense of a history to the display arrangements.

19 Certainly since the 1980s it has been forced to be more self-aware, by a broadly based critique of its positivist framework. This critique is represented in Britain by works such as Robert Lumley, ed., *The Museum Time Machine: Putting Cultures on Display* (London: Comedia/Routledge, 1988), and Peter Vergo, ed., *The New Museology* (London: Reaktion Books, 1989).

20 The other thing we have is oral history. The orality of most museums' institutional cultures has struck me often throughout my career.

21 Cited in Edward Miller, *That Noble Cabinet: A History of the British Museum* (London: Deutsch, 1973), 222.

22 This lack of interest in aesthetic quality as grounds for classification is associated by Breckenridge with the "cabinet of curiosities" tradition that "represented an eclectic aesthetic of mercantilism soon to be displaced by one of imperialism in which collecting served as a sign of connoisseurship, and hence of control. Value in wonder cabinets was derived less from an object's aesthetic associations, and more from its uniqueness that was the product of its decontextualized presentation" (Breckenridge, "Aesthetics and Politics," 199).

23 What follows depends on Miller, "Appendix C: The Keepers of the Departments," in *That Noble Cabinet*, which is not always easy to interpret.

24 See Franks's entry in Sir Leslie Stephen and Sir Sidney Lee, eds., *The Dictionary of National Biography, Volume 22: Supplement* (Oxford: Oxford University Press, 1901), 665–668; see also Miller, *That Noble Cabinet*, 313–316. Both stress how Franks used his considerable personal wealth and his activities as a private collector to benefit the British Museum.

25 Hobson's *Times* obituary of 7 June 1941 is reprinted in *Transactions of the Orien-*

tal Ceramic Society 18 (1940–41): 9–10, and is followed by Bernard Rackham, "Mr R. L. Hobson's Contribution to the Study of Chinese and Chinese Ceramics," ibid., 11–13.

26 "The Apollo Portrait: Basil Grey," *Apollo* 129 (1989): 41.

27 This decision was driven to an extent by the need for a separate identity as a means of raising private-sector funding in Japan for the museum's activities.

28 William Anderson, *Descriptive and Historical Catalogue of a Collection of Japanese and Chinese Paintings in the British Museum* (London: Longmans and Co./B. Quaritch/Trubner and Co., 1886).

29 Lawrence Smith, "Collection of the Japanese Arts in the British Museum," in *Daiei hakubutsukan hitsuzō Edo bijutsu ten* (Tokyo: Tokyo Municipal Museum of Art, 1990).

30 What follows depends largely on Anthony Burton, "The Image of the Curator," *Victoria and Albert Museum Album* 4 (London: 1985), 373–387.

31 Rubert Faulkner and Anna Jackson, "The Meiji Period in South Kensington: The Representation of Japan in the Victoria and Albert Museum," in Oliver R. Impey and Malcoln Fairley, eds., *Meiji mo Takara: Treasures of Imperial Japan* (London: Kibo Foundation, 1995), pp. 152–195.

32 Quoted in Ernst Gombrich, *The Sense of Order* (London: Phaidon, 1979), 56. Owen Jones somewhat modified his views in his *Examples of Chinese Ornament, Selected from Objects in the South Kensington Museum and Other Collections* (London: S. & T. Gilbert, 1867).

33 Robert Skelton, "The Indian Collections: 1798 to 1978," *Burlington Magazine* 120 (1978): 302. Purdon Clarke, prior to his appointment as director, had been the architect of the Indian Court at the 1878 Paris international exhibition, and keeper of the Indian section from 1883. During 1881–1882 he traveled extensively in India, acquiring 3,400 artifacts, specifically designed to be an exhaustive and encyclopedic taxonomy of Indian manufacturing, with particular attention paid to place of origin within the empire.

34 I can find no documentation of the reasons behind this major move; they remained entirely within the oral culture of the museum and are now (by the retirement of everyone involved) outside even that. Thus a contingent step comes to seem like a "natural" development.

35 Thus the Department of Sculpture (later Architecture and Sculpture) produced almost no scholarship on any aspect of the extensive Chinese collections it held, and the level even of internal cataloging was exiguous for much of the period. The Department of Metalwork was more conscientious in its internal practice but still produced little work on China. The same would be true of Furniture and Woodwork, with the exception of Lt. Col. E. F. Strange (1862–1929), who published a pioneering *Catalogue of Chinese Lacquer* in 1925. On Strange's career see Craig Clunas, "Whose Throne Is It Anyway? The Qianlong Throne in the T. T. Tsui Gallery," *Orientations* 22 (1991): 44–50.

36 See William Bowyer Honey's obituary (by Bernard Rackham) in *Transactions of the Oriental Ceramics Society* (hereafter cited as *TOCS*) 29 (1954–55): 9–10, and Bernard Rackham's obituary (by John Ayers) in *TOCS* 35 (1963–64): xxiii–xxiv.

37 Laurence Binyon et al., *Chinese Art* (London: Kegan Paul, Trench, Trubner, 1935).

38 H. Granville Fell, "Chinese Art at South Kensington," *Connoisseur* 103 (1939): 223, 225. The photograph accompanying this display is of the Tang-Song section of the gallery, dominated visually by sculpture, (though including one of the early painted textile banners from Dunhuang) and with separate cases for metalwork and ceramics, in the manner of departmental apartheid that determined display policies in the Victoria and Albert Museum well into the 1970s.

39 Waley worked for the British Museum from 1913 to 1930 and produced a catalog of the Dunhuang paintings in 1931, which is still reckoned of some value today. Waley represented the exceptional figure of the self-taught genius and remarked quite correctly in 1923 that it was simply impossible to learn in London the kind of Chinese needed to equip one for a study of Chinese

painting (though the idea of going to China to learn it was equally rejected) (T. H. Barrett, *Singular Listlessness: A Short History of Chinese Books and British Scholars* [London: Wellsweep Press, 1989], 47).

40   Described by his entry in *Dictionary of National Biography* as "poet, art-historian and critic," Laurence Binyon remained very much the fin-de-siècle aesthete in his views, a man for whom his work on *The Painting of the Far East* (1908) was but one strand in a career equally devoted to Western art, to his practice as a poet, and even as a playwright, who enjoyed critical success with his historical dramas *Attila* (1907) and *Arthur: A Tragedy* (1923, with music by no less a figure than Edward Elgar!) (L. G. Wickham Legg and E. T. Williams, eds., *The Dictionary of National Biography, 1941–1950* [Oxford: 1959], 79–81). Binyon was a much more famous figure in his day than his present reputation allows and certainly merits a full-length biographical treatment.

41   One difference between the orientalist scholars described by Edward Said and the practice of an orientalist art history by Binyon and his contemporaries is that no emphasis was put on command of the relevant literary sources or linguistic resources. Neither Binyon, Hobson, nor Honey knew Chinese. (Waley of course did, but famously "never went to China," preferring to retain the Tang dynasty as a country of the mind.) Nowhere in any source of the period is this implied to be a lack. The key to understanding "Chinese art" in this schema lies not with the "Chinese" part of the equation but with a universalist ideal of the aesthetically sensitive individual. This contrasts markedly with the situation in the United States, where beginning in the nineteenth century, Asian (albeit usually Japanese) scholars with a command of the traditional connoisseurship literature had been employed in major museums or accepted as mentors by major collectors like Freer, and where promising young scholars like Archibald Wenley and Laurence Sickman were sent to China to acquire language skills. This cannot but

have influenced the development of collections in Britain away from the study of painting (where linguistic resources have been seen as relatively more important) toward those areas in which it was felt (wrongly) that lack of a knowledge of the Chinese language was no impediment.

42   Binyon, C.H., D.Litt., L.L.D., *The Spirit of Man in Asian Art* (rpt., Cambridge, Mass.: Dover, 1936), 16.

43   Ibid., 7.

44   Ibid., 21.

45   Bushell had been medical officer with the British legation in Peking, where he had acquired an impressive familiarity with traditional Chinese connoisseurship, including the written sources in Chinese, in the major area of interest to him, namely Chinese ceramics. Although never paid by the South Kensington Museum, he acted as its agent in Peking in the early 1880s, choosing objects for its collections and spending the sum of £250 on his own authority. The fact that Bushell could deploy Chinese texts in his study of art – at a time when the only employee of a national museum to have any knowledge of the language was the librarian Lionel Giles (1875–1958) – gave his work a particular orientalist authority, which has led to its continued citation into the present day. Bushell's expertise was valued in the United States also, where he cataloged the collection of the Baltimore magnate W. T. Walters (Cohen, *East Asian Art*, 18; see also Rose Kerr, "The William T. Walters Collection of Qing Dynasty Porcelain," *Orientations* 22 [April 1991]: 57–63). Although documentation survives concerning Bushell's purchases for the museum, all correspondence with him regarding the commissioning of *Chinese Art* was destroyed in the early 1960s, as part of continuous and systematic "weeding" of museum records.

Giles was the son of Herbert Giles, who succeeded Sir Thomas Wade as second professor of Chinese at Cambridge in 1897. "Young Giles" worked largely on the Chinese manuscript material from Dunhuang, shipped to the British Museum Department of Oriental Manuscripts and Printed Books, by Sir Aurel Stein in 1907.

46 S. W. Bushell, C.M.G., B.SC., M.D., *Chinese Art*, 2 vols. (London: 1904), 2: 104.

47 The shift had begun before the war, with the Burlington Fine Arts Club *Exhibition of Early Chinese Pottery and Porcelain*, 1910. Hobson was responsible for the catalog introduction, and George Eumorfopoulos was the leading lender.

48 Gotlieb, " 'Vitality' in British Art Pottery and Studio Pottery," *Apollo* 127 (1988): 163–167.

49 This has been the subject of considerable research in recent years. See, among others, James Clifford, *The Predicament of Culture*.

50 No trace appears as yet of a rebirth of the arts. Georges Soulié de Morant, *Histoire de l'art Chinois de l'Antiquité jusqu'à nos jours* (Paris: Payot, 1928), 261.

51 Breckenridge, "Aesthetics and Politics," 203–204.

52 *Nominal File: J. P. Swift*, Victoria and Albert Museum Registry. From its acquisition to the removal of the collections at the coming of World War II, the throne was the main focus in a gallery (room 42) devoted to Chinese and Japanese lacquer and woodwork. It is singled out as the most significant item in the room in *The Victoria and Albert Museum: Brief Guide* (London: 1924) and *The Victoria and Albert Museum: A Short Illustrated Guide* (London: 1937). For a fuller discussion of the circumstances of the acquisition see Clunas, "Whose Throne Is It Anyway?"

53 Stewart, *On Longing*, 135.

54 On Eumorfopoulos see L. G. Wickham Legg, ed., *Dictionary of National Biography, 1931–40* (Oxford: 1949), 260–262 (the entry is by Basil Gray). His obituary (by Hobson) is in TOCS 17 (1939–40): 9–10. On David (by Harry Garner), see TOCS 35 (1963–64): xxi–xxii. There is valuable material on David's career as a collector in Lady David, "Introduction," in *Percival David Foundation of Chinese Art: A Guide to the Collection*, ed. Rosemary E. Scott (London: 1989), 9–26. See also Anthony Lin Hua-Tien, "An Interview with Lady David," *Orientations* 23 (1992): 56–63.

55 "Rules," TOCS 1 (1921–22): 5. The *Transactions* remain almost the only source for the history of the society.

56 The history of the trade in Chinese art in London remains to be written and would necessarily depend on access to the records of current or defunct businesses, records that are not publicly accessible. Relations between dealers and museums have certainly undergone considerable changes in the period under study. Bluett and Sons was established in 1884, remained a family business until 1988, and went out of business in January 1993 (Caren Myers, "Saint Bluett's," *The Antique Collector* [June 1993]: 80–81).

57 Gray, "The Royal Academy Exhibition of Chinese Art, 1935–36, in Retrospect," TOCS 50 (1985): 11.

58 Cohen calls it an "extraordinary stimulus to the study of Chinese art.... For China, it was an almost unimaginable public relations success" (*East Asian Art*, 122–123). He shows too how the failure of H. E. Winlock, director of the Metropolitan Museum, to bring the show to New York reflected a "tilt" in American foreign policy against China and toward Japan at that precise moment.

59 Gray, "Royal Academy Exhibition," 33.

60 S. H. Hansford, *The Study of Chinese Antiquities*, An Inaugural Lecture Delivered on 15 May, School of Oriental and African Studies, University of London (London: 1956), 3.

61 Yetts had no academic background in Chinese art history. He was fifty-two when he took the post, and had previously enjoyed a distinguished medical career in the Royal Naval Medical Service, as medical officer of the British Legation, Peking (coincidentally Bushell's old post) and as Medical Officer of the Ministry of Health. He never studied the Chinese language in any British institution, and his knowledge of written classical Chinese is presumably owing to the efforts of private tutors in Peking. While still an employee of the ministry he began to write on Chinese art subjects, chiefly the bronzes that were now much more readily available and more widely appreciated on the London art mar-

ket. His earliest pieces are all basically puffs for bronzes in the collections of the major dealers – Bluett's, Yamanaka, C. T. Loo – but in 1925 he contributed a piece on bronzes to a special Chinese art issue of *The Burlington Magazine*, edited by Roger Fry. Yetts may well have been collecting and dealing in Chinese art in his own right, since he became a member of the Oriental Ceramic Society in 1925, when wealthy individuals still made up almost all of its seventeen-strong membership ("Dr Walter Perceval Yetts, C.B.E.," *Times*, 15 May 1957 [obituary]. This obituary is almost certainly by Howard Hansford. Harrie A. Vanderstappen, ed., *The T. L. Yuan Bibliography of Western Writings on Chinese Art and Archaeology* (London: Mansell Information/Publishing Ltd., 1975) has a full listing of Yetts's prolific output.

62 Wen Fong, "The Study of Chinese Bronze Age Arts: Methods and Approaches," in *The Great Bronze Age of China*, ed. Wen Fong (New York: Metropolitan Museum of Art/Alfred A. Knopf, 1980), 20–34. Loehr was a pupil of Ludwig Bachhofer (1894–1976), who in turn had been trained by Heinrich Wolfflin (1864–1945). Loehr taught at the University of Michigan from 1951 to 1960 and at Harvard from 1960 to 1974.

63 *Times*, 15 May 1957.

64 It has been suggested to me that it was the language requirements necessary for the advanced study of China that made a connection with the School of Oriental and African Studies seem desirable, but it is hard not to speculate that the objects of study that Yetts and Hansford chose for themselves seemed uncomfortably "low" and "antiquarian" to the rigorously "high" European tradition of the Courtauld.

65 Hansford, *Study of Chinese Antiquities*, 4.

66 Ibid., 11.

67 See Cohen, *East Asian Art*, 160–168, on Bachhofer and the "sinology" versus "art history" debate in American academia.

68 "Art of the Far East – In the V&A's New Primary Collection," *Illustrated London News*, 20 September 1952, 469.

69 When the Far Eastern Department was created in 1970, it was a Deputy Keeper of Ceramics, John Ayers (b. 1922, joined the museum in 1950), who was its first head.

70 Gray's obituary (by William Watson) in TOCS 53 (1988–89): 9–10 is not without inaccuracies. Basil Gray was Laurence Binyon's son-in-law and the last great "orientalist" of the British tradition, writing with equal fluency on Chinese and Persian art. His obituarist in the *Independent* newspaper, the Islamicist Michael Rogers (formerly in the British Museum, now David Khalili Professor of Islamic Art in the School of Oriental and African Studies), proclaimed it one of Gray's great strengths that his aesthetic sense was not clouded by a knowledge of any Asian language. Gray worked with curators such as R. Soame Jenyns (1904–1976; obituary in TOCS 41 [1975–77]: xxiv) and William Watson (b. 1917, British Museum 1947–1966, Head of the PDF 1966–1983).

71 Skelton, "Indian Collections," 303.

72 The T. T. Tsui Gallery of Chinese Art opened at the Victoria and Albert Museum in 1991, and the Joseph Hotung Gallery of Oriental Antiquities opened at the British Museum in 1992.

12

Introduction to *Art/Artifact: African Art in Anthropology Collections*

Susan Vogel

This is not an exhibition about African art or Africa. It is not even entirely about art. *Art/Artifact* is an exhibition about the ways Western outsiders have regarded African art and material culture over the past century. A central issue is our classification of certain objects of African material culture as art and others as artifacts. Our categories do not reflect African ones, and have changed during this century. An examination of how we view African objects (both literally and metaphorically) is important because unless we realize the extent to which our vision is conditioned by our own culture – unless we realize that the image of African art we have made a place for in our world has been shaped by us as much as by Africans – we may be misled into believing that we see African art for what it is.

In their original African setting most works of art (I use our phrase for the moment, but more on that later) were literally viewed differently from the way we see them. Masks were seen as parts of costumed figures moving in performance, or seen not at all. Figures often stood in dark shrines visible to only a few persons, and then under conditions of heightened sensibility. Other objects were seen only swathed in cloth, surrounded by music, covered with offerings or obscured by attachments. Most sculpture could be seen only on rare occasions. As Arthur Danto (1988) says, the primacy of the visual sense over all others is particular to our culture: African objects were made to belong to a broader realm of experience. If we take them out of the dark, still their movement, quiet the music, and strip them of additions, we make them accessible to our visual culture, but we render them unrecognizable or meaningless to the cultures they came from.

To understand these objects better we must consider the intersection between the ways we see them literally, and the metaphorical vision our culture has of them.

Most visitors are unaware of the degree to which their experience of any art in a museum is conditioned by the way it is installed. As the enshrinement of African sculptures in the Michael Rockefeller wing at the Metropolitan Museum in the early part of this decade subliminally communicated the aesthetic and monetary worth of African art, so do anthropological, art historical or other kinds of installations color the viewer's estimation of

From Susan Vogel, *ART/Artifact: African Art in Anthropology Collections* (New York: Museum for African Art, 1988), pp. 11–17. Reprinted by permission of the Museum for African Art.

what he sees. The conditioning begins with the selection of what is to be displayed. Because today the forms and materials of art are frequently the same as those of non art objects, the setting or context in which art is displayed may be its most evident defining characteristic. A pile of tires in front of a museum is to be viewed as art where the same pile in a gas station clearly is not (figure 12.1). The very presence of an African stool in an art exhibition makes assertions about African material culture. The museum exhibition is not a transparent lens through which to view art, however neutral the presentation may seem.

Museum installations have naturally reflected the philosophies and attitudes of their organizers from the time they first began. One of the first Western settings for African objects was the "curiosity room." French, German, and English scientists and amateurs had formed collections of exotic, natural and manmade wonders since the Renaissance. Most curiosity rooms made no allusion to the original cultural context of objects, and implied little aesthetic intent or competence on the part of their makers. *Art/Artifact* exhibits such a room recreated from The Hampton Institute's first presentation of its ethnographic collection in the 1870s (Vogel 1988). Such "curiosity" collections rarely separated botanical, zoological, and geological specimens from cultural artifacts, and often mixed together objects from different places.

"Curiosity rooms" were often private, but during the third quarter of the nineteenth century, museums of natural history opened to the public in many American and European cities. With a strongly educational mission from the outset, these museums presented didactic exhibitions using their specimens to illustrate prevailing theories, as they do today. It was the midtwentieth century – relatively late in the history of Western collecting – before African sculptures made much of an appearance in art museums. Once they did, it became necessary to determine which objects were properly

Figure 12.1 Installation view of Alan Kaprow's *Yard* (1961) reconstructed in 1984 for the Whitney Museum of American Art's exhibiton *Blam! The Explosion of Pop, Minimalism and Performance 1958–1964*

art and should be displayed in art museums, and which were artifacts that belonged in natural history museums.

The category of African objects defined as art has steadily expanded throughout the twentieth century. Virtually all of the African art works we now know were once classified as artifacts. The problem of distinguishing between the two categories has proven remarkably resistant to clear-cut solutions, and continues to bedevil those who collect and exhibit African and the other "Primitive" arts.

The question arose from several historical circumstances. It originated in the fact that during the 1880s and 1890s, when the first African museum collections were being formed in Europe and America, the almost universally held definition of art excluded non-naturalistic traditions. Early African collections were generally made in the field and included large numbers of utilitarian objects, biological and geological specimens, and other things of a purely scientific interest. Separating the small number of sculptures from this mass, was made more problematic by the fact that the continuum of objects runs unbroken from freestanding figures, for example, to figures that are incorporated in staffs or musical instruments to staffs or instruments with fine nonrepresentational decorations, to rudely formed, purely functional staffs and instruments. The material – usually wood – provided no obvious demarcation between fine and applied arts.

No help came from the African peoples who produced the objects. They did not distinguish between art and other manufactured objects, and rarely had a word that could be translated as "art." Early writers made much of this fact which was still being regularly mentioned at the time of the "Primitivism" exhibition in 1984. Because the creators of these objects were not making a claim for their status as artists or for their works as art, and since their products generally failed to correspond to the art made in Europe at the time, most objects were classified as ethnographic specimens and sent to anthropology museums.

In natural history museums African artifacts were used to illustrate different aspects of culture (figure 12.2). At the end of the last century, many thinkers considered African and other "Primitive" cultures to be living fossils,

contemporary ancestors that had preserved early stages in the evolution of culture. African artifacts were seen as providing a precious glimpse into the past of human development, the dawn of consciousness, and the roots of art – as the word "primitive" implies. Cultural evolution was believed to have reached its zenith in late nineteenth century Europe. Though the theory of an evolution of culture has been a minority point of view in the twentieth century, most natural history museums still deal mainly with "low cultures" and exotic cultures and exclude "high cultures" and familiar ones such as those of the United States and Western Europe. (I do not wish to imply that the museums today regard their subjects as primitive, but simply to point out that their focus on the study of certain culture areas was established at a time when those were prevailing attitudes, and that they still study essentially the same areas.) In all cases, anthropology museums have continued to use their collections as sources of information about culture.

Art museums have tended to view their collections from the opposite perspective using information about the cultural setting to understand the work of art. The different orientations of the two kinds of museums is immediately visible in the ways they have acquired and displayed their collections. Anthropology museums have prized large field collections which combine extensive documentation with duplication. Because they sought what was typical of the culture rather than what was unique, they often exhibited (more in the past than today) vast series of closely similar objects, often arranged typologically (i.e. weapons, masks, cups).

In contrast, art museums have not traditionally been concerned with documentation, but have preferred the unique object, valuing originality and invention – the qualities that separate art from craftsmanship in Western definitions. Art museums have accordingly purchased works one by one (or acquired collections that were formed that way) and have avoided redundancy.

During the four or five decades that art museums have been dealing with ethnographic art, however, the separation between the anthropological and the art historical approaches has narrowed. Anthropologists are increasingly

Figure 12.2 The 1910 African Hall of the American Museum of Natural History combined ethnography and zoology, and was organized geographically. Note the novel use of the color transparencies placed in window boxes, to give the viewer a sense of context. Neg. no. 32926. Courtesy Department Library Services. American Museum of Natural History

sensitive to the aesthetic dimension of the objects in their care, as art historians have become alive to the vast amount of anthropological information that they can use to understand art. This has tended to make their respective museums' installations resemble each other more than ever before.

The crowded presentation of the old fashioned natural history museum grew out of a desire to show many typical examples, but it also reflected the generally cluttered aesthetic of the period. It is interesting, however, to note that one of the earliest exhibitions of African sculpture in an art gallery presented it much as art museums do today – isolated for aesthetic contemplation, completely removed from its cultural context or any suggestion of use.

A photograph of Alfred Steiglitz' 291 Gallery exhibition of African art in 1914 already shows an African art purified of its functional look (figure 12.3). The Fang sculpture seen standing on a pedestal is a reliquary guardian originally attached to a box of ancestral bones for the purpose of warding off intruders. Here it appears cleansed of bark and bones, and the dowdy aura of the ethnographic specimen. The impulse to strip African art of its visible cultural context has roots in the desire to make it resemble art of the West and conform to our definition of what art is. An essential quality of Western art is that it exists for its own sake, that it has a higher ambition than to be useful in any pedestrian sense. That African art is functional – even when its function is spiritual as in the case of the Fang guardian figure – can appear to compromise its status as art.

The corpus of nearly a thousand bronzes seized in the Kingdom of Benin and brought to Europe in 1891 was the first African material that Westerners generally recognized as art

Figure 12.3 Installation view of Stieglitz' 291 Gallery, New York City, 1914–1915

(Vogel 1988: 55). No other African work then known so closely fit the European category of art: the bronzes were produced by a technically complex process; they were representational and moderately naturalistic; some plaques and altar groups seemed to depict scenes. Hundreds of Benin bronzes were auctioned for high prices soon after they arrived in Europe. Nevertheless, most were acquired by museums of ethnography.

The introduction of African art around 1907 into the circle of avant garde artists in Paris, and the subsequent transformation of their art led to the creation of a European art that resembled some African works. This in turn led people in advanced circles to accept many kinds of African sculpture as art. In an extremely gradual process, artists, then scholars, museums, and the general public have progressively redefined certain kinds of African artifacts as art. The process seems to be led by artists whose nonrepresentational, then abstract, and finally pseudo-artifactual works, have been followed at each stage by the acceptance of more and more African objects as art

(figure 12.4). This process may now have come as far as it legitimately can. Western artists have been making pseudo-artifacts for some time – nonfigurative objects apparently useful in some unknown ritual, or private culture. Many resemble "Primitive" architecture, ritual sites, altars, weapons, traps, tools and so forth, mainly of an extremely unadorned kind. Repeating the process that has continued through much of this century, we can look again at the African artifacts that they resemble and regard the artifacts as art. But should we? And if not, then have the earlier shifts in definition between art and artifact been equally inappropriate?

Opinions differ: they even differ on whether an art-craft definition is worth discussing. And there are still those who say we do not yet know the first thing about how to look at African art or artifacts. The originating cultures, however, tell us certain things about problematic objects that cannot be ignored.

In Africa the experience of any given work of art varied from person to person, and was

Figure 12.4 Untitled, 1977. Ana Mendieta. From Fetish Series. Earth-body work of sand, sticks and water, executed at Old Man's Creek, Iowa City, Iowa. Photograph courtesy of the New Museum of Contemporary Art, New York City

closely tied to the circumstances in which it appeared. When an African artist created a sculpture, he almost always made it for a particular purpose, a specific audience, and often for a single location. The object's profound meaning was known in greater or lesser degree to that original audience who understood it with varying nuances of emphasis.

For example, a men's society mask might be regarded as entertaining and possibly intimidating by uninitiated youths; initiated men would identify with it as an expression of their power and would understand its deeper spiritual and social meaning gradually as they rose through levels of initiation; women and members of different clans, courtiers or commoners might view it respectively as ugly and menacing, a glorious manifestation of their group, or as awesomely sublime. An artist could fix mainly on the details of manufacture

and the skill of the artist. Those who did not belong to the original audience, such as Africans from a neighboring area, might see the sculpture as unknown and alien, or might mistakenly interpret it in terms of their own differing traditions.

Only the original audience could experience the work of art in its fullness, and their experience was multifarious. Further, that experience changed over time. The villagers who today watch a masquerade performance may perceive in it things the originators never foresaw, and may only dimly understand certain symbols that have become remote since the masquerade was created. This was probably always true as generation succeeded generation. (In some measure, of course, the same can be said of all art made in a time or place different from the viewer's.) How, then, are we to see African art? The only context available to most Westerners is the museum. If the original African experience was variable and can be only imperfectly simulated outside its culture, then a museum presentation can only be arbitrary and incomplete.

When at the end of the nineteenth century African art came to the attention of the West, it was mounted – both in the art world and in ethnological circles – the way Greek, Roman, Chinese, and other antiquities were displayed at the time: that is, figures set off by square or rectangular pedestals; masks and heads on necklike blocks; some masks hung on the wall like relief sculptures. (Masks, of course, are not relief sculptures; they are the front of a composition that included the wearer's whole head – a realization that complicates rather than elucidates the display problem for a museum.) Recognizing that the methods we adopt to display African sculptures are arbitrary and remote from the ways in which they were meant to be seen forces us to reexamine our displays.

How would African art be shown if it had reached us for the first time in the 1980s? Museums are conservative institutions and have changed their displays very little in the past half century or more – aside from reducing the density of exhibits and increasing the labels. The presentation of the art of our own time, however, has changed considerably.

Partly under the influence of African and other "Primitive" arts, twentieth century sculptors have tended to create works that

Figure 12.5 The Arches, 1959. Alexander Calder. Painted steel. Collection of Whitney Museum of American Art, New York City. Gift of Howard and Jean Lipman 82.44. Photograph by Jerry L. Thompson

Figure 12.6 The Freedman, 1863. John Quincy Adams Ward. The Metropolitan Museum of Art. Gift of Charles Anthony Lamb and Barea Seeley Lamb in memory of their grandfather Charles Rollinson Lamb, 1979 (1979.394). Photograph by Jerry L. Thompson

stand in the viewer's space; earlier works usually carried their own space with them, in their own scale. A small bronze horseman stood on a small bronze patch of earth, for example; a monumental marble figure stood by a huge marble tree trunk. In contrast, African and Modern sculptures were generally not meant to be isolated from the viewer by a frame or base, but to invade, to share his environment. African figures do not create their own scale or space, but intrude into ours and establish their size in relation to the human body. They are large or small, they dwarf us or make us giants by cohabiting our space. If our reference were the art of our own time, and not that of a century ago, we might want to show African sculpture without barriers or mounts.

In the exhibition is a repousse brass head made in the royal court of Abomey (Vogel 1988: 53). It is either an unfinished work, or all that remains of a complete figure; in its present state it could not have been a significant or useful object in Abomey, and would almost certainly not have been displayed. How must we display it? The curatorial impulse is to mount it upright on a block, but since it has become meaningless in terms of its original culture, and has now become an artifact of our culture, could we validly show it simply lying on its side? That would give it a certain resonance with works of Western art (notably Brancusi's "Sleeping Muse": figure 12.7) and would be a statement about the place this African head occupies in our inventory of cultural objects.

There is no single right way for us to exhibit the head from Abomey or any African object – only ways that are more or less illuminating, beautiful, instructive, arbitrary; faithful to this or that school of thought. We exhibit them for our own purposes in institutions that are deeply embedded in our own culture. There is nothing strange or wrong about that. It is simply a given.

In the exhibition is a large, interesting-looking, honey colored bundle of rope with regular knots visible beneath the binding, and some thick black encrustation on one side (Vogel 1988: 175 and figure 13.2). Placed under the spotlights of an art museum it looks like a work of modern art, though it is smaller than most. It is in fact a hunting net made by the Zande people of Zaire and collected for the American Museum

Figure 12.7 Sleeping Muse. Constantin Brancusi. Bronze. The Metropolitan Museum of Art. The Alfred Stieglitz Collection, 1949 (49.70.225)

of Natural History by Herbert Lang in 1910. For the Zande its purpose and meaning were straightforward – to catch animals in communal hunts that brought meat to the village. However symbolically or metaphorically the Zande conceptualized hunting, no expressive intent is apparent in this artifact. (In Danto's (1988) formulation its meaning was its purpose.) Furthermore, its present configuration is not its intended one; to be useful or even to be examined by the Zande it would have to be unfurled. The intriguing black encrustation is accidental, perhaps tar from the ship that brought it here.

In evaluating the hunting net, its Zande makers and users would probably have been concerned with workmanship, the toughness and uniform thickness of the rope, the regularity of the knots, and the evenness of the openings – all qualities necessary to its functioning. Most African languages have a single word that means good, useful, well made,

beautiful, suitable. This net would probably have merited that word. But it would probably not have been considered interesting to look at. Though it bears a spurious resemblance to works of Modern art, the net cannot itself be considered a work of art.

Also in the exhibition is a needle case made by the Lozi people of Zambia which consists of a series of finely wrought iron needles with twisted ends and polyhedron terminals pushed randomly into a tightly wrapped fiber case (Vogel 1988: 185). We can admire the efficiency of the case which protects the points of the evidently precious needles, the variety of their forms and decoration, and we can also see an expressive dimension in the irregular way they have been thrust into the case. But that would be a false reading of this object because, like the rope net, it is not in its intended configuration. The needles were meant to be used singly; their present position and grouping is as temporary and accidental as that of any pincushion or pile of tomatoes in the kitchen. The Lozi might have been interested in the various kinds of ornamentation on the needle's tips, and of course in how sharp they were. I doubt they would have wasted time on other visual aspects of this object.

A great wooden bowl from Wum in the Cameroon Grasslands is also a functional object – probably intended to hold elements of chiefly regalia during displays – but it is also a masterful sculpture (Vogel 1988: 58). The body of a male figure wraps ingeniously around the bowl and cradles it on his knees; his arms merge progressively into the bowl itself until his hands lose all volume and become only lines incised into the bowl's surface. The breadth of his shoulders and knees, out of all proportion to his slender torso, suggest energy, protection, stability. The artist who carved this bowl made a functional object whose expressive form takes it beyond the net, or the needle case into a realm our culture calls art.

But the people of Wum almost certainly classified it in quite a different way. They saw in this sculpture a useful object, a symbol of their kingdom, an heirloom; an expression of the continuity and security of their state. Ordinary people probably differed about the artistic quality of the work, for its forms are unusual and exaggerated. Kingdoms had more than one such bowl, all equivalent in function and expressive of the same values. Some surely recognized this one for the superior expression that it is, though our information on such questions is woefully thin.

Whether the Wum bowl is art, whether the hunting net, or the Lozi needles are art or artifact is strictly our problem. The makers of humble African nets, needles, stools and mats that we term artifacts have not somehow aspired to sophistication and the status of art and failed. They never for a minute lost sight of the fact that these were simply useful, wellmade objects. The question and the categories are ours.

African cultures do not isolate the category of objects we call art, but they do associate an aesthetic experience with objects having certain qualities. The aesthetic experience is universal – with or without a word that describes it. Africa is only one of a great number of world cultures that created and recognized art while lacking a word like our "art". As

Blier points out, before the sixteenth century the English word "art" referred primarily to the idea of practical skill.[1] The Latin root *ars* has its source in the word *artus* meaning to join or fit together. Both the Italian term *arte* and the German word *kunst* were linked to the idea of practical activity, trade, and knowhow. Arthur Danto's definition (Danto 1988: 38) is well suited to the art of our own time, but does not entirely answer the African situation. "To be a work of art," he argues, "is to embody a thought, to have a content, to express a meaning. . . . "

In African cultures numerous natural and manmade objects embody complex meanings including, for example, certain leaves, animals, shells, and metals. Motifs woven into textiles and mats, incised on the human body, or painted on walls are named and significant. The shapes formed by sacrificial blood or wine poured on the earth carry meanings. The basket of bones, the pan of sacrificial materials, the lump of clay at the center of a shrine may be the most highly significant element there, even when flanked by sculpted figures. Like the baldaquin, the monstrance and the altar itself in a Catholic church, African sculptures often embellish shrines whose most complex meanings are embodied in nonaesthetic objects like the Catholic host. Danto's definition holds true of African works of art, but fails to separate them from much else in the culture. It leaves out the aesthetic dimension.

Though African languages do not have a word for art, they have many words that indicate artistry; words for embellished, decorated, beautified, out of the ordinary. Sometimes there are two words for the same type of object: one for the natural or plain example, another for the embellished or manmade one. (A naturally occurring separation between the front teeth has one name, and is beautiful, but less so than the cosmetic separation produced by filing, which has another name.) Many Africans make a distinction between the product of artistry, and the routine object on the basis of the beauty of the object, and the care and skill that went into making it beautiful. I do not know how they would classify the deliberately rough, ferocious or ugly sculptures made by artists (that we would consider art) that do not fit into the definition I have concocted here.

Where their definition corresponds to a dictionary definition of art is in the sense of skill and the requirement that there be something deliberate, and manmade about the beauty of the object. In traditional African thinking, art is a sign of culture and man's ability to fashion the merely useful to his desire.

NOTE

1   Suzanne Blier (1988), "Art Systems and Semantics: The Question of Stylistic Taxonomy in West Africa," *American Journal of Semiotics* 6(1): 7–18.

REFERENCES

Blier, Suzanne. 1988. "Art Systems and Semiotics: The Question of Art, Craft, and Colonial Taxonomies in Africa." *American Journal of Semiotics* 6(1): 7–18.

Danto, Arthur. 1988. "Artifact and Art". In Susan Vogel, ed., *ART/Artifact: African Art in Anthropology Collections*. New York: Centre for African Art and Prestel Verlag.

Vogel, Susan, ed. 1988. *ART/Artifact: African Art in Anthropology Collections*. New York: Centre for African Art and Prestel Verlag.

13

Vogel's Net
Traps as Artworks and Artworks as Traps

Alfred Gell

A good deal of discussion in the philosophy of art, visual art particularly, at the present time, has to do with the problem of defining the idea of an 'artwork'. When is a fabricated object a 'work of art' and when is it something less dignified, a mere 'artefact'? There are (at least) three possible answers to this question. It may be said that a work of art can be defined as any object that is aesthetically superior, having certain qualities of visual appealingness or beauty. These qualities must have been put there intentionally by an artist, because artists are skilled in activating a capacity present in all human beings, i.e. the capacity to respond aesthetically to something. This theory is not one I propose to discuss here, although it is still widely held, especially by the general public, who tend to think that visual attractiveness, or beauty, is something they can recognize automatically.

The second theory holds that artworks are not, as the 'aesthetic' theory holds, distinguished by any external quality. A work of art may not be at all 'beautiful' or even interesting to look at, but it will be a work of art if it is interpreted in the light of a system of ideas that is founded within an art-historical tradition. Call this the 'interpretive' theory. The great

critical merit of the interpretive theory over the 'aesthetic' theory is that it is much more attuned to the realities of the present-day art world, which has long abandoned the making of 'beautiful'-looking pictures and sculptures in favour of 'concept' art, e.g. of the exhibition of gallery assemblages like Damien Hirst's dead shark in a tank of formaldehyde (figure 13.1, to be discussed later) – not an object that could be called appealing, nor a work of any excellence in terms of craftsmanship. But Hirst's shark is a highly intelligible gesture in terms of contemporary art-making, not a stunt or a symptom of insanity. It is a work thoroughly grounded in the post-Duchampian tradition of 'concept' art and, as such, is capable of being evaluated as good art, bad art, middling art, but definitely art of some kind. Proponents of the 'aesthetic' theory have difficulties with this kind of work, to say the least, and may be inclined to deny that it is art at all, but in that case they may be accused by critics and artists, rightly to my way of thinking, of reactionary tendencies.

Finally, there is a more radical version of the 'interpretation' theory, which, provides the third possible answer to the question 'what is an artwork?'. This theory, known as

From *Journal of Material Culture* 1 (1) (1996), pp. 15–38. Sage Publications, 1996. © Sage Publications 1996. Reprinted by permission of Sage Publications Ltd.

Figure 13.1 Damien Hirst's shark: *The Impossibility of Death in the Mind of Someone Living*, 1992

the 'institutional' theory, claims, like the 'interpretive' theory, that there is no quality in the art-object, as material vehicle, that definitively qualifies it to be, or not be, an artwork. Whether it is or not is dependent on whether or not it is taken to be one by an art world, i.e. a collectivity interested in making, sharing and debating critical judgements of this type. The difference between the interpretive theory and the institutional theory is that the institutional theory does not presuppose the historical coherence of interpretations. A work may be in origin unconnected with the mainstream of art history, but if the art world co-opts the work, and circulates it as art, then it *is* art, because it is the living representatives of this art world, i.e. artists, critics, dealers and collectors, who have the power to decide these matters, not 'history'. This view is the one put forward by a noted American philosopher of aesthetics, George Dickie (1974, 1984). It is a theory that does not seem to have the support of anything like a majority of Dickie's philosophical colleagues, but that is perhaps because it is a sociological theory rather than a truly philosophical one – a theory about what is (really) considered art, rather than what ought (rationally) to be considered art. But the objectionableness of Dickie's theory from the standpoint of traditional aesthetics is precisely what constitutes its appeal to the anthropologist, since it bypasses aesthetics entirely in favour of a sociological analysis much of the kind this discipline would provide anyway (Bourdieu, 1984). None the less, the merits of the 'institutional' theory of art as a contribution to philosophical aesthetics must be as-

sessed independently of its usefulness as a starting point for sociological study of the art world.

The points at issue between these various theories were brought very much into focus at an exhibition, 'ART/ARTIFACT', mounted at the Center for African Art, New York, in 1988, under the direction of the anthropologist Susan Vogel. (I never saw this exhibition, but it received a detailed review in *Current Anthropology* outlining its contents and layout; see Faris (1988), who makes certain critical comments that I take up later.) The first exhibition space was entitled 'The Contemporary Art Gallery' (whitewashed walls, spotlights) and the star item on display was a striking object (figure 13.2) – a Zande hunting net, tightly rolled and bound for transport. Susan Vogel presumably displayed this item in this way because New York gallery-visitors would be spontaneously able to associate this 'artefact' with the type of artwork that they would have looked at in other galleries, or at least seen illustrated in newspapers and magazines. (The closest immediate analogy is with the string-bound sculptures of Jackie Windsor, see figure 13.3). Faris (1988: 776) mentions Nancy Graves and Eva Hesse as further parallels.) Vogel's choice of this particular item was a curatorial masterstroke, for which she deserves much praise, and the 'net' provoked an equally masterly catalogue essay by the American critic and philosopher of art, Arthur Danto (1988), which was published in the exhibition catalogue. What Vogel wanted to do was to break the link between African art and modern art 'Primitivism' (the Picasso of *Les Demois-*

Figure 13.2 Zande hunting net, bound up for transport, Central Africa. Courtesy of the American Museum of Natural History. Neg. no. 3444(2). Photograph by J. L. Thompson

Figure 13.3 Bound Square by Jackie Windsor, 1972

elles d'Avignon, pseudo-African masks by Modigliani, Brancusi, etc.) and suggest instead that African objects were worthy of study in a more expanded perspective, including the dominant art-style in New York in the 1980s, i.e. concept art, represented by the likes of Jackie Windsor et al. Vogel's catalogue essay-

ist, Danto, had reasons for wishing to resist this move, inasmuch as he was not persuaded that the hunting net was, or could ever become, art. 'Institutionally' speaking, the net had indeed become art in the sense that it had been exhibited as such by Vogel, and we may be sure it was received as such by a significant, and very gallery-educated, segment of the visiting public. I would hazard that had Dickie, rather than Danto, written the catalogue essay, the 'net' would have been celebrated precisely as an instance of the way in which an art world creates its artworks by labelling them as such. But Danto, on the other hand, devoted his essay to proving that the 'net's' affinities with contemporary concept art were only superficial.

In this essay I want to do two things: first, to consider Danto's proposed distinction between 'artefacts' and true works of art; and, second, to mount a little exhibition of my own (unfortunately consisting only of text and illustrations) of objects that Danto would consider artefacts but which I consider candidates for circulation as works of art, even if they were not intended to be 'works of art' by their originators, who indeed probably lacked this concept altogether. If I persuade my public, and if the institutional theory is true, i.e. art is what I and enough like-minded people say it is, then a new category of art objects is about to be born. Or not, as the case may be. . . . And especially not according to Danto, to whose arguments I must now turn.

Danto is responsible for both the interpretive and institutional theories of art, in that it was he, originally, who introduced the expression 'art-world' into philosophical aesthetics (Danto, 1964). But whereas Dickie (1974) developed Danto's ideas in the sociological direction outlined above, so that being a 'work of art' becomes a matter of social consensus among the art public, Danto tends towards a more idealist view of art, with many explicit references to Hegel in his later work. Danto's position is that art objects are such by virtue of their interpretation, and that interpretation is historically grounded. He has written two very important and well-received studies on the philosophy of modern art along these lines (1981, 1986). I agree with Danto's output in many, probably most, respects; but I am forced to say that the weaker points in Danto's version of interpretive theory emerge rather visibly in the anthropological, cross-cultural context of his 'Art/Artifact' essay.

According to Danto, there are no characteristics that an object can have which make that object a work of art; the 'objective' difference between a real Brillo box and a mock Brillo box by Warhol is not what is responsible for the fact that only the latter is a work of art.

Indistinguishably similar objects could be differentiated such that one would be an artwork and the other not. (This is exhaustively discussed in Danto, 1981.) But there is a big difference between the kind of interpretation, context, symbolic significance, etc. that an object must have if it is to be an artwork, compared to that attached to a non-artwork or 'mere' artefact. The interpretation must relate to a tradition of art-making that has internalized, reflects on and develops from its own history, as western art has done since Vasari, and maybe before. According to Danto (and I am entirely persuaded by this) modern 'concept' art corresponds to the total take-over of the 'image-making' side of art by the 'reflecting on history' side of art: concept art is the final convergence of art-making, art history, art philosophy and art criticism in a single package. However, the key concept here is the notion of a progressive, cumulative tradition (Geist, spirit, etc.). What is Danto to do when New York gallery-goers seem to want to enthuse over a hunting net as if it was the latest production of Geist in the person of Jackie Windsor or her ilk? Can contemporary art swallow extraneous objects in this way? Is the absence of an identifiable maker, and any recognizable 'artistic' intention on his or her part, an obstacle? Danto cannot but assume a critical position because intention, meaning and groundedness in a discrete, self-reflexive tradition is essential to his understanding of contemporary art, and indeed all western post-Renaissance art. The Zande hunter who made or commissioned the net did not participate in the historic frame of reference to which Windsor's similar-looking work refers, so the analogy between them is misleading. Nor could it be alternatively argued (Danto does not even consider this possibility) that the 'artist' here is Vogel, who is presenting the 'net' as a 'ready-made' in the tradition of such Duchamp prototypes as the shovel, coat rack, urinal, etc. – because Vogel is not presenting herself as a second Duchamp, but as a museum curator, offering us something to admire made in Africa, by an anonymous 'artist' who is certainly not Vogel herself.

Danto's dilemma is, essentially, that his interpretive theory of art is constructed within the implicit historical frame of western art, as was its Hegelian prototype. If he says that nothing that comes from without the historical stream of western art (which is certainly a broad stream) is 'art' in his sense, then he is certainly open to an unwelcome charge of Eurocentricity; but if he admits that exotic objects that do not participate in the *Geist* of western art are nonetheless art, how is he to exclude the 'net'? And if he allows the 'net' to be included, what is left of the explanatory value of the historically grounded interpretation, and the art/artefact distinction that is founded on it? The philosopher is truly ensnared in Vogel's net, fulfilling, at long last, its function, if not in the originally intended way.

There is only one way out for the idealist under these circumstances; he must assume that there are underlying interpretive or symbolic affinities between all true works of art in all traditions. The Zande net is to be excluded in Zande terms, because in Zande culture, as in all possible cultures, art objects have to have a particular type of symbolic significance, which a mere hunting net could safely be assumed to be lacking. Having been excluded (presumptively) by the Zande, it cannot be included by the New Yorkers, because to do so is to contradict their own principle of 'no interpretation – no art'; having agreed that not just any Brillo box but only a Warhol Brillo box is 'art', they have to accept that this net, in Zande terms, is no Warhol, but just any old net.

But how to specify the basis of the affinity between (qualifying) African artworks and western artworks, and the non-affinity between the Zande net and either of these? Danto argues that 'great' African sculpture was recognized as on a par with Donatello, Thorwaldsen, etc. by a process of 'discovery' that he likens to scientific discovery, carried out by Picasso, Brancusi, Roger Fry and their contemporaries; this greatness was always there but had been obscured by prejudicial canons of taste associated with colonialism. But this kind of African art was produced, it is implied, by individual, highly talented and discriminating sculptors, who had specific artistic (aesthetic) intentions that they carried through in their work, which ultimately became accessible to the non-African public via the efforts of sympathetic westerners. However, this approach to the incorporation of African art into the Danto scheme of things

carries with it a certain risk of aestheticism – and is not Danto the one responsible for telling us that what makes art art, is not any external (aesthetic) characteristic it may possess? So Danto is obliged to change tack, and consider an instance in which there might be African 'art' that would not be obviously different, in any external or visible respect, from African non-art, a stipulation not applicable to famous examples of African sculptural art, whose art-object status is never in doubt, for Danto at least.

Danto is a philosopher, so he does not take the obvious course of turning to the tomes upon tomes that have been written on material culture in Africa – instead he obeys his disciplinary imperative and indulges in a *Gedankexperiment*, in which he happens to be a particularly skilled practitioner. He imagines that there are two related, contiguous, but historically divergent African tribes, whom he names the Pot People and the Basket Folk, respectively. To outward observation the material productions of these two tribes, which include both pots and baskets, are pretty much identical. But the Pot People revere Pot makers, who are their priests and wise men, and the making of pots is a sacred activity that recapitulates cosmogeny, since God was a potter who formed the earth out of mud. The Pot People also make baskets, for utilitarian purposes, but they do not regard basket-making as a particularly noble activity. On the other side of the hill, among the Basket Folk, things are otherwise; here God was a basket-maker who wove the world from grass, and it is pots that are considered merely utilitarian. So here the basket makers are the wise men of the tribe and the potters are mere technical specialists, artisans.

Danto maintains that even if only the most minute examination enables the museum experts to distinguish the pots and baskets of the Pot People from the pots and baskets of the Basket Folk, the difference in the spirit in which potting is engaged in among the Pot People is sufficient to ensure that their pots are works of art, as opposed to the Basket Folk's pots, which are not (and vice versa for their respective baskets). The pots of the Pot People and the baskets of the Basket Folk belong in the prestigious *Kunsthistorisches Museum;* the baskets of the Pot People and the pots of the Basket Folk in a quite different collection, the *Naturhistorisches Museum*. The works in the Art History Museum emanate from Absolute Spirit, they are vehicles of complete ideas, stemming from, and illuminating, the human condition in its full historic density and fatefulness, whereas the objects in the Natural History Museum are means towards ends, implements that help human beings to live out their material lives – they are, in another Hegelian expression, only part of 'the Prose of the World'.

Danto, by implication, excludes the hunter's net on the grounds that it is 'prose' in object-form, and it will be seen that he draws a particularly sharp distinction, on the basis of his thought-experiment, between art objects and artefacts. But, as with all such experiments, one is entitled to ask whether it is realistic. Anthropology ought to be able to pronounce on these matters, since Danto's experiment is clearly meant to evoke real ethnography as the prototype for useful expository fictions. According to Faris, in his review of the exhibition, anthropology is only too willing to oblige with copious corroborating instances of wise men uttering Dantoesque things – and that is the problem. He roundly denounces Danto's piece for promoting tainted orthodoxy, both art-historical and anthropological. Modernists like Danto are

> paralysed by the acceptance of all cultural tyrannies and the consequent blindness to specific tyrannies [so that] they frequently fall into the most banal of humanist sentiment and idle gush about expressive and emotive power.... [T]hey do so largely in acceptance of the anthropological enterprise – the notion that, for example, African objects cannot be fully understood without indigenous Africans in the specific cultural setting that produced them.... Danto might agree, and while it is trivially true that context is relevant to meaning, it cannot be accorded axiomatic value, particularly as such context and such meaning have been structured by anthropology. (Faris, 1988: 778)

Faris argues that this kind of liberalism ostensibly receives the productions of the ethnographic Other on the Other's terms, but in fact only does so if the Other comes up with something acceptable – consistent with an existing concept of Absolute Spirit, perhaps. Danto's

imaginary ethnographies of Pot- and Basket-cosmogeny reveal exactly what kind of anthropological story-telling he would find congenial, but in reality anthropologists and indeed their informants have never been slow in providing just this sort of thing. Faris's Foucauldian point is that the whole anthropological enterprise is slanted towards finding the sort of wise men Danto endows with the power to distinguish between art and non-art, because we want to pin these objects down and attribute to them fixed, controllable meanings. I agree with Faris that Danto's (fictional) wise men are palpably projections of authority, and that they deserve to be unmasked. But unfortunately Faris does not really grapple with the 'art object' vs. 'artefact' distinction, except to indicate that it is subject to continuous redefinition (cf. Clifford, 1988: 224) and can be hardly disentangled from issues of ideology and power.

Danto himself has more to say on the subject than simply that wise men can provide the interpretations that make true artworks fragments of Absolute Spirit. In the second half of his essay he dwells on the idea that artefacts are 'incomplete' whereas artworks embody complete, self-sufficient ideas. Citing Heidegger, he remarks that an artefact is always part of a *Zeugganzes* – a system of tools, a technical system forming a whole. There cannot be a hammer by itself; a hammer implies nails to be hammered, wood to hammer them into, saws to shape the wood, and so forth. The net (implicitly) is only a component of the Zande hunting *Zeugganzes*, and has no meaning in itself. However finely crafted, an object like a net, a hammer, or even a very decorative door-hasp or other example of applied art, is incapable of conveying the kind of idea that distinguishes the art object, which always addresses the universal:

> It would be baffling were someone to say such things [pertaining to universal truths] about knives or nets or hairpins, objects whose meaning is exhausted in their utility. Universality belongs after all to thoughts or propositions, and no one would have supposed that knives or nets or hairpins express universal content. They are what they are used for, but artworks have some higher role, putting us in touch with higher realities: they are defined through the possession of meaning. They are

to be explained through what they express. Before the work of art we are in the presence of something we can grasp only through it, much as only through the medium of bodily actions we have access to the mind of another person. (Danto, 1988: 31)

But even Danto is forced to qualify this, since it is obviously the case that the bulk of the art comprising the western art tradition was not produced to be appreciated by an art public, but to fulfil instrumental purposes. Religious pictures serve liturgical functions (as altarpieces, aids to piety), portraits convey likenesses, statues dignify public spaces and glorify rulers, and so forth. The same is even more glaringly true of African products of the kind Danto is prepared to concede artwork status to; not one of them was made to be admired as an independent artwork rather than as an adjunct to public ceremony – ceremonies that cannot be exported when the artworks are exported. In short, not just nets but things like African masks are part of *Zeugganzes*, too. Danto deals with this problem by admitting that

> until very recent times [and even now, presumably, in Africa] artworks enjoyed double identities, both as objects of use and praxis, and as vessels of spirit and meaning. African art, once exported, loses its former functions, but retains its latter ones. One does not want to make placelessness one of the defining attributes of art, because that would disenfranchise as art the artworks of Primitive cultures. In their own societies these works have a place, but it would not be the *kind* of place they have in the *Zeugganzes* in their dimensions as tools in system of tools. The important point is that the whole practical life of those societies could go forward if the society had in fact no works of art . . . granted that works of art play roles in ritual that are believed to have practical efficacy. (Danto, 1988: 29)

This is surely a puzzling statement, even for a philosopher. Danto wishes to say that artworks have meaning apart from their use, and insofar as they are art they are not useful but meaningful. The self-same objects do have uses, though, in rituals of presumed efficacy. Now we could subtract the artworks and 'practical life' would still be able to continue, minus artworks, because the self-same objects,

in their guise as tools or artefacts, would still be there to fulfil their previous extra-artistic functions. This is surely casuistry. How could African masks be deployed in a ritual context as instruments of efficacy and not simultaneously have whatever cultural-interpretative significance they would have to have, according to Danto's own theory, to qualify as artworks? The proposed separation between instrumentality and spirituality is not feasible. And if artworks are implements of a kind (which would not I think be disputed by African carvers) then is it not also conceivable that implements might not also be artworks of a kind?

When you come down to it, the reason that Danto excludes the 'net' as art is that he cannot imagine a wise man who might be able to tell him a tale sufficiently compelling to induce him to think otherwise; he assumes that because it is a net, and nets are used for hunting, and hunting is a means of obtaining food, ergo, the net is a mere tool, like a cheese-grater. In this he reveals lack of familiarity with African ethnography where most of the hunting is described as taking place either as part of specific rituals (initiations, annual festivals, etc.) or at the very least in a highly ritualized manner, certainly not as a routine means of obtaining the staff of life. So had the 'net' been properly documented at the time of its collection (*c.* 1910) it is most likely that it would have figured ritually as an attribute of the 'hunter' role in the collective drama of the ritual hunt – or at least one cannot exclude this possibility – in which case it would be functioning in a way not too different from any other item of ritual paraphernalia, such as a mask.

Meanwhile, one is able to know that wise men in Africa are prepared to tell stories to anthropologists that reveal not only that hunting is ritually important (as a source of augury, an ordeal for the youth, and so on) but that the means of hunting, i.e. nets, or in this case, traps, are metaphysically significant. The source I use here is Boyer's (1988) account of wise men, chanters of magical epics, *mvet*, among the Fang of West Africa. Boyer is explicitly trying to understand the nature of 'traditional' wisdom, and in the course of his enquiries he comes to know a certain expert chanter, Ze, with whom he holds long discussions on the nature of wisdom:

Like wild animals, and like *evur* (wisdom/ magical power) *mvet* (epic) is a thing of the forest, in that it is evanescent; you think you can get hold of it, but it escapes, and it is you who gets caught. It was with Ze that I pointed out that at a certain point the complexities of *mvet* were often being compared to traps. In response, he told me the following story:

'In my youth I got to know the Pygmies well. The Pygmies belong to the forest, they are not village people like us. . . . I often went hunting with the Pygmies, they have special traps for every kind of animal, that is why they obtain so much game. They have a special trap for chim- panzees, because chimpanzees are like human beings: when they have a problem, they stop and think about what to do, instead of just running off and crying out. You cannot catch a chimpanzee with a snare because he does not run away [and thus does not pull on the run- ning-knot]. So the Pygmies have devised a spe- cial trap with a thread, which catches on the arm of the chimpanzee. The thread is very thin and the chimpanzee thinks it can get away. Instead of breaking the thread, it pulls on it very gently to see what will happen then. At that moment the bundle with the poisoned arrow falls down on it, because it has not run away like a stupid animal, like an antelope would.' (Boyer, 1988: 55–6, my translation)

This is not a dumb hunting anecdote, but Ze's way of communicating to Boyer (among other things) the basic Faustian problem about knowledge, a problem that is no less salient for the Fang of the Cameroonian rain forest than it is for the professors at MIT.

It seems unquestionable, on the basis of this testimony that for this Fang wise man, the idea of a 'trap' is a master metaphor of very deep significance, a refraction of Absolute Spirit if ever there was one. But let us bear in mind Faris's strictures against wise men, who may be considered not to be talking about utilitar- ian traps, traps in prose, but about imaginary, spiritual traps, traps as tropes, not common or garden traps. The Fang wise man does not produce any traps for Boyer's inspection. Can we move one step on from Boyer's text, to the point at which we could mount an exhibition, in a gallery, of animal traps, and present this to the public as an exhibition of artworks?

Let us leave wise men out of it for the pre- sent and ask ourselves what animal traps re- veal about the human spirit, even in the absence of native exegesis. Do animal traps, in their bare, decontextualized presence, tell us no more than that human beings like to consume animal flesh?

In order to allow you to arrive at a judge- ment, I offer the accompanying illustrations, drawn from the ethnological literature on traps. Take the arrow trap (figure 13.4). Re- member that Danto says that looking at a work of art is like encountering a person; one encounters a person as a thinking, co-present being by responding to his or her outward form and behaviour – similarly one responds to an artwork as a co-present being, an em- bodied thought. Now imagine encountering the arrow trap, not (one hopes) as the victim is going to encounter it, but as a gallery-goer encounters an 'installation' by the latest con- temporary artist. In those circumstances, and without additional context, what might the sensitive gallery-goer intuit as the thought, or intention, in this artwork?

There would be nothing amiss, I think, should the imaginary visitor to our exhibition see here, in the arrow trap, a representation of human being-in-the-world. It is a representa- tion that the narrow-minded might prefer to censor and repress, were they only aware that the trap *could be* a representation. For it shows being-in-the-world as unthinking, poised vio- lence, which is not perhaps a pretty thought, but not for that reason an untrue or inartistic one. Initially, a trap such as this communicates a deadly absence – the absence of the man who devised and set it, and the absence of the ani- mal who will become the victim (the artist has indicated this victim in the background of the illustration). Because of these marked ab- sences, the trap, like all traps, functions as a powerful sign. Not designed to communicate or to function as a sign (in fact, designed to be hidden and escape notice), the trap nonetheless signifies far more intensely than most signs intended as such. The static violence of the tensed bow, the congealed malevolence of the arrangement of sticks and cords, are revelatory in themselves, without recourse to convention- alization. Since this is a sign that is not, officially, a sign at all, it escapes all censorship. We read in it the mind of its author and the fate of its victim.

This trap is a model as well as an implement. In fact, all implements are models, because

Figure 13.4 Arrow trap, Central Africa; sketch by Weule

they have to be adapted to their users' characteristics, and so bear their imprint. An artificial leg is a model of a missing real leg, a representation that functions as a prosthesis. The arrow trap is particularly clearly a model of its creator, because it has to substitute for him; a surrogate hunter, it does its owner's hunting for him. It is, in fact, an automaton or robot, whose design epitomizes the design of its maker. It is equipped with a rudimentary sensory transducer (the cord, sensitive to the animal's touch). This afferent nervous system brings information to the automaton's central processor (the trigger mechanism, a switch, the basis of all information-processing devices) which activates the efferent system, releasing the energy stored in the bow, which propels the arrows, which produce action-at-a-distance (the victim's death). This is not just a model of a person, like any doll, but a 'working' model of a person. What carving, it is surely reasonable to ask, which only shows us our outward lineaments, actually reveals as much about human being as this mechanical device? Much more of what there actually is to a human being is present here than in any carving, but because it is not an obvious instance of an 'art' object, it is never to be looked at in this light.

Moreover, if we look at other traps, we are able to see that each is not only a model of its creator, a subsidiary self in the form of an automaton, but each is also a model of its victim. This model may actually reflect the outward form of the victim, as in the comical giraffe trap shown in figure 13.5, which delineates, in negative contour, the outlines of the lower half of a giraffe. Or the trap may, more subtly and abstractly, represent parameters of the animal's natural behaviour, which are subverted in order to entrap it. Traps are lethal parodies of the animal's *Umwelt* (figures 13.6, 13.7). Thus the rat that likes to poke around in narrow spaces has just such an attractive

Figure 13.5 Giraffe trap drawn by Wood

Figure 13.6 Rat trap, Vanuatu; sketch by Bell

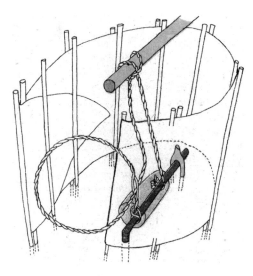

Figure 13.7 Trap from Guyana; sketch by Roth

cavity prepared for its last, fateful foray into the dark (figure 13.6). Of course, it is not really the case that the trap is clever or deceitful; it is the hunter who knows the victim's habitual responses and is able to subvert them. But once the trap is in being, the hunter's skill and knowledge are truly located in the trap, in objectified form, otherwise the trap would not work. This objective knowledge would survive even the death of the hunter himself. It would also be (partially) 'readable' to others who had only the trap, and not the animal lore that was reflected in its design. From the form of the trap, the dispositions of

the intended victim could be deduced. In this sense, traps can be regarded as texts on animal behaviour.

The trap is therefore both a model of its creator, the hunter, and a model of its victim, the prey animal. But more than this, the trap embodies a scenario, which is the dramatic nexus that binds these two protagonists together, and which aligns them in time and space. Our illustrations cannot show this because they either show traps awaiting their victims, or victims who have been already entrapped; they cannot show the 'time structure' of the trap. This time structure opposes suspended time, the empty time of 'waiting', to the sudden catastrophe that ensues as the trap closes. This temporal structure varies with the kind of trap employed, but it is not hard to see in the drama of entrapment a mechanical analogue to the tragic sequence of hubris–nemesis–catastrophe. Consider the doomed hippopotamus (figure 13.8) lulled into a sense of false security by sheer bulk and majesty. How many tragic heroes have suffered from the same hubristic illusions and have invited the same fate? If the chimpanzee who falls for Boyer's trap is Faust, perhaps this hippopotamus is Othello. The fact that animals who fall victim to traps have always brought about their downfall by their own actions, their own complacent self-confidence, ensures that trapping is a far more poetic and tragic form of hunting than the simple chase. The latter kind of hunting equalizes hunters and victims, united in spontaneous action and reaction, whereas trapping decisively hierarchizes hunter and victim. The trapper is God, or the fates, the trapped animal is man in his tragic incarnation.

It therefore seems to me that, even without ethnographic context, without exegesis from any wise men, animal traps such as these might be presented to an art public as artworks. These devices embody ideas, convey meanings, because a trap, by its very nature, is a transformed representation of its maker, the hunter, and the prey animal, its victim, and of their mutual relationship, which, among hunting people, is a complex, quintessentially social one. That is to say, these traps communicate the idea of a nexus of intentionalities between hunters and prey animals, via material forms and mechanisms. I would argue that

Figure 13.8 Hippopotamus trap drawn by Boteler

walls project virtual images of the equally aseptic surrounding gallery into the shark's biological domain. A distant echo of the upper (biological) and lower (mechanical) halves of Duchamp's *Large Glass*? – no doubt – but also a reflection on our power to immobilize elemental forces, which nonetheless always seem potentially liable to escape. Even Hirst's shark, as dead as a dead thing can be, is still residually alive, watching and thinking, or seems to be, because it keeps its eyes open and stares at us. One day it is going to get out.

It would be appropriate to place the shark alongside this bark-painting scene from Morphy's *Ancestral Connections* (figure 13.9) showing the painting of a trapped shark, visually nearly identical to Hirst's installation in the Tate. The Yolnngu produce this painting during funerary rituals, and it refers to the up-river journey of a mythical ancestral shark, which was temporarily trapped on the way, but which escaped. This painting refers to the deceased's clan affiliations, and metaphorizes

Figure 13.9 Coffin lid being painted with the image of a trapped shark. Photograph by Howard Morphy

this evocation of complex intentionalities is in fact what serves to define artworks, and that suitably framed, animal traps could be made to evoke complex intuitions of being, otherness, relatedness. The impact of these traps, now being presented as artworks, might however be increased if they were exhibited in conjunction with western artworks (of which it is easy to find numerous examples) that seem to occupy the same semiological territory.

The work of Damien Hirst, the most media-exposed of younger British artists in recent times, seems to be a case in point. In fact, it was Hirst's notorious Turner Prize exhibit at the Tate Gallery in 1992 that first induced me to start thinking about traps as art objects. Consider Hirst's shark in a tank of formaldehyde (figure 13.1). This work captivates because of the profound contrast between the gigantic, ultra-biological fish and its aseptic glass cage, or trap (recalling Eichmann at his trial, trapped in a glass box) whose reflective

the journey of the spirit towards the ancestral country, and the need to transfer power to it (via funerary ceremonies) so that it, like the ancestral shark, can burst out of the 'traps' that threaten to impede its progress. The episode of the shark being trapped, and escaping, is enacted by the participants. These eschatological ideas are, of course, specifically Yolnngu, but I would submit that the surface similarity between Hirst's work and the Yolnngu work are not just superficial, and that a metaphor is being deployed here that is accessible cross-culturally in a highly transformed, but still readable, way.

Meanwhile, to reinforce the point that Hirst's work is in a rather deep way about traps, and the network of complex intentionalities that the notion of entrapment sets up, I should simply describe another of Hirst's works in the same exhibition, which actually incorporated a working trap device. I refer to the installation consisting of a decaying sheep's head in a glass box, which breeds maggots, which turn into flies, which then become victims of a butchers'-shop type fly trap, which attracts the flies by violet light on to high-voltage electrified wires, on which they die. A trap within a trap, victims within a victim: as anthropologists we should be the first to recognize redundancy within the mythological code as a means of underlining the dialectical message, which in this case is to induce the spectator to identify him- or herself with the victims in this assemblage (the dead animal, the maggots, the flies) and at the same time with the vicious God who has set this rigmarole of a world in motion, the maker of traps, Hirst, you, me . . .

Hirst would not be the only western contemporary artist whose work would be on display at the exhibition of traps. Next to the arrow trap, for instance, I might install the work by the concept artist Judith Horn (figure 13.10), consisting of two shotguns suspended from the gallery ceiling, which periodically blast one another with red, blood-resembling liquid, drawn off from tanks above them. Evidently, at one level, this is a commentary on the senselessness of war, but the key to this work is not so much the theme of mutual violence as the marked absence of its perpetrators – precisely the theme I identified earlier in relation to the arrow trap. In fact, Horn's installation directly

Figure 13.10 High Noon by Judith Horn

relates to the type of 'class war' man-traps (shotguns triggered by tripwires) that were set to deter poaching on shooting estates in times past.

Additional examples of post-Duchampian artworks (even work by Duchamp himself, such as the *Trébuchet* of 1917) that could figure in this exhibition could easily be selected, but Hirst and Horn will do for now. It is not that I would insist that a trap from Africa and the latest work of Damien Hirst are instances of the same kind of thing at all, but only that each is capable, in the context of an exhibition, of synergizing and drawing meaning out of the other. They are not the same, and are not entirely different or incommensurable either; they are, in Marylin Strathern's (1991) phrase 'partially connected'.

Nor do I suppose that for an African trap, or a trap from any other exotic part of the world, to function as an artwork it is actually necessary or desirable for the ethnographic context to be stripped away. The artistic meaning of certain traps can often only be established ethnographically, and this makes essential a textual component to any satisfactory exhibition of 'trap' artworks – but there is no need to apologize for this; since Duchamp it has gone without saying that written notes and commentary in the form of interviews and suchlike are necessary for the comprehension of contemporary artworks – just as a knowledge of neo-Platonic philosophy is necessary for a true appreciation of Renaissance art, I would say

(Wind, 1957). I simply happen to have no exegesis for the arrow trap, for instance, but this trap is so graphic it hardly needs any. With certain other traps it is essential.

Take, for instance, the angling trap from Guyana, illustrated in Roth (1924), see figure 13.11. I would hardly have regarded it as a particularly artistic trap unless Stephen Hugh-Jones had informed me (pers. comm.) that the equivalent type of fishing trap among the Barasana (in neighbouring Colombia) is known as the trap 'which turns fish into fruit'. Given this information one sees at once how wittily metaphysical and magical this trap is. One moment the fish is placidly swimming along belonging (so it thinks) to the animal kingdom and then, bang, before it knows what has happened it is a vegetable, dangling from the branches of a tree, to be plucked like any other fruit by a passing Indian. What a come-uppance, in more senses than one! This transubstantiation recalls the (dead) sheep's head/maggot/fly/ (dead) fly transubstantiations in Hirst's installation discussed above, but more radically, in that the fish moves between kingdoms, while the sheep's head, rather more literally, only moves between orders. Certainly, this point would not occur to a non-Barasana art public without textual clues – but once the clue is provided one does not need a PhD in anthro-pology to enjoy the joke, nor, I think, to be led to reflect on its deeper implications.

Another instance (which must be the last) of a trap that can function as an artwork only with the assistance of a certain degree of exegetical material is the Anga eel-trap described in a recent paper by Pierre Lemonnier (1992). This trap consists of a long cylinder of rolled-up tree-bark, bound together with numerous coils of rattan, reinforced with wood and provided with an ingenious sprung trapdoor. Eels are trapped in elongated traps like this in many parts of New Guinea and, indeed, elsewhere. What is significant about the Anga trap is the context in which it is made, and the care which is lavished on it, which could not be apparent to the uninstructed. Lemonnier's Anga trap eels in traps like these in the context of mortuary ritual, specifically, at the end of the period of mourning, when the mourners must be revived in preparation for their return to ordinary life. Feasting on eels is efficacious at this time, not just because eels are excellent, valued food; but also because eels are associated with the penis of the founding ancestor, detached because it was superfluously long. They are thus a source of spiritual vitality as well as superior nourishment, not that these categories can be completely dissociated in local terms. Were this all, the traps themselves might still

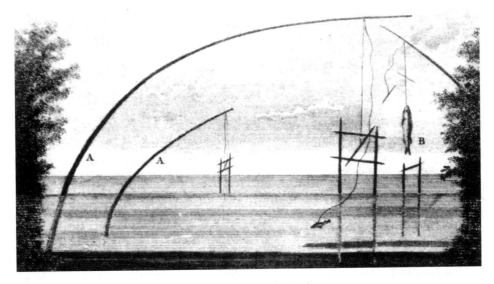

Figure 13.11 Spring-hook fishing trap, Guyana; sketch by Stedman

be considered mere implements, because the fact that eels are sacred to the Anga does not necessarily also mean that the means of obtaining eels are sacred, or in any way extraordinary. Even the fact that the traps are constructed in the course of a ritual, with much magical attention being given to them, might not suffice to take them outside the ruck of common objects. But what Lemonnier can show – and this, very probably, would only be apparent to an anthropologist, poised between the Anga world and the western one, not a native – is that it is actually in the fabrication of the traps that the Anga construct their notion of the 'power' inherent in eels. The traps are made of strips of bark bound together with hoops of cane and provided with a trapdoor at the wider end. What Lemonnier notices is that the cane 'binding' hoops are far stronger, more numerous and more carefully made than would be needed to restrain a few eels, and, similarly, the trapdoor is much sturdier than strictly necessary. Thus it is the trap, rather than the real eel, that carries the message of eel-power. As a symbolic artefact that captures and contains eel-power, it functions, metonymically, to empower the eel, by virtue of its own sturdiness and strength. Indeed the trap, which is shaped to accommodate and attract eels, is a representation of an eel, both in the already-mentioned sense of being an objectification of eel behavioural lore, but also more directly, in that it is itself eel-like (eel-ongated), phallic, ingestive and reproductive.

There could not be a clearer refutation of the thesis that would consign things like animal traps to the status of 'mere' artefacts, by comparison to ancestor-carvings and the like (which the Anga, incidentally, do not make) as candidates for artwork status. If the Anga embody their ancestors in fabricated form, it is surely in the form of traps such as these (as well as other artefacts, such as initiation temples). These traps are 'images of the ancestors' in the sense that they contain, embody and communicate ancestral power. Moreover, they make possible its realization of ancestral presence in the here and now as few conventional images may be said to, not 'in spite of' the fact that they are also useful implements for catching eels, but *because* of this fact. We in the West have longed for (and fantasized about) statues or images that would move, or bless, or make love, but,

for centuries, always in vain. The Anga, by contrast, have 'images' of ancestral power that actually accomplish work, actually nourish those who make them, and so achieve a goal that has always eluded our artists, waylaid as they have been by the need for realistic representation of (surface) forms.

Conclusion

Suppose, then, that such a hybrid exhibition of animal traps from far and wide, interspersed with relevant western artworks, were to be presented to the gallery public. What might that imply for the problem with which I began this essay – the dispute concerning the criteria for artwork status? I hope that I might have said enough to convince at least some people that such a conjunction would not be wholly inopportune. The institutional theory of art would at this point immediately 'enfranchise' a large array of artefacts – hitherto consigned to the *Naturhistorisches Museum* – to a place in the *Kunsthistorisches Museum*, assuring them a quite different audience and reception, since by being successfully circulated as artworks, these works would become nothing less. Would that be a retrograde step?

Speaking as an anthropologist concerned with art, rather than as an art critic or a mouthpiece for Absolute Spirit, I believe that this would be a welcome development. The worst thing about the 'anthropology of art' as at present constituted is precisely the way in which it has inherited a reactionary definition of art, so that it more or less has to concern itself with objects that would have been classified as 'art' or, more likely, 'craft' at the beginning of this century, but has little or nothing to do with the kinds of objects (installations, performances) that are characteristically circulated as 'art' in the late 20th century. In effect, 'art' for the anthropology of art consists of those types of artefacts one might find on display as 'art' only in a very sleepy provincial town which (as most of them do) boasts a 'gallery' where one finds folksy ceramics, carvings and tufted woollen tapestries, not to mention innumerable still-lives and Palmeresque rural idylls. The tradition of middlebrow art that produces and consumes these things is of course indestructible, but why should the ethnographic Other be deemed a producer of 'art' only if he or she produces work that is generically analogous to such reactionary dross, even if individual works of 'primitive art', so circumscribed, are actually of the highest quality. The reason for the persistence of this state of affairs – which may, however, be unravelling as I write (see Weiner, 1994) – lies in the continuing hold of the 'aesthetic' notion of artworks over the anthropological mind (Maquet, 1986), since it is this definition of artworks that ensures that only 'aesthetically pleasing' carvings, paintings, pots, cloths, etc. are to count as 'art'.

The move I advocate is the abandonment of the aesthetic notion of artworks by the anthropology of art (Gell, 1992), which alone would permit the kind of direct confrontation described above, between the artefacts of non-western peoples and the productions of post-Duchampian artmaking, i.e. the central tradition of contemporary art, properly speaking, not the *ersatz* to be seen in provincial arts-and-crafts galleries. One should accept the essentially liberating premise of the institutional theory of art, which has arisen precisely to accommodate the historic fact that western artworks no longer have an aesthetic 'signature' and can consist of entirely arbitrary objects, like dead sharks in tanks of formaldehyde, and so on.

Do I mean that any object of human manufacture whatsoever can be circulated as an artwork? Is this what is implied by the 'institutional' theory of art? Potentially, perhaps, yes; but this has been trivial, in terms of contemporary art theory, since 1917, when Duchamp exhibited his notorious urinal (or *Fountain*). That was in the time of my grandfather, and the time of the great-grandfathers of today's artists, such as Damien Hirst. So if selecting and exhibiting arbitrary objects as 'art' were all that defined the post-Duchampian tradition, there would be little left to expect from it by this late stage. Actually, things are otherwise; Duchamp's ready-mades were carefully selected and thematically tightly integrated to his two major projects (the *Large Glass* (1915–23) and the *Waterfall* (1944–66)). What is interesting about Duchamp's ready-made art objects was never the objects themselves, but Duchamp's reasons for selecting them (divulged in the course of a life-long strip-tease performance) and the same is true for the art produced by his many followers.

The apparently 'arbitrary' objects of concept art are only *apparently* arbitrary, and they all work, if they do work, because they have complex (Dantoesque) historic and iconographic resonances, of which the gallery public is, to a greater or lesser extent, made aware. They are objects that are scrutinized as vehicles of complicated ideas, intended to achieve or mean something interesting, difficult, allusive, hard to bring off, etc. I would define as a candidate artwork any object or performance that potentially rewards such scrutiny because it embodies intentionalities that are complex, demanding of attention and perhaps difficult to reconstruct fully (cf. Kant's notion of the 'free play of cognitive powers').

Thus it takes more to make a post-Duchampian artwork than merely exhibiting it in a gallery – an interpretive context also has to be developed and disseminated. In this respect the purely institutional theory of the artwork is less than satisfactory because it has nothing to say about the criteria that govern the creation of the kinds of contextual resonances to which the educated gallery public are sensitive. To this extent Danto is right to insist on the priority of interpretability in the constitution of the artwork. What is wrong with his theory, at least so far as the artwork vs artefact distinction is concerned, is its dependence on an over-idealized distinction between 'functional' artefacts and 'meaningful' artworks. This is a legacy of post-Enlightenment philosophers such as Hegel, but it obscures the view of any art world other than the one Hegel had specifically in mind. Perhaps contemporary gallery artworks do nothing but evoke meaning; but most artworks have political, religious and other functions which are 'practical' in terms of local conceptions of how the world is and how humans may intervene in its workings to their best advantage. Artworks can also trap eels, as we have seen, or grow yams (Gell, 1992: 60). The 'interpretation' of such 'practically' embedded artworks is intrinsically conjoined to their characteristics as instruments fulfilling purposes other than the embodiment of autonomous 'meaning'.

A half-way house between the 'institutional' and 'interpretive' theories therefore seems to me the best option. The institutional theory of art is amenable to the idea that artworks can be 'arfefacts' securing a range of human purposes, so long as they are simultaneously deemed interesting as art to an art public. But the institutional theory has a problem in that it is less clear about the kinds of criteria that dictate whether candidate objects will or will not be selected as artistically 'interesting'. The Danto–Hegelian conception of an autonomous art 'Geist' will not enfranchise any but a narrow and unrepresentative range of human productions, and fails to account for the rather successful artwork candidacy of Vogel's 'net' except as the result of a category mistake on the part of the art public. A broader notion of interpretability, encompassing the objectification of 'complex intentionalities' in pragmatic and technical modes, as well as the project of communicating autonomous symbolic meaning, seems to me to overcome the problems contained in both the 'interpretive' and 'institutional' theories of art.

What the 'anthropology of art' ought to be about, in my opinion, is the provision of a critical context that would enfranchise 'artefacts' and allow for their circulation as artworks, displaying them as embodiments or residues of complex intentionalities. Anthropology should be part of art-making itself, insofar as art-making, art history and art criticism are a single enterprise nowadays. Partly this would consist of the provision of relevant ethnography (such as provided by Boyer, Hugh-Jones, Lemmonnier, mentioned earlier) and partly the discovery of connections between complex intentionalities in western artworks and the kind of intentionalities embodied in artworks and artefacts (now recontextualized as artworks) from elsewhere. This would be a one-sided transaction in art-making, in the sense that essentially metropolitan concepts of 'art' would be in play, not indigenous ones; but objects, as Thomas (1991) has shown are 'promiscuous' and can move freely between cultural/transactional domains without being essentially compromised. This they can do because they have indeed no essences, only an indefinite range of potentials.

So was Vogel's net an artwork? I believe that the New York gallery-goers who took it for one were not mistaken. Nor were they entirely swayed by the mere fact that they were institutionally invited to see it as one, by the gallery setting and the chance rhymes between the Zande net and the work of well-known western concept artists such as Jackie Windsor. They were also, I am sure, responding to the very notion of a 'net' and the paradoxical way in which this net had been itself caught, and tightly bound, within a second net. This recursive metaphor of capture and containment would have been itself enough to give them pause, halt them in their passage, and induce them to stand and stare, like Boyer's fated chimpanzee. Every work of art that works is like this, a trap or a snare that impedes passage; and what is any art gallery but a place of capture, set with what Boyer calls 'thought-traps', which hold their victims for a time, in suspension? Vogel's net was set with care, and in it she captured, besides sundry philosophers and anthropologists – including this one – a large part of the question 'what is art?'.

REFERENCES

Bourdieu, Pierre (1984) *Distinction: A Social Critique of Judgements of Taste*, trans. Richard Nice. London: Routledge & Kegan Paul.

Boyer, Pascal (1988) *Barricades mystérieuses et Pièges à Pensée: Introduction à l'analyse des épopées Fang*. Paris: Société d'Ethnologie.

Clifford, James (1988) *The Predicament of Culture*. Cambridge, MA: Harvard University Press.

Danto, Arthur (1964) 'The Artworld Journal of Philosophy', *Journal of Philosophy* 61: 571–84.

Danto, Arthur (1981) *The Transfiguration of the Commonplace*. Cambridge, MA: Harvard University Press.

Danto, Arthur (1986) *The Philosophical Disenfranchisement of Art*. New York: Prentice Hall.

Danto, Arthur (1988) 'Artifact and Art', in *ART/ARTIFACT: African Art in Anthropology Collections*. Exhibition Catalogue. New York: Center for African Art and Prestel Verlag.

Dickie, George (1974) *Art and the Aesthetic*. Ithaca, NY: Cornell University Press.

Dickie, George (1984) *The Art Circle: A Theory of Art*. New York: Havens.

Faris, James (1988) 'ART/ARTIFACT: on the Museum and Anthropology', *Current Anthropology* 29(5): 775–9.

Gell, Alfred (1992) 'The Technology of Enchantment', in Jeremy Coote and Anthony Shelton (eds) *Anthropology, Art and Aesthetics*. Oxford: Oxford University Press.

Lemonnier, Pierre (1992) 'The Eel and the Ankave-Anga: Material and Symbolic Aspects of Trapping', draft article, unpublished.

Maquet, Jaques (1986) *The Aesthetic Experience: An Anthropologist Looks at the Visual Arts*. New Haven, CT: Yale University Press.

Morphy, Howard (1991) *Ancestral Connections: Art and an Aboriginal System of Knowledge*. Chicago: Chicago University Press.

Roth, Walter (1924) 38th Annual Report of the American Bureau of Ethnology.

Strathern, Marylin (1991) *Partial Connections*. Savage, MD: Rowman Littlefield.

Thomas, Nicholas (1991) *Entangled Objects*. Cambridge, MA: Harvard University Press.

Weiner, J. (ed.) (1994) 'Aesthetics is a Cross-cultural Category', Group for Debates on Anthropological Theory. Manchester University, Department of Anthropology.

Wind, Edgar (1957) *Pagan Mysteries in the Renaissance*. Oxford: Oxford University Press.

Part III

Aesthetics across Cultures

Introduction

It is not easy to understand why aesthetics has been so neglected in anthropology, nor why the application of the concept of aesthetics to the anthropological study of art has been so controversial (see the protagonists in Ingold 1996, the arguments of Gell 1998, and the response by Layton 2003:449). While particular aesthetic judgments and ideas of beauty will vary between (and within) cultures that does not mean that the concept of aesthetics is irrelevant for cross-cultural research. Indeed we would argue that it is necessary. As with any cross-cultural category it is necessary to divorce it from any particular culture's ideational system, and to define aesthetics in general terms and not associate it with a particular culture's ideational system, without losing sight of its core meaning. Aesthetics is centered on the effect(s) that form (broadly defined to include shape, texture, light and shade, taste and smell and so on) has on the senses. Aesthetics involves the perception of qualities, and the evaluation, interpretation, and response to qualitative aspects of form. A study of aesthetics also requires an understanding of the way that aesthetic factors motivate the production of artworks and the purposes to which they are put. Aesthetics concerns the sensual aspects of objects but it is not confined to the beautiful.

While it is possible as Morphy argues, that humans universally sense some aesthetic effects across place and time – shininess, symmetry, and asymmetry, for example – they are experienced and interpreted differently according to cultural context and the position of the responder. A particular aesthetic effect may inspire fear in the New Guinea Highlands and evoke feelings of spiritual joy and ecstasy in a Catholic mass. The shield that terrifies the opponent may give the bearer a sense of health, well-being and strength (see O'Hanlon's chapter). The aesthetics of art has to be explored in the context of the particular society that produces it. While there may be overlaps in the evaluations of the same works by members of different cultures, such overlaps need to be demonstrated rather than presumed.

Farris Thompson's analysis of Yoruba aesthetics was the first detailed published analysis of the aesthetic judgments made by African artists and their indigenous audience. His analysis enables non-Yoruba to look at the works from a Yoruba perspective, and to see and evaluate them on that basis rather than in terms of the aesthetic system of their own society. Thompson has developed a hybrid vocabulary based in part on the terminology used by European art historians to describe the structure and formal composition of sculptures but modified to respond to Yoruba criteria. While aesthetics cannot be reduced to the idea of beauty Thompson develops his analysis as a precursor to understanding Yoruba concepts of beauty, and exploring the ways in which the concept articulates with religious and moral values (see Boone (1986) for a complementary analysis of the aesthetics of Mende masquerade). Thompson suggests that this opens the way for aesthetic discourse between Yoruba and non-Yoruba art historians. It is interesting to compare Farris Thompson's analysis with Bateson's analysis of a Balinese painting (ch. 4). While Bateson does not provide the kind of detailed exegesis about Balinese aesthetic criteria that Thompson does for the Yoruba, the conclusions that both draw about the relationships between aesthetics and a moral order show remarkable parallels. There is a sense in which the aesthetic dimension of objects is thought to provide a means of apprehending general structurings of value and the core metaphysics of particular societies – metaphysical and phenomenological aspects of the culture that cannot be easily communicated in everyday language. However because it so easy to read values into art objects on the basis of one's own aesthetic experience it is vital to approach the topic from the basis of a rigorous analysis of the objects in the context of the cultures which produce them. Munn's (1986) analysis of qualities (such as heaviness and lightness) in Gawan society from a semiotic and phenomenological perspective provides an exemplary analysis of value creation processes in the Massim.

While Morphy and Farris Thompson focus on art objects, broadly defined, Coote makes the important point that aesthetics can intervene in virtually all aspects of the daily life of a society. Indeed in the case of the Nilotic peoples of southern Sudan he argues that there is an absence of what are conventionally understood to be art objects. Aesthetics and aesthetic valuations are however important in everyday life and in patterning people's experience. While it is true that under a broader definition of art Nilotic society is rich in poetry, song, and ritual performance, the more general point that Coote is making is an important corrective to those who restrict their exploration of aesthetics to recognized art objects. While in some societies art may provide a central focus for aesthetic discourse, aesthetics is likely to be much more pervasive as a factor in people's lives and it is important that anthropologists should approach aesthetics from this broader perspective. It is as important to analyze the aesthetics of furniture design and the motor car – and cattle – as it is to focus on the object set aside in the art gallery for reflective contemplation. Firth's analysis of Tikopean headrests (ch. 5) complements Coote's analysis well.

Aesthetic factors are often important determinants of action and integral to the effectiveness of an event, as well as to the personal appeal of an object. Aesthetics can be integral to value creation processes and be important determinants of a cultural trajectory. Analyzing the aesthetics of material culture in archaeological or historical contexts can provide important avenues for interpretation. Lechtman's chapter (15) on Andean "gold" objects demonstrates how analyzing objects from an aesthetic perspective can reveal important components of systems of value which in this case influence the technological trajectory of a society.

REFERENCES

Boone, Sylvia Ardyn, 1986 *The Radiance from the Waters*. New Haven: Yale University Publications in the History of Art.

Gell, Alfred, 1998 *Art and Agency: an Anthropological Theory*. Oxford: Oxford University Press.

Ingold, Tim, ed. 1996 1993 Debate: Aesthetics is a Cross-Cultural Category. In *Key Debates in Anthropology*. London: Routledge.

Layton, Robert, 2003 Art and Agency: A Reassessment. *Journal of the Royal Anthropological Institute* (N.S.) 9: 447–464.

Munn, Nancy, 1986 *The Fame of Gawa: A Symbolic Study of Value Transformation in a Massim (Papua New Guinea) Society*. Cambridge: Cambridge University Press.

14

Yoruba Artistic Criticism

Robert Farris Thompson

There exists in Subsaharan Africa, locked in the minds of kings, priests, and commoners, a reservoir of artistic criticism. Wherever tapped, this source lends clarity to our understanding of the arts of tropical Africa. The Western scholar may assign value to a work which would elicit equal praise in the compound of a traditional king, assuming the work and critics were from the same African society, but he cannot assume that the reasons for his choice are present in the mind of the native critic.

Africans may admire works of art, or categories of artistic expression, which a Westerner, in the ethnocentric conviction that he had mastered all the relevant issues, might pass over in ignorance. African criticism enriches, in these cases, our sense of definition. By definition I mean the identification and characterization of expressive media which, like African dancing, might pass largely unanalyzed through the filter of Western scholarship. Conversely, consideration of African judgment of African art protects the student from the dangers of reading into a work of art aesthetic principles which might not be present in the native imagination.

More important is the fact that African aesthetics opens onto African sensibility. Aesthetic criticism suggests the relation of art to emotional ideals. These ideals, in turn, reveal the hidden unities which impose meaningful design upon the face of a culture. The mosaic may, of course, be apprehended only in fragments by members of the society.

Contexts of Yoruba artistic criticism

Yoruba art critics are experts of strong mind and articulate voice who measure in words the quality of works of art.

Yoruba artistic criticism may occur at a dance feast where the excellence of sculpture and motion becomes a matter of intense concern. In Iperu-Remon, Nigeria, "loads" (headdresses) for the Orò cult are judged competitively on the basis of sculptural and choreographic appeal. Similarly, in Ajilete, Nigeria, "battles of dance" decide which quarter at a given festival has triumphed and brought glory to the town. The elders of Igogo-Ekiti critically observe the dance movement of young men who aspire to the honor of carrying the senior headdresses of the local Epa cult. Young men of legitimate birth, physical, moral, and artistic powers are chosen. In this way festivals provide a setting of criticism.

In addition to the cult context, where critical acuity seems to increase under the stimulus of expressive sounds and sights, artistic criticism

From Warren D'Azevedo (ed.), *The Traditional Artist in African Societies*, 2 (Bloomington: Indiana University Press, 1973), pp. 19–61, 435–454. Reprinted by permission of Indiana University Press Ltd.

seems to flourish among the Yoruba in those situations where money provides auxiliary excitement or agitation. In the market, workshop, and other places, the quality of a work of art can become the essence of commercial transaction. Here aesthetic products again meet articulated conventional tests of quality. An apprentice, for example, who has attempted to sell an indifferent example of his work to a bona fide patron may find himself called into the workshop of the village master where the master criticizes him (Cordwell 1952: 292). The master indicates, either by carving a new piece or by improving the finish of the unsatisfactory work, proper control and care. He tells the carver what went wrong with the work and warns him to do better. The criteria of the master are frequently regarded as trade secrets, which explains why so few have been shared in the past with Westerners.[1]

Mutual criticisms among sculptors are an especially sensitive source of information about Yoruba aesthetics. When a master carver impugns the abilities of a lesser carver, his gestures and facial expression can be as eloquently derisive as his words. Alaga of Odo-Owa, for example, dilated his nostrils with disgust when he met a carelessly rendered *Ẹpa* headdress at Egbe: "Á! À! the juju gourds are unpleasingly lumpy. The face of the man is crooked. *Ó burú tó bẹẹ̀ gẹ* – it's as bad as bad can be."

Apart from important chiefs and mutual friends, Yoruba critics will not criticize with style and precision unless it is made financially worth their while. This does not mean that they are professional. It simply means that Yoruba live traditionally in a world of money, personal honor, and entourage. By acts of generosity a Yoruba leader proves to his entourage that he is worthy of their acclaim. By the same token, the Western student proves by remuneration that he merits the honor of shared qualitative data. The size of a Yoruba ruler's entourage is a mark of his generosity and importance (Bascom 1951: 496); the quality of the data of the field worker may reflect the amount of money allocated to aesthetic research. This is in character with the importance that Yoruba give to spending money on oral skills. Drummers, for example, find livelihood in the praise of rich men, and one woman of Ikare has earned 75 pounds a year in rec-

ompense for prayer of surpassing beauty and force.[2]

The oral art of criticism also moves within the sphere of money. It is certain, moreover, that few traditional Yoruba make gratuitous statements of opinion on any subject in the presence of foreigners. No informant ever discussed with me the notion of multiple souls, but this did not mean that such a belief was not indigenous, as the researches of P. Amaury Talbot (1926: 261–2) and William Bascom (1960) attest. We must therefore weigh the following report with special care:

> I have never heard a spontaneous discussion on the form, proportion or expression of a piece of sculpture – although I have lived twelve years in Yoruba country and have moved a great deal among priests and worshippers in shrines full of religious carvings. (Beier 1963: 6)

This does not imply an absolute lack of spontaneous discussion in aesthetic merits in Yorubaland. It may mean that outside the festival, the commercial transaction involving sculpture, the admonitions of master to apprentice, the mutual criticisms among sculptors, and so forth, it is rare. Entrance into a shrine full of carving clearly does not guarantee an audience with a traditional critic. After all, do Roman Catholics analyze the aesthetic merits of cathedral images when at worship?

A Westerner may be lucky enough to overhear some fragment of spontaneous criticism. By chance I observed a mother of twins abuse an apprentice because he had brought her an image which she said did not resemble a human being. Again by chance I observed the head of the Mẹko Gẹlẹdẹ cult motivate his hired carver, by worriedly knitting his brows, to rectify certain proportional improprieties.

Is it possible to distinguish criticism to paying outsiders from in-group criticism? In both instances critics name abstractions and cite common terminology in order to define the qualities which distinguish aliveness from, say, woodenness. However, it seems likely that critics who are also master carvers may rise to a higher level of nuance and precision in their conversations about quality. In point of fact, some sculptor-critics use a set of analytical verbs which are as sure in effect as the defining strokes of their adzes. These verbs grant them the power to measure the relative weight and shading of linear properties with an accuracy which might well provoke astonishment in the West.

As in the professional jargon of the social scientist, the proliferation of conceptual vocabulary among the better Yoruba critics "corresponds to an intensely sustained attention toward the properties of reality." This is an instance of Lévi-Strauss' important observation that in their appetite for objective knowledge we have one of the most neglected aspects of the thinking of those whom some still dare to call primitive (Lévi-Strauss 1962:5).[3]

Cross-cultural identification of the critic

Yoruba qualitative criteria are consensual. This means they are matters of opinion, widely shared, but perhaps only fully comprehended by the guardians of philosophic thought. The best example of the latter are the priests of the divination cult. Yoruba aesthetic criteria are perhaps best nuanced by sculptor-critics who lend to their words their special insights of process and form. But the roots of the criteria lie with the common people without whose supporting testimony the fabric of aesthetic thought loses conviction and certainty.

Aesthetics among the populous Yoruba people is thus the sum of simple statements about artistic quality and the sum of the verbal characterizations which qualify these statements. When the qualifications are weighed it is found that the simplicity of the vocabulary is only apparent. On the other hand, a Westerner might validly draw from random audiences the following conclusion:

I have seen people dancing and singing for a new work of art – but its merits as *art* are not normally discussed. It is possible to hear comments on the craftsmanship. Slovenly surface treatment in a piece of sculpture, and any kind of quick careless work will be condemned. (Beier 1963:6)

What looks like art criticism is here interpreted as conversation on craftsmanship. Nevertheless, *collective* rationalizations reveal true consciousness of aesthetic bearing. Yoruba, for example, consider haste indelicate. Delicacy is almost universally recognized as an important quality in the aesthetic systems of the world.

Identification of the African critic

The art critic in a traditional African society may be identified first on the basis of whether he has voiced elements which imply a theory of elegance or excellence in art. Secondly, one notes whether the critic successfully applies this theory to particular cases. In the process, it is possible to distinguish the critic from the appreciator (Ballard 1957:194).

Appreciators identify with a work of art; in their vision the physical facts are in sharp focus, while aesthetic facets are blurred. An example: one evening while the harmattan blew chill into the air, a young man attempted to evaluate a twin statuette by the light of a native lamp. He dealt with the practical virtues of the cap depicted on the image's head; its flaps, he said, protect one from the cold. He had identified with the subject matter. A critic emerged from the shadows around the lamp and criticized the appreciator's lack of insight. He made comments about posture and vigor and qualified one of his standards. Appreciators only identify. Critics both identify (richly reflecting cultural preoccupations) and criticize (on the basis of relative formal elegance).

The most important criterion of identification of African critics is that their standards of judgment be qualified. Estimation of quality on grounds of coiffure may, if no further reasons are given, reflect associative values. Coiffure characterized in terms of delicacy of line and spacing does indeed constitute aesthetic criticism.

Judgments of better or worse imply an aesthetic when they are qualified and if the qualifications prove to be fairly systematic. Whatever else true criticism is, it is an applied aesthetic. Traditional African critics may qualify their remarks with subordinate clauses, as it were, in which the reasons behind each choice are spelled out and where, ideally, the reasons for the reasons are also given. At one end of the continuum of judgments one monitors the simple statement that such-and-such a work is "good"; in the middle one finds characterizations of aesthetic flavor, for example, "the features are handsome"; at the opposite end of the continuum one encounters aesthetic substance, as when a critic remarks on the delicacy of the modeling of lips.

One meets surprises. One may discover a rationale which is wholly "cultural" in flavor.

Thus an Oke-Iho critic found fault with the carved image of a devotee in a shrine because the face was not beautiful. Why? Because the mouth was carved open. Why this objection? Because a fly (one of the traditional messengers of evil) might enter the mouth or dirt collect within the oral cavity (Yoruba fear imprecations uttered when the mouth is dirty, especially early in the morning).

Associative values, even of the most magico-religious nature, and true aesthetic sensibilities are not mutually exclusive any more than possession of the skill of reading and writing prevents one from worshiping the traditional Yoruba gods.

Yoruba Art Critics: Their Character and Contribution

The presence of sculpture in Yoruba country, together with a tradition of artistic criticism, provides a basis for the understanding of the relation of African sculptors to art itself.

As Bohannan has commented, definition of artistic criticism depends upon study of critics, not artists (see Smith 1961:94):

> I was wrong in my field work because, Western fashion, I paid too much attention to artists, and when artists disappointed me I came away with nothing. When I return I shall search out the critics. There are as many reasoned art critics in Tiv society as there are reasoned theologians or political theorists, from whom we study Tiv ideas about their religion and politics.

Bohannan's conclusions gave direction to my program of study. He taught me to expect little from artists as informants on quality. Early in my field work I asked a Yoruba sculptor which were his finest works and was not surprised to hear that all of his works were fine. At the end of my field work I returned to his compound. This time he spoke of form and quality in sculpture although he still evaded analysis of his own works. What had opened his lips about quality? Rapport, *per se*, had little to do with it. What had happened was this: thanks to conversations with critics I now possessed some of the vocabulary of the Yoruba aesthetic. The sculptor confronted with the critical language of his peers is the sculptor partially disarmed.

The collapse of "primitive art"

Criteria of primitivism in the main do not apply to the traditional Yoruba, which means that one must rethink the status of the arts and criticism of this important African people. For example, here are some of the characteristics of "primitive culture" (Hsu 1964: 1) non-literacy, 2) small-scale settlements, 3) isolation, 4) lack of historical records, 5) low level of technical achievement, 6) social relations based primarily on kinship, 7) nonindustrialization, 8) lack of literature, 9) relative homogeneity, 10) nonurban setting, 11) general lack of time reckoning, 12) moneyless economy, 13) lack of economic specialization, and 14) endowment with an overpowering sense of reality where everyday facts have religious and ritual meaning.

Only four of these criteria really apply to the Yoruba. It is true that Yoruba were nonliterate before the coming of the Europeans to their shores. They based their social relations primarily on kinship (and they still do). They were not industrialized; they were endowed with an overpowering sense of reality (many still are). But their cities were not small in scale, nor were they isolated. Yoruba urbanism, Bascom (1959:29–44) indicates, predates the European penetration and probably was ancient. Court singing kept historical records alive (Biobaku 1955). The technical achievement of the Yoruba craftsmen is an historic fact.[4] Equally complex were and are the many genres of the rich oral resources of traditional Yoruba literature – hunters' ballads, ancestral songs, praise poems, divination verses, proverbs, and so forth.[5] Yoruba traditionally had a sense of time reckoning and a cowrie-shell currency.[6] Economic specialization, both in degree and incidence, was striking. If some traditional Yoruba are endowed with an overpowering sense of reality, it is difficult to see where their attitude differs from that of clergymen or philosophers in the West.

The issue of nonliteracy and industrialization seems important only to those for whom it is important to preserve the concept of "primitive art." Lack of factories and a high incidence of illiteracy have never prevented scholars from classifying the world of Gothic France as a civilization.

It is possible to stress, as definitively "primitive," the "absence of any concept of political organization, which is necessary before man-power can be trained and utilized for the construction of roads, aqueducts, or monumental architecture" (Wingert 1962:6). However, we know from the history of Yoruba architecture that a mighty rampart, the *eredo*, surrounded the inner kingdom of the Ijebu (Lloyd 1962:15–22). The ancient holy city of Ilé-Ifè was superbly walled. Monumental royal architecture, necessitating politically organized units of communal labor, adorned the ancient cities of the Ekiti.[7]

It is interesting that a recent artistic geography of "primitive art" excludes the arts of the Andes. Is Great Benin or Ancient Ifè more primitive than Chan-Chan? The separation of the civilizations of the world into great, in contrast to primitive, categories of culture appears meaningless when applied to the complex Guinea Coast cultures, but also when applied to simpler societies. The collapse of "primitive art" as a workable concept is nigh.

Once the mask of primitivism falls, what will we see? We may discover that the vision of African aesthetics as rudimentary or functional only projected our own weakly developed means of verbalizing the visual constituents of fine African sculpture. It is just possible, for example, that Yoruba critics surpass all but the most professional of Western students of Yoruba art in fluency of verbalization. To match the level of competence with which a Yoruba cultivator estimates artistic quality, one would have to deal with a specialist of Western art. Wherever and whenever Yoruba critics of Yoruba sculpture analyze sculpture, they do so with conviction and swiftness of verbalization.

Yoruba critics: selection and profession

Artistic criticism was not requested in any village or town until data about carvers, dating of works, names of woods, and so forth had been collected. This art historical research served as a kind of lure. Potential critics moved in the curious crowds of bystanders which always formed around the writer, his wife, and assistant. The crowd was then asked, while pieces of sculpture brought out for study were still in the sunlight, was someone willing to rank the carvings for a nominal fee and explain why he liked one piece over another? Owners sometimes immediately made clear that they did not want to participate – "put it to another person," a twin image owner protested once. Almost without fail someone would step forward and immediately begin to criticize the sculpture. The rare delays did not stem from lack of verbal skill. Rather some informants were simply afraid that their efforts would not really be compensated. Others wished to study the works with care in the light, turning them around and testing their profile and mass. The volunteer-critics were, with two exceptions, male.

Eighty-eight critics offered their services.[8] None was a full-time professional, as far as could be determined, but as two entries in Bowen's *Grammar and Dictionary of the Yoruba Language* of 1858 – *amęwa* "to be a judge of beauty" and *męwa* "to be a judge of beauty" – broadly suggest traditional Yoruba have long had a concept which substantially overlaps our own notion of the connoisseur.[9]

But if Yoruba critics are not professionals, many of them prove to be leaders of opinion in other areas. Sixteen informants were village chiefs, nine were heads of traditional cults, four presided over quarters of towns, fifteen were artists, eleven were in trade, and seven were in the employ of the Nigerian government. All drew upon their importance or self-esteem as the basis for their authority. In the male-oriented Yoruba world it was not surprising that only two women appeared as critics. But also many of the images under discussion were twin images, and women are the owners of these images. As such, they were understandably reluctant to rank their own possessions.

Yoruba criticism is not the prerogative of kings or of politically important persons. Almost anyone is free to criticize art if he (or she) so desires. Thus 20 cultivators, some of them of very humble economic means, balanced the simplicity of their material possessions against the riches of their mind. Their powers of qualitative characterization compared favorably with the commentaries of kings. Neither king nor commoner, however, could improve upon the insights of the sculptor-critics of Northern Ekiti. If the excellence of criticism is intellectually ranked among the Yoruba, the ranking depends upon the critic's individual talent and degree of familiarity with the forms of art.

Name, approximate age, village, profession, and religion were tabulated insofar as possible. In this way it was discovered, for example, that practicing Christians and Muslims used the same criteria by which worshipers of traditional Yoruba gods judged art. But only 19 exclusively Christian and five exclusively Muslim responded. The remainder (64 critics) were practicing devotees of one or more of the traditional Yoruba gods.

The variable of ownership seems pertinent. Of a total of 88 informants, only 32 actually owned the pieces of sculpture under discussion. They may have possessed sculpture in their own compounds but none of them offered to fetch and analyze their own possessions. This suggests that Yoruba more readily evaluate sculpture when it belongs to somebody else.

Nevertheless, 32 critics saw no harm in ranking their own possessions provided they were paid for doing so. But no mother of twins was ever persuaded to judge her own twin statuettes. Years of ritual had made these images seem alive. In point of fact, twin mothers handle their statuettes lovingly. Some explain that they are alive. One cannot expect a mother in such circumstances to play favorites. To do so is positively dangerous: the spirit of a slighted twin may strike the mother with sterility or cause her to "swell up" and die. In the Aworri bush village of Ayobo, a middle-aged critic had begun an interesting recital of the "proper" physiognomy of the *ibéjì* face when suddenly he cut himself short and became silent. When asked to resume the thread of his argument, he refused and stated firmly: "We cannot so abuse these *ibéjì*. We are afraid of what they might do to us."

The artist as self-critic

An American photographer was once asked to rank and edit his works for an exhibition catalogue. He replied bitterly that he would rather edit his own children. There is little reason to believe that less emotion attaches to the works which Yoruba sculptors create or that they might rank in public their own works with pleasure. Compare Bohannan's experience among the Tiv: he asked a calabash carver which was his favorite design, and the artist reasonably replied that he normally liked the one he was working on, so he liked them all.

Yoruba carvers had a stock reply for Justine Mayer Cordwell when she asked them to evaluate their preference of one form over another: "I do whatever the customer orders." In the light of this and similar admissions heard in Yoruba country from carvers, it seems likely that when sculptors rank their works equally, they do so with an eye to commercial advantage and that, in any event, inability to criticize their own works is shammed. I did not embarrass the Alaga of Odo-Owa (formerly known as Bamgboye) with direct questions about the qualities of his recent work, but I could not fail to note the enthusiasm with which he led me around the *Epa* headdresses which he carved before 1955 and which were of good quality and the sadness which came into his face when he stood before his last *Epa* headdress, at Obo Ayegunle, carved in 1959 when his physical strength had declined.

It is significant that the carvers and blacksmiths who served as critics judged the work of rivals and not their own handiwork. Their gusto and precision might well have evaporated had they been asked to analyze their own creations. Nevertheless, one Yoruba sculptor, Bandele Areogun, has proved willing to criticize (at least retrospectively) his own works.[10]

Identification of basic criteria

Conversation with the critics was straightforward. When an Egbado critic observed that the lineage marks on the face of an image pleased him, a simple pointing question, *nítorí kíni* (Why?), sufficed to elicit an aesthetic response.

All responses were translated into English in the following manner: 1) the field interpreter wrote out a verbatim text of the critic's comments on the spot and checked it with him, 2) the field interpreter and the author wrote out together a rough translation of the comments on the spot and checked it with the critic, 3) the translations were evened out and polished at the author's base at Lagos or Ilé-Ifè, 4) finished typescripts of vernacular text and English translation were rechecked for accuracy and searched for nuances of idiom and vocabulary by Mr. Samuel Adetunji of Ilesha in New Haven, Connecticut.

When I analyzed the comments of the 88 critics, common denominators of taste emerged, representing the rationale behind the individual choices. This rationale is the "Yoruba aesthetic."

Yoruba Aesthetic Criteria

Eighteen indigenous criteria of sculptural excellence are presented in this section. Each criterion, a named abstraction, defines the categories of elegance by which Yoruba recognize the presence of art. No single Yoruba provided all these ideas. Canonical notions developed by the investigator were discussed with individual Yoruba sculptors who sometimes added important insights or refinements of their own.

Before examining the criteria in detail the general Yoruba notion of the aesthetic will be discussed.

The Yoruba notion of the aesthetic

To speak of a native aesthetic presupposes basic questions. First, have the Yoruba a notion of the aesthetic? The answer, as might be plain by now, is "yes." Artistic sensibility, mixed with a hint of the hierarchy of the beautiful, is a clear power of the following verse from the oral literature of divination:

Anybody who meets beauty and does not look
    at it will soon be poor.
The red feathers are the pride of the parrot.
The young leaves are the pride of the palm tree.
The white flowers are the pride of the leaves.
The well-swept verandah is the pride of the
    landlord.
The straight tree is the pride of the forest.
The fast deer is the pride of the bush.
The rainbow is the pride of heaven.
The beautiful woman is the pride of her husband.
The children are the pride of the mother.
The moon and the stars are the pride of the sun.
Ifa says: beauty and all sorts of good fortune
    arrive.
                              (Beier and Gbadamosi 1959:30)

Discrete visual phenomena intersect: beautiful possessions (verandah, wife, children) whose quality the owner maintains or protects; ephemeral beauty (leaves, flowers, rainbows) at its prime; the beauty of more permanent things, earthly and celestial, which a sensitive man does not take for granted. Prize these things, the god of divination warns, for mental richness creates material wealth.

Aesthetic impulse alone brought together these felicities; their unifying aspect was beauty. The poem has the effect of an *aide-mémoire*: it safeguards, as it were, the natural resources of Yoruba aesthetic experience.

It is clear that a classification of visual powers, systematically developed, does not constitute mere function or utility. On the contrary, the moral is clear: aesthetic sensibility brilliantly embarks a man upon his career.

This poem, as well as other passages which might be cited from the oral literature of the Yoruba, refutes the old assumption that Africans lack experienced appreciation of natural beauty for its own sake. Yoruba, for instance, greatly admire the quality of verdancy which is implicit in one line of the poem and explicit in the common phrase, *ilẹ̀ yìí tútù yọ̀yọ̀*, "this land is verdant" (Abraham 1958: 658).[11]

If it is accepted that Yoruba truly appreciate physical beauty, the next question is: have the Yoruba a notion of aesthetic quality in sculpture; have they precise criteria by which to analyze the constituents of the beautiful in plastic expression? The answer again is yes. The plastic order of Yoruba sculpture is so striking as to stimulate an immediate awareness of its concrete manifestations in the minds of native critics. They speak fluently of the delicacy of a line, of the roundness of a mass. This eliminates the general question of whether or not Yoruba identify the aesthetic components of form.

Art as use: the pidgin English of African aesthetics

Few old-fashioned ethnologists dreamed that the peoples they investigated experienced aesthetic responses. And they never dreamed that "primitive man," himself conversant with art and noting few men of like experience among the emissaries from Europe he met in the nineteenth century, might be addressing to Westerners the same reproach.

Some traditional Yoruba seem to assume a white man's ability to perceive aesthetic import in art is weak or underdeveloped. One illustration must suffice: asked why he was most proud of a certain carved divination dish, a diviner at Ilobi replied: "It is a container of good divination things." Outwardly, he was "incapable of aesthetic analysis." But inwardly, he had assumed that utility was the only trait a foreigner might comprehend. When assured of the true direction of the inquiry, he spoke at once of quality.

The alleged lack of aesthetics among ethnographic peoples may well have derived from a kind of conceptual pidgin which arose when "civilized" and "primitive" man met and spoke of art, neither believing the other capable of aesthetic analysis. Thus, as Bohannan observed, the Tiv weaver keeps his best piece for his mother-in-law and sells his worst piece to foreigners who, presumably, would not know the difference (See Smith 1961: 92). The Fon brass caster sells the coarsest of his creations to foreigners and excellent pieces in traditional styles to indigenous patrons (Herskovits 1938: 358).[12] An Anago Yoruba wood sculptor, although locally noted for an especially sensitive handling of earth colors, permits enamel paint to be splashed in garish patterns over commissions for Westerners, obliterating the fine cuts of his knife, because "that is what those Europeans like." In the process, Western and African prejudices are mutually reinforced.

Yoruba qualitative criteria

Midpoint Mimesis

A value of Eastern art is exemplified by the story of the dragon which was painted with such aliveness that the creature flew out of the ink and into the air. The Western parallel tells of the birds who pecked at painted fruit. "What is the similar African story?" Mr. Kenneth Murray (1961: 100) has asked.

The following African version, a precious fragment of the oral literature of the Yoruba, documents equal attention to shape, detail, and vitality, but these Western-sounding preoccupations dissolve in a solvent of native irony.

Motinu and the Monkeys is a fable about a beautiful girl, Motinu, who meets a magnificently handsome man near the Yoruba city of Ọwọ. The man is actually a monkey in disguise who tricks Motinu into marrying him and moving to his forest eyrie where he transforms himself back into his true state and the hapless girl is forced to drum dance music and fetch wild corn for her captor and his chattering friends. By chance Motinu meets a hunter, when alone in the woods one day, and he promises to rescue her. The hunter's stratagem is a capsule rendering of the traditional Yoruba notion of mimesis:

On his return to Owo, the hunter called on a woodcarver in the town. He described to the carver Motinu's hairstyle, and tribal markings and asked him to make eight little images of her. When these had been carved and painted, the hunter carried them to the bush when he knew he would find Motinu alone, and then together,

they set out quickly for Owo. Every few miles, the hunter dropped one of the carvings in a conspicuous place along the track. (The hunter) knew that these images would delay the monkeys when they tried to follow them. . . .

When the monkeys reached the first image they were very curious indeed and sat down to chatter and argue.

"What is this," they said, "that bears such a strong resemblance to Motinu?" . . . growing tired of it, they threw it away into the bush and went on in pursuit of their lost Motinu . . . Each image they came to exasperated the monkeys more and more, and when they came upon one they would pounce on the image in anger and smash it up, chewing the pieces afterwards till nothing remained. By this means Motinu and (the hunter) were able to escape. (Fuja 1962:47–49)

This fable, to begin with, qualifies the degree of realism Yoruba critics desire: the village connoisseurs are pleased by conventionalized human faces sharpened with touches of individuality (lineage marks and coiffure). The monkeys, unlike the birds of the West, were not deceived. There was no reason that they would be, for one of the aims of the Yoruba sculptor is to strike through the individual personality of men and women to arrive at general principles of humanity.[13]

The monkeys puzzled over the images and, in a sense, appreciated their mimetic qualities – "What is this, that bears such a strong resemblance to Motinu" – but never did they confuse art with reality. Thus the fable summarizes Yoruba mimesis: the formulation of general principles of humanity, not exact likeness. Light touches of portraiture (hair, scars, dress) redress the balance in favor of individuality, yet not to the degree where even the vilest monkey cannot distinguish likeness from equivalence. Mimesis to modern traditional Yoruba means the cultivated expression of resemblances (*jíjọra*), not likenesses. It is "midpoint mimesis" between absolute abstraction and absolute likeness.

This is brought out by the vocabulary of the 20 critics who applied this criterion to their arguments. A single sentence, *Ó jọ ènìyàn* (It resembles a person), was the modal expression although an alternate phrasing, *Ó dàbí ènìyàn* (It looks like a person), was also heard. A healthy recognition of the limitations of illusion is implied in the verb *jọ*. Witness the common phrase, *ó jọ bẹ̀ẹ̀* (It *seems* to be the case). It is therefore significant that Yoruba critics qualify mimesis with a phrase which makes clear a desire for generalization. They did not say that carvings resembled specific personalities.

Hypermimesis

Some of the reasons why Yoruba art comprehends mimesis as a process sited somewhere between abstraction and exact likeness can be found in the critic's rationale for disapproving of a work. Amos Tutuola plants one clue in his Yoruba folk novel, the *Palm-Wine Drinkard*, which is based upon traditional mythic themes. At one point the hero of the novel encounters his own portrait in wood and is frankly terrified (Tutuola 1952:68):[14] "Our own images that we saw there resembled us too much." There can be something sinister about absolute mimesis. Why? One reason seems magical. A master carver of Ẹfọn-Alaiye, Owoeye Oluwuro, told me that a traditional *Ẹfọn* sculptor, before he initiated any important commission involving the carving of human eyes, mouth, and nose, had to make a sacrifice of sugarcane, dried maize with red palm oil, and pigeon to prevent the entrance of ugliness into his carving. What kinds of ugliness? A wrinkled man's wrinkles, a warty man's warts. If his adze slipped, as it were, and he began to carve the unpalatable truth in some of the faces which he saw around him, the danger existed that these very features might be transmitted to the face of his next-born child.

To one Yoruba critic a slight hint of individual expression sufficed to incur censure: "[One carving's mouth] comes out to form a laugh. That is bad." The lips of an ideal statue ought to be pursed. Such lips reflect impersonal calm.

Perhaps the most decisive factors behind the limitations placed upon mimesis in Yoruba art are aesthetic ones: the assumptions of the native critic (that sculpture be smooth, youthful, erect, and so forth) would be violated by direct rendering of the rough skin, gaunt appearance, and ruined posture of an elderly man.

Excessive abstraction

Related to the notion of mimesis, on a negative grid of disapproval, is the notion of excessive abstraction. Fine sculpture, to the Yoruba, is not too real, but neither does it absolutely depart from natural form. For example, a North Oyo critic stated that "if a person's ears were all round like that they would talk about him" and condemned a work of art while he went on to laud another piece with relatively realistic ears.

Carvers are amused by apprentices who fail to imprint human quality upon the principal masses of their work. Bandele Areogun once studied a carved house column by Ayantola of Odo-Ehin and commented derisively:[15] "It looks like an *àpótí*," and then laughed. In making this comparison with *àpótí*, a common Yoruba term for box, Bandele had impugned the ability of his rival to enliven brute timber with human presence.

Visibility

Twenty-nine critics stressed this quality. A master sculptor, the Alaga of Odo-Owa, heartily concurred with their emphasis: "One knows from the visibility of the face and other parts of the image whether the work is beautiful." The artist used, as did some of the critics, the precise Yoruba word for visibility, *ìfarahọ̀n*.

Some critics phrase the idea without refinement and simply assign importance to sculpture of full, well-finished, organic details. Thus a critic of Tede: "the tribal marks are well cut...I like the eyelashes, they help make the face attractive...the hairdress is exact...all five fingers are complete...all five toes are complete. The other carvers did not show the toes so visibly."

But sculptors lend to their criticism a vocabulary of astonishing accuracy and range. Their works describe, to begin with, the stages of the process of carving. Bandele Areogun of Osi-Ilorin distinguishes four divisions in the making of sculpture:[16] 1) the first blocking out, 2) the breaking of the initial masses into smaller forms and masses, 3) the smoothing and shining of the forms, 4) the cutting of details and fine points of embellishment into the polished surfaces of the prepared masses.

Alaga of Odo-Owa views the process slightly differently: 1) the measuring of the wood, 2) the blocking out of the head, occiput, chest, torso, buttocks, thighs, legs, and feet in that order, 3) the smoothing and polishing of all masses, 4) the incising of details into the polished masses. Alaga insists that "above the shoulders the head must be readily visible." Visibility as criterion therefore is an assignment of the initial stages of adzework (are the major masses visible?) and the terminal stages of knifework (are the smaller embellishments and linear designs visible?).

The privilege of visibility must not be abused; as the Alaga told me, a sculptor must not only block out a schematic eye (yọ ojú) which provides a gross visibility and relief, he must also "open" the eye (là ojú) with sensitive lining. Visibility refers, therefore, to clarity of form and to clarity of line.

Let us consider the last quality first. Linear precision is largely a matter of knifework, whereas plastic clarity is summoned from the brute mass of the chunk of the log by means of adzework. Although knifework falls under Bandele's fourth category of fífín in Osi-Ilorin, this final stage cannot be described solely by means of the root verb fín, which means to carve or incise. Bandele uses an extended set of special verbs, each with its own nuance:[17] 1) là, which refers to the "lining" of eyes, mouth, fingers, ears, and toes, 2) lọ, which refers to the "grooving" of brass bracelets, 3) gé, which refers to the cutting of waistbeads and other forms of beads, 4) fín, which refers to the "incising" of coiffure, sash fringes, and special patterns and designs.

Bandele criticizes, for example, the lack of visibility of a certain cult container by means of these special verbs: "The mouth remains; they have not lined it. They have not incised the sash. They have grooved the sash."

The fact that a lexicon of linear qualities exists suggests the depth of the Yoruba aesthetic. Bandele uses verbs of line to estimate swiftly those carvers who have (or have not) liberated fine points of human appearance from the larger masses of the wood.

Alaga of Odo-Owa and Mashudi Latunji, who works in the faraway town of Mẹkọ in the province of the Ketu, use much the same sort of verbs Bandele employs in their criticisms. Like their colleague, the latter artists criticize the finishing of small detail, the rendering of its visibility, in terms of lining and incising and grooving but they criticize the cutting of coiffure and interlace patterns with the verb dì, which means, literally, to tie. Alaga insists one may judge the excellence of the rendering of cloth in sculpture by means of

the verb sán. Thus: Ó sán bàntẹ dádá – "He rendered the loincloth well." This refers, literally, to the tying on of the garment.

The apparent lack of specialized vocabulary in the criticisms by non-carvers might suggest that Yoruba criticism is intellectually stratified. Bandele, the sculptor, said: "They have not lined the eyes." But a carpenter (with no artistic pretensions) said: "The beautiful face has eyes which have lids and the ugly faces have lidless eyes." Yet all critics of Yorubaland hold the artist responsible for as complete a grid as possible of human anatomic coordinates. Carvers seek to express generalized principles of humanity. They must carve them, nonetheless, with ultimate sharpness of clarity and focus.

Thus the notion of linear connoisseurship is highly developed among traditional Yoruba. Symptomatically, the art of cicatrization in traditional times was of paramount importance, both as mark of lineage membership and aesthetic concern. Verbs of linear analysis in sculpture find a parallel in the language of the cicatrix specialist. This professional, like sculptors, has a verb for different visual effects. He cuts (bu) àbàjà marks, slashes (sá) kẹkẹ marks, digs or claws (wa) gòmbó marks, and splits open (là) Èfọn marks (Abraham 1958:301).

Relation of verb to sculptural effect seems meaningful. Kẹkẹ marks are bold; when they are faint, they are allegedly called gòmbó, a fact which might be conveyed by the concept of slashing the former and clawing the latter. Èfọn marks indeed seem to split open the flesh of the cheek.

Since antiquity, Yoruba have adorned their cheeks with lines. They associate line with civilization. "This country has become civilized" literally means in Yoruba "This earth has lines upon its face" (Abraham 1958:399). "Civilization" in Yoruba is ilàjú – face with lined marks. The same verb which civilizes the face with the marks of membership in urban and town lineages civilizes the earth: Ó ṣá kẹkẹ; Ó sáko (He slashes the kẹkẹ marks; he clears the bush). The same verb which opens Yoruba marks upon a face, opens roads and boundaries in the forest: Ó lànòn; Ó là à*àlà; ó lapa (he cut a new road; he marked out a new boundary; he cut a new path). In fact, the basic verb to cicatrize (là) has multiple associations of the imposing of human pattern upon the disorder of nature: chunks of wood, the human face, and the forest are all "opened," like the human eye, allowing the inner quality of the substance to shine forth (Abraham 1958:399, 400, see also 602 as to *șá*).

This history of associations with the tradition of cicatrization sharpens the eye of the Yoruba critic and gives the sensitive noncarver the knack of talking about clarity of line with conviction. For example, an Aworri critic insisted that the coiffure on what he considered inferior sculpture was "too faint" and that the lines of good sculptural versions of hair must be seen. An Ijesha critic with a single comment – "the eyes really show on *Èfòn* pieces" – went to the heart of his taste for linear visibility.

Another sample criticism: Ojelabi of Oluponon admired an image because the face was "visible" and there was "a boundary line for the hair." These comments and many others which could be cited prove that noncarvers, with the simple verb *hòn* (becomes visible), are able to defend their tastes when judging sculpture which does or does not satisfy local feelings about linear visibility.

Visibility, as has already been pointed out, also refers to clarity of form. An Ijebu cultivator judged one twin image excellent on the ground that its forehead was "more visible than the other [piece]" – (*Otowá ó hòn jù eléyi lọ*). At Șepeteri a critic admired the nose on an image because it was readily visible. The taste for crispness of form affects the criticism of abstract shapes and ornament as well: a young citizen of Ajasse-Ipo viewed four carved door panels in the palace of the local chief and found the criterion of visibility the decisive means of distinguishing the best patterns. As in the discussion of line, plastic clarity is expressed by the verb *hòn* or grammatical units constructed from this verb.

Artistic integrity is also a factor which must be taken into account. This point might not have been documented but for the comment of a critic from the west of Igbomina country who singled out the sharp visibility of an image and added that "If you want to marry a person you have to see the body completely." Plastic and linear clarity become a matter of candor: all parts of the body are presented to the court of the eye. Visibility in this sense means that the honest carver has nothing to hide; he nakedly exposes his imagination. He does not conceal an inability to portray a complicated hairdress under a cap or headtie.

To Bandele of Osi-Ilorin the head and the hands of images are the essential aspects of plastic clarity. "Don't we," he asked Kevin Carroll didactically, "look at the face at the top of the *Epa* headdress first and then we look at the hand? Those two places we first take notice of. The body is not so difficult." If the face and the hand of the *igi* (superstructure) are carved with proper conscientiousness the carving will become readily visible and therefore good and therefore beautiful.

Shining smoothness

Yoruba who invoke the quality of visibility simultaneously invoke the quality of luminosity. Alaga of Odo-Owa told me that when he finishes a work of art he stands back to examine the "shine" of the work, the polished surfaces and the shadows in between the lines of incisions.

This taste for luminosity appears to have considerable historical depth. We may infer that the Yoruba-influenced city of Great Benin reflected, as early as 1668, the Yoruba quest for luminosity in art (in this case architecture) as visual stimulus, for early explorers duly documented the extraordinary polish of the earthen red walls of Benin (Roth 1903:160–1).

Eleven modern Yoruba critics shed light on the nature of this canon. Onamosun of Iperu recalled: "When my father (Taiwo Olejiyagbe) objected to low quality in my early work he sometimes lashed me with a flywhisk. I did not make any serious slips of quality after I got the hang of carving from observing my father's work day after day. But if he told me to carve an image very smoothly and I failed to comply, I would be punished. The smoothing (*ișé dídón*) was done with a knife, with the side of the knife" (figure 14.1) An Aworri lineage head asserted that smoothness was a matter of skill: he praised the straightness of the hand of a sculptor and then commented upon his luminous touches of polish.

Headmen at Ilogbo-Aworri and Ipole-Ijesha made clear that they demanded smoothness and shining qualities in sculpture. Speaking of cheeks, a priest of Erinle at Oke-Iho said: "The cheek (of this image) is beautiful; it is not swollen but rather shining" (*Eèkée ó dára, kò wú, șùgbón ó dón*).

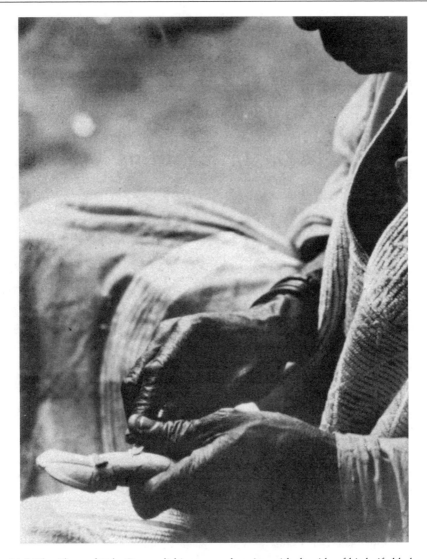

Figure 14.1 The Alaga of Odo-Owa polishing a woodcarving with the side of his knife blade

Creative enjoyment of art by Yoruba critics relates to the notion of luminosity in remarkable ways. Thus a cultivator at Odo-Nọpa in the kingdom of the Ijebu:

> One image is ugly and can quickly spoil. Its maker did not smooth the wood. Another image was carved so smoothly that one hundred years from now it will still be shining, if they take proper care of it, while the ugly image will rot regardless.

One might compare this fragment of criticism (which seems to raise luminosity to talismanic powers of preservation) with a more idealized Yoruba notion of beauty as "guard" or "amulet," which is present in the pages of the novels of Amos Tutuola. Here is a passage from his *Palm-Wine Drinkard*:

> If bombers saw him in a town which was to be bombed, they would not throw bombs on his presence, and if they did throw it it would not explode until this gentleman would leave that town, because of his beauty. (Tutuola 1952:25)

When Yoruba critics discuss luminosity, they almost unfailingly use the verb *dọ́n*. The qualities conjured by the verb intermesh with aesthetic implications associated with the initial stages of carving. Thus Bandele.[18] "We know a carver's work is good if he has blocked it out well and by the shining smoothness of the wood" (*t'o ba ti bu ona, ti o ba ti lena ona lile da.. nipa igi didọn*). Onamosun of Iperu and Bandele explain that *iṣẹ́ dídọ́n* technically mean the smoothing of the forms of sculpture, respectively with a knife of Rẹmọn and with a knife and chisel in Northern Ekiti. Kevin Carroll has informed me that the old smoothing-tool in Ekiti dialect was called *unkan* and consisted of a handle and cutting edge formed from one iron bar. Bandele's phrasing refers to the Yoruba sculptor's intent to smooth down the surface of his wood so that it reflects light and seems to shine, as if from an inner source. The smoothness-shining duality emerges as both cause and effect. Surfaces are so smoothed that they give back the lights of intelligence which went into their making.

We are now prepared to suggest the background of one of the most striking of the habits of the Yoruba artist – his penchant for carving facial traits in (to academic Western tastes) excessive relief. The issue cannot be treated, of course, apart from other notions of quality. Linear and plastic clarity combine with shining smoothness to illumine the artistic intent behind this habit of carving.

The rounded shapes of the face of a Yoruba image have been smoothed so as to reflect light whether in sunlight or in shade. Eyes in protrusion cast meaningful shadows against the glowing surfaces of the face. The ink of shadow is calculatingly spilt below or above the eyes (according to the source of light), the better to mark off their form against the shine of the face, the better to make them "readily visible" (figure 14.2). The short durational values of Yoruba music propel sculpture in the dance with staccato movements that blur the vision. Shadow against shining surfaces acts as a countereffect to this blurring.

Moreover, Yoruba appreciate distinct intensities of shadow. I have observed Alaga turning a carved comb around in sunlight, testing the beat, as it were, of its rhythmic shadowed incisions. I have also observed a critic at Tede turning a twin statuette around in the sunlight, turning the image around several times, observing the flow of shadows.

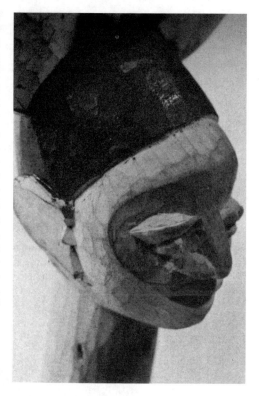

Figure 14.2 A carving by Owoeye of Efon-Alaiye, 1960

Yoruba recognize that deliberate excrescences and edges in sculpture cast darkened silhouettes which may be "read," as an abstract image, at considerable distance by an observer. Moreover, in the blur of the dance or under the shadows of a verandah, refinements of form must be made readily visible. Alaga tells us that the shadows between or within incisions and the shadows beneath or above relief are beautiful against the polished surfaces of the whole of a sculpture.

The eye primed to appreciate the canon of shining smoothness, as the foil of shadow, distinguishes master from apprentice in works of art. The adzemarks of the master, where the edges show, shine, while the adzemarks of the apprentice lack formal separation and do not shine.

We must be careful to point out that Yoruba seem to prefer the relative or moderate enunciation of any given criterion. An absolute polish, mirror-like and glittering, is as foreign to their art as is sculpture in which no attempt whatsoever has been made to polish surfaces. Moreover, as Kevin Carroll has usefully reminded me, the woods which Yoruba sculptors use are generally smooth in texture. And even the moderate or generalized shining of Yoruba sculpture is broken in some areas with crosshatching, and other designs, sometimes extensively.

One of the most interesting extensions of the Yoruba taste for luminosity is the depiction of clothing. Because Yoruba artists devoutly desire to create well polished surfaces that reflect large amounts of light, they do not treat substances, which in reality are soft, with realistically softened textures. When a Yoruba carves a headtie, turban, cap, or gown, he exaggerates its bulk and polishes it to a high sheen. Drapery conventionally has a consistency which resembles sheet-metal far more than it does cloth. The soft twists of the turban of the Muslim cleric – a favored theme in recent *Gẹlẹdẹ* carving of the Yoruba southwest – harden in the hands of a sculptor. Loose, or folded twists of female headties (*gèlè*) stiffen into architectonic forms. Èṣù, the trickster, in one instance wears a cloth cap which in sculpture becomes as unyielding as an iron helmet.

Thus the Yoruba aesthetic hardens and polishes the representation of the soft substances of life so that they will shine in harmony with the luminous whole of the image, so that the edges of a turban or a gown will cast the same strong shadows cast by eyes in expressive relief or by multifaceted foreheads and torso areas. Just as the sound of hard, metallic percussion dominates much Yoruba music – Yoruba iron bells and gongs are distinctive because of their high pitch (King 1961:11)[19] – so the creation of hard, almost metallic polished surfaces dominates Yoruba sculpture. With respect to representations of clothing, and even hair, Yoruba sculptors discover luminosity by thickening widths and polishing surfaces and sides.

A verandah post by Alaga which he carved for the house of a chief at Ekan-Meje *ca.* 1931 demonstrates most tangibly to what extent he successfully acquired the aesthetic of luminosity.[20] The distinction between the smooth radiance of the head and coiffure of the central figure and the duller lustre of the unfinished structural support above the head of the figure is decisive (figure 14.3): Hair, cloth, and flesh glow with equal intensity.

Figure 14.3 Verandah post carved by the Alaga of Odo-Owa, 1931

The Yoruba sense of luminosity is especially refined. Hunters in Yorubaland are sensitive to this quality and have, for example, a word (*rekina-rekina*) to describe the glittering effect of sunlight shining on wind-ruffled water.[21] And in their ballads and salutes hunters generally admire the gleaming surfaces of the pelt of a wild beast as they might have admired, when in town, the luminous refinements of a carved image.

Emotional Proportion

Yoruba notions of proportion form a dialogue between the permissive and the prescribed. Critics countenance certain dimensional liberties when they are charged with traditional sanction of aesthetic expression. Critics approve sculptural compositions set in "social perspective" where the sculptor indicates seniority by gradations of scale. At all times, however, critics rank sculpture upon a theory of relative proportion. The members of a king's entourage must be carved in proportion to one another, regardless of their scale in relation to the monarch.

A Ketu paradigm: the late Duga of Mẹko finished, probably before 1955, a striking headdress for the local cult of Gẹlẹdẹ. The headdress is surmounted by an Àlùfáà (the Muslim cleric), carved standing in a canoe with a helper (figure 14.4). Two teakettles flank the canoe. The cleric counts his beads. The size of his rosary is overpowering; the beads fill his hands as a chunky width of Manila hemp rope might fill them. This is a splendid example of fusion of proportion and empathy. The usage of "emotional proportion" contrives to communicate the psychological importance of a thing, as opposed to strict measurement. Duga enlarged the beads of the cleric for at least two purposes: 1) so that they would "read" easily in the motion of the dance, 2) in conformance with their role in the important Islamic ritual of *dhikr* – "telling beads" – in solitary communion with Allah and the Prophet (Trimingham 1961:93). The size of the rosary translates its fascination in the eyes of non-Muslim Yoruba who recognize the power *dhikr* acquires from use in initiation and cult practice.

Duga framed the canoe bearing the cleric and helper between two teakettles. These are strikingly out of proportion to the cleric and the canoe, but they are convincingly related to the dimensions of the head of the mask which serves as infrastructure. All Yorubaland has observed Muslim cattle-drivers from the north of Nigeria halt by the sides of roads and streets to pour ablutions from teapots. Recognition of the teakettle as a mark of modern Islam in West Africa would be immediate. Their symbolic dimensions are no more startling than the diminutive or heightened renderings of the Christian cross which are not taken as literal measurements of the True Cross but are tokens of faith.

Yoruba share a notion with Heraklitus: a man's character is his fate. Yoruba sculptors

Figure 14.4 Wooden headdress of the *Gẹlẹdẹ* cult, representing the Muslim cleric. Carved by Duga prior to 1955

enlarge the human head to mark its importance as the seat of character, the part conversant with destiny. Heads, as wisdom symbols, mark the visual climax. But exaggeration of the head must not be ludicrous.

In the clear-cut instances of standing figures, the components of judicious proportion are swiftly identified by critics. Alaperu of Iperu minced no words: "The thighs are too thick for the body." Of a certain carver's work he said: "Bako carves figures with eyes too open. The lower part of the lid is too stretched out" (figure 14.5). A minor lapse of conception by the hand of the local master, Onamosun, did not pass unremarked: "Actually the height of the figure shows some grace. So far as I look at the cheeks and the nose I like what I see. Only the eye is a bit out of proportion" (figure 14.6). Significantly, the proportion of the head (which was slightly exaggerated) was not mentioned.

The criticism of Abinileko of Otta provided another source of Yoruba thinking about proportion in carving. Abinileko, who in 1964 presided over the Oruba quarter of the capital of the Aworri subtribe, had been a tailor in his

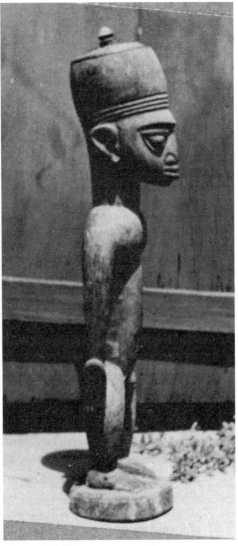

Figure 14.6 Image by Onamosun of Iperu, 1940

Figure 14.5 Twin by Bako from Iperu, 1940

youth and kept a cloth measuring tape in a wooden chest as a memento. He applied this measuring instrument to a judgment of the relative merits of the works of Labintan and Salawu, two sculptors of Otta. The basis of his judgment were two Gẹlẹdẹ headdresses which he took down from nails on the walls of his parlor. "Labintan is the better carver," Abinileko began, tapping the best headdress with a stick. Breadth (ibú) was to his mind an import-

ant variable. Labintan had conceived a human nose, for example, with pleasingly moderate measurements while Salawu had not. The critic reached for his measuring tape and marked off two and a half inches for the breadth of the ugly nose, one and a half for the finer nose.

He then compared mouths. Labintan's was two inches long, Salawu's three. He commented: "Labintan's mouth looks like the mouth of a person but Salawu's does not" (Ẹnun tí Lábíntán rí bi tí ẹnu ènìọn, sùgbón tí Salawu kò jọ ènìọn).

He dissected further deficiencies: "Salawu's forehead is too close to the edge of the head-gear. The distance from cap to the top of the nose is too short." He buttressed this point with a measurement: two and a half inches described the distance between nose and hat in the image by Labintan, one and a half for Salawu.

Precise measurements are by themselves merely descriptive. But the critic analytically used measurement as a means of arriving at a concrete notion of proportion.

Moderation in small things, not too broad the lips, not too short the forehead, might be suggested as the sum of these notions. The use of a Western instrument here does not vitiate the traditional grounding of this exercise, for the measuring tape was simply a replacement of African prototypes. Thus Ketu sculptors use the length of the blade of their knives as a rough module to secure the proportion and symmetry. Finally, Kevin Carroll has observed Bandele of Osi-Ilorin "often use a measure of hand length, finger length, and knuckle length."

As he wove his way through a complex argument about the aesthetic merits of *Eyinlè* cult figures, an Oke-Iho critic made several observations which help us to understand how Yoruba view the proportion of facial traits. The critic liked one chin because it was not short (*kò kúrú*). He condemned the dimensions of another sculptor's version of the human chin with metaphor: "It is not beautiful. The chin rushes into its house" (*Kò dá; àgbòn kó sílé*). The lower lip of the mouth on this piece was neglected; the lower margin of facial outline and the lower lip had been made to coincide, as in a mode prevalent among the Western Ijo. The fine piece, on the other hand, displayed a suitably fleshy chin. The metaphor was apt: the chin of the inferior face did indeed seem to rush into the mouth and disappear.

The same critic found the lips of one figure "decently proportioned" (*Ó wa mogi-mogi*) and "terrible" on another figure. The "terrible" mouth was too big.

In conclusion, man is the module. As Alaga told me: "if the image represents a big man, the eyes must be big, if the image is small the eyes must be small." But inspiration and imagination are part of the process: "These measurements we use," Mashudi told me, "God gives them to us. No one is using the white man's

instruments when they carve at Mẹko. We take our measurements from our heart."

Positioning

This concept overlaps the notion of proportion. Alaperu, for instance, analyzed the proper placement of parts of the body: "The ears are good, well-fixed, not too far down, not too far up." Eleven critics made similar commentaries. Jogomi of Ajilete laid equal stress upon the correct placing of the navel. Otuṣoga of Odo-Nopa was disgruntled by a nose which he felt had been placed too high upon a face.

Yoruba hunters attach importance to elision in recitals of their traditional ballads. Thus a Yoruba was once documenting the ballad of the monkey when another Yoruba interrupted: "No. Do not write it so, it does not sound sweet like that" (Collier 1953). The latter informant then proceeded to elide eight words to satisfy his tastes. On the other hand, there were many words which he did not run together, for as the distinguished late authority on Yoruba linguistics, Professor R. C. Abraham, was forced to admit, there is no underlying principle about elisions (Abraham 1958:xxxi).

By the same token, Ogidi of Igogo-Ekiti imitates the natural position of the shoulders and navel in his sculpture, but he connects the upper lip to the edge of the nose. One elides things for the sake of visual concord but there does not seem to be a fixed principle. Other North Ekiti carvers take pains to separate the nose from the lips.

Composition

The aesthetic spacing of things in relation to one another is a complication of the art of siting. Positioning of traits by means both mimetic and emotional becomes a more elaborate task of relating individuals (sometimes individuals, things, and animals) within a single composition.

On a minor level Yoruba composition means the pleasing articulation of limbs in spatial terms. Alado of Ado-Awaiye characterized his pleasure in the graceful placement of the hands of a figure which embellished his own divination container. The curve of the wrist and the arm, the naturalness of the gesture, were stated as pleasing qualities.

Onamosun of Iperu reported that "one of the things that people are talking about when they see my work is my carving of the hands without detaching them from the body, with the outer side of the hand flat." The design element to which the carver refers is one of the striking qualities of his mode of figural composition (figure 14.6).

Olodoye of Ijero-Ekiti briefly adumbrated a few compositional qualities. He liked the suppleness of the placement of a child within a mother's hand and he also expressed pleasure in the placement of a twin on the mother's back. Unfortunately, he did not qualify these remarks. It is possible that a cultural factor, namely the Yoruba intense appreciation of motherhood and children, guided his remarks more than aesthetic discernments.

As to free siting, critics did not discuss the matter but it seems probable that blendings of permissive and prescribed actions again apply. For instance, the members of a senior person's entourage are carefully positioned, normally, so that when seen full-front they do not obscure the view of their master.

Delicacy

Sixteen critics spoke of this quality, one of the few aesthetic notions for which we have scraps of nineteenth-century literary evidence. Thus the explorer Richard Lander in 1830: "The natives of that part of Africa appear to have a genius for the art of sculpture. Some of their productions rival in point of delicacy any of a similar kind I have seen in Europe" (Quoted in Allison 1956:18). Lander was an ethnocentric outsider but his disadvantages did not preclude a striking observation at an early date of one of the informing qualities of Yoruba sculpture.

Samuel Johnson, himself a Yoruba, understood the relevance of delicacy to the appreciation of other Yoruba arts. Here is a comment on coiffure written in the 1890's:

Hair is the glory of the woman. Unmarried ones are distinguished by their hair being plaited into smaller strips, the smaller and more numerous the plaited strips the more admired. (Johnson 1921:101)

Traditional connoisseurs of the arts of hairdressing today still nod in agreement with the notion of delicacy and closeness of spacing. The more closely spaced the braids, the more braids can be made to embellish the head. This taste informs the commentaries of modern

traditional critics of Yoruba sculpture. Thus an Egbado diviner at Ilobi characterized the aesthetic appeal of a certain divination dish in terms of its numerous faces and their diminutive eyes. "Small eyes" (*ojú kékeré*), he added, make an image resemble a person.

Delicacy of eye cut and lining was a concern of an Egbado and an Ijesha critic. The former liked the eyes of a twin image at Ajilete because the lids were thin (*ipénpéjú tíńrín*); the latter remarked the pleasing smallness of eyes and used the identical phrase employed by the Ilobi diviner, *ojú kékeré*. An Ijebu critic isolated the element of delicacy in the aesthetic character of a carved version of hairstyle. He stressed the sensitive rendering of the plaits, saying literally that the "cuts" or "lines" were thin.

Smallness suited the tastes of the Ijebu critic when applied to the field of linear ornament. Smallness of anatomic mass provoked a different reaction. The critic denounced the slimness of an *ibéjì*'s arm with the same adjective with which he had praised fineness of line: *Èyìí tíńrín jù lọ* (This one is thinner than the other). A thin line is beautiful, a very thin mass is not. Thus one must take pains to plot the usage of verbs which predict quality in Yoruba criticism according to context and subject matter. Linear delicacy is a matter of admiration. But excessive delicacy or thinness in the portrayal of human mass is condemned. It may be that the latter quality is associated with the sinister, as suggested by a phrase in the pages of the Yoruba novel *Simbi and the Satyr of the Dark Jungle* (Tutuola 1955:73): "Their bodies were withered for fear." Ideally, the human frame in Yoruba sculpture is carved with attributes full, vigorous, and fleshy. It is the shape of confidence.

To return to linear finesse: a carpenter of Ṣepeteri used an interesting verb in relation to this quality when he admired an especially sensitively carved *ibéjì* and remarked that the coiffure was "just like a crown," an appropriate simile for its well-finished elegance of form. He refined his remark with a verb which seems to conjoin the notions of delicacy in coiffure which Samuel Johnson had documented some 74 years before. "I like the lines of the hairstyle," he said, "[Each] is small and tightly spaced" (*Ó wẹ dáda*). The verb *wẹ*, according to Mr. Samuel Adetunji, describes both delicacy of line and spacing.

Yoruba critics require delicacy in portrayals of human morphology. An Ajilete critic liked the ears on an image because they were small; an Oke-Iho critic voiced the same thought with the same phrase (Ó kéré). This speaker condemned versions of ears which were "conspicuously" (Ó hòn gbagadagbagada) visible. This is interesting because it not only qualifies the notion of grossness as the opposite of delicacy, but it also refines the notion of visibility. Elements which are conspicuous – too visible – are indecorous. The aesthetic import of kéré, like tínrín, depends upon context. There is a difference between a delicate nose and a nose which is simply too small. The vanishing nose is censured with the phrase Ó kéré.

Thus four words, at least, form the Yoruba vocabulary of delicacy: 1) kékeré, "small," referring to delicacy of mass; 2) kéré, "is small," referring to delicacy of mass in the context of approval; excessive diminution of proportion in the context of disapproval; 3) tínrín, "narrow," referring to delicacy of line, both as to fineness of outline and as to sensitivity of grooving or incision patterns (Tínrín when applied to mass may acquire a negative denotation); and 4) wé, literally "is slender," referring to linear delicacy in a special sense – tiny lines spaced closely together in neat parallel incisions.

Clear-cut definitions of the verbs' meanings emerge in contexts in which subtle sculpture stands beside brutal works. Taiwo of Ajilete said of sensitively incised lineage marks: "That cicatrization pattern pleases me. It is tiny and spaced tightly together and not conspicuously big" (Ilà nã wùn mi. Ó wé dáda. Kò tóbi gbagadagbagada).

Yoruba oppose in their diction the synonyms and antonyms of the delicate as skillfully as, in their traditional songs, the manifestations of romantic and practical love are opposed, as in the stanza "love is of many kinds, one love says 'if you die let me die with you,' another love says 'if you buy the soup I will buy the yam!' " The antonyms of the delicate in the parlance of Yoruba critics are "big" and "blunt," as illustrated by the peculiarly expressive phrase tóbi gbagadagbagada (conspicuously big). The dull or blunted edge is not aesthetic. The fine edge *is* aesthetic. This notion overlaps to a great extent Western notions. Thus a common dictionary definition:

Fine. 1. Exquisitely fashioned; delicate ME. 2. Not coarse; delicate in structure, a texture . . . very thin or slender.

Roundness

Fourteen critics defined roundness as an aesthetic handling of carved outlines and full spherical mass. As regards curved outlines the comment of an Igbomina critic is a useful introduction: "I prefer the chin of one image – the other is flat and sharp – for the best chin is moderate." Examination of the images he held in his hands as he judged them revealed that what he meant by "moderate" was pleasingly rounded, not angular.

The idea of full spherical mass was explored by Alaga of Odo-Owa. Alaga explains that the ideal form of the "pot mask," which serves as the helmet of the Epa feast dancer, is rounded. He made signs of disgust when he stood before an Epa headdress in Yagba territory which he felt failed to measure up to this standard. Alaga elaborated: "The pot-mask is not beautiful; it is not finished, it is not rounded" (Kòkò kò dá; Kò şe pé; kò şe róbótó). He referred to his own work as model. Failure to round major and minor masses not only destroys art, in Alaga's opinion, it can impair the prime mimetic function of art. Thus he found that small calabashes on the same headdress were lumpily rendered and therefore not realistic and not beautiful. Calabashes must be specially rounded.

Mashudi Latunji spoke of the rounding of the forms of good Gelede masks. He alleged that carvers "invent" roundness after close observation of reality: "We use our eyes to observe how things are round." There is art historical truth to what he says. The basic roundness of Yoruba art is especially evident in the art of Ketu, the ancient Yoruba town under whose cultural influence Mashudi's own town of Meko lies. Mashudi has indeed used his eyes to absorb the penchant for rounded mass which characterizes the style range of Ketu.

The unified rounding of small masses in relation to larger masses is a hallmark of fine style. In Egba sculpture the eye often flattens to follow the curve of the temple. Ogundeji of Iseyin, in contrast to the Egba solution, rounds the sphere of the exaggerated eyes he carves so that when viewed in profile they are congruent with the rounded mass of the forehead. Ogidi of Igogo-Ekiti vividly rounds off all elements of his images; his works stand on rounded limbs; concave lines articulate arms from rounded torso; convex lines articulate fusions of loin and legs. Each marked division of mass is achieved with fluent curvilinearity.

Criticism of human buttocks where represented in sculpture brings the Yoruba love of rounded shapes into focus. Jogomi of Ajilete likes his buttocks rounded and "human." By inhuman he means sharp protrusion. The head of the Shango cult in Ila-Orangun made the same distinctions. Departure from the idea of the rounded rump met with amusing ribaldry in an Ijebu village: "If a man wants to copulate, or if a man wants to have an affair, he would quickly and easily be able to do what he wants to do [with this image] as its buttocks resemble those of a real person. But the second [image], its rump is raised up, its rump [stands up] high at the back" (Ó se dó fún okùnrin, ti ó bá jẹ wípé okùnrin ba fẹ̀ bá lò pò, ó lè tètè rí ṣe ng kan ti ò fẹ nítoríwípé ìdí rè dàbí ti ènìòn. Ṣùgbón èkejì ìdí rè wà lókè, kole rete di gíga èyìn ni ìdí rè wà.)

Protrusions

A pleasing bulge, as opposed to displeasing or incompetent bulges, may be denoted by the verb of action, yọ, "sprouted," qualified by an appropriate adverb. Thus a critic of Ṣepeteri extolled the tactile structure of a nose quite simply: "It bulges" (Ó yọ gbuñgbu). "You can hold the beautiful nose with your fingers," he added, "you cannot do this with the unattractive nose." This criterion seems to distinguish the sculptural from the schematic. Moderate bulges are thus an accepted part of roundness.

Nonpleasing protrusions

A definite vocabulary defines this negative taste. The modal response of the critics was ó yọ síìta, "it protrudes," and it was used, for example, by critics at Oke-Iho and Ilobi to portray, respectively, a jutting forehead and a jutting chin. The verb is rooted in the currency of abuse, as in the Yoruba phrase "he is troublesome" (Ó yọnun), meaning literally, "he is mouth-protruding."

The verb yọ by itself, of course, is neutral; adverbs shade the quality of the protrusion.

Thus *ètèērèé yọ dòdò* describes a pendulous lip, *ó lẹnun dòdò* a drooping mouth (Abraham 1958:141).[22] Here the adverb *dòdò* denotes a sagging curve of flesh. An Aworri critic used this word to characterize what he felt was wrong with the pectorals of a male *ibéjì* image. A deliberate usage of this effect in Yoruba art occurs in satiric sculpture for the *Egungun* cult. One mask, now in the collection of the Nigerian Museum, lampoons a nineteenth-century enemy of the Yoruba, the Dahomean, with a striking depiction of sagging jowls.

Sinister bulges

In general, rounded masses define Yoruba sculpture. Excessively curved swellings are not, however, looked upon with favor. One critic declared that swollen cheeks were bad art and puffed out his own cheeks in demonstration.

The verb this critic employed to denote swelling (*wú*) has sinister connotations. *Oríìmí wú*, literally "my head is swollen," means "I remember something which makes me apprehensive" (Abraham 1958:673).[23] *Orí wíwú*, "the remembrance of a terrifying event," is another example.[24] Then there is the singularly cheerless phrase, *Á wú kó tó bẹ*, "Things will be worse before they are better."[25]

Amos Tutuola draws upon this folk fear of unusual swelling in his *Palm Wine Drinkard*:

> I noticed that the left hand thumb of my wife was swelling out as if it was a buoy, but it did not pain her. [A] child came out from the thumb. He began to talk to us as if he was ten years of age. I was greatly terrified. I was thinking in my mind how we could leave the child in the farm and run to the town, because everybody had seen that the left hand of my wife had only swelled out, but she did not conceive in the right part of her body as other women do. (Tutuola 1952:31; see also p. 32)

An excrescence which is sited "in the right part of the body," forming the "obstetric line" which defines the belly of a pregnant woman, does not of course generate fear, although it is infrequently seen in Yoruba sculpture. At least one obviously pregnant woman appears as a theme, carved, with humorous intent, for the *Epa* feasts of the town of Ipoti-Ekiti. Outside of the context of rational expectation a swelling shape recalls pathology and is to be feared.

An Egbado mother warned Kenneth Murray once that if he kicked an *ibéjì* image about, as he was kicking about an abandoned celluloid European doll, he would swell up and die. A strange bulge of earth in the court of the priest of Orò at Iseyin is held dangerous: "if someone steps on Ota Orò they will swell up and die immediately." Fear of swelling, in fact, may well be diffused throughout West Africa.

Under the pressure of similar beliefs, an Ijebu cultivator immediately related the swollen upper arms of an *ibéjì* figure to pathology: *Ó tún wú bí ẹní pé ó dùn* "It is swollen doubly like a person in pain." An oral literary reflection of this visual prejudice is the ballad of the Scarlet River Hog or *Túùkú*: "River-Hog, a swelling has ruined your beauty" (*Túùkú, kókó ba ojú jẹ,* literally, "river-hog protuberance spoils face") (Abraham 1958:656).[26]

Pleasing angularity

Roundness is not an immutable law. One of the strengths of the Yoruba aesthetic is its flexibility. Yoruba critics may waive their tastes provided that novel departures are phrased with richness of human expression. Mr. William Fagg (1962) of the British Museum once told me: "The Yoruba roundness is not to be found in the works of Agunna of Oke Igbira. Agunna is more ascetic, concentrating the chin and the mouth into one point."

Within the style range of Ẹfọn-Alaiye, for example, there is a mode (much favored by chiefly patrons in Ilesha) whereby the chin is crisply pointed. Samuel Adetunji, a native of Ilesha, has described the effect: "You really notice the chin on *Èfọn* carvings. They carve chins which look like a blade." To Eṣo of Ipole-Ijesha *Èfọn* chins were "pointed" (*ṣóṅṣó*).

Ṣóṅṣó thus describes the sculptural concentration of human attributes into points. It is a usage slightly elevated from common speech where the verb acquires an occasionally whimsical tinge, as in the phrase "he has a pointed nose." But *ṣóṅṣó* implies something more than a physical state, according to Samuel Adetunji. In its most refined nuance, the verb connotes boldness; it reflects character. Eṣo of Ipole invoked this special power of the word. This was entirely in keeping with the heroic stance and pose of fine Ẹfọn-Alaiye sculpture. The bold sharpness of the *Èfọn* chin seems to be a prerogative, interestingly enough, of the general-

ized representations of mounted warchiefs and kings in the Ilesha area.

The elements and counter elements of the Yoruba notion of roundness briefly reviewed include canonic roundness described as *róbótó*; pleasing bulges are greeted with the phrase *ó yọ gbuṅgbu*; negative bulges described by a language apparently borrowed from abuse; sinister bulges fall under the verb *wú*; and, finally, one aspect of a pleasing angularity, at least, is characterized by the word *ṣóṅṣó*. Yoruba in general admire roundness but will accept sharp, angular, or bulbous shapes if these present aesthetic credentials which are clearly legible. Eṣo of Ipole, for example, not only detected the expression which went into the making of an abstract mode of *Èfọn* chin, but he measured its visual impact with a verb nuanced with boldness.

Straightness

This quality ranks with roundness as a geometric trait of essential character in fine sculpture. Yoruba define straightness as upright posture and, by extension, balanced alignments and symmetry. When Bandele of Osi-Ilorin was asked by Kevin Carroll why he used to stand back from his work at Oye-Ekiti and look at it from a distance the sculptor replied: "We were looking at the straightness of the work" (*Gígún iṣé l'a nwò*), "So that it would not be crooked" (*Kí ò máà wó*) (Father Kevin Carroll, personal communication).

Sculpture must stand erect. This is one of the first demands made upon an apprentice striving to master the art of sculpture. At a later point in his career he can assume that the problem of straightness has been mastered, and he can concentrate his energies upon more challenging aspects of form. But in the beginning (and perhaps forever for third-rate carvers) the matter of alignment is a matter of paramount concern. Bandele confessed his own fledgling uncertainties: "I did not look to the quality of shining smoothness but to the straightness. If you will remember I wasn't as good then as I am now. At that time I did not know the art of blocking the main shapes out of the wood as I do now" (Father Kevin Carroll, personal communication).

If Bandele's enunciation of the problem is enlivened with memories of the mastery of process and form, the noncarving critics' detections of this quality are equally to the point. The head man of Ilogbo told me that he found the stooped posture of an *ibéjì* not beautiful (*kò dá*). In Central Ekiti a critic liked the back of an *ibéjì* because it was straight, while the back of a rival piece was not straight (*ò gún*) and, therefore, inappropriate.

I observed Ajanaku, a fine blacksmith of Efon-Alaiye, at work in his workshop on an iron staff. The staff was surmounted by an iron bird with an iron plume sprouting from the back of its head. The blacksmith in the last stages of the work attended to the straightening of the neck of the bird and to the straightening of the staff supporting the bird. He took the staff in his tongs and placed it in the sand upright and studied it critically before he was satisfied with the *gígún* (straightness) of the total effect.

That the testing of the staff for straightness was a mental process which did not operate at a subconscious or subliminal level, in a manner suggested by Ralph Linton (1958:11–12), was clearly demonstrated the next time Ajanaku was visited. On this occasion one of the sons of the blacksmith took over the anvil.

The straightening of the bird's neck was not to the taste of the father. Ajanaku softly told his son to reheat the neck of the bird in the furnace and to straighten it out, so that it would not be crooked (*Kí ò mà wó*). The son complied. In the glowing "charcoal" of palm kernels he turned the neck of the bird around several times, holding the object with his tongs. With pincers freshly moistened in water he bent the neck of the bird, now cherry-red, just behind the crest behind the bird's neck. At last the neck was suitably erect. Ajanaku smiled. He then told his son to bend the wings of the bird slightly down; this formed a pleasing visual contrast to the rigid axis of the neck and spike.

Here a blacksmith is communicating with verbal commands a canon of straightness tempered with contrast. Pointing commands are the means of the qualification of canons. Mere physical example does not suffice. At some point the master must put into words what has gone wrong.

Symmetry

The calming virtues of symmetry are a constant in Yoruba art. The serene lips of a twin image find reflection in the balanced disposition of the image's hands. When a woman kneels and presents her offering in a container, her hands fold symmetrically around the bottom of the object; when a warrior sallies forth on his mount his hands, if free, touch the reins at precisely mirrored points. Even the theme of a bird pecking a snake, potentially a scene of random coils and agitated posture, becomes, in the hands of Duga of Meko, a concrete manifestation of pure form in even-sided resolution.

Alaga spoke of the nature of symmetry from a sculptor's point of view. Quite characteristically, he inextricably merged the concept with notions of straightness and siting. "One always positions the ears equal to each other," he asserted, "and one always keeps the ears and the eyes on the same line." He continued: "But there are some carvers [laughter] who are like small children and these put the ear on the jaw and do not think of the place of the eyes at the time they block out the ears and the mouth."

A sculptor in Ketu declared that a good carver never works without careful measurements either by adze-nicks or knifed incisions on the log, so that he can balance one effect against another as forms emerge from the raw chunk of the wood. One works quickly, he explained, but one does not work so hastily that one blocks out shapes which are not "straight." As a model of his ideal, he pointed to his own work, a headdress representing a market woman with wares on a tray atop her head. The wares were symmetrically disposed in a criss-cross of minor and major masses.

The critics made comments about straightness in the sense of symmetry, though not with the sophistication of carvers' commentaries. They spoke, for example, of the symmetry of lips, and one critic traced with his finger imaginary lines as he discussed the symmetrical disposition of facial traits and headtie on a Thundergod dance wand.

Straightness is extremely important in what might be phrased the *Ẹpa* cult aesthetic. Here it is canonic among the dancers who carry headdresses during feasts. The canon not only reflects the practical necessity of avoiding the dangerous tilting of the heavy superstructures during the ceremony but also links the pronounced straightness of the architectonic forms of the sculpture to the postures of the dance.

Allusions to the importance of straightness may be found in classical Yoruba poetry. One example is the sixth line of the divination verse quoted near the beginning of this paper. Another exists in the class of Yoruba poems known as àròfọ̀ (literally jokes, as in the term aláàròfọ̀, witty person) which are verses aimed at abstract subjects. As their title implies, they probe the assumptions of daily life with irreverence:

Why do we grumble because a tree is bent
When, in our streets, there are even men who
    are bent?
Why must we complain that the new moon is
    slanting
Can any one reach the skies to straighten it?
                        (Hodgkin 1960:326)[27]

Sculptors, however, are more committed than the makers of the oral arts. But they may approach the canonical with equal levity in the prescribed areas of moral inquisition, satire, and psychological warfare.

Skill

Yoruba esteem skill. There are suitable means of phrasing the rare knowledgeability of the artist. A frequent source is the oríkì, or praise name. Oríkì are attributive names. They express a man's most noble qualities, real or imagined. For males they often bear heroic connotations. Thus the oríkì of a sculptor may allude not only to his skill but magnify the quality on an heroic scale.

Consider the oríkì of Taiwo of Ilaro, an excellent sculptor who died around 1920 and whose early twentieth century work is found in the study collections of the Royal Ontario Museum at Toronto. In the province of the Egbado, Taiwo was widely known under his attributive name of Onípàsọ́nọ̀bẹ which means possessed of a knife like a whip.[28] It is a miniature poem in praise of artistic cunning. Such was the skill of the late Taiwo that he summoned shapes, as with a whip, out of brute wood with his knife and made the shapes do as he bid them.

Ephebism

This is perhaps the most important criterion. It is, in a sense, the resolution of all the canons in combination. Ephebism means, broadly, the depiction of people in their prime. In accordance with this canon, critics pose this question: Does the image make its subject look young?

Yoruba sculpture is a mirror in which human appearances never age. In Ipokia, for example, an old priest pointed to a robust image and said with pride: "That stands for me." Yoruba art idealizes seniority. Divination poetry tells us wisdom is the finest beauty of a person.[29] Ergo, what could be more appropriate than to flatter the moral beauty of the elders with the physical beauty of the young?

Moreover, the actual physiognomy of the senior devotee often resists the flawless seal of Yoruba sculptural form. To imitate the masters of Yoruba life and religion as they really are would deny the Yoruba idea of sculpture from self-realization.

Critics led me to these conclusions. Thus the wife of the village blacksmith at Ilishan: "I like that carving – it makes the Ọba look so young." Study of the carving she criticized validates her judgment. Cheeks are firm, stance is sure, chinline is strong. The waist is slim and youthful, and the chest is muscular, if slightly androgynous.

At Shaki an Egungun worshipper pursed his lips and parried a request for artistic criticism of twin images with a question: "Between a beautiful young woman and an old woman which would you prefer for a wife?" The expected reply was given. The informant was amused for he had led his interrogator into corroborating his argument. "I like one image best," he then stated, "because it is carved as a young girl while the other three are like old women."

This ranking was one of the very few which did not coincide with the opinion of the present writer. Three twins which seemed slender and youthful to the writer and his wife were the very pieces which seemed old to the informant. What caused the divergence of views? The informant pointed to the breasts. The breasts of the "old" women were high, as if shrunken and withered, while the breasts of the "young" girl hung down and gave the impression of fullness.

A more important reason, however, was probably the erosion of features through ritual washing. The facial traits of the "old" pieces had been somewhat worn away by time and use. It is of interest that the informant was not swayed by the sumptuous money garments, made of cowries, which adorned two of the nonfavored *ibéjì*.

A critic of Ilogbo-Aworri immediately censured the hunched shoulders and fleshy pectorals of an *ibéjì* image. Good images, he said, were carved as youths, not old men. A critic at Ifaki-Ekiti made substantially the same point and added "The chest of a young man should look like this," pointing to a hard, polished surface. "It is beautiful because it makes the image look young."

Critics characterized the alleged age of an *ibéjì* (female) at Ṣepeteri on the basis of breasts. A favored image had breasts of equal length. "It resembles a young girl" (Ó dàbí ọmọnge). A rejected image had breasts which sagged, with the right breast longer than the left, a not infrequent phenomenon among Yoruba mothers whose children have favored one nipple over the other while nursing. Asiru of Ṣepeteri made this point concrete: the most elegant *ibéjì* possessed breasts of the same length and consequently resembled a young woman.

Abinileko of Otta established that ephebism can control the judgment of *Gẹlẹdẹ* masks: "Labintan's chin looks like the chin of a young man, but that of Salawu resembles someone who is middle-aged" (Àgbọ̀n ti Lábíntán dàbí ti ọdọ́mokùnrin, ṣùgbọ́n ti Salawu dàbí ti àgbàlágbà). The main source of satisfaction with Labintan's image was that it had the look of a young boy.

The vocabulary of ephebism is simplified. It consists essentially of the key verb *jọ* (resembles) in combination with substantives denoting the quality of being young. Ephebism, as criterion, is a logical interpretation of certain of the visual constituents of Yoruba sculpture. For example, roundness connotes the vigorous period of existence, for human faces tend to become angular in old age.

Coiffure also points in the direction of youth. *Irun àgògo*, a bridal mode of the nineteenth-century Oyo, is frequently used in sculpture.[30] The high-keeled structure of the hair to a Yoruba immediately recalls the fresh beauty of the bride.

Mashudi of Mẹko reveals that one motive for the use of ephebism is commercial advantage:

If I am carving the face of a senior devotee I must carve him at the time he was in his prime. Why? If I make the image resemble an old man the people will not like it. I will not be able to sell the image. One carves images as if they were young men or women to attract people.

The Yoruba aesthetic qualifies the notion that Africans never seem to carve their subjects as of any particular age. The intent of the Yoruba sculptor is to carve a man at the optimum of his physical beauty between the extremes of infancy and old age. Even where a beard indicates maturity the brow of a Yoruba sculpture may glow with the freshness of early manhood (figure 14.7).

Seen as a whole, the Yoruba aesthetic is not only a constellation of refinements. It is also an exciting mean, vividness cast into equilibrium. "The parts of this image are beautiful," an Oyo elder once said, "because they are equal to one another." Each indigenous criterion is a paradigm of this fundamental predilection. Thus mimesis, as traditional Yoruba understand it, is a mean between absolute abstraction and absolute likeness; the ideal representational age is the strong middle point between infancy and old age; the notion of visibility is a mean between faint and conspicuous sculpture; light is balanced by shade. That beauty is a kind of mean is explicitly stated by Tutuola in *Feather Woman of the Jungle*: "She was indeed a beautiful woman. She was not too tall and not too short; she was not too black and not yellow."

Yoruba color preferences extend these beliefs. One schoolboy once stated on a questionnaire given by Justine Cordwell that his favorite color was blue because "it usually gives some attraction to the eyes. It is midway between red and black. It is not too conspicuous as red and it is not so dark as black. It is cool and bright to see." He spoke with the full authority of his ancestors. Most significant was the notion of blue, a highly favored traditional Yoruba color, as a mean between red and black.

Yoruba sculptors impose a truce upon the elements of their works, the elements themselves expressed in moderation. Even in the field of Egungun sculpture, where in order to suggest visitations from the world of the dead much license is allowed, one finds bestial and human attributes coexisting in a dignified manner because they have been balanced. Then, in turn, the sculpture will be balanced

Figure 14.7 Yoruba *Gẹlẹdẹ* headdress

Figure 14.8 Headdress of the *Egungun* cult, from Anko

on the top of a dancer's head, and he himself will probably make symmetrical gestures with a pair of flywhisks as a countereffect to his occasional impassioned twirlings.

Increase and fertility are important preoccupations. But of themselves they constitute no more than the instincts of a beast. Yoruba artistic criticism seems to be saying that force or animal vitality must be balanced by ethics, the moral wisdom of the elders. Ethics in this special sense would be the peculiarly human gift of finding the tolerable mean between the good and the bad, the hot and the cold, the living and the dead, to safeguard man's existence.

NOTES

1 Thus Cordwell (1952:292): "none of the master carver informants would become more explicit about what it was that they would say to another carver in pointing out why and how the carving was not good."

2 Ikare informants told me very simply that beauty of voice is also considered by those who judge the quality of oral skills.

3 Thus: "Comme dans les langues de métier, la prolifération conceptuelle correspond à une attention plus soutenue envers les propriétés du réel."

4 See Murray (1938?). As to one of the monuments of Yoruba metallurgy see Williams (1964:152). "[The 'anvil' of Ladin], a drop-shaped block of iron 30 inches high with a girth of 41 1/2 inches, still stands in the compound of the Oni of Ife. It was believed by Frobenius to be of cast iron, a claim which would suggest furnaces capable of generating temperatures in the region of 1,550°C. The block on close inspection, however, appears to have been built up from lumps of wrought iron which in any case represents a high degree of metallurgical skill."

5 An excellent survey of Yoruba literary types is *Yoruba Poetry* by Beier and Gbadamosi (1959).

6 As documented by D'Avezac (1845:78): "markets...operate on a money basis – based on the cowrie shell, called *owwo*." On pp. 81–83 D'Avezac discusses the Ijebu Yoruba concept of the week, month, and year.

7 See, for example, Roth (1903:157–191). See also Weir (1933: par. 101). "The official residence of the Ologotun is maintained by the townsfolk and the share of the work is allocated as follows: (1) By all the town (a) the entrance gate to the forecourt known as *enu geru* (b) the forecourt

known as *ode gbaragada* (c) the second court known as *ode useroye* (2) By the Uba quarter (a) the court for council meeting known as *ode ayigi*." Weir documents similar information in his *Intelligence Report on the Ikerre District of the Ekiti Division of the Ondo Province* (Lagos: 31 December 1933).

8 I have since this time interviewed many more critics. Eventually I hope to plot differences of taste by ethnic sub-group, though the task may prove difficult.

9 Bowen (1858). *Amèwa* seems formed of a *mòn èwà* "Knower (of beauty," just as "lawyer" (*amòfin*) is literally a "knower (of the) law" (*A mòn òfin*).

10 Quoted in a personal communication to the author from Father Kevin Carroll of the Roman Catholic Mission, Ijebu-Igbo.

11 The details of spelling are taken from Abraham (1958). Thus, for example, I spell "*enia*" as he does, phonetically *enion*. Abraham's *Dictionary* is likely to stand for years as a standard reference and to facilitate thus the easy use of his intricately organized materials, I have used frequently his own system of orthography.

12 Thus: "Most of these commercial pieces exhibit a lack of feeling so marked that they can easily be distinguished from the figures made for Dahomeans, on which time and effort are lavished in the best traditional manner." Compare Kenneth Murray's experience with Suli Onigelede, a woodcarver of Lagos, circa 1946: "Suli...had some ibeji (twin statuettes)... unfortunately he smothered them in bright green enamel as he thought that Europeans would like them so, in spite of my instructions to use native colours" (Murray, unpublished manuscript).

13 Cf. a brief summary of the problem of portraiture in African sculpture may be found in Bohannan (1964:152–3).

14 These are described as real portraits "for remembrance."

15 For these and other remarks by Bandele I am indebted to the kindness of Father Kevin Carroll who shared the insights of this famous son of Areogun of Osi-Ilorin in a letter dated February 29, 1964.

16 Father Carroll has published the Ekiti Yoruba terms for these stages in his

"Three Generations of Yoruba Carvers," *Ibadan* no. 12 (June 1961), p. 23.

17   These are points from tape-recorded conversations with Bandele which Father Carroll has shared with me.

18   Quoted in a personal communication from Father Kevin Carroll.

19   King (1961:11). Bells and gongs are made "visible" to the ear, as it were, because of their high pitch.

20   Nigerian Museum, Lagos (KCM 381). The housepost once stood in a courtyard in the house of the Elegbe.

21   Collier ("Yoruba Hunter's Salutes," p. 54): "Some hunters say *rekina-rekina* which I understand to mean "glistening" or "glittering" – like the sun shining on wind-ruffled water, I was told..."

22   See *dòdò* (Abraham p. 141).

23   *Wú* (Abraham p. 673).

24   *Ibid.*

25   *Ibid.*, p. 672.

26   Abraham's translation has greater focus than an earlier version of the ijala of the Red River Hog by F. S. Collier, who rendered the Yoruba "animal...with swelling on his face."

27   From E. L. Lasebikan, "The Tonal Structure of Yoruba Poetry," *Présence Africaine* no. 8–10 (1956), p. 49.

28   Mr. Kenneth Murray collected this information at or near Ilaro.

29   Cf. Beier and Gbadamosi (1959:30): "Wisdom is the finest beauty of a person. /Money does not prevent you from becoming blind/ Money does not prevent you from becoming mad."

30   *Agogo* coiffure also, of course, denotes subservience to a deity.

REFERENCES

Abraham, R. C. 1958 *Dictionary of Modern Yoruba.* London: University of London.

Allison, Philip 1956 The Last Days of Old Oyo. *Odù* 4:18.

Ballard, Edward G. 1957 *Art and Analysis.* The Hague: Martinus Nijhoff.

Bascom, William 1951 Social Status, Wealth and Individual Differences Among the Yoruba. *American Anthropologist* 53(4):490–505.

—— 1959 Urbanism as a Traditional African Pattern. *Sociological Review* 7(1):29–43.

—— 1960 Yoruba Concepts of the Soul. In A. F. C. Wallace (ed.), *Men and Cultures.* (Selected Papers of the Fifth International Congress of Anthropological and Ethnological Sciences) Philadelphia: University of Pennsylvana Press. Pp. 401–10.

Beier, Ulli 1963 *African Mud Sculpture.* Cambridge: Cambridge University Press.

Beier, Ulli and Bakare Gbadamosi 1959 *Yoruba Poetry.* Lagos: Black Orpheus.

Biobaku, Saburi O. 1955 The Use and Interpretation of Myths. *Odù* 1:12–17.

Bohannan, Paul 1964 *Africa and Africans.* Garden City, N.Y.: Natural History Press.

Bowen, T. J. 1858 *Grammar and Dictionary of the Yoruba Language.* Washington, D.C.: Smithsonian Contributions to Knowledge.

Collier, F. S. 1953 Yoruba Hunters' Salutes. *Nigerian Field* 18(2): 1.

Cordwell, Justine Mayer 1952 Some Aesthetic Aspects of Yoruba and Benin Cultures. Unpublished doctoral dissertation, Northwestern University, Evanston, Ill.

D'Avezac, M. 1845 Notice sur le pays et le peuple des Yebous en Afrique. *Mémoires de la Société Ethnologique,* II. Paris.

Fagg, William 1963 *Nigerian Images.* London: Lund Humphries.

Fuja, Abayomi 1962 *Fourteen Hundred Cowries: Traditional Stories of the Yoruba.* London: Oxford University Press.

Herskovits, Melville J. 1938 *Dahomey,* Vols. I and II. New York: J. J. Augustin.

Hodgkin, Thomas 1960 *Nigerian Perspectives: An Historical Anthropology.* London: Oxford University Press.

Hsu, Francis L. K. 1964 Rethinking the Concept 'Primitive.' *Current Anthropology* 5(3): 169–78.

Johnson, Samuel 1921 *The History of the Yorubas.* Lagos: Church Missionary Society Bookshop.

King, A. V. 1961 *Yoruba Sacred Music from Ekiti.* Ibadan: Ibadan University Press.

Lasebikan, E. L. 1956 The Tonal Structure of Yoruba Poetry. *Présence Africaine* 8–10.

Lévi-Strauss, Claude 1962 *La Pensée sauvage.* Paris: Librairie Plon.

Linton, Ralph 1958 Primitive Art. In William Fagg and Eliot Elisofson (eds.), *The Sculpture of Africa.* New York: Praeger. Pp. 9–17.

Lloyd, Peter C. 1962 Sungbo's Ersko. *Odù* 7:15–22.

Murray, Kenneth 1938? Native Minor Industries in Abeokuta and Oyo Provinces. Unpublished manuscript. Lagos.

—— 1961 The artist in Nigerian tribal society: A comment. In Marian W. Smith (ed.), *The Artist in Tribal Society*. New York: Free Press of Glencoe.

Roth, Ling 1903 *Great Benin*. Halifax: F. King and Sons

Smith, M. W. (ed.) 1961 *The Artist in Tribal Society*. Proceedings of a symposium held at the Royal Anthropological Institute. London: Routledge and Kegan Paul.

Talbot, Amaury 1926 *The Peoples of Southern Nigeria*. Vol. II. London: Oxford University Press.

Trimingham, J. Spencer 1961 *Islam in West Africa*. London: Oxford University Press.

Tutuola, Amos 1952 *The Palm-Wine Drinkard*. London: Faber and Faber.

Weir, N. A. C. 1933 *An Intelligence Report on Ogotun District, Ekiti Division, Ondon Province*. Lagos.

Wingert, Paul S. 1962 *Primitive Art: Its Traditions and Styles*. New York: Oxford University Press.

15

Style in Technology: Some Early Thoughts

Heather Lechtman

In 1973, Arthur Steinberg and I suggested that it would be fruitful, particularly for archaeologists who deal almost exclusively with material culture, to investigate technological style as a phenomenon as well as the manner in which individual styles of technology relate to other aspects of the cultures in which they occur.

> In asking what is the cultural component of technology, we are also asking what can technology tell us about culture? We must be concerned not only with the bodies of skill and knowledge of which Merrill (1968) speaks, not only with the materials, processes, and products of technology, but also with what technologies express. If we claim that technologies are totally integrated systems that manifest cultural choices and values, what is the nature of that manifestation and how can we "read" it? . . .
> We would argue that technologies also [like visual art, music, dance, costume, gesture] are particular sorts of cultural phenomena that reflect cultural preoccupations and that express them in the very style of the technology itself. Our responsibility is to find means by which the form of that expression can be recognized, then to describe and interpret technological style.
> (Lechtman and Steinberg 1973)

I organized the symposium "Style in Technology" to stimulate interest in the concept of technological style, to see how useful it might be in interpreting cultural data, whether ethnographically or archaeologically assembled, and to elicit some concrete examples of the stylistic component of technology as it functions in specific cultural contexts. . . .

By style I refer to the formal, extrinsic manifestation of intrinsic pattern. The oft-cited distinction used by linguists between *langue* and *parole* is precisely that distinction between pattern and style. The ordered, redundant phenomena that constitute the patterned structure of all culture are expressed as style in verbal, visual, kinesic and technological behavior. Style is the manifest expression, on the behavioral level, of cultural patterning that is usually neither cognitively known nor even knowable by members of a cultural community except by scientists who may have analysed successfully their own cultural patterns or those of other cultures.

One of the most useful expressions of the relationship between pattern and style is given by Cyril Stanley Smith (1978:16) who considers style as a phenomenon which is dependent upon structure and is hierarchical in nature.

From Heather Lechtman and Robert S. Merrill (eds.), *Material Culture: Styles, Organization and Dynamics of Technology. Proceedings of the American Ethnological Society for 1975* (St. Paul: West Publishing Company, 1977), pp. 3–20.

Style is the recognition of a quality shared among many things; the quality, however, lies in structure on a smaller scale than that of the things possessing the quality...

The part/whole relationships that produce the externally-visible quality called style seem to be closely analogous to the relationship between internal structure and externally-measurable property that distinguishes one chemical phase from another.... Bulk properties of matter such as density, color, conductivity, crystal structure or vapor pressure by which a chemical phase is identified are not a property of any of the parts, (though they would not exist without them) but rather are external characteristics depending on the *pattern of interaction* between the atomic nuclei, electrons and energy quanta and the extension of this pattern by repetition throughout the entire volume of the phase concerned. (italics mine)...

Style is hierarchical; it resides at all levels, or rather between any inter-relatable levels.

Two features of style emerge from Smith's model of the structural nature of all systems, whether physical, biological, or social: 1) within any system "it is the relationships of communication, not the parts themselves, that lock in to reinforce and stabilize a larger pattern..." and it is our perception of the formal arrangement of those interrelationships that we recognize as style; 2) the particular patterns of relationships among interacting parts are different at different levels within the system, thus style is hierarchical and its manifestation depends upon where we locate to observe the interactions.

For example, a crystal exists at one level of structural hierarchy higher than that of the ordered arrays of atoms which comprise it. Crystallinity, as an identifiable property, represents a physical style of matter. It is a style dependent upon the *repetition* of the local symmetries of the unit cell throughout the crystal. Though the essence of crystallinity lies in the unit cell, the crystal is the extension of this. The physicist who studies the internal structure of the atom does not see the unit cell, and the crystallographer who studies the symmetries of the unit cell does not necessarily see the crystal as defined by their extension and the limits of their extension. Different styles become observable at different levels of the hierarchy of aggregation. (Smith 1978). The properties identifying crystal grains in the aggregates studied by the metallurgist or the polyhedral crystals studied externally by the traditional mineralogist represent a new state of things, a style emerging at a higher level from the patterns of atomic interaction at lower levels.

Scholars rarely experience any difficulty in talking about style or in describing its formal elements when we are considering objects, that is, the physical products of certain types of behavior. The large majority of studies in art history are predicated upon the scholar's ability to group works of art by their formal, stylistic properties. Archaeology is similarly dependent upon the use of stylistic categories of artifacts which are derived from study of their formal characteristics. What we haven't seemed to recognize or at least paid much attention to is that the activities themselves which produce the artifacts are stylistic. "Material culture is the name given to the man-made physical products of human behavior patterns..." (R. Spier 1970:14); and it is precisely those behavior patterns that constitute the style of technology. Technological behavior is characterized by the many elements that make up technological activities – for example, by technical modes of operation, attitudes towards materials, some specific organization of labor, ritual observances – elements which are unified nonrandomly in a complex of formal relationships. It is the format or "package" defined by these relationships that is stylistic in nature, and it is the style of such behavior, not only the rules by which any of its constituent activities is governed, that is learned and transmitted through time.

Leone's analysis (1973) of Mormon town plans and fences as well as his discussion of Mormon "sacred technology" in his symposium paper here (1977:87–107) are excellent illustrations of technological style. He sets out the characteristic web of interactions of certain "pieces" of Mormon technology with the culture's ideology, religion, and social structure and provides the principle he believes underlies those interactions. That principle is "mutually exclusive compartmentalization: the use of categories whose closest members have no contact with each other" (see p. 102). The building of fences – fences that separated house from house and therefore family from family, sheep and goats from horses and cattle, natural predators from everything domesticated, and wind-borne sands from the farmyard and garden (1973:143–4) – was an ecological necessity in the semi-arid Utah plains, in that fences "... separate[d] competitive niches from each other and protect[ed] all artificially created niches from the universally destructive wind" (1973:144). But the building of fences was important also because behind his fence a Mormon could raise a garden, could make the desert bloom, could demonstrate his worth before his God. "The state of a man's yard is the state of his religion" is the way one Mormon expressed the relationship (Leone 1973:147). Fences were crucial for subsistence but also were fundamental to religious and social life. Leone argues further that the physical compartmentation of the Mormons' world, the parceling out of that world through the technology of fence building, created the kind of cultural environment in which the individual grew up and that that environment must have had a cognitive effect upon him. "This environment is a result of the way Mormons have had to think about their world and of what the Mormon idea-system was and has become. If fences are a piece of enabling... - technology, then it is reasonable to suppose that the technology enables them to think in certain ways, as well as to grow crops in certain ways. As a result, this system of technology should have cognitive consequences" (1973:147). Leone goes on to describe what some of those consequences are and concludes that "... fences enable them [Mormons] to redeem the earth and manipulate and act out the categories used to deal with the world" (1973:148), categories that are essentially exclusive and incompatible. The technological style observed in Mormon fencing and town planning is an expression, on the level of technological behavior, of an underlying cultural pattern of "mutually exclusive compartmentalization." The technology incorporates and transmits the principle itself.

Style can be thought of, then, as the sensible manifestation of pattern; and technological style is expressed "emic" behavior based upon primarily "etic" phenomena of nature: copper melts at 1083°C and, after cold working, re-crystallizes at about 300°C, but why a culture technically capable both of casting and of forging copper elects one of these manufacturing techniques to the exclusion of the other is not explained by these properties of the metal. If, through appropriate study, we can describe the elements of any given technological style and can determine the relationships among them, in other words if we can successfully define the style, what can we then say about the intrinsic cultural pattern or patterns of which it is an expression? This issue is vital to archaeological research, for the single subsystem of a once-living culture that archaeologists can reconstruct and understand almost in its entirety is the technological subsystem. Binford (1962: 218) has observed, "It has often been suggested that we cannot dig up a social system or ideology. Granted we cannot excavate a kinship terminology or a philosophy, but we can and do excavate the material items which functioned together with these more behavioral elements within the appropriate subsystems." But what we can and do excavate are technologies. Furthermore, it is wholly within our capability to determine accurately the technical events that went into the manufacture of the kinds of items to which Binford refers, from the gathering of the natural resources through the various stages of processing, alteration, and final rendering of the artifact. These events are all behavioral, and they proceed in a formal way. I am calling technological style that which arises from the formal integration of these behavioral events. It is recognizable by virtue of its repetition which allows us to see the underlying similarities in the formal arrangement of the patterns of events.

An example to illustrate the argument I have been developing might be helpful. It comes from my work in the field of pre-Columbian metallurgy. Although I have presented the data and the issues surrounding them before (Lechtman 1971, 1973, 1979), the problems raised remain to be solved, and the case seems an instructive one for the present discussion.

When one considers the development of metallurgy in the Andean area prior to the Spanish invasion, one is struck by the nature of the alloy systems that dominated the course of Andean metallurgy for at least two millennia. They are remarkable when compared with the alloys used by other ancient culture areas that practiced sophisticated metallurgy, for example, the Near East, Europe, China, both because they are so different from those others and because they appeared on and were a primary stimulus to the Andean metallurgical scene long before alloys of bronze were produced by Andean metalworkers. Whereas the other great prehistoric traditions of metallurgy were founded upon the utilization of copper and, very early, of copper-arsenic and/or copper-tin bronze, the production of bronze was a relatively late development in Andean metallurgy. It was preceded by two thousand years of experience, at a high level of technical sophistication, with a variety of copper-based alloys that were developed for the colors they would impart to the artifacts made from them. These deliberate alloys (as distinct from naturally occurring ones), of copper-silver, copper-gold (usually referred to as tumbaga), and copper-silver-gold, were not exclusive to Andean metalworkers. They were utilized by other peoples prehistorically, but only occasionally, and nowhere else did they form the backbone of the indigenous metallurgy, influencing markedly the course of its own internal development.

The colors the early Andean metalworkers wanted to achieve were the colors of silver and gold. When objects were made directly from either of these precious metals, the color was attained automatically. But objects made from other metals – copper, for example – could be given the desired appearance by providing them with a surface layer of metallic silver or gold. The usual way of gilding or silvering metal objects, as such surface coating is called, the method utilized by the ancient metallurgies of the Old World, is to apply a thin layer of the metal directly to the object's surface. For example, gold in the form of thin foil or leaf, in the form of a fine powder, in molten form, or as an amalgam with mercury, was applied to metal objects to provide them with surfaces of gold.

The Andean process for achieving the same end is almost the reverse of that just described. Rather than placing the precious metal upon the surface of the object, as an added element, nonintegral with the object itself, they placed the precious metal within the bulk of the object by incorporating it as one of the constituents of the original alloy from which the object was later fabricated. For example, an alloy of 80 percent copper and 20 percent gold contains the gold in solid solution, distributed homogeneously throughout the alloy. The alloy does not look golden; rather it is a distinctly coppery color, and an object made of such an alloy would appear as copper. But the gold is present internally and can be made manifest at the object's surface by treating the surface so that the copper there is removed selectively, leaving the gold in place. The gold is "developed" at the surface by eliminating the other components of the alloy – copper or minor constituents such as silver or lead – at the surface and leaving only the gold coating layer. The Andean peoples devised various alloy systems and associated techniques for chemically treating the surfaces of those alloys in order to obtain gold- and silver-looking objects. The first such alloy seems to have been a simple copper-silver binary system which gave a silver surface to objects made from it. Tumbaga then appeared (copper-gold) and eventually the ternary copper-silver-gold alloy that is so characteristic of north Andean metallurgy as practiced by the Kingdom of Chimor whose master goldsmiths were brought to Cuzco by the conquering Inca to work for the royal lineage.

The principle of incorporating within a metal object the constituent which was later to become its most important external quality was the governing idea that stimulated the invention of a whole group of alloy systems in ancient Peru. The idea spread from Peru to the peoples of Colombia where it was adopted and adapted to a technical tradition of handling metal that was almost diametrically opposed to the Peruvian tradition (casting in Colombia vs. forging in Peru). It was an idea to which Andean metallurgy was committed for the major part of its history and through which some of its most inventive developments took place. These considerations suggest that the principle itself was a powerfully motivating one. Its application resulted in a metallurgical style unique to the Andes.

This metallurgical style, based upon processes of surface enrichment and depletion, has been identified through laboratory studies on large numbers of metal objects from the Andean culture area. The majority of these were used for ceremonial or political purposes – as funerary masks applied to mummy bundles, large expanses of metal sheet that lined the interiors of palace and temple walls, small plaques sewn to garments for status display, figurines, decorative vessels, and so forth. That gold and silver should have been the colors desired is consistent with the obviously fundamental role those metals played in Andean cosmology and statecraft. Our best evidence is from the Late Horizon (ca. 1470–1532 A.D.) when gold and silver were the exclusive property of the Inca, that is, of the state. The royal lineage was believed to have issued directly from the sun, the first Inca being the son of the sun. Gold was considered the "sweat of the sun," silver the "tears of the moon." Ritual performed for the sun cult was one of the most important of the priestly functions. But neither the weaving of these materials throughout the religious and cosmological orders nor their political manipulation accounts for the particular metallurgical style that was the Andean response to a desire for gold- or silver-looking objects. Nor, for that matter, do any of the other explanations that have been offered, particularly for the widespread use of the copper-gold alloy tumbaga, account for the evolution of the technological style. William Root (1951) argued that although tumbaga may have been used because it was easier to cast such an alloy than it was to cast copper; it made objects harder because copper-gold alloys are harder than either copper or gold alone; it economized on gold because a small amount of gold within the alloy was sufficient to create a gold surface and, therefore, a "gold" object; the most likely reason for its use was simply that those who made and used the alloy preferred the color of gold to that of copper. Even though the constellation of tumbaga may have been composed of some or all of these factors, they seem to me to fall short of explaining what appears to have been an overwhelmingly central tendency, a pattern of Andean metallurgical development. We can recognize the technological style. But what does it express? What gave it the tenacity it most certainly had such that Andean metalworkers seem to have been locked into a style of operating, though with evident opportunity, within that convention, to be inventive.

I have suggested (Lechtman 1979) that what lay behind the technological style were attitudes of artisans towards the materials they

used, attitudes of cultural communities towards the nature of the technological events themselves, and the objects resulting from them. The basis of Andean surface enrichment systems lies in the incorporation of the essential ingredient into the very body of the object. The essence had to be present though invisible. The style is a playing out of the notion that:

> the essence of the object, that which appears superficially to be true of it, must also be inside it. The object is not that object unless it contains within it the essential quality, even if the essence is only minimally present. For without the incorporation of the essence, its visual manifestation is impossible.... Although ideological considerations may have had little to do with the initial working out of [the technical] procedures, I feel sure that the way in which the Andean peoples perceived such processes or at least the objects that resulted from their use had a great deal to do with the way in which the technology emerged and matured. Belief systems and attitudes toward materials supported the technology and gave rise to further developments along similar lines. (Lechtman 1979:32)

The technological performance was supported by a set of underlying values. I have suggested what I think one of those values or standards may have been, as I interpret it from that portion of the performance which is purely technical, the events of production that remain part of the physical structure of the object.

Examples such as this one indicate that it is possible to determine the technological styles that underlay particular sets of artifacts of archaeological study. The much more difficult step is to argue from a confident understanding of the style of technological behavior to more fundamental, deeper cultural patterns which informed that behavior. Yet, if we could do that, archaeology would have a powerful tool for getting closer to those aspects of past cultures that cannot be determined directly – for example, the realm of ideology, values, philosophy – yet whose imprint should be accessible through the study of behavior as it is observed in the material record. "The objects man has learned to make are traditionally termed material culture. Culture is intellectual, rational, and abstract; it cannot be material, but material can be cultural and "material culture" embraces those segments of human learning which provide a person with plans, methods, and reasons for producing things which can be seen and touched" (Glassie 1968:2). What are our chances for success in determining the "plans" and "reasons" behind technological behavior as those are revealed in the artifacts themselves?

In the example of Andean metallurgy just cited, how do I know that my interpretation is correct, as plausible as it may seem from my frame of reference? Does my ethnocentrism come between me and the data? And even if we can get at the standards *for* technological behavior by looking at patterns *of* technological behavior (see Keesing 1969:208), what is there to suggest that those same standards inform any of the other interacting subsystems of culture?

The view of culture as cognitive code which is separate and distinct from material artifacts and behavior has been most forcefully represented by Goodenough. In fact, Keesing (1969:207) considers the "... effective theoretical separation between cultural codes – cognitively based normative systems – and their enactment in behavior..." one of the major breakthroughs in social anthropology of recent years. In essence, Goodenough (1964) argues that there are two domains in culture, the ideational and the phenomenal, the latter being an artifact of the former. He states that the phenomenal order of events, of behavior, of artifacts within a human community:

exhibits the statistical patterns characteristic of internally stable systems, as with homeostasis in the living organism. Similar, but never identical, events occur over and over again and are therefore isolable as types of event and patterned arrangement. Certain types of arrangement tend to persist and others to appear and reappear in fixed sequences. An observer can perceive this kind of statistical patterning in a community without any knowledge whatever of the ideas, beliefs, values, and principles of action of the community's members, the ideational order.... The ideational order, unlike the statistical order, is nonmaterial, being composed of ideal forms as they exist in people's minds, propositions about their interrelationships, preference ratings regarding them, and recipes for their mutual ordering as means to desired ends. (Goodenough 1964:12)

Whether or not one subscribes to this view, I would argue, on the basis of Smith's model, that the patterns of behavior we see depend upon the level at which we isolate them for study and at which they exhibit style. To the extent that style is hierarchical, the scale of resolution at which we can study behavior may not be the same as the scale at which ideation operates, but one is a manifestation of the other and there must be a structural connection between the two. While it may be extremely difficult to arrive at the underlying structure in culture below the level at which we perceive technological style, for example, the persistent attributes of the style relate to a formal arrangement of operations and that arrangement, in itself, carries a heavy load of meaning. Communication among the parts of a system are the backbone of style, but the style as a whole, once perceived, is itself a form of communication.

Despite the primacy of language as *the* human means of communication and the *sine qua non* of culture, no one would argue that it is the sole device for the sharing of socially acquired knowledge nor that verbal communication functions best in transmitting all varieties of messages. As Frake has pointed out, what we want to do is both to describe socially meaningful behavior and to discover the rules behind such behavior. The entire domain of socially interpretable acts and artifacts, that is, the total domain of "messages" is the concern of ethnography which "seeks to describe an infinite set of variable messages as manifestations of a finite shared code, the code being a set of rules for the socially appropriate construction and interpretation of messages" (Frake 1964:132). Implicit in the equation of "socially interpretable acts and artifacts" with "messages" is the understanding that a shared cultural code is expressed along a variety of communication channels, among which are reckoned acts of behavior and artifacts. In that case, archaeology can address itself to at least some of the behavioral and all of the material elements which make up the total domain of messages within a community. Artifacts are the products of appropriate cultural performance, and technological activities constitute one mode of such performance. What I have called the style of technological behavior is the rendering of appropriate technological performance. The style itself is the rendition, and the measure of its appropriateness, as determined archaeologically at least, lies in its reiteration. Furthermore, it is the synthesizing action of the style, the rendering of the performance, that constitutes the cultural message. Technologies are performances; they are communicative systems, and their styles are the symbols through which communication occurs. The relationships among the formal elements of the technology establish its style, which in turn becomes the basis of a message on a larger scale.

I would argue further that what is communicated through the expression of technological style is not communicable verbally, despite Frake's skepticism that "... it [is] difficult to conceive of any act, object, or event which can be described as a *cultural* artifact, a manifestation of a code, without some reference to the way people talk about it" (1964: 133). Bateson (1972:137) credits Anthony Forge for the remark by Isadora Duncan: "If I could tell you what it meant, there would be no point in dancing it." Recent studies of indigenous art are providing increasing evidence for the use of nonverbal systems of expression to communicate fundamental ideas about the natural and social order. In his studies of Abelam flat painting, Forge (1973) has indicated that some of the messages the art carries do not seem to operate at a conscious level, but rather that there is a "grammar" of painting which is as unconscious as is the grammar of spoken language. The styles of the painting, he argues, are systems of meaning, systems of communication which " ... unlike those to which we are used, exist(s) and operate(s) because [they are] not verbalized and probably not verbalizable, [they] communicate(s) only to those socialized to receive [them]" (1973:191). Similarly, Nancy Munn has documented, in a series of provocative articles (1964, 1966, 1973), the method by which Walbiri communicate principles of cosmic order through their spatial arrangements, in media of two and three dimensions, of the traditional elements of their visual vocabulary. She points out, however (1973:216, note 1), that such iconographic systems may be given somatic form in dance or the enactment of ritual. I do not think it far fetched to suggest that part of the communicative aspect of technologies lies in the somatic

nature of their performance which involves not only the articulation of body and tool or body and material but the exemplification of skill. The case is stated elegantly by Hallowell (1968:235).

> Systems of extrinsic symbolization necessitate the use of material media which can function as vehicles for the communication of meanings. Abstraction and conceptualization are required since objects or events are introduced into the perceptual field as *symbols*, not in their concrete reality. Thus systems of extrinsic symbolization involve the operation of the representative principle on a more complex level than do processes of intrinsic symbolization. In case of *Homo sapiens*, extrinsic symbolic systems, functioning through vocal, graphic, plastic, gestural, or other media, make it possible for groups of human beings to share a common world of meanings and values. A cultural mode of adaptation is unthinkable without systems of extrinsic symbolization.

Technologies are such symbolic systems. A good example in support of this argument is given by M. J. Adams' work (1971, 1973) on the island of East Sumba, Indonesia. Dyed textiles are not only the major "visual art" of the island but are also exceptionally important as ceremonial costume, as wealth in ritualized gift exchange, and as sacred objects (1971: 322). Adams describes the technical procedures and work schedules that are associated with the production of textiles, from the planting of the cotton seeds to the final weaving of the ikat designs into the cloth. At each stage of production she shows the close relationships between the activities undertaken in the work routine and phases in the Sumbanese life cycle, especially those which relate to the physical and social maturation of women. "In myth, ritual and social rules on Sumba, the stages of textile work are consistently linked to the progressive development of individual human life. These stages provide an overarching metaphor for the phases of the Sumbanese life cycle" (1971:322). It is not only that, as Adams argues, the procedures and schedules of work provide metaphoric schema for other symbolic systems, but that the technological acts themselves constitute a symbolic system.

There is no question, then, that we can excavate artifacts and reconstruct the technologies behind them. In doing so, we may discover specific technological styles which are renderings of appropriate technological behavior communicated through performance. The culturally accepted rules of the performance are embodied in the events that led to the production of the artifact. We should be able to "read" those events, if not all of them at least those of a technical nature, by laboratory study of the materials that make up the artifacts in question. The history of the manipulation of those materials is locked into their physical and chemical structure; the methods of materials science can interpret that technical history.

Having come thus far, what remains is the task of describing the relational order between the symbolic, technological events, and that which they symbolize – of coming to grips with decoding the technological system of communication. The interpretation of symbolic content in archaeological data is extremely difficult. We can rely upon the fact that the formal relationships that exist in any iconographic scheme or that constitute a technological style are rarely if ever dictated solely by the environment. They largely reflect cultural choices. That a particular community tills in a certain way or pots in another or builds in yet another is certainly affected by the nature of the soil and micro-climate, the clay, or the building materials available. But those are immutable conditions in and around which people elaborate technological behavior along lines that are meaningful socially, economically, and ideologically. The rules behind their choices are what we are after.

Although I have been talking about "technological style" as a phenomenon, that should not imply that any given cultural community is characterized by only one such style. In fact, several styles may operate synchronically, each having developed as it did as a result of a multitude of factors including the nature of the technological "task" itself (the building of irrigation ditches as opposed to the construction of a ceremonial dance mask), the social group performing the technological activity or for whom it is performed (e.g. commoner/elite, peasant/landlord, men/women), the cultural subsystem in which the technological events primarily operate (social, technological, ideological), the properties of the environment

being manipulated by the technology, and so on. As Binford has argued, the artifacts one studies or the class of items they represent "... are articulated differently within an integrated cultural system, hence the pertinent variables with which each is articulated, and exhibit concomitant variation are different" (1962:219). Technological behavior is manifest in all activities in which the natural or social environment is directly manipulated, but the style of that behavior may be different according to the particular integration of the technological complex within any given subsystem of the total cultural scene. Styles for the production of mundane goods may be different from styles for the manufacture of sacred objects; elite styles may be different from folk styles. In attempting to decode the message carried by technological style we must be cognizant that the message may not be the same for each style encountered within a given cultural community. The intriguing questions are: when the styles *are* the same, when the message *is* reiterated, a) what is the message; and b) what are the socio-cultural circumstances that stimulate styles which bear similar messages? For example, will we tend to find that, despite the obvious differences in technique between women who weave sacred or ritual garments and men who cast ritual vessels for use in the same ceremonies as the cloth, the styles in which these otherwise disparate technologies operate are based on similar underlying patterns of technological behavior because what each expresses has to do with what the ritual expresses? Will technologies within the ideological subsystem tend to be stylistically alike because of the relationships they bear to the underlying ideology? Or are we more likely to find that we cannot always apply the same sorts of categories Binford (1962) uses for artifacts to technologies, that is, technomic, sociotechnic, ideotechnic categories based on the primary functional context of the artifact or, in this case, of the behavior? My guess is that technological styles will appear similar wherever the message they carry relates to idea systems, values, orientations that cross-cut the social, technological, and ideological realms of a society. In fact, archaeological identification of similar technological styles within these various subsystems should point to a message widely expressed throughout the culture and, perhaps, give us a better handle on what that message may have been, of how to reconstruct that portion of the cultural code which is manifest in the style. Perhaps both specific styles relating to specific cultural spheres and intracultural styles exhibiting a similar expression in many of those spheres will prove to be characteristic of styles in technology.

Returning to my earlier question, if we allow ourselves to interpret the meaning of technological style once we have defined the style, how do we know that our interpretations are correct? If it is true that technological styles are both meaningful in themselves and are manifestations of cultural codes, then a style which seems indigenous (as opposed to introduced from the outside), persistent, and stimulative, may have served as the model for the expression of "message" in other media or in other subsystems of the culture than those in which it is first observed and for which it seems particularly characteristic (as, for example, the style of metallurgical technology). The problem for the archaeologist is where to look for the evidence. Does one begin with another technology, one which appears of similar importance and which one suspects was designed in part to bear ideational content (in the Andes this would unquestionably be the production of cloth) to see if the style of that system is organized around a similar model and is expressive of similar preoccupations? Will we find, as in the case of Andean metallurgy, that the model applies primarily to behavior the products of which, the artifacts, are primarily operative in the social or ideological subsystems of the total cultural system? Does *cumpi* cloth, the finest textiles woven for the Inca by the specially chosen and trained *aclla* female weavers or the male *cumbicamayocs*, display in its structure or the manipulation of its materials the same patterns of formal relationships that underlie the style of the royal metallurgy? Or does it make more sense to look not at another creative technological complex but rather at a different system of communication, one which relies upon technological input but whose focus is elsewhere, the realm of "art," for example? If we were to seek the aesthetic locus of a culture, in the sense that Maquet (1971) uses that concept, and were to investigate the symbolic and expressive

content of that locus or elements within it through study of its remaining artifacts, would we find similar patterns indicative of ideas such as the incorporation of essences, reiterated in the locus structure? Testing hypotheses that have to do with the message content of sets of artifacts is exceedingly difficult, but I think we must make the attempt if we expect to make any headway in understanding the interplay between ideas and performance in the technological sphere of life. That we must proceed cautiously, avoiding the obvious pitfalls, has been amply stressed by others as well (e.g. in the work of Friedrich 1970 and White and Thomas 1972).

I have dwelt at some length with the concept of style in technology as that concept applies to archaeological situations, because archaeology must constantly explore new strategies for mining its artifacts for all that they are worth. My feeling is that systems of technology, as reconstructed primarily from evidence provided by laboratory study of artifacts, are worth more than we have sought from them. I am suggesting that one tactic we might exploit is the study of technologies as systems that proceed in a stylistic manner, some of the elements of which we can determine with little error. Defining the parameters of a particular style may help in eliciting from the technology information about its own symbolic message, and about cultural code, values, standards, and rules that underlay the technological performance. It is obvious that the ideas I have set forth here must be tested through ethnographic fieldwork. That may not be easy, at least in the case of many of the traditional societies whose technologies have undergone more rapid change than other aspects of life as a result of Western economic imperialism. When the technology involved is a Western imposition or import, there is little reason to suspect that any of the traditional sets of values still inform modern technological behavior. But we might still find clues in those areas of life that were not central to Western development schemes, in the traditional arts, for example. If systems of beliefs are reflected in objects of art, they ought also to be reflected in the processes by which art objects are produced. Perhaps it is in the technology of art that we might look for evidence of the symbolic content and code-bearing nature of technology. On the other hand, we ought also to investigate the technologies of modern, industrial societies where, although the data may be more complex and difficult to assess because of our closeness to it, we may have a better chance of observing the kinds of relationships I have tried to define.

I would encourage anthropologists – whether they practice ethnography or archaeology – to reconsider the richness of technological behavior and to explore that behavior not only as moderator between society and the natural world but as an important vehicle for creating and maintaining a symbolically meaningful environment. The maintaining of particular technological styles has probably always been one of the effective ways by which communities have enculturated values through nonverbal behavior.

REFERENCES

Adams, Marie Jeanne 1973 Structural Aspects of a Village Art. *American Anthropologist* 75:265–279.

—— 1971 Work Patterns and Symbolic Structures in a Village Culture, East Sumba, Indonesia. *Southeast Asia* 1:321–334.

Bateson, Gregory 1972 Style, Grace, and Information in Primitive Art. In *Steps to an Ecology of Mind*. G. Bateson, ed. Pp. 128–156. San Francisco: Chandler.

Binford, Lewis R. 1962 Archaeology as Anthropology. *American Antiquity* 28:217–225.

Friedrich, Margaret Hardin 1970 Design Structure and Social Interaction: Archaeological Implications of an Ethnographic Analysis. *American Antiquity* 35:332–343.

Forge, Anthony 1973 Style and Meaning in Sepik Art. In *Primitive Art and Society*. A. Forge, ed. Pp. 169–192. New York: Oxford University Press.

Frake, Charles O. 1964 Notes on Queries in Ethnography. In *Transcultural Studies in Cognition*. A. K. Romney and R. G. D'Andrade, eds. *American Anthropologist* 66, part 2, no. 3:132–145.

Glassie, Henry 1968 *Patterns in the Material Folk Culture of the Eastern United States*. Philadelphia: University of Pennsylvania Press.

Goodenough, Ward H. 1964 Introduction. In *Explorations in Cultural Anthropology*. W. H. Goodenough, ed. Pp. 1–24. New York: McGraw-Hill.

Hallowell, A. Irving 1968 Self, Society, and Culture in Phylogenetic Perspective. In *Culture – Man's Adaptive Dimension*. M. F. Ashley Montagu, ed. Pp. 197–261. New York: Oxford University Press.

Keesing, Roger M. 1969 On Quibblings Over Squabblings of Siblings: New Perspectives on Kin Terms and Role Behavior. *Southwestern Journal of Anthropology* 25:207–227.

Lechtman, Heather 1979 Issues in Andean Metallurgy. In *Pre-Columbian Metallurgy of South America*. E. P. Benson, ed. Pp. 1–40. Washington, D.C.: Dumbarton Oaks.

—— 1973 The Gilding of Metals in Pre-Columbian Peru. In *Application of Science in Examination of Works of Art*. W. J. Young, ed. Pp. 38–52. Boston: Museum of Fine Arts.

—— 1971 Ancient Methods of Gilding Silver – Examples from the Old and the New Worlds. In *Science and Archaeology*. R. H. Brill, ed. Pp. 2–30. Cambridge, Mass.: M.I.T. Press.

Lechtman, Heather and Arthur Steinberg 1973 The History of Technology: An Anthropological Point of View. In *The History and Philosophy of Technology*. George Bugliarello and Dean B. Doner, eds. Pp. 135–160. Urbana: University of Illinois Press.

Leone, Mark P. 1973 Archeology as the Science of Technology: Mormon Town Plans and Fences. In *Research and Theory in Current Archeology*. Charles L. Redman, ed. Pp. 125–150. New York: John Wiley.

Leone, Mark P. 1977 The Role of Primitive Technology in Nineteenth Century American Utopias. In *Material Cultures: Styles, Organization and Dynamics of Technology*. Proceedings of the American Ethnological Society for 1975. St. Paul: West Publishing Co.

Maquet, Jacques 1971 Introduction to Aesthetic Anthropology. *Current Topics in Anthropology* 1, module 4:1–38.

Merrill, Robert S. 1968 The Study of Technology. In *International Encyclopedia of the Social Sciences*. David L. Sills, ed. Vol. 15:576–589. New York: Macmillan.

Munn, Nancy D. 1973 The Spatial Presentation of Cosmic Order in Walbiri Iconography. In *Primitive Art and Society*. A.

Forge, ed. Pp. 193–220. New York: Oxford University Press.

—— 1966 Visual Categories: An Approach to the Study of Representational Systems. *American Anthropologist* 68:936–950.

—— 1964 Totemic Designs and Group Continuity in Walbiri Cosmology. In *Aborigines Now*. M. Reay, ed. Pp. 83–100. Sydney: Angus and Robertson.

Root, William C. 1951 Gold-Copper Alloys in Ancient America. *J. of Chemical Ed.* 28:76–78.

Smith, Cyril Stanley 1978 Structural Hierarchy in Science, Art, and History. In *On Aesthetics in Science*. Judith Wechsler, ed. Pp. 9–53 Cambridge, Mass.: MIT Press.

Spier, Robert F. G. 1970 *From the Hand of Man*. Boston: Houghton-Mifflin.

White, J. P. and D. H. Thomas 1972 What Mean These Stones? Ethno-taxonomic Models and Archaeological Interpretations in the New Guinea Highlands. In *Models in Archaeology*. D. L. Clarke, ed. Pp. 275–308. London: Methuen.

16

"Marvels of Everyday Vision"
The Anthropology of Aesthetics
and the Cattle-keeping Nilotes

Jeremy Coote

> The current idea that we look lazily into the world only as far as our practical needs demand it while the artist removes this veil of habits scarcely does justice to the marvels of everyday vision.
>
> E. H. Gombrich, *Art and Illusion*

Introduction

This essay is written out of a conviction that progress in the anthropological study of visual aesthetics has been hampered by an undue concentration on art and art objects. The cattle-keeping Nilotes of the Southern Sudan make no art objects and have no traditions of visual art, yet it would be absurd to claim that they have no visual aesthetic. In such a case as this, the analyst is forced to attend to areas of life to which everyday concepts of art do not apply, to attend, indeed, to 'the marvels of everyday vision' (Gombrich, 1977: 275) which we all, not just the artists and art critics amongst us, experience and delight in. It is my contention that such wide-ranging analyses will produce more satisfactory accounts of the aesthetics of different societies – even of those with art traditions and art objects. With this in mind, then, I present the cattle-keeping Nilotes of the Southern Sudan as a sort of test-case for the anthropology of aesthetics.

The Anthropology of Aesthetics

While it is generally recognized that aesthetics concerns more than art and that art is about more than aesthetics, anthropologists, along with philosophers and aestheticians in general, have tended to work on the assumption, made nicely explicit in the 'Aesthetics' entry in the *New Encyclopaedia Britannica* (Pepper, 1974: 150), that 'it is the explanation that can be given for deeply prized works of art that stabilizes an aesthetic theory'. In their accounts of the aesthetics of other cultures, anthropologists have concentrated on materials that fit Western notions of 'works of art', at times compounding the problem by making the focus of their studies those objects which are 'deeply prized' by the Western anthropologist,

From Jeremy Coote and Anthony Shelton (eds.), *Anthropology, Art and Aesthetics* (Oxford: Clarendon Press, [1992] 1995), pp. 245–273. Reprinted by permission of Oxford University Press.

rather than those most valued by the people themselves. Moreover, what has passed for the anthropology of aesthetics has often been little more than talk about such 'art'; for many years, anthropologists' or art critics' talk, more recently, indigenous talk as systematized by the anthropologist.

While one doubts that works of art are ever deeply prized for their aesthetic qualities alone, it is probably true that in Western societies, and in others with highly developed art traditions, aesthetic notions are most perfectly manifested in works of art, and are given their most refined expression in that type of discourse known as the philosophy of art. But the aesthetic notions so manifested and refined are those of members of the art world, not necessarily those of the general population. For most of us – or, perhaps more accurately, all of us most of the time – our aesthetic notions have more to do with home decorating, gardening, sport, advertising, and other areas of so-called 'popular' culture. The presence of art having become almost a defining feature of Western notions of the civilized, anthropologists have been loath to say of any other society that it has no art. There is, it is true, probably no society that has no art-form at all, but there are certainly societies with no visual art traditions. A Western preoccupation with the visual has led both to the undervaluation of the poetic, choreological, and other arts, and to the widening of the definition of visual art so as to embrace all those objects or activities which have 'artistic' or 'aesthetic' qualities. So, for example, body decoration has been reclassified as art in recent years. While I have no fundamental objection to 'art' being defined in such broad terms, I find it more satisfactory to talk rather of the aesthetic aspect of a society's activities and products.

All human activity has an aesthetic aspect. We are always, though at varying levels of awareness, concerned with the aesthetic qualities of our aural, haptic, kinetic, and visual sensations. If art were to be defined so broadly as to encompass any human activity or product with an aesthetic aspect, then none could be denied the status of art. This seems to me unwarranted; the possible insight seemingly captured by such an argument is adequately caught by saying that all human activity has an aesthetic aspect.

I am encouraged in arguing for such a view by a trend that seems to characterize some recent anthropological and philosophical literature, a trend towards recognizing that aesthetics may be usefully defined independently of art. The anthropologist Jacques Maquet, for example, has argued repeatedly (e.g. 1979: 45; 1986: 33) that art and aesthetics are best treated as independent. Among philosophers, Nick Zangwill (1986: 261) has argued that 'one could do aesthetics without mentioning works of art! Sometimes I think it would be safer to do so.' And T. J. Diffey (1986: 6) has remarked how it is not just philosophers of art who require a notion of aesthetics; philosophers of religion require one too, and 'a notion of it as that which has no especial connection with art, but which, rather, is closer to perception'. Diffey regards 'aesthetic experience' as an as yet 'inadequately understood expression', as a term 'that extends thought, stretches the mind and leads us into new and uncharted territory' (ibid. 11). The task of philosophy, as he sees it, is to clarify and explicate what ordinary language has already 'inchoately discovered'. It is my view that rather than waiting for the clarifications and explications of philosophy, the anthropology of aesthetics should follow such ordinary language usage, disconnect itself from art, and get closer to perception.

I hope that what is meant by this admittedly vague contention will become clearer through the course of this essay. It might be thought too easy to have recourse to 'everyday usage', for probably any definition at all can be supported by judicious selection from the flux of everyday language. I am able, however, to adduce here non-specialist usages of 'aesthetic' and its cognates by three of the authors whose writings on the peoples of the Southern Sudan are drawn on in this essay. These authors do not discuss aesthetics as such, but make passing references which I find significant. Evans-Pritchard (1940a: 22) refers to 'those aesthetic qualities which please him [a Nuer] in an ox'. Elsewhere, Jean Buxton (1973: 7) tells us that 'marking and patterning are very highly estimated in the Mandari visual aesthetic', and John Burton (1981: 76) refers to a particular cattle-colour configuration as being 'the most aesthetically pleasing for the Atuot'. In none of these cases does the author explain what he or she means by the term. They can all be taken to be using the term in an everyday sense which they expect their readers to understand. I take them to mean by an 'aesthetic' something like 'the set of valued formal qualities of objects' or 'valued formal qualities of perception'.

The anthropology of aesthetics as I see it, then, consists in the comparative study of valued perceptual experience in different societies. While our common human physiology no doubt results in our having universal, generalized responses to certain stimuli, perception is an active and cognitive process in which cultural factors play a dominant role. Perceptions are cultural phenomena. Forge touched on this some twenty years ago when he wrote (1970: 282) concerning the visual art of the Abelam of New Guinea:

What do the Abelam see? Quite obviously there can be no absolute answer to this question: it is impossible literally to see through the eyes of another man, let alone perceive with his brain. Yet if we are to consider the place of art in any society...we must beware of assuming that they see what we see and vice versa.

I should argue that, more than just being wary of making assumptions, we must in fact make the attempt to understand how they see. The study of a society's visual aesthetic, for example, should be devoted to the identification of the particular qualities of form – shape, colour, sheen, pattern, proportion, and so on – recognized within that society, as evidenced in language, poetry, dance, body decoration, material culture, sculpture, painting, etc. A society's visual aesthetic is, in its widest sense, the way in which people in that society see. Adapting from Michael Baxandall's studies of Western art traditions (1972: 29 ff.; 1980: 143 ff.) the phrase 'the period eye', anthropologists might usefully employ the notion of 'the cultural eye'. It is a society's way of seeing, its repertoire of visual skills, which I take to be its visual aesthetic, and it is with this that I believe the anthropological study of visual aesthetics should be concerned. Such an anthropology of aesthetics will be a necessary complement to any anthropology of art, for it surely must be essential to any anthropological consideration of art, however conceived, that an attempt is made to see the art as its original makers and viewers see it.

The study of aesthetics as it is taken here is to be distinguished from both art criticism and the philosophy of art. These disciplines are concerned with aesthetics, but not exclusively so. The evaluations of art criticism involve considerations of form, but also of content and meaning. The philosophy of art tends towards analysing the relations between art and such matters as the True and the Good, matters which are beyond the formal qualities of works of art. It is perhaps worth emphasizing that practices similar to those of Western art criticism and philosophy are to be found in other cultures. These practices are worthy of study in their own right. According to the terminology adopted in this essay, however, they are not the aesthetics of a society, but its art criticism or its philosophy.

The Cattle-keeping Nilotes

The cattle-keeping Nilotes need little introduction here. This essay focuses on the Nuer, Dinka, Atuot, and Mandari of the Southern Sudan, concerning each of whom there is a substantial and easily accessible literature, while making passing reference to the closely related Anuak of the Southern Sudan and the more distantly related Pokot and Maasai of East Africa. The Nuer and Dinka in particular are well known to all students of anthropology.[1] What does perhaps require some explanation is their being taken together as 'the cattle-keeping Nilotes'. The million or so people who are referred to by the names 'Nuer', 'Dinka', 'Atuot', and 'Mandari' do not compose a homogeneous society – but then, neither do any of the four 'peoples' themselves. There are, for example, variations in the ecological situation, economic life, degree of political centralization, and particularities of religious belief and practice both within and between these peoples.

However, they also share many social and cultural features, not least of which is the importance of cattle in their lives.[2] Cattle are not just a food source, but a central factor in all aspects of their social and cultural activities, being used to mediate social relationships through the institutions of bride-wealth and bloodwealth, as well as to mediate man's relationship with God through their role as sacrificial victims. Moreover, the Nuer, Dinka, Atuot, and Mandari share a common history,[3] live in geographical proximity, and have extensive interrelations across the 'borders' that might be supposed to exist between them.

The picture of Nilotic visual aesthetics painted here is an analyst's abstraction. It is founded on the current state of anthropological knowledge concerning the group of peoples which provide the ethnographic focus, peoples who are related linguistically, historically, geographically, and culturally. Further research may reveal significant differences between and amongst the aesthetics of these four peoples. It might, however, also reveal significant similarities between these four peoples and other Nilotic-speaking peoples. The analysis presented here is ahistorical. This is for the sake of convenience only. A full understanding of an aesthetic system must include the historical dimension. I hope to be able to deal with aesthetic change among the Nilotes elsewhere.

Nilotic Aesthetics

Little attention has been paid by scholars to aesthetics amongst the Nilotic-speaking peoples of Southern Sudan and East Africa.[4] In his thesis on Western Nilotic material culture, Alan Blackman (1956: 262–73) devotes a chapter to 'Aesthetics', but only to discuss representational art – or, more accurately, the lack of it. Ocholla-Ayayo's discussion (1980: 10–12) of 'Aesthetics of Material Culture Elements', in his account of Western Nilotic Luo culture, is a purely theoretical account of the abstract notion of beauty and its relation to value, appearance, use, and society, drawing on thinkers such as Santayana, without entering into a discussion of the particularities of Luo aesthetics as such. Harold Schneider's short but often quoted article on 'The Interpretation of Pakot Visual Art' (1956) is the best-known contribution to the study of Nilotic aesthetics, and is worth commenting on at some length.

Schneider defines his terms rather differently from how they are defined here. He defines 'art' as 'man-made beauty', but recognizes that what the Pokot themselves find beautiful should not

be assumed by the analyst but has to be discovered. To do this, he analyses the meaning and use of the Pokot term *pachigh*, which his interpreter variously translated as 'beautiful', 'pretty', 'pleasant to look at', and 'unusual'. *Pachigh* is distinguished from *karam*, which means 'good', and which Schneider glosses as 'utilitarian'. The Pokot apply the term *pachigh* to non-utilitarian, aesthetically pleasing objects of the natural world or of non-Pokot manufacture, as well as to the non-utilitarian embellishments of Pokot utilitarian objects. Cattle, for example, are utilitarian (*karam*), but the colours of the hides are *pachigh* (ibid. 104). People are also *karam*, though a woman 'may have aspects of beauty such as firm round breasts, a light, chocolate-coloured skin, and white even teeth' (ibid. 104); and a fully decorated man may be referred to as beautiful but 'it is clear that they mean only the aesthetic embellishments' (ibid. 105).

Through his analysis of the term *pachigh*, Schneider is able to identify what it is that the Pokot find aesthetically pleasing, but he tells us little about *why* these particular objects and embellishments are considered *pachigh*. In recognizing that what is of interest is not a category of objects – art – but a category of thought – aesthetics – Schneider makes an important contribution – being 'forced' to, perhaps, by the very lack of Pokot art – but he tells us little about what characterizes this category of thought, merely listing those objects to which it is applied. While he refers in passing to contrast, which is discussed below – and to novelty, which I hope to discuss elsewhere – the discussion of aesthetic qualities, the very stuff of aesthetics, is not developed. It is on the aesthetic qualities which Nilotes appreciate, rather than on the category of objects in which these qualities are observed, that this essay concentrates.

For Nilotic-speaking cattle-keepers, cattle are the most highly valued possessions. This analysis of Nilotic aesthetics is, therefore, centred on cattle. The importance of cattle for the Nilotes is well known, and I do not propose to summarize the literature here. I wish to concentrate on the perceptual qualities of cattle as they are appreciated by their owners. These concern the colour configuration and sheen of the hide, the shape of the horns, and the bigness and fatness of the body including particularly the hump (see figure 16.1). These are discussed first, and then their ramifications into other areas of Nilotic life are traced.

Of primary importance for this discussion are the cattle-colour terminologies which are so characteristic of the cattle-keeping peoples of East Africa.[5] Nilotic languages in general have many terms to describe the colour configurations of cattle. Even people who no longer keep cattle or depend upon them materially may maintain cattle-colour terminologies. The Anuak, for example, who, according to Evans-Pritchard (1940b: 20), can only have been a pastoral people 'a very long time ago', still based their metaphorical praise-names upon cattle-colour configurations when Lienhardt studied them in the 1950s (Lienhardt 1961: 13n.). Cattle-colour terms rarely refer to pure colours or shades of colours, but rather to configurations of colours or, in a loose sense of the term, patterns.

For the Western Dinka, Nebel (1948: 51) recorded twenty-seven terms, while for the Ngok Dinka, Evans-Pritchard (1934) recorded thirty. For the Nuer, Evans-Pritchard (1940a: 41–4) showed that there are 'several hundred colour permutations' based on ten principal colour terms multiplied by at least twenty-seven combination terms. In his 1934 article on Ngok Dinka terms, he promised that he would publish a full account of Nuer terms, a promise repeated in *The Nuer* (1940a: 44). The fact that the promised lengthy analysis, of what he noted in 1940 was a 'neglected' subject (ibid. 41 n.), has never appeared suggests how difficult such an analysis would be. Indeed, the application of the abstract terminology to real animals is not always straightforward for Nilotes themselves. According to Deng (1973: 96), 'the colour-patterns are so intricate among the Dinka that frequent litigation centres on their determination'. And Ryle has described (1982: 92) – in interesting terms, given the subject of this essay – how

When discussing the colour pattern of an animal – as they do for hours – the Dinka sound more like art critics than stockbreeders. For instance, when does *mathiang* – dark brown – become *malual* – reddish brown? If the animal has brown patches, are they large enough to

Figure 16.1 Dinka ox of the *marial* configuration; Bekjiu, near Pacong, Agar Dinka. Photograph by Jeremy Coote, February 1981

make it *mading* or are they the smaller mottling that identifies *malek*?

Such discussions are a matter of both appreciation and classification, perhaps more akin to the discussions of antique-dealers or wine connoisseurs than to those of art critics.

It is not necessary to analyse these terminologies at length here. It is sufficient to identify briefly the principles underlying the perceived configurations. For Mandari, the colours red, white, and black have much symbolic importance (Buxton, 1973). With cattle, however, they are not so interested in pure colours; what is important is that an ox should be piebald or variegated. When a piebald is born, its owner is delighted and the beast is set aside as a display ox (ibid. 6). Similarly, Ryle has described (1982: 93–6) the 'hopeful expectation' that attends the birth of a new calf amongst the Agar Dinka. He relates how in one instance Mayen, the cow's owner, 'was ecstatic, beaming with pleasure and singing snatches of song, because the calf was a much desired *marial*'. It is the destiny of such well-marked male calves to become 'song', or 'display' oxen, being castrated when they are eight or nine months old. Animals with the most highly valued configurations are thus excluded from breeding. Ryle was told that one cannot anyway predict the occurrence of such colour patterns, 'and therefore there is no point in trying to breed for them' (ibid. 93; cf. Howell *et al.*, 1988: 282). For the Western Dinka Lienhardt (1961: 15) records how, when a male calf of a highly valued configuration is born, 'it is said that... the friends of its owner may tear off his beads and scatter them, for his happiness is such that he must show indifference to these more trivial forms of display'. If the dam that has produced the well-marked calf is a good milch cow, Dinka may find it hard to choose whether to keep the calf for stud purposes, knowing that it is likely to produce further good milch cows, or castrate it for display. They may hope that the dam will produce another, not so well-marked, male calf later, and castrate the one it has already produced. Mandari also choose their stud bulls from the progeny of good milch cows. All other things being equal, they will choose well-coloured ones; but, significantly, not the piebald or variegated but the plain black

or red calves, trusting that these will produce offspring which are well-marked (Buxton, 1973: 6).

In fact, most cattle are not well-marked. Buxton noted that the majority of Mandari cattle are a nondescript white (ibid.), and my own experience would support this. Amongst the Agar Dinka to the west, the situation is much the same; greyish, off-white cattle are preponderant, as aerial photographs have demonstrated.[6] That they are relatively rare helps to explain why well-marked beasts are valued to such an extent that the Agar Dinka, for example, 'will trade two or three oxen of unexceptional colourings for one particularly desirable beast, if the owner is willing to part with it' (Ryle, 1982: 92). It follows that it is the cattle of less aesthetic interest, as well as those beyond breeding, which are marketed by those Nilotes, such as some Atuot, who have entered the incipient Southern Sudanese cattle trade (Burton, 1978: 401).

The sheen of the hides is also appreciated and valued. Though sheen is not a factor in cattle-colour terminologies, its appreciation can be amply illustrated by the amount of time and effort expended in the grooming of cattle, and by frequent reference to it in poetry and song. An Atuot song, for example, includes the words: 'the back of my ox is as white as the grazing in the new grass' – the image, as Burton explains (1982: 274), being 'of morning dew glittering in the sunlight'. A song by Stephen Ciec Lam, a Nuer, refers to 'my sister's big ox/ whose glossy hide shines against the compound' (Svoboda, 1985: 32). Another by Daniel Cuor Lul Wur, also a Nuer, refers to an ox whose hide 'is like the sun itself: he is the ox of moonlight' (ibid. 19). And yet another by Rec Puk relates how 'Jiok's hide is as bright as moonlight,/ bright as the sun's tongue./ My Jiok shines like gold,/ like a man's ivory bracelet' (ibid. 11). In this last example, specific comparison is made between the white-on-black cattle-hide and the whiteness of the ivory bracelet shining against the black Nuer skin.

The training of ox-horns is practised by cattle-keeping peoples all over the world. Nilotes cut the horns of young display oxen so that they grow into shapes which their owners find particularly pleasing. They are cut with a spear at an oblique angle, and the horns grow back against the cut.[7] To describe such horn shapes the Nuer have six common terms, as well as 'several fancy names' (Evans-Pritchard, 1940a: 45). In combination with the cattle-colour configuration terms, these considerably increase the number of possible permutations to specify individual beasts – logically, to well over a thousand. As can be seen in figure 16.2, the horns may also be adorned with buffalo-tail hair tassels to accentuate the effect. When Burton (1982: 279) was carrying out his fieldwork among the Atuot, such tassels were exchanged at the rate of one tassel for six cow-calves. Cutting also thickens the horns, and large and heavy horns are especially characteristic of display oxen among the Mandari (Buxton, 1973: 7).

Appreciation of horns is expressed in song. A Dinka song, for example, tells of an 'ox with diverging horns,/ The horns are reaching the ground;/ The horns are overflowing like a boiling pot' (Deng, 1972: 84). The range of imagery is vast: Cummins (1904: 162) quotes a Dinka song in which an ox's horns are said to be 'like the masts of ships' – presumably referring to the masts of sailing ships which once plied the Nile and its tributaries. Horns are also sometimes decorated with ash, when oxen are exchanged in bridewealth, for example, the effect being to make them stand out more against the dull background of sky and landscape.[8]

In his discussion of the Nuer attitude to their cattle, Evans-Pritchard (1940a: 22) referred to 'those aesthetic qualities which please him [a Nuer] in an ox, especially fatness, colour and shape of horns'. And, according to him (ibid. 27), it is fatness which is most important, for 'colour and shape of horns are significant, but the essential qualities are bigness and fatness, it being considered especially important that the haunch bones should not be apparent'. He goes on (ibid.): 'Nuer admire a large hump which wobbles when the animal walks, and to exaggerate this character they often manipulate the hump shortly after birth.' This admiration of humps is shared by the Dinka and Atuot. A Dinka song (Deng, 1972: 81) has the lines: 'My ox is showing his narrow-waisted hump./ The hump is twisting like a goitered neck,/ Staggering like a man who has gorged himself with liquor;/ When he walks, the hump goes on twisting/ Like a man traveling on a camel.' Another Dinka

Figure 16.2 Dinka man with decorated song-ox. Photograph by Survival Anglia, 1975

song, quoted by Cummins (1904: 162), refers to an ox whose hump is 'so high that it towers above the high grass'.

The qualities of bigness and fatness are also referred to in songs. An Atuot song recorded by Burton (1982: 272) refers to the ox which is the subject of the song as 'the mahogany tree', thereby likening the size of the ox to the tree. Another Atuot song (Burton, 1981: 107) tells of an ox which is said to be 'so large like an elephant'. A Dinka song recorded by Cummins (1904: 162) tells of an ox which is 'so big that men can sit and rest in his shadow'. It should be stressed that bigness and fatness are not appreciated because they will lead to a better price at market, or to a larger meal on the death or sacrifice of the animal: cattle are primarily a feast for the eyes, and only secondarily a feast for the stomach.

Before going on to trace some of the ramifications of these elements of Nilotic 'bovine' aesthetics into the Nilotes' appreciation of, and action in, the world, it is worth making the attempt to understand why the particular perceptual qualities identified are so appreciated.

The appreciation of a large hump and of bigness and fatness are presumably at least partly explicable as indicators of healthy and well-fed beasts. And the same can presumably be said for the appreciation of sheen – it indicates a sleek and healthy hide; though it should be noted that sheen is perceptually exciting in and of itself, so its appreciation can be understood as a particular manifestation of the universal appreciation of brightness.

The appeal of horn shapes is not difficult to understand in the field. One quickly learns to appreciate the variety of trained and untrained shapes in a forest of horns in the cattle camp. Both the symmetrical and the asymmetrical curving shapes of Nilotic cattle horns have great visual appeal, especially when they are seen moving through space as the cattle move their heads, and when the arcs the horns make in the air are exaggerated by the swinging movements of the tassels. Fagg (e.g. 1973) has drawn attention to the frequent use of exponential curves in African art: the Nilotic appreciation of the curving shapes of cattle horns can be seen as yet another instance of this theme in African aesthetics.

As with horns, the appeal of particular cattle-colour configurations cannot be explained by reference to the healthiness or well-being of well-marked beasts. The majority of such beasts, though, are likely to have larger body proportions than other beasts, as the majority of well-marked beasts are castrated, and neutering encourages body growth. They also spend no energy in sexual activity and much less than uncastrated cattle in fighting; so their body growth is further encouraged and they remain physically unblemished. In general, more care is lavished on them by their owners, and one can expect this to have a beneficial effect on their health and well-being. Well-marked beasts are thus also likely to be big and fat, and vice versa. It would, however, be a strange argument which explained the appeal of well-marked beasts by the fact that they are healthier, when their being healthier depends upon their being well-marked.

As aestheticians stabilize their theories by explaining why highly prized works of art are so valued, the explanation for the Nilotes' appreciation of well-marked cattle might be sought in what they value most highly. For the peoples who are the focus of this essay, it is bold pied markings. For the Western Dinka at least, it is in particular the black-and-white configurations *majok* and *marial* (Lienhardt, 1961: 15). The former is most simply described as a black animal with a white chest, the latter as a black animal with a white flash on its flank. Black-and-white configurations provide strong contrasts. Buxton offered an explanation of the appeal of such contrasts, noting (1973: 7) that 'marking and patterning are very highly estimated in the Mandari visual aesthetic; and the strong contrast markings of black on white, red on white, or a combination of all three, stand out so strikingly in a landscape devoid of strong colour that the importance given to it can be readily understood'. Such an explanation can only be partial at best, but when one remembers that the vast majority of cattle are a nondescript white, the appeal of strongly contrasting black-and-white or red-and-white markings can be appreciated more readily.

The visual stimulation offered by both black and red markings amongst a herd of greyish cattle is not to be doubted. It might be expected, then, that it should be the pure black or red beasts which are most highly valued. This is not the case, for while the appreciation of well-marked beasts should be understood in the context of a dull and pale landscape and herds preponderantly off-white in colour, it is the contrast of black and white or red and white in the single beast which provides the greatest aesthetic satisfaction. The individual beast, then, provides the locus for stimulating visual experience.

Aesthetics in the Wider World

Having introduced some elements of Nilotic aesthetics, it is possible to trace their ramifications in the Nilotes' appreciation of, and action in, the world in which they live.

The cattle-colour terms are associated with a wide range of phenomena apart from cattle. At its most simple, this involves the recognition of connections between, for example, the ox *makuac* – that is, an ox of the *kuac* configuration – and the leopard, *kuac*. In their poetic imagery, however, the Nilotes go beyond these relatively straightforward linguistic connections to more complex associations. Evans-Pritchard recorded (1940a: 45) some 'fanciful elaborations of nomenclature' among the Nuer where, for example, 'a black ox may be called *rual mim*, charcoal-burning or *won car*, dark clouds'. And amongst the Western Dinka, according to Lienhardt (1961: 13), a man with a black display ox may be known not only as *macar* 'black ox', but also as, for example, '*tim atiep*, "the shade of a tree"; or *kor acom*, "seeks for snails", after the black ibis which seeks for snails'.

It is not just that Nilotes make metaphorical connections between cattle-colour configurations and other phenomena; it is not just poetic play. In a real sense they see the world through a sort of grid or matrix of cattle-colours:

> The Dinkas' very perception of colour, light, and shade in the world around them is . . . inextricably connected with their recognition of colour-configurations in their cattle. If their cattle-colour vocabulary were taken away, they would have scarcely any way of describing visual experience in terms of colour, light, and darkness. (Lienhardt, 1961: 12–13)

This is not, of course, to say that they could not perceive the black ibis or the shade of a tree if it were not for the existence of black oxen, but it is to say that their visual experi-

ence and appreciation of the ibis and the shade is inseparable from their appreciation of the *macar* colour configuration in cattle.

Those cattle-colour terms, such as *makuac*, which are clearly related linguistically to natural phenomena, are no doubt derived from the term for the phenomenon and not vice versa. Presumably the Dinka called the leopard *kuac* before they called the spotted ox *makuac*. However, the *kuac* configuration in cattle is not called after the leopard because of some significance of the leopard as such, but because it is like the pattern to be found on *kuac*. Children will learn the names of cattle-markings, and apply them to natural and cultural phenomena, before they ever see the source of the name of the markings. A Dinka child will know what *kuac* means as a marking pattern, and will be applying it to cattle and to spotted cloth, for example, well before he or she ever – if ever – sees a leopard. The visual experience of young Dinka is focused on cattle and their markings, and the cattle-colour terminology is learned through listening to daily discussions about cattle. As Lienhardt (ibid. 12) writes, 'a Dinka may thus recognize the configuration in nature by reference to what he first knows of it in the cattle on which his attention, from childhood, is concentrated'. This fact is of greater significance than the possible historical origins of the terms.[9] That the Nilotes' visual perception of their natural and cultural world is thus shaped by their interest in, and experience of, the colour configurations of their cattle is amply attested, both by their complex cattle-colour terminologies and by the rich poetic and metaphorical elaborations of these terminologies by which associations are made between the most diverse visual experiences and cattle-colours. These associations are not by any means always obvious; part of the pleasure of composing and singing songs is in making creative connections which one's audience has to work at to comprehend.

That these associations are not made only in poetic contexts, however, is shown by Lienhardt's remark (1961: 19) that Dinka 'frequently pointed out to me those things in nature which had the *marial* colour-configuration upon which my own metaphorical ox-name was based'. One might expect a man to become particularly attuned to the colour-configuration of his own name or song ox, but, as

Lienhardt's anecdote makes clear, this attuning is not exclusive; Dinka recognize and appreciate a wide range of colour-configurations. Agar Dinka friends called me Makur, explicitly referring to the dark rings around my eyes like the black patches round the eyes of the ox *makur*. Other Agar to whom I was introduced immediately grasped why I had been so called.

It is not just in their perception of their world, and their poetic expressions concerning it, that we can trace these elements of the Nilotic aesthetic. They can also be traced in the ways in which Nilotes act in the world. For example, they decorate their bodies with ash, the decoration being always (as far as I know) non-representational, but very commonly geometric.[10] Buxton tells us (1973: 401) that among the Mandari 'young people decorate their faces with white ash to imitate the facial markings of oxen and cows'. This is what one might expect to be the case for the Nilotes in general, though I know of no other report of such decoration as conscious imitation. The appearance of ash-covered bodies is, in any case, not unlike the colour of the majority of poorly marked, greyish cattle. Even if it is the case that when they decorate themselves with ash they are not consciously imitating the markings of cattle, it is surely not too much to assume that the appreciation of the markings of cattle and of the ash-covered bodies are similar, and that the former affects the latter.

More clearly, perhaps, the black-and-white animal skins, like that of the colobus monkey, which are part of 'traditional' Nilotic dress, can be seen as reflecting the contrasts appreciated in cattle-hides.[11] In recent years it has been possible for Nilotes to buy plastic accoutrements with which to adorn themselves; the man pictured with his ox in figure 16.2 is wearing a striking black-and-white plastic leopard-skin belt.

The contrasts that Nilotes appreciate in their cattle, and in the world around them, they also achieve in their decorative work. Mandari incise patterns on pots and gourds and blacken them with the heated point of a knife or spear, and contrasts are also made by rubbing white clay or ash into black or red surfaces. Black-and-white contrasts can also be seen in the frequent use of ivory bracelets in body decoration: as noted above, the whiteness of the ivory gleams against the wearer's black skin.

Necklaces and bracelets made of indigenous materials such as wood and shell are also characterized by black-and-white contrasts.[12] It seems that contrast continues to be an important aspect of the aesthetics of beadwork, even with the immense range of hues now available in imported plastic beads.[13]

The forked branches erected in cattle camps, like the Agar Dinka example in figure 16.3, are decorated by the removal of alternate sections of bark to produce a banded, hooped, or straked effect.[14] In the 1980s, Mandari had access to acrylic paints, and took to painting the tall poles they erect in cattle camps. Instead of stripping alternate sections of bark to produce the desired effect, the whole bark was stripped off and alternate sections painted black and white, or, as in one example I saw, bright red and brilliant yellow.

The asymmetrical branching shape effected by horn-training can be seen in the tree branches erected as shrines amongst the Dinka, Mandari, and Atuot.[15] Although, as

Figure 16.3 Forked-branch cattle-post in an Agar Dinka cattle-camp. Photograph by Jeremy Coote, February 1981

Figure 16.4 Forked-branch shrine in an Apak Atuot homestead, near Aluakluak. Photograph by Jeremy Coote, February 1981

can be seen in figure 16.4, they also have a practical purpose, in that their shape makes them suitable to lean spears against and hang things from (Lienhardt, 1961: 257–60), it seems unlikely that shapes so reminiscent of the trained horns of oxen are accidentally so. One is encouraged to think that the resemblance is deliberate by the fact that the place marked by such forked-branch shrines is known amongst the Dinka as 'the head of the cattle-hearth' (ibid. 258); and Cummins (1904: 158) recounts a Dinka myth of origin in which it is said that where God lives there is a tree 'that is leafless with only two branches, one to the right and the other to the left like the horns of a bull'. For the Atuot, at least, 'the imagery of the spreading branches is consciously associated with the horns of a cow sacrificed on the occasion when the power was brought into the homestead' (Burton, 1979: 105 n.).

Whatever the case with forked-branch shrines, there can be no doubt that in other areas of life the representation of horns is conscious. Both symmetrical and asymmetrical shapes are imitated and represented. Some Nilotic scarification patterns can be seen as being based on cattle-horns; perhaps even the forehead marks of some Dinka and Mandari might be seen in this way.[16] Amongst Agar Dinka, at least, it is not unusual to see cattle-horn-shaped scarification on various parts of the body.[17]

After initiation, Nuer youths endure much pain and discomfort to imitate the horns of their oxen. They render useless their left arms by fixing a set of bracelets to them. This temporary deformation holds down their left arms as the left horns of oxen are trained downwards (Evans-Pritchard, 1956: 256–7).[18]

Lienhardt describes various ways in which Dinka imitate cattle in stylized action, remarking (1961: 16) that 'a characteristic sight in Western Dinkaland is that of a young man with his arms curved above his head, posturing either at a dance or for his own enjoyment when he is alone with his little herd'. Such posturing has been illustrated frequently and can be seen here in figure 16.5 where, as they dance at a sacrifice, Agar Dinka women raise their arms above their heads in imitation of the horns of cows.[19] This curving of the arms in imitation of cattle is, for the Dinka, 'one of the forms of "handsomeness" (*dheng* [or *dheeng*]), a bodily attitude which the Dinka consider graceful' (ibid. 16); it is 'a gesture of pride and triumph' (ibid. 269).

Evans-Pritchard (1940*a*: 38; cf. 1956: 251) colourfully describes how

> when a Nuer mentions an ox his habitual moroseness leaves him and he speaks with enthusiasm, throwing up his arms to show you how its horns are trained. 'I have a fine ox,' he says, 'a brindled ox with a large white splash on its back and with one horn trained over its muzzle' – and up go his hands, one above his head and the other bent at the elbow across his face.

In one type of Atuot dance, 'men leap high into the air with their arms outstretched, imitating the girth and pattern of the horns of their personality oxen' (Burton, 1982: 268). Even when ox songs are sung in a sitting position a Dinka 'holds his hands up as the horns and moves his head and body in imitation of the ox' (Deng, 1972: 83).

Figure 16.5 Agar Dinka dancing at a sacrifice, near Pacong. Photograph by Jeremy Coote, February 1981

Horn shapes are also found in Nilotic ornament. MacDermot (1972: pl. opp. p. 49) illustrates Thiwat, a Nuer man, wearing two leopard teeth fastened to a piece of leather around his neck, the resultant shape being very reminiscent of horns. Fisher (1984: 42) illustrates a Nuer wooden necklace with a central forked pendant 'shaped to resemble cows' horns'. She also illustrates (ibid. 54, 57) ivory pendants 'shaped like cows' horns' suspended from bead necklaces. And Ray Huffman (1931: fig. 3.6, opp. p. 17) illustrates a 'two-pronged wristlet' – in fact a ring – in which the shape formed by the prongs is again reminiscent of the horns of an ox.

It is not just horns which are imitated. In dance, it can be the whole animal, or groups of animals. In the same Atuot dance as that referred to above, young women imitate cows. Burton (1982: 268) describes it as follows:

a line of six or eight young women forms directly in front of the drummers. Here they perform a movement which attempts to imitate the slow gallop cows make as they saunter across a pasture. A girdle of colored beads reaching well above their heads sways back and forth, suggest-

ing the manner in which the hump of a cow shifts back and forth when running.[20]

Deng (1972: 78–80) discusses a number of dances in which men and women act out the roles of bull, ox, and cow. And Lienhardt (1961: 17) describes a Dinka dance which is based upon 'the running of oxen with cows in the herd'. In considering fully the aesthetics of such dances, we should have to take into account more than just the purely visual; the major element is presumably the kinetic experience of the dancers themselves, though there are oral, and aural, elements too (ibid.). The visual appearance of cattle – the horns, the hump, and the general posture – are imitated as part of a more complete imitation the analysis of which is beyond the scope of this essay.

Nilotes have no developed tradition of figure sculpture or painting. There are, however, examples of modelling and drawing in which the aesthetic elements identified above are manifested. Through an examination of such models and drawings, we can deepen our understanding of the ideal forms in terms of which actual cattle are assessed and appreciated.

The making of clay, mud, or baked-earth models of cattle is a common occupation of Nilotic children. Generally speaking, the models are made by children for children's play, as is illustrated by the Dinka boy featured in a Survival Anglia film (1983) and in figure 16.6 here.[21] Amongst the Nuer, children play games with their oxen, 'taking them to pasture and putting them into byres, marrying with them and so on' (Evans-Pritchard, 1937: 238; cf. 1940a: 38), and Deng (1972: 60) tells of Dinka children making cattle camps using either shells or clay figures as cattle.[22] Such mud oxen may have their horns decorated with tas-

sels in imitation of the real-life song oxen, as has the one at furthest left in the group illustrated in figure 16.7. They may also be coloured with ash or charred wood (Huffman, 1931: 65; Blackman, 1956: 273) in imitation of the markings of real animals.

In the examples illustrated in figure 16.7,[23] it is evident that what are emphasized and exaggerated are the hump, the horns, and the general fatness of the body: the head, legs, and hooves are of much less importance. A most satisfying example of such exaggeration, in which these features have been abstracted to produce a form which at first sight it takes a little imagination to

Figure 16.6 Dinka boy modelling a mud cow. Photograph by Survival Anglia, 1975

Figure 16.7 Nuer mud toy cattle; collected by E. E. Evans-Pritchard in the 1930s (all but one, far right, labelled 'Anuak', though they are almost certainly all Nuer). Pitt Rivers Museum, Oxford (d.d. Evans-Pritchard 1936)

Figure 16.8 Pokot mud toy cattle; collected by Jean Brown in the 1970s. Pitt Rivers Museum, Oxford (1978: 20.194-8)

see as a whole beast, are a group of five mud cows collected by Jean Brown among the Pokot in the 1970s and illustrated in figure 16.8. While not from a people within the particular focus of this essay, they are so striking that they are well worth illustrating here. In these examples, the aesthetically central aspects of the physical form of cattle – the fatness of the body, the hump, and the horns – have been brought together to produce a form which, though it bears little resemblance to the form of the animals themselves, is in itself aesthetically pleasing. That such models are made by children for children's play, or, as in the Pokot case, by mothers for their children, does not lessen

their interest for an understanding of Nilotic aesthetics. They can be taken as an indication of what is aesthetically pleasing for the older brothers of these children, that is, for themselves when they grow up.[24]

Two-dimensional representations of cattle as illustrated in figure 16.9 are found on external hut walls amongst the Agar Dinka. Although there are reports of such mural drawings amongst the Nuer (e.g. Evans-Pritchard, 1937: 238; Jackson, 1923: 123–4), there are no published illustrations to provide comparative examples. They may be compared, however, with the figures of cattle incised on gourds by the Anuak as illustrated in figure 16.10. Here the

Figure 16.9 Agar Dinka hut-wall drawings of a young man with two tasselled oxen (*majok* left; *makuac*, right); near Pacong, Agar Dinka. Photograph by Jeremy Coote, February 1981

Figure 16.10 Anuak gourd bowl, incised with figures and decorative designs; collected by E. E. Evans-Pritchard in the Southern Sudan in the 1930s. Pitt Rivers Museum, Oxford (1936.10.79)

cattle have triangular humps, and the colour configurations on their rectangular bodies are geometrically stylized.[25] They are more reminiscent of flag designs than the configurations actually found on cattle. If clay modelling reflects the Nilotic appreciation of the physical qualities of bigness and fatness, then the geometricized representations of cattle on gourds and walls can be seen to reflect the importance of colour configurations. That the bodies are rectangular and the configurations geometricized suggests that the cattle-colour classification represents a set of ideals which can be abstractly stated – or represented – even though real cattle only ever approximate to them.

Aesthetics and Society

So far I have discussed some of the qualities of perceptual experience recognized and appreciated by Nilotes. Little reference has been made to 'art', 'beauty', or 'the good', which are so often taken to be defining terms of the aesthetic. Nor has reference been made to those traditional concerns of anthropology, such as social organization and social structure, to which analysts have attempted to link aesthetics. The discussion of elements of visual appreciation in a given culture is an end in itself, contributing to an understanding of what it is to be a member of that culture.

Nevertheless, I shall try to address, albeit briefly, some of the wider concerns often discussed in what has been taken elsewhere to be the anthropology of aesthetics. My concern is to bring out what I take to be the implications for the anthropology of aesthetics of the material presented above.

As for 'art', I have referred to body decoration, mural drawing, and clay modelling, all of which might well have been discussed under a heading of 'art'. I indicated my response to such an approach in the introduction to this essay. Such activities as body decoration and clay modelling have an aesthetic aspect, as all human activity does, and it is the aesthetic aspect of these activities which has been of concern in this essay. No good purpose would be served for the anthropology of aesthetics, as I understand it, in separating such activities as 'art', or in restricting any discussion of aesthetics to them.

As for 'beauty', it is hoped that the terminology adopted in this essay avoids the problems that beset attempts to use such vague terms in accounts of other cultures. An understanding of the aesthetic qualities which we have identified is, of course, relevant for any understanding of Nilotic ideas approximating Western notions of beauty. For example, Lienhardt (1963: 87) quotes a Dinka song in which the singer compares his own 'dazzling array' – glossed by Lienhardt as 'shining beauty' – with that of the ugliness of 'a big coward' to whom a girl in whom the singer is interested has been promised by her father: 'This dazzling array is a poor man's truculence, ee/ [That her father] gives her to that big ugly coward to play with, ee/ This dazzling array is just truculence'. The words for 'dazzling array' and 'ugly' are, in fact, the cattle-colour terms *marial* and *malou*. As noted above, *marial* is one of the most highly valued black-and-white configurations signifying a black ox with a white splash on its flank. *Malou* is a grey ox, the implication in this context being dullness – *lou* is the Dinka name for a large bustard, probably the visually uninteresting kori bustard (*Ardeotis kori*) (Nebel, 1979: 52, 56). That *rial* combined with *nyin*, 'eye', is the Dinka term for 'to dazzle' gives some indication of the Dinka conceptualization of the visual stimulation of the *rial* black-and-white configuration (ibid. 76). In some contexts, 'pied' and 'beautiful' might be

virtually interchangeable: Deng (1972: 63) quotes a song in which some young girls are said to wear 'pied and beautiful beads'.

But what is aesthetically pleasing and what is beautiful are not necessarily the same thing. A better appreciation of Nilotic ideas concerning beauty can be achieved through a discussion of indigenous concepts, such as the Dinka notion *dheeng*, mentioned in passing above. In a discussion of the virtues and dignity of a 'gentleman', Deng (1972: 14) glosses the term as follows:

> *dheeng* . . . is a word of multiple meanings – all positive. As a noun, it means nobility, beauty, handsomeness, elegance, charm, grace, gentleness, hospitality, generosity, good manners, discretion, and kindness. The adjective form of all these is *adheng*. Except in prayer or on certain religious occasions, singing and dancing are *dheeng*. Personal decoration, initiation ceremonies, celebration of marriages, the display of 'personality oxen', indeed any demonstration of an esthetic value, is considered *dheeng*. The social background of a man, his physical appearance, the way he walks, talks, eats, or dresses, and the way he behaves towards his fellowmen are all factors in determining his *dheeng*.

In the context of this essay it is the perceptual qualities contributing to *dheeng* which are of significance, and some of these, as they relate particularly to cattle, have been identified. But it is clear from Deng's discussion that for the Dinka there is more to 'beauty' than meets the eye.

It is also in the notion of *dheeng* that aesthetics and morality are linked. What is morally good is expected to display valued aesthetic qualities, and what displays valued aesthetic qualities is expected to be morally good. It is recognized, however, that this is far from always being the case. A Dinka man is *adheng* if he has social status, whether ascribed or achieved, if he is virtuous in his relations with others, or if he is physically attractive. Ideally, these three aspects should go together, but Dinka recognize that they do not always do so.

Some of the recent literature in the anthropology of aesthetics attempts to relate aesthetics to social organization or social structure. As presented here, Nilotic aesthetics seems rather to be a contingent product of these cattle-keepers' experience of the world which they inhabit, and to have little to do with any social facts. In his account of the aesthetics of the Fang of Gabon, Fernandez (1971: 373) claims to identify basic principles of opposition and vitality at work in Fang society and culture: 'in both aesthetics and the social structure the aim of the Fang is not to resolve opposition and create identity but to preserve a balanced opposition'. This is achieved in the social structure, he argues, through complementary filiation, and in their ancestor statues through skilful aesthetic composition. Should it not be possible to make such a profound summation concerning the material presented in this essay?

To some extent, one's answer to such a question depends upon one's intellectual temper. No doubt many would find it intellectually satisfying to relate the high value of piedness to the segmentation of Nilotic political structure and to the divided world of Nilotic cosmology. The combination of black and white, or red and white, in the pied ox, the argument might run, is valued because it fits with the principles of the social organization and religious thought. It is probably the case that an intellectually diverting picture of the anthropological material concerning Nilotic aesthetics could be constructed along such lines. But what would it mean? That social structure and cosmology are products of aesthetic principles, or that aesthetic principles, and cosmology, are products of social structure, or that they are all products of underlying principles? For anyone wishing, despite these ontological puzzles, to make links of this sort, there are some suggestive facts in the ethnography to which one might point. They do not, however, stand up to closer inspection.

There is, most famously, the Nuer leopard-skin priest, amongst whose duties it is to resolve conflicts between disputing factions, and to act as an intermediary between man and God. Is it not, therefore, most suitable that he is the *leopard-skin* priest? The leopard-skin is pied, and combines within itself the opposites of black and white. However, the priest is not usually known by this title by the Nuer themselves. The more usual title can be translated as 'earth (or soil) priest'; as Evans-Pritchard (1956: 291) points out, 'the leopard-skin title

is taken only from his badge [of office] whereas the earth title is derived from a symbolic association with the earth of deeper significance'. He is, therefore, not in fact a leopard-skin priest, but a priest of the soil who wears a leopard-skin as a badge of office. There is no hint that the Nuer regard a pied skin as suitable, *qua* its piedness, for a priest who is in an intermediate position and whose duty it is to resolve disputes. There is no reason to suppose any more profound reasons for the wearing of the leopard-skin than the symbolic associations of the leopard itself, which are beside the point here, and that it is a visually attractive and bold material symbol.

While Nilotes do not, in general, picture God to themselves,[26] Lienhardt relates (1961: 46) how some Western Dinka conceive of Nhialic, God, or Divinity, as being pied:

> Some people claim to have had visions of Divinity. Two youths, at different times, told me that their mothers had once seen Divinity... In one vision Divinity was seen as an old man, with a red and blue pied body and a white head. In the other he appeared as a huge old man, with a blue-green body (the colour of the sky) and again a white head. Other Dinka who have heard of such visions seem usually to be agreed that in them the body of Divinity is strikingly pied, but with a white head, a mark of age and venerability.

The blue-green body, it is worth noting at the outset, is not pied blue and green, but a single blue-green colour – the colour of the sky, *nhialic*, in which Divinity is conceived as living. The red-and-blue pied configuration is not found in cattle, but represents one of the strongest perceptual contrasts. It is an extreme form of piedness. Among the Atuot, similarly, one of the powerful spirits of the sky, the power of rain, is 'usually referred to by its ox-name *awumkwei*', and according to Burton (1981: 76), 'this color pattern is the most aesthetically pleasing for the Atuot; it signifies a boldly marked black and white animal, with a fully white head and red nose'.

That Nhialic and Awumkwei should be thought of as pied is not surprising, given how much the Dinka and Atuot value such configurations. The high aesthetic value of pied configurations, whether in cattle or elsewhere, is sufficient reason for Divinity to be thought of as pied, when Divinity is thought of as displaying any perceptual qualities at all.

Lienhardt (1961: 46) goes on to explain that 'white oxen or oxen boldly marked with white are especially appropriate for sacrifice to Divinity'. Significantly, it is not the piebald which is especially suitable, but the white ox – or, in the case of the piebald, one that is marked with white. Similarly for the Mandari, Buxton's careful and sophisticated analysis of their colour symbolism (1973: esp. 385–94) makes it clear that, despite the high aesthetic valuation of variegated beasts, they have no symbolic importance and no especial place in sacrifice over and above their being cattle like any other. The appropriateness of different colour configurations for sacrifice to different divinities – or Divinity – amongst the Dinka, however, is exemplified in a number of cases in Lienhardt's study. In particular, the black-and-white configurations in cattle are especially suitable for sacrifice to the free-divinity Deng, which is particularly associated with celestial phenomena such as rain, thunder, and lightning. It is, however, not the piedness as such which makes beasts of black-and-white configurations suitable for sacrifice to Deng, but rather the imaginative connections between the quality perceived in the black-and-white ox and the quality of the lowering skies: 'the black-and-white configurations in cattle...impress themselves upon the minds of the Dinka as does the lightning in dark, overcast skies which signifies the activities of Deng' (Lienhardt, 1961: 162). The symbolic action is thus inexplicable without an understanding of the workings of the Dinka imagination, and our appreciation of the workings of the Dinka imagination involves, I should argue, an appreciation of Dinka aesthetics.

Conclusion

Cattle provide the primary aesthetic locus of Nilotic society. This is a given of their pastoral life-style and the well-documented centrality of cattle in their lives. The particularities of the Nilotic aesthetic relate to their deep appreciation of the physical qualities of their cattle and their ideals of bovine form. Their appreciation of cattle-colour configurations can be understood in the context of the environment in which the cattle are perceived, and as a particular instance of the universal appeal of

contrast, manifested here in the appreciation of black-and-white and red-and-white beasts in herds of mostly off-white, greyish cattle. Elements which have their origins in this 'bovine' aesthetic can be traced through the ways in which Nilotes perceive, appreciate, enjoy, describe, and act in their world.

The underlying assumptions of this essay are that, all other things being equal, people act in the world to maximize their aesthetic satisfaction, and that an awareness of this aspect of human activity may help us to understand what we might otherwise seek to explain with reference to social structure, cosmology, symbolism, etc. I do not imagine that I have established beyond doubt the worth of these assumptions here, but I hope that I have provided at least an insight into how the Nilotes of the Southern Sudan take pleasure in the lives they lead, as well as into some of the marvels of their everyday vision.

NOTES

1   For the Nuer, see Evans-Pritchard (1940*a*); for the Dinka, Lienhardt (1961); for the Atuot, Burton (1987); and for the Mandari, Buxton (1973).

2   See, for the Nuer, Evans-Pritchard (1940*a*: 16–50); for the Dinka, Lienhardt (1961: 10–27); and for the Mandari, Buxton (1973: 5–11).

3   This includes the war currently being waged in the Southern Sudan, in which Nuer, Dinka, Atuot, and Mandari have been involved as combatants, victims, and refugees.

4   In his comprehensive overview of the literature on 'African Aesthetics', Van Damme (1987) mentions only one work on a Nilotic people, Schneider (1956) on the Pokot. Klumpp (1987) includes a brief discussion of Maasai aesthetics. There are a number of works which discuss body decoration, material culture, and so on amongst Nilotic peoples; this literature contains material relevant to the study of aesthetics, but rarely discusses aesthetics specifically.

5   See e.g. Turton (1980) on the Mursi.

6   For illustrations, see e.g. Ryle (1982: 17, 26–7, 34–5, 139); Howell et al. (1988: 287, 288, pls. 21, 22); and fig. 16.1 here,

in which the 'background' of off-white cattle is an accidental feature of the photograph. The veterinary officer Grunnet (1962: 7) claimed that 60% of Dinka cattle were 'greyish white or dirty white'.

7 On Nuer practice, see Evans-Pritchard (1940a: 37–8; 1956: pl. xiii, opp. 256); for the Dinka, see Lienhardt (1961: 17), and the illustrations in Ryle (1982: 65, 94–5), and in Howell et al. (1988: 205, pl. 18); for the Atuot, see Burton (1981: fig. A, opp. 36); and for the Mandari, see Buxton (1973: 7, pl. 1, opp. 6).

8 For an illustration, see Ryle (1982: 39).

9 The fact that similar patterns are highly valued by geographically contiguous peoples who do not keep cattle – such as the Uduk (James, 1988: 28–9) – suggests that these elements may have been part of Nilotic aesthetics even before the Nilotes became cattle-keepers. This is, however, irrelevant to an understanding of the appreciation of such patterns by Nilotic cattle-keepers today, which is founded in their daily experience of their cattle.

10 For illustrations, see e.g. Ryle (1982: 62–5).

11 See e.g. the photograph of a Dinka wearing a colobus monkey skin and other finery in Howell et al. (1988: 205, pl. 18).

12 For illustrations, see e.g. Fisher (1984: 42).

13 Schneider (1956: 105) noted the importance of contrast in Pokot beadwork, and Klumpp (1987) has discussed the importance of both contrast and complementarity in contemporary Maasai beadwork. I hope to discuss Nilotic beadwork at length elsewhere.

14 See also e.g. the post illustrated in Buxton (1973: pl. 2, opp. 78).

15 For the Dinka, see Lienhardt (1961: pl. vi, opp. 176); for the Mandari, see Buxton (1973: 54, fig. 1; pl. 7, opp. 371; and app. ii at 419); for an Anuak example, see Evans-Pritchard (1940b: pl. ivb, opp. 40).

16 For illustrations, see, for the Dinka, Fisher (1984: 48, 50, 52); for the Mandari, Caputo (1982: 366).

17 For illustrations, see Ryle (1982: 7, 18, 70–1).

18 For an illustration, see Evans-Pritchard (1956: pl. xii, opp. 234).

19 For other illustrations, see, for the Dinka, Deng (1972: 18); Ryle (1982: 15, 58–9); Lienhardt (1961: pl. 1, opp. 16); and the various sequences including dances interspersed throughout the film Dinka (Survival Anglia, 1983), especially the sacrifice sequence.

20 For illustrations of such girdles, or corsets, see Fisher (1984: 50, 51); Howell et al. (1988: 205, pl. 18).

21 Lienhardt (1961: 264), however, found mud models of bulls hanging in a shrine he visited.

22 Lienhardt (1963: 82) also refers to children playing at cattle-herding with snail-shells. I do not know what form these shells have, but I should not be surprised if they resembled in some ways the schematized cattle forms represented in the abstracted Pokot examples in fig. 16.8.

23 These examples are in the Pitt Rivers Museum, Oxford, and were collected by Evans-Pritchard. All but one are inscribed as having been collected among the Anuak, but it is almost certainly the case that they were all collected among the Nuer.

24 In his discussion of Dinka arts, Caravita (1968: 366) suggests that painting and sculpture remain undeveloped and marginalized because they are the work of people, that is, women and children, who are marginalized within Dinka society.

25 Huffman (1931: 69) remarks that the figures drawn by Nuer children and those incised on gourds by Nuer women always have rectangular bodies.

26 Evans-Pritchard (1956: 123) says that 'Nuer do not claim to see God', while, according to Buxton (1973: 19), Mandari say 'Creator has not been known or seen', and among the Atuot, according to Burton (1981: 138), ' "God the Father" is never said or imagined to exist in any physical form'.

REFERENCES

Baxandall, Michael (1972). *Painting and Experience in Fifteenth-Century Italy: A Primer in the Social History of Pictorial Style*. Oxford: Oxford University Press.

Baxandall, Michael (1980). *The Limewood Sculptors of Renaissance Germany*. New Haven, Conn.: Yale University Press.

Blackman, A. A. (1956). 'The Material Culture of the Nilotic Tribes of East Africa'. B. Litt. thesis, University of Oxford.

Burton, John W. (1978). 'Ghost Marriage and the Cattle Trade among the Atuot of the Southern Sudan', *Africa*, 48(4): 398–405.

—— (1979). 'Atuot Totemism', *Journal of Religion in Africa*, 10(2): 95–107.

—— (1980). 'The Village and the Cattle Camp: Aspects of Atuot Religion', in Ivan Karp and Charles S. Bird (eds.), *Explorations in African Systems of Thought*. Bloomington: Indiana University Press, 268–97.

—— (1981). *God's Ants: A Study of Atuot Religion*. Studia Instituti Anthropos 37. St Augustin, Germany: Anthropos Institute.

—— (1982). 'Figurative Language and the Definition of Experience: The Role of Ox-Songs in Atuot Social Theory', *Anthropological Linguistics*, 24(3): 263–79.

—— (1987). *A Nilotic World: The Atuot-Speaking Peoples of the Southern Sudan* (with a foreword by Francis Mading Deng). Contributions to the Study of Anthropology, No. 1. New York: Greenwood Press.

Buxton, Jean (1973). *Religion and Healing in Mandari*. Oxford: Clarendon Press.

Caputo, Robert (1982). 'Sudan: Arab–African Giant', *National Geographic*, 161(3): 346–79.

Caravita, Gianni (1968). 'L'arte dei Dinka', *Africa* (Rome), 23(3): 350–69.

Cummins, S. L. (1904). 'Sub-Tribes of the Bahr-el-Ghazal Dinkas', *Journal of the Royal Anthropological Institute*, 34: 149–66.

Deng, Francis Mading (1972). *The Dinka of the Sudan*. New York: Holt, Rinehart & Winston.

—— (1973). *The Dinka and their Songs*. Oxford Library of African Literature. Oxford: Clarendon Press.

Diffey, T. J. (1986). 'The Idea of Aesthetic Experience', in Michael H. Mitias (ed.), *Possibility of the Aesthetic Experience*. Martinus Nijhoff Philosophy Library 14. Dordrecht: Nijhoff, 3–12.

Evans-Pritchard, E. E. (1934). 'Imagery in Ngok Dinka Cattle-Names', *Bulletin of the School of Oriental and African Studies*, 7(3): 623–8.

—— (1937). 'Economic Life of the Nuer: Cattle', *Sudan Notes and Records*, 20(2): 209–45.

—— (1940a). *The Nuer: A Description of the Modes of Livelihood and Political Institutions of a Nilotic People*. Oxford: Clarendon Press.

—— (1940b). *The Political System of the Anuak of the Anglo-Egyptian Sudan*. London School of Economics Monographs on Social Anthropology, no. 4. London: Lund, Humphries.

—— (1956). *Nuer Religion*. Oxford: Clarendon Press.

Fagg, William (1973). 'In Search of Meaning in African Art', in Anthony Forge (ed.), *Primitive Art and Society*. London: Oxford University Press, 151–68.

Fernandez, James W. (1971). 'Principles of Opposition and Vitality in Fang Aesthetics', in Carol F. Jopling (ed.), *Art and Aesthetics in Primitive Societies: A Critical Anthology*. New York: Dutton, 356–73 (first published 1966).

Fisher, Angela (1984). *Africa Adorned*. London: Collins.

Forge, Anthony (1970). 'Learning to See in New Guinea', in Philip Mayer (ed.), *Socialization: The Approach from Social Anthropology*. ASA Monographs, no. 8. London: Tavistock, 269–91.

Gombrich, E. H. (1977). *Art and Illusion: A Study in the Psychology of Pictorial Representation*, 5th edn. Oxford: Phaidon (first published 1960).

Grunnet, N. T. (1962). 'An Ethnographic–Ecological Survey of the Relationship between the Dinka and their Cattle', *Folk* (Copenhagen), 4: 5–20.

Howell, Paul *et al.* (1988). *The Jonglei Canal: Impact and Opportunity*. Cambridge: Cambridge University Press.

Huffman, Ray (1931). *Nuer Customs and Folklore* (with an introduction by D. Westermann). London: Oxford University Press.

Jackson, H. C. (1923). 'The Nuer of the Upper Nile Province', *Sudan Notes and Records*, 6(1): 59–107; 6(2): 123–89.

James, Wendy (1988). *The Listening Ebony: Moral Knowledge, Religion, and Power among the Uduk of Sudan*. Oxford: Clarendon Press.

Klumpp, Donna Rey (1987). 'Maasai Art and Society: Age and Sex, Time and Space, Cash and Cattle'. Ph.D. thesis, Columbia University, New York.

Lienhardt, Godfrey (1961). *Divinity and Experience: The Religion of the Dinka*. Oxford: Clarendon Press.

—— (1963). 'Dinka Representations of the Relations between the Sexes', in I. Schapera (ed.), *Studies in Kinship and Marriage: Dedicated to Brenda Z. Seligman on her 80th Birthday*. Royal Anthropological Institute Occasional Paper No. 16. London: Royal Anthropological Institute, 79–92.

MacDermot, Brian Hugh (1972). *Cult of the Sacred Spear: The Story of the Nuer Tribe in Ethiopia*. London: Hale.

Maquet, Jacques (1979). *Introduction to Aesthetic Anthropology*, 2nd edn. Other Realities 1. Malibu, Calif.: Undena Publications (first published 1971).

—— (1986). *The Aesthetic Experience: An Anthropologist Looks at the Visual Arts*. New Haven, Conn.: Yale University Press.

Nebel, Arthur (1948). *Dinka Grammar (Rek-Malual Dialect) with Texts and Vocabulary*. English text rev. by C. W. Beer. Museum Combonianum 2. Verona: Missioni Africane.

—— (1979). *Dinka–English, English–Dinka Dictionary: Thong Muonyjang Jam Jang Kek Jieng, Dinka Language Jang and Jieng Dialects*. Museum Combonianum 36. Bologna: Editrice Missionaria Italiana (first published 1954).

Ocholla-Ayayo, A. B. C. (1980). *The Luo Culture: A Reconstruction of the Material Culture Patterns of a Traditional African Society*. Studien zur Kulturkunde 54. Wiesbaden: Steiner.

Pepper, Stephen (1974). 'Aesthetics', in *New Encyclopaedia Britannica: Macropaedia*, i. Chicago: Beaton, 149–63.

Ryle, John (1982). *Warriors of the White Nile: The Dinka*. Amsterdam: Time-Life.

Schneider, Harold K. (1956). 'The Interpretation of Pakot Visual Art', *Man*, 56: art. 108, 103–6.

Survival Anglia (1983). *Dinka*. The Vanishing Tribes of Africa 3. Film. Norwich: Survival Anglia.

Svoboda, Terese (trans.) (1985). *Cleaned the Crocodile's Teeth: Nuer Song*. Greenfield Center, NY: Greenfield Review Press.

Turton, David (1980). 'There's No Such Beast: Cattle and Colour Naming among the Mursi', *Man*, n.s., 15(2): 320–38.

Van Damme, Wilfried (1987). *A Comparative Analysis Concerning Beauty and Ugliness in Sub-Saharan Africa*. Africana Gandensia 4. Ghent: Rijksuniversiteit.

Zangwill, Nick (1986). 'Aesthetics and Art', *British Journal of Aesthetics*, 26(3): 257–69.

17

From Dull to Brilliant
The Aesthetics of Spiritual Power among the Yolngu

Howard Morphy

Content is a glimpse of something, an encounter like a flash.

Willem de Kooning

Introduction

In this essay I shall consider aspects of the aesthetics of Yolngu art. I am concerned primarily with a category of painting produced by men, but I place my analysis in the broader framework of the aesthetics of Yolngu ritual.[1] The Yolngu are an Australian Aboriginal people, renowned in the anthropological literature as the Murngin, who live in northeast Arnhem Land, a coastal area of northern Australia.

'Aesthetics' is a rubric term with no simple, universally acceptable, definition. It is easier to state the kind of things it is about than it is to provide a neat definition of what it is. Hence I will begin by briefly considering what I think an essay on Yolngu aesthetics should be about. Aesthetics is concerned with how something appeals to the senses – in the case of paintings, with the visual effect they have on the person looking at them. An aesthetic response concerns sensations or feelings that are evoked or caused in the viewer looking at a painting – a

positive emotional response, one that can be associated with feelings of pleasure, but which is not necessarily interpreted as pleasure. An aesthetic effect may be additional to some other kind of property of an object, for example, its communicating functions or practical properties. The aesthetic effect may be complementary to some other kind of property of an object or necessary to its fulfilling some other function. For example, an object may be aesthetically pleasing in order to draw a person's attention to it so that some other function may be fulfilled or message communicated. An aesthetic effect may arise out of the way some other purpose of the object is achieved, for example, through the perfect functional utility of a chair, the simplicity of an idea, or the elegance of a solution to a problem.

Aesthetic properties are often properties of objects which require them to be seen in a particular way by viewers who, because of their background or personality, are able to appreciate them – a relationist perspective that may be reduced to: beauty is in the eye

From Jeremy Coote and Anthony Shelton (eds.), *Anthropology, Art and Aesthetics* (Oxford: Clarendon Press, 1992), pp. 181–208. Reprinted by permission of the University of California Press.

of the beholder and the light in which the object is seen (cf. Morawski, 1974: 23). In an extreme form, however, I reject this subjectivist position, for while an artist familiar with his or her audience may try to create an object which elicits a particular response from the audience, the creator of an object is never the complete master of its aesthetic potential. With the audience the artist thinks he or she knows, it is always going to be difficult to know if the intended effect has been achieved because of the difficulties involved in communicating the emotions. The artist may find an unfamiliar audience responding in unintended and unpredictable ways to quite different attributes of the object from those he was conscious of creating. Some have argued that it is precisely the potential of objects to be aesthetically or expressively productive beyond the control of their creator that makes them into works of art. Whitford (1981: 7) writes of the artist Egon Schiele: 'Only minor artists manage to say all they wish to and major artists frequently express things they did not intend to or were even unaware of.'

This essay will focus primarily on the aesthetics of Yolngu art for Yolngu people. I am not concerned with the aesthetics of Yolngu art for a European audience or market, though there is some overlap in response in the two cases, and European evaluations of different works of art can be related to Yolngu ones. However, although I am focusing on the aesthetics of Yolngu art for Yolngu, I am not concerned with Yolngu aesthetics in the strictest sense of the term. For by Yolngu aesthetics I would understand a body of theory about art which is reflexive and concerned with the theory of response to works of art and with art-critical practice. The Yolngu have neither aestheticians nor art critics in this sense. Indeed, even by using a looser definition it is arguable that the Yolngu do not have an indigenous aesthetics, in that there is little overlap between Yolngu ways of talking about objects that Europeans call art and Europeans' way of talking about the same objects. Yolngu are unlikely to say of a painting that it is beautiful or well balanced, or that it conveys a particular emotion relative to another painting. The terms Yolngu use when talking about art do have some overlap with those Europeans employ, but more often their critical focus seems

different. Aesthetic motivations are seldom acknowledged by the Yolngu as a purpose behind the production of works of art. However, the Yolngu clearly are concerned to produce effects on the senses by which the success of the work can be judged and which Europeans would interpret as aesthetic effect. Indeed, I do not wish to exclude the possibility that Yolngu art may have certain expressive characteristics that are universal in their effect, and which have been utilized by artists of many different cultures throughout time. Such properties are properties of form that may have an effect on the senses in an analogous way to the effect of heat on the nerves – in other words, they do not have to be interpreted in order to have an impact. When interpreted, indeed, they may be understood in very different ways in different cultural contexts; and as aesthetic characteristics they may be evaluated differently in different traditions and in the context of different valuational criteria.[2] In the case of Yolngu art, at a general level what Europeans interpret as an aesthetic effect Yolngu interpret as a manifestation of ancestral power emanating from the ancestral past.

'Aesthetic' as I have employed the term implies the existence of a scale of judgement, or at least a standard that has to be achieved or properties that have to be created in an object if it is to be successful. In other words, some works can be judged failures as works of art. It also implies the possibility that some artists produce work that is in general considered to be better than that of other artists, and that they can hence be considered better artists. Both these propositions challenge conventional wisdom about Yolngu art which would have it that any, indeed all, Yolngu can paint, that no specialists are recognized, and that none is considered better than others.[3] However, it is this conventional view that is wrong. Some individuals are recognized as more skilful painters than others, and it is these individuals who are chosen to paint on ceremonial occasions in preference to others. The role taken by the individuals will, it is true, be justified on other grounds – for example, that as sisters' children they are the appropriate persons to do the painting, or that they belong to a mother's mother's clan, and mother's mother's clan members always do that particular kind of painting.[4] However, there are usually a number of other people, who fit the social specifications for performing the role equally well (if not better), who will never be seen producing a painting. These people's status is not diminished by the fact that they never paint, and they may well excel in other areas of ritual performance – for example, as leading singers or dancers.

The idea that the artist's skill is unrecognized by the Yolngu may have arisen partly because the individual appears to gain no status or reward for his role as an artist, and because his performance of that role is seldom attributed to any special skill he possesses. When asked directly, however, people readily acknowledge that some people paint better than others. By this Yolngu do not mean that they are more creative than other artists, for individual creativity is denied; rather, they refer to differential skill. Consistent with this, Yolngu, when criticizing a work of art, or explaining why a person does not paint, usually refer to a technical rather than a cognitive deficiency, as, for example, 'He knows all about painting, it's just that his hand shakes too much when he holds the brush'. (Unless, of course, a person has failed to learn the design correctly, in which case he has simply made a mistake which must be rectified.) Certainly, the ideology that individual creativity has no role in Yolngu art can be challenged and is indeed false, but as far as public comments are concerned, individual creativity has no positive role. If a person is said to have invented a design, then that is in itself a negative comment on it. Implicitly, however, artistic creativity is recognized, and those artists who are asked to paint on ceremonial occasions are frequently ones whom Europeans would label as creative.

Before considering the aesthetics of Yolngu paintings, it is necessary to consider what kinds of objects paintings are to the Yolngu: for if paintings vary cross-culturally, it is partly on the basis of the different meaning of these objects to members of different cultures. Their significance affects the way in which an object is seen and also what its emotional effect is interpreted as being: a ray of light may convey the awesome power of nature or, alternatively, be understood as the power of God.

Yolngu Paintings and the Creation of *Bir'yun*

Yolngu paintings are referred to as *mardayin miny'tji*. Neither word has a direct equivalent in English, but I will begin by considering the meaning of *miny'tji* as it overlaps in meaning with the English word 'painting'. *Miny'tji* can be roughly glossed as 'a painting' although, as we shall see, it is semantically more complex than this. The act of painting can be described by using either the phrase *miny'tji dja:ma* (painting work) or the compound verb *miny'tji-yarpuma* (jabbing or spearing paint). An artist can be described as 'a person having painting work' (*miny'tji-dja:mamirri yolngu*) or 'a person who jabs paint' (*miny'tji-yarpunhara yolngu*). These phrases refer to what I shall show to be two separate components of the meaning of the word *miny'tji*: design and colour. Thus *miny'tji* can be used adjectivally to describe anything that appears colourful, like the wings of a butterfly or a lump of yellow ochre used as pigment. *Miny'tji* can also be used to refer to any regularly occurring pattern or design, whether it is natural or cultural in origin. The pattern made by interlocking sections of a turtle's shell, the thin spirals engraved by insects on the bark of the scribbly gum, and the chequer-board pattern in black and white on the cone shell are all alike *miny'tji*, as are blazons on a car door and designs on a can of baked beans.

The distinction between natural and cultural designs must not be too rigidly conceived, as things which are called *miny'tji* are all believed to be the result of consequential action; *miny'tji* are meaningful designs (see also Stanner, 1960: 102). The design on the back of a turtle is seen as its design in much the same way as the design painted on a human body is seen as belonging to and representing a clan. A myth, for example, explains the origin of the pattern on the turtle's shell, how it was put there, and why it takes the form it does. Myths explaining the form of natural designs are analogous to those relating to cultural designs; indeed, natural and cultural designs are frequently seen as two manifestations of the same thing. The patterns on the back of the long-necked fresh-water tortoise (*minhala*), for example, are believed to have resulted from water-weed clinging to the shell of an ancestral being in the form of a tortoise, as it moved along the bottom of the river at Ga:rn-garn. Ga:rngarn was also the place where Bar-ama, one of the major ancestral beings of the Yirritja moiety, emerged from the ground. He, though human in form, also came out of the water with the water-weed clinging to his body and falling from his arms in streamers. The pattern of the weed on his body became the clan design of the Dhalwangu (figure 17.1). It is the same as shell designs on representations of the tortoise. The majority of designs are be-lieved to have originated in a similar way,

being naturally occurring designs isolated by their connection with a particular ancestral being. (Moreover, when it is realized that many ancestral beings were transformed from animals into men and from animate to inani-mate forms, and that natural designs bear wit-ness to the reality of these transformations, then the distinction between natural and cultural designs is largely irrelevant as far as Yolngu understandings are concerned.)

The word *mardayin* can be roughly trans-lated as 'sacred law'; indeed, that is how it is

Figure 17.1 Yangarinny Gumana, *Long-Necked Freshwater Turtle at Ga:rngarn*, 1976, Yirrkala; ochres on reinforced paper board. The painting represents the sea's flood-waters carrying debris of wood and logs along the river. Streamers of weed are attached to the limbs of the turtle. Photograph by Howard Morphy, private collection

referred to by Yolngu when speaking English. The *mardayin* consists of sets of songs, dances, paintings, sacred objects, and ritual incantations associated with ancestral beings. The *mardayin* refers to the actions of ancestral beings in creating the land and in instituting the practices of Yolngu life. Yolngu ceremonies involve the use of the *mardayin* to recreate ancestral events and the use of their powers to serve particular ends. To the Yolngu, the *mardayin* are not only the means of expressing ancestral events, but also part of the essence of the ancestral beings themselves. They provide a means of becoming directly involved with the ancestral past.

Ancestral designs are among the main manifestations of ancestral beings which can be reproduced by humans. The same design may take many forms: it may be produced as a sand sculpture, as a design in string, or in painted form as a body painting, bark painting or painting on a ceremonial post. Details of the design will vary according to the medium used and the space available.

Yolngu paintings are ancestral designs or manifestations in three senses. Firstly, the designs are ones that originally appeared on the body of the ancestral being they represent, and were designated by that ancestral being as part of the sacred law (or property) of the group of human beings who subsequently occupied the land with which the design is associated. Continued ownership of that land is thereafter conditional on maintaining the rituals associated with the land (see Morphy, 1988). Secondly, paintings encode meanings that refer to the events in the ancestral past that resulted in the creation of the landscape, including, of course, events that led to the creation of the design itself. Finally, designs are ancestral in that they are thought to contain the power of the ancestral being concerned and provide a source of ancestral power for use in ritual. The power of the design may be used for a specific purpose, for example, when painted on a coffin-lid it may assist the soul of the dead person on its journey to the lands of the dead. Or it may be used in a more general way to increase the fertility of the land or to strengthen the participants in a ceremony.

To summarize the argument so far, Yolngu paintings are ancestral designs which are the property of clans and which contain spiritual power. The functions of Yolngu paintings relate directly to these properties. Paintings are produced in ceremony as part of the recreation of ancestral events, as a demonstration of rights held by a clan in *mardayin* and land, and as a source of spiritual power. Aesthetic factors would seem at first hardly to enter the picture as far as the concept of paintings is concerned, or, indeed, in relation to their use. In the majority of cases, paintings that have taken many hours or even days to paint are covered up or destroyed within hours or even minutes of their completion. Coffin-lid paintings, for example, are carried out in a restricted context. Apart from the artists, hardly anyone appears to look at the painting except occasionally to see whether it is finished or not. Senior men with rights in the painting may occasionally look at it and offer instruction on a point of detail. Other men may occasionally offer assistance in finishing off the painting with cross-hatching, especially if time is getting short. As soon as the painting is completed, it is covered up with a sheet of cloth and will never be seen again. A body-painting's fate is usually similar. A painting that has taken eight or nine hours to complete may be rubbed out shortly after its completion in order that the person may return to the public arena. The majority of paintings like this are seen in their full glory for a fleeting second, and even then by a restricted set of people. It is inappropriate for women and un-initiated men to show too much interest in the ceremonial production of paintings. Although the majority of paintings are done in contexts that are only semi-restricted, where they could be observed by anyone who tried to look, people tend to avert their eyes. Hence much of people's experience of painting consists of images fleetingly glimpsed out of the corner of the eye.

On reflection, however, there is no reason why a painting has to be seen for aesthetic factors to be important in its production and in its effect. For example, a painting may only have to be known to be a type of object that is aesthetically powerful for it to achieve its purpose; it may not be necessary for it to be seen to be so. There are contexts in which paintings are displayed publicly and in which everyone has the opportunity to look at them. For example, mortuary poles that are erected in memory of a dead person have designs painted on them which are similar to those painted on coffin-lids. Their aesthetic effect is known, and hence the aesthetic effect of coffin paintings is, or may be, taken for granted. What this does suggest in the case of coffin paintings, however, is that gaining an aesthetic response from an audience is not part of the intention of the artist (as few people view the painting), and that the painting must be being produced for some other purpose. As far as the body-paintings are concerned, the aesthetic value of the art may be enhanced by the limited extent to which it is seen in its pristine state by the majority of people. Long, contemplative viewing is not the only way to appreciate a painting. The brief glimpse from the corner of the eye may, indeed, produce an aesthetic effect in harmony with the way Yolngu art is intended to be experienced and understood.

What, then, is the Yolngu artist trying to produce when he produces a painting in a ritual? What effect is he trying to create, and by what criteria is his work going to be judged? I would argue that the artist is guided by three objectives: to produce a correct design, to produce an ancestrally powerful design, and to produce a painting which enhances or beautifies the object it is painted on. The setting of the correct design is primarily associated with the first stage of painting, the drawing of the basic outline pattern which constrains the final form the painting will take. It is important that the design should be an acceptable representation of the ancestral design, in that other knowledgeable people are prepared to accept it as the correct form of the design. In outline form the design, although it is a sign of a particular ancestral being or set of ancestral beings, is relatively safe and free of ancestral power. At this stage the painting is referred to as 'dull' or 'rough'. The power and beauty of the painting are acquired through the painting process, and in particular are associated with the final stages of the painting. They are produced by qualities of the painting that are quite separate from correct form, though a painting that does not possess correct form could not, for the Yolngu, have other qualities.

In order to understand the aesthetics of Yolngu art, it is necessary to examine the painting process in some detail, particularly in relation to Yolngu understandings of the transformations that occur in the appearance of paintings as they progress.

Yolngu paintings are composed of a number of components of different types organized in a particular way. There is a base colour (figure 17.2), then various internal subdivisions, figurative representations, geometric background patterns, and cross-hatching.[5] For the purposes of this discussion, however, it is necessary to distinguish only between cross-hatching and the other components, which can be referred to as the underlying design. The underlying design is produced by outlining the figurative and geometric components of the painting in yellow ochre (or occasionally black) on a red background (figure 17.3).

The initial production of other components is played down in relation to cross-hatching. Thus artists assert that it does not matter if you draw the figurative representations roughly or

Figure 17.2 A circumcision ceremony at Yirrkala, July 1974. The artist begins to outline a design on the initiate's body, which has already been painted with red ochre. Photograph by Howard Morphy

Figure 17.3 A circumcision ceremony at Yirr-kala, July 1974. A number of boys are having designs painted on their chests prior to being circumcised. The painting is done to the accompaniment of songs. Sacred dilly bags decorated with rainbow lorikeet feathers are hung in the branches of the trees above the initiates' heads. Photograph by Howard Morphy

Figure 17.4 A circumcision ceremony at Yirr-kala, July 1974. After the designs are outlined in yellow, cross-hatching begins. Photograph by Howard Morphy

the clan design quickly (as long as you do this correctly): 'you draw them roughly because you are going to cover them up' (figures 17.4 and 17.5). In fact, the initial 'drawing' of a painting will usually be completed within an hour, with up to a week being spent in cross-hatching. Indeed, as the painting progresses it undergoes considerable transformation. Because cross-hatching always overlaps the outlines of figurative representations, their size is gradually reduced and the outline changed through the course of the painting. Thus the figures are initially drawn larger than they finally appear. Before cross-hatching, the painting looks dull, consisting of yellow and black on red, and it is often difficult to discern its structure. After cross-hatching, the successful painting attains a shimmering brilliance, and

its separate components become clearly defined (figure 17.6).[6]

The transformation of a painting from a rough dull state to a clearly defined and bright state through the process of cross-hatching is clearly recognized by the Yolngu. The two main criteria employed in judging a painting, apart from the matter of its correctness, are its brightness and the clarity of its cross-hatched lines.[7] If the cross-hatched lines are too thick or if they run into each other, then the painting will be criticized as being 'too rough'; if there is a preponderance of black in the painting, then it may not be bright enough.

It is the quality of brilliance that is associated in Yolngu art with ancestral power and with beauty. I will consider its association with ancestral power first. The importance of the concept of 'brilliance' was first noted by the anthropologist Donald Thomson in his unpublished field notes (1937). The Yolngu word Thomson translates as 'brilliant' is *bir'yun*. *Bir'yun* can be termed an aesthetic

Figure 17.5 The artist Narritjin Maymuru finishing a painting, Canberra, October 1978. A brush of human hair (*marwat*) is gently drawn across the surface of the painting to produce the fine cross-hatched lines. Photograph by Howard Morphy

Figure 17.6 Welwi Warnambi *Dhuwa Moiety Wild-Honey Painting*, November 1974, Yirrkala; ochres on woven reinforced paper board. This painting captures the Yolngu aesthetic of brilliance and clarity. Photograph by Howard Morphy, private collection

property, as it operates independently of specific meanings encoded in a painting, although, as we shall see, it interacts with them. *Bir'yun* is a particular visual effect. Thomson (ibid. 5 Aug.) writes that the mundane or secular meaning of *bir'yun* refers to intense sources and refractions of light, the sun's rays, and to light sparkling in bubbling fresh water, as in:

> *gong ngayi walu bir'yu-bir'yun   marritji*
> ray   its   sun   scintillate-scintillate go
> 'the sun's rays scintillate'

Applied to paintings, *bir'yun* is 'the flash of light, the sensation of light one gets and carries away in one's mind's eye, from a glance at *likanpuy miny'tji*' (ibid. 4 Aug.). The *bir'yun* of a painting is the visual effect of the fine cross-hatched lines that cover the surface of a sacred painting: 'it's the sensation of light, the uplift of looking at this carefully carried out

work. They see in it a likeness to the *wangarr* [ancestral past]'.

Thus *bir'yun* is the shimmering effect of finely cross-hatched paintings which project a brightness that is seen as emanating from the *wangarr* beings themselves – this brightness is one of the things that endows the painting with ancestral power.

In the past, paintings with fine cross-hatching were, in an unmodified form, restricted to closed contexts. These paintings were referred to as *likanpuy miny'tji*. Men painted with *likanpuy miny'tji* would have to have the design removed, or at least obscured, before returning to the main camp or public ceremonial ground. Most commonly the painting was modified by smearing the cross-hatched infill, reducing the fineness and separation of the cross-hatched lines to a smudge of pigment. They would be transformed back from a bright to a dull state. Thus, although some aspects of the form of the painting remained discernible, it had lost its brilliance (*bir'yun*) and, through losing this, had lost

some of its ancestral power. It had lost, according to one of Thomson's informants, 'its
likeness to the *wangarr*'.

There is, in fact, a category of paintings
which has no cross-hatching. Such paintings
are referred to as *bulku miny'tji* or 'rough'
paintings. These consist of the outline shapes
of clan designs and are painted during the
public phases of ceremonies. They are in
many respects *likanpuy* paintings without the
cross-hatching – in other words, paintings in
their dull form or mode. This is explicitly recognized by the Yolngu. One of Thomson's informants described *bulku* paintings as being
mali nhangu likanpuy miny'tji – shades or
shadows of *likanpuy* paintings – whereas
likanpuy paintings can be described as *mali
wangarr* – shades of the ancestral world.

Bir'yun represents a generalized spiritual
power associated with the *wangarr*, which all
likanpuy paintings can potentially possess, irrespective of the clan or moiety to which they
belong. Each painting, however, is more
closely associated with one ancestral being or
set of ancestral beings than it is with others,
and, depending on the clan and ancestral being
concerned, *bir'yun* may have more specific
connotations. For example, Thomson records
that the *bir'yun* of a Gupapuyngu clan *birr-
kurda* (wild honey) design expressed the light
of fresh water and the light of eucalyptus in
flower. He quoted an informant saying of it,
ngoy ngamathirri, ngoy kitkitthun, which he
translates as 'the light that makes the heart go
happy, makes it smile'. Although a reasonable
free translation, it is a little misleading, as *ngoy*
refers to something more abstract than the
heart, and is better referred to as 'the seat of
the emotions', which Yolngu locate in the region of the gut. In myth, the wild honey ancestor is closely associated with fresh water and
with eucalypt flowers that provide the nectar
for Yirritja moiety bees. The meanings 'fresh
water' and 'nectar' are encoded in elements of
the design. Hence the visual effect of the painting, *bir'yun*, is integrated with semantic aspects of the painting, enabling it to express
characteristic properties of the *wangarr* being
that it represents (see figure 17.7).

A second source of spiritual power, blood,
is associated with similar qualities in ritual
as the fine cross-hatched lines. In Warner's
(1958: 274) description of blood-letting in the

Figure 17.7 Dula Ngurruwutthun, *Yirritja Moiety
Wild-Honey Painting*, February 1975, Yirrkala;
ochres on woven reinforced paper board. This
painting is similar to that referred to by Thomson
in his field notes. The diamonds represent the
structure of the hive and various components of
the wild-honey mythological complex. Photograph by Howard Morphy, private collection

Djungguwan ceremony, it seems that both
the process of blood-letting and the blood itself
are associated with feelings of happiness and
joy. The blood of initiates is drawn from the
elbow (*likan*) and collected in a paper-bark
basin. Warner (1958: 276) quotes an informant
saying 'when [the initiate] gets up he'll be very
quick and feel very light; and he will be very
happy because the blood running out of him
will make him that way' (cf. Munn, 1986:
191). Later the blood is used to paint sacred
designs on the bodies of the participants, and
white down is stuck on to the blood and highlights the design. The blood is now sacred
blood, the blood of the *wangarr*. The blood is
painted only on the initiated men, and it gives
them strength: 'it makes us feel easy and comfortable and it makes us strong' (Warner, 1958:
277). But to women the blood is dangerous, for
contact with it will cause sores, and it is too
strong to be painted on the neophytes.

The language used to talk about the blood echoes the language used to talk about the qualities of the painting and its effect. In the blood-letting the feelings of lightness and happiness, perhaps induced in part by the loss of blood and the power of the occasion, are interpreted as ancestral power and are subjectively experienced as ancestral power by the initiate. *Bir'yun* is also interpreted as ancestral power, and the cross-hatched designs when painted on the body of the initate may become an objectification of those very feelings associated with blood-letting that the individual has come to interpret as the experience of that power. The visual effect of *bir'yun* is both a complementary source of such experiences and an objectification of related experiences which cumulatively create the felt reality of ancestral power.

In the majority of cases *bir'yun* is associated with positive emotions such as joyfulness (*wakul*) or happiness (*ngamathirri*). However, Thomson gives one example in which it appears to express negative emotions. This concerns the *bir'yun* of Ma:rna, the shark ancestor (figure 17.8). Thomson records that the *bir'yun* from paintings of the shark can also be referred to by a more specific term, *djawarul*. Djawarul is the proper name of a sacred well created by the *wangarr* shark, at the place where the shark was killed by Murrayanara. *Djawarul* refers to the 'flash of anger in the shark's eye – the blaze of anger of the shark killed by stealth'. The spirit of the shark is dangerous (*mardakarritj*), and was described as *miringu ma:rr*, 'the power of vengeance'. This is, of course, by no means inconsistent with Yolngu concepts of ancestral power. *Ma:rr* is a positive force associated with happiness, strength, health, and fertility, but it is also associated with death, and can always have a dangerous dimension. *Ma:rr* can be dangerous to anyone who is spiritually weak, to young people, to people suffering bereavement, to people recovering from serious illness, and, to an extent, to women as a category. It can also give strength to participants in an avenging expedition. If someone who is vulnerable sees a sacred object or painting, their sickness and eventual death may result. This is one of the reasons why paintings were, and sometimes still are, smeared before they are displayed in public,

and why people avoid looking directly at paintings that are being produced. The 'flash of anger in the shark's eye' is a powerful image that captures this aspect of ancestral power; it reinforces some of the danger that surrounds that power, and contributes to its strength.

To summarize this section, Yolngu artists aim to create a particular visual effect in their paintings which is referred to as *bir'yun*. *Bir'yun* is thought of as a shimmering quality of light which engenders an emotional response. The response is associated with phrases that in the context of contemporary European art would be interpreted as being concerned with an aesthetic appreciation of the work as art, to do with feelings of lightness, joy, happiness, and power. In the Yolngu case, however, the emotional effect is interpreted as representing or being a manifestation of ancestral power. It is almost as if ancestral power is encoded in paintings by way of the emotional response it engenders in the viewer – a process that is probably widespread in religious art.

The Ritual Value of Brilliance

The aesthetics of Yolngu paintings is part of a more general aesthetics associated with Yolngu ritual and symbolism in which bright contrasts with dull and is associated with manifestation of the *wangarr*. The raw materials that are used to produce the surface finish on ceremonial objects or in decorating the human body, that is, red and yellow ochres, blood, pipe clay, rainbow lorikeet and cockatoo feathers, beeswax, and animal fats, all have properties of shininess and brightness. Frequently, within these categories particularly bright examples are considered most powerful, and are selected for use in preference to others. The most highly prized red ochre, and one that is traded throughout Arnhem Land, is a purple-coloured rock that produces a naturally burnished finish. It has the effect of providing a rich sheen to the painted surface. Other natural substances that are thought to be ancestrally powerful include blood and fat. These are both substances that, when applied to the human body in ritual, provide it with a sheen. The most prized fat is the rich yellow fat found round the liver and kidneys of animals such

Figure 17.8 Ma:w' Mununggurr, *Djapu Clan Shark Painting*, November 1974, Yirrkala; ochres on bark. This is by the artist who painted the Marakulu woman's coffin lid (see p. 315). Photograph by Howard Morphy

as shark and sting-ray, in the tail of goannas and kangaroos, and in the limbs of tortoises and turtles. Such fat, as well as being collected for ritual purposes, is a highly valued food resource that is thought to have restorative properties and to be a sign of health in the animal. Animals without fat may, indeed, be rejected as food. As far as the human individual is concerned, people who are plump and sleek are thought to be healthy, and may be thought to be endowed with spiritual power. Thomson (1975: 7) reports that to be too fat can be dangerous because it arouses fear and jealousy in others.[8]

The qualities of brightness are precisely those that are taken up when materials such as parrot feathers, red ochre, or fat are incorporated in Yolngu song and poetry, and their association with spiritual power is often referred to. For example, one of the key songs of Dhuwa moiety ritual refers to the Djan'kawu sisters hanging their dilly bags, decorated with the orange and green feathers of the rainbow lorikeet, in the branches of a casuarina tree, at the end of the day. The feathers are caught in the rays of the evening sun which intensifies their redness. As Ian Keen (1977) has shown, this particular song has many possible translations and evokes a series of complementary images and associations. One based on a translation by Wandjuk Marika is as follows:

> Rainbow lorikeet climbing the Djuta.
> Drying its feathers in the rays of the sun
> Children of the Djan'kawu ... shining[9]

Towards the end of the Djan'kawu sisters' journey is a place, Djiriniwuruma, on the mainland north of Milingimbi. There they laid down their dilly bags, which were transformed into a rock formation which, according to the Yolngu, radiates red and blue colours in the sunlight and produces coloured reflections in the waters of the swamps (Berndt, 1976: 164).

Within songs, and sequences of songs, it is possible to identify an underlying structure of content progressing from dark and dull to light and brilliant that is analogous to the transformation that takes place in the process of painting. A particularly good example is at the climax of the Goulburn Island series of songs that belongs to the Dhuwa moiety in north-east Arnhem Land. The Goulburn Island song cycle recounts the seduction of a group of western Arnhem Land women by the long-penised men of Goulburn Island. Their relationship was consummated amidst the cabbage palms beside a wide lagoon adjoining the Arafura Sea. The verses I quote follow on immediately from this idyll. The translated text is from Berndt (1976: 66) with some abridgements:

1

From those fighting clubs, assembled in rows
  come the Western clouds...
Dark rain clouds and wind, rising up in the
  west...
Clouds that spread all over the sky, spreading
  across the country
They spread all over the sky
Dark rain clouds they come rising up.

2

Thunder rolls along the bottom of the clouds, at
  the wide expanse of water,
Thunder shaking the clouds.
Large snake at the billabong edged with bamboo,
'I make the crash of thunder – I spit and the
  lightning flashes'.

3

The tongues of the lightning snake flicker and
  twist
Flashing above the people of the Western clans
All over the sky their tongues flicker.
Lightning flashes through the clouds, flash of the
  Lightning Snake.
Its blinding flash lights up the palm leaves
Gleams on the cabbage palms, and on the shining
  semen among the leaves.

Analagous transformations or movements from dull to brilliant, from dark to shining, occur within the ritual process itself. Many Yolngu rituals operate to enhance the spiritual power of individuals and the community. One of the ways in which this is done is by making people into sacred objects or representations of the *wangarr* by making them shine. The bodies of initiates are rubbed with ochre and fat and then decorated with feathers and *likanpuy* paintings. In such a state they become like the ancestral beings. Such a state is not achieved in a single ceremony but as a result of participating in a number of ceremonies during which the individual is progressively associated with the *wangarr* (cf. Keen, 1978: 229). For example, in the case of circumcision, the initiate will first take part in a ceremony in which his body is simply rubbed in red ochre. On subsequent occasions increasingly elaborate paintings will be put on his body until finally, at his circumcision ceremony, his body will be painted from his head to his knees with *likanpuy* paintings infilled with fine cross-hatching. The whole process will take place over a period of several years, and can be seen to involve a movement from dull to brilliant just like that which takes place with the production of a single *likanpuy* painting.

Aesthetics and Yolngu Ritual Performance

So far I have been dealing almost exclusively with the aesthetics of form; but aesthetics can also be concerned with content, with the way in which a particular idea is expressed, with the appropriateness of an image to a particular event.

Some aesthetic effects associated with particular genres, for instance catharsis in tragedy, are centrally concerned with content. Content is integral to the aesthetics of Yolngu ritual, as it is for reasons of content that the particular ritual component is chosen. The individual component has aesthetic qualities independent of context, but aesthetic effects also arise out of the way in which elements of the ritual are structured and joined together in a sequence in relation to the themes and objectives of the particular ceremony. In order to understand this aspect of the aesthetics of Yolngu art, it is necessary to look briefly at the semantics of ritual components and the way in which they are integrated within ritual performance.[10]

Components of Yolngu ritual are, as mentioned earlier, the *mardayin*: the songs, dances, paintings, incantations, and ritual actions that are associated with the actions of ancestral beings in the ancestral past that resulted in the creation of the landscape. The components can be used in many rituals of different types, in each case being joined with other components in ways that reflect the themes of the particular ceremony. For example, the same painting could be painted on a boy's chest prior to circumcision, on a coffin-lid for a primary burial ceremony, and on a memorial post for a Djungguwan ceremony (which is in part a regional fertility ceremony). In an abstract sense, the painting or any other ritual component has meaning independent of any context in which it is embedded. To use a concept of Schechner's (1981), a Yolngu painting is (in two senses) stored ancestral behaviour. First, it is an ancestral design that originated through actions in the ancestral past, and is indeed thought of as a manifestation of the being concerned. Secondly, the

painting encodes meanings that refer to the ancestral events concerned, events which resulted in the transformation of the landscape in a particular locality. I will refer to the latter as the iconographic meaning of the component. In ceremonies, the iconographic meaning becomes the raw material for the creation of a metaphor or analogy that is appropriate to the performance of a particular ritual event. The purpose for which the painting is selected will affect which aspects of its iconographic meaning are emphasized and influence the way it is understood in the ceremony as a whole. To illustrate this point I will use an example taken from a mortuary ritual.

Yolngu believe that a person has two kinds of spirit: *birrimbirr* and *mokuy*. The *birrimbirr* spirit is the one associated with the *wangarr* ancestral beings, and on a person's death it returns to the ancestral domain. One aspect of it returns to the clan lands of the deceased, while another goes to one of the Yolngu lands of the dead. The *mokuy* spirit is an evil spirit or ghost; it must be driven away on a person's death or it will return to haunt the living.

One of the principal themes or objectives of burial ceremonies is the guiding of the *birrimbirr* spirit of the dead person back to the reservoirs of spiritual power in the clan territory. The journey of the *birrimbirr* spirit provides the ordering theme of the ceremony, and affects which ritual elements are selected and the order in which they are performed. In primary burial, the moving of the body from the place of death to the grave provides the framework for enacting the journey of the spirit from the place of death to the place where it will rejoin the clan's ancestors. The ceremony consists of a series of key events: making the coffin, painting the coffin-lid, carrying the coffin to the body, placing the body in the coffin, carrying the body to the grave, and finally burying it in the ground. Each of these events is, or can be, performed in a ritual way, accompanied by song, dance, and incantation. The ritual chosen is both appropriate to the event and associated with a stage of the spirit's journey. For example, when the coffin is moved to the body, a dance may be performed which represents the flood waters of the wet season tossing hollow logs along a water-course at a place half-way between the place of death and the final destination of the spirit. When the coffin is lowered into the grave, a dance may be performed that represents the *wangarr* beings at the spirit's journey's end. What happens to the body is an analogue for what happens to the soul. The coffin painting is incorporated within the structure, both in its purpose and through its integration with other ritual elements.

Frequently the coffin painting represents a central place on the journey of the *birrimbirr* soul. Ritual episodes which precede the nailing of the lid on the coffin refer to earlier stages of the journey, episodes which follow it represent the final stages of the journey. Sometimes the subject or content of the coffin painting may have little connection with the other episodes of the ritual except as a marker of a particular stage on the journey. On other occasions the content of the painting chosen may be interwoven, or connected with the content of subsequent episodes, to create a continuity of symbolic action that flows through the ceremony as a whole.

On one occasion a Marrakulu clan woman died at Yirrkala. Her spiritual home was at Trial Bay many kilometres to the south. Her mother's mother's group, the Djapu clan, were responsible for organizing the ceremony, and the painting chosen for the coffin-lid belonged to their clan. The painting represented the shark at Wurlwurlwuy, inland from Trial Bay (see figure 17.8). The iconographic meaning of the painting refers to a chunk of ancestral law that includes many ancestral actions and their consequences. The shark, as it rushed headlong inland from Djambarrpuyngu country in Buckingham Bay where it had been speared by an ancestral harpoon, created the river at Wurlwurlwuy. The shark was caught in a fish-trap at Wurlwurlwuy, but escaped by breaking it apart. The shark's body was transformed into various features of the environment including, for example, the trees that line the river bank. In the ceremony, many of those events were referred to in the songs that accompanied the painting of the coffin-lid. However, in the performance as a whole only certain events were singled out and represented in detail, events that became core metaphors for the two journeys that were to take place, the journey of the body to the grave and the journey of the woman's spirit to its spirit home. The shade in which the coffin was painted represented the fish-trap in the river. A trellis of sticks was built at the entrance to the shade representing the barrier wall of the fish-trap. When the body was placed in the coffin, it represented the shark caught in the fish-trap. The time came to move the body, and dancers acting as sharks held the coffin and burst out of the shade, smashing down the wall of sticks. The shark had escaped from the fish-trap and torn it to pieces. The coffin was then carried forward to the vehicle that was to drive it to the cemetery, in a dance that represented the rush of water released from behind the broken-down wall of the fish-trap. In the context of the mortuary ritual, the sequences of action were an analogue for the journey of the woman's spirit, the shark's breaking out of the fish-trap symbolizing the soul's struggle to leave the body and the struggle of the journey ahead. The energy of the shark and the power of the waters represent the power of the ancestral forces summoned to help the soul on its way.

The shark bursting out of the fish-trap functioned as the structuring performative metaphor that enabled the spirit's journey to be accomplished.[11] The principles of selection are concerned centrally with the appropriateness of the mythical episode to the ritual task that has to be accomplished and indirectly with those aspects of the human condition that the ritual is concerned with structuring. Thus in many respects they are equivalent to the aesthetic principles involved in the construction of Western drama. By this argument, the success of the ritual, in the subjective sense of engendering positive emotions in the participants, should depend on such factors as the success of the core metaphors, the extent to which they are integrated within an overall flow of ritual action, and the sense of coherence that the ritual has as a whole.

The same ritual episode can, of course, be associated with a number of different themes of a ceremony. In the burial ceremony for the Marrakulu woman, episodes associated with the shark not only were concerned with the journey of the woman's spirit but also had quite different connotations in relation to a second major theme of Yolngu mortuary rituals – the expression of grief and anger. Mortuary ceremonies provide a context for expressing anger towards anyone who is thought to be responsible for the death, whether through neglect or by sorcery. The shark provides an appropriate focus for these sentiments. The shark, like the mourners, had been wounded, he by a spear, they by bereavement, and he, like they, felt angry. The dancers who carried the coffin from the shade and who broke down the fish-trap had fighting bags gripped tightly in their mouths. The shark dance is a dance of aggression carried out after a member of a clan has been killed, prior to setting out on an avenging expedition. Performed in the mortuary ceremony, it has a cathartic effect, bringing out the emotions of anger and diffusing them or directing them outside the group. This aspect of the ritual is recognized explicitly by some Yolngu:

> Before the body had been laid to rest, you are very angry. You feel wild, you break down, you are against the songs, the body, everything. If you just bite the dilly bag, hold yourself, make yourself still, you'll be settled down. But if you suspect someone has caused the deaths – then everyone bites the dilly bag, that's your connection, your power up from the dilly bag. You put into your mind all of your thoughts, and you connect everything to your power, and then you fight another man.[12]

In this respect the shark dance can be understood to be cathartic in the Aristotelian sense of 'arousing negative emotions in order to have some therapeutic effect on the audience's mental health, and thereby giving a pleasurable sense of relief, to reach a state echoed in Milton's phrase from *Samson Agonistes* "in calm of mind all passion spent" ' (Beardsley, 1975: 64).

Conclusion

It is my hypothesis that *bir'yun* is an effect that operates cross-culturally. Its impact may be modified by environmental factors, by individual and cultural experience of different visual systems; the way it is experienced may vary on an individual basis according to certain neurophysiological factors; but basically it is an effect which transcends particular cultural contexts. The shimmering effect of the crosshatching, the appearance of movement, the sense of brightness are all attributes of Yolngu

art that can be experienced independently of any other knowledge about Yolngu paintings. They are attributes of Yolngu art as natural objects in much the same way as they are attributes of the sea glistening in the evening sun. However, Yolngu paintings are not natural products but cultural products, and the shimmering effect of the painting is integrated within the system of art as a whole to produce objects that are to be understood in a particular way. It is at this point that relativism enters aesthetics, for the way the *bir'yun* is understood by the Yolngu is quite different from the way a similar effect is to be understood, for example, in Bridget Riley's paintings. *Bir'yun* has a place in a Yolngu system of art that integrates it with other components, formal and semantic, in a unique system. The aesthetics of Yolngu art as it appears to the Yolngu cannot be apprehended directly by an outsider, but must be subject to the same process of translation that characterizes the work of anthropologists in general. However, I leave open the possibility that at the level of form and structure there is a component of the aesthetic that is relatively autonomous, and which consists of elements that can become incorporated in particular aesthetic systems regardless of time and space *and* for the same reason – that is, they produce effects that human beings find stimulating.[13]

In conclusion I will attempt to bring some of the threads of my argument together, focusing on aesthetic aspects of the shark painting. This painting possesses *bir'yun*, brilliance that is thought of as the power of the *wangarr* shark shining like a light from the painting.[14] The light is real in that it is an effect of the technique of painting; its interpretation is a cultural one. The interpretation of the brilliance, what it is understood to represent, is influenced by the images of the shark that are enacted in ritual and by what is known of the shark as an animal, its natural fierceness and power, enhanced by images of the wounded animal trapped in the fish-trap. In the ritual a series of expressive components, the brilliance of the painting, the effect of the music and the dancers, the clouds of dust they kick up, and the smashing down of the trellis of sticks, can all be related to a particular content, the shark ancestor in the context of myth and ritual. The components are effective independently (though in different ways to different people, depending on what they see, know, and experience of the particular events). *Bir'yun*, the shining effect of the painting, can, as we have seen, create sensations of movement, light, and joy. The well-chosen ritual episode can likewise, through its content, have a direct effect on the mental state of the participants, as was the case with the cathartic effect that the aggressive action of the shark dancers had on the feelings of the mourners. We can see how in such contexts the general expressive effect of *bir'yun* can become focused on a particular element of the content of a ritual, and how the two for a moment become interacting components of the shark ancestor. The relationship between form and content is a two-way one. The content gives a particular meaning to the flash of light or to the stamping feet of the dancers, yet the flash of light or cloud of dust in turn may emphasize or enhance a particular content, presenting it in a striking way that associates it with the emotions felt at the time. Such effects, feelings, and understandings, when, for example, they are associated with the shark ancestor, may enhance the latter's believability and, indeed, are interpreted as emanating from the shark, enabling people to experience its power. It is aesthetic effects in combination with cognitive understandings that give concrete form to an abstract conception, and enable people to use that conception for particular purposes.

In some respects my argument echoes Durkheim's (1954) and, more particularly, Radcliffe-Brown's (1964) theory of the role of the emotions in ritual. Radcliffe-Brown's analysis of Andamanese dancing came to conclusions which are similar to mine concerning *bir'yun*. He saw the rhythmic movements of the dancers directly creating feelings of pleasure and inner power that could be interpreted as religious feelings: 'the mental state of the [ritual] dances is closely related to the mental state that we call aesthetic enjoyment' (Radcliffe-Brown, 1964: 251). However, Radcliffe-Brown then went on to link this with a fairly straightforward Durkheimian argument. The Andamanese dance is a pleasure but it is also an obligation willingly undertaken: 'dance produces a condition in which the unity, harmony and concord of the community are at a maximum and in which they are intensely felt by every member. It is to produce the condition that is the primary social function of dance' (ibid. 252). Radcliffe-Brown made no attempt to analyse the cultural meanings of Andamanese dances.

Radcliffe-Brown's functionalist reductionism not only detracts from the original insight by oversimplifying the purposes and effects of ritual action, it also makes the specific content and form of the ritual action largely irrelevant. The analogy he draws throughout the section is between Andamanese dances and the waltzes of European ballrooms – an amusing dig at the Establishment, perhaps, but otherwise unhelpful. The Andamanese dances could consist of anything. What I hope I have shown in the case of the Yolngu is that the selection of ritual components for a ceremony is centrally concerned with matters of content as well as form. Both form and content are associated with aesthetic effects. The selection of dances and paintings is a creative act, undertaken to achieve a ritual purpose. The possibility of the act depends upon a belief in ancestral beings, but selection is also motivated by objectives that can be thought of as aesthetic – the successful ritual act is also successful theatre. The appropriateness of the images to the objectives of the ceremony may well enhance belief in the effectiveness of the ritual; but I certainly do not believe that the power of ritual can be reduced to aesthetic effects, or that such effects are produced in order to create feelings of social solidarity.

NOTES

1   Although in the past the paintings I write about were exclusively produced by adult men and rarely even glimpsed in unmodified form by women and uninitiated men, today the ritual context has opened out to a considerable extent and women have much greater access to them. Women today produce paintings for sale as part of the local art and craft industry, and in some rare cases have produced paintings in ceremonial contexts to which they had previously been denied access. (See Morphy and Layton, 1981 for a discussion of Yolngu responses to the marketing of their art; and for a detailed analysis of changing categories of Yolngu art, see Morphy, 1977.)

2   Morawski (1974) provides a good discussion of valuational criteria that is relevant to a cross-cultural study of aesthetics. I agree with Morawski (ibid. 174) that 'Aesthetic judgements concern emotions and conations and, even if they refer to some objective qualities, there is no possibility of verifying them by means of measurement operations'. Hence objectivity in evaluations must depend on 'universality' which may be confined to one social group or culture or which may be spread across the whole of humanity.

3   This point of view is e.g. largely put forward by Mountford (1961: 8).

4   For a discussion of rights in paintings, see Morphy, 1978.

5   For a more detailed discussion of the structure of Yolngu art, see Morphy, 1977; 1989.

6   Jones and Meehan (1978: 27), in their excellent analysis of the Anbarra concept of colour, show how, in a neighbouring group, colour terminology is structured on the opposition between light and brilliant colours (-gungaltja) and dark and dull colours (-gungundja). They give many examples of the way in which these concepts are applied to objects in everyday contexts. It is clear from their analysis that degree of saturation is not in itself sufficient to determine the allocation of a colour to a particular class, since red is preferentially included in the -gungaltja category relative e.g. to greens and blues of the same hue. Brilliance is discerned in certain red objects, such as blood, sunset, and red ochre, and is not discerned in objects of other colours which have the same hues. Although Jones and Meehan do not make the point explicitly, the association between brilliance (-gungaltja) and manifestations of ancestral power is clearly revealed by their analysis.

7   In 1988 Bandak Marika, a Yolngu artist who has become a print-maker, discussed with me ways in which her art followed on from traditional Yolngu practice. She had been taught that in European print-making practice you begin with the lighter colours and gradually build up to the darker colours; as a Yolngu she could not do that, but had to begin her prints with the darker colours and end up with the lighter ones. She also said that in the successful Yolngu painting, when it was finished, everything became clear and well-defined, echoing the words that Narritjin Maymuru, a leading Yolngu artist, had used to me a decade earlier in discussing the process of Yolngu painting. He pointed out that towards the end of the painting process, when most of the cross-hatching had been completed and before the figures had been redefined with a thin outline, the painting often looked messy, but suddenly at the very end everything turned out all right and the painting became 'clear'. This simultaneous expression of clarity through shimmering brilliance lies at the heart of Yolngu aesthetics.

8   Thomson's 1975 article provides an excellent discussion of the Yolngu concept of spiritual force or ma:rr, in its various manifestations, supported by detailed Yolngu exegesis.

9   The translation comes from Ian Dunlop's film In Memory of Mawalan (1976). The film is of public phases of a Dhuwa moiety Nga:rra ritual that focuses on the journey of the Djan'kawu sisters. The film provides impressive illustrative material for anyone wishing to glimpse the power of Yolngu aesthetics. Djuta is the name for a species of tree and also for a sacred digging-stick.

10 A detailed analysis of the structure and semantics of Yolngu ritual is to be found in Morphy, 1984.

11 I use 'performative metaphor' in the sense developed by Fernandez (1972; 1977). A performative metaphor is a metaphorical idea that is performed through ritual action and by which certain objectives are said to be achieved. Fernandez sees performative metaphors operating on emotional states and altering them in a process similar to catharsis: '[People] come into a cult with some constellation of feelings – isolation, disengagement, powerlessness, enervation, debasement, contamination – from which they need to move away. [Metaphors] by persuasion and performance – operate upon the minds of the member allowing him eventually to exit from the ritual incorporated,

empowered, activated, euphoric' (Fernandez, 1972: 56).

12 This statement was made by Narritjin Maymuru following the burial ceremony of a child who died at Trial Bay in 1976. The burial ceremony was filmed by Ian Dunlop and is the subject of his *Madarrpa Funeral at Gurka'wuy* (1989). Narritjin's statement refers to the 'Yellow Ochre Dance' which is shown in the film (see also Morphy, 1984: 77 ff).

13 The idea that aesthetic values may be objective is quite compatible with aesthetic relativism: different valuations are not necessarily opposed subjective judgements, but can be complementary responses based on different understandings and perceptions of the same thing or different attributes of the same thing. Access to the aesthetic values of other cultures requires learning about them. McDowell has discussed this issue in an essay on objectivity and aesthetic value in which he writes (1983: 3): 'Our appreciating what we do need not preclude our supposing that there are different values, to which we are perhaps insensitive, in the artefacts of remote cultures – as if, when we take the value we find in the objects we appreciate to be really there in them, we use up all the room the world might afford for aesthetic merit to occupy. In fact it is remarkable, and heartening, to what extent, without losing hold of the sensitivities with which we begin, we can learn to find worth in what at first too alien to appreciate.'

14 *Bir'yun* is a manifestation of what using Munn's (1986) terminology we might refer to as a 'qualisign'. Munn's qualisigns are qualities (such as lightness or heaviness) that can be applied to different things across contexts, and which operate as signs. In the Yolngu case, it seems that lightness as a qualisign is associated with ancestral power, and that intense sensations of light are felt as manifestations of that power. Interesting confirmation of the experiential dimension of the dark–bright opposition and the association of light with ancestral power is provided by Chaseling's account (1957: 168) of a Yolngu sea voyage: 'Makarola told me that he had been overtaken by darkness when returning with his family after a day's fishing. A strong wind arose and the canoe was blown out to sea, waves half-filled it, and whilst wives and children baled frantically in the darkness, he toiled to keep the dugout into the wind. Makarola then remembered his totem and called on it for help. He said that in that instant he saw a "bright light" which filled his head. By the light he was assured that they would be brought safely to land.'

REFERENCES

Beardsley, Monroe C. (1975). *Aesthetics from Classical Greece to the Present: A Short History*. Studies in the Humanities 13. Tuscaloosa, Ala.: University of Alabama Press (first published 1966).

Berndt, Ronald M. (1976). *Love Songs of Arnhem Land*. Melbourne: Nelson.

Chaseling, Wilbur S. (1957). *Yulengor: Nomads of Arnhem Land*. London: Epworth Press.

Dunlop, Ian (director) (1979). *Madarrpa Funeral at Gurka'wuy*. Sydney: Film Australia.

—— (director) (1981). *In Memory of Mawalan*. Sydney: Film Australia.

Durkheim, Émile (1954). *The Elementary Forms of the Religious Life*, trans. Joseph Ward Swain. London: Allen & Unwin (first published 1915).

Fernandez, James W. (1972). 'Persuasions and Performances: Of the Beast in Every Body... and the Metaphors of Everyman', *Daedalus*, winter 1972: *Myth, Symbol, and Culture*, 39–60.

—— (1977). 'The Performance of Ritual Metaphors', in J. David Sapir and J. Christopher Crocker (eds.), *The Social Use of Metaphor: Essays on the Anthropology of Rhetoric*. Philadelphia: University of Pennsylvania Press, 100–31.

Jones, Rhys, and Meehan, Betty (1978). 'Anberra Concept of Colour', in L. R. Hiatt (ed.), *Australian Aboriginal Concepts*. Canberra: Australian Institute of Aboriginal Studies, 20–39.

Keen, Ian (1977). 'Ambiguity in Yolngu Religious Language', *Canberra Anthropology*, 1(1): 33–50.

Keen, Ian (1978). 'One Ceremony One Song: An Economy of Religious Knowledge among the Yolngu of North-East Arnhem Land'. Ph.D. thesis, Australian National University, Canberra.

McDowell, John (1983). 'Aesthetic Value, Objectivity, and the Fabric of the World', in Eva Schaper (ed.), *Pleasure, Preference, and Value: Studies in Philosophical Aesthetics*. Cambridge: Cambridge University. Press, 1–16.

Morawski, Stefan (1974). *Inquiries into the Fundamentals of Aesthetics*. Cambridge, Mass.: MIT Press.

Morphy, Frances (1983). 'Djapu: A Yolngu Dialect', in R. M. W. Dixon and Barry J. Blake (eds.), *Handbook of Australian Languages*, iii. Canberra: Australian National University. Press.

Morphy, Howard (1977). ' "Too Many Meanings": An Analysis of the Artistic System of the Yolngu People of North-East Arnhem Land'. Ph.D. thesis, Australian National University, Canberra.

—— (1978). 'Rights in Paintings and Rights in Women: A Consideration of Some of the Basic Problems Posed by the Asymmetry of the "Murngin System" ', *Mankind*, 11(3): 208–19.

—— (1984). *Journey to the Crocodile's Nest: An Accompanying Monograph to the Film 'Madarrpa Funeral at Gurka'wuy'* (with an afterword by Ian Dunlop). Canberra: Australian Institute of Aboriginal Studies.

—— (1988). 'Maintaining Cosmic Unity: Ideology and the Reproduction of Yolngu Clans', in Tim Ingold, David Riches, and James Woodburn (eds.), *Hunters and Gatherers, ii: Property, Power and Ideology*. Oxford: Berg, 249–71.

—— (1989). 'On Representing Ancestral Beings', in Howard Morphy (ed.), *Animals into Art*. One World Archaeology 7. London: Unwin Hyman, 144–60.

—— and Layton, R. (1981). 'Choosing among Alternatives: Cultural Transformation and Social Change in Aboriginal Australia and the French Jura', *Mankind*, 13(1): 56–73.

Mountford, Charles P. (1961). 'The Artist and his Art in an Australian Aboriginal Society', in Marian W. Smith (ed.), *The Artist in Tribal Society: Proceedings of a Symposium held at the Royal Anthropological Institute*. Glencoe, Ill.: Free Press.

Munn, Nancy D. (1986). *The Fame of Gawa: A Symbolic Study of Value Transformation in a Massim (Papua New Guinea) Society*. Cambridge: Cambridge University Press.

Radcliffe-Brown, A. R. (1964). *The Andaman Islanders*. Glencoe, Ill.: Free Press (first published 1922).

Schechner, R. (1981). 'Restoration of Behaviour', *Studies in Visual Communication*, 7(3): 2–45.

Stanner, W. E. H. (1960). 'On Aboriginal Rites, 3: Symbolism in the Higher Rites', *Oceania*, 31(2): 100–20.

Thomson, Donald (1937). Field notes. Museum of Victoria, Melbourne.

—— (1975). 'The Concept of "Marr" in Arnhem Land', *Mankind*, 10(1): 1–10.

Warner, W. Lloyd (1958). *A Black Civilization: A Social Study of an Australian Tribe*, rev. edn. New York: Harper.

Whitford, Frank (1981). *Egon Schiele*. London: Thames & Hudson.

Part IV

Form, Style, and Meaning

Introduction

The analysis of form must be central to the anthropology of art. Art can usefully be approached as the intervention and experience of expressive and meaningful forms in the context of human social action. The form of objects is what creates their affective potential and in part explains their meaningfulness and impact in context (see Kingston 2003). Forms are a resource, forms have histories, forms may identify groups or regions, epochs, religious identities, castes and class. Form can be used to trace relationships over time, to identify cultural trajectories, to research processes of transmission, to demonstrate or problematize the boundaries around social entities. Form and style are bridging concepts that link the anthropology of art with other disciplines, in particular art history (see Schapiro 1953; Sieber 1969:106), archaeology (Deetz 1967), and studies of material culture in general (Ucko 1969). Theories of form and style often transcend the boundary between dry methodology and bold metaphysics (Focillon 1989 and Kubler 1962 provide rich examples).

Where possible, form must be placed in the context of action to learn how it is experienced. The baskets that Guss writes about are integrated within the way of life of the Yekuana society as a whole. They are seen in the process of manufacture, the patterns on them are revealed as food is consumed, they are experienced differently according to where a person is seated and how light falls on the object. The patterns on the basket will have a different significance to, and a different impact on, the viewer depending on gender, individual experience, and personality, the nature of the occasion, and so on. However, although form has to be placed in context in order to be fully understood this does not mean that the form of an artwork has no meaning out of context, nor does it make formal analysis of artworks methodologically less significant. Form in context may be how objects are generally experienced; the forms themselves, however, have *relative autonomy*. In this latter sense, form is linked to style, which can be one of the factors influencing and giving coherence to the trajectory of a form. The analysis of form provides a means of understanding how the objects are made, how they work and how forms are passed on and transformed over time. The analysis of form must include an understanding of the technical processes by which objects are manufactured, both in terms of formal instruction and the embodied behaviors that facilitate production and that may be part of the ways they are experienced.

The analysis of form is one of the ways the anthropologist can discover what kind of objects these works of art are. The oppositions that are often made between different methods of analysing form in art – semiotic, aesthetic, functional, agentive – are false ones. Artworks are both multidimensional and diverse. As O'Hanlon shows, it has proved unproductive to analyze the design variations on Highland shields as components of a language-like system of communication. That is not the basis of the system and it has not proved the most productive approach to Highland New Guinea art. The forms of Highland art must be understood on a different basis. The analysis of form in this case can reveal affective and expressive dimensions of Highland shields and trace the origins of some of the designs. Australian Aboriginal art on the other hand has been productively analyzed as a system of encoding meaning, as Nancy Munn's pioneering analysis shows. Munn is able to show how systems of representation with different properties are used to communicate meanings in fundamentally different ways (for a fuller analysis see Munn 1973). However Aboriginal art can also be approached from an aesthetic, expressive performative perspective and its form must be understood in the context of its production, use and performance.

While ideally the formal analysis of art should be complemented by detailed ethnographic observations of the production and use of art in context guided by interpretative exegesis from the artists themselves and other members of their society, fieldwork is no substitute for the analysis of form. The analysis of form, through for example works in museum collections, can extend the database available to the anthropologist, enabling her/him to see changes over time and gain knowledge of a far wider range of forms than the duration of fieldwork usually allows. Formal analysis can also provide the basis for understanding the ways in which meaning might be encoded in the art, and what the affective properties of the object might be – setting up a dialogue between the object and the analyst that can be productively tested through participant observation and by interviewing the producers of the art. Often in the case of archaeological cultures and early ethnographic collections the analysis of form provides the main means of access to the ideational systems and performative practices that produced the art in context. The museum collections of Northwest Coast Native American art are better documented than most, and the chapters by Rosman and Rubel (ch. 19), and Jonaitis (ch. 20) show how analysis of the forms of the art can provide insights into different aspects of Northwest Coast society at the turn of the 19th century. Rosman and Rubel show how different styles of art reflect and create the seasonality of Kwakiutl society while Jonaitis reconstructs the experience of shamanic performance through an analysis of the iconography of Tlingit masks.

Style and meaning are clearly important concepts in the anthropology of art. Style is a widely used term in studies of art and material culture across disciplines (see Shapiro 1953 for a penetrating and broad-ranging discussion of the concept). It is not easy to define and indeed is often left undefined. It is often used simply as a way of summarizing salient formal similarities between objects that form part of the same set. It refers to coherent relationships in the form of sets of objects that differentiate them from other sets. It can be applied cross-culturally or across time but also to contemporaneous sets of objects existing within the same society. Style can be fashion but it can also reflect differences in the meaning of objects (for example, as indices of class and status) or be the product of different ways of encoding meaning, as Munn shows for Aboriginal Australia and Rosman and Rubel for the Northwest Coast (see also Morphy 1977).

Meaning intersects with style. Style is an equally difficult and important concept because of the different senses in which it is used. In the analysis of form in art it is important to adopt the broadest perspective on meaning and to be open to all the ways in which art objects might work as meaningful forms (see e.g. Friedrich 1986, and Morphy 1991: chs. 6–8). The study of meaning requires an analysis of *how* something means as much as *what* something means – it requires the analysis of systems of representation and of encoding, the study of affect, of purposive aspects of the object, what it does and what it is thought to be. In the study of art analysis of meaning involves the interrogation of form in context. Much unproductive discussion has come from the failure to recognize that different art objects, and different styles of objects that are produced, used, interpreted, and experienced in different social and cultural contexts, function in fundamentally different ways.

REFERENCES

Deetz, James, 1967 *Invitation to Archaeology.* New York: Natural History Press.

Focillon, Henri, 1989 *The Life of Forms in Art.* New York: Zone Books.

Friedrich, Paul, 1986 *The Language Parallax: Linguistic Relativism and Poetic Indeterminacy.* Austin: University of Texas Press.

Kingston, Sean, 2003 Form, Attention and a Southern New Ireland Life Cycle. *Journal of the Royal Anthropological Institute* (N.S.). 9:681–708.

Kubler, George, 1962 *The Shape of Time: Remarks on the History of Things.* New Haven and London: Yale University Press.

Morphy, Frances, 1977 The Social Significance of Schematisation in Northwest Coast Art. In *Form in Indigenous Art: Schematisation in the Art of Aboriginal Australia and Prehistoric Europe.* Peter Ucko, ed. Canberra: Australian Institute of Aboriginal Studies.

Morphy, Howard, 1991 *Ancestral Connections: Art and an Aboriginal System of Knowledge.* Chicago: University of Chicago Press

Munn, Nancy, 1973 *Walbiri Iconography.* Ithaca: Cornell University Press.

Schapiro, Meyer, 1953 Style. In *Anthropology Today.* Alfred Kroeber, ed. Chicago: University of Chicago Press.

Sieber, Roy, 1969 Comments. In *Tradition and Creativity in Tribal Art.* Daniel Biebuyck, ed. Pp. 192–203. Berkeley: University of California Press.

Ucko, Peter, 1969 Penis Sheaths: a Comparative Study. *Proceedings of the Royal Anthropological Institute for 1968.* Pp. 27–67.

18

Visual Categories
An Approach to the Study of Representational Systems[1]

Nancy D. Munn

I

Culturally standardized systems of visual representation, like other sorts of cultural codes, function as mechanisms for ordering experience and segmenting it into manageable categories. While this orientation toward the examination of pictorial art has recently been emphasized by the art historian E. H. Gombrich (1960), it has not to date been taken up by anthropologists, who might well extend current studies of cultural categories and schemes of classification to include it.

In this paper, intended to be exploratory, I use the notions of "element" and "category" to discuss some classificatory aspects of pictorial systems. While my illustrations are drawn primarily from the graphic art of the central Australian Walbiri[2] and from bark paintings made at Yirrkalla[3] in northern Australia, supplemented by examples from other societies, it is my contention that an approach based on the definition of contrastive units and meaning ranges is relevant to any system of culturally standardized representations (two or three dimensional) where one can identify discrete, recurrent units through which visual contrasts are made.[4]

In figure 18.1, I have assembled some visual schemata from Walbiri sand drawings and designs on sacra and from Yirrkalla bark paintings of northeast Arnhem Land that exemplify two familiar sorts of schemata occurring in Australian art. Each schema shown here is an irreducible unit, used to stand for certain meaning items, examples of which are listed under it.[5] All the schemata are iconic in the sense that some feature of likeness characterizes the relation between the visual form and its meanings, and this feature is intrinsic to the functioning of the graphic system. Put another way, each schema provides a "structural equivalent" for its object within a particular system of such equivalents (cf. Arnheim 1954: 132). I therefore use the term "representation" in its broad sense to cover all these visual elements regardless of the character of the visual similarity between the element and its referents.[6]

All the items that can be represented by one schema constitute what I shall call a *visual category*. By this term I mean any range of meaning items represented either by a single, irreducible visual schema (as in figure 18.1) or by a unitary combination of more than one such schema (as in figure 18.2). Categories

From *American Anthropologist* 68 (1966), pp. 936–950. Berkeley: University of California Press, 1966. Reprinted by permission from the American Anthropological Association.

A. Continuous Meaning Ranges

Yirrkalla

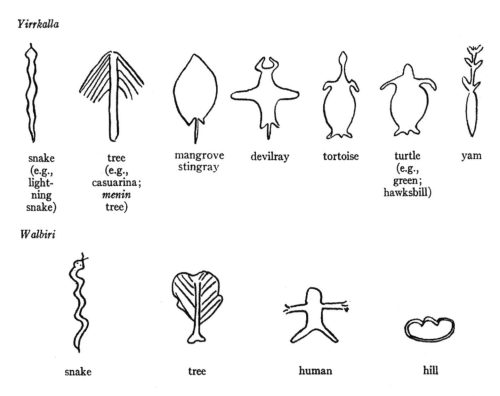

| snake (e.g., lightning snake) | tree (e.g., casuarina; *menin* tree) | mangrove stingray | devilray | tortoise | turtle (e.g., green; hawksbill) | yam |

Walbiri

snake   tree   human   hill

B. Discontinuous Meaning Ranges—*Walbiri*

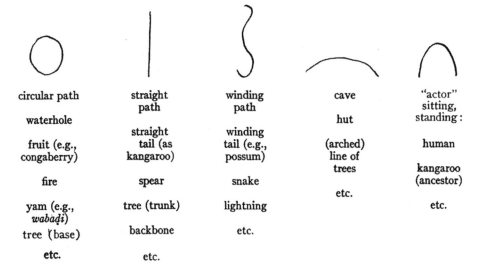

circular path	straight path	winding path	cave	"actor" sitting, standing:
waterhole			hut	
fruit (e.g., congaberry)	straight tail (as kangaroo)	winding tail (e.g., possum)		human
fire	spear	snake	(arched) line of trees	kangaroo (ancestor)
yam (e.g., *wabaḍi*)	tree (trunk)	lightning		etc.
tree (base)	backbone	etc.	etc.	
etc.	etc.			

Figure 18.1 Elementary visual categories

defined by schemata of the first sort – the fundamental elements of a graphic system – I call *elementary categories*. Those defined by unitary constructions of more than one element I call *composite categories*.

As an example of an elementary category, consider the tree from Yirrkalla paintings depicted in figure 18.1a. In the literature on the paintings, a meaning provided by the informant in a particular instance – for example, "mangrove tree" or "casuarina" – is generally noted. However, the published data do not give enough information to determine with any certainty whether this particular "tree" schema can be used to depict any variety of tree distinguished by informants (so that all varieties would in effect belong to the one visual category), or whether the conventions restrict it to some varieties and not others. Moreover, a cursory examination of Yirrkalla paintings indicates that the painters use a number of slightly different schemata for trees. A tree can be drawn, for instance, with the branches extending upward rather than down, or with curved branches rather than straight ones. The problem is whether these and other variations in form are simply free variants – either standardized alternatives or idiosyncratic variations subject to the invention and whim of the painter – or rather indicators of some regular change in the meaning of the element. And, if the latter, do these changes refer to class inclusion (for example, are only certain kinds of trees drawn with curved branches)?

Only by more precisely determining the range of inclusion of each visual term can one come to predict the usage of the visual elements and to recognize and interpret innovations that may occur. Ideally, one should be able to define the semantic limits, or rules of use, for a particular schema; the specific meanings or referents will vary within these limits. If a standard schema comprehends a relatively general category such as "tree," an informant might use it to specify a casuarina tree in one instance, a mangrove in another; or he might say that it is just "a tree." The specific meaning depends upon the informant's selection from a range of possible meanings.

The degree of generality of the visual terms in a single system will vary, of course, as the examples from Yirrkalla art in figure 18.1a

suggest. Thus, the outline of a snake can probably be used for all varieties distinguished by the aborigines, but what appear to be more specific distinctions are illustrated by the occurrence of contrasting schemata for stingrays and devilrays and for freshwater turtles (tortoises) on the one hand and green and hawksbill turtles on the other.[7] For the Walbiri elements, the meaning ranges of examples in figure 18.1a and 18.1b also reflect different degrees of generality, as will become clear later.

The proper functioning of some representational systems depends quite directly upon a rather wide variability in the specific meanings possible for each schema, i.e., upon a relatively high degree of category generality. For instance, in a discussion of objects used in divination among the Ndembu of Northern Rhodesia, Turner (1961:8 ff.) describes a figurine that represents in simple outline the forms of a man, a woman, and a child. Turner points out that the diviner may interpret this figure in various ways. In one instance he may say that it represents a chief and his kin (man = chief; woman, child = kin); in another, a headman and his kin; in still a third, witches. The man, woman, and child can be an elementary family, but more commonly they are interpreted as "co-members of a matrilineage"; further, the particular relationships within the matrilineage, and thus the specific kin represented, will vary with the diviner's interpretation. As Turner remarks, "all kinds of groups, relationships and differences of status can be expressed by this symbol" (1961:9). Turner emphasizes that this sort of "multireference," as he calls it, characterizes all the divinatory objects.

The use of relatively general visual categories is well known to Western art historians; many examples can be cited from medieval European and Byzantine art. Thus Weitzmann (1947:156), writing of certain early Christian book illuminations, comments that the "formula" for a Byzantine emperor was used "wherever a ruler or high dignitary was to be represented": "... Joseph in Egypt, or Pharaoh himself, King Saul, King David, or King Solomon all look alike, because the same convention was used for each of them." Similarly, Gombrich (1960:68–69) says of the "Nuremberg Chronicle": "... we find the same woodcut of a medieval city recurring with dif-

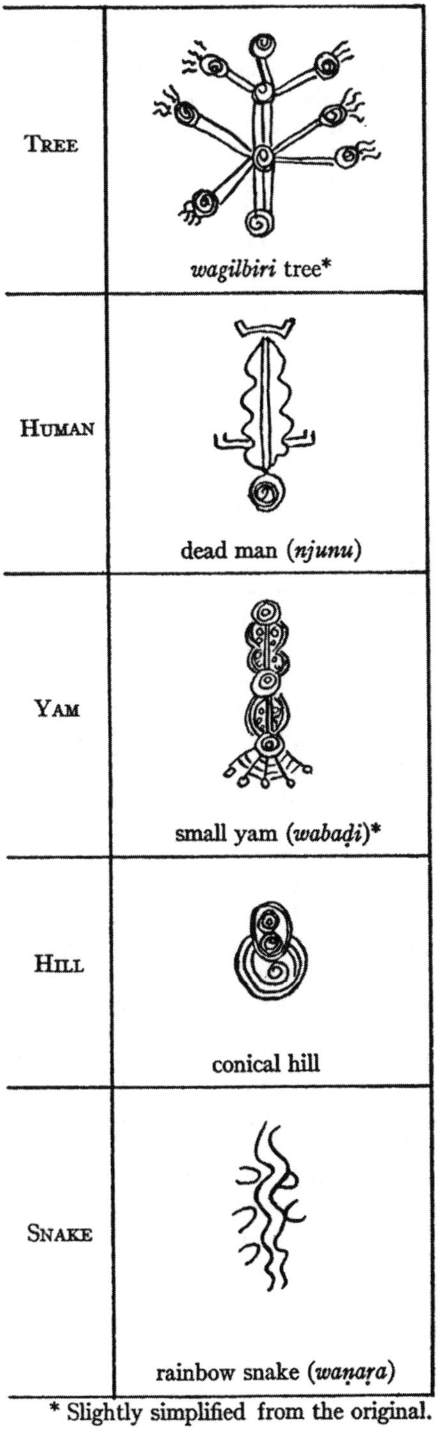

TREE	*wagilbiri* tree*
HUMAN	dead man (*njunu*)
YAM	small yam (*wabaḍi*)*
HILL	conical hill
SNAKE	rainbow snake (*waṇaṛa*)

* Slightly simplified from the original.

Figure 18.2 Composite visual categories – Walbiri

ferent captions as Damascus, Ferrara, Milan and Mantua.... we must conclude that neither the publisher nor the public minded whether the captions told the truth. All they were expected to do was to bring home to the reader that these names stood for cities." For each such fairly general visual term, the specific meaning relevant to a particular usage can be communicated in different ways. The oral identifications of the Ndembu diviner have been mentioned; in literate societies the parallel device is the use of written inscriptions. The Carolingian scholar Alcuin (quoted in De Bruyn 1946, 1:283) states this function succinctly: "Represent a woman holding an infant on her knee. If there is no inscription how does one know if she represents the Virgin with Christ or Venus with Aeneas, Alcmene with Hercules, Andromica with Astyanax?"

To turn to the schemata in figure 18.1b, the problem of category generality is presented here in a special form. These schemata cover highly general categories, each of which includes a variety of different classes of phenomena. The circle, for instance, can be used to specify a waterhole (or, when required by context, a particular waterhole at a named place), fire, fruits of various kinds, and other items. In ordinary usage, as in a sand drawing accompanying conversation, only one of these meaning classes is relevant at a time. For example, a circle between two facing arcs might in one instance specify two (particular) persons sitting at a waterhole and, in another, two persons sitting at a fire; these individuals might be human beings or ancestral persons such as kangaroo men or any other class of mobile being recognized by the Walbiri. The point is that the persons using the system select in each instance a specific meaning from the range of possible meanings.

The visual category comprehended by the circle consists of all "roundish" or "closed," nonelongate phenomena. Items of a straight, elongate form like spears and straight paths are represented by a straight line. Elongate, winding forms like snakes and lightning are represented by a meander line. These categories are so broad that an indefinite variety of phenomena can be pictured by each element; the Walbiri schemata characterize an object by a basic defining feature of shape. Pictures of this kind reduce objects to their limiting features rather than elaborate their visual particu-

larities (hence they have often been confusingly labeled "abstract" or "geometric").

Thus, the meaning ranges of the Walbiri elements shown in figure 18.1b are not restricted to species of things, such as "trees," "yams," or "turtles"; rather, they intersect class or species distinctions of this kind. The circle, which conveys the "roundness" or "closedness" of an object, can portray equally well a yam, say, or the base of a tree (standing for the tree as a whole in some Walbiri usages). In the Yirrkalla idiom a yam is represented by a more specialized form, which cannot also depict a tree. Rather, the pictures for "yam" and "tree" contrast as separate elements in the system.

Borrowing a label from linguistics, I have called meaning ranges of the type exemplified in 18.1b *discontinuous* since they include heterogeneous classes of meaning items, only one of which is relevant at a time. As we shall see, however, Walbiri also make use of metaphoric linkages in some segments of the graphic system, so that more than one of these classes of items can be applicable in a single instance.

Meaning ranges of the 18.1a elements, on the other hand, I have called *continuous* since they do not cover heterogeneous classes of meaning items. A "tree" schema might be used for different varieties of trees, but cannot also represent waterholes, fires, and other such classes of phenomena.

As figure 18.1a indicates, elements with continuous meaning ranges do occur in Walbiri art; this system also uses "footprints," most of which (for example, kangaroo or dog prints) have continuous ranges. Conversely, what appear to be discontinuous categories occur also in the Yirrkalla system. The emphasis upon highly general elementary categories with discontinuous ranges is, however, an outstanding characteristic of central Australian art; as we shall see, Walbiri art is elaborated on principles that "play" upon this feature.

One may infer that an art like the Walbiri, functioning primarily with discontinuous elementary categories, could operate with a smaller number of elements than one relying largely on continuous categories. Where the meaning ranges are discontinuous, it is theoretically possible to increase the number of classes of phenomena represented without expanding the repertory of visual elements. Walbiri women, for instance, represent the

Australian billy-can in their sand drawings by a circle rather than by creating a specific schema to picture it, for the billy is readily fitted into the category of "roundish," "closed" forms represented by the circle. Or let us suppose that, using the elements of this system, we wanted to portray a car. We might decide to represent the whole car as a circle; or, alternatively, we might treat the wheels as circles and the axle and body of the car as a line. We would then have to combine the circles and the line in an appropriate arrangement, but we still would not have increased the number of basic elements or elementary visual categories. On the other hand, if we were using elements of the continuous type, we would have to create a separate schema to picture a car, and so we would add to the number of visual elements in the system.

Ethnographic examples of pictorial systems relying primarily upon discontinuous categories, other than the central Australian, can only be identified tentatively from the descriptive literature. It seems probable, for example, that the parfleche decoration of the Arapaho Indians described by Kroeber (1902), and examined by Boas (1927:88 ff.) along with other similar systems, is of this kind. The elements in this art are lines, triangles, rectangles, and other basic forms, which are combined into a limited number of standardized arrangements. A single element can stand for a variety of different meaning items: a triangle, for instance, can stand for items such as "mountain," "tent," and "body-part of a person"; elongate items like paths, however, are represented by lines.

Kroeber was impressed by the variety of meanings for each element. Thus, in describing a particular bag, he says:

It will be noticed that identical white spots mean on different sides of the bag respectively snow-patches and turtle-eggs. What signification they have depends in each case on the symbolic context. Similarly a three pronged figure...often signifies the bear's foot, but here, when adjacent to a turtle-symbol, a turtle's foot. Such representation of different objects by the same symbol – or such different interpretation of the same figure...is constantly found...[1902:83].

There is an interesting similarity between Kroeber's description of the Arapaho design meanings and the semantic descriptions of central Australian designs by early observers. In both cases, meanings were thought to be highly variable without any discoverable intrinsic patterning; extrinsic "context" and the informant's personal whim were the only limiting factors. Davidson (1937:91 ff.), for instance, stressing the "inconstant character" of design meanings in central Australian art, pointed out:

For the geometrical designs...we find great differences in meaning. A group of concentric circles or a spiral...are often interpreted as representing a totem center, the totemic animal or plant, a waterhole or some other natural feature of the terrain,...the imprint in the earth left by a person's buttocks, the intestines of an animal or bird, an egg, or other things or places...[1937:95].

In my opinion, it is very likely that the Arapaho system, like the central Australian, makes wide use of elements with discontinuous meaning ranges and that it has, therefore, a discoverable semantic structure.[8] If this is the case, then it would be useful to reconsider Boas' classic treatment of the semantic variability of such designs in the light of the present discussion.

II

I now turn to composite categories in Walbiri art. I mean to illustrate both the pictorial possibilities of a system using discontinuous elementary categories and one of the ways in which it can provide an organizing pattern or structure through which separate classes of phenomena – in this case totemic phenomena – can be ordered.

My examples are drawn from men's totemic designs, since it is within this genre of Walbiri art that the potentialities of the graphic system are most fully realized. Each design is connected with one of the totemic ancestors whose travels created the country, and it pictures various features of the species to which the ancestor belongs. A single ancestor is generally represented by more than one design. A few designs are connected with "mythical" beings not directly associated with the creative ancestors, but like them classified in terms of the subsection and descent systems.[9] One example in figure 18.2, the "dead man," is of this sort.

Figures 18.1 and 18.1b illustrate two different ways of representing similar phenomena, both of which occur in Walbiri art. In 1a are elements comprehending continuous categories; except for the figure of a human being, each was identified by an informant as a totemic design or part of a design. In figure 18.2 are examples of the more typical Walbiri designs: composite constructions of circles, lines, and additional constituents. These constructions actually yield continuous categories on the order of "snake," "tree," "yam," etc.

For present purposes it is sufficient to note the general order or class of phenomena and the particular variety represented by the designs in figure 18.2 (*wagilbiri* tree, small yam, etc.), but a more detailed consideration of meaning ranges and of the degree of exclusiveness or visual distinctiveness of the constructions would be necessary for an accurate assessment of the categories. For example, the meander line combined with a particular arrangement of arcs appears to be restricted to representations of rainbow snakes, while similar but not identical configurations occur for other snakes. Although the meander line is also used in the closely related designs for rain – where it may specify lightning, say, or rain falling – the snake arrangement of arcs and meanders does not occur in rain designs, and two informants in fact distinguished rain and rainbow snake on this basis.[10]

Thus, through the combination of different selections of elements into various arrangements, a system that works with highly general elementary categories of the discontinuous type can yield composite categories with continuous meaning ranges. This mode of representation can provide pictorial detail as easily as one using elementary continuous categories. The depictions of trees in figures 18.1a and 18.2 are structurally different – the former is a single, unbreakable unit; the latter has hierarchical structure since it is made by combining more than one element into a unified pattern – but the latter also pictures the roots, trunk, branches, and leaves in an appropriate arrangement.

In the representations of figure 18.1a the different pictures cannot be broken down into any shared constituent parts, and the Walbiri representations of a snake, tree, human, and hill do not bear any significant similarity to each other. Nothing in the observable form of the pictures would convey to us that these phenomena might have anything in common. But in the typical totemic designs of figure 18.2 it is precisely the similarity between representations of different phenomena that strikes us. These similarities are of two kinds: shared terms or elements and shared types of arrangements. The relatively distinctive constructions can be resolved into constituent elements, of which the circle and the straight or meander line occur either singly or together in all the pictures. Other elements, such as the arc, also occur in more than one design. Thus the composite categories covering classes such as "tree" or "yam" can be broken down into elementary categories partially shared with other designs.

The constructions also share common arrangements. We may distinguish one sort in which a central unit consisting of a circle (or series of circles) and line sequence is accompanied by various elements ranged around or adjoined to the sequence. The pictures of the tree, man, and yam are of this kind. In another sort of arrangement the central unit consists of a circle or line (in the example, a meander line) with surrounding or adjoined elements; "conical hill" and "rainbow snake" are the examples. I call the central parts of these designs the *core* and the surrounding elements *adjuncts*. Walbiri themselves, when making these designs, generally draw the core elements first and then add the surrounding elements, but the core-adjunct analysis and description derives from my examination of semantic and structural features of the designs rather than from any explicit Walbiri analysis.[11] While other types of constructions occur in the totemic designs, this core-adjunct type is basic to the system as a whole and has the widest distribution among the different totems.

The designs in figure 18.2 can all be broken down into core and adjunctive parts. Elements functioning as the core are always circles or lines or both. Elements that may fill the adjunctive slot are widely variable; they include the circle and straight line as well as, more commonly, other elements in the system. In table 18.1 the vertical columns show both the core and adjunctive positions and the visual elements from the designs in figure 18.2 that occur in each position. The elements and positions illustrate a kind of vocabulary and grammar, in terms of which a design can be constructed.

The horizontal columns show the assemblage of parts (from figure 18.2) that are relevant to a particular totem species. For example, the dead man consists of backbone, buttocks, ribs, arms, and legs. The backbone and buttocks are treated as the core; while ribs, arms, and legs function as adjuncts. The arrangement of parts is handled in terms of a general pattern common to designs for other phenomena. Moreover, the backbone, buttocks, and ribs belong to larger categories: the backbone to a category of elongate items that can all be represented by the line, the buttocks to a contrasting category of "roundish" items represented by the circle, and the ribs to still another broad category of plural, semicircular items represented by arcs. Only the arms and legs are pictured by elements with a very limited distribution in the designs as a whole. Different parts of the dead man are thus reclassified into broad visual categories (roughly: roundish, elongate, and semicircular segments) common to other species as well.

In effect, to picture an object in this system one dissects it into two parts: on the one hand, a central stem or torso-like part such as the tree trunk and its roots, the snake's body, the main portion of the hill; on the other, its ap-pendage-like parts such as tree branches and leaves, the pearl shells associated with the rainbow snake (which he is said to send out with the rain), and the conical tip of the hill.

Since the body or torso-like parts are of two kinds – elongate items (meandering or straight) such as the snake and yam stem, and closed, roundish items such as the hill and yam tubers – there is an additional dual classification into elongate and roundish segments of the torso implicit in the structure of the system. This classification is reinforced by an explicit Walbiri metaphor. Walbiri equate the elongate parts with the paths of these totemic beings (tree trunks and yam stems, for instance, are also ancestral paths), and all the roundish parts with their camp sites (for example, the yam tuber is the camp of the yam). This metaphor functions to reinforce the unity of each visual category since varied items in the same category are metaphorically identified as "the same thing" (see also Munn 1962).

Table 18.1 can now be read as the outline of an analysis and classification of phenomena. This classification, implicit in the structure of the totemic designs, suggests the sort of dissection and reordering of different totemic species in terms of a common structure discussed by Lévi-Strauss (1962). One of his examples is the description of totemic animals in the ritual

Table 18.1   Core–adjunct construction

	Core		Adjunct					
	○	|	○	|	}}}	))	⊐	○○ ○○
Tree (*wagilbiri*)	tree roots (and branch junctures)	trunk	branch tops (camps)	branches (paths adjoining main track)	leaves			
Human (dead man)	buttocks	backbone			ribs	legs, arms		
Yam (small yam)	yam tubers (= hills)	underground stem			roots (also: lines = roots)	small tubers		
Hill (conical)	hill		conical tip (small camps)					
Snake (rainbow snake)		snake's body			pearl shells			
	Camp	Path						

chants of the Osage Indians. Lévi-Strauss points out that the different animals connected with the Osage clans are described in the texts in a way that effectively analyzes these species into a "system of invariant characters supposedly common to all the species" (1962:193).

Thus, in the Osage chants the puma asserts that he has black feet, a black muzzle, and a black tail. According to Lévi-Strauss, all the other totemic animals and birds are similarly described, and items such as beaks and noses are equated. The different totems are in effect broken down into a set of corresponding parts: the muzzle or nose-like parts, including the bear's muzzle, the eagle's beak, and other such items; the feet-like parts, including the bear's feet, the eagle's claws, and so on. In addition, all these items are said to be black, a feature that (because of certain symbolic associations important to the Osage) is stressed as being common to all the animals.

On the one hand, each of these totemic species is distinctive and functions as the symbol of a particular clan; on the other hand, each can be analyzed into a set of parts shared with the other totemic animals and intersecting these species differences. As Lévi-Strauss points out, there is "a sort of ideal dismemberment of each species that re-establishes... the totality on another plan" (1962:195).

Much the same may be said of the Walbiri designs. On the one hand, totems of different species can be represented by contrastive designs.[12] On the other hand, a common structure and shared visual categories intersecting these differences reorder the different species in terms of a common pattern. This reordering provides a kind of visual comparison and analysis. A construction of the core-adjunct type can in theory be used to represent any totemic species, which could thus be analyzed and reassembled in the terms I have described.

The reliance upon graphic elements comprehending highly general visual categories with discontinuous meaning ranges together with the use of a limited number of construction types (of which I have discussed the most widely used one) makes it possible to represent an indefinite variety of totemic species without necessarily increasing the visual complexity of the system. Since the number of Walbiri totem species is exceedingly large (Meggitt [1962: 205] counted over 150 totems for the Walbiri

as a whole, some of them belonging to the same species), this graphic economy is of some functional significance.

The design structure that I have described also meshes with Walbiri cosmology. Walbiri regard each major totemic ancestor as an individual with a particular set of locale associations; the individual belongs to a species, and a cluster of attributes (including characteristic behavioral as well as formal attributes) stereotypes each species, marking it off from others. But all species of ancestors also share certain important attributes: for example, all made camps and left track-marks in the country (Munn 1962, 1964). These shared attributes are criteria of the class of totemic ancestors.

This interplay between similarity and difference, unity and plurality, is also plotted in the design system, as I have briefly suggested, although a more precise examination of the links between design structure and these principles in the cosmology is outside the scope of my paper. To the extent that the design structure conveys an organization inherent in the cosmology, the designs function as visual models that present these principles, as it were, directly for inspection. Bober (1956–57:84) comments on this kind of function when he describes certain circular schemata or *rotae* in a medieval school book as "visual instruments" because of "their peculiar capacity to give visual expression to broad syntheses of a given subject; to show correlation between its parts." In this sense, Walbiri designs can also be called "visual instruments."

III

In his recent review of ethnoscientific studies, Sturtevant (1964:107) has pointed out that since "non-linguistic communication systems are also structured... it seems wise not to restrict the meaning of ethnoscience to the study of terminological systems." Although he suggests that "complex aesthetic phenomena" may be one of the possible candidates for structural analysis, Sturtevant does not mention visual representations as such. In the present paper I have attempted to show that the concepts of elementary unit and category can be illuminating in the analysis of representational systems. I have distinguished a type of visual category that includes radically different, "discontinuous" classes of meaning items from one in which the included items are relatively homogeneous or "continuous." In the Walbiri case I have shown how the use of discontinuous elementary categories as a basic organizing principle affects certain features of the larger representational structure.

One implication of this paper is that representational systems, or aspects of them, could be compared cross-culturally along structural rather than simply stylistic dimensions. It is interesting to consider, for example, how an art handles the problem of contrasting a series of related individuals or classes of phenomena such as totemic ancestors, a pantheon of gods, or saints. I have described one solution to this problem, that characteristic of Walbiri totemic designs.

Some additional notes may be helpful in suggesting a comparative context. Where the elementary categories are continuous (rather than primarily discontinuous, as in the Walbiri case), schemata for members of the series may be systematically differentiated by sets of contrastive features, such as clothing, position, etc., elaborated across the series. Thus, in medieval European art the portrait "type" of each saint is differentiated by a cluster of traits involving clothing, beard, and hair style; these traits are components of the elementary schema (the human figure), unlike emblems, which are *added to* the unit. A less systematic, but similar mode of specification is suggested by Ray for Alaskan Eskimo carvings: "selected diagnostic characteristics of animals are of primary concern to the contemporary carvers.... The carvers differentiate the white fox from the red fox, for example, by making the legs of the former shorter, and they indicate the differences between polar bear and brown bear by the smaller size of the brown bear's palms and the greater amount of fur on the polar bear's front legs" (1961:144).

Another device, that of adding diacritical emblems to a representation, is familiar from diverse arts. Emblems, such as the corn or arrows often held by the personae of Navaho sand paintings, are the distinctive attributes of certain individuals or social categories, for instance, the category "warrior." Emblems may also occur along with featural contrasts, as in later medieval depictions of saints or in Indian images of the Divine Buddhas. In all these examples the prob-

lem is one of showing the distinctive features of a number of individuals or separate categories of beings who also share common characteristics. The particular solution chosen will, of course, be framed, as in the Walbiri case, in terms of the wider representational structure.

The questions I have raised lead to more general issues in the study of pictorial codes. What structural devices are widespread in such codes, and how does iconicity itself limit the possible ordering techniques employed cross-culturally? To answer these and related questions we must refine the current ethnographic tools used in describing the representational arts. Indeed, the ideal that Conklin has voiced with respect to language could well be applied to the study of visual representations: "accurate and productive ethnography... [must go] beyond the identification and mere cataloguing of linguistic forms to the point where crucial structural semantic relations can be described systematically" (1962: 86). The substitution of "representational" for "linguistic" in this statement would aptly sum up the viewpoint of the present paper.

NOTES

1 This paper is a revised version of one given at the 1964 meetings of the Australian–New Zealand Association for the Advancement of Science in Canberra. At the time, I was in Australia under the auspices of the Australian Institute of Aboriginal Studies. I am grateful to Robert J. Smith and Victor W. Turner for reading and commenting upon an earlier draft of the present paper.

2 Research among the Walbiri was supported by a Fulbright grant and carried out under the auspices of the Australian National University between 1956 and 1958 at Yuendumu settlement, Northern Territory (central Australia), where primarily southern Walbiri were in residence. The social organization of the Walbiri is described by Meggitt (1962). Further details of the graphic system, the social processes in which it is embedded, and the cosmological significance Walbiri attach to their totemic designs (see part II of this paper) are given in Munn (1962, 1963, 1964).

3 The Yirrkalla elements are after illustrations of bark paintings in Mountford

(1956: pls. 112A, 96B, 106B, 108B, 119A, 119C, 115A). Other major sources illustrating Yirrkalla paintings are Berndt (1964) and Elkin, Berndt, and Berndt (1950).

4   A few examples of well-developed representational systems are the paintings and carvings of the northwest coast Indians, Navaho sand paintings, ancient Mayan sculpture and painting, certain African figurine systems like the Ashanti goldweights, Yoruba religious carvings, and masking systems like those of the Dogon or the Pueblos. The religious sculpture and painting of medieval Europe and Byzantium and of Indian Buddhism and Hinduism furnish additional examples of highly elaborate iconographies. All of these arts, although varying in complexity, are built upon the principle of discrete, recurrent contrasts.

5   The published examples of Yirrkalla schemata for lizards, turtles, and human beings appear in some instances to consist of a separable schema for "arms" (or "arms" and "legs") combined with a "body" schema. The typical Yirrkalla element, however, is a contour of the whole figure, and it is not clear whether internal segmentation may also occur. For present purposes, I regard these representations as unbreakable units exemplifying the schematic type discussed in the text.

6   A narrower use of the term "representation" is sometimes made. Thus Beardsley (1958:270 ff.) treats circles and similar visual forms as nonrepresentational and merely "suggestive" because of their relatively generalized visual properties. According to his definition, "design x" can be said to depict or represent "object y" when "x contains some area that is more similar to the visual appearance of y's than to objects of any other class" (1958:270). The circle, he suggests, has a shape sufficiently general for it to stand for various classes of species of phenomena such as plates, moons, etc. "But it is no *more* like a moon than it is like a plate, and so it cannot really be said by our definition to *depict* [i.e., represent] any of these things" (270). In effect, Beardsley's argument arbitrarily restricts representation to object classes of a certain level and kind of generality, as he himself makes clear in his sub-

sequent argument. Yet, as I discuss later, a visually simple form like the circle can certainly provide a pictorial equivalent for a class of objects – in the case of the Walbiri circle, a class of "closed," nonelongate, or roundish objects – and one must grant that a circle used in this way would then meet Beardsley's definition of "representation." A more far-reaching criticism, however, is that the pictorial value of the circle or of any other visual form can only be determined by examining the particular system of visual-semantic contracts of which it is a part. One can, in fact, conceive of a pictorial system in which the circle is used to stand for (let us say) waterholes only, with contrasting elements serving to represent classes such as moons or plates. In such a system, the circle would function as a pictorial likeness for waterholes and no other class of objects. On this view, the iconic value of a visual element is relative to its position in a particular system of conventions and cannot be defined outside of a system.

7   The English labels used here are the ones that serve to translate native terms as given in Mountford (1956): "green turtle," *gariwa*; "hawksbill turtle," *kouwaradji*; "fresh-water turtle" or "tortoise," *mimala*. Native terms also distinguish the two kinds of rays. I have no information, however, that would indicate whether Yirrkalla aborigines distinguish more general groupings, roughly comparable to our "turtles" or "rays," either by inclusion in a single verbal category or by other grouping techniques. It is of some interest that in the Yirrkalla string figures collected by McCarthy (1960: figs. 176, 178), the distinctive feature of the tortoise is again the long neck, and the whole figure is constructed quite differently from that shown for the green turtle.

8   The element arrangements in Arapaho designs provide additional evidence for this hypothesis. Although the same or similar types of constructions can in different instances refer to very different objects or object-complexes, the construction *resembles* the specified objects in each instance. One common construction, for example, consists of two "mirror-image" segments

with a connecting element or "juncture." This can specify various items: examples are "two frogs with heads in scum" (scum = juncture from either side of which the legs and bodies of the frogs extend); a turtle (carapace = juncture from which the claws extend). See Kroeber (1902: fig. 28; pl. XII, fig. 4). The systematic iconicity of a construction over a range of very different phenomena is one index of internal semantic order in the designs. Walbiri constructions operate very similarly (see above, part II).

9 Rights over ancestral totems and their associated designs are held by patrilineal groups; the totems are classified in the same father-son subsection couple as the groups that have rights over them.

10 Not all categorical contrasts can be determined as clearly from my data as those for rain and rainbow snake and related species; nevertheless, the typical designs for certain well-known totem species contain clear-cut visual contrasts. In the case of less well-known totems the problem of analysis is more complex. In addition, not all designs available for a totem contain features distinguishing the species. Some designs, for instance, are part of a highly generalized graphic idiom that can be used for any totem. Thus, designs of differing degrees of generality or distinctiveness occur.

11 The criteria used for designating parts of designs as core or adjunct, and occasional ambiguities giving rise to problems in the analysis of particular designs, are not discussed here. Compositional features from other parts of the system suggest, for instance, that the branches in table 18.1 could perhaps be analyzed as core rather than adjunctive elements. Difficulties of this sort, however, are outside the scope of this paper, which aims only to call attention to an organizing structure implicit in the representational system.

12 Walbiri designs do not constitute a "heraldry" in the strict sense of this word. A single patrilineal group has rights over a number of totemic species, and designs for these species do not necessarily share common visual features marking them off from designs representing totems controlled by other groups. Segmentation in the social structure cannot be "read off" from critical visual contrasts between designs or relevant sets of designs.

REFERENCES

Arnheim, R. 1954 *Art and visual perception.* Berkeley, University of California Press.

Beardsley, M. C. 1958 *Aesthetics: problems in the philosophy of criticism.* New York, Harcourt Brace.

Berndt, R. M., ed. 1964 *Australian aboriginal art.* Sydney, Ure Smith.

Boas, F. 1927 *Primitive art.* Oslo, H. Aschehoug. Reprinted 1955, New York, Dover; page references to this edition.

Bober, H. 1956–7 An illustrated medieval school-book of Bede's "De natura rerum." *Journal of the Walters Art Gallery* 19–20: 65–97.

Conklin, H. 1962 Comment on C. Frake, "The ethnographic study of cognitive systems." In *Anthropology and human behavior.* Washington, D. C., Anthropological Society of Washington.

Davidson, D. S. 1937 A preliminary consideration of aboriginal decorative art. *Memoirs of the American Philosophical Society,* vol. 9. Philadelphia.

De Bruyn, E. 1946 *Études d'esthétique médiévale.* 3 vols. Bruges, de Tempel.

Elkin, A. P., R. M. Berndt, and C. M. Berndt 1950 *Art in Arnhem Land.* Melbourne, Cheshire.

Gombrich, E. H. 1960 *Art and illusion: a study in the psychology of visual representation.* Bollingen Series XXXV.5. New York, Pantheon.

Kroeber, A. L. 1902 The Arapaho. *Bulletin of the American Museum of Natural History,* no. 18. New York.

Lévi-Strauss, C. 1962 *La pensée sauvage.* Paris, Plon.

McCarthy, F. 1960 The string figures of Yirrkalla. In *Records of the American-Australian scientific expedition to Arnhem Land,* vol. 2: *Anthropology and nutrition.* C. P. Mountford, ed. Melbourne, Melbourne University Press.

Meggitt, M. 1962 *Desert people.* Sydney, Angus and Robertson.

Mountford, C. P. 1956 *Records of the American-Australian scientific expedition to Arnhem Land*, Vol. 1: *Art, myth and symbolism.* Melbourne, Melbourne University Press.

Munn, N. D. 1962 Walbiri graphic signs: an analysis. *American Anthropologist* 64: 972–984.

—— 1963 The Walbiri sand story. *Australian Territories* 3:37–44.

—— 1964 Totemic designs and group continuity in Walbiri cosmology. In *Aborigines now.* M. Reay, ed. Sydney, Angus and Robertson.

Ray, D. J. 1961 *Artists of the tundra and the sea.* Seattle, University of Washington Press.

Sturtevant, W. C. 1964 Studies in ethnoscience. *American Anthropologist* 66, no. 3, pt. 2:99–131.

Turner, V. W. 1961 Ndembu divination, its symbolism and techniques. *Rhodes Livingston Papers*, no. 31. Manchester, Manchester University Press.

Weitzmann, K. 1947 Illustrations in roll and codex: a study of the origin and method of text illustration. *Studies in Manuscript Illumination*, vol. 2. Princeton, Princeton University Press.

19

Structural Patterning in Kwakiutl Art and Ritual

Abraham Rosman and Paula G. Rubel

The investigation of meaning in art is a topic of longstanding interest in anthropology. Several anthropological studies of art have shown how it can convey significant themes within a society. For example, in her study of Walbiri iconography Munn (1973) likens this graphic or representational system to a language and attempts to derive meaning by relating art to the wider sociocultural order. She links the affective load carried by designs to their instrumental function in bringing about desired ends. Similarly, Witherspoon (1977) holds that Navajo art expresses the concepts, states and conditions of happiness, goodness and well-being which comprise the Navajo understanding of their way of life. The meaning of Navajo art, according to Witherspoon, is obtained by elucidating the relationship between the characteristics of a work of art (such as a rug or sand painting) and Navajo values, as expressed through the semantic aspects of language. Like Munn and Witherspoon, Forge (1966; 1967; 1973), in his study of Abelam art, sees art as part of a system of communication whose purpose is to convey concepts and values. Art, for Forge, is similar to language. In examining the sociopolitical position of the Abelam artist, he shows how artistic productivity relates to the attainment of leadership positions.

In this article, we shall examine messages conveyed in Kwakiutl art relating to basic themes in their culture. In our analysis, we shall adopt a structuralist perspective derived from the work of Lévi-Strauss. His approach to art is the same as that which he adopts in his analyses of kinship and mythology. As in these other areas, art is seen as a form of communication. The meaning of an element lies in its position within a relational system, as it does in language. Lévi-Strauss observes that 'as is the case with myths, masks, too, cannot be interpreted in and by themselves as separate objects. Looked upon from the semantic point of view, a myth acquires sense only after it is returned to its transformation set' (1979: 12). This is also the case for masks.

The richness of the ethnographic record and the striking quality of the art have stimulated some interesting analyses of Northwest Coast material. Using some of Boas's ideas from *Primitive art*, which we ourselves discuss below, F. Morphy (1977) characterizes symbolic or schematic art as the utilization of a series of features to represent certain animal forms which in turn function as visual representations of social groups. She distinguishes this kind of symbolic art from what she calls 'realistic' art. Faris (1983) sees the function of elaborate aesthetic display at potlatches as a

From *Man* 25 (4) (1990), pp. 620–639. Reprinted by permission of Blackwell Publishing.

way of emphasizing status in the political-economic sphere. Vastokas (1978) has used a cognitive approach in her examination of Kwakiutl art to demonstrate the presence of general organizational principles such as bilateral symmetry and tripartite structure, but she does not deal with the relationships between the principles embodied in the art and other aspects of Kwakiutl culture.

We intend to explore the question of meaning in Kwakiutl art dating from the turn of the century, by relating the art to a basic division in Kwakiutl ritual and culture between *baxus* (secular) and *tsetsequa* (sacred). This distinction was made by the Kwakiutl themselves and was expressed in a division of the year into two periods, each with its own appropriate rituals and social structure. A wide variety of carved and painted objects were used and these played an important role in these rituals.

This article is about art as anthropologists define it, just as they define religion, kinship and economics. Essentially, these are Western analytical categories. The objects of Kwakiutl material culture which we shall be discussing will be treated analytically as art objects, in the same way that shell money is treated as an economic object. By calling them 'art objects' we do not mean to imply that they cannot simultaneously be viewed analytically as religious objects, economic objects or objects encoding kinship relations. These objects obviously have a variety of meanings and associated behaviours in the world of the Kwakiutl. During the last century, many of the objects we will be considering were removed from their Kwakiutl context, shorn from the drama, music and dance with which they were associated, to be displayed in the static contexts of the world's most famous museums. In these museums, the objects acquired new and different meanings.

In this article, we suggest that the pervasive distinction between *tsetsequa* and *baxus* is reflected in the art in three ways: 1) Kwakiutl art objects can be classified into two sets corresponding to this distinction. Art objects in one set are used at one time of year, and in one set of ceremonies, while the objects in the other set are similarly limited in their use. 2) There are systematic stylistic differences between the art of *baxus* and the art of *tsetsequa*. 3) Stylistic elements characteristic of each of the two sets can be paired. Thus, one stylistic element of a *baxus* piece may be paired with another stylistic element in the piece in the *tsetsequa* realm with which it corresponds. In establishing such correspondences, we work within a structuralist paradigm which seeks to determine the underlying patterns linking superficially distinct cultural domains.

Social Organisation and Ceremonial Life of the Southern Kwakiutl

We begin with a discussion of the relevant ethnographic material. This discussion is based primarily on Boas's ethnographic description of the Southern Kwakiutl around Fort Rupert. Boas's first visit to British Columbia occurred in 1886, and, beginning in the 1890s, he conducted fieldwork among the Kwakiutl, observing the Winter Ceremonial in 1895 and subsequently publishing on it and other topics in 1897. This source, along with the voluminous ethnographic data obtained later by Boas and Hunt in the form of texts, gives us a picture of Kwakiutl culture in the last decades of the nineteenth century.

By the time of Boas's first visit to the Kwakiutl, they had experienced almost a century of contact with Europeans. When Vancouver and Manzies, the first Europeans to describe the Kwakiutl, visited the Nimkish village in 1792, its inhabitants were already in possession of Spanish muskets, the result of direct or indirect trade in otter skins. Regular trading relations with Europeans, specifically with the Hudson's Bay Company, began soon after that. The Kwakiutl knew the fur market very well, succeeded in getting the highest prices for their furs, and were regarded as competitors by the Hudson's Bay Company (Codere 1950: 21 sqq.; 1961: 438). In 1849, the first Hudson's Bay trading post was set up with the founding of Fort Rupert. Those Kwakiutl groups that moved to Fort Rupert acted as mediators in the trade between the company and other Indians, became wealthy as a result, and were able to potlatch more frequently (Codere 1961: 455). Fort Rupert remained the most important settlement until 1881, when an agency and mission were set up at Alert Bay, bringing to the Kwakiutl the Royal Canadian Mounted Police, a school, sawmill and canneries. By this time the Kwakiutl were also involved in commercial fishing and lumbering. Though the first Canadian legislation to prohibit the potlatch was passed in 1876, it was not strictly enforced, and the 1890s – when Boas did his fieldwork – marked a period of increase in the frequency and elaboration of potlatches and winter ceremonials. We shall be concerned with the art and ritual of this period.

In order to understand the difference between the art of *tsetsequa* and the art of *baxus* we must go into some detail about this basic division in Kwakiutl ritual and culture.[1] The Kwakiutl division of the year into two distinctive and contrastive periods is reflected in many aspects of their life. The summertime, called *baxus*, is the period when people are involved in economic activities and when potlatches are held. Boas glosses the term *baxus* as 'profane', but we characterize it as the secular period. *Tsetsequa*, which means 'secrets', is the winter period (Boas 1897: 418). During this time, the Kwakiutl believe that a supernatural power is present in and around the villages, which sanctifies all activities. This is the period during which the winter ceremonial is held. In this article, we refer to this time as the sacred season. When the sacred season begins, quarrels, sickness and unhappiness are forgotten. According to Boas, 'the Indians express this alternating of seasons by saying that in summer *baxus* is on top, the *tsetsequa* below, and vice versa in winter' (Boas 1897: 418).[2]

During *baxus*, Kwakiutl tribes are subdivided into *numayms*, cognatic descent groups (see Rosman & Rubel 1971). These cognatic descent groups are organized according to basic principles of kinship which are different from those that organize social groups during the *tsetsequa* winter season. One set of myths, found in the family histories collected by Boas, gives details about the origin of the *numayms* from particular ancestors, along with names and rites which belong to each *numaym* (Boas 1921). For every *numaym* there exists a complete series of ranked names and associated potlatch seats. Each individual can claim *numaym* membership through either his mother or father, and individuals may belong to more than one *numaym*. Residential factors result in individuals usually having a single primary *numaym* affiliation. By bestowing a name owned by a *numaym* on a child at a potlatch, the *numaym* formally lays claim to

that child. The inheritance of chiefly position, embodied in a name and a seat, is based upon a rule of primogeniture. This division of Kwakiutl society into *numayms* with chiefs, ranked positions and family histories is operative during *baxus*.

Since *numayms* and the myths that tell of their origins are associated with *baxus*, potlatches marking the transfer of such names and the telling of myths associated with them are held in the summer, during the *baxus* period. Potlatches are occasions when guests from other tribes and *numayms* are called to witness the validation of membership and rank in a *numaym* by the bestowal of names which have been handed down from the first ancestors. At potlatches, the myth associated with the name is re-enacted, frequently dramatized with masks and other ritual paraphernalia. The rights to use the crests, masks and other forms of decoration are embodied in the myths. As one of the chiefs recounted at a potlatch, 'Indeed, indeed that is the speech to make at the first meeting of these great tribes, for we are told by our ancestors that we are to follow the road they made for us to be walked on.... These are the great names of my chief who lived before me, for you, tribes. Now I will tell the history, the myth of our great chief' (Boas 1921: 191–3). Here the Kwakiutl chief is collapsing myth and history into a single diachronic record. In Boas's *Family histories*, he does the same. These histories often begin with an eponymous ancestor who is a bird or an animal, and who is soon transformed into a man, and they then continue up to the time when George Hunt recorded them.

The sacred *tsetsequa* season is introduced by a liminal period. After the announcement that a winter dance is to be held, all must be cleansed and abstention from sexual intercourse is observed. During this time, the whistles which represent the voices of the spirits of the winter dance sound closer and closer to the village, and people use names and songs appropriate to the summer for the last time. When the initiates are captured by the spirits and disappear, the liminal period has ended and *tsetsequa* has begun.

In discussing the relationship between the two seasons, Boas states: 'Thus, at the beginning of the winter ceremonial the social system is changed.... During this period, the place of the clans [*numayms*] is taken by a number of societies, namely, the groups of all those individuals upon whom the same or almost the same power or secret has been bestowed by one of the spirits' (1897: 418). The origins of the secret societies are embedded in a set of myths which are different from the myths about the origins of the *numayms*. Secret society myths relate to the acquisition by ancestors of special supernatural powers. These have been transmitted to their descendants for generations. They are acquired through initiation into the secret societies, which takes place during *tsetsequa*, the sacred period. Boas likens this initiation to the vision quest of the Plains Indians, in which individuals isolate themselves and, through starvation, deprivation and sometimes mutilation, attempt to induce a trance during which a supernatural being appears to them and then becomes that individual's guardian spirit and protector. On the Plains, the number of guardian spirits was unlimited, since each man had his own spirit. Among the Kwakiutl, individuals inherited the equivalent of guardian spirits.

> From the legends which I have told, it appears that these spirits appeared first to the ancestors of the clan, and I have stated that the same spirits continue to appear to the descendants of these mythical ancestors. The number of spirits is limited, and the same one appeared to ancestors of various clans [*numayms*] of different tribes. But in these cases he gave each of his protégés his powers in a slightly different form.... the spirits give new names to the men to whom they appear, but these names are in use only during the time when the spirits dwell among the Indians – that is, in winter. Therefore from the moment when the spirits are supposed to be present, all the summer names are dropped, and the members of the nobility [meaning Kwakiutl of the highest rank] take their winter names.... Thus the *ha mats'a*, *nu mal*, bear dancers, etc., form each one society, which consists of a limited number of names, because members of the society each derive their membership from the initiation of one of the ancestors of the nobility (Boas 1897: 418–19).

Since they are based on different principles of organization, membership of the secret societies cuts across that of the *numayms*. Rights

to become an initiate in a particular secret society follow the same rules as *numaym* membership, and secret society membership can be acquired through one's mother or father. However, rights to secret society membership are also transferred through marriage and can even leave a *numaym*. Repurchase of the bride by her father (representing her natal *numaym*)[3] almost invariably includes the transfer of winter ceremonial rights from the father to his daughter's husband. This usually means that such rights are being transferred to the daughter's son. The option exists, however, for a son-in-law to give those rights to another heir of his, such as his sister's child. In such a situation the privileges may be passing from one *numaym* to another. Boas points out that the *hamatsa* first came to the Kwakiutl through marriage, not more than a century before his first fieldwork among them. Since the ceremony of initiation into the secret societies is exceedingly expensive, it may be combined with a marriage repurchase at a potlatch. However, secret society initiation ceremonies could only be held in the winter during *tsetsequa* and the marriage repurchase potlatch would be held, in this case, at the same time. Boas gives no information to indicate that the Kwakiutl were concerned by this penetration of *baxus* into *tsetsequa*. If marriage repurchase is held at a potlatch during the summer, the box containing the winter ceremonial privileges remains closed and under a blanket, and is not opened until the winter ceremonial is held.

Kwakiutl tradition relates that when ancestors obtained their spiritual protectors they were also given both the right to perform certain dances, and certain secret songs. When the initiate emerges from seclusion and performs his song and his dance, he is re-enacting the myth of how his ancestor first acquired the spirit. According to Boas, when the initiate wears his mask and ornaments, 'he personates the spirit' (1897: 396). In this, the initiate has crossed a dividing line and become *nau'alak*, supernatural.

Boas presents a list of the spirits with whom the ancestors were originally in contact. These spirits are still present today and it is they who capture the initiates. There are several major spirits, but *Baxbakualanuxsiwae* seems to be the most important, since the spirits whom he controls dominate the winter ceremonies. *Bax-bakualanuxsiwae* is a cannibal who lives in the mountains and is always hunting men. Associated with him are the following subordinate spirits: *hamatsa* (a cannibal, in whom *Baxbakualanuxsiwae* has instilled the desire to eat human flesh), *hamshamtses* (a less violent cannibal), *nontsistalal* (devourer of fire), *nane s Baxbakualanuxsiwae* (the cannibal grizzly bear), *kinqalalala* (his female slave who procures human flesh for the *hamatsa*), *qominoqa* (his wife or servant who also procures flesh for the *hamatsa*), *hoxhoku* (a fabulous bird who eats men's brains), *haialikilal* (a friend of *Baxbakualanuxsiwae*). An initiate comes into contact with either *Baxbakualanuxsiwae* or any of his subordinates during his initiation, and then becomes the personification of one of the subordinates, the same one that his ancestor personified. Each of these supernatural creatures has his own song and dance. In addition, there are other spirits, such as *nulmal* and *qoaxqoaxualanuxsiwae*, the cannibal raven, and still another class of spirits associated with *winalaqilis*, the war spirit, who are important in the winter ceremonies.

Initiates who personify the spirits discussed above become members of the higher-ranked category of secret societies, known as 'the seals'. This includes the *hamatsa*, *hamshamtses*, *kinqalalala*, *nulmal*, *nane*, etc. (Boas 1897: 419). The remaining societies are *ququtsa*, 'the sparrows', subdivided into small groups on the basis of age and sex. Just as *numayms* are ranked with respect to one another during *baxus*, the secret societies are also ranked, with the *hamatsa* on top. Boas points out how the order of seating at a *tsetsequa* ceremony indicates the ranking of societies.[4]

The subdivisions of the *quequtsa* (sparrows) have animal names. The reason for this sheds light on the Kwakiutl conception of the relationship between humans and animals. Boas notes: 'the Indians give the explanation that the ceremonial was instituted at the time when men still had the form of animals.... The present ceremonial is a repetition of the ceremonial performed by the man animals or, as we may say, a dramatization of the myth. Therefore the people who do not represent spirits, represent these animals' (1897: 420–1). Two of the female societies are called *qaqaqao*, 'hens', and *mosmos*, 'cows'. According to

Boas, 'The present societies of the women are quite new, as is shown by their names – hens and cows. The former were called until about twenty years age *waxwaxoli*' (1897: 419). The winter ceremonies were constantly changing as a result of dances and rituals introduced from other tribes, either through intermarriage or through conquest. These new women's groups are simply another example of this process. The introduction of new dances and rituals meant that the repertoire of dances and secret society personages for each Kwakiutl tribe was somewhat different.

Membership in the higher ranked secret societies also confers 'the right to eat human flesh' (Boas 1897: 337). This refers primarily to the *hamatsa*. During the winter ceremonial which Boas observed, members of the *hamatsa* society bit people and simulated the eating of human flesh. However, George Hunt, Boas's informant, told that his father had witnessed the killing of a slave from Nanaimo in the early days of Fort Rupert. The slave's body was cut apart and given to the highest *hamatsas*, and the face of *Baxbakualanuxsiwae* was carved on a rock on the beach where the body was eaten. The slave's wife cursed the killers, and within five years they all died (1897: 439).

The winter ceremonial begins with the abduction of the initiates by the spirits. This is dramatically described as follows:

Suddenly the roof of the house shook violently. At the same time, a boy was seen on the entrance of the house being wafted up and down. He hung perfectly limp while he was flying to and fro. Suddenly he had disappeared. After a short time his bloody clothing and his head ring of red cedar bark fell down through the roof, and soon the bloody clothing of a girl also fell down.... Three of our youths have been taken away by the spirits. Now our winter ceremonial shall begin (Boas 1966: 189).

During his seclusion, the initiate acquires knowledge about his supernatural spirit and its magical gifts. The purpose of the winter ceremonial is to bring the youth back and to exorcise the spirit which has seized and possessed him. To do this, the members of all the secret societies perform their winter ceremonial songs and dances, wearing masks and full costumes and using ceremonial

paraphernalia, such as rattles. The winter ceremonial is held in a special dance house called
lo'peku, meaning 'emptied' because it has been
emptied of everything profane. The uninitiated
can only enter the house when dances are
being performed, and they must stay at the
left side of the entrance.

There is a relationship between the Kwakiutl
winter ceremonial and shamanism. Initiation of
novices in the winter ceremonial is analogous in
all details to that of a shaman, and 'Among the
Kwagul [a Kwakiutl tribe] the participants are
all called "shamans..."' (Boas 1966: 135,
172). The shaman is active during the portion
of the winter ceremony devoted to the exorcism
of the spirit from the initiate.

The relationship between animals and humans takes different forms during *baxus* and
during *tsetsequa*. The ancestral familial relationship between animals and humans is acted
out during *baxus* when family histories are
dramatized at potlatches. In these family histories, ancestors are described as the descendants of 'supernatural' animals. Boas refers to
'the numerous tales of ancestors who came
from heaven, took off their masks, and became
men, for in all these cases the mask has
remained the crest of the clan' (1897: 337).[5]
During *baxus*, men hunt and eat animals, who
may in fact be linked to their ancestors, asking
the spirit of the hunted animal not to be
offended and to send other animals in the future to be hunted.

In contrast to *baxus*, during *tsetsequa* the
winter ceremonial enacts the relationship between humans and their secret society spirits.
These spirits are special forms of supernatural
animals, like Cannibal Raven, Cannibal Grizzly Bear, or other 'fabulous creatures', as Boas
calls them, who, during *tsetsequa*, capture and
'devour' the initiates. After their 'deaths' and a
period of seclusion, initiates are 'reborn' during the *tsetsequa* ceremony. It is as though
animals and humans have two aspects – one
manifested during *baxus* and the other during
tsetsequa – which are inversions of one another. As Reid points out, during *baxus* humans hunt, kill and eat animals, while during
tsetsequa the supernatural animal spirits associated with secret societies hunt and devour
human beings (Reid 1976).

Boas's ethnographic data deal with the
Southern Kwakiutl around Fort Rupert, but

there appears to be a basic structure common
to all Kwakiutlan-speaking groups. In 1940
Drucker made a study of secret societies, covering those parts of the Kwakiutl area not dealt
with by Boas. He looked primarily at the Heilt-
suk-speaking Wikeno, Bella Bella and Xaihai,
and the Xaisla (Haisla), all Northern Kwakiutl
groups. His research indicated that there was a
degree of variation between the ritual systems
of the Northern and Southern Kwakiutl. He
observes that, 'Instead of the single "winter
ceremonial" of the Southern Kwakiutl which
Boas describes, the northern tribes had two or
three distinct ceremonial systems...The general pattern of all of the rituals was the same'
(1941: 227). All these groups had a series of
dances in the fall, referred to by Drucker as
'Shamans' Series' (*tsitsiqua*), which include
most of the elements of the winter ceremonial
described by Boas. They also had a different
series of dances in the spring called *dluwulaxa*
or *mila*, which were usually held in conjunction with potlatches. Drucker notes that the
key word *tsitsiqua*, which is used among the
Northern Kwakiutl (with some variations) for
the Shaman's Series of dances and among the
Southern Kwakiutl (*tsetsequa*) for the winter
ceremonial, is the Heiltsuk word for shaman.
Both Drucker and Boas point out that some
Southern Kwakiutl tribes, Koskimo, Blunden
Harbour, and Neeweetee (La'Lasiqoala in
Boas's text, 1895: 621) had two distinct series
of dances, like the Northern Kwakiutl. However, most of the Southern Kwakiutl had incorporated these rituals into one *tsetsequa*
ceremonial conducted only in the winter.

It is clear from the foregoing discussion that
the Kwakiutl organized their life differently
during the two seasons of *baxus* and *tsetsequa*.
The social structures during the two periods of
the year were distinct and the mythic supports
for these distinct structures were enacted
through the staging of different ceremonials
during each period. Individuals had one name
which was used during *baxus* and another
name which was used during *tsetsequa*, implying that each person had a 'summer' and a
'winter' form. Boas presents the two forms of
organization operative at different times of the
year as if they were quite distinct. However,
there are certain underlying principles which
they both share. One of these is the principle of
rank, which has one manifestation during

baxus, where chiefs make their names – and those of their *numayms* – great by potlatching, and another during *tsetsequa*, when humans don masks and are transformed into supernatural creatures which are ranked with respect to one another. Although descent from ancestral animals is enacted in potlatch ritual and depicted in crest art, these animals are not significant in the claims to rank asserted in the potlatch. Rank in this *baxus* context is the product of human relationships established through a succession of potlatches. During *tsetsequa*, by contrast, when the *numayms* are not operative, the secret societies which replace them are ranked and the seating in the ceremonial house graphically expresses this rank system. The masks worn by individuals in *tsetsequa* are immediately identifiable as representing supernatural creatures with particular rank positions in the hierarchy, though the origin of the hierarchy of spirits and their organizations is not known. In contrast to *baxus*, where rank is the product of relationships among humans, during *tsetsequa* rank is a product of the relationship between humans and the supernatural. Nevertheless, those of chiefly rank in the different *numayms* are also the ones with access to positions in the highest-ranked secret societies. Moreover, the same animals, though in different manifestations, feature in both forms of social organization. Marriage is another principle which breaches the boundary between these forms. Thus, though the rituals of winter and summer have an oppositional relationship to one another, there is also a degree of commonality and interpenetration.

Opposition and Transformation in Kwakiutl Art

The art of the Kwakiutl demonstrates the same division which we have discussed above. The art embodied in the masks and ritual paraphernalia that are used in initiation to secret societies, through form and style, proclaims itself to be the art of *tsetsequa* and thus differentiates itself from the art of *baxus*. As will be demonstrated below, in style *baxus* constitutes the unmarked category and *tsetsequa* the marked category. Together, they form a transformation set. Though the two categories of art share many of the same visual character-

istics, and portray different forms of the same animals, an additional characteristic marks the art of *tsetsequa*.

In Boas's early work, *Primitive art* (1955 [1927]), he discusses the art of the Kwakiutl, together with the art of other Northwest Coast societies. He uses the concept of style which he defines to include technical processes, form elements, and systems of arrangement of those form elements. The latter two relate to the nature of representation and to the meaning of the art. Boas's analysis focuses on the conceptualization of a single category of 'living things', which includes humans, animals, and forces of nature such as wind, echo, sun and moon, monsters and mythological creatures. These are all personified in an anthropomorphic manner in the art by being given a face. Thus, octopuses, snails, mosquitoes and dragonflies are all depicted with faces. The faces of animals and humans appear very similar, but the placement of ears differentiates them. Humans have ears on the sides of the head and animals' ears are on the top of the head. In nature, hawks do not have external ears or mouths separate from their beaks; however in Kwakiutl art, they are portrayed with ears and mouths below their sharply curving beaks. When a mask contains a hawk's beak and ears placed on the side of the head, it is a representation of a 'human'-hawk or mythical man-animal, meaning an ancestor of humans. When the hawk as an animal is being represented artistically, the ears appear on the top of the head. By an artistic device, the Kwakiutl readily recognize the difference between hawk as a man-animal, and hawk as a supernatural bird.

The Kwakiutl also distinguish different animal forms according to whether they inhabit the land, the sea or the air. This distinction is reflected in their art in that land animals are portrayed with paws; creatures of the sea with fins; creatures of the air have feathers. The faces of creatures of the air are also modified in that beaks may replace mouths or be added as in the case of the hawk. Animals of the sea include fish and sea mammals in a single category.

Kwakiutl art reflects the notion that animals and humans are interchangeable. As shown above, the Kwakiutl believe that in mythic times the ancestors of men were animals. When these animal-ancestors removed their masks, they became human beings and ancestors of particular *numayms*.[6] The mask became the crest of the *numaym* and just as the mythic animals removed their masks and became humans, present-day humans don the masks and become their eponymous animal ancestors in dramatizing the origin myths of their *numayms* during potlatches. The unity of man and animals is also illustrated by the fact that the winter ceremonial was said to have come to the Kwakiutl when humans were man-animals (*nu'xnemis*) and still had animal form. During the winter ceremonial, the initiate returning from the period of seclusion wears the mask of, and personifies, the supernatural animal of the secret society. During both times of the year, masks are the means by which men transform themselves into different manifestations of animals.

H. Morphy has noted that 'different cultures select different features of animals when representing them in art' (1989: 5). In Kwakiutl artistic representations of animals, what is portrayed is not necessarily what we consider to be most distinctive about that animal, but rather the essential characteristics of the animal from the Kwakiutl point of view. Boas shows how these characteristics represent distinctive features which mark the separation of animals from humans, and one animal from another in Kwakiutl art. For example, in masks and other artistic portrayals, the eagle is symbolized by a large curved beak with its point turned downward, the killer whale is symbolized by the large dorsal fin, blow hole, and large head with elongated nostrils, round eye and large mouth with teeth, and the bear is symbolized by large paws, a large mouth with teeth and protruding tongue, a large nose and a sharp upward turn from snout to forehead.

Monsters and mythological creatures are represented in the art by combining the distinctive features of one type of creature, for example, wolf, bear or raven, with those of another, for example, killer whale, to produce a Sea Bear, a Sea Wolf or a Sea Raven. Such monstrous creatures represent combinations which cross boundaries. As Morphy notes in his discussion of Fabulous Beasts, 'composite animals can have a cultural reality that may be more revealing than representations of known species because they create sets of species that cross-cut our categories and force us to ask

questions about the relationships between those creatures in the cultures concerned' (Morphy 1989: 5). The 'Fabulous Beasts' of the Kwakiutl cut across their categories as well as ours. The combinations are not however limitless in that there are apparently no mythological creatures which combine features of land and air forms, such as flying bears or flying wolves. Rather, characteristics of creatures of the sea are always combined with characteristics of one of the other two categories.

It is not clear why, for the Kwakiutl, anomalous creatures can cross certain boundaries and not others. Kwakiutl myths recount how humans frequently visit the undersea villages of the killer whale and the sea lion. It is interesting to note that creatures the Tlingit consider anomalous such as the land otter, which lives in two different domains, are associated with shamans and are portrayed on rattles used in shamanic performances (Jonaitis 1986: 89–90). This association of shamans with anomalous creatures also seems to hold among the Kwakiutl. The beings from whom the Kwakiutl shamanic initiate receives his power include such anomalous creatures as lizard, toad, frog and loon. These creatures all occupy more than one domain, either land and water or air and water (Boas 1966: 135).

Our hypothesis about the distinction in Kwakiutl art between that associated with *baxus* and that associated with *tsetsequa* is supported by an examination of the objects depicted in Hawthorn's *Kwakiutl art* (1979). The book is a broad-ranging study of Kwakiutl art objects which comes close to representing a compendium of every kind that the Kwakiutl produced. Hawthorn's work draws upon the collection of the University of British Columbia Museum. The material in the book is based upon information from Kwakiutl informants coming to the Museum, rather than on Hawthorn's own fieldwork. Many of the objects were made in the twentieth century, while others came from 'family collections they [the Kwakiutl] were no longer using, as many families abandoned the potlatch feasts and gift giving that had been the core of their social life' (1979: viii).[7]

For Hawthorn, meaning is equated with function, as it was for Malinowski. The many kinds of utilitarian objects such as hooks, halibut knockers and whistles are categorized on the basis of their uses. Masks are discussed in terms of the person or thing personified, which is identified by a Kwakiutl term, and their ceremonial settings and mythic associations are often provided. These constitute their meaning.

Hawthorn notes that 'the beings associated with the winter dances are rarely portrayed outside of these dances and rarely, if ever, shown in representations of lineage myths; but are reserved for the most sacred parts of the winter ceremony' (1979: 29). Many of the best-known Kwakiutl mask types – Crooked Beak (figure 19.1), Cannibal Raven (figure 19.2), and Nulmal or Fool Dancer (figure 19.3) – are used only during the *tsetsequa* period. In contrast, other types, such as the Raven (figure 19.4) and Grizzly Bear (figure 19.5) masks representing family crest myths, are used only during *baxus*.

Rattle types and other kinds of decoration also fall into one or the other of these two categories, according to Hawthorn (1979:

Figure 19.3 Nulmal mask. Boas (1897: pl. 34)

94). During *tsetsequa*, the round rattles are shaken by the *he'liq a* or healers to pacify the *hamatsa* when he emerges from seclusion and begins biting people's flesh. They are frequently in the shape of a skull (see figure 19.6), and sometimes in the shape of a human head. The chief's raven rattle (see figure 19.7) appears to have come to the Kwakiutl originally from the Haida and Tsimshian, by way of the Heiltsuk (Boas 1897: 629–30). This type of rattle was used in ceremonies in which the dancers were not supernaturally possessed in the way in which they were during *tsetsequa*. They wore masks representing mythological ancestors and in these ceremonies they re-enacted family myths (Hawthorn 1979: 49, 94). The raven rattle contrasts with the round type of rattle used in *tsetsequa*. From Hawthorn's information it would seem to be associated with *baxus*.

Sound is a significant element in Kwakiutl ritual drama. According to Hawthorn, 'the use of sound to characterize the ever present

Figure 19.1 Crooked beak mask. Hawthorn (1979: 207). Courtesy UBC Museum of Anthropology, Vancouver, Canada (1973 A17138).

Figure 19.2 Cannibal raven mask and dress. Boas (1897: pl. 31)

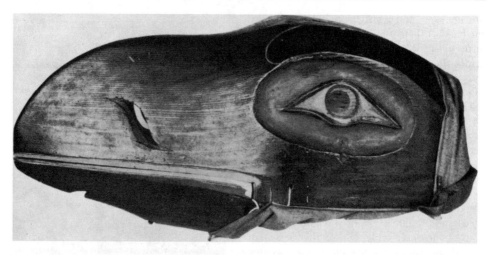

Figure 19.4 Raven mask. Hawthorn (1979: 207). Courtesy UBC Museum of Anthropology, Vancouver, Canada (1970 A5270).

Figure 19.5 Grisly (Grizzly) bear mask. Boas (1909: pl. L)

supernatural spirits among humans was a very important part of the winter society dances' (1978: 94). The voices of the spirits are represented by whistles. As noted above, the sound of whistles becoming louder signifies the approach of the spirits and the beginning of the winter ceremonial season. Carved batons were beaten on long planks to keep time for the singers and dancers. Whistles, batons, and clappers in use during *tsetsequa* are not used in *baxus*. Red cedar bark decorations and the double-headed *Sisiutl* serpent motif are used only in *tsetsequa*, while helmet head-dresses and the chief's ceremonial staff are apparently used only in *baxus*.

The division is not absolute since feast dishes, some ladles and spoons seem to be used in both *baxus* and *tsetsequa*. *Dzonokwa*

as a mythic figure has several manifestations which are associated with both *baxus* and *tsetsequa*. Boas notes that the *Dzonokwa* of the clan legends is a wild woman who lives in the woods and steals children in order to eat them. *Dzonokwa*, in this instance, would appear to be cannibalistic during *baxus*, relating, no doubt, to her anomalous status. This form of *Dzonokwa* is represented on many house posts and masks (Boas 1897: 372). The *Dzonokwa* of the *tsetsequa* ceremony is a member of the seal society, who lumbers to her seat guided by a rope, and is otherwise always asleep. She is attired in a bear-skin, to which the mask is attached (Boas 1897: 479). Hawthorn adds still another vision of *Dzonokwa*, important in the potlatch, as a male wealth-giver, carrying a basket in which the chief's coppers were stored before distribution. The portrayal of *Dzonokwa* in masks remains the same, sunken eyes and round protruding mouth, though these masks represent totally different aspects of *Dzonokwa* in *baxus* and in *tsetsequa*.

There is a special room for the initiates within the house used for the winter ceremonial. Boas includes a picture which shows an unmasked *hamatsa* initiate emerging from this room through the mouth of a depiction of a cannibal raven (see figure 19.8 for a diorama depicting this). In the picture, the novice is coming out for his first dance. Having been devoured by the cannibal spirit, the initiate emerging from the room is depicted as being

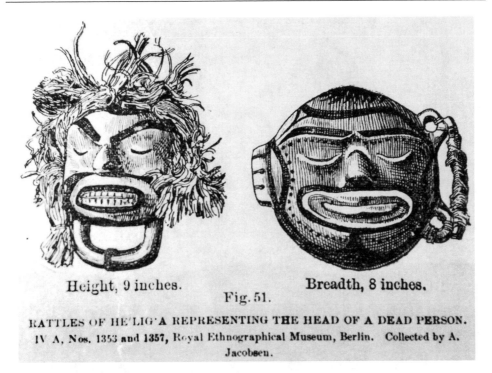

Height, 9 inches.   Breadth, 8 inches.

Fig. 51.

RATTLES OF HE'LIG'A REPRESENTING THE HEAD OF A DEAD PERSON.

IV A, Nos. 1353 and 1357, Royal Ethnographical Museum, Berlin. Collected by A. Jacobsen.

Figure 19.6 Rattles used during winter ceremonial. Boas (1897: 435)

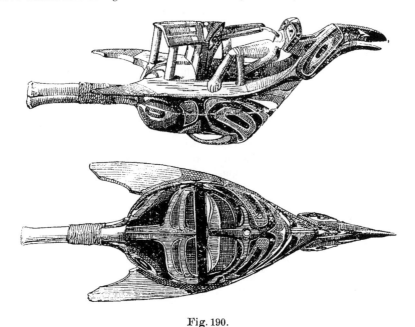

Fig. 190.

RAVEN RATTLE.

Length, 13 inches; blue, black, red.

IV A, No. 427, Royal Ethnographical Museum, Berlin. Collected by A. Jacobsen.

Figure 19.7 Raven rattle. Boas (1897: 623)

Figure 19.8 Initiate emerging from the secret room, inside the special dance house of the winter ceremonial. Boas (1897: 446)

regurgitated by the raven. After this, he seems to re-emerge from the side of the room wearing the mask of the cannibal raven which is supposed to be growing out of his body (Boas 1897: 446–7). The *numaym* house stands in sharp contrast to this (see figure 19.9). The house front and its totem pole are elaborately decorated with family-owned crests, all associated with *baxus*. The *numaym* house personifies the order and equilibrium of the secular world. In contrast, the house of the winter ceremonial epitomizes the supernatural.

The period of the winter ceremonial is one in which the boundaries of the society are permeable. The initiate bursting through the raven's mouth of the sacred room personifies disorder, the unruly disorder of the shaman.[8] *Nulmals*, the Fool Dancers who help the *hamatsa* to enforce the rules of the ceremonial also illustrate this disorder (see the *nulmal* mask in figure 19.3). They are filthy, their enormous noses dripping with snot, and they run about throwing stones, hitting people with sticks, breaking boxes, kettles, houses and canoes,

and tearing and soiling beautiful new clothing which offends them. As Boas notes, they 'act the madman in every conceivable way' (1897: 466–7). If *baxus* is a time of sanity and orderliness, then *tsetsequa* is a time of madness and creative disorder. Not only is there a division between the two times of the year, but also there is a significant qualitative difference between them.

During *tsetsequa*, the Kwakiutl live in the world of the supernatural, an exaggerated and distorted world which the shaman experiences as a result of deprivation or the taking of hallucinogenic drugs. His vision of this world is conveyed in the art used during *tsetsequa* through grotesqueness and exaggeration. Just as *baxus* and *tsetsequa* are in an inverse relationship with one another, so also are the styles of art associated with these two times of the year in a transformational relationship. But this relationship is of a different type. As we have pointed out, certain features of the animal are singled out and used for the representation of that animal in a metonymic fashion.

Fig. 18.

HOUSE FRONT OF THE CLAN G·I·G·ILQAM, NIMKISH.

Figure 19.9 House front of a *numaym* house, Nimkish. Boas (1897: 378)

In the form of the animal which is portrayed in the art of the secret societies during *tsetsequa*, one of those features is exaggerated and made grotesque. The features which represent the various animal forms portrayed during *baxus* can be said to constitute the unmarked category. The exaggeration of a single feature which characterises the art of *tsetsequa* makes it the marked category.

Within the category of birds, raven and eagle form a contrastive pair, distinguished solely by the shape of the beak. When portrayed in art, the eagle's beak is sharply curved and the raven's beak is straight. This is the way they are represented in masks used in *baxus* (see figures 19.4 and 19.10). When depicted in masks associated with *tsetsequa*, beaks are exaggerated, so that the beak of the raven becomes very long, as in the mask of the cannibal raven (figure 19.2). One would also expect that the curved beak of the eagle would be transformed into a grotesquely crooked beak of something equivalent to a cannibal eagle.

However, neither Hawthorn nor Boas makes reference to a supernatural entity, cannibal eagle, or illustrates a mask depicting such a creature. Instead, Hawthorn lists under the category of 'Hamatsa Bird-Monster Masks' the *Galokwudzuwis* (Crooked Beak), of which she has many illustrations. However, she does not see Crooked Beak as a monster form of eagle. There are two masks pictured in Boas (1897) which are clearly of the same type as Hawthorn's 'Crooked Beak' (figure 19.11, compare with figure 19.1). In the text and in the captions he identifies these as masks of *Baxbakualanuxsiwae*, who was mentioned earlier as the chief cannibal spirit, in whose house the other spirits lived (1897: 448, fig. 77, plate 30). In contrast to Boas, Hawthorn states that the presence of *Baxbakualanuxsiwae* is made known through whistling sounds and that he is invisible (1979: 45). Hence there are no objects depicting *Baxbakualanuxsiwae* in her book. By pointing out the common feature shared by all depictions of *tsetsequa* animal

Figure 19.10 Baxus form of eagle, representing the 'Ancestor of the Clan (Tsetselwalagame)', Nimkish. Top: mask in closed position. Bottom: mask in open position. Boas (1897: pl. LI)

forms, that is exaggeration and distortion, our analysis shows that there is a relationship between the artistic representations of two forms of bird-creatures with curved beaks. One is the eagle, which is the representation of a lineage ancestor in its *baxus* form. The *tsetsequa* counterpart with its exaggerated beak is the Crooked Beak (whether it represents *Baxbakualanuxsiwae* or his helper *Galokwudzuwis*).

Wolf and bear are contrasted within the category of land animals by virtue of the different ways the snout is portrayed in masks. The bear's snout is short and blunt (see figure 19.5), while that of the wolf is elongated with the nose raised at the end (figure 19.12). Features of snout and mouth are exaggerated in the forms of these animals portrayed in the *tsetsequa* winter ceremonial (figures 19.13 and 19.14).

Concluding Discussion

In this article we have been concerned to stress the importance not only of the ideas which Kwakiutl art encodes, but also of the stylistic features employed to express them. We have tried to shed light on the underlying structure of the art, as it relates to aspects of cognitive structure. In Ucko's terms, we have tried to make inferences 'from visual images about the ways the people who created and used the art thought about the relations between humans and animals' (Ucko 1989: xii). The cognitive structure to which the structure of the art is related is as follows: the Kwakiutl envision a world of living beings in which humans, animals and forces of nature exist on a single continuum. Alongside this world is another, consisting of supernatural, spiritual beings, which are seen only when humans are in contact with the supernatural. This is the world they see themselves entering during the *tsetsequa* winter ceremonials. While the everyday world of *baxus* is controlled and orderly, the world of the supernatural they enter during *tsetsequa* is relatively unrestrained and disorderly, though it has an order of its own. The Kwakiutl see a cyclical relationship between the two: they take turns in being on top. This seems to us to contrast with a vision of the supernatural as inchoate and 'becoming', in which the orderly distinctions of the natural world are not yet established.

Two concepts of time seem to be involved here. As conceived during *baxus*, time is ongoing with a present and a past. It includes a

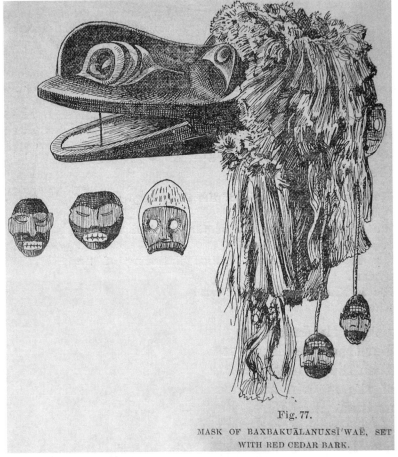

Fig. 77.

MASK OF BAXBAKUĀLANUXSĪ'WAĒ, SET
WITH RED CEDAR BARK.

Figure 19.11 Masks of *Baxbakualanuxsiwae* (Boas 1897: top, pl. 30; bottom: fig. 77). The two masks in Boas (1897) of the 'Crooked Beak' type (cf. figure 19.1)

former time when ancestral animals were transformed into men and a present during which men re-enact the myth of how this occurred at potlatches within a current sociopolitical context. However, today they are no longer in contact with the spirits of those ancestral animals. *Tsetsequa* is in a sense 'out of time' or timeless. The spirits that initiated the ancestors are still present today, and they devour the present-day initiates just as they

Figure 19.12 Wolf mask. Boas (1909: pl. XLII)

Figure 19.13 Grisly (Grizzly) bear mask, Dzawad-Eenox tribe. Boas (1909: pl. LII)

devoured their ancestors. The organization of the secret societies of *tsetsequa* is renewed and

recreated under the tutelage of the supernatural spirits each winter.

We have demonstrated how the structure of these ideas is reflected in Kwakiutl art. Just as the supernatural world represents a transformation of the 'real' world, the stylistic devices in the art for portraying the beings of that supernatural world represent exaggerations of their 'real' counterparts. The exaggeration of one element has metonymically come to stand for the whole.

As we noted earlier, men and animals are unified on the most abstract level. On a lower level of abstraction (in both life and in art) men are separated from animals. This first occurred when ancestral animals were transformed into men. In a process analogous to giving birth, men were separated from their animal ancestors. In the normal course of events, during *baxus*, men eat animals, incorporating the animals into themselves and begging their pardon for having to eat them.[9] During *tsetsequa*, initiates eat men, and in the process are human no longer but 'become' supernatural animals. The boundaries separating men, associated with culture, from animals, associated with nature, are breached in the ritual and the art becomes the means for breaching the boundaries, since the wearing of masks is the device that enables men to cross over into the other category. When they don

Figure 19.14 Wolf masks worn by dancers in the Walasaxa Wolf Dance during the winter ceremonial. Boas (1897: pl. 36)

tsetsequa masks, they are also able to carry out tabooed behaviour – to eat other men.

Leach's ideas about the relationship between art and the category of taboo are clearly relevant to this analysis. He writes of how art makes possible the crossing of cultural boundaries, and how meaning is to be found in showing the way in which art 'may be saying what may not be said' (Leach 1973: 227). Elsewhere, he argues that things which are intrinsically ambiguous with regard to a significant boundary are sacred and are therefore given exaggerated treatment (Leach 1983: 256). The art of the Kwakiutl winter ceremonial crosses just such a boundary, and the elements of grotesqueness of that art are an illustration of the stylistic use of exaggeration to portray that which is sacred. The cannibalistic creatures who devour human initiates, portrayed artistically in the winter ceremonial, demonstrate the way in which Kwakiutl art deals with tabooed topics – through distortion.

The distinction made by Pasztory (1982) between shamanic art and non-shamanic art is also relevant to the present discussion. She has noted that art on the Northwest Coast associated with shamanism is often made more grotesque and distorted in order to express the emotional content of the trance state. This differentiates these objects from 'more socially motivated' ones (1982: 12). Pasztory's explanation of the grotesqueness of shamanic art would also seem to account for the grotesqueness of *tsetsequa* art. Boas had earlier pointed to the same kind of contrast in the art of Siberian peoples. He calls attention to the distinction between the crude decoration on the clothing of shamans and the finely detailed appliqué work on the fishskin clothing worn by people on festive occasions among the Gold tribes of the Amur River area in Siberia (1955: 67).

Pursuing this point, Jonaitis (1983) observes that the shamanic art style among the Tlingit is characterized by crudeness and disregard for the conventions of crest art, because it constitutes a visual representation of the supernatural. With regard to the stylistic oppositions between shamanic and secular art, she notes that 'those shamanic art works that are antithetical to artistic standards are not examples of "bad art", but instead visual symbols of the shaman's participation in the realm of the

spirit. When the shaman wished to indicate his sacred status during his curing rituals, he displayed to the community art works that did not adhere, perhaps intentionally, to secular conventions of artistry' (1983: 131). In a later, more comprehensive work on the art of the Northern Tlingit, she sees an important distinction between secular or 'crest' art displayed at potlatches and the art of the shaman used in shamanic performances, noting both stylistic and iconographic differences (Jonaitis 1986: 25, 26, 32–3). This distinction which Jonaitis makes for Tlingit art, and the oppositional relationship she sees between the two kinds of art and associated ritual, has obvious relevance to the Kwakiutl distinction between *baxus* and *tsetsequa*. However, while Tlingit shamanic art is distinguished by the deliberate crudeness of its execution, in Kwakiutl *tsetsequa* art it is not crudity but exaggeration and distortion that signify the realm of the supernatural.

Lévi-Strauss long ago recognized that the exceptional feature of Northwest Coast art was the way in which it synthesized the serenity exemplified by Chartres and the carnival atmosphere of the amusement park (Lévi-Strauss 1943: 180). We have tried to illuminate the ways in which these contradictory images are employed in the art of the Kwakiutl. The art of *tsetsequa* conveys this contradictory feeling of both awe and buffoonery. The element of buffoonery, however, is entirely absent from the art of *baxus*. The stylistic and representational contrasts in the art associated with the two seasons epitomize the differences that the Kwakiutl themselves recognize between them. Together with the forms of social organization and ceremonial life enacted in each season, the art objects of the Kwakiutl only make sense – as we have shown – when seen as part of a complex transformational set.

NOTES

1 The use of the present tense in this discussion denotes the ethnographic present.

2 This distinction between secular and sacred is at odds with Goldman's (1975) conclusion that *all* of Kwakiutl life, including the potlatch, should be encompassed within the religious sphere.

3 At a marriage, goods passed from the bride's *numaym* to that of the groom at a potlatch. Some time later, usually after a child was born, another potlatch was held at which the bride's *numaym* gave goods to the groom's. Boas refers to this second potlatch as the repurchase of the bride.

4 'The order of seats which prevails in summer is also suspended and a new arrangement takes place. The seal society have the seats of honor in the rear of the house, and among them the highest hamatsa has the first seat, in the middle of the rear of the house. At both sides of the hamatsa society sit the bear dancers and other members of the seal society. At the extreme ends of this society sit the *nulmal*, the messengers of the hamatsa. The killer whale and rock cod societies sit in front of the seal society... The henelk and the whale society sit next to the nulmal....' (Boas 1897: 436).

5 An example of this is the family history of the *numaym* Maamtagila, which begins, 'I shall first talk about Matagila, the Grey Seagull. It is said that he was flying along inside of Gwadze. Then he took a rest at Kodagala. Then he desired to have what was a pretty beach and he took off his bird mask and became a man' (Boas 1921: 938).

6 In the mythology of some South American societies, such as the Ge, all creatures were originally human until the divinity turned some of them into animals (Wilbert & Simoneau 1984). This represents a different point of view of animal-human relations from that of the Kwakiutl.

7 Hawthorn further notes that 'with the achievement of greater prosperity and the return of open potlatching, materials came in from the southern Kwakiutl less frequently' (1979: xiv). The Kwakiutl now store their ceremonial regalia at two museums which they have established at Quadra Island and Alert Bay. These museums also contain the potlatch material seized by the Canadian Government in 1922, which has now been repatriated.

8 We owe this insight to Tim Ingold.

9 Walens considers the theme of hunger and orality to be central to Kwakiutl culture. Control of hunger is the mark of humanization. The ritual taming of the *hamatsa's* desire to eat human flesh is seen as 'a metaphoric extension of child socialization' (Walens 1981: 15, 137).

REFERENCES

Boas, F. 1897. *The social organization and secret societies of the Kwakiutl Indians* (Report of the U.S. National Museum for 1895). Washington, D.C., Smithsonian Institution.

—— 1909. *The Kwakiutl of Vancouver Island*. Memoir of the American Museum of Natural History, vol. 8, part 2; Publication of the Jessup North Pacific Expedition, vol. 5, part 2.

—— 1921. *Ethnology of the Kwakiutl*. 35th Annual Report of the Bureau of American Ethnology, Washington, D.C.

—— 1955 (1927). *Primitive art*. New York, Dover.

—— 1966. *Kwakiutl ethnography* (ed.) H. Codere. Chicago: University of Chicago Press.

Codere, H. 1950. *Fighting with property* (Monogr. Am. ethnol. Soc. 18). Locust Valley, N.Y.: J.J. Augustin.

—— 1961. Kwakiutl. In *Perspectives in American Indian culture change* (ed.) E. Spicer. Chicago: University of Chicago Press.

Drucker, P. 1941. Kwakiutl dancing societies (*Anthrop. Rec.* II, 1938–1940). Berkeley: University of California Press.

Faris, J.C. 1983. From form to content in the structural study of aesthetic systems. In *Structure and cognition in art* (ed.) D. Washburn. Cambridge: Univ. Press.

Forge, A. 1966. Art and environment in the Sepik. *Proc. R. anthrop. Inst.* 1965.

—— 1967 The Abelam artist. In *Social organization: essays presented to Raymond Firth* (ed.) M. Freedman. London, Chicago: University of Chicago Press.

—— 1973. Style and meaning in Sepik art. In *Primitive art and society* (ed.) A. Forge. London: Oxford University Press.

Goldman, I. 1975. *The mouth of heaven: an introduction to Kwakiutl religious thought*. New York: John Wiley.

Hawthorn, A. 1979. *Kwakiutl art*. Seattle: University of Washington Press.

Jonaitis, A. 1983. Style and meaning in the shamanic art of the northern Northwest Coast. In *The box of daylight: Northwest*

Coast Indian art (ed.) B. Holm. Seattle: University of Washington Press.

—— 1986. *Art of the Northern Tlingit*. Seattle: University of Washington Press.

Leach, E. 1973. Levels of communication and problems of taboo in the appreciation of primitive art. In *Primitive art and society* (ed.) A. Forge. London: Oxford University Press.

—— 1983. The gatekeepers of heaven: anthropological aspects of grandiose architecture. *J. anthrop. Res.* 39, No. 3.

Lévi-Strauss, C. 1943. The art of the Northwest Coast at the American Museum of Natural History. *Gazette des Beaux-Arts*.

—— 1979. *The way of the masks*. Seattle: University of Washington Press.

Morphy, F. 1977. The social significance of schematisation in Northwest Coast American Indian art. In *Form in indigenous art* (ed.) P.J. Ucko. New Jersey: Humanities Press.

Morphy, H. 1989. Introduction. In *Animals into art* (ed.) H. Morphy. London: Unwin Hyman.

Munn, N. 1973. *Walbiri iconography*. Ithaca: Cornell University Press.

Pasztory, E. 1982. Shamanism and North American Indian art. In *Native North American art history* (eds) Z. Methews & A. Jonaitis. Palo Alto, CA: Peak Publications.

Reid, K.S. 1976. The origins of the Tsetsequa and Baxus: a study of Kwakiutl prayers, myths and ritual. Thesis, University of British Columbia.

Rosman, A. and P. Rubel 1971. *Feasting with mine enemy: rank and exchange among Northwest Coast Societies*. New York: Columbia University Press.

Ucko, P. 1989. Foreword. In *Animals into art* (ed.) H. Morphy. London: Unwin Hyman.

Vastokas, J. 1978. Cognitive aspects of Northwest Coast art. In *Art in society* (eds) M. Greenhalgh and V. Megam. New York: St Martin's Press.

Walens, S. 1981. *Feasting with cannibals*. Princeton: University Press.

Wilbert, J. and K. Simoneau 1984. *Folk literature of the Ge people*. Los Angeles: U.C.L.A. Latin American Center Publications.

Wingert, P. 1949. *American Indian sculpture: a study of the Northwest Coast*. New York: J.J. Augustin.

Witherspoon, G. 1977. *Language and art in the Navajo universe*. Ann Arbor: University of Michigan Press.

20

Sacred Art and Spiritual Power
An Analysis of Tlingit Shamans' Masks

Aldona Jonaitis

Among the Tlingit of southeastern Alaska, the shaman plays a prominent role in assuring the survival of his group: he cures the sick, controls the weather, guarantees success in warfare and banishes malevolent supernaturals such as witches.[1] To achieve these ends, the shaman manipulates a variety of spiritually potent objects, such as charms, batons, knives and rattles. Among the most important of these articles are the face masks which the shaman dons at both private healing ceremonies and public displays of power, transforming himself into the spirit-helpers each mask represents.

The Tlingit call these spirit-helpers *yek*. Masks depict a wide variety of both zoomorphic *yek*, such as land otters, devilfish or octopus, hawks, ravens, wolves, and kingfishers, as well as anthropomorphic *yek* such as angry men, peacemakers, chiefs, old men and young women. Understanding the meaning and function of a single mask presents no problem: each represents one of the shaman's spirit assistants which can assume the form of either a human or an animal. During a healing ceremony or power-displaying ritual, the shaman puts on a mask and turns into that *yek*, behaving like a bird, a wolf, a young woman, or an angry man, depending on the identity of the spirit on the mask. The Tlingit shaman, however, does not wear just one mask at these ceremonies, for he owns a set of several masks, and wears them in a series.

The shaman's sequential donning of a set of masks and consequent transformation into a series of different beings raises several questions. The first involves the contents of these sets: is there some quality to a set of masks, some recurrent pattern observable among the masks, some special relationship between the masks, that we can identify as the principle which organizes the assortment of masks in a set? The second question involves the ritual consequences of wearing masks sequentially: even though we know that a mask is a highly potent shamanic article in its own right, does the act of donning a set of masks result in some special dimension of power that the donning of a single mask would not provide? The answers to both of these questions which are, as we shall see, interconnected, is yes. We propose that the process of wearing a set of masks organized according to an identifiable principle facilitates the shaman's acquisition of

From Zena Mathews and Aldona Jonaitis (eds.), *Native North American Art History: Selected Readings* (Palo Alto, CA: Peek Publications, 1982), pp. 119–136.

power and enables him to complete his tasks successfully.

To prove this assertion, we will focus on one particular set of masks which were owned by a shaman of the X̣at'kA' ayi kin group, who lived in the Yakutat area during the nineteenth century (figures 20.1 through 20.8). How we have access to this and other sets of shamanic masks is of interest. During the late nineteenth century, an extraordinary individual, Lieutenant George T. Emmons of the United States Navy traveled up and down the Alaskan coast, recording aspects of Tlingit culture and collecting examples of their art. He knew that the Tlingit buried shamans along with their sacred implements in small grave houses which were far from the villages. Emmons, or his associates, located these graves and removed their contents. He then sent these pieces, along with copious notes on their meaning and function, to various museums across the country.

It is most fortunate that we have available for study this particular set of a shaman's masks, since it was found in a particularly elaborate grave. This X̣at'kA' ayi shaman had, at his disposal, not only eight masks but also thirty-four other objects such as rattles,

cedar bark neckrings, ivory necklaces, bone charms, knives, clubs, carved figures, a comb, and various pieces of twigs, shells, roots, and parts of dead animals. Emmons sent this entire kit to the Field Museum of Natural History in Chicago, where it is available for study.[2]

The eight masks from this kit depict a variety of *yek* in both human and animal form. Three masks are animals: a wolf (figure 20.1), a kingfisher (figure 20.2), and a hawk (figure 20.3); two are humans: an old woman (figure 20.4) and a Tlingit spirit (figure 20.5); and three are humans associated in some way with animals: a Tlingit spirit with a devilfish (octopus) coming out of his mouth (figure 20.6), a spirit of a Tlingit shaman with a headdress of a composite land otter and devilfish (figure 20.7), and an angry spirit with ears of a bear (figure 20.8).

Why does the shaman have *yek* in both human and animal forms? According to the foremost contemporary interpreter of Tlingit culture, Frederica de Laguna (1972:682, 835–6; 1973:227), a *yek* is the ghost of a dead person which can assume either zoomorphic or anthropomorphic shape. Ghosts of warriors who died in battle appear at times as birds, ghosts of people who died normal

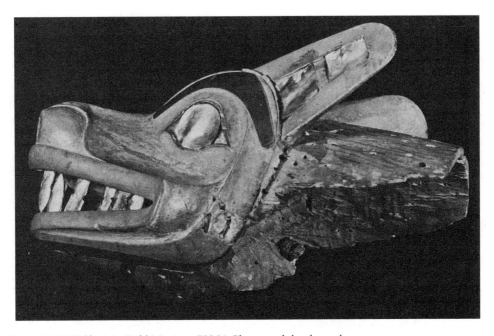

Figure 20.1 Wolf spirit. Field Museum 79254. Photograph by the author

Figure 20.2 Kingfisher spirit. Field Museum 77844. Photograph by the author

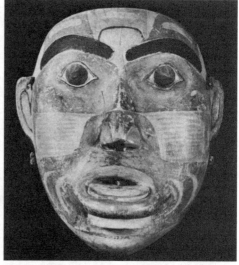

Figure 20.3 Hawk spirit. Field Museum 77843. Photograph by the author

Figure 20.4 Spirit of an old Tlingit woman. Field Museum 79255. Photograph by the author

Figure 20.5 Tlingit spirit. Field Museum 79257. Photograph courtesy of Field Museum of Natural History, Chicago

Figure 20.6 Tlingit spirit with a devilfish coming out of its mouth. Field Museum 79253. Photograph by the author

deaths may take the form of land animals, and ghosts of drowning victims are sometimes visible as sea animals. In the view of the Tlingit,

such metamorphosis from human to animal form occurs on a regular basis in the supernatural world.[3]

Although on occasion a shaman inherits *yek* which were originally possessed by an ancestral shaman, most often he must acquire his *yek* on an initiatory vision quest, a solitary expedition of approximately eight days into the woods or onto deserted beaches. During this event, the supernatural beings which are to become this shaman's spirit-helpers approach him in zoomorphic form and drop dead at his feet. Since, for the Tlingit, spiritual potency, knowledge of the sacred world, and profound curative powers are all contained within the tongues of these creatures, the novice shaman excises the tongue of each *yek*-animal and ties them all to a bundle of twigs. This bundle becomes one of the shaman's most valuable possessions. By the time his vision quest is over, the shaman has acquired about eight tongues, and thus has at his service eight *yek* which he then portrays in both human and animal form on his numerous artworks.[4]

We should point out here that eight is a highly significant number for the Tlingit. As we have seen, our sample set contains eight masks; the novice shaman embarks on an eight-day vision quest and collects eight tongues. Eight appears in other contexts as well: a chief must host eight potlatches to properly validate his status; a young girl must undergo ritual seclusion for eight seasons (two years); the human body is "symbolically formulated in terms of the 'eight joints' or 'eight big bones' " (de Laguna 1954:175–76). For the Tlingit, eight appears to be the number of totality, completion, and wholeness. Considering the importance that the Tlingit ascribe to that number, we must assume that it is not accidental that the Dry Bay set contains eight masks; presumably, this indicates a complete set.[5]

We propose that the identity of those masks is also not accidental. As we have already mentioned, two basic types of mask occur in the set: those that depict humans and those that depict animals. Humans and animals are complements of one another, that is, although each is a distinct order of living being, both together constitute the entirety of living beings. Complementary pairs, such as human/animal, form a whole. As we analyze the contents of the Dry

Figure 20.7 Spirit of a Tlingit shaman with representations over the forehead of combination land otter and devilfish. Field Museum 79256. Photograph by the author

Figure 20.8 Angry spirit wearing bear's ears. Field Museum 77845. Photograph by the author

Bay set, several other complementary pairs become evident: there is a female mask as well as several male masks; both an old spirit and some young ones; and a malevolent, angry spirit along with some benevolent beings. Since animals from the three cosmic levels of air, sea, and land occur in this set, we also have a complementary triplet. All eight masks belong to subsets composed of members which have complementary relations with each other. Let us now look more closely at the five subsets which constitute the illustrated kit.

Animal/Human

The most fundamental complementary pair in this kit is animal/human. Since *yek* can appear either way, it is not surprising that masks depict them in both forms. However, as we analyze the manner in which the Tlingit artist renders each version of *yek*, it becomes evident that he by no means delineates with any clarity the dividing line between animals and humans. Indeed, we can interpret the Tlingit carver's depiction of *yek* on masks as an expression of the intimate relations between humans and animals in the spiritual world.

In the Dry Bay kit, only four masks illustrate beings which fall clearly into the categories "human" or "animal." The old woman (figure 20.4) and the Tlingit spirit (figure 20.5) are straightforward anthropomorphic faces; the wolf (figure 20.1) and the kingfisher (figure 20.2) are relatively naturalistic zoomorphic images. By incorporating both human and animal elements, the other four masks convey the interconnections between these two complements. Around the mouth of the Tlingit spirit in figure 20.6 are strands of devilfish suckers which appear to be integral parts of his facial features; on the brow of the shaman spirit in figure 20.7 are composite land otter/devilfish creatures; instead of human ears, the angry spirit in figure 20.8 wears the ears of a bear. None of these masks is strictly human; neither is the hawk mask (figure 20.3) solely animal, since its face is actually that of a human whose nose has become pointed and somewhat beak-like. As depicted on these masks, the whole world of living beings is not composed of two dualistically opposed halves but is instead formed of a series of beings which we can place on a continuum, from animals that look like animals through animals that look human and humans affiliated with animals to humans unaffiliated with animals.

Animals of the Air/Animals of the Land/Animals of the Water

For the Tlingit, there are three levels that constitute the entire cosmos. Ghosts that died in different fashions inhabit each level, assuming the animal form appropriate to their level. In the illustrated kit, the whole, tiered universe is represented by the kingfisher and hawk of the air, the wolf and land otter of the land, and the devilfish of the sea.

Several of these animals are not entirely restricted to the cosmic level in which they reside. For example, the kingfisher dives beneath the surface of the water, temporarily becoming a being of the sea, the land otter swims in the water as easily as it runs on the land, and the devilfish sometimes climbs onto wet rocks and damp sand.[6] Unlike the wolf and hawk which remain on one level most of the time, these three animals straddle cosmic levels. Thus, among the animals in this kit, we can discern a continuum of beings analogous to the continuum proposed above in respect to humans and animals, namely: animals of the air/animals of the air and water/animals of the land/animals of the land and water/animals of the water and land.

Male/Female

Every living species is composed of the fundamental complementary pair of male and female. In the Dry Bay kit, most anthropomorphic masks depict male spirits, but one, shown in figure 20.4, illustrates a female. As is conventional in Tlingit art, the labret indicates femininity. Although the masks in this kit are clearly one sex or the other, there is a kit, found near Chilkoot by Emmons and donated to the American Museum of Natural History (numbers 19/850–53) in which gender is somewhat blurred. This kit contains a mask of an "old dead woman" (19/851) as well as one of a man (19/850, ill. Wardwell 1978, pl. 5) which Emmons describes as "one of eight brothers, one a hermaphrodite." Although it does not appear that this mask depicts that hermaphrodite itself, its intimate

relationship to a being of questionable sexuality implies that, in the case of the American Museum of Natural History kit at least, the demarcation between male and female is not so clearly defined as it might be.

Old/Young

Any human community consists of individuals whose ages range from very youthful to quite aged. To express this type of wholeness, the Dry Bay kit has some masks with full, fleshy faces (figure 20.5) and wide open, energetic mouths (figures 20.6, 20.8)[7] which convey dynamic youthfulness, and one, the old woman mask (figure 20.4) whose barely-opened mouth, surrounded by painted lines, communicates great age.[8]

Malevolent/Benevolent

This last pair concerns the temperament of the mask spirits. We can contrast the hostile, aggressive character of the angry spirit (figure 20.8) whose bear's ears suggest warfare[9] with the more placid, sedate old woman (figure 20.4) and Tlingit spirit (figure 20.5) whose face seems emotionally neutral. In other kits, such differences in disposition are even more clearly spelled out: in the American Museum of Natural History there is one kit (E/396–403) that includes both an "angry man" (E/397) and a "peacemaker" (E/401), both illustrated in de Laguna(1972, pl. 192), and a second kit (E/1591–1601) that contains an "angry man" (E/1592, illustrated in de Laguna, 1972, pl. 202) as well as a "good natured spirit" (E/1597).

The eight masks from the Dry Bay kit compose five subsets. Some masks belong to more than one subset, such as the old woman which forms part of the complementary subsets male/female, animal/human, old/young, and malevolent/benevolent. The masks of a subset are not necessarily in polar opposition to each other since they often occupy specific points in a continuum. An example of this is the series of masks from animal to human that together constitute an entire or whole entity. For this reason we have specifically used the term "complementary subsets" instead of "dualistic groupings." We can approach neither the masks within the subsets nor the subsets themselves in a simplistic manner, because both are complex and multi-referential. As scholars such as Claude Lévi-Strauss (1963, 1966), Victor Turner (1967, 1969, 1974), and Barbara Myerhoff (1974) have discussed at great length, a potent and effective symbol system is characterized by such complexity.

Since we have established that there is an organizational principle in the set of masks from Dry Bay, it is necessary now to explore the ritual significance of this principle. We propose that this particular organization of masks facilitates the successful completion of the shaman's responsibilities during masking ceremonies. To prove this, we must first examine the occasions during which the shaman wears masks so that we can identify the significance of complementary subsets in terms of those rituals.

The Tlingit shaman wears his mask at both private healing ceremonies and public displays of power. In both of these events, the main purpose of masking is to enable the shaman to control malevolent supernaturals, particularly witches. To provide a sense of what the Tlingit shaman faces, we have the following description of the Tlingit witch by de Laguna (1972: 728).

> The witch was feared and loathed because there was no antisocial, evil or unnatural act of which he was not believed capable: dishonesty, shamelessness, incest, mysterious powers of locomotion or of bodily transformation and, above all, corroding spite and jealousy that made him cause the illness or death of those he envied.

These despicable but dangerous beings are local villagers – usually men – whom other witches had recruited.

Witches apparently cause disease either by performing some magical ritual over the food leavings, hair, nail parings or bits of clothing of the victim, or by magically injecting an object into the victim. In order to cure a bewitched individual, the Tlingit shaman performs a variety of acts: he sings, dances, shakes rattles, beats drums, manipulates some of his supernaturally potent items, such as the charms, batons, knives and amulets from his large kit, massages the ailing part of the patient's body, sucks out the disease-inducing object, and tries to determine which member of his village performed the witchcraft. This last act has an element of brutality to it, since once the shaman has identified the guilty witch, he has his associates capture him, then bind and torture him by withholding food, forcing him to drink salt water, and beating him, until he confesses.[10] Once the witch confesses, the patient recovers. It is during this lengthy and complex process of healing that the shaman dons his set of masks, which appear to confer on him the power needed to overcome the forces of the witch.

Emmons has provided us with a description of how one particular shaman from Angoon wears his eight masks (Thomas Burke Memorial Washington State Museum 1344–1351). When a family calls on this shaman to cure an ailing member, he comes to their house and dons a series of four masks, transforming himself into the four *yek* they represent. At that point, he demands and receives payment, and then checks the condition of his patient. If the patient has recovered, the shaman's task is completed; however, if the patient still is ill, the shaman requests more payment and dons his other four masks. Apparently, the power which the shaman receives from his set of masks is cumulative: on some occasions, when an illness is not especially severe, the power from four masks is sufficient to ensure a cure, while on other occasions of more serious affliction, the shaman needs the additional power which only the total of eight masks will provide. There is apparently an ever-expanding "circle" of power surrounding the shaman which increases in proportion to the number of masks he has put on.

The masking process creates an aura of supernatural potency for the shaman at the other event during which he wears masks, the great public power display held during the winter. The following description of such a ritual is taken from a note on shamanism by Emmons in the Provincial Archives, British Columbia:[11]

> As winter is a time of festivity and feasting with the Thlinkets, and in ancient days when the power of the Doctors was greater and to preserve this power it was necessary to constantly keep themselves before the people so on many occasions shamans danced before the clan assembled. The drums together with dancing sticks and the Doctor's rattles accompanied the chant which told of the power of the

evil spirits, the mischief they had done and the strength of the doctor to subdue them and bring them under his control, and as he danced he constantly changed his headdress, each one representing some spirit and as his clan recognized another mask they would vary the chant so throughout the shaman's wardrobe of masks, so the more numerous and elaborate the shaman's wardrobe of masks, the greater his power to a great degree.

In this quote, Emmons specifically mentions that the more masks the shaman owns, the more powerful he is.

We could perhaps at this point terminate our discussion with the following solution to our question of why a Tlingit shaman owns a set of masks: if one mask embodies a certain amount of power, then the quantity of power is approximately doubled by two masks, tripled by three masks, and so on. Although this equation may be true, it avoids a fundamental question that must now be posed: why does a mask, which is really a piece of wood carved to depict an animal or human, become the embodiment of spiritual strength which is transferred to the shaman when he wears it? We cannot say that a mask has this kind of potency because the shaman who owns it says so, for individual shamans do not determine the efficacy of their paraphernalia.

Marcel Mauss, in his significant work on shamanism and related phenomena, *A General Theory of Magic* (1972, first published 1902/03), pointed out the very important point that it is never the shaman or "magician" who ascribes qualities of supernatural power to either himself or the implements he manipulates; it is instead the social group to which the shaman belongs that decrees what is and what is not spiritually potent. As Mauss explains in this book, the manner in which the social group invests an individual with the ability to fulfill the role of shaman is complex, subtle and often not explicit. The manner by which the Tlingit ascribe spiritual potency to their shamans' masks is similarly subtle and involves the actual process of wearing masks specifically organized into complementary subsets.

To understand how the groupings of Tlingit masks in kits facilitate acquisition of shamanic power, we must first review some anthropological theory on the relationship between spiritual potency and social order. This theory is based on the writings of two of Mauss' contemporaries, Arnold van Gennep (1960, first published 1909) and Emile Durkheim (1965, first published 1912), who state that humans organize their world into two complementary orders, the profane and the sacred. The profane order, governed by an assortment of secular rules and structured according to clearly defined component parts, is the relatively safe and secure realm of everyday life. The sacred world is the antithesis or reversal of the profane: that which is ordered in the profane realm becomes disordered in the sacred; that which is defined becomes anomalous; that which is heterogenous becomes homogenous.[12] It is necessary to bear in mind that the sacred world is not necessarily geographically separate from the profane, as is the case in the western concept of heaven and earth, for the sacred and profane can be quite close to one another; what matters is that they remain separate. For a human to enter and exit the sacred realm, which is by definition dangerous, he must follow strict procedures which van Gennep termed rites of passage.[13]

In addition to being dangerous, the sacred arena is also profoundly powerful. If an individual wishes to have some of this power invested onto himself, he must in some way incorporate an antithesis to social order, since, as we mentioned above, that which embodies the sacred is actually a reversal of some element of the profane. By virtue of the masks he wears during healing and power-displaying ceremonies, the Tlingit shaman experiences just this sort of reversal of secular order. To explain this, let us describe the shaman's position in the profane structure of his society and the kinds of reversals he experiences to that structure.

When the shaman is not practicing some ritual, he is living in a society rigidly structured according to definite rules, such as rules of status that determine one's place in the hierarchy, rules of marriage which govern whom one may or may not marry, rules of economic exchange which dictate how one produces and distributes goods and services, even rules of etiquette which specify where one sits at a potlatch.[14] These rules, which assure the smooth functioning of Tlingit secular life, are based on the clear definition of every individual's rank, kinship affiliation, sex, age, role and place of residence. The Tlingit shaman too participates in this group, for he is a male member of a certain age of a ranked house group in a specific village married to a woman from the opposite moiety. Thus, we can assert that in terms of these qualities, any Tlingit shaman is firmly entrenched in the profane order of his society.

There are, however, other qualities which set the Tlingit shaman somewhat apart from his group. Whereas the layperson is relatively neat in appearance, the shaman has ragged nails and long, snarled, uncut hair. Clans store their crest objects such as boxes, spoons, and Chilkat blankets inside the lineage houses, but shamans store their paraphernalia out-of-doors, bringing them into houses only during healing seances. And, according to Oberg (1973:95), while gift-giving is the proper mode of payment for services rendered within the group, a shaman bargains with his customers, something only done at other times with strangers and foreigners. When he dies, the shaman – like the one from Dry Bay whose masks we are now studying – is carried to a grave house far from his village and entombed therein. Laypersons, in contrast, are cremated, and their ashes placed in a repository behind their lineage house. These oppositions to secular order place the shaman into the sacred realm.[15]

One might, at this point, suggest that there is a contradiction here: how can the shaman be both in his profane order *and* in the sacred domain? This is, however, not a contradiction at all; the ability of the shaman to reside in both the profane realm of social structure and the sacred world of the spirits defines his role and distinguishes him from the layperson.[16] This intermediate position, however, does not invest the shaman with abundant power; it is far too close to the profane order for that bestowal to happen. As we shall see, it is the process of masking which removes the shaman far enough from secular order so that his spiritual potency is adequate for the tasks he must perform.

As an example of this process of acquiring power by a series of acts that progressively remove a shaman from the temporal realm, let us hypothesize a scenario of the Dry Bay shaman wearing his set of masks. He starts off

as a member of profane society, but then in a sequence transforms himself into an old woman, a younger man, an angry man, a spirit associated with a devilfish, a spirit affiliated with both a land otter and a devilfish, a hawk, a kingfisher, and a wolf. During this process, the shaman effectively disregards all the rules of social order which govern his group: he becomes several different beings of different ages living in different locales. He blurs the distinctions – so crucial to profane order – between complements: by becoming both man and woman, he confuses the differentiation between the sexes; by becoming both human and animal, he confounds the distinction between nature and culture; by becoming animals of the three cosmic levels, he obscures geographic separations; by becoming old and young he blurs linear time; by becoming malevolent and benevolent, he confuses personality-types. He does all this while wearing several masks which in themselves confound the distinctions between complements.

This blurring is a kind of reversal of secular order. As the shaman dons more and more of these masks, he successively obscures the distinctions and definitions that are the foundations of profane existence. As he distances himself from social structure, he becomes more and more a member of the antithetical realm of the sacred and acquires as a consequence more and more of the supernatural efficacy it embodies. It is thus the process of donning a series of masks which are organized into complementary subsets that confers spiritual power upon this Dry Bay shaman.

On the basis of the information provided so far, one could argue that the pattern of masks in the Dry Bay kit is exceptional, that the particular organization we have discussed is accidental and will not hold true for other kits of masks. We propose, however, that the complementary subsets of our illustrated kit adhere to an organizational model of other Tlingit mask kits. To prove this basic principle, we have available nineteen other kits of masks, most of which were collected by Emmons. The contents of these kits fall into the same five subsets already mentioned as well as two others, namely, dead/alive and Tlingit/foreign.[17] Table 20.1 lists the source and contents of these kits and the complementary subsets they contain; note that only two kits contain

Table 20.1 Tlingit mask kits[a]

Kit no.	Present location and source	Subjects of masks, references to illustrations	Complementary subsets
1.	Field Museum (FM) 77843–77845; 79253–79257 (8 masks) Dry Bay, Yakutat subdivision	hawk, kingfisher, angry spirit, Tlingit spirit with devilfish coming out of mouth, wolf, old Tlingit woman, Tlingit shaman, Tlingit spirit (all illustrated here)	animal/human; land/sea/air; male/female; old/young; benevolent/malevolent
2.	FM 79249–79250; 77885–77888 (6 masks) Alsek R., Yakutat subdivision	very old man, old woman, dead shaman with mice on cheeks, young woman, sculpin, old man (Wardwell 1964, pl. 13)	animal/human; male/female; dead/alive; old/young
3.	American Museum of Natural History (AMNH) E/340, 342, 343, 345 (4 masks) Dry Bay, Yakutat subdivision	cold north wind, (de Laguna 1972, pl. 180), land otter man (de Laguna 1972, pl. 180, Wardwell 1978, pl. 6) old man (de Laguna 1972, pl. 180, Wardwell 1978, pl. 7), angry man (de Laguna 1972, pl. 180)	animal/human; old/young
4.	AMNH E/396–403 (8 masks) Dry Bay, Yakutat subdivision	devilfish (de Laguna 1972, pl. 192), angry man (de Laguna 1972, pl. 192), dog (de Laguna 1972, pl. 190), land otter man (Wardwell 1964, pl. 10, de Laguna 1972, pl. 191; King 1979, pl. 81), peacemaker (de Laguna 1972, pl. 192), chief (de Laguna 1972, pl. 191) angry spirit (de Laguna 1972, pl. 192)	animal/human; land/sea/air; malevolent/benevolent
5.	AMNH E/409–417 (9 masks) Dry Bay, Yakutat subdivision	good natured spirit (da Laguna 1972, pl. 188, Wardwell 1978, pl. 4), drowned man turning into land otter (de Laguna 1972, pl. 189, Wardwell 1978, pl. 3), singing shaman (de Laguna 1972, pl. 189), Tlingit (de Laguna 1972, pl. 188), dead man (de Laguna 1972, pl. 188, Wardwell 1978, pl. 2), shaman (de Laguna 1972, pl. 188), shaman, raven (de Laguna 1972, pl. 189), sculpin (de Laguna 1972, pl. 188)	animal/human; land/sea/air; dead/alive
6.	AMNH E/653–657 (5 masks) Peril Straits, Sitka subdivision	hawk, sun, young man who lives above, head man of cloud spirits, old woman	animal/human; male/female; old/young
7.	AMNH E/1490–1493 (4 masks) Hot Springs, Sitka subdivision	dead Tlingit woman, three dead Tlingit men	male/female

(continued)

Table 20.1 (continued)

Kit no.	Present location and source	Subjects of masks, references to illustrations	Complementary subsets
8.	AMNH E/1591–1601 (11 masks) Alsek R., Yakutat subdivision	puffin (Boas 1927, Fig. 207, de Laguna 1972, pl. 201), angry man (de Laguna 1972, pl. 202) sun (de Laguna 1972, pl. 202), small freshwater fish (de Laguna 1972, pl. 202), shaman who lives under earth, warrior (de Laguna 1972, pl. 201), wolf (de Laguna 1972, pl. 200, Wardwell 1978, pl. 17), chief, ice man (de Laguna 1972, pl. 200), young woman who lives in woods – a "good spirit" (de Laguna 1972, pl. 202), good-natured spirit.	animal/human; land/sea/air; male/female; malevolent/ benevolent
9.	AMNH E/1625–1631 (8 masks) Dry Bay, Yakutat subdivision	"eight women, four old, and four young, who live in the clouds" (de Laguna 1972, pls. 206, 207; Boas 1927, Fig. 210)	old/young
10.	AMNH E/1654–1660 (7 masks) Akwe R., Yakutat subdivision	Tlingit with frog spirit, kingfisher, dead Tlingit (de Laguna 1972, pl. 197), angry man (de Laguna 1972, pl. 197), woman (de Laguna 1972, pl. 197), dead shaman, young girl (de Laguna 1972, pl. 197)	animal/human; male/female; dead/alive; malevolent/ benevolent
11.	AMNH E/2358-2361 (4 masks) Angoon, Killisnoo subdivision	land otter, man, old man, old woman	animal/human; male/female; old/ young
12.	AMNH E/2683-2690 (8 masks) Berner's Bay, Auk subdivision	devilfish (Wardwell 1978, pl. 8), sun dog, spirit living in a lake, land otter, porpoise, trout canoe, spirit living in stars, deer.	animal/human; land/sea/air
13.	AMNH 19/850-53 (4 masks) Chilkoot area, Chilkat subdivision	one of eight brothers, one a hermaphrodite (Wardwell 1978, pl. 5), dead woman, eagle (Vancouver 1967, pl. 11), wolf (Feder 1971, pl. 36)	animal/human; male/female; dead/alive
14.	AMNH 19/881-888 (8 masks) Killisnoo subdivision	Athapaskan chief, Haida man, eagle, Athapaskan, old woman, owl, moon, Athapaskan	animal/human; male/female; young/old; Tlingit/foreigner
15.	AMNH 19/868, 870, 872, 874, 876, 880 (6 masks) Yakutat subdivision	Athapaskan (de Laguna 1972, pl. 184), Athapaskan woman with hawk bill (de Laguna 1972, pl. 184), Athapaskan man (de Laguna 1972, pl. 186), Tlingit (de Laguna 1972, pl. 184), owl (de Laguna 1972, pl. 184), mosquito (de Laguna 1972, pl. 185)	animal/human; male/female; Tlingit/foreigner

16.	Thomas Burke Museum (TBM) 2029-2036 (8 masks) Yakutat subdivision	hawk, shaman with fighting headdress, old man, bear with land otter/devilfish on chin (Inverarity 1950, pl. 77, de Laguna 1972, pl. 181, Jonaitis 1980, pl. 2), land otter-man, wolf, mosquito, singing shaman with land otters on face	animal/human; land/sea/air; old/young; malevolent/benevolent
17.	TBM 1344-1351 (8 masks) Angoon, Killisnoo subdivision	sea gull, dogfish, brown bear, old Tlingit woman, moon, land otter-man, eagle, owl	animal/human; land/sea/air; male/female; old/young
18.	Princeton University Museum of Natural History 3911, 3922, 3923, 3957 TBM 2256, 2271 (6 masks).[b] Yakutat, Yakutat subdivision	hawk (Baird, 1965:8, Collins et al., 1973, pl. 302, de Laguna 1972, pl. 174) shark (Baird 1965:8, de Laguna 1972, pl. 174), devilfish (Baird 1965:8, de Laguna 1972, pl. 174, Collins et al. 1973, pl. 301, Furst 1973/74, p. 51, King 1979, pl. 86), singing man (de Laguna 1972, pl. 174, King 1979, pl. 88), singing man (de Laguna 1972, pl. 174), very old Tlingit woman (de Laguna 1972, pl. 174)	animal/human; male/female; young/old
19.	Bureau of American Ethnology neg. nos. 3089-a-1 and 3 (4 masks) Alsek R., Yakutat subdivision	cross spirit, spirit put on in war with frog, raven, land otter-man, starfish painted on cheeks (all in Swanton, 1908, lvii, de Laguna 1972, pl. 194)	animal/human; land/sea/air; malevolent/benevolent
20.	Kit described by Emmons in Provincial Archives, Victoria (8 masks) Kluckwan, Chilkat subdivision	shaman, spirit which enters shaman through palm of the hand, dead spirit, dead woman, woman, kingfisher, devilfish, sculpin	animal/human; male/female; dead/alive

[a] Emmons collected kits 1–17 and the Thomas Burke Museum masks from kit 18. Professor William Libbey of Princeton University collected the first four masks in kit 18 (see Baird 1965, for more information on this kit). Kit 19 are models of masks Swanton obtained (see Swanton 1908, pp. 467–68). Kit 20 is a list of masks described by Emmons in his notes in the Provincial archives.
[b] De Laguna (1972:692) asserts that these masks originally came from the same kit but ended up in different museums.

one subset (numbers 7 and 9), and two contain two subsets (numbers 3 and 12), while the other sixteen contain between three and five subsets. This distribution of masks is, in all probability, not random; indeed, it strongly indicates that the Tlingit shaman, consciously or unconsciously, must transform into several beings which have complementary relations with each other in order successfully to heal the sick and display his power.[18]

Let us conclude with a brief reflection on the process by which a Tlingit shaman acquires power. When we described the masking ritual of the shaman from Angoon, we pointed out how the shaman put on four masks and accrued a certain amount of power, and then put on four more, gaining yet more power. Evidently, the first four masks removed the shaman a certain distance from social order and invested him with the amount of potency that may have been enough to ensure a cure. If not, the next four masks removed him even farther and pushed him more deeply into the realm of the sacred.

Van Gennep (1960:26) notes that groups perceive strangers or outsiders as "sacred, endowed with magico-religious powers and supernaturally benevolent or malevolent." In order to prevent such potency from overwhelming the group, the stranger must be ritually incorporated into that group by "an exchange of gifts, an offer of food... or the provision of lodging" (van Gennep 1960:28). In contrast, the Tlingit shaman experiences the opposite of this, for he actually *becomes* a stranger to his group in the process of masking. The power he accrues in this process enables him to assure the survival of his group by combatting the forces of witchcraft. Once he has done that, the Tlingit shaman can remove his last mask, cease being a stranger to his group, and return to secular order, having once again succeeded in controlling the malevolent forces that threaten society.

NOTES

1 Since the main authorities on Tlingit culture agree on most aspects of shamanic practice, I present here a synthesis of the data on shamanism from the following sources:

Krause 1956, pp. 194–203, Swanton 1908, pp. 463–69, Olson 1961, pp. 207–16, Olson 1967, pp. 110–15, de Laguna 1972, pp. 669–725, Oberg 1973, pp. 17–21, and notes by G. T. Emmons in the American Museum of Natural History, Field Museum of Natural History, Thomas Burke Memorial Washington State Museum, and Provincial Archives, Victoria, B.C.

2 It is not at all clear who actually collected the eight illustrated masks. The curator of Northwest Coast anthropology at the Field Museum, Ronald Weber, makes the following comments: "[This collection] was collected by Emmons but appears to have been received from Spuhn who was a Hudson's Bay Company agent. Spuhn may have actually done the collecting over a number of years.... It is not fully clear to me that it was Emmons who invaded the Dry Bay grave house. It may have been Spuhn or it may have been the Tlingit people who brought the pieces to Spuhn to be sold" (letter, Jan. 8, 1981). If it was indeed Spuhn who sold the pieces to Emmons, who then sold them to the Field Museum, it is still clearly Emmons who provided the documentation on them.

3 Numerous Tlingit myths relate episodes of metamorphosis (see Swanton 1909). In addition, two supernatural beings can undergo metamorphosis with extreme ease: witches, who turn into birds or other animals, and land otters, which are animals that were once human and which endeavor to transform other humans into land otters. For more information on witches and land otters, see Krause 1956, pp. 186–88; 200–01, Swanton 1908, pp. 469–71, Swanton 1909, pp. 29–33; 187–89, Olson 1961, pp. 216–18, Olson 1967, pp. 115–16, de Laguna 1954, pp. 187–89, de Laguna 1972, pp. 727–55.

4 The depiction of a long tongue, probably the symbol of transference of spiritual power and possession of curing ability, appears on numerous shamanic art works, such as masks (Maurer 1977, pl. 493), rattles (Johnson 1973, pl. 31), and charms (Harner and Elsasser 1965:100).

5 Of the twenty kits studied here (see table 20.1), eight (40%), contain eight masks and 5 (25%) contain four masks. Being one-half

of eight, four is also significant to the Tlingit. Since 65 percent of all kits contain four or eight masks, we must conclude that these are the desirable numbers of masks in a kit.

6 For more information on the significance on the land otter and the devilfish in Tlingit art, see Jonaitis 1978 and 1980.

7 Emmons (American Museum of Natural History E/411 and 19/874, Thomas Burke Memorial Washington State Museum 2030) sometimes describes these open-mouthed faces as individuals who are "singing." It should be mentioned here that there are a variety of mouth-forms possible on these shaman's masks, namely, closed (fig. 2), slightly open (figs. 4, 5, 7), slightly open and revealing teeth (figs. 1, 3), wide open and diamond-shaped (figs. 6, 8), wide open and circular (Swanton 1908, pl. lviii, de Laguna 1972, pl. 194), and open to reveal something inside, like a tongue (de Laguna 1972, pl. 188, Wardwell 1978, pl. 2) or another being (Dockstader 1966, pls. 87, 88, Coe 1977, pl. 267). It is not clear what meanings, if any, these mouth-forms have.

8 Deeply incised or painted lines all over a face also indicate age; see Collins et al. 1973, pl. 300 and Wardwell 1978, pls. 7 and 11.

9 Tlingit warriors sometimes wear headdresses that represent the ears of a bear; see Wardwell 1978, pls. 15 and 16 for illustrations of examples.

10 The binding and torturing of a witch is a frequent image on the so-called "oyster catcher rattle," an instrument which is, according to Emmons (notes, Provincial Archives, Victoria, British Columbia), particularly efficacious against witches. Illustrations of such rattles can be found in Collins et al. 1973, pls. 349, 351 and Maurer 1977, pl. 494.

11 Lt. Emmons occasionally lapsed into poor grammar in these notes; I have left in all such errors.

12 A great deal of contemporary anthropological literature that has its theoretical roots in the writings of Durkheim, van Gennep and Mauss analyses, from numerous perspectives, the relations between the sacred and profane. See, for example, Leach 1961, Douglas 1966, 1975, Turner 1967, 1969, 1974, 1978, Rigby 1968, Hieb 1972, Babcock 1978.

13 For a study of the symbols of art which accompanies such a rite of passage, see Jonaitis 1981.

14 For more detailed information on Tlingit social structure, see Krause 1956, pp. 62–173; Swanton 1908, 415–50; Olson 1967, pp. 5–110; McClellen 1954; Averkieva 1971; de Laguna 1972, pp. 293–545, 579–651; Oberg 1973, pp. 23–54; Testart 1976.

15 For two students of Tlingit culture, these differences from the norm indicate the shaman's alienation from his group. McClellen (1954:95) states that the shaman is an individualist who "often acts without regard to the usual moiety and sib structuring," and Oberg (1973:20) asserts that "totemism was social and integrative while shamanism was individual and disintegrative." It is wrong to assume that the shaman's divergence from certain social norms is in any way destructive; such behavior is necessary for the shaman to complete his tasks.

16 Myerhoff (1976) and Halifax (1979) both point out that this straddling of sacred and profane is a characteristic aspect of shamanism.

17 Death can be portrayed by a skeletal face (Maurer 1977, pl. 493) and by a face with a protruding tongue, which indicates that the soul is leaving the body via the tongue (Wardwell 1978, pl. 2). Foreigners, such as Haida and Athapaskans, sometimes appear no different from Tlingit. However, sometimes an Athapaskan is shown with a nose pin (de Laguna 1972, pl. 181 and King 1979, pl. 92).

18 That this is not a random patterning is indicated by comparing the distribution of *yek* images on masks to those on the highly potent charms (see Jonaitis 1981, appendix III); whereas only 28 percent of charms depict *yek* anthropomorphically, 70 percent of masks represent human faces. We must assume that the artist was in some way interested in presenting a broad range of human types who could fall into the subsets we have described here. Nowhere among charms or any

other items of shamanic paraphernalia do we have this particular assortment of beings whose age, sex and other characteristics are so specifically spelled out. Even the small forehead maskettes (see Wardwell 1978, pls. 19–22), also found in graves but apparently not so potent as masks, do not have these subjects. Unfortunately for this study, we do not have a large enough assortment of secular potlatch masks for comparison. However, other types of secular art do not fall into the shamanic mask-patterns either.

REFERENCES

Averkieva, Julia P. 1971 "The Tlingit Indians." In *North American Indians in Historical Perspective*, ed. Eleanor Leacock and Nancy Lurie, New York, Random House, pp. 317–42.

Babcock, Barbara 1978 "Introduction." In *The Reversible World*, ed. Barbara Babcock, Ithaca, Cornell University Press, pp. 13–36.

Baird, Donald 1965 "Tlingit Treasurers: How an Important Collection Came to Princeton," *Princeton Alumni Weekly*, Feb. 16, pp. 6–17.

Boas, Franz 1927 *Primitive Art*. Oslo, H. Ashehoug and Co.

Coe, Ralph T. 1977 *Sacred Circles: Two Thousand Years of North American Indian Art*. Kansas City, Nelson Gallery Foundation.

Collins, Henry B., Frederica de Laguna, Edmund Carpenter and Peter Stone 1973 *The Far North*. Washington, D.C., National Gallery of Art.

Dockstader, Frederick 1966 *Indian Art in America*. Greenwich, Conn., New York Graphic Society.

Douglas, Mary 1966 *Purity and Danger*. London, Routledge & Kegan Paul.

—— 1975 *Implicit Meanings*. London, Routledge & Kegan Paul.

Durkheim, Emile 1965 (First published 1912) *The Elementary Forms of Religious Life*. New York, Free Press. Translation of *Les formes élémentaires de la vie réligieuse*. Paris, Felix Alcan.

Emmons, George T. n.d. Catalogs E and 19, Department of Anthropology, American Museum of Natural History, New York.

—— n.d. Collection notes, Thomas Burke Memorial Washington State Museum, Seattle, Washington.

—— n.d. Collection notes, Field Museum of Natural History, Chicago.

—— n.d. Notes, Provincial Archives, Victoria, British Columbia.

Feder, Norman 1971 *American Indian Art*. New York, Harry N. Abrams, Inc.

Furst, Peter 1973–1974 "Roots and Continuities ," *Arts Canada* 30, pp. 33–60.

Halifax, Joan 1979 "Into the Níerika," In *Shamanic Voices: A Survey of Visionary Narratives*, ed. Joan Halifax, New York, E. P. Dutton, pp. 1–34.

Harner, Michael J. and Albert B. Elsasser 1965 *Art of the Northwest Coast*. Berkeley, Robert H. Lowie Museum of Anthropology, University of California at Berkeley.

Hieb, Louis A. 1972 "Meaning and Mismeaning: Toward an Understanding of the Ritual Clown." In *New Perspectives on the Pueblos*, ed. Alfonso Ortiz, Albuquerque, University of New Mexico Press, pp. 163–96.

Inverarity, Robert B. 1950 *Art of the Northwest Coast Indians*. Berkeley, University of California Press.

Johnson, Ronald 1973 *The Art of the Shaman*. Iowa City, Iowa, the University of Iowa Museum of Art.

Jonaitis, Aldona 1978 "Land Otters and Shamans: Some Interpretations on Tlingit Charms," *American Indian Art Magazine*, 4 (1), pp. 62–66.

—— 1980 "The Devilfish in Tlingit Sacred Art," *American Indian Art Magazine*, 5 (3), pp. 42–47; 77.

—— 1981 "Tlingit Halibut Hooks: An Analysis of the Visual Symbols of a Rite of Passage," *Anthropological Papers of the American Museum of Natural History*, 57 (1).

Laguna, Frederica de 1954 "Tlingit Ideas About the Individual," *Southwestern Journal of Anthropology*, 10, pp. 172–91.

—— 1972 "Under Mount Saint Elias: The History and Culture of the Yakutat Tlingit," *Smithsonian Contributions to Anthropology*, 7.

—— 1973 Notes on objects in *The Far North*, Henry B. Collins, Frederica de Laguna, Edmund Carpenter, and Peter Stone, Washington, D.C., National Gallery of Art.

Leach, Edmund 1961 "Two Essays Concerning the Symbolic Representation of Time." In *Rethinking Anthropology*, New York, The Humanities Press, pp. 124–36.

Lévi-Strauss, Claude 1963 (First published 1958) *Structural Anthropology*. New York, Basic Books. Translation of *Anthropologie structurale*, Paris, Plon.

—— 1966 (First published 1962) *The Savage Mind*. Chicago, University of Chicago Press. Translation of *La pensée sauvage*, Paris, Plon.

King, J. C. H. 1979 *Portrait Masks from the Northwest Coast of America*. London, Thames and Hudson.

Krause, Aurel 1956 (First published 1885) *The Tlingit Indians*. Seattle, University of Washington Press. Translation of *Die Tlinkit-Indianer*, Jena.

Maurer, Evan M. 1977 *The Native American Heritage*. Chicago, Art Institute of Chicago.

Mauss, Marcel 1972 (First published 1902/03) *A General Theory of Magic*. New York, Norton Library. Translation of "Esquisse d'une théorie générale de la magie," *L'Année sociologique*.

McClellen, Catherine 1954 "The Interrelationships of Social Structure with Northern Tlingit Ceremonialism," *Southwestern Journal of Anthropology*, 10, pp. 75–96.

Myerhoff, Barbara 1974 *Peyote Hunt: The Sacred Journey of the Huichol Indians*. Ithaca, Cornell University Press.

—— 1976 "Balancing Between Worlds: The Shaman's Calling," *Parabola*, 1, pp. 6–13.

Oberg, Kalervo 1973 *The Social Economy of the Tlingit Indians*. Seattle, University of Washington Press.

Olson, Ronald L. 1961 "Tlingit Shamanism and Sorcery," *Kroeber Anthropological Society Papers*, 25, pp. 207–20.

—— 1967 "Social Structure and Social Life of the Tlingit in Alaska," *Anthropological Records of the University of California*, 26.

Rigby, Peter 1968 "Some Gogo Rituals of Purification: An Essay on Social and Moral Categories." In *Dialectic in Practical Religion*, ed. Edmund Leach, Cambridge, Cambridge University Press, pp. 153–78.

Swanton, John R. 1908 "Social Conditions, Beliefs and Linguistic Relationship of the Tlingit Indians," *26th Annual Report of the United States Bureau of American Ethnology*, pp. 391–485.

—— 1909 "Tlingit Myths and Texts," *United States Bureau of American Ethnology, Bulletin*, 39.

Testart, Alain 1976 "Milieu naturel, mythologie, et organisation sociale: le principe de la classification dualiste chez les Tlingit de la côte nord-ouest de l'Amérique du Nord," *Social Science Information/Information sur les sciences sociales*, 15 nos. 2–3, pp. 415–26.

Turner, Victor 1967 *The Forest of Symbols*. Ithaca, Cornell University Press.

—— 1969 *The Ritual Process*. Bungay, Suffolk, U.K., Penguin Books, Ltd.

—— 1974 *Dramas, Fields and Metaphors*. Ithaca, Cornell University Press.

—— 1978 "Comments and Conclusions," In *The Reversible World*, ed. Barbara Babcock, Ithaca, Cornell University Press, pp. 276–96.

Van Gennep, Arnold 1960 (First published 1909) *The Rites of Passage*. Chicago, University of Chicago Press. Translation of *Les rites de passage*.

Wardwell, Allen 1964 *Yakutat South*. Chicago, Art Institute of Chicago.

—— 1978 *Objects of Bright Pride: Northwest Coast Indian Art From the American Museum of Natural History*. New York, Center for Inter-American Relations and the American Federation for the Arts.

Vancouver Art Gallery 1967 *Arts of the Raven*. With essays by Wilson Duff, Bill Holm and Bill Reid. Vancouver, Vancouver Art Gallery.

21

All Things Made

David M. Guss

Tidi'uma

While the Yekuana, like many tribal peoples, have no fixed category corresponding to the Western concept of "art," they do distinguish between objects manufactured within the guidelines of traditional design and those that simply arrive without any cultural transformation or intent. *Tidi'uma*, from the verb *tidi*, "to make," are the collective artifacts of the culture, the sum total of everything one must learn to make in order to be considered a Yekuana. These are the essential items, from canoes and graters to houses and baskets, the things that not only distinguish the Yekuana as a society but incorporate the symbols that allow them to survive. *Mesoma*, on the other hand, is simply "stuff," the undifferentiated mass of goods that the Yekuana have acquired through either trade or chance. Often referred to by the Spanish term *coroto*, these objects, such as tin cans and plastic buckets, have none of the magical power or symbolic meaning associated with *tidi'uma*. And though a person may occasionally try to disguise a commercially manufactured object with a layer of skillfully applied *ayawa*, *mesoma* remains a synonym for any insipid or alien object.

For the Yekuana, the distinction between *tidi'uma* and *mesoma* is an important one, as it recognizes culture as something to be made. Unlike the prefabricated *mesoma* that arrives from the outside lacking either significance or resonance, the objects classified under the term *tidi'uma* are all handmade. They represent not only the collective resources of the culture but also a conviction that culture is something to be created daily by every member. Through the complex arrangement of symbolic elements incorporated into the manufacture, design, and use of each one of these objects, *tidi'uma* are able to take on a metaphoric significance that far outweighs their functional value. The semiotic content of every artifact demands that the maker participate in a metaphysical dialogue, often articulated with no more than his hands. Implicit in the growth of every individual as a useful member of society, therefore, is the development of his intellectual capacity. For in learning how to make the various objects required for survival, one is simultaneously initiated into the arrangements underlying the organization of the society as a whole. Just as ritual actions may be said to necessarily accompany all material ones, the symbols incorporated into the manufacture of all *tidi'uma*

From *To Weave and to Sing: Art, Symbol and Narrative in the South American Rain Forest* (Berkeley: University of California Press, 1989), pp. 69–85, 90–91, 231–232, 247–262. Reprinted by permission of the University of California Press.

require that every functional design participate in a greater cosmic one. Hence, to become a mature Yekuana is not only to develop the physical skills demanded of one's gender, but also the spiritual awareness that the preparation of these goods imparts. In a society that has no special category for a work of "art," there can be no object that is not one. Or, put another way, to become a true Yekuana is to become an artist.

As if to acknowledge the close relation between technical and esoteric skills, the Yekuana often speak of the development of manual expertise as analogically indicative of other more intangible qualities. The fact that those who create the most skillfully crafted objects are also the most ritually knowledgeable members of the community is a truism every Yekuana recognizes.[1] In order to manufacture even the simplest objects of everyday use, the maker will need to be familiar with the symbolic arrangements necessary to their completion. As these objects become more complicated, so too must the esoteric knowledge incorporated into their design. Of all the artifacts the Yekuana manufacture, no other demonstrates this simultaneously incremental development of technical and ritual competence as does basketry. The most pervasive of all Yekuana art forms, basketry may not only be used to chart the growth of an individual but of an entire community as well. A shibboleth of tribal identity, the Yekuana state that "a person who does not make baskets is just like a criollo," and emphasize that the authenticity or "Yekuananess" of other villages may be judged by the quality of their weavings.

Of all the material activities required of a Yekuana, there is almost none that, in one way or another, does not demand the use of a basket. Whether it be simply to fan a fire or to carry a piece of game, all actions carried out by both men and women in some way incorporate an object woven from a cane, palm, vine, or twig. The largest number of these baskets are those utilized in the complex transformation of poisonous yuca into edible cassava. Although this group of baskets is used exclusively by the women, all but one of them, the *wuwa*, is manufactured by the men. Referred to in sacred chants as *amunkayedono*, "that which hangs from the back," *wuwa* are proportionately designed so as to evenly distribute their

enormous loads between the bark tumpline hanging from the head and the contoured basket resting against the back. Used primarily in gardening to transport tubers and remove weeds, the sturdy *wuwa* is the woman's all-purpose carrying basket, an extension of her body without which she is rarely seen leaving the village. *Wuwa* are used to gather firewood, carry fish and game, and to transport household goods on expeditions. Taking longer to make than any basket manufactured by the men, *wuwa* are characterized by a form of construction restricted to the women alone. This is the twining technique, wherein the flexible weft elements of the basket are wrapped horizontally around those of a stationary, vertical warp. To reinforce this structure, both elements are secured to a heavy vine called *amaamada* (*Hubebuia pentaphylla*), which is coiled along the inside of the entire basket.[2]

Differing from the twining technique used to make *wuwa* is that of twilled plaiting, the method employed for the manufacture of the four additional baskets that men must weave for women in order for them to process yuca. Of the four, the most simple is the *wariwari* or firefan (figure 21.1). Made of thin strips prepared from the outer part of a tall itirite cane called *ka'na* (*Ischnosiphon* sp.), the *wariwari*, like all twilled plaiting, is created by passing these equally-sized strips over and under one another at ninety-degree angles. Although monochromatic, patterns can be derived by alternating the regularity with which warp and weft elements pass above or below one another. Unlike twining, there is no inner frame or sewn element, tension being maintained solely by the tightness of a weave that never permits a weft element to cross over more than three warps.[3] While referred to as firefans, *wariwari* also serve as spatulas with which to control the cooking of cassava. For this purpose, the large square variety, called an *u yanakato* or "cassava turner," is preferred, as its long straight edge is capable of easily gliding under the enormous loaves to both turn them over and remove them from the grill. The *watto yamatoho* or "fire beater," a triangular firefan to which a short handle is attached, is less versatile and may be limited in use to the family hearth. Because of the simplicity of both of these firefans, *wariwari* are usually the first objects a Yekuana boy learns to weave as he approaches

Figure 21.1 Firefan or *wariwari* of the *yamatoho* variety. Courtesy Helga Adibi (Wilbert, 1972)

the age of ten and begins to contemplate life in the inner male circle.

Much more demanding to make are the large round trays that are used to carry pressed yuca from the house to the grill and to catch it as it is sifted through another basket immediately prior to cooking. Referred to as *waja tingkuihato*, a name emphasizing their close relation with the *tingkui* or yuca press, these highly durable baskets may be up to three or more feet in diameter. While woven of the same unpainted *ka'na* as the firefans, the *waja ting-*

kuihato are plaited in a variety of simple patterns, the most common of which is the concentric square design known as *fahadifedi* or "armadillo face." Once the body of this basket has been completed, it is set inside two interlocking hoops prepared from the branches of a tree called *fumadi*. The edges of the basket are pulled through and the ends, in groups of three to five, are tightly twisted and then sewn onto the *fumadi* as a thick piece of *kurawa* fiber is passed through the perimeter and with a circular stitch used to bind the two pieces of the "frame" (*chähudu*) together (see figure 21.6). A smaller, but otherwise identical version of this monochromatic basket serves as a plate for those undergoing fasts. Commonly known as *Kutto shidiyu* or "frog's bottom," this ritually indispensable basket will be discussed at length at a later point.

Serving as a companion to the *waja tingkuihato* is the slightly smaller *manade* basket. Woven and finished with the same materials and patterns, the plaiting in this basket is not closed but rather is left with small openings between the strips. It is through these gaps that the pressed yuca is forced, resulting in a fine flour which is then sprinkled over the grills to be cooked as cassava. Fitting perfectly into the *waja tingkuihato* it is used with, the *manade* may also be employed elsewhere as the need for fine sieves demands.

The fourth and final in this group of baskets is the *tingkui* or yuca press itself. Often referred to by its Spanish name, *sebucan*, this basket, because of its awkward materials and complicated, reinforced ends, is among the most difficult for any Yekuana to master. Although made of *ka'na* the individual strips are much longer and wider, resulting in a finished basket strong enough to be suspended with up to 125 pounds of freshly grated yuca in it. Averaging six feet in length, the *tingkui* is constructed in the form of a long sleeve with the top open and loops at either end. When filled with grated yuca, it is hung from the top one and a pole is inserted into the bottom. As pressure is periodically applied to this pole, the prussic acid in the pulp is extracted through the tightly plaited sides and a poison-free, dry white mass created. It is this mass which is now ready to be forced through the *manade* in anticipation of the final stage of cassava preparation.

Although the *wariwari, waja tingkuihato, manade*, and *tingkui* comprise a special category of baskets set apart from all others, they represent but a few of the many that every Yekuana male must learn how to make. There are also baskets made for carrying, storing, caging, hunting, fishing, eating, dancing, fighting, playing, and trading. Among these others, the most commonly used is the *tudi*, the men's carrying basket, an open-backed rectangular basket carried by a bark strap around the shoulders (figure 21.2). Manufactured with either a tightly plaited or open lattice-work weave, the *tudi* is used to transport everything from game and fish to personal effects and provisions. Should a man be caught away from home without a *tudi* and have need to transport something, a quickly improvised basket called a *duma* is woven in minutes from whatever palms are at hand. Using a bent branch as a frame, the temporary *duma* backpack is discarded as soon as the load reaches the village. Also used to transport goods, though not as a backpack, are the *mahidi* and *dakisa* baskets (figure 21.3). Differing from one another

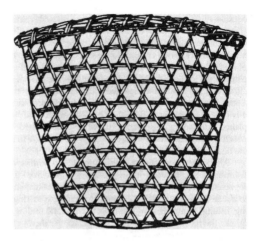

Figure 21.3 Mahidi. Courtesy *Antropológica* (1976)

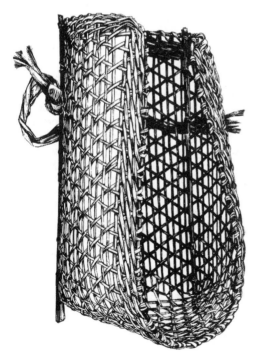

Figure 21.2 Men's carrying basket or *tudi.* Courtesy Helga Adibi (Wilbert 1972)

mainly in size, these valise-like baskets are woven in the same hexagonal weave as the open-style *tudi*. Yet instead of being attached to a frame, a wide-mouthed rim is simply fashioned from the loose ends of the body. When the *mahidi* is used to transport game and produce, or the smaller *dakisa* captive birds, this rim is closed to serve as a convenient handle.

Another basket used to cage small animals, as well as to store peppers, cotton, and other items, is the diminutive *cetu* (figure 21.4). This elegant basket, approximately the same size as the *dakisa*, is made from strips of the *muñatta* vine (*Anthurium flexuosum*). The same material used to make *wuwa, muñatta* is sturdier, if less flexible than itiriti (*ka'na*). As such, it provides the wicker sides and coiled handle of the *cetu* with a strength and durability that far exceeds its functional importance. This cannot be said for another wicker-style basket constructed of *muñatta*. This is the *mudoi* or fish creel, which must be strong enough to withstand nights on end wedged between rocks in the shallows of rivers. Constructed of differing sizes of *muñatta* or sometimes of the even stronger *amaamada*, the *mudoi* consists of a large bottle-shaped frame as well as a flexible inner one through which unsuspecting fish enter and are trapped.

There are several baskets made not for daily use but for ceremonial occasions alone. Amongst these is the *fwemi*, a feathered crown worn by the men during the three-day Garden

Figure 21.4 Cetu. Courtesy *Antropológica* (1976)

woven directly around the game or fish which returning villagers must ceremonially carry. Tightly plaited from the fresh San Pablo leaves (*maahiyadi*) that give it its name, the *maahi* is constructed with a loop so as to attach it firmly to one's wrist. This is an important feature, as those returning to the village in a *waseha* ceremony must have *maahi* dangling from their arms in order to show the success of their journey. Pride, however, soon turns to mayhem as those arriving are attacked and, after a struggle, relieved of their prizes.

A similar, though more substantial basket is the *ahadaño*. Translated as "from the arm" (from *yahadi*, "arm"), this basket, made from *muñatta* and lined with leaves, is also tightly woven around a prize of fish or game. It is used only during one particular dance, which occurs during the first morning of the *Wasai yadi* festival to welcome home returning travelers. At a given signal, these travelers, all dancing with large *ahadaño* dangling from their biceps, are attacked by the women, who steal the baskets away from them. As with the *maahi*, the *ahadaño* are discarded as soon as the food inside them has been consumed.

One last basket closely associated with ceremonial use is the *amoahocho*, a five to seven-inch long replica of the *tingkui* yuca press. This miniature, though not required for any precise ritual purpose, is a favorite game of young people with which to capture the opposite sex during festivals. Functioning exactly like a Chinese finger game, anyone who inserts a finger finds it harder to escape the more he or she tries. Thus, it recalls the manner in which Wanadi captured his own wife, Kaweshawa, and as such explains why *amoahocho* are also referred to as *Wanadi hinyamo otohüdi* or "to catch Wanadi's wife."

The final group of baskets manufactured by the Yekuana are the bichromatic plaited ones that have received far more critical attention than any other Yekuana artifact. Referred to by the Hameses as "the pinnacle of Yekuana artistic achievement" (1976:17), it is also this tradition that Koch-Grünberg singled out for praise during his 1911–1913 expedition. Never particularly sympathetic to the Yekuana, he concedes that these baskets are "true works of art which far surpass through the fineness of the plaited strips and in all other aspects of their workmanship the similar products of their east-

Festival. One of the most beautiful Yekuana artifacts, the structure of the *fwemi* succinctly restates the symbolism acted out in this annual dance. The transformation of Wanato and the bird people responsible for planting the first garden into an organized group of horticulturists – the So'to or Yekuana – is woven into the crown worn at the festival commemorating this event. For, like the garden and house, the *fwemi* consists of two concentric circles: an outer natural one of macaw, parrot, harpy eagle, and currasow feathers and an inner, humanly manufactured one of rigid, carefully coiled *ka'na*.

A much more simply fashioned basket, used in both the *Wasai yadi ademi hidi* and *Atta ademi hidi* as well as in the ceremonies for a newborn child and a newly harvested *conuco*, is the *maahi*. This small, packet-like basket is

ern neighbors and the tribes of the Río Negro" ([1924] 1982:289).[4] While the Yekuana also place this group in a special category apart from all other basketry, it is for reasons other than the aesthetic ones that have attracted the notice of Western visitors.

All bichromatic twilled plaiting is made from one of two types of cane, the thick, bamboolike *wana* (*Guasdua latifolia*) or the taller, slender *eduduwa* (unidentified). While *wana* yields strips noted for their whiteness and strength, *eduduwa* has almost twice as much space between nodes, permitting longer strips and hence larger baskets. After the materials have been chosen and cut, the green skin is scraped off with the back of a knife and the cane set out to dry. The basket maker now goes off to gather the bark of one of several trees. Scraping the pulp inside of this bark together, a moist raglike mass is formed, which is then passed along the underside of a cassava grill to collect the *fwa-tadi inhadoniya*, "the ash below." The resultant black dye is used to paint the outside of one half of the cane. After the cane is allowed to dry, the basket maker begins to prepare the strips, each a sixteenth- to an eighth-of-an-inch wide, from eighth-of-an-inch wide, from both the painted and unpainted material. By carefully notching around the top of the cane, over two dozen fine strips can be removed from each piece, every one to be redivided and scraped before final use.[5]

The prepared strips, known as *setadi*, can be used to make one of three types of baskets: a round, slightly concave serving tray, a box-shaped telescoping basket, or the cover basketry used to sheathe weapons (figure 21.5). Regardless of which is made, the plaiting technique follows the same formula. A small number of white and black strips are lapped together at right angles to create a corner. Then, after laying down additional white ones to enlarge the size of the warp, the blacks are individually inserted, with the number of white elements covered or revealed by each determining the final design. In no instance should a black ever cover more than five of the whites, as to do so would undermine the overall strength of the basket. This rule, along with the need to place all weft elements at a ninety-degree angle to the warps, is a technical determinant that every basket maker must incorporate into his design.

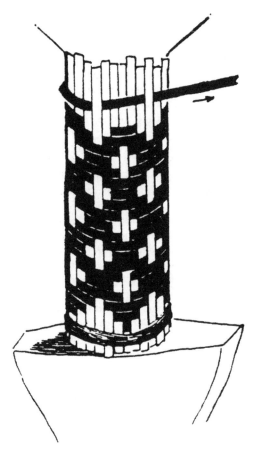

Figure 21.5 Cover basketry. Roth (1924)

Of the three forms of bichromatic basketry, the simplest by far is the cover basketry used to sheathe the handles of all traditional Yekuana weapons. Referred to as *wayutahüdi*, this covering is plaited in simple designs directly onto the carved wooden weapons, producing a seamless effect. The only finishing is the wrapping of fine strips of *kurawa* fiber around the loose ends of both top and bottom to prevent unraveling.

Much more complicated is the manufacture of the telescoping basket, referred to as such because of the two parts that slide into one another. Found throughout the Guianas, this basket is also commonly described as a *pegall*, a name claimed by Roth to be "the Creole corruption of the Carib term *pagara* or *pagala*" (1924:345). To the Yekuana these baskets are known as either *kungwa* or *amato*. Made only by the most skilled craftsmen, this basket is completely double-plaited, with the outer parts bearing any of a variety of designs and the inner monochromatic. Woven into the shape of a box with reinforced edges, the bottom is slightly smaller than the top in order to fit inside it. When finished, the *kungwa* is hung from a rafter by a long piece of *kurawa* looped tightly around it and, unless made for trade, used to store such personal ritual objects as healing gourds, *maada*, quartz crystals, magic stones, and tobacco.

The final group of bichromatic plaited baskets is also the most frequently manufactured. These are the *waja*, the circular serving trays used as plateware for the cassava eaten at every meal. Better known than any other Yekuana basket due to their popularity as trade items, the different *waja* may incorporate up to thirty designs recombined in an infinite variety of ways. Because of this pronounced graphic element and the need to distinguish it from the other *waja* – the monochromatic *waja tingkuihato* – this basket is also referred to as a *waja tomennato* or "painted" *waja*. But a dramatic graphic element is not the only thing that distinguishes these baskets from one another. Though similarly shaped, the "painted" *waja* is just a third the size of the other, measuring in most instances only ten to fourteen inches in diameter. The two baskets are also made of completely different materials, one of *ka'na* and the other of either *wana* or *eduduwa*. And finally, each basket is finished with a different technique (figure 21.6). The *waja tingkuihato*, made to carry heavy loads during the processing of yuca, is finished with a self-selvage, incorporating the twisted ends into the final design of the rim. The more delicate *waja tomennato*, on the other hand, has a separately woven finishing band which, once attached, gives this basket a grace and refinement not to be found in any other.

A Cycle of Baskets

Marriage

The importance of basketry in every aspect of Yekuana life makes it a natural yardstick with which to measure the maturity and character of a developing male. As one masters the different skills required of every adult member of the society, he will also have to learn how to make the baskets necessary to accomplish these tasks. Basketry therefore becomes a significant indicator in the general growth and competence of an individual, used to chart not only practical knowledge but also status and identity. That this is the case is revealed in a variety of beliefs, many of which concern marriage. For to properly support a wife, one must be able to make the baskets that enable her to work. Hence, Yekuana regularly state that a boy is not ready for marriage until he is capable of making every basket, and will refuse to accept one for a son-in-law who is not. This view is articulated in a commonly repeated motif found throughout Yekuana mythology. In it, a young man has just married into a strange family. While his bride is attractive and loving, the father-in-law is an evil cannibal looking for a pretext to kill the boy. He commands his new son-in-law to weave a stack of *tingkui* baskets in a single day, an impossible task whose failure will be used as an excuse to kill him. But the young man is a shaman with supernatural powers, and with the help of other beings, usually birds, he weaves the baskets and, after carrying out several other miraculous deeds, kills not only the father-in-law, but the bride as well (de Civrieux 1980:88). While this story is, of course, a fearful exaggeration of marriage and the anxiety-provoking household realignment it represents for males, it nevertheless reaffirms the inevitable initiatory role of basketry in becoming a husband.

For the Yekuana the consecration of a marriage is a subtle and private affair. Lacking the public ceremonialism associated with festivals, it is an event that goes all but unnoticed, except by those immediately associated with it. Yet, despite this apparent lack of public recognition, the Yekuana attach tremendous importance to the marriage event, particularly as it affects the male. Unlike the bride who has recently undergone an *Ahachito hato* initiation, the man has no other ritual marking his transition from adolescence to manhood. True, he has gone into the circle of unmarried males at the age of ten or eleven, but now he is ready to move out of it to become part of an entirely new family. For matrilocal marriage means that it is the man who will have to shift his allegiance from biological parents to spousal ones. While his bride remains in the same secure environment she has

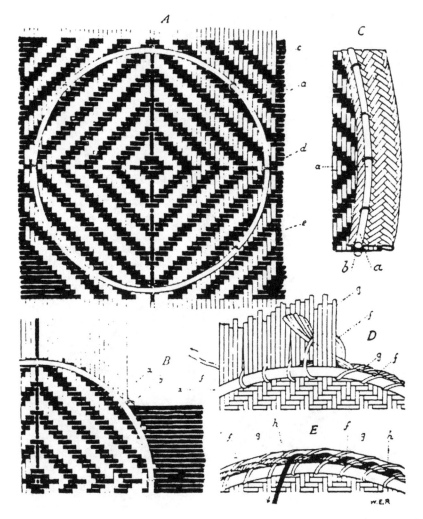

Figure 21.6 Waja finishing techniques: A. The finished body of a *waja tomennato*, the "painted" *waja*, before trimming. Note the plaiting technique – weaving is diagonal from the bottom of the image to the A at the top. B. The *chähudu* frame bands temporarily fixed to the body as the loose ends of the strip are cut away. C. A close-up of the attached finishing band sewn tightly between the *chähudu*. Made from the same materials as the body, this separately woven monochromatic band is called a *chahiyü* or "lips," a name describing the manner in which it grabs the edge of the basket. D. Self-selvage technique of the *waja tingkuihato* wherein a finished edge is made of the coiled ends of the basket itself. E. *Kurawa* being sewn around the *chähudu* bands to keep the edges and frame in place. Roth (1924)

known since birth, the groom faces the most radical transition he will ever undergo. The symbols surrounding marriage acknowledge this "rebirth" into a new family just as they test the young man's willingness to accept its authority.

While marriages may be contracted for either personal or political reasons, the ideal one is always between cross-cousins, a union which permits both partners to remain in their native village. Once proposed, the marriage is discussed by the parents, with particular importance given to the views of the girl's. Unless they are convinced that their future son-in-law will be hardworking, faithful, and obedient, they will not agree. After both

Figure 21.7 Juan Castro weaving a basket, Parupa, 1977. Photograph by David M. Guss

parties have given their consent, they approach the chief, who calls the entire community together for an open meeting. Only after every person in the village has had a chance to speak is the couple allowed to marry. The girl is now permitted to enter the *annaka*, where she removes the young man's hammock and rehangs it next to her own. When he enters the private quarters of his new family that evening, his bride offers him a gourdful of *sukutuka*, a beverage made from cassava and water. That night they eat nothing else, simulating the fast that begins every major life-cycle transition.

Although the couple now lives as husband and wife, the ceremony is not necessarily over. The man must first weave his bride a series of baskets in a strictly prescribed order. The first one he weaves for her shortly after moving is the *Kutto shidiyu*, the "frog's bottom" variation of the *waja tingkuihato*. Much smaller and more finely made than the otherwise identical *waja tingkuihato*, this "wedding basket" will be the only one the couple uses to eat from over the coming year. As such, it symbolizes their status of newness and rebirth, just as the simple meal of *sukutuka* did on the first night

Figure 21.8 Juan Castro's son Pedrito starting a "painted" *waja*. Photograph by David M. Guss

of their marriage. For although the couple does not undergo an actual fast, the *Kutto shidiyu* basket is the one used in fasting, especially by those involved in the three major fasts of life-cycle transition. These fasts – for the *ahachito bato*, the birth of a child, or the death of a close relative – are ordered according to the foods that a baby first ingests, working up from the simplest meal of *sukutuka* to the most "toxic" one of peccary. During the entire year that one is on this restricted diet of a "newborn," he or she may only take food from a *Kutto shidiyu* basket and never from a "painted" *waja*. Because of this, the *Kutto shidiyu* is not only a powerful symbol of rebirth but also of purity and health.

The next basket every new husband makes is the *tingkui*, the complicated yuca press that is among a woman's most important daily tools. In weaving this basket, the young man quickly affirms his competence to an ever-wary household, which will be testing him in its own way with other improvised commands. Then reversing the order in which he learned to weave them, the man makes a *waja tingkui-hato*, a *manade* sieve, and a *wariwari* firefan. Only when all of these have been completed does he begin to construct the enormous wooden apparatus from which the *tingkui* baskets are hung. This *tingkuiyedi*, which will require the aid of some of his in-laws to build, will be used not only by the man's wife, but by the other women of the household as well. Now, after a full year, the husband is ready to make his final basket, a "painted" *waja* to replace the *Kutto shidiyu* the couple has used since the beginning of their marriage (figure 2.8). But first he goes to consult his father over the design he should choose, for whichever one he gives her will be the basket the man must make for his wife throughout the course of their marriage. This does not mean that he will never weave other baskets to either trade or give as gifts to friends. Yet for his wife he may only make the design woven into the *waja tomennato* given to her at the end of the first year of their marriage. If he should ever do otherwise and his wife eats from the basket, she will die. As a result, a man contemplates seriously before deciding which basket to weave. Often he chooses one that his father or grandfather has made for one of their wives. In this sense, a *waja* design may assume the importance of a family crest passed on from generation to generation. But this is not how the Yekuana characterize it. For them it is the realization of a couple's identity, defining what until then has been an amorphous and transitional relation, as symbolized by the blank image of the *kutto shidiyu* fast basket. With the gift of the *waja tomennato*, however, this period comes to an end. The couple is now accepted as a separate entity, ready to begin a family of its own. As long as they remain together, the special images woven into this "painted" *waja* will be a clear statement of the strength and uniqueness of their bond.[6]

While the completion of this cycle of baskets may represent the conclusion of a year-long marriage ritual, it is by no means the end of the husband's education as a basket maker.

From this point on, his basketry will graduate into a new level of meaning and expertise. As a married man, he will begin to disassociate himself from the *modeshi* who hang their hammocks at the center of the roundhouse. He will be expected to take on more responsibilities now, carrying out tasks for his father-in-law and even leading work parties of his own. Soon he will start to speak at meetings, sitting with the elders as they discuss the affairs of the village late into the evening. And like them, he will spend more and more of his time making baskets, not just the ones needed by the women of his household or by himself, but baskets made as a means of meditation and expression. This is not to say that these baskets are any less functional than others he has made. Certainly every basket will at least find a place as an item of trade. Yet, as a man matures, his interests begin to turn more toward the metaphysical and hence toward basketry, particularly the *waja tomennato*. For beyond serving the Yekuana as plateware, these baskets incorporate a complex system of symbols that acts as an index and key to the rest of the culture. Yekuana men appreciate this, using these baskets as a discipline to penetrate the mysteries of their society and world. It is no surprise, therefore, that as a man enters into the serious study of *Watunna* and other esoteric lore, it is basketry that accompanies him, a fact which also explains why the most accomplished ritual singers and most skillful basket makers are inevitably one.

[...]

The Poetics of Basketry

As one begins to observe, the problem of understanding Yekuana basketry is the problem of understanding traditional art forms within the framework of small, tribal societies in general. Unlike the works of contemporary Western artists, those produced by the Yekuana are not so easily dismissed by a formalist discussion. Although the affective properties of shape, color, and tension are of course issues, they diminish in importance as one begins to explore the remarkable resonance implicit in every aspect of the work. At the same time, a functionalist approach, to which so much of "primitive art" has been reduced, captures only a fraction of the power and meaning of objects that regularly resist classification. Commenting on this same problem, Clifford Geertz writes that the study of these art forms must first uncover "the distinctive sensibility" out of which they grow:

> This realization, that to study an art form is to explore a sensibility, that such a sensibility is essentially a collective formation, and that the foundations of such a formation are as wide as social existence and as deep, leads away not only from the view that aesthetic power is a grandiloquence for the pleasures of craft. It leads away also from the so-called functionalist view that has most often been opposed to it: that is, that works of art are elaborate mechanisms for defining social relationships, sustaining social rules, and strengthening social values. (1976:1478)

By extending itself into every aspect of the culture, the "primitive" work of art succeeds in recreating it, justifying Geertz's conclusion that "a theory of art is at the same time a theory of culture, not an autonomous enterprise" (ibid.:1488). Such a conclusion naturally demands that all analyses recognize the greater dimensionality of this work. While ignoring neither the formalist nor functionalist concerns, the main focus must be on the "total system of symbols and meanings" (Schneider 1976:208) that leads back to the society that produced it and which it, in turn, reproduces. For ultimately the real question is not *what* art means but *how*. In studying the Yekuana baskets this question cannot be fully answered until each of the converging symbolic systems is identified and analyzed. These include the narrative element – the stories the Yekuana tell concerning the baskets and other artifacts. Running like a subtext through each of the baskets' different features, these tales and chants provide us with the closest approximation we have of a native exegesis of these phenomena. Of course, the most striking element to be examined is that of the graphic designs woven into the surface of the baskets. Yet no less important is the technology of the baskets. Organized around the gathering, preparation, and weaving of the various basketry materials, these aspects comprise a separate, but complementary set of symbols to be studied. Finally, there is the question of the basket's use, its function in daily life, the rituals that permit

it, the prohibitions that prevent it. Only when all of these elements have been considered – the narrative, graphic, technical, and functional – can the baskets be viewed in their true cultural context. Only then can one begin to recognize the same configuration of symbols constellated around such other cultural forms as the house, garden, and dress. By replicating the organization of symbols articulated in these and other forms, the baskets provide yet another expression of the Yekuana conceptualization of the universe. As such, one might say the ultimate subject matter of the baskets is culture itself. For like "all things made" (*tidi'uma*), they are intended as portraits of the society that inspired them.

NOTES

1   It is this same congruence of ritual and technical skills that Arvelo-Jimenez refers to when she discusses the attributes required of a chief:

> There are two ways in which a headman is distinguished from the commoners. The first is the duties he has to the villagers; the other is the unusual combination of wisdom in handling people, technical proficiency and ritual wealth. This enables a man to aspire for village headmanship and to lead his political followers to believe he is well suited for that office. This is why a headman has to be really proficient in the arts and crafts of his society. He has to be a hard worker. He has to be ritually affluent and perform ritual services at the request of his fellow villagers. He is supposed to be a wise and peaceful individual capable of influencing people to adjust differences.... He must be a generous man and have a natural following. (1971:233)

2   All basketry terminology follows as closely as possible that of J. M. Adovasio, *Basketry Technology: A Guide to Identification and Analysis* (1977). In agreement with Adovasio as well is the definition of basketry as a "technique of manufacture. Specifically, all forms of basketry are manually assembled or woven without a frame or loom" (ibid.:1). In putting the emphasis on technology and materials rather than function and form, this simple

definition closely parallels that of the Yekuana. It also permits the inclusion of such "un-basketlike" forms as hats, firefans (matting), and covering basketry. For more detailed descriptions of the actual manufacture of the different baskets, see Roth 1924, Hames and Hames 1976, and Henley and Mattéi-Muller 1978.

3   As various people have pointed out, to speak of a true warp and weft, that is, an inflexible, passive element and a pliable, active one, may be more of a convention than anything else when discussing twill plaited basketry, as each element is capable of a certain amount of movement and manipulation. Cf. Roth: "Each element of the weft passes over and then under two or more warp elements; in Guiana twilled basketry the warp and weft would appear to be sometimes indistinguishable" (1924:140).

4   For a full discussion of Koch-Grünberg's complicated relationship with the Yekuana see Guss 1986b. So ambivalent is his attitude that even his praise of Yekuana basketry is undermined by his subsequent statement that "their weavings do not owe their origin to any conscious artistic sentiment but to a simple manual dexterity they have learned from tribes of a higher level, perhaps the Guinau, now degenerated" ([1924] 1982:292).

5   For a detailed description of the preparation of these cane strips, see Roth 1924: 137–39.

6   If a man has more than one wife, as permitted by the Yekuana rules of polygamy, he makes each one a basket with her own design. As such, the emphasis is placed on the identity of the couple rather than on that of just the husband.

REFERENCES

Adovasio, J. M. 1977 *Basketry Technology: A Guide to Identification and Analysis.* Chicago: Aldine Publishing Company.

Arvelo-Jimenez, Nelly 1971 *Political Relations in a Tribal Society: A Study of the Ye'cuana Indians of Venezuela.* Latin American Studies Program Dissertation Series, no. 31. Ithaca, N.Y.: Cornell University.

de Civrieux, Marc 1980 *Watunna: An Orinoco Creation Cycle.* Ed. and trans. David M. Guss. San Francisco: North Point Press.

Geertz, Clifford 1976 "Art as a Cultural System." *Modern Language Notes* 91:1473–99.

Hames, Raymond B., and Ilene L. Hames 1976 "Ye'kwana Basketry: Its Cultural Context." *Antropológica* 44:3–58.

Henley, Paul, and Marie-Claude Mattéi-Muller 1978 "Panare Basketry: Means of Commercial Exchange and Artistic Expression." *Antropológica* 49:29–130.

Koch-Grünberg, Theodor 1982 [1924] *Del Roraima al Orinoco,* vol. 3. Trans. Federica de Ritter. Caracas: Ediciones del Banco Central de Venezuela.

Roth, Walter E. 1924 *An Introductory Study of the Arts, Crafts, and Customs of the Guiana Indians.* Thirty-eighth Annual Report of the U. S. Bureau of American Ethnology (1916–17). Washington, D. C.: Smithsonian Institution.

Schneider, David M. 1976 "Notes toward a Theory of Culture." In *Meaning in Anthropology,* edited by Keith H. Basso and Henry A. Selby. Albuquerque: University of New Mexico Press.

Wilbert, Johannes 1972 *Survivors of Eldorado: Four Indian Cultures of South America.* New York, Washington, London: Praeger Publishers.

22

Modernity and the "Graphicalization" of Meaning
New Guinea Highland Shield Design in Historical Perspective

Michael O'Hanlon

Introduction

If the major concern in studies of the anthropology of art and of material culture over the last three decades has been with 'meaning' (Coote & Shelton 1992: 4), then the dominant models or metaphors in terms of which that meaning is to be disclosed have undoubtedly derived from language. Art, material culture (and, of course, much else beside) have endlessly been 'read', their constituent forms and designs compared to linguistic units of different orders, and analysed for their combinatorial rules to see what 'messages', thus 'decoded', they 'communicated' (see, for example, Barthes 1973; Sahlins 1976; Layton 1981).

More recently, however, what had always existed as a muted countercurrent to the linguistic analogy has been foregrounded. Miller (1987: 95–6), for example, has argued that the imposition of linguistic models has had the effect of 'subordinating the object qualities of things to their word-like properties'. McCracken (1988: ch. 4) has disputed the appropriateness of a linguistic analogy even when applied to its heartland territory of

dress, so often analysed as 'the language of clothing'. Earlier, Ong (1982) had delineated the 'chirographic' mindset which hides from us the extent to which literacy has pervaded our understanding and, as Gow (1990) has shown, can lead to misdirected efforts to find a semantic and representational key to indigenous design. Gell (1992: 43) has similarly alluded to the defects of an iconographic approach which 'treats art as a species of writing, and which fails ... to take into consideration the presented object, rather than the represented symbolic meanings'. More broadly, and beyond anthropology, Stafford (1993: 463) has traced what she regards as our inhibiting tendency to 'see images linguistically' back to the eighteenth century when, she argues, perceptual apprehension became established as 'an inferior gnosis' to non-visual, written modes of knowing.

It would be a mistake, however, to polarize the issue and to reject linguistic analogies as fervently as they were initially embraced. As Morphy (1994: 665) remarks, 'many of the theoretical controversies in the analysis of art ... have resulted from a failure to recognize

From *Journal of the Royal Anthropological Institute* 1 (1995), pp. 469–492. Reprinted by permission of Blackwell Publishing.

the multidimensional nature of objects and the immense variety of ways in which meanings can be represented'. Quite possibly, aesthetic systems may differ empirically in the degree to which they are language-like and thus in the extent to which linguistic models are helpful in understanding them (O'Hanlon 1989: 19). Before finally accepting or rejecting such a model, one would also want to be clear as to the specific aspect of language to which the object-world is being compared: whether it is the fact that language is structured, or that it is communicative, or that its rules have been internalized by native speakers whose knowledge of them is thus often held unconsciously, or the representationalism which underlies the distinction between signifier and signified.

My purpose here, though, is less to reassess whether linguistic models were originally the best ones for analysing the object world than to examine a contemporary counterpart to that argument and, in doing so, to touch on the still neglected topic of aesthetic change. The point I want to make is a simple one. It is that if indeed we have been unduly concerned with the notion of 'reading' objects, with attributing word-like properties to design and motif and interrogating them for their meaning by virtue of those properties, then the same broad influences which made that seem the approach to take are also likely to be having an effect locally. In other words, whether or not such linguistic analogies were originally appropriate, subsequent changes – and here I have in mind the impact of literacy, the explosion of goods and advertising and other specific aspects of modernity[1] sketched below – may be making them so.

One goal of this article is to examine this through a remarkable category of objects: the battle shields used by the Wahgi, a people of the Western Highlands Province in Papua New Guinea. What makes these shields especially interesting is their discontinuous and mutating history. Once a defining feature of Wahgi warfare, the shields effectively vanished as the Australians suppressed local fighting in the years following 'first contact' in the 1930s. Then, after three decades in latency, the shields were reinvented for the renewed warfare of the 1980s, but now with designs whose older communicative modality had been given a new graphical dimension engendered by the inter-

vening encounter with modernity. Finally, changing military technology is again leading to the disappearance of shields among some Wahgi groups, while radically changing their significance among others. In fact, not the least interesting aspect is how this one object charts the history of the Wahgi from the precolonial era through the colonial period to the present.

This leads into the second issue which I wish to explore through these data: that of recontextualization. I borrow the term from Thomas (1991), who uses it in his account of the transfer of artefacts – the borrowings, the expropriations, the general mutual entanglement through objects – which occurred between Whites and Islanders during the early colonial phase in the Pacific. In part, Thomas is concerned to draw attention to the way in which artefacts may be locally appropriated, shift their meanings and generally be put to new uses as they move across colonial boundaries. He thus challenges our tendency to treat artefacts as 'essences that have merely been moved physically from places of origin' (1991: 186); as he succinctly puts it: 'To say that black bottles were given [to natives in trade] does not tell us what was received' (1991: 108). At the same time, Thomas emphasizes that the extent to which artefacts *do* get recontextualized depends upon historical and political circumstances; here he is anxious to avoid merely replacing the thesis of overdetermination by the global system with an equally lopsided celebration of the appropriative capacities of local agency.

Wahgi shields allow the issue of recontextualization to be considered from a novel, though analogous, perspective. In the instances discussed by Thomas, the disjunctions are mainly spatially generated: objects produced in one part of the world are potentially recontextualized as they are exchanged or traded in a very different one. I will be looking at some examples of such spatial recontextualization, but shields also provide an opportunity to consider the same issues when the disjunction is temporal. These are objects revived in the same place, but in a very different time: a postcolonial world of changed technology, new imagery and fresh visual forms. But for this to be appreciated, it is first necessary to say something about the Wahgi, about warfare and about the shields themselves.

The Wahgi: Pre-pacification Warfare and Weaponry

The Wahgi Valley can be imagined as a gigantic corridor, whose walls are great mountain ranges and along the broad floor of which the Wahgi River meanders from west to east. The Wahgi people themselves mostly dwell in the central section of this valley, where traditionally they lived in dispersed settlements scattered along the valley walls, preferring to avoid the humid and marshy river plain. The people are organized in localized exogamous patriclans, many of which are grouped into tribes, and some into dispersed phratries. While there is some linguistic and cultural variation between Wahgi living on either side of the river, and east to west along the valley walls, their mutual similarities are greater than their resemblances to their Hagen and Simbu neighbours. First encountered by the celebrated Leahy-Taylor patrol in 1933, we owe our earliest extended anthropological accounts of the Wahgi to the missionary-linguist Luzbetak (e.g. 1954) whose work was mainly done on the North Wall of the valley, and to Reay, whose long-term field research was conducted in the southeast corner of the Wahgi cultural area (e.g. Reay 1959).

Drawing upon their accounts, but also upon my own fieldwork in the northwest corner of the Wahgi area, I have earlier given a picture of local society as incorporating a latent structural contradiction (O'Hanlon 1989; 1992). On the one hand, there was a hypostatization of group (particularly clan) strength and solidarity: a preoccupation all the stronger for being allied to the fear that the purportedly solidary group in fact harbours aggrieved, self-interested and treacherous members. Their suspected witchcraft, illicit consorting with enemy clansmen, or even merely their undisclosed anger are thought of as imperilling not only the security of the group but also the individual health and well-being of their fellow members. On the other hand, the sources of health and well-being are also traced *beyond* the clan, to the group from which an individual's mother originally came, and, more remotely, to the subclans from which mother's mother, father's mother, mother's mother's mother, etc., came. All these external matrilateral connexions are actually referred to as 'source people', whose continuing goodwill towards their 'cuttings' needs to be secured through making life-cycle payments to them. Because Wahgi clans tend to intermarry repeatedly over the generations, the supposedly unified clan is likely to contain a number of blocks which (following Meigs [1984: 13]) I term 'shadow communities', each composed of people who acknowledge the same common external 'source' clan.

One of the circumstances in which this latent structural contradiction manifested itself was in warfare, endemic in the pre-contact period. Ideally, affinally and matrilaterally related groups did not fight but at times they fell out, sometimes bitterly. Reay (1987) has contrasted the relatively secular nature of Engan warfare with the strongly religious orientation of Wahgi fighting, in which success was felt to depend upon securing the support of clan ghosts. I subsequently elaborated this point on the basis of my own research on the North Wall (O'Hanlon 1989: 51–2, ch. 3), drawing particular attention to the way in which warfare involves the ritual heightening of the links between fellow clansmen, with a concomitant problematization of their extra-clan relationships. I suggested that the intensification of clanship was manifested particularly in the ritually-charged charcoal in which warriors coated themselves before battle, and which was said not only to render them terrifying but also to make them *indistinguishable*. I also found similar evidence of ritual heightening in the prebattle emphasis that clansmen should confess outstanding grievances and misdeeds perpetrated against each other. On the other hand, the problematic status of extra-clan links in such circumstances is registered in the ritual precautions which a man must take against his *own* clansmen when their opponents are his 'source' people.

Overall, I attempted to draw attention to the moral dimension to Wahgi warfare, illustrating how fighting was at once the context for scrutinizing the state of crucial social relationships and the ultimate divination as to whether all outstanding issues in those relationships had been repaired. Many of these points have been gratifyingly sustained and elaborated in the most recent work on Wahgi warfare by Muke (1993), himself a native Wahgi speaker, who provides a more formal analysis of

contemporary shields from the South Wall of
the Wahgi than I am able to do here. Muke's
work also provides support for one aspect of
Harrison's (1993) lucid re-analysis of Melanesian warfare, in which he questions the background Western assumption that conflict
escalation corresponds to a progressive breakdown or abandonment of social controls.
Muke's account is certainly a corrective to
any tendency to think of Wahgi warfare merely
as an uncontrolled 'descent' into Hobbesian
chaos. He brings out the extent to which warfare developed through regulated stages, substantially under the participants' control, as
they negotiated with each other to fill the cast
of ritual roles which warfare entails.

The relevance of the foregoing will emerge
in due course; at this point it is useful to move
towards a consideration of the shields themselves. The Wahgi make a terminological distinction between fighting (*nganmal*) and
warfare proper (*opo*), and between the
weapons appropriate to each. Traditionally, if

fighting occurred at all within a group
(whether clan or tribe), weaponry was ideally
restricted to long staves and to the parry
shields used to fend off blows from them
(Aufenanger 1957). 'Warfare', in contrast, involved the use of spears, stone axes, bows and
arrows, and of the massive battle shields with
which I am concerned here.

The earliest mention of Wahgi battle shields
in the literature actually comes from Taylor's
original 1933 patrol diary. The entry for
12 April, written while the patrol paused for
a few days near Kerowil on their first passage
along the Valley, reads: 'About mid-day a
native from a settlement near the river passed
by, carrying his shield and a spear, going along
so it appeared to help some friends in a
dispute. I persuaded him to go back with
his shield after M.J. Leahy had taken
several photographs'. As is apparent from
Leahy's photographs (figure 22.1), traditional
shields comprised a single plank of wood,
roughly the height of a man, decorated with

Figure 22.1 Wahgi shield, topped with cassowary plumes, 12 April 1933. M.J. Leahy Collection, roll
47, National Library of Australia

ochre paints and adorned above with cassowary plumes. Shields were generally made from *tapi* wood (*Albizia* sp): *kumbrapi*, the term for a shield, literally means '*tapi* wall'. Although *tapi* is a fast-growing wood, the size of Wahgi shields meant that their average weight was relatively great: around 9 kg. Indeed, Wahgi men sometimes assert that it was only the ancestral assistance which they invoke before a battle which enabled them to manoeuvre for long periods carrying their shields over rugged ground.[2]

Almost all Wahgi shields were decorated. The designs, which were executed by the individual warrior in ochre and charcoal, were generally large and bilaterally symmetrical.[3] In a paper which launched the best known debate on New Guinea shield adornment, Leach (1954: 105) declared with reference to Trobriand shields that 'Primitive designs are usually representational' (see also Glass 1986). Certainly, the models of ethnographic art which I took with me to the field predisposed me to think that Wahgi designs and their constituent motifs – whether on shields or elsewhere – must 'represent' or 'mean' something.[4] Though Wahgi shield designs are mostly geometric in appearance, and there proved to be no terms for designs as totalities, the constituent motifs were given names which at least suggested to me the possibility of an underlying symbolic scheme. Figure 22.2 shows the individual motifs recorded, along with translations of the words used to describe them.

The salience of bird-related terms among the motifs provoked one train of thought. Attention has, of course, frequently been drawn to the ramifying sets of associations made in many Highlands cultures between people and birds (e.g. Goldman 1983). In Wahgi, the associations are specifically between *men* (and it is they, after all, who are the warriors) and birds. Thus, only men are named after birds, and it sometimes used to be said that after death men turned into birds (O'Hanlon 1989: 94). Furthermore, warriors do of course wear a variety of plumes – although to the extent that there is a focus upon any specific bird species in warfare it is directed towards the cassowary and the Raggiana bird of paradise, rather than the 'owls' or generic 'bird's feet' which are among the names given to shield motifs. A second potential theme lay in the recognition,

quite explicit in this case, that there is an underlying link between shields and their bearers (Muke 1993: 208–9), and some shield motifs do indeed correspond to body parts, with 'head', 'arms', 'stomach' and 'legs' identified – even if the 'v' shape often found at the *bottom* of a shield design is sometimes identified as 'red *head*'. In a rather less literal way, Muke has drawn attention to parallels between a variety of traditional shield motifs, military formations in which the shields are used, and Wahgi social and religious themes: for example, between the rectangles found on some shields, and the similar 'openness' of public arenas such as ceremonial grounds and battlefields; and between circles as a shield motif, and aspects of Wahgi religious life (1993: 20–1, 219–20).

However, it seems from Muke's fairly careful phrasing that these are correspondences to which he, as an analyst, is pointing, rather than any ready local exegesis, which is my concern here. I certainly came to find the process of trying to wring significance from such clues to be as unsatisfactory, as I suspect my patient informants did, at least in so far as the goal of the exercise was to uncover some conscious and shared local perception of the significance of shield designs and their constituent motifs. Different respondents would sometimes give different names to the same 'motif', or see as a single motif what others had distinguished as separate ones. Not even I, let alone my informants, could readily advance plausible links between warfare and others of the motifs ('waxing moon', 'spider's web', 'red head', etc). And even were I able to conjure up significance at this level, it would leave unexplained the fact that most shield decoration was a *combination* of such motifs.

Two disclaimers must be registered at this point. First, these negative findings do not, of course, exclude the possibility of a formal analysis which might well yield regularities and significances of which Wahgi themselves were not consciously aware. Indeed Muke, in his role as an insider who can yet bring an external analytical perspective to bear, has gone a considerable way in this direction in pointing to the kinds of formal correspondences noted above. However, as indicated, my concern here is with ready local exegesis, rather than

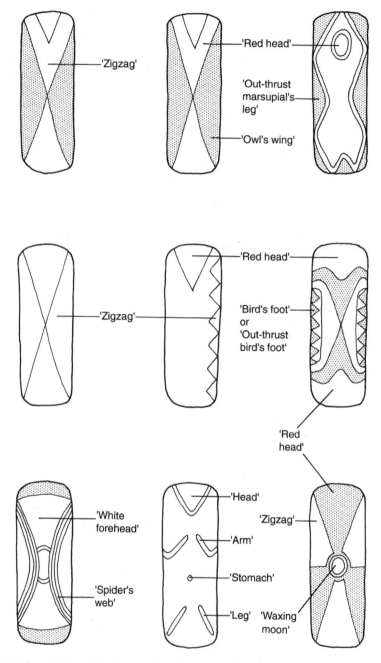

Figure 22.2 Wahgi shield motifs; drawing by Rebecca Jewell

with any unvoiced meanings. Secondly, the possibility could not be excluded that I might have found more graphical meaning being attached to these designs and motifs had I been investigating them during warfare, rather than (as was the case) in the abstract, largely well away from the battlefield. But in the absence of such an opportunity, I could only make an informed guess, which was that if traditional designs *did* possess more graphical significance than emerged from my inquiries, that meaning was at most embryonic. On balance, I was forced to conclude that what I wished to read as 'symbolic' was little more than a set of fairly rough and ready mnemonics, used to recall and refer to design motifs. To read very much more into them was an artefact only of my own chirographic presuppositions about design.

At one level, my failure to locate such meaning should, of course, have come as no surprise: the dedication with which earlier writers have inquired about the conscious graphical significance of New Guinea Highland shield designs as totalities is equalled only by the regularity with which they, too, have found themselves forced to report that it is almost entirely absent. Lowman (1973: 26, 29), for example, writes of Maring shield design that 'What is represented . . . cannot be considered important for there was rarely consensus as to what object was actually being represented. . . . One gets the impression that the iconic forms in the designs are projected or interpreted, rather than intended', and Ryan (1958: 248) refers to the 'complete lack of Mendi interest in any interpretation of their shield-designs' (see also, Cranstone 1968; Sillitoe 1980).

This is not, of course, to suggest that codes of the kind I was searching for are in themselves foreign to the Wahgi. Such codes exist, for example, in the realm of dream interpretation, where individual images *are* recognized to denote particular meanings. Again, in the verbal realm, rich systems of metaphors are found in oratory and in song and these may also take a three-dimensional form, so that an orator at a bridewealth ceremony can fiddle with twigs to indicate that the bride is unattractively stick-like. It is simply that such codes for interpretation really did not seem to be extended, except in the most rudimentary fashion, into the realm of two-dimensional shield motifs and designs.[5] The only specifically graphical significance which informants, when pressed, *would* accord to shield designs lay in the remark made by a number of men that their shield designs helped identify them, so that any maternal kin on the opposing side would know to avoid them, while their own clansmen would recognize them if they were in trouble and hasten to their aid.[6] Muke (1993:

105–6) has similarly noted that the shield design of a 'deviant' clansman might be betrayed to the enemy by his own side, so identifying him to be killed in battle.

Only later during my original fieldwork did I come to understand that there was one quite different way in which shield surfaces *were* locally thought of as meaningful, one which Muke's (1993: 206 sqq.) work has since borne out and amplified. Essentially, the overall appearance of shields – whether they looked bright, vivid and glowing or seemed unimpressively dull, ashy and pale – was read as a reflection of the inner moral condition of the warriors with respect to those issues of concealed treachery, unconfessed anger and unhonoured debts mentioned earlier. As warriors emerged from their pre-fight rituals, spectators were said to evaluate the appearance both of shields and of the shield-bearers more generally. If the men of a clan did not impress, they would be advised to go back into seclusion and talk through and confess outstanding issues since, until these were resolved, there was no point in fighting as the clan would inevitably lose. On the other hand, I was repeatedly told that the appearance of clansmen whose internal relations were harmonious, and whose relations with their allies and opponents were free of grievances which could be deployed against them, would be so overwhelming that I would be unable even to bear looking at such warriors.[7]

Here it is important to note that while shields, and the appearance both of warriors and of decorated dancers more broadly, were indeed assessed in this way, such evaluations also had an active existence apart from the occasions which were said to give rise to them. They served as an idiom in terms of which clansmen debated moral issues, attributing their past defeats to specific delicts or predicting future victories in the light of subsequent revelation of hitherto concealed transgressions. From this perspective, shield designs – mediated through evaluations made of their lustre or dullness – had at least as much impact upon the shield carriers' *own* group as they did upon the enemy whom they were overtly supposed to influence. But for present purposes, the more basic point is that while shield surfaces *were* locally meaningful, their conscious significance to the Wahgi was not *graphically* based. As I have expressed it elsewhere (O'Hanlon 1989: 21) in discussing the politics of aesthetic appraisal, indigenously recognized significance was located at the level of evaluation rather than structure.

Pacification, and the Later Resurgence of Highlands Fighting[8]

Much of the discussion of traditional shields so far derives, however, not from personal observation but from talking to Wahgi and from the drawings which I asked them to make for me of shield designs: for by the time I began fieldwork in 1979 virtually no shields were to be seen.[9] As the quotation cited earlier from Taylor's patrol report indicates, the incoming Australians had, from the very first, been concerned to stop intergroup fighting, an end they sought partly through enjoining clans to burn their weapons. A measure of pacification had already been achieved by the late 1930s and this was swiftly consolidated after the hiatus caused by the second world war. Restrictions on White residence in the Wahgi area were lifted in 1947 (Luzbetak 1958: 55), allowing missionaries to lend their weight to peace-making. Warfare was certainly categorized as 'bad' in the accounts Wahgi later gave me of Biblical events: they told me that warfare was among their traditional practices which God gave to Lucifer when the latter was cast down from Heaven; equally, the support which ancestral ghosts are thought to lend to warriors is referred to as *tantan pake tom*: 'the help of "satans" '. The Australians established their subdistrict headquarters at Minj on the South Wall in 1952, and instituted systematic patrolling, aimed both at producing detailed demographic information and stamping out any remaining intergroup fighting. Corrigan, the Assistant District Officer at Minj, felt able to note in his South Wahgi patrol report of 1952–3 that he did 'not think that any embers of martial ardour continue to glow' in the area.[10]

It is also clear that, as happened in neighbouring parts of the Highlands, intergroup tensions and competitiveness formerly expressed in warfare were now partly re-channelled into the system of ceremonial exchange. The Australians had imported enormous quantities of shells, the indigenous

valuable, to pay for food and labour and, from the late 1940s, they introduced a money economy, whose coins and notes were also quickly drawn into the local exchange system. At first, Wahgi men sought this wealth through working as carriers on patrols to the newly opened-up Southern Highlands, and as labour migrants on the Highlands Labour Scheme (Heaney 1989). But coffee, initially introduced by expatriate planters in the mid-1950s, was soon adopted as a cash crop by many Wahgi. Coffee income was ploughed not only into ceremonial prestations but also into the other proliferating expressions of modernity. These included the tinned fish, rice and other goods which could now be purchased in the trade stores which were established all along the Wahgi road network, itself being expanded to provide access for coffee buyers' vehicles. They also included the taxes which were introduced during the 1960s, and school fees. By the 1980s, most men of middle age and below had had at least some schooling, and most young men were at least partially literate in Pidgin. Their reading matter was a mixture of religious material, newspapers and comics: the strip cartoon hero Phantom was especially popular in Papua New Guinea at this time (Wheeler 1988: 47), and a large folk painting of him adorned the façade of one of the bulk-stores in the Wahgi town of Banz.

Wahgi purchasing power was greatly boosted by the quintupling of coffee prices which followed the frosting of the Brazilian crop in 1975. The increased income was spent on vehicles (Toyota pickups were particularly popular), on further trade store goods (such as the ubiquitous Cambridge cigarettes, whose manufacturers sponsor the Cambridge Cup, a national rugby league championship) and on alcohol, the colonial prohibition on indigenes drinking having been lifted in 1962. Beer is by far the most popular drink, and cartons of South Pacific and San Miguel beer were incorporated in intergroup prestations. Advertisements for 'SP', 'Cambridge' and other products became a pervasive part of the visual environment, whether painted on the front of bulkstores in Wahgi towns, ornamenting the goods themselves – purchased for re-sale in local tradestores – or decorating the cardboard packaging which is recycled in Wahgi house construction.

By the 1970s, however, more planned and organized fighting was again taking place in parts of the Highlands. The reasons for the upsurge in fighting, and the extent to which it constituted a 'revival' or was so different in form and cause as to have little in common with pre-contact warfare, have of course been much debated. At one level, as A.J. Strathern (1977: 143) has noted, the exchanges and ceremonies into which intergroup tensions were diverted during the colonial period also functioned to keep alive the structure of older enmities and alliances. At another level, as he makes equally plain, aspects of modernity were also implicated in the renewed warfare, whether merely as precipitating factor or as underlying cause. Cash-cropping increased pressure on land; the proliferation of vehicles, especially in the context of beer drinking, led to road deaths which in turn led to intergroup fighting when negotiations for compensation broke down. Initially, the Wahgi area escaped relatively lightly but from the early 1980s, albeit in limited parts of the valley, large numbers of Wahgi were again periodically to be seen engaged in set piece battles, lasting days or weeks, their traditional fighting dress of charcoal and cassowary plumes now complemented or replaced by cut-off jeans, T-shirts, and protective innovations such as crash helmets and hard hats.

The Shield Reinvented

At first, shields were either little made for the renewed Wahgi warfare, or were fairly rapidly confiscated and burned by police: I certainly encountered none before 1981. But as fighting became more widespread and prolonged, substantial numbers of shields were again to be seen. In what follows, I shall mainly be discussing the shields used in two wars which took place in 1989: those between Senglap and Dange tribes on the North Wall of the Wahgi, and between Konumbka and Kondika on the South Wall – two conflicts which, as will emerge, took very different courses. In both cases the wars were over by the time of my 1990 return visit to the Wahgi, and my information derives solely from examining the shields and from interviews, particularly with Senglap men. However, the Konumbka-Kondika conflict is described in detail in

Muke's thesis, and that of Bruce (1992). I also draw to a lesser extent on my own experience of seeing shields in use during an earlier return visit to the Wahgi, when I watched a battle in the 1986 war on the South Wall between Konumbka and Koleka on the one side and Ngeneka on the other.[11]

While many of the reinvented shields were much as their pre-contact predecessors had been described to me, others showed changes. Some of these were technical. The replacement of stone axes by steel led most men to feel that the older cane mesh was no longer sufficient to protect the shoulder-sling mounting from an axe blow; stouter materials (often pieces of metal) were therefore substituted for cane mesh. By the mid-1980s, a few Wahgi men were experimenting with all-metal shields, often salvaged from pick-up carcasses. A decade before, Enga warriors had tried using corrugated iron shields (serious fighting had resumed much earlier there), but had discarded them since they apparently caused arrows to ricochet so erratically that they endangered men of the shieldbearers' own side (Meggitt 1977: 57). In the Wahgi case, however, metal shields were retained and were in fact produced in increasing numbers. This was partly in anticipation of a radical change in Wahgi warfare – one which was to sweep shields from the South Wall battlefields and to transform their significance in the North – discussed in the next section.

Some of the designs on the reinvented shields were of the kind that had been described to me as traditional, though most were now executed in acrylic paints rather than ochres, or were stencilled with spray paints. But many shields, particularly those decorated by young men, showed differences indicative of a radical expansion in the way in which designs functioned as communicative forms. One striking change was the inclusion of new motifs which differed from traditional designs not only in being explicitly figurative but also in being overtly motivated with regard to the warfare in which they were being used. Thus traditional motifs inconsistently glossed as 'red head' or 'bird's foot', terms having no obvious relation to warfare, were now complemented by instantly identifiable images of axes or spears (figure 22.3), it being readily explained that these were represented as weapons which killed opponents; one shield

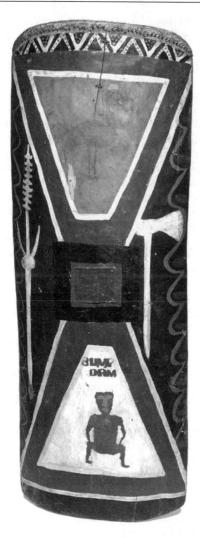

Figure 22.4 Contemporary metal shield, Wahgi Konumbka tribe, picturing flames (near base) and fanged image intended to terrify. The inscription also includes the date of the war in which it was used ('89'), the name of the bearer ('Kunump'), and a discreet advertisement for the skills of Kaipel Ka, the part-time sign painter who decorated it ('Quality signs. Call in at Talu, KK sign')

Figure 22.3 Contemporary wooden shield, Wahgi Kondika tribe, including explicit graphical representations of spear (left), axe (right) and inscription '*Bump Dam*'

was decorated with a graphic image of a hawk (*ka kip*), talons outstretched, because the bearer was from the hawk sub-subgroup (Kipkanem) of Senglap tribe; another shield (figure 22.4) included a painting of flames, said to refer to the warriors' 'hot bellies'; some of the shields belonging to Konumbka tribe were decorated with images of fish, an ironic allusion to their Kondika opponents' vain boast that they would drive Konumbka back into the Wahgi River where their bodies would be consumed by fish.

Words and lettering, similarly motivated, were also incorporated into the new designs. Where some Konumbka shields featured images of fish, others instead included the words '*WAGI PIS*' ('Wahgi fish'), registering the same taunt verbally. Some warriors printed their names on their shields, while other shields had numbers inscribed on them, either the date of the war or numbers with specific symbolic significance. Many shields from the Senglap subgroup of Gilgalkup, for example, were inscribed 'Six 2 Six', which all over New

Guinea generally refers to a 'social', an all-night party, but in the context of warfare became a Gilgalkup boast of their capacity to fight all *day* long. Other shields included the figure '7', because the shape was said to be similar to that of an axe, and axes symbolized internecine warfare. Internecine warfare in turn evokes a Pidgin expression '*Nau wantok kaikai wantok*' ('Now buddy slays buddy') and a Dange shield had these words superimposed on its traditional design.

These changes in design clearly spring broadly from the Wahgi encounter with literacy and, as will emerge, with exogenous iconography in the form of trade store advertisements and labels on cans and packets. This is so not simply in the self-evident sense that you have to see words before you can start using them to decorate shields, but rather in the sense that ideas of reading, of inspecting graphical marks for their significance *as graphical marks*, leads to people thinking of motifs and designs as potentially significant in new ways. As I have tried to bring out, this really does not seem to have been the case in the past, when the significance of shield designs lay not in their graphical nature but in whether they were assessed as glossy and glowing, or dull and ashy.

This is not, of course, to suggest that motivated symbolism as such was foreign to Wahgi before modernity: as we have seen, it existed in codes for dream interpretation, in ideas about omens and signs, as well as in the elaborate verbal forms common to many other Highlands cultures. But it barely seems to have featured so far as *graphical* marks were concerned. What I am arguing is that the encounter with literacy and with figurative iconography introduces – or at least greatly boosts and valorizes – the potent notion that motifs are significant *by virtue* of being graphical marks. In fact, one might suggest that Wahgi were becoming 'graphicate', coining the neologism to emphasize that 'literacy' and 'iconography', more usually contrasted, are here both part of a broader process whereby people become attuned to the semantic potential of graphical marks in general.[12] It is clear that this new way of thinking was most developed in instances when shields were decorated by literacy-professionals such as local sign-writers and school-teachers. In some cases, such individuals were commissioned to decorate others' shields as well as

their own. For example, Kaipel Ka, a talented part-time sign-writer from Senglap tribe, painted the shields not only of men of his own subgroup of Gilgalkup but also those of Senglap Baiman, his maternal kin. But while this new thinking was most developed in such cases, it was also evident in many shields from both the North and South Walls of the valley.

But if the figurative, motivated nature of such designs was novel, the ideas they expressed were often familiar. The new designs included, for example, representations of heroes such as Phantom and invocations of Superman. As Muke (1993: 226) acutely observes, these figures represent moral uprightness: so that where in the past the ancestral support which rewarded moral virtue was testified by whether a shield appeared glossy, glowing etc., it could now also be asserted through explicit representations of 'good guys'. Equally, ancestral support could now be graphically inscribed on shields, as it was on some Kondika shields which bore the words '*Bump Dam*' (figure 22.3), a reference to Kondika's collective ancestral spirit, Bump (Bruce 1992: 33). Again, the terror said to have been inspired in spectators by the sight of charcoaled warriors was now complemented by shield designs which included ghoulish figures that were explicitly intended to be frightening (figure 22.4). Alternatively, war in its post-contact sense of a specifically sinful activity was registered on one shield which was reported to incorporate a picture of Satan, while on other shields the inscription of the group's name was followed by the letters 'NK', standing for *ngal kes*, 'bad child'.[13]

Just as figurative and motivated designs became a vehicle for conveying 'traditional' themes in fresh graphical ways, so modernity also paved the way for further innovations with local resonance. One such aspect of modernity is the example it offers of multiple copies of things, whether hundreds of identical beer advertisements or of rugby league teams all clothed in the same team uniform. This is what seems to have stimulated three subgroups of Senglap tribe (Olkanem, Gilgalkup and Baiman) each to adopt a design said to be common to all men of that subgroup. The impression of co-ordination was amplified by the fact that the different subgroups' designs were each executed by a single individual. At one level this is a distinct break with pre-contact practice in which, as I have noted, it was sometimes claimed that a function of shield designs was to *distinguish* the individual shield bearer from his fellow clansmen. But at another level there is an elective affinity between the notion that the charcoal donned for warfare merges the identity of its wearers, rendering them indistinguishable, and the notion of co-ordinating a group's shield design. Again, a graphical dimension is added to something formerly achieved in nongraphical ways.

The 'team' origin of co-ordinated shield design was most explicit in the case of the Senglap subgroup of Olkanem, all of whose shields (figure 22.5) were said to have the same design based around the Cambridge Cup, the sponsored rugby league trophy mentioned earlier. Here it is also worth noting that the individual who decorated these Olkanem shields explained his use of the word 'Squad' on the shield as a reference to the Wahgi norm that men should fight in their respective groups, not mixed in with other 'lines': a sporting-cum-military inscription was thus used to emphasize the ideal of unity that was formerly expressed only through wearing charcoal. An even more obvious reference to team metaphors was provided by the inscription on a Karapka[14] shield used in their 1989 war against Dange. It read DANGA MURUKS *VS* KARAPKA SP BROTHERS, 'Muruks' and 'SP Brothers' being typical names of Papua New Guinean rugby league teams: the fighting between the two thus being explicitly portrayed as a league match.

Closer examination showed that not every man of the three Senglap subgroups who each claimed to have co-ordinated their respective shield designs had in fact done so. One reason for such non-conformity returns us to the rival loyalties an individual owes to maternal kin. For example, Kaipel Ka, the Senglap shield decorator mentioned earlier, painted his own shield not with the 'Six 2 Six' design used by the rest of his Gilgalkup agnates (figure 22.6) but with the design associated with his Baiman maternal kin, who had asked him to co-ordinate *their* shield designs (figure 22.7) around versions of an advertisement for South Pacific lager. Thus the new intra-group co-ordination of shield designs adopted by some Senglap subgroups furnished a fresh graphical way in which a man could mark his alternative commitment to his maternal kin.

The explanation which Kaipel gave me of the iconography of the 'SP' design (figure 22.7) is also an excellent illustration of the overtly motivated and graphically meaningful thinking which, I am arguing, modernity stimulated Wahgi to extend to shield decoration. Kaipel explained that he had been asked by his matrikin to incorporate a representation of a beer bottle on all their shields, to make the point that 'it was beer alone which had precipitated

Figure 22.5 Contemporary wooden shield, Senglap tribe, Olkanem subgroup; the spray-painted designs include an axe and (top left) a bird of paradise perched upon a rugby ball

Figure 22.6 Most members of Senglap Gilgalkup co-ordinated their shield designs around an inversion of the sociality normally expressed by 'Six 2 Six'

this fighting'. (Beer had been implicated in the road death which lay at the root of the warfare.) However, rather than incorporating an image of a bottle, Kaipel decided instead to make the point by decorating the entire surface of the shield with a design based upon the advertisement for South Pacific beer (he may also have been prompted to do this by the formal similarity between the rounded vertical shape of a beer can or bottle and that of a shield[15]). I also asked Kaipel why he had decorated this and other Senglap shields with a border of red triangles. Here he explained that senior Senglap men had instructed him to incorporate in the shield decoration the design (typically triangular) from a quite separate ceremonial ornament, known as *geru* (O'Hanlon 1989: 102). This was to allude to the fact that, following earlier warfare, Senglap and their Dange opponents had initiated taboos against eating or drinking with each other (*geru*-wearing involves such taboos). The best way he thought he could do this, Kaipel told me, was to adapt to the purpose the rather similar triangular design associated with

the packaging on the *other* well-known local beer, San Miguel.

The Shield Outmoded and Transformed

The overt co-ordination of shield designs obvious among some Senglap groups did not, however, take place everywhere. It was not so evident in the other war which took place in 1989, that between Konumbka and Kondika on the South Wall of the valley.[16] This is not because team idioms are any less important on the South Wall: indeed, Bruce (1992: 71) reports that the first major clash of the Konumbka-Kondika war was actually sparked off at a rugby league match between two tribe-based teams. But in another respect, the Konumbka-Kondika fighting was becoming very much *less* game-like: later the same year, and for the first time in Wahgi warfare, guns were used in battle.

Firearms were not in themselves new to the Wahgi. A number of local men had long been

Figure 22.7 Kaipel's own shield was unusually intricately decorated with a locally modified version of the advertisement for South Pacific lager ('SP No. 1 Beer')

licensed to own shotguns for hunting but they never appear to have been used in the sporadic fighting which persisted even during colonial times. This was probably partly because gun-owners, who were anyway sometimes ex-government employees, knew that such illicit use of their weapons would speedily be traced. But the use of shotguns in pre-1989 fighting seems also to have been prohibited by a 'ritualization' (Strathern 1992: 233) of the kind that re-directed most intergroup tensions into ceremonial exchange in the first place. When I asked Wahgi men in 1981 whether shotguns

were ever used in warfare, they had vehemently denied it, giving three reasons: people were frightened of shotguns, they told me, there was a strong taboo against their use, and they were not traditional Wahgi weapons.

The incorporation of guns into South Wall warfare at the end of the 1980s thus represented a considerable shift, albeit one which some Hagen groups had made three years earlier (Strathern 1992).[17] Initially, however, the great majority of Wahgi firearms were home-made and their effectiveness did not always match their ingenuity. Constructed from metal piping strapped to carved wooden stocks, they fired shotgun cartridges, using as the firing pin a nail driven by a strip of rubber from a car inner tube. In the earliest of the Konumbka-Kondika engagements in which these 'home-mades' were used, their impact appears to have been quite limited. Shields certainly made their carriers highly visible and a number were wounded by pellets. However, there was a perception that by throwing himself backwards a shield carrier could deflect the pellets, while the home-made guns could be quite lethal to their users, at least one of whom was killed when his weapon blew up in his face.

But once the ritual restriction on gun use had been breached, Konumbka and Kondika engaged in a desperate search for further factory-made firearms for their respective arsenals. While much rumour and uncertainty surrounds the topic, Wahgi to whom I spoke in 1990 were quite clear that by then warriors had access to a range of manufactured weapons, grenades among them, either said to be smuggled from Irian Jaya or to have been obtained from the police, whether by theft, loan or sale. When warfare resumed between Konumbka and Kondika some weeks after their first bout, the impact of enhanced weaponry was immediately apparent. Muke (1993: 255) records that seven Kondika were fatally shot, all of them shield carriers; as he notes, it was clear that shields had been transformed from protective devices to liabilities which too often served merely to advertise a target. Certainly, when I talked to Konumbka and Kondika men the following year, by which time peace had at least temporarily been made, they stressed that shields had had their day; when next they fought, they said, it would be individually, using firearms. And in the latest mid-Wahgi warfare of which I have knowledge, the fighting between Kurupka and Maiamka since 1992, shields were not used at all. This was a pure gun fight, with ambushes being the norm and field encounters limited to skirmishes (John Burton, pers. comm).

On the North Wall, in contrast, ritual restraints remained in place throughout the 1989 war between Senglap and Dange. People emphasized that they had made a pact to use only traditional weapons: spears, bows and arrows, axes and shields. Guns were excluded from the fighting, specifically because the opposing sides feared that their adoption would lead to wholesale slaughter. This mutual restraint survived despite a number of conventional battle deaths on either side. Here, then, shields were retained as the primary defensive weapons of war, and a visible symbol of reciprocal forbearance. It is notable that while Konumbka and Kondika were eager to sell me as many as possible of their now redundant shields for a museum collection I was making at the time, Senglap men declared that I ought only to be permitted to purchase a limited number, since they might have need of them in the future.

Conclusion

It is perhaps appropriate that my account of an artefact with so discontinuous a history should itself have considerable gaps. I have not been able to deal in any detail with shield use in practice, with the causes of warfare, or with why the fighting should have taken a more severe turn on the South Wall of the Wahgi than it did on the North. My main focus has been upon the relationship between modernity and certain changes to shield design as a communicative form. Pursuing this has raised a number of instances which bear upon the second of the topics raised at the outset, that of recontextualization.

Let me begin by summarizing the material on the latter. I have considered a number of potential opportunities for what I have termed spatial recontextualization. This did take place in the area of shield design where, as I have shown, advertising material and other exogenous designs have been incorporated to re-express distinctively local issues. Manufactured guns, in contrast, were not recontextualized: once the ritual restraints against their use had been breached, their adoption effected a fundamental change in the patterns of local warfare. But I have also suggested that shields, with their unusual discontinuous history, raise the possibility of an alternative kind of recontextualization, temporal rather than spatial. Here I hope my point is already sufficiently clear. When initially reinvented, shields served their original purpose as the major defensive weapons used in warfare, their adoption signifying a recognized move from less formalized fighting to warfare proper. But within a few years, and with the arrival of factory-made guns, shields were radically recontextualized. From marking fullscale warfare, shields shifted their meaning entirely, their use coming to express, rather, the ritual restraint of combatants who had mutually agreed to eschew the use of firearms. Indeed, in so far as they are part of a set of arrangements which mitigate the effects of warfare, these shields with their unusually elaborate ornamentation, are themselves a 'ritualization', paralleling the earlier shift from warfare to ceremonial exchange.

My major concern in this article, however, has been to document what seems to me the decisive expansion in communicative modality which shield decoration itself underwent as a consequence of the encounter with modernity. I have traced how an original system, in which a range of information was thought of as communicated through the overall assessment of shield surface, has been complemented by one in which meaning is *graphically* inscribed, whether in the form of the new motivated, figurative designs or through writing itself. Furthermore, as I have attempted to bring out, there are strong parallels between what is expressed under the two different modalities. Thus moral virtue can now also be registered through incorporating images of 'good guys' like Superman or Phantom; ancestral support can be alluded to through written inscriptions; the ideal of clan unity, previously marked through common charcoal body covering, can now also be expressed through the adoption of a common shield design, on the analogy of a team or squad; while this in turn provides a new graphical way in which a man can register his innate connexion to his 'source' people by adopting the same design around which they have co-ordinated *their* shields.[18] In fact, the use by Wahgi warriors of this new graphical form to re-express local issues is in a wider sense another instance of spatial recontextualization.

More broadly, what this same material also points up is a relatively unexamined area in the anthropology of art and material culture. It is regularly reported that this or that aesthetic tradition, hitherto largely abstract, is now beginning to incorporate writing, or to become more representational than it was in the past. With a few outstanding exceptions (e.g. Neich 1990) there has been a temptation to footnote such instances as self-explanatory, or even as sad if inevitable examples of 'contamination', rather than seeing them – as I have tried to do here – as potentially indicative of a shift in communicative modality, a shift which may yet be deployed to do 'traditional' things.

As might be anticipated, such literature as *has* focused upon this point tends to relate less to production for local use, as is so with Wahgi shields, than to art forms caught up in the tourist nexus. In either case, we can see the literature as mapping a range of alternative possibilities. Dussart (n.d.: 11), for example, has described what at first sight might appear to be a similar move from abstract to representational designs in contemporary Australian acrylic painting. However, as she makes clear, this is an illusion: the apparently abstract Western Desert motifs (unlike those on Wahgi shields) actually are representational and meaningful – if one knows the code. It is because non-local purchasers of the acrylics do not know the code, and thus fail to understand the Dreaming embodied in the painting, that the painters have shifted to overtly figurative and iconographic motifs in an effort to make it more 'readable'. But once designs do shift in the direction of being graphically representational, another possibility arises, that of their incorporating a sequential or temporal dimension, rather as does a strip cartoon. This has not happened in the case of Wahgi shields (except in so far as incorporating dates and allusions to past taunts entails a degree of temporality). It does, however, appear to be taking place in another New Guinea Highland form, this time from Irian Jaya, as ancestral *sabalhe* boards are transformed from 'ritual' to 'pictorial' art under the impulse of production for outsiders (Gunn and Manembu 1995).

Another permutation is provided by Gow (1990) in his analysis of a Piro text which recounts the story of the first native man from this area of eastern Peru to claim that he could read. Scanning salvaged newspapers, this man, Sangama, would announce that cargo was en route to the Piro from downriver. But what appears to emerge from an examination of this text is that, for Sangama, it was not the graphical marks written *on* the newspaper which he felt to be communicative: these he assimilated to Piro woven, painted and engraved designs which are *not* representational but to do with the visual control of surfaces. Rather, for Sangama, it appears to have been the paper itself, imaged as a female shamanic spirit, which was communicating to him. This case, then, is in a sense the inverse of the Wahgi one: where the Wahgi adopt from the West a new graphical modality as a fresh way of communicating what they had hitherto expressed in non-graphical ways, the Piro assimilate the new graphical mode to an older non-representational tradition of designs, but imagine the paper substrate as communicating by analogy with local shamanic practice.

A final possibility arises when a local design tradition comes up against a determination – even more resolute than my own initially was – that the constituent designs *must* have some graphical significance. Price (1989: 115 sqq.) describes the conviction on the part of exoticist writers that the motifs on Maroon calabashes had a hidden erotic symbolism. One urban Surinamer has produced a symbol dictionary which Maroons themselves now find helpful to point to when pressed by Westerners wishing to know 'the meaning' of their designs.

Recently, Morphy (1994: 677) has cogently pointed to the way in which, of late, 'art has increasingly been inserted into the space between indigenous peoples and the developed world'. As this process continues, the relationship between local and exogenous ways of seeing which the foregoing cases raise seems likely to become of increasing interest and complexity. As we view local designs through chirographic spectacles, so local people, themselves influenced by such modes of interpretation and responding to the need to produce work that is meaningful according to Western canons, may shift visual modality and perhaps eventually begin to interrogate what were originally non-graphical designs for their graphical significance. The widely noted incorporation of representational designs and of odd bits of writing within local art forms deserves to be assessed from this perspective, rather than routinely being footnoted as oddities.

Finally, let me return briefly to the Wahgi case and ask what happens to all the expressions of clan solidarity, of moral virtue and of matrilateral affiliation, when the adorned bodies and shields from which these were read have disappeared, as is happening on the South Wall of the Wahgi where warfare is increasingly conducted through ambushes or by gunmen in cut-off jeans, T-shirts and hard-hats with only a smear of charcoal across the face. The short answer is that I do not know. My suspicion, however, is that at least for a while appearance will continue to be thought of as morally significant, even if it is increasingly restricted to being an idiom in terms of which issues are debated rather than being actively assessed on the battlefield.

NOTES

1   Of course, the term 'modernity', which earlier tended to be used merely as a synonym for 'modern-ness', has more recently been the focus for extensive theoretical debate, and has come to refer to a more profound and problematic – if still diffuse – existential condition: see, for example, Miller (1994) for a valuable discussion of the term in relation to contemporary Trinidad. My own use of 'modernity' as shorthand for a somewhat haphazard set of effects and manifestations is not intended to return the term to its earlier usage. Indeed, there is a parallel between the 1976–83 oil-boom which enhanced the term's applicability to Trinidad, and the boom in coffee prices at the same time in Highland New Guinea. More particularly, I see the present article as contributing to the anthropological examination, which Miller (1994: 68) also urges, of the balance between global homogenization and local appropriation.

2   I am unclear about what proportion of men traditionally carried shields in battle. My initial impression was that most did, an impression supported by Taylor's (1933: 29, 45) characterization of Wahgi as 'spear' rather than 'bow and arrow' fighters. However, in recent warfare relatively few warriors carried shields and Muke's (1993: 95) information suggests that the division between 'shield carriers' and 'arrow men' is a longstanding one.

3   Designs were sometimes also delineated in punctuate (see also Lowman 1973: 22).

4   One casualty of this preoccupation with what shields 'communicate' has been the provision of equivalent information on how shields were actually carried and used. For example, the fullest single contemporary study of any Melanesian shield type is probably Lowman's (1973) well-known analysis of Maring shields which stresses their role in communicating messages about warriors' size, numbers, etc. to their opponents. But otherwise suggestive though Lowman's account is, her description and diagram (1973: 24) of how a shield was supported omits a vital sling and, if followed, would actually have left the shield slung over the warrior's *back* and in no position either to protect him or to communicate anything to his opponents. Brief details of Wahgi shield use and shield support mechanisms – which are similar to those on Maring shields – are given in O'Hanlon 1993: 64 ff.; see also O'Hanlon (1995). One might, in fact, see in the fixation with shield design a contemporary analogue to the aestheticization of weaponry which Knauft (1990: 259–60) detects in many early anthropological accounts.

5   In fact, the only instance that comes to mind of motivated graphical significance explicitly being attributed to any traditional Wahgi design is given by Luzbetak (1954: 106) and later Reay (1959: 161), who record that the triangular motifs on the ceremonial *geru* boards symbolize the vulva/ fertility. This is not something that was ever volunteered to me, though Salisbury (1959: 50–51), writing of the Siane, similarly reports that *geru* board designs possessed motivated graphical significance.

6   Ryan (1958: 243) similarly records of Mendi shield designs that, while they did not function as escutcheons proper, they had a similar identificatory aspect.

7   O'Hanlon (1989: ch. 6) discusses the range of terms used in evaluating the decorated appearance.

8   A more detailed account of post-contact Wahgi history from the perspective of Komblo tribe in particular is given in O'Hanlon (1993).

9   During my first period of fieldwork on the North Wall of the Wahgi (May 1979–August 1981) I saw only two shields, both being used at a Provincial Government celebration in July 1981.

10 Shields similarly disappeared around this time, and for the same reasons, from the material repertoire of neighbouring peoples (Nilles 1953: 3; Strathern and Strathern 1971: 102; Lowman 1973: 8; P. Brown, pers. comm). In the Wahgi case, this impression of an artefact utterly falling out of existence must disguise odd instances in which, at least for a while, men deliberately concealed shields from the colonial authorities for fear of being suspected of fighting; furthermore, shield storage places were anyway sometimes ritually restricted, hidden from all but the most determined outsider (Aufenanger 1957: 632; 1959: 8). Shields can also be re-used as beds, and a number must have survived for a while in this capacity.

11 Burton (1990) provides an account of the same battle, and goes on to contrast it with the gun warfare which shortly followed it.

12 I am particularly grateful to Alfred Gell for crystallizing my thoughts in this direction, though I have preferred the neologism 'graphicate' to his suggestion of 'figurate'.

13 I have not myself seen either of these; I am grateful to Charles Clay for information about the former and to Alphonse Dire for the latter.

14 This is, in fact, an antique term for Senglap tribe.

15 An observation I owe to Jeremy Coote. A shield shown in one of John Muke's photographs (1993: plate 12) from a different war actually appears to have been carved in the shape of a bottle, or perhaps to have the giant image of a bottle taken from an advertising hoarding fastened to its front.

16 Muke (1993: 224–5, 243 ff.) does, however, discern a degree of co-ordination of different groups' shield designs in terms of colours. I am unclear, though, whether this is an intentional marking-out or is the by-product of the fact that the men of a given group will tend to decorate their shields together and are likely to draw communally on whatever paint stocks they happen to possess.

17 See also Hutchinson (1996) for a brilliant analysis of some of the transformations, both tactical and symbolic, which flowed from the inclusion of guns in warfare in quite another part of the world, Nuerland. Her account raises many tragically pertinent questions with regard to the more recent introduction of guns into Wahgi fighting.

18 In drawing attention to these parallels, I am not suggesting that the shift towards 'graphicalization' identified in this article has had no effect on meaning. In a stimulating comment on an earlier draft, Foster, for example, asks whether such co-ordinated shield designs as 'Cambridge Cup' (fig. 22.5) are less the expression of a traditional Wahgi concern with group solidarity so much as the expression of an emergent identity based around the consumption of new national products (pers. comm; see also Foster 1995). My emphasis has been upon the former, because what those Wahgi men with whom I discussed the matter commented upon was the collective aspect to team games and its parallel to clanship, rather than the commodity which the trophy's sponsors happened to sell. However, fresh idioms carry their own entailments, and Foster is undoubtedly correct in pointing to the potential for new identities (though, as it happens, there is also an *indigenous* Wahgi notion which recognizes that co-consumption of the same product generates a measure of shared identity: this is registered in the practice whereby two people will call each other by the name of any foodstuff which they have shared).

REFERENCES

Aufenanger, H. 1957. The Parry shield in the Western Highlands of New Guinea. *Anthropos* 52, 631–3.
—— 1959. The war-magic houses in the Wahgi Valley and adjacent areas (New Guinea). *Anthropos* 54, 1–26.
Barthes, R. 1973. *Mythologies*. St Albans: Paladin.
Bruce, R.G. 1992. The study of law and order in Papua New Guinea: social deviance and identity among the Kuma-Kondika of the South Wahgi. Thesis, University of Cambridge.
Burton, J. 1990. Tribal fighting: the scandal of inaction. *Res. Melanes.* 14, 31–40.
Coote, J. and A. Shelton 1992. Introduction. In *Anthropology, art and aesthetics* (eds) J. Coote and A. Shelton. Oxford: Clarendon Press.
Corrigan, B. n.d. Minj Patrol Report no. 3 of 1952/3.
Cranstone, B.A.L. 1968. War shields of the Telefomin sub-district, New Guinea. *Man* (N.S.) 3, 609–24.
Dussart, F. n.d. Disembodiment of a body painting. Paper presented at ASA IV Decennial Conference session on 'Visual representations and systems of visual knowledge', 27 July 1993. Ms.
Foster, R. 1995. Print advertisements and nation making in metropolitan Papua New Guinea. In *Nation making: emergent identities in postcolonial Melanesia* (ed.) R. Foster. Ann Arbor: University of Michigan Press.
Gell, A. 1992. The technology of enchantment and the enchantment of technology. In *Anthropology, art and aesthetics* (eds) J. Coote and A. Shelton. Oxford: Clarendon Press.
Glass, P. 1986. The Trobriand code: an interpretation of Trobriand war shield designs. *Anthropos* 81, 47–63.
Goldman, L.R. 1983. *Talk never dies: the language of Huli disputes*. London: Tavistock Publications.
Gow, P. 1990. Could Sangama read?: the origin of writing among the Piro of eastern Peru. *Hist. Anthrop.* 5, 87–103.
Gunn, M. and Niesje Manembu. 1995. *Sabalhe ancestor boards of the Yali, central Irian Jaya: a transformation from ritual to pictorial art*. *Baessler-Archiv* 43(1): 127–165.

Harrison, S. 1993. *The mask of war: violence, ritual and the self in Melanesia*. Manchester: Univ. Press.
Heaney, W.H. 1989. Circular labor migration and entrepreneurship in the Wahgi Valley, Papua New Guinea. Thesis, Columbia University.
Hutchinson, S. 1996. *Nuer dilemmas: coping with money, war and the state*. Berkeley: University of California Press.
Knauft, B.M. 1990. Melanesian warfare: a theoretical history. *Oceania* 60, 250–311.
Layton, R. 1981. *The anthropology of art*. St Albans: Granada Publishing.
Leach, E.R. 1954. A Trobriand Medusa? *Man* 54, 103–5.
Lowman, C. 1973. *Displays of power: art and war among the Marings of New Guinea* (Mus. prim. Art Stud. 6). New York: Museum of Primitive Art.
Luzbetak, L.J. 1954. The socio-religious significance of a New Guinea pig festival. *Anthrop. Q.* (N.S.) 2, 59–80, 102–128.
—— 1958. The Middle Wahgi culture. *Anthropos* 53, 51–87.
McCracken, G. 1988. *Culture and consumption: new approaches to the symbolic character of consumer goods and activities*. Bloomington: Indiana University Press.
Meggitt, M.J. 1977. *Blood is their argument: warfare among the Mae-Enga tribesmen of the New Guinea Highlands*. Palo Alto: Mayfield.
Meigs, A.S. 1984. *Food, sex and pollution: a New Guinea religion*. New Brunswick: Rutgers Univ. Press.
Miller, D. 1987. *Material culture and mass consumption*. Oxford: Basil Blackwell.
—— 1994. *Modernity: an ethnographic approach*. Oxford: Berg.
Morphy, H. 1994. The anthropology of art. In *Companion encyclopedia of anthropology* (ed.) T. Ingold. London: Routledge.
Muke, J.D. 1993. The Wahgi *Opo Kumbo*: an account of warfare in the central Highlands of New Guinea. Thesis, University of Cambridge.
Neich, R. 1990. Maori figurative painting: tradition and innovation in the search for identity. In *Art and identity in Oceania* (eds.) A. Hanson and L. Hanson. Honolulu: Univ. of Hawaii Press.

Nilles, J. 1953. The Kuman people: a study of cultural change in a primitive society in the central Highlands of New Guinea. *Oceania* 24, 1–27.

O'Hanlon, M.D.P. 1989. *Reading the skin: adornment, display and society among the Wahgi*. London: British Museum Publications.

—— 1992. Unstable images and second skins: artefacts, exegesis and assessments in the New Guinea Highlands. *Man* (N.S.) 27, 587–608.

—— 1993. *Paradise: portraying the New Guinea Highlands*. London: British Museum Press.

—— 1995. Medusa's art: interpreting Melanesian shields. In *Protection, power and display: shields of Island Southeast Asia and Melanesia* (ed.) A. Tavarelli. Boston: Boston College Museum of Art.

Ong, W.J. 1982. *Orality and literacy: the technologizing of the world*. London, New York: Routledge.

Price, S. 1989. *Primitive art in civilized places*. Chicago: Univ. of Chicago Press.

Reay, M.O. 1959. *The Kuma: freedom and conformity in the New Guinea Highlands*. Melbourne: Univ. Press.

—— 1987. The magico-religious foundations of New Guinea Highlands warfare. In *Sorcerer and witch in Melanesia* (ed.) M. Stephen. New Brunswick: Rutgers Univ. Press.

Ryan, D'A.J. 1958. Some decorated fighting-shields from the Mendi Valley, Southern Highlands district of Papua. *Mankind* 5, 243–9.

Sahlins, M. 1976. *Culture and practical reason*. Chicago: Univ. of Chicago Press.

Salisbury, R.F. 1959. A Trobriand Medusa? *Man* 67, 50–1.

Sillitoe, P. 1980. The art of war: Wola shield designs. *Man* (N.S.) 15, 483–501.

Stafford, B.M. 1993. Presuming images and consuming words: on the visualization of knowledge from the Enlightenment to postmodernism. In *Culture and consumption: the world of goods* (eds) J. Brewer and R. Porter. London: Routledge.

Strathern, A.J. 1977. Contemporary warfare in the New Guinea Highlands – revival or breakdown? *Yagl-ambu* 4, 135–46.

—— 1992. Let the bow go down. In *War in the tribal zone: expanding states and indigenous warfare* (eds) R.B. Ferguson and N.L. Whitehead. Santa Fe: School of American Research Press.

Strathern, A.J. and M. Strathern 1971. *Self-decoration in Mount Hagen*. London: Duckworth.

Taylor, J.L. 1933. *Mount Hagen Patrol Report*. Australian Archives A7034, item 56.

Thomas, N. 1991. *Entangled objects: exchange, material culture and colonialism in the Pacific*. Cambridge, MA: Harvard Univ. Press.

Wheeler, T. 1988. *Papua New Guinea: a travel survival kit*. South Yarra: Lonely Planet Publications.

Part V

Marketing Culture

Introduction

To address the question of marketing or the sale of art – in part, a question of audiences and how to bring work to them – the process through which marketing is learned and in what context must be considered. The boundaries between contemporary art, tourist art, and what Nelson Graburn (ch. 23) calls "Fourth world arts" are becoming increasingly vague. Objects that are sold may be intentionally produced for sale as fine art or as souvenirs, but they may also be older objects or those produced originally for a range of indigenous functions. While the international art market ensures that objects circulate continually through a system of non-indigenous galleries, museums, and collectors, objects have long been and continue to be exchanged or sold within indigenous systems. Objects that circulate outside the original community have both didactic functions, as a central means through which an audience learns about a culture, and economic functions, through which producers can adapt to a local or global market economy while retaining certain cultural practices. The groundwork for the study of tourist art set out in the essay by Graburn has continued more recently with a collection assembled by Phillips and Steiner (1999). Since the distinctions between Western and non-Western have become increasingly untenable, a comprehensive anthropological analysis of art for sale must also address this process in a broad context – ranging from the study of the market for work by contemporary indigenous artists trained in art schools to the interpretation of the roles of international auction houses in the sale of European art.

The perceptions of the viewer and the expectations of the market continue to reflect certain stereotypes, and objects are often created to satisfy those tastes (see Bourdieu 1984 for an important sociological study of taste and Price 2001 for an analysis of Western tastes for "primitive art"). The souvenir, for example, has become a convenient and potent way for tourists to symbolize their connection (however cursory) to a place or a culture. Phillips demonstrates how the production of material for the market acts as both a process of conservation and cultural adaptation in Native American art (see Phillips 1998 for the complete study from which our selection is excerpted). On one level, the demands of the market have had undoubted influence on forms and practices through the tourists' desire to create an "authentic" Indian experience through the acquisition and display of objects (see Hill 2002 and Babcock 1995 for related approaches to authenticity in Native American art). Yet the adaptation of materials and styles for different forms of production and use also reflect the strength and adaptability of traditional forms such as beadwork and basketry. After long resistance, many museums are slowly beginning to collect and display the new forms of material culture that have incorporated non-indigenous materials and been used for trade or as souvenirs.

Steiner's work demonstrates the complex relationship between producers and buyers through his analysis of the role of the middlemen who make a living by ensuring that the tastes of the market are satisfied through the manipulation of objects (this subject is explored in greater length in Steiner 1994). The presentation, description and alteration of African objects to suit the tastes of the market reflects the desire among collectors for older pieces that have been used in an indigenous context (see MacClancy 1988 for an analysis of related tastes in the British art market). These tastes have created an extensive market for copies and forgeries of objects made in traditional styles. Related questions concerning the authenticity of objects produced in any cultural context are central to the art market and its creation of value (see Benjamin 1968 for a seminal study relating to this topic and Handler 1986 on the relationship between sincerity and notions of cultural authenticity). Yet the criteria for judging authenticity vary considerably for objects from different cultures. Categories of objects may be sold and still continue to have ritual meaning (see Myers ch. 27 and Dussart 1997). Copying, forgery, or the adherence to prescribed forms may be viewed differently depending on the system of production and the expectation of the audience. The same art market that demands qualities such as originality and innovation in Western art, may expect African or Native American art to be produced anonymously in recognizable and often stereotypical forms. Similar objects produced for use within their indigenous context may also involve a degree of copying since a class of objects must retain certain characteristics if they are to serve particular ritual functions. Copying may also serve as a method of training and a challenge for artists as is the case in China where copies of paintings hold very high value (see Fu 1991:33–36 for examples of the many types of copies and the reasons why Chinese painters produce them).

As producers become increasingly aware of the interests of the market, more individual or cooperative efforts are being made to sell directly – the sale of Inuit art (Graburn 2004), and Aboriginal Australian painting (Morphy 1991; Myers 2002;) have become particularly prominent in recent decades. The main motivation for the sale of art may be economic but it is often part of wider social processes of engagement, adjustment, and transformation. The sale of art has implications for the control of knowledge as the objects are traded beyond the boundaries of a society. On the one hand, the sale of art may help educate outsiders and promote wider understanding of the way of life and values of members of a society; on the other hand, it may have consequences on the internal structure and dynamics of the society itself. The commodification of art may be one of the ways in which members of a society work through complex processes of social change. Anthropologists who study art can play a role in mediating between the artists and the market, facilitating the communication of cultural meaning and value through art. The market is not always comprised of those who are knowledgeable. Indeed, it is often made up of the ignorant or the simply curious; some who want to learn more (even if without permission) and some who do not.

REFERENCES

Babcock, Barbara, 1995 Marketing Maria: The Tribal Artist in the Age of Mechanical Reproduction. In *Looking High and Low: Art and Cultural Identity*. Brenda Jo Bright and Lizi Bakewell, eds. Tucson: University of Arizona Press.

Benjamin, Walter, 1968 The Work of Art in the Age of Mechanical Reproduction. In *Walter Benjamin, Illuminations*. Hannah Arendt, ed. New York: Schocken Books.

Bourdieu, Pierre, 1984 *Distinction: A Social Critique of the Judgement of Taste*. Cambridge: Harvard University Press.

Dussart, Francoise, 1997 A Body Painting in Translation. In *Rethinking Visual Anthropology*. Marcus Banks and Howard Morphy, eds. Pp. 186–202. New Haven: Yale University Press.

Fu Shen, C. Y., 1991 *Challenging the Past: The Paintings of Chang Dai-chien*. Washington: Smithsonian Institution Press.

Graburn, Nelson H. H., ed. 1976 *Ethnic and Tourist Arts: Cultural Expressions of the Fourth World*. Berkeley: University of California Press.

Graburn, Nelson H. H., 2004 The Invention of Authentic Inuit Art. In *Beyond Art/Artifact/Tourist Art: Social Agency and the Cultural Value(s) of the Aestheticized Object*. Nelson Graburn and Aaron Glass, eds. Special issue, *Journal of Material Culture* 9(2):141–159.

Handler, Richard, 1986 Authenticity. *Anthropology Today* 2(1): 2–4.

Hill, Richard W., 2002 Blood Work: Debating Authenticity of Indian Art. *Native Americas* 19(1/2):56–61.

MacClancy, Jeremy, 1988 A Natural Curiosity: The British Market in Primitive Art. *Res. Anthropology and Aesthetics* 15:163–176.

Morphy, Howard, 1991 *Ancestral Connections: Art and an Aboriginal System of Knowledge*. Chicago: University of Chicago Press.

Myers, Fred, 2002 *Painting Culture: The Making of an Aboriginal High Art*. Durham: Duke University Press.

Phillips, Ruth B., 1998 *Trading Identities: The Souvenir in Native North American Art from the Northeast, 1700–1900*. Seattle: University of Washington Press.

Phillips, Ruth and Christopher Steiner, eds. 1999 *Unpacking Culture: Art and Commodity on Colonial and Postcolonial Worlds*. Berkeley: University of California Press.

Price, Sally, 2001[1989] *Primitive Art in Civilized Places*. Chicago: University of Chicago Press.

Steiner, Christopher B., 1994 *African Art in Transit*. Cambridge: Cambridge University Press.

23

Arts of the Fourth World

Nelson H. H. Graburn

The concept of the Fourth World, which has already been the title of two books (Whitaker 1972; Manuel and Poslums 1974),[1] is a particularly appropriate one for the study of anthropology and for the majority of the peoples whose arts are discussed in this book. The Fourth World is the collective name for all aboriginal or native peoples whose lands fall within the national boundaries and technobureaucratic administrations of the countries of the First, Second, and Third Worlds. As such, they are peoples without countries of their own, peoples who are usually in the minority and without the power to direct the course of their collective lives.

Not only are they no longer isolated or autonomous peoples as they perhaps once were, but their arts are rarely produced for their own consumption or according to their own unmodified tastes. In many ways these peoples have become dependent part-societies (Graburn 1967) whose very thought and culture reflect the differences from, and accommodation to, the realities of the majority peoples surrounding them. Thus, the study of the arts of the Fourth World is different from the study of "primitive" art, characteristic of most earlier anthropological writings, for it must take into account more than one symbolic and aesthetic system, and the fact that the arts may be produced by one group for consumption by another. The study of Fourth World arts is, par excellence, the study of *changing* arts – of emerging ethnicities, modifying identities, and commercial and colonial stimuli and repressive actions.

Attitudes Toward Fourth World Arts

This volume, then, concerns one of the most neglected fields within the disciplines of anthropology and art history. It involves the study of what used to be called "primitive" art in the changing sociocultural context of the modern world, a world in which small-scale nonindustrial societies are no longer isolated and in which holistic cultures with their inner-directed traditional arts have almost ceased to exist.

These arts were only "discovered" to have aesthetic value during the last century (Goldwater, in Biebuyck 1969). Before this, although they were collected, it was only for their curiosity value. They were first seriously and widely appreciated by disaffected Western artists, who took them as a form of innovative inspiration without realizing their inherent conservatism.

From Introduction to *Ethnic and Tourist Arts: Cultural Expressions from the Fourth World* (Berkeley: University of California Press, 1976), pp. 1–30, 372–393. Reprinted by permission of the University of California Press.

This is the first point where one might say that (segments of) Western society "needed" primitive arts. Perhaps this need coincided with the bankruptcy of the academic art world, and more importantly, with the increasing secularization, standardization, and industrialization of Euro-America. This early interest in and collection of works of primitive art, however, (see Gerbrands 1957:25–64; Claerhout 1965), was without appreciation of their cultural context. In many cases the agents of colonialist powers, after they had overcome some of their revulsion toward the subject peoples, collected arts and crafts as souvenirs of their sojourns in the service of the empire (see especially Bascom in Graburn 1967a: ch. 17). These souvenirs might have been actual examples of the traditional arts of the local peoples and occasionally were commissioned models of such items. Even in the former instance, however, the colonial agents were usually unable to tell whether the items they had bought were truly traditional or whether they were specially made and modified for the souvenir market.

As "civilized societies" come to depend more and more upon standardized mass-produced artifacts, the distinctiveness of classes, families, and individuals disappears, and the importation of foreign exotic arts increases to meet the demand for distinctiveness, especially for the snob or status market. One gains prestige by association with these objects, whether they are souvenirs or expensive imports; there is a cachet connected with international travel, exploration, multiculturalism, etc. that these arts symbolize; at the same time, there is the nostalgic input of the *handmade* in a "plastic world," a syndrome best described in Edmund Carpenter's "Do You Have the Same Thing in Green? or Eskimos in New Guinea" (1971). But for many items of commercial art, this very demand often leads to a proliferation and a mass production that vitiates the prestige and usefulness in the very snob market for which the new arts were invented – thus, "success breeds failure" is a new version of the adage "familiarity breeds contempt."

The Anthropology of Art

Falling well within the major boundaries and goals of traditional anthropological theory, this study is an enquiry into the nature of social integration, in the Durkheimian sense (1893), and of course, the converse, differentiation. Our attempts to understand both integration and differentiation have often been expressed as the study of structure, social or cultural, depending on the levels. Integration and differentiation are but two sides of the same coin, essential to the processes of solidarity within groups and between parts of groups, or between groups that go together to form a part of larger entities. These groups, or segments of society, are called by many names: classes, castes, tribes, ethnic groups, identity groups, etc., all of which are tending to merge in the contemporary world. The arts of these peoples have been called "primitive" art and "folk" art, depending on whether the creators are, respectively, members of a recently conquered group or of the long-familiar "lower classes" of complex societies.

Though the terms "primitive" and "folk" art may have been satisfactory for the purposes of nineteenth-century Europeans, it now seems clear that such categories are hopelessly inadequate for any contemporary description (see Gerbrands 1957:9–24). Indeed, they are often taken to be either prejudicial or patronizing slurs upon the arts and artists in question. Even the label "art" itself reflects the elitist traditions of "high civilizations" concerning the value of arts vs. crafts, the importance of creativity and originality, and specializations and distinctions that emerged in Europe and China. As J. Maquet (1971) has clearly shown, aesthetic productions may be (1) *art by destination*, that is to say, they may have been intended by their producers to be art per se or to have a primarily aesthetic locus, or (2) they may be *art by metamorphosis*, in which case they are deemed art sometime *after* they were originally made (often as a result of the changing standards and preferences of the consumer). A special case of "art by metamorphosis" occurs when objects produced in one society are transported to another and labeled as "art." That the object may have been intended for such external consumption is itself an indication of the special relationship that exists between the art-producing peoples of the Fourth World and the tourists and art-consumers of the West; it is this relationship that provides much of the subject matter for this volume. (See, for instance, my article

"I like things to look more different than that stuff did," 1976b).

As Maquet so aptly remarks (1971:16) "Outside our showcases, there is no primitive art, particularly not in the nonliterate societies where museum and gallery objects have been created." The concept of "primitive" art is a particularly Western concept, referring to creations that we wish to call art made by peoples who, in the nineteenth century were usually called "primitive," but in fact were simply previously autonomous peoples who had been overrun by the colonial powers. The descendants of these peoples are no longer autonomous, nor are they necessarily preliterate, and their arts – the arts of the Fourth World – are rarely free of the influences of the artistic traditions of the dominant societies that engulfed them.

Similarly, "folk" art was a concept invented in the nineteenth century by which the literate upper classes of such stratified societies as those in Europe and India could label the arts and crafts of the lower classes, the often non-literate rural peoples who followed local as well as national traditions. Nations are no longer organized along such feudal lines, and most classes of people are no longer illiterate; moreover, even if they were, most of them are now exposed to national and international traditions and tastes, through radio, travel, marketing networks, and increasing worldwide standardization. Today, the term "folk" art is used for those remnants of local traditions that have broad appeal, that represent the continuing traditions of handmade things, and that are not officially part of the art establishment or the avant-garde. Hence, our book deals with the descendants of the primitive arts and the transformations of some folk arts. Many, if not most, of these arts are made for appreciation and consumption outside of the society of creation, contrasting with the internal orientations of primitive and folk arts in the past. That these processes are not confined to minority cultures in a capitalist environment is well illustrated in Kaplan and Baradulin (1975).

Although the general purpose of this book is to explore the forms, functions, and meanings of Fourth World arts in their changing sociocultural contexts, the increasing importance of this "special relationship" between producer and consumer should be kept in mind as the reader proceeds through the various chapters.

For this is not only an *art* book, it is an *anthropological* book as well. The reader, then, is urged not only to evaluate the various objects herein discussed in terms of their "artistic significance," but also to consider his own "emotional investment" in the objects, perhaps his own unintentional or unconscious distortions of the work of art and the artist. This suggestion can be taken as a methodological *caveat*, a reminder that *all* people (even the "primitives") tend to want to make the unfamiliar less frightening and more "understandable" by bending it to their own preconceptions. The danger is that what often results is not the world as we know it, but the world as we would have it.

The Changing Arts of the Fourth World

In stratified societies that consist of dominant and conquered strata, the arts of the latter peoples may be of two major types: (1) Those arts – the inwardly directed arts – that are made for, appreciated, and used by peoples within their own part-society; these arts have important functions in maintaining ethnic identity and social structure, and in didactically instilling the important values in group members. (2) Those arts made for an external, dominant world; these have often been despised by connoisseurs as unimportant, and are sometimes called "tourist" or "airport" arts. They are, however, important in presenting to the outside world an ethnic image that must be maintained and projected as a part of the all-important boundary-defining system. All human social groups, from the family to the United Nations, need symbols of their internal and external boundaries; the practical and decorative arts often provide these essential markers.

Most of the societies that are described in this book have undergone some form of change or acculturation that has been defined as "those phenomena which result from groups of individuals having differing cultures coming into first-hand contact, with subsequent changes in the original culture of either or both groups" (Redfield, Linton, and Herskovits 1936:149). Thus, they could be called the "arts of acculturation," which I have defined elsewhere as "art production, which differs significantly from traditional expressions in form, content, function, and medium, and which also differs from the various forms of art production indigenous to ever-growing 'civilization' " (1969:457). This broad category embraces those forms that have elsewhere been labelled transitional, commercial, souvenir, or airport arts, but it also includes certain novel noncommercial art forms.

Building on a previous classification (Graburn 1969), we may attempt to outline some of the differing directions taken by the processes of artistic change, as illustrated in this book:

1. Extinction

The decline or disappearance of the indigenous art form has, surprisingly, rarely been described. One case is illustrated ... by Biebuyck's description of the demise of Lega *bwami* sculpture [Biebuyck, in Graburn 1976a:ch. 19].

2. Traditional or functional fine arts

The persistence of a traditional art form can be accompanied by some changes in technique and form, or even show incorporation of a few European-derived symbols and images. As long as these changes do not seriously disturb the transmission of symbolic meaning, and hence the culturally appropriate satisfactions, these may still be called functional or contact-influenced traditional arts (May 1974:1–6). They are exemplified by some of the pottery made for home consumption at Laguna (see Gill, in Graburn 1976a:ch. 5) and other Pueblos, by the temple and wall paintings of Rajasthan (see Maduro, in Graburn 1976a:ch. 13), or by the larger bark paintings of traditional beliefs made by the aborigines at Yirrkala, Arnhem Land (see Williams, in Graburn 1976a:ch. 13). In chapter 16 (Graburn 1976a) Mead describes the still-traditional carvings and buildings of the New Zealand Maori, which serve the minority community, but are made with metal tools and modern paints, by artists with government-sponsored university instruction in the arts.

3. Commercial fine arts

Many art forms similar to the above may be called commercial fine arts or pseudo-traditional arts (May, ibid.) because, although they are made with eventual sale in mind, they adhere to culturally embedded aesthetic and formal standards. The better of the Peruvian gourds described by Boyer (in Graburn 1976a:ch. 10), some of the Shiaibo pottery described by Lathrap in Graburn 1976a: ch. 11, and Australian aborigine and Maori productions fall into this category. Commercial arts range almost imperceptibly from the truly functional, such as Asmat *biche* poles and Melanesian *malanggan*, which may be sold to anthropologists or collectors after ritual usage, through considerably modified forms, such as Huichol yarn paintings to objects with less meaning and lowered standards, such as those described in our next category.

4. Souvenirs

When the profit motive or the economic competition of poverty override aesthetic standards, satisfying the consumer becomes more important than pleasing the artist. These are often called "tourist" arts or "airport" arts and may bear little relation to the traditional arts of the creator culture or to those of any other groups. Akamba wood carvings (see figure 23.1), Seri ironwood carvings (see Ryerson, in Graburn 1976:ch. 6, the bark paintings of Xalitla (see Stromberg, in Graburn 1976:ch. 8), or even the ebony carving of the Makonde of Tanzania (see figure 23.6) are innovations or novelties, with specific dates and recorded origins that indicate they have been made within the past 20 years! The rationalization of production and the standardization or simplification of design of many souvenir arts have tended to give all commercial, contemporary arts a bad name. The symbolic content is so reduced, and conforms so entirely to the consumers' popular notions of the salient characteristics of the minority group, that we may call these items ethno-kitsch, paralleling Dorfles' concept of porno-kitsch (1969: 219–223).

5. Reintegrated arts

Not all contemporary arts fall on a simple continuum between traditional arts and European arts. Cultural contact between dominant and minority peoples has often led to fertile new forms, developed by taking some ideas, materials, or techniques from the industrial society and applying them in new ways to the

Figure 23.1 East African Akamba souvenirs, with anthropomorphic handles; female bust; and warrior figures; all mid-twentieth century. Courtesy of the Lowie Museum UCLMA 5–5946, 5–5947, 5–10205, 5–3856.

needs of the small-scale peoples. These arts are new syntheses, such as the colorful *mola* blouses (see Salvador, in Graburn 1976a:ch. 9) that the Cuna Indians of Panama made after they were introduced to imported textiles, needles, and scissors. In the American Southwest, the traditionally mobile Navajo hunters learned weaving from the sedentary Pueblo Indians, adapted sheepherding from the colonial Spanish, and themselves developed a unique weaving tradition (see Kent, in Graburn 1976a:ch. 4) to fill their needs for clothing and saddle blankets. Later, these textiles in turn came to be sold to white Americans. We might say that this art form went from a new inte-

grated synthesis to a Navajo tradition to a form of highly valued commercial art.

6. *Assimilated fine arts*

There are an increasing number of instances where the conquered minority artists have taken up the established art forms of the conquerors, following and competing with the artists of the dominant society. These are characteristic of extreme cultural domination and hence a desire to assimilate. Excellent examples are most of the Plains and Southwest Indian painting (Brody in Graburn 1976a:ch. 3; and 1971) and the water-color productions of the Australian Aborigine painter, Namatjira (see figure 23.2), and the Hermansburg school (Batty 1963).

7. Popular arts

The assimilation of previously colonialized peoples to the arts and traditions of the dominant European powers can also take another turn. An artistic elite has arisen whose arts often take the forms of European traditions, but in content express feelings totally different, feelings appropriate to the new cultures that are emerging among the leaders of the Third World. Thus, there are painters and poets in Mozambique, such as Malangatana (Schneider 1972), who express in European terms African feelings about art and life, and in the former Belgian Congo, now Zaire, there is a genre called *arts populaire* (Szombati-Fabian and Fabian 1975) that records for the modern Africans their feelings about their ancestral tribal past, their domination by harsh Belgian colonists, and their present developing and urbanizing country. Such phenomena are not properly the subject of this book, for these people are moving from

being powerless Fourth World minorities to being powerful leaders – if not majorities – of their own Third World countries.

We may now summarize these processes in [a]...two-dimensional diagram of the various art forms of the Fourth World (table 23.1). Moving from top to bottom, we pass from arts made for the peoples of the minority cultures themselves, to those made for export to outgroups and foreign markets; moving from left to right we pass from arts made purely according to traditional aesthetic and formal criteria (even if made with new techniques and materials in some cases) to, at the far end, arts that fall squarely within the traditions of the dominant powers. In the center column are those arts specially developed from a synthesis of native and European forms, or even complete innovations created out of the unique contact situation.

Not all contemporary arts of Fourth World peoples fit the above scheme neatly. Many art forms fit more than one category at the same time, as they are quite purposefully multifunctional. For instance, to teach their young men

Figure 23.2 Water color painting by the Australian artist Albert Namatjira, *The Ancient Ghost Gum of Temple bar* (1943). Namatjira painted landscapes in his aboriginal homeland, in the style of white artist Rex Battarbee. Courtesy of Mrs. R. H. Croll, and the Australian Consul General, San Francisco.

Table 23.1 Aesthetic-Formal Sources and Traditions

Intended Audience	Minority Society	Novel/Synthetic	Dominant Society
Minority Fourth World	Functional Traditional e.g., Lega, Maori marae, some pueblo pottery	Reintegrated e.g., Cuna molas, Pueblo kachinas	Popular e.g., Zaire, Mozambique, Navajo jewelery
External Civilizations	Commercial Fine e.g., Maori woodcarving, New Guinea shields	Souvenir Novelty e.g., Seri, Makonde carving; Xalitla amate	Assimilated Fine e.g., Santa Fe Indian painting, Namatjira watercolors, Eskimo prints

their beliefs about Dreamtime, aborigine men in Australia (see Williams, in Graburn 1976:ch. 15) make bark paintings of "important scenes," which they sell, along with other paintings to museums and rich collectors. They also, however, produce small portable and relatively meaningless barks for the tourist trade. One might diagram the processes as follows:

Traditional barks		
Hunting scenes	Suitcase souvenirs	Namatjira watercolors

In this fashion we might, in fact, diagram many of our other cases, noting the movement of the art form over time, e.g., as the functions and techniques change:

Worn	Cuna molas	Western dress
For sale	Tourista molas	

Pueblo pottery	Revivals	Manufactured utensils
Sale	Souvenirs	

This kind of diagram represents only the arts of the contact situation produced by the no-longer isolated groups. If we could imagine a third dimension, below the diagram would be the uninfluenced traditional arts of tribal and small-scale societies. Moving with the flow of

time, we would find contact first in the upper left-hand square – contact-influenced traditional arts. As cultural contact and accommodation increased, any of the other art forms could arise; the one on the top right, which is usually the last, is where the minority peoples have reassumed some power of autonomy and have undergone considerable assimilation. At that point, they have become consumers of arts from traditions outside their own, often borrowed from the dominant powers themselves, but still produced by their own elites. Then the formerly powerless Fourth World peoples may pass up and out of the diagram, to become a self-governing national elite in the First, Second, or Third World.

We should also note that the arts of the dominant cultural traditions – at a third level above the surface of the diagram – often dip down, as it were, and use, steal, or copy ideas from Fourth World arts. This ranges all the way from Picasso's reproduction of the sculpture of West African peoples under colonial domination, to Dutch textiles based on Indonesian *batiks*, to the process of commissioning poor village people to mass produce "art" according to Western notions of what the consumer thinks "folk" art is like (Hirschmann 1976). These processes, of course, have serious repercussions on the arts of the Fourth World peoples and even on their cultural self-image [see later section, " Borrowed Identity"].

Process and Change

Now let us consider in more detail the process of change involved in the emergence of new art forms, noting how particular kinds of arts have been subject to certain forces and trying to explore why some contemporary arts look much the same the whole world over.[2] Although many of the same cultural and technical forces are operating on both the functional, internally directed arts and on the commercial, made-for-export arts, we shall consider them separately, starting with the former.

Functional, noncommercial arts

These arts, which are those most meaningful to the creator peoples, include the only slightly modified contact-traditional arts, completely borrowed foreign popular arts, and the innovative and syncretistic reintegrated arts. Just because arts are made for local consumption and are never intended for outside peoples or for external display or trade, does not mean that they do not change. Two major sets of forces are at work: material and technical opportunities, and cultural and formal influences.

Material and technical changes: All societies that are in contact with each other eventually exchange materials, items, and ideas. If two societies are in long-term contact, and are at greatly different economic and technological levels, great modifications are introduced into the material culture of the less-developed societies. All peoples, save the most spartan, may seek easier ways to carry out their essential activities, from growing crops to making idols. The great woodcarving peoples discussed in this book – the Maori and the Northwest Coast Indians – adapted their stone-blade tools so they could use metal blades and started using manufactured pigments for their important ceremonial houses and monuments during the eighteenth and nineteenth centuries. As a result, they could more easily fell and sculpt great trees, which led to a consequent florescence in architecture and the woodcarver's arts. Today these peoples make use of the latest in blades, power tools, and long-lasting paints in refurbishing and renewing these ceremonial houses and monuments (see figure 23.3).

Similarly, the traditional painters, such as the Brahmins of Nathdrawa and the aborigines of Yirrkala, sometimes take to commercial brushes and pigments, or at least use better

Figure 23.3 At the Kwakiutl village of Alert Bay, Vancouver Island, the James family carves an enormous totem pole for the tribe. The motifs, though traditional in style, are a selection from sub-tribal forms. The pole, donated by a lumber company, is made in two parts bolted together, which at 170 feet is the tallest in the world, 1971

methods of making the paints stick. Foreign materials are substituted for hard-to-obtain native objects, such as imported beads for porcupine quills, freeing artists from the problems of gathering and preparation and allowing them to concentrate on design and execution – and greater production. Metals and manufactured items often come "prepackaged" and last much longer than native items. Although this may benefit the arts and crafts in some ways, it might also destroy such social relationships as a traditional one between materials suppliers and artists.

Often traditional arts and crafts are in direct competition with imported manufactured items. Cheaply reproduced pictures, for example, reduce the sales of such artists as the painters of Rajasthan, who – following the edict "If you can't lick 'em, join them" – now sell their paintings to calendar companies in

Bombay, who in turn reproduce and sell them by the thousand. Practical arts, such as carriers and containers, are often the first to go: if their prime functions are utilitarian rather than aesthetic and ritual, they are replaced by lighter and stronger, but even less aesthetic, imports; but this is not always the case, as Gill informs us (in Graburn 1976a:ch. 5) – Laguna Pueblo wares are not really replaceable.

The assimilation to popular arts – the copying of foreign art traditions from schooled and stratified "civilization" – sometimes occurs in that painful period of rank imitation that follows a people's loss of independence. The caps, badges, clothes, and songs of the conquerors are imitated by the conquered as though power and prestige will follow. And novelty and a taste for the exotic do not seem to be an exclusive characteristic of the conquerors: Canadian Eskimos decorate their drab wooden houses with *Life* magazine pictures and plastic flowers from Hong Kong. The Indian villagers of the Andes wear local "ethnic" clothes that are imitations of sixteenth-century Spanish dress. The Navajo "borrowed" silver jewelry from the Spanish, and Hopi Kachina dolls are probably imitations of the apparently magic *santos* that the Spanish Catholics brought to the Southwest.

Totally new forms arise with the access to new materials. Eskimos now wear parkas that deviate from their traditional skin garments because of the advantages and disadvantages of the wool duffle and Grenfell cloth that they import; Cuna molas were developed from body-painting and basketry designs, via painted skirts, with the advent of cotton cloth, scissors, needle, and thread. The Cuna have also adopted certain very bright color schemes, just as some American Indians have dyed the feathers in their headdresses, Pueblo and Peruvian potters have come to use brightly painted designs, and the Iwam of New Guinea have developed even more complex painting styles with greater contrast on their shields.

Other modified functional or reintegrated arts include African masks, which have in many areas long incorporated trade items, such as beads, nails, cloth, and even European symbols (Bravmann 1974; Bascom 1973). Modern American Indian costumes have "traditionally" contained imported items. Eskimo skin parkas have been decorated with beads, coins, spoons, and trinkets; the Cuna

have used English cotton prints, and so on. As these Fourth World peoples decorate their lives with manufactured items, perhaps they might say that we are the makers of their "folk" or "primitive" arts!

New materials and tools become available as they are invented and improved, but mainly as transportation and trade become more widespread. As I have emphasized elsewhere in this book, the same routes that carry in these industrial products carry out those very arts that are our subject matter.

Cultural changes: More important than the availability of new materials and techniques is the advent of new ideas and tastes. Contacts with foreign peoples, education, literacy, travel, and modern media so broaden the ideas and experiences of Fourth World peoples that they may *want* to change, break away from, or enlarge upon their previously limited traditions.

It is these ideas that not only build up new arts, but that are eventually destructive of old traditions. Missionaries and governments have destroyed many art traditions around the world, but neglect and competing ideas have destroyed just as many. The potlatch was banned for the Northwest Coast Indians so totem poles were no longer raised; but new forms of prestige, derived from occupations and commerce, also destroyed the prestige system that was the underpinning of the ceremonial and art traditions of these same Indians. Totem poles are still made and raised (figure 23.3), but not with the same frequency, pomp, and complex nuances of meaning that formerly obtained. African masks and New Guinea *biche* poles and long houses have been burned by outsiders, but some have also been burned by African and Melanesian converts to the new iconoclastic religions of Islam and Christianity. Indeed, it has often been said that traditional religions are the raison d'être for local art traditions, and, though this is not universally true (for secular beliefs such as rank and power are also expressed), the death of the local religion often coincides with the demise of the functional arts. World religions may substitute no comparable expressions or they may be a cover for growing secularism, the turning away from the magic and the spiritual to a more drab life based on material and individual satisfactions. If no one wants to dance in rituals, the masks are not made; if all are equal – or equally downtrodden – then distinctions of rank and ancestry will not be expressed in elaborate costume and paraphernalia. Education, political bureaucracy, and a materialist orientation tend to turn Fourth World peoples into pale imitations of the masses of the larger societies that have engulfed them. The persistence of traditional arts and crafts depends on: (1) continued demand for the items, (2) availability of the traditional raw materials, (3) time to work and lack of competing attractions, (4) knowledge of the skills and the aesthetics of the arts, (5) rewards and prestige from peer-group members, (6) the role of the items in supporting the belief systems and ritual or gift-exchange systems. Much as we are nostalgic about these loved arts, people do not go on making them for our pleasure if our society and technology have destroyed the incentive to do so. They go off and become bus drivers or betel-nut sellers (Maduro in Graburn 1976a: ch. 13 p. 243).

But not all change is destruction. We have talked about the impact of materials and techniques, and ideas flow along the same channels. Many up-to-date functional arts are constantly changing, incorporating and making explicable new ideas and events. The Maori took up a version of European dress as a mark of status in the nineteenth century, adopting imported ideas to make bandoliers and bodices, which they wear along with their more traditional clothing (Mead, in Graburn 1976a: ch. 16). The Cuna portray the Kennedys (Dawson, Fredrickson and Graburn, 1974), political parties, and space ships in their molas; the Indonesians incorporate rockets and supermen into their batiks, and portray Nixon and the Communists in their *ludruk* dramas (Peacock, 1968); the Hopi make Mickey Mouse Kachina dolls (Carpenter 1972, coverpiece) and Africans include modern themes in the mud architecture of their gas stations (Beier 1960). As outsiders we might not like such phenomena, or bemoan the "lack of tradition." But this *is* tradition; it is as real to the peoples now as the spirits of skulls and amulets were to their ancestors one hundred years ago. If Eskimos are Christian, they want to make crosses and altar-pieces for themselves, as they used to make ivory-tooth charms. When the Navajo made textiles for

themselves and for local consumption (and not for the national collectors' market), they made them to their own liking, with imported bright cochineal and indigo dyes and unravelled bayeta (Kent, in Graburn 1976a: ch. 4, p. 88); it is only recently that outsiders taught them to find and use muted, local natural dyes.

European and Western society in general, while promoting and rewarding change in its own arts and sciences, bemoans the same in others. They project onto "folk" and "primitive" peoples a scheme of eternal stability, as though they were a kind of natural phenomenon out of which myths are constructed. Much as Lévi-Strauss (1963) has shown that these peoples use "nature" as a grid against which to demarcate their experience, so the rulers of the world have used the powerless and the exotic as "nature" by which to demarcate their "culture."

Commercial and tourist arts

Though there are many instances where traditional arts and exact model crafts have been sold for souvenirs and curios, most commercial arts are modified somewhat, or even invented, for the purposes of sale. In the first diagram above, we have separated the types: commercial fine arts, souvenir arts, and assimilated arts. Sources of change incorporated into commercial arts come from both without and within, according to the tastes of the buyers and the efforts of the producers.

Perhaps the commercial fine arts – the pseudo-traditional arts – follow most closely the changes previously outlined for the functional arts, involving the use of materials and techniques for elaboration of form and color. The commercial fine arts are generally those demanded – more as status objects than as memorabilia – by people who wish to get "close to the native" spirit (not body of course) by having "genuine," "authentic" artifacts to show. The buyer, at this point, does not have to understand the symbolism or the iconography of the item, he only has to find it aesthetically acceptable and visually authentic. Closeness to what is believed to be traditional by the collector's reference group is the goal.... Thus the forces on the artist who makes traditional objects for sale usually point in the direction of some historical recorded model of what is "the real thing." Even here the accepted model of "traditional" changes over generations in the culture of the collectors; objects that would be deemed too innovative at one time are later found acceptable; collectors or museum curators who reject items as too new or mere junk, often pay high prices for the same objects later on. "Classic period" Navajo blankets, or even Haida argillite miniatures (Kaufmann, in Graburn 1976a: ch. 2), were deemed "trade stuff" for decades, but are now worth hundreds of dollars apiece. One wonders if it is aesthetic tastes or market values that have changed?

Fourth World artists who depend on sales for a living – the Canadian Eskimos, some Pueblo Indians, Xalitleños, the people of Yirrkala, the Makonde, and many others discussed in this book – find the constraints of their belief system sometimes lead them away from mere reproductions of their believed-in functional arts. Since these latter arts may be sacred, artists would not, as Kaufmann shows for the Haida (Graburn 1976a: ch. 2), make models of important functional items until their culture had been so destroyed and secularized that such things had lost their original value. In Central Australia, for example, the Aranda did not sell, or even show, their *churingas* to whites until the missionized and educated young saw the opportunity to make a shilling or two. Thus: (1) Tourist arts may be strictly separated from other arts on the grounds that to do otherwise would be a sacrilege, thereby forcing those involved in commerce to choose less sensitive items to make for sale: the people of Laguna Pueblo make pottery for sale but never include ritual and gift pieces among their ware. (2) The arts may have a dual purpose: the Australian aborigines use their bark paintings of important scenes (Williams, in Graburn 1976a: ch. 15) to teach their beliefs to their children, and then sell the paintings to the missions and dealers; similarly, the Cuna wear their valued (though secular) molas until they are worn out or their themes are "dated," and then sell them to visitors or in Panama. (3) Though apparently identical objects are made both for ritual purposes and for sale, the artists may keep them separate in their heads: the santeros of Cordova, New Mexico, make wooden *santos* for religious worship, and make the same or similar items for sale, but call the latter *monos*,

"mere dolls, models" (Briggs 1974). (4) The commercial success may lead to secularization: the Huichol Indians of Nayarit, Mexico, used to make small wool-pressed-into-beeswax paintings on bits of board as offerings in their peyote cult rituals (Furst 1968–69). As these grew in size and popularity, some of the Huichol grew wealthy and famous and left their rural homeland. Now, many apostate Huichol make yarn paintings that have no intrinsic spiritual value but simply illustrate interesting aspects of their beliefs (see 23.1).

The market itself is the most powerful source of formal and aesthetic innovation, often leading to changes in size, simplification, standardization, naturalism, grotesquery, novelty, and archaism. Souvenirs or trade objects for the mass market must be (a) cheap, (b) portable, (c) understandable, and (d), as D. Ray (1961) has shown us for Alaskan Eskimo ivory carvings, dustable! Sometimes it helps if they are useful, for at least then the owners will know what to do with them and they will have some inherent meaning in the home environment of the traveller (figure 23.1).

Makers must compete with each other and with imported souvenirs (plastic totem poles, post cards, manufactured items), always keeping an eye on low unit cost. This in turn may lead to small sizes, such as Yirrkala souvenir barks, small Cuna mola panels, or Ainu "couple" dolls, which are easily stored, sold, transported, or bought in number by visitors for gifts. Similar forces are also behind the manufacture of not just small souvenirs, but miniatures of beautifully made traditional items, such as California Indian basketry (Dawson, Fredrickson and Graburn, 1974; figure 6), Laguna pottery, and some Indian paintings.

Miniaturization also has several advantages: applicability for decorative use; economy of materials; a doll-like, folkloristic quality not associated with the real article. Though miniaturization makes some arts more salable, the opposite, increase in size, may be considered more economical by the artists: for instance, Eskimo soapstone sculptors and Cordova *santeros* (Briggs 1974) calculate that far less time and effort is spent making large, expensive carvings than the more typical small ones – they just can't sell so many of them!

Economic forces lead not only to changes in size, but also to simplification of form and decoration. The fewer steps that are involved, the more the artisan will be able to produce, and the lower the unit price. If artisans specialize in different stages of the production, they may become more skilled at each and a sort of "production line" is set up, as with the family division of labor of the Kamba woodcarvers or the bark-painters of Xalitla. Simplification is aided by the fact that the buyer does not know the meaning of the omitted detail (such as the painted colors on Asmat items) or may not even be aware that there was more to the traditional objects than the ones in the shop.

Large-scale souvenir production methods, such as those of the "factory" that makes Makonde pieces at Mtwara, Tanzania (Stout 1966), those used in the craft shops of the Ainu (Low, in Graburn 1976a: ch. 12) or even those used by Canadian Eskimos, sometimes employ power machinery to ease and speed up operations. This may not lead to a lowering of standards, but it might well lead to a uniformity or standardization of product that will make it less salable and less admired as a handicraft. The Naskapi-Cree of Ungava (see also below; figure 23.4), however, made things so well by hand that a middle-class audience thought they were machine made and wouldn't buy them.

Beyond the raw forces of "unit cost" are more subtle matters of content and taste, which force peoples to produce for sale things that are acceptable to a public that already has its preconceptions of what is typical and appropriate. For instance, the travelling public of the Western world seems to believe that souvenirs should match the skin color of their producers, particularly that black people should produce black art objects. Although the early Kamba items (figure 23.1) were in light-colored wood, the nearby Makonde make things in ebony (figure 23.6), as do the Bini in Nigeria; and the Papuans of the Sepik

Figure 23.4 Robbie Dick hand painting "Cree Craft" rattles and drums, in the Great Whale River Indian-Eskimo Cooperative, 1970. Note the "authenticating" models on the wall and the degree of perfection

Figure 23.6 Modern Makonde commercial sculptures of ebony wood. Left: naturalistic *bindamu* sculpture of man and boy; right: abstract *shetani* (spirit) sculpture, expressing the "exotic" often demanded of primitive arts, Tanzania, 1971. Collection of the author, courtesy of Gail Suzuki.

Figure 23.5 Miniature middle Sepik ancestor figure, black stained light-colored wood, 1969. Collection of the author, courtesy of Karl Heider.

(Figure 23.5), who don't have any dark woods at all, dye or shoe polish their souvenir arts. The buying public also emphasizes "valuable" materials such as ebony and mahogany in the tropics, shiny brown ironwood from the Mexican Indians (Ryerson, in Graburn 1976a: ch. 6) and argillite and ivory from the Alaskan Indians and Eskimos respectively. Eskimo sculptures made of dark green serpentine are inherently more attractive than those made of

a gray soapstone, and are often bought for their material rather than their workmanship.

The subject matter and form of commercial arts must symbolize to outsiders a few central characteristics or beliefs about their makers. Two opposite trends have been pointed out, particularly for African arts, by Bascom (in Graburn 1976a: ch. 17) and Ben-Amos (in Graburn 1976a: ch. 18). The major tendency is toward naturalism, the simple portrayal of some being, person, or object in such a way as to be understood and recognized by someone who is not too familiar with the culture. Crafts and models, such as the Seri animals and birds and Eskimo sculptures, are also prime examples of this trend. As Ben-Amos has explained it: "Tourist art . . . operates as a minimal system which must make meanings as accessible as possible across visual boundary lines...[a] reduction in semantic level of traditional forms, expansion of neo-traditional secular motifs, and utilization of adjunct communicative systems" (1973: 9). Thus, Ben-Amos demonstrated that tourist arts are like an obvious visual cross-cultural code, rather like pidgin languages are when used in trade. At this level, we might say that their content consists of signs rather than symbols.

Similarly, reproductions of everyday objects and portraits of village life are an important part of other commercial art forms. This need for understanding and realism, combined with the romantic impulse, is behind the popularity of certain completely non-native assimilated arts. Namatjira, an Aranda, took up watercolor painting (figure 23.2); the Santa Fe Art Studio for Indians produced a much appreciated style by presenting selected aspects of Indian life in a familiar genre.

The opposite trend is toward grotesqueness or exoticism, arousing in the minds of the millions living dreary, affluent, "civilized" lives the fears and excitement of exploration, the unknown, and the untamed. Sometimes this leads merely to giganticism, the exaggeration of features or the creation of something "larger than life". More often it encourages the definite effort to promote repulsion, awe, terror, or the inexplicable, cashing in on the Westerner's ambivalent attitudes toward exotic peoples. The Makonde of Tanzania, who only recently took up ebony carving because of poverty and displacement from Mozambique, have made the best use of this trend: they have developed two entirely new tourist art forms (figure 23.6), the *bindamu*, purely realistic forms that are recognizably African, and the *shetani* or spirit forms, which are semi-abstract. Similarly, the peasants of Ochumicho have found that there is a greater tourist demand for their "devil" figures than for their traditional whistles. Even the Canadian Eskimos feel that they are encouraged to make imaginative or mythological figures by the white buyers. Grotesqueness is an exaggeration of unfamiliar or distorted features; although it is not naturalistic, it is not abstract either. The latter quality is rare in commercial arts, in spite of the tendency toward simplification; realism is generally dominant, although

the Seri, perhaps (Ryerson, in Graburn 1976a: ch. 6), prefer abstract human figures. Here too, some of the Canadian Eskimos feel that buyers force them to make more abstract sculptures than they presently like.

What the outside world recognizes as ethnicity is a small bundle of overt features. A few things are selected for souvenir purposes – black skin, hunting prowess, traditional occupations, or past glories. These are the things that get exaggerated by the market, and sometimes feed back to the creator people. Though they may know that they are not as portrayed in the stereotypic arts, over the years the demand is bound to have an influence on a people's own self-image. Eskimos and Australian aborigines are "taught" by the powers that be that they are "naturally" good artists; Africans are "supposed" to be woodcarvers, and, even where they are not, as in East Africa, they take up the métier and become good at it! When stereotypes are constantly played out in commercial arts, a people may come to believe the same things about themselves or their past as the outside world does. Numerous examples in this book, however, testify to resistance to this process.

With the Western world's search for the primitive, the handmade, the rare, and the authentic, the search inevitably turns to the past. There is a well-developed cult of the authentic that translates as the cult of the antique for both Western and non-Western arts: things "stand the test of time," "come from a long ancestry," "mature," and grow rare and more valuable. So artists, promoters, and dealers are often faced with the question of preserving, reviving, or reproducing ancient or dying arts. In some circumstances this is a happy feature, for as D. Crowley (1970) has shown, Africans believe old masks lose their vigorous powers just at the time that Europeans deem them valuable. This may lead to the sale of old masks, or to the wholesale faking and antiquing of objects (see Bascom, in Graburn 1976a: ch. 17; Carpenter 1972; Crowley 1970).

Revivals and modifications of traditional crafts for sale is almost as common as straight faking or invention of new genres. The Asmat, once so famous for their ancestor poles and canoe prows, were forbidden to make them by their Indonesian colonizers. At the behest of the United Nations, they are now making simpler (but better-finished) models of their former arts

(Schneebaum 1975). Even more tragic is the case of the Naskapi-Cree peoples of Great Whale River and the eastern James Bay. These northernmost Algonkian Indians had suffered by comparison with their neighbors, the Eskimos, whose soapstone carving had been well received and promoted and had brought both fame and a good income. The efforts of the Indians to sell soapstone carvings, wood carvings, dolomite carvings, and souvenirs had been relative failures. The white and Indian staff of the Fédération des Coopératives du Nouveau Québec devised a new genre, marketed as "Cree Craft," that was scaled to a lower price bracket than the Eskimo sculptures and reflected the ethnicity and environment of the Indian creators. These artifacts included decorated copies of full-size aboriginal utensils and models of larger items, all of which had been in use until recently. All were made of local woods – black pine, spruce, tamarack, or birch – which were logged and worked by handknife by the men of this area. They were made for sale and decorated by two or three young men, using aboriginal motifs, symbols, and color combinations applied with imported brushes and acrylic paints. Though well made and promoted and sold for a very low price, the market for them soon fell off and the Naskapi-Cree were told to stop producing for the already swollen warehouse inventory.

In contrast, the closely related Cree peoples at the southern end of James Bay continue to make souvenir carvings for sale. These are not promoted through the cooperative or other middlemen, and only a few Cree who want to pursue this occupation spend much time on it. Older men, such as Johnny Blueboy, whittle wall plaques, cozy "northern scenes," and model birds and animals, producing a genre of crafts that is closer to plastic models from Japan or Middle America than it is to anything aboriginally Indian (figure 23.7). Yet the demand from local whites and visitors continues and generally outstrips supply. The agents of change are the makers and buyers themselves; there are no promoters and no one has to guess or research the market.

Perhaps we should unravel some of these value-laden terms. *Revival* refers to the attempted re-creation of an art form that has fallen into disuse (such as Cree Craft); it may involve slight modification of the form and

Figure 23.7 "Cree Craft" wooden ladle, Naskapi-Cree, 1970, and Canada goose wall plaque by Johnny Blueboy, James Bay Cree, 1972. Collection of the author, and of the Lowie Museum, #UCLMA 2–56502.

probably does not re-create the context of the original manufacture. *Faking* refers to the manufacture of something valuable (and often past) by whatever means – including antiquing in a termite mound or by drilling holes or using rotten materials – and passing it off as authentic (see Crowley ibid.). *Reproduction* refers to approximately the same phenomenon, the re-creation of something old or valuable by whatever means, so that the final object resembles the original, even if it is made of entirely different materials, but not claiming that it is original. *Archaism* is a tendency to make things that look old, or resemble to some degree an ancient tradition, without actually reproducing some particular object: archaism is attractive both commercially, to tourists who buy Mexican pots or paintings that have Aztec themes, and noncommercially, to governments who are trying to create a national "ethnicity" out of some glorious past (see later section on "Borrowed Identity").

Thus commercial arts at all levels are subject to more contingencies than internally important arts. They have to satisfy the aesthetics of the foreign consumer as well as the producer, if possible; they have to project a clear image, either ethnically relevant or suitably exotic; they have to be transportable and not too fragile and resemble some genre that is deemed worth collecting by outsiders. These forces are very similar to those experienced by pockets of "folk" artists within the First World itself – such as the artisans of Appalachia or counterculture artists of Telegraph Avenue, Berkeley (Levin 1976) – for they too have to make a living and have their own "ethnicity" to project and protect. The many solutions to these problems lead to sometimes disheartening, often ingenious, and occasionally exciting new art forms.

[...]

Art, Communication, and Ethnicity

All peoples surround themselves with material objects that express their individual identity and their identity within a social category [...] The means by which material items express identity is through *symbols*. Symbols – visual, verbal or aural – are arbitrary expressions that *stand for* something; they are arbitrary because usually there is no necessary connection between the content of the sign or word and the object or category for which it stands. Thus, symbols are conventional devices by which we recognize something. Their only limitation is that the bearers and the viewers (or transmitters and receivers) must "speak the same language," that is, agree on the meaning conveyed.

Social identity such as ethnicity needs to be conveyed for two different purposes: for the members of the in-group – that is, for the other people of the same group who wish to get together; and for members of the outgroup – that is, for people whose relationships depend upon their being different. [...] In brief, all societies contain social categories within which members are similar, but between which they are different but complementary; these categories are marked, often by material symbols, to enable society to function and for people to know how to behave properly toward each other. If a society is stratified, as most are to some degree, then possessing or wearing certain symbols are marks of prestige leading to deferent behavior by other members. Ethnicity is an increasingly important form of identity in a pluralistic world where communication, education, and travel allow every group knowledge of and access to almost every other.

Internal identity

People of small societies have usually maintained their social subdivisions with material symbols and paraphernalia, often in the form of clothing and ritual objects. These are guides to appropriate behavior for other members of the group and mark differences as gross as those between the sexes, or as fine as those between ranks of Samoan aristocracy. Yet within one symbol system the mutual recognition of differences reinforces the shared set of beliefs and group membership. Under the threat of external political and economic forces, Fourth World societies often feel the need to retrench, or at least to emphasize their native customs and values, especially when up against pressure from missionaries or attractive but disruptive material offerings.

[...]

External identity

What were once relatively independent societies have become Fourth World minorities, overrun by and up against the more powerful peoples who have taken charge of the world. The need for external distinctions, as well as the maintenance of internal order, has become more complicated. With the recent increase in world travel and communications, not only are people seen directly by visiting strangers, but also their artifacts have penetrated to the ends of the earth. As transistor radios and plastic flowers have found their way into the homes of the most far-off Third and Fourth World peoples, by the same routes *their* productions are known in the shop windows and living rooms of much of the middle-class industrial world.

[...]

Commercial works of art have often become the mere souvenirs of fleeting visits of far-off places, for though their distinctive features are much simplified, these items are all the tangible evidence the traveller needs to recall the reality of the trip. ...

But it is not only the buyers who ordain what they wish to believe in; the makers of these movable symbols also wish to express values important to themselves. Thus a Fourth World people's "image" in the eyes of the rest of the world is often as strongly influenced by their portable arts and crafts as by what they actually do in some remote and forgotten homeland or reservation [...] The commercial arts of these small populations may be made for outsiders only (as in three of these four cases), but they carry the message: "We exist; we are different; we can do something we are proud of; we have something that is uniquely ours." The accommodation between the demand and the traditional features of the culture often produces a narrowing or stereotyped notion of what constitutes the important parts of their ethnicity – i.e., what they have as against what other ethnic groups possess [...]

Often the subject matter of models and souvenirs presents assets, achievements, and artifacts that are the pride of the group, embodying the style or glamor of the culture. Tourists and other buyers are often interested in the same positive features. [...]

When the desperation of poverty and the forces of the market cause people to churn out items that have no connections with their traditional belief system and do not reflect their previous standards of craftsmanship, one feels that the messages conveyed do not express pride and joy, but instead are saying: "We are forced into this to make a living; this is not us; these are not our standards; this is you using us for cheap labor." But we must not always be so cocksure that the creators feel as we might in the same predicament. They may well have their own standards within the new genre ... they may be proud of their competitive ideas and innovations ... They may keep separate in their minds the standards of what they have to sell quickly from what they really enjoy doing when they can afford it.[...]

Borrowed identity

But the world moves on: people do not always retain fixed images of themselves or their value to the outside, and new symbols and materials may have greater prestige than the older ones – especially if they are brought by powerful and prestigious outsiders. Symbols of identity may be borrowed, stolen, or even exchanged. Groups may wish to enhance their prestige in their own or others' eyes by taking on the materials, symbols, and regalia of other groups – almost as though a magic power could rub off by imitation; such phenomena are always

part of the numerous cargo and millenarian cults around the world [...]

Numerous examples could be cited to illustrate the process by which objects and symbols of one culture have been taken over by another to such a degree that they became part of the public identity of the borrowing group.

[...]

A further step is taken in this process of borrowing when a previously colonized group comes to power and takes as part of its public identity the arts of its less-educated tribesmen, or even of other still-dominated Fourth World peoples. [...]

Perhaps even more widespread than the above type of borrowing is the almost universal proclivity of modern First, Second, and Third World nations to collect and display the arts of their present and past minority peoples as symbols of their national identity.

[...]

A recent cursory survey of the contents of various ethnic arts stores and United Nations gift shops shows that these processes of borrowing the identity of minority peoples – perhaps at the very same time as repressing other aspects of their cultures – is international. Nations choose obscure but exotic cultural features to present as their ethnic markers to others. [...]

One fascinating aspect of artistic expressions of identity in this ethnically complex world is the attempt of one group to portray members of another group using the creator group's symbolic and artistic traditions and attaching importance to those features that are important to the in-group rather than the out-group. This generally results in stereotypic portrayals that are satisfactory to the in-group but hilarious or insulting to the outsiders portrayed. We all know the most obvious examples from American literature depicting ethnic subgroups; and the Western world's explorers, for another example, stereotyped the rest of the world in such a way that we can even tell the time period and the cultural influences governing the artist by the way a portrait was drawn. But this also has not been a one-way process. The Europeans themselves were often portrayed with scathing penetration in the media of the peoples being explored (Burland and Forman 1969); every group, in fact, has conventional and accepted portrayals of its neighbors and enemies (see Lips 1937) [...]

NOTES

1 Vine Deloria, in his foreword to the second of these two references, traces the evolution of consciousness of the differences between the Third and the Fourth World. The term was also used in a more limited, but slightly incorrect, fashion by Berreman (1972:396), who wrote " 'fourth-world' colonialism, i.e., exploitation inflicted by 'third-world' (non-Western) people on their internal minorities, analogous to that they have often experienced themselves at the hands of 'first-' and 'second-world' colonialists (Western noncommunist and communist nations respectively)."

In recent popular journal articles economists have been quoted as dividing the underdeveloped nations into Third and Fourth worlds, solely on the basis of average per capita income. Not only is this at odds with the original (1955 Bandung conference) political and structural intent of the division into First, Second, and Third worlds, but it produces perhaps temporary and anomalous divisions of contiguous poor nations on the basis of ill-reported and hard to calculate income statistics. I here assert that "non-nations" – native peoples subject to internal colonialism – logically form a politico-structural Fourth World category, though they may soon emerge as independent nations in their own right.

2 Some of the ideas and examples in the following sections were generated during the research and writing for *Traditions in Transition* (Dawson, Fredrickson, and Graburn 1974).

REFERENCES

Bascom, William 1973 *African Art in Cultural Perspective: An Introduction*. New York: W. W. Norton.

Batty, Joyce D. 1963 *Namatjira, Wanderer Between Two Worlds*. Melbourne: Hodder and Stoughton.

Beier, Ulli 1960 *Art in Nigeria*. Cambridge: Cambridge University Press.

Ben-Amos, Paula 1973 "Pidgin Languages and Tourist Arts." Paper prepared for the Advanced Seminar in Contemporary Developments in Folk Art, School of American Research, Santa Fe, N. Mex. Manuscript copy on file at Temple University, Philadelphia.

Berreman, D. G. 1972 "Race, Caste, and Other Invidious Distinctions in Social Stratification," *Race* 13:385–414.

Biebuyck, Daniel P. (ed.) 1969 Introduction to *Tradition and Creativity in Tribal Art*, pp. 1–23. Los Angeles and Berkeley: The University of California Press.

Bravmann, R. A. 1974 *Islam and Tribal Art in West Africa*. London: Cambridge University Press.

Briggs, C. L. 1974 "Folk Art Between Two Cultures: The Wood-Carvers of Cordova, New Mexico." University of Chicago (ms).

Brody, J. J. 1971 *Indian Painters & White Patrons*. Albuquerque: University of New Mexico Press.

Burland, C., and W. Forman 1969 *The Exotic White Man: An Alien in Asian and African Art*. New York: McGraw-Hill.

Carpenter, Edmund C. 1971 "Do You Have the Same Thing in Green? or, Eskimos in New Guinea." Paper delivered at the Shell Program on the Canadian North. Scarborough, Ontario, 28 January. Mimeo.

—— 1972 *Oh What A Blow that Phantom Gave Me!* New York: Holt, Rinehart and Winston.

Claerhout, G. A. 1965 "The Concept of Primitive Applied to Art," *Current Anthropology*, vol. 6, pp. 432–438.

Crowley, Daniel J. 1970 "The Contemporary-Traditional Art Market in Africa," *African Arts* 4:1:43–49, 80.

Dawson, L. E., Vera-Mae Fredrickson, and N. H. H. Graburn 1974 *Traditions in Transition: Culture Contact and Material Change*. Berkeley, California: Lowie Museum of Anthropology.

Dorfles, Gillo (ed.) 1969 *Kitsch, the World of Bad Taste*. New York: Bell (translated from the 1968 original Italian edition).

Durkheim, E. 1893 *The Division of Labor in Society*. New York: Free Press (1948) (translated from the original French edition).

Furst, Peter T. 1968–69 "Myth in Art: A Huichol Depicts his Reality," *Quarterly* 7:3:16–25. Los Angeles: Los Angeles County Museum of Natural History.

Gerbrands, Adrianus A. 1957 *Art as an Element of Culture: Especially in Negro-Africa.* Leiden, Netherlands: E. J. Brill.

Goldwater, Robert 1964 *Senufo Sculpture from West Africa.* New York: The Museum of Primitive Art.

Graburn, Nelson H. H. 1967 "Economic Acculturation and Caste Formation." Paper delivered at the Annual Meetings of the Southwestern Anthropological Association, 24 March, San Francisco.

—— 1969 "Art and Acculturative Processes." *International Social Science Journal* 21:457–468. Paris: U.N.E.S.C.O.

—— 1976a *Ethnic and Tourist Arts: Cultural Expressions from the Fourth World.* Berkeley: University of California Press.

—— 1976b "I Like Things to Look More Different Than That Stuff Did: An Experiment in Cross-Cultural Art Appreciation," in V. Megaw, ed., *Art Artisans and Society.* London: Duckworth.

Hirschmann, Niloufer I. 1976 "The World in a Paper Bag," *Kroeber Anthropological Society Papers*, no. 47.

Kaplan, N. I. and V. A. Baradulin, 1975 "Yakuts Folk Crafts," *Soviet Anthropology and Archeology* 13:74–86 (translated from *Sovetskaia etnografia* 1, 1969).

Levin, Claudia L. 1976 "The Effects of Commercialism on the Telegraph Avenue Artisan," *Kroeber Anthropological Society Papers*, no. 48.

Lévi-Strauss, Claude 1963 *Totemism* (trans. R. Needham), Boston: Beacon.

Lips, Julius 1937 *The Savage Hits Back.* New Haven: Yale University Press.

Manuel G. and M. Poslums 1974 *The Fourth World: An Indian Reality.* New York: Free Press.

Maquet, J. 1971 *Introduction to Aesthetic Anthropology.* Reading, Mass.: Addison-Wesley.

May, R. J. 1974 "Tourism and the Artifact Industry in Papua New Guinea." Paper presented at the Workshop on the Impact on Pacific Island Countries of the Development of Tourism, East-West Center, Hawaii.

Peacock, J. L. 1968 *Rites of Modernization: Symbolic and Social Aspects of Indonesian Proletarian Drama.* Chicago: University of Chicago Press.

Ray, Dorothy J. 1961 *Artists of Tundra and Sea.* Seattle: University of Washington Press.

Redfield, Robert, R. Linton, and M. J. Herskovits 1936 "A Memorandum on Acculturation," *American Anthropologist* 38: 149–152.

Schneebaum, Tobias 1975 "A Museum for New Guinea," *Craft Horizons*, 35:2, 36:88–89.

Schneider, B. 1972 "Malangata of Mozambique," *African Arts*, 5:40–45.

Stout, J. Anthony 1966 *Modern Makonde Sculpture.* Nairobi: Kibo Art Gallery Publications.

Szombati-Fabian, I., and J. Fabian 1975 "Art, History and Society: Popular Art in Shaba, Zaïre." Manuscript copy at Wesleyan University, Middletown, Conn.

Whitaker, Ben (ed.) 1972 *The Fourth World.* Eight reports from the Field work of the Minority Rights Group. London: Sidgwick & Jackson.

24

The Collecting and Display of Souvenir Arts

Authenticity and the "Strictly Commercial"

Ruth B. Phillips

The complete degeneration of an ancient art from the beautifully designed pouches into the strictly commercial articles made for sale at Niagara Falls around 1900 is all too evident in this exhibit.

Text panel, Museum of the American Indian, New York, 1970s

Art made after contact is just as important to understanding as the ancient forms of expression. Each generation of Native peoples leaves its impressions about life through its art. As the circumstances around Native communities changed, their art also changed. This is why Native art today is as legitimate as older work in presenting Native world views.

Text panel by Richard W. Hill, National Museum of the American Indian, New York, 1994

The study of any visual art tradition is limited by the nature of the object record that has survived through extant example, graphic or photographic depiction, and verbal description. For Native North American arts, as for other arts that have been classified as "primitive," ethnographic museums have been by far the most important repository. These largely nineteenth-century foundations have absorbed nearly all the collections of curiosities made during the seventeenth and eighteenth centuries. In the twentieth century a smaller group of fine-art collectors also began to acquire Aboriginal objects, though in much smaller numbers. Although we have become relatively adept at reading museums and their exhibitions as texts (Karp and Levine 1991; Hooper-Greenhill 1992), less attention has

From *Trading Identities: The Souvenir in Native North American Art from the Northeast, 1700–1900* (Seattle: University of Washington Press, 1998), pp. 49–71, 287–289, 311–325. Reprinted by permission of the University of Washington Press.

been paid to the anatomy of collections as historically contingent object records that permit or exclude certain representational possibilities.[1] In this chapter I will examine in detail the dynamics that affected the collecting of souvenir art, in order to assess the kind of object record upon which the detailed studies that follow must necessarily be based. This exercise is valuable because it reveals a central contradiction that has run like a fault line through standard museum representations of Native art and culture. This contradiction arises directly from unresolved conflicts between the romanticized, dialectical notion of the modern and the primitive, and a persistent discomfort with the logical consequences of commoditization.

The changing scholarly and popular paradigms of authenticity that were discussed in chapter 1 of my book have intervened to create an object record of souvenir arts that differs in important ways from the record that exists for other Native North American art. For Aboriginal people, the primary value of souvenir arts lay in their use as exchange commodities that provided basic subsistence. Almost everything that was produced was sold, and it is rare to find historical pieces in Native communities today unless they have been recently collected. (Private photograph collections held in Native communities, however, often contain pictures of the souvenir arts made and sold by earlier generations.) Among Western collectors, in contrast, souvenir arts have been alternately prized, disguised, or banished altogether. The inconsistent and erratic way in which souvenir arts are represented and identified in both ethnological and fine-art collections directly reflects the ambivalence of Western collectors toward not only indigenous commoditization but also stylistic hybridity.

There is today a general recognition that colonial museums are situated within two particular paradigms of knowledge, "natural history" and "rare art collecting," which dominated the "Museum Age" that lasted from about 1840 to 1930 (Sturtevant 1969; Stocking 1985: 7–8).[2] Museum collections, like other archives, are historical deposits produced by complex, diachronic, processes of textual negotiation. They are, furthermore, intertextual products not just of two but at least four distinct collecting projects. In addition to the roles played by the professional ethnologist and the rare art collector, two other important actors intervened, the Native American collector-agent and the tourist-collector. Although the roles played by science and art in museum formation are widely acknowledged, those played by the ordinary consumer and the "other" are not.

The collecting practices of scholars working in northeastern North America are particularly revealing of these dynamics because of the early development of tourism in the region. The Museum Age coincides almost exactly with the period during which souvenir art production became the economic mainstay of many northeastern Aboriginal communities. I will argue that objects which displayed the traces of Aboriginal peoples' negotiation of Western artistic and economic systems had to be excluded from formal programs of collecting and exhibiting in order to support the standard museum representation of Native Americans as other, as marginalized, and as premodern. Their exclusion served two sets of mutually contradictory interests: those of the romantic primitivists seeking an escape from industrial modernity, and those of the economic developers seeking hegemony over Indian lands and resources. The same elaborate set of fictions, constructed within the colonial discourse of the museum, served the interests of both groups.

Colonial Displays and Competing Authenticities

This discourse is not yet history. In many museums in Europe and North America, displays informed by late-nineteenth-century ideologies remain on view. The largest single museum collection of Native American objects, founded as the private collection of a wealthy New York businessman, George Heye, at the beginning of this century, is representative. This museum, now the National Museum of the American Indian and part of the Smithsonian Institution, is currently in a process of transformation, but as late as the early 1990s the old displays – last reinstalled in the early 1960s – remained on view, continuing to transmit their colonial messages.[3] The visitor found to the left of the main doorway and centrally placed in the large section devoted to the Indians of the Woodlands a large case entitled "Iroquois Women." The main case label read: "The Iroquois Woman Tilled the Fields, Owned Her Home, and Chose the Chiefs." In secondary relation to this text, placed beneath it and lettered in smaller print, was a label reading: "Using Quills, Beads and Ribbons Skillfully, She Decorated Her Leggings and Moccasins." Placed next to these texts was an unusual group of female "False Face" masks and craft objects categorized according to medium – bark, basketry, or beadwork. Despite the assertion of the role of an Iroquois woman as a major economic producer, "home owner," and political power broker, she thus was effectively represented in standard Western patriarchal terms as a craft producer.[4] The partial nature of the Heye display was also the product of the Western stress on objects, on "seeing," and on "art" that is fundamental, as Alpers (1991) has pointed out, to the museum. In ethnographic exhibits the emphasis on the object has promoted a focus on technologies of making over nonmaterial aspects of culture, such as kinship or political activities, which are far more difficult to narrate through objects.

What was offered as a representation of the Iroquois woman was a linear historical account of her production of beadwork:

In early times, Iroquois women use[d] dyed porcupine quills for decoration, and when White traders introduced glass beads, the traditional quillwork designs were used in a similar technique. In the mid-1700s, foreign influences, particularly learned in French Canadian convents, brought new and bold floral designs into fashion.

But continued White contact resulted in the abandonment of traditional Iroquois art concepts. New patterns, which expressed contemporary tourist tastes, were adopted. The complete degeneration of an ancient art from the beautifully designed pouches into the strictly commercial articles made for sale at Niagara Falls around 1900 is all too evident in this exhibit.

The narrative presented here is standard and familiar. It inscribes colonial concepts of race and purity through its insistence on the detrimental effects of "foreign influences" and "White contact." Contact is tightly linked to an inevitable cultural decline leading toward a

vanishing point "around 1900." After this portentous date a silence falls, the stillness of death signifying the disappearance of the Indian, which has been foretold in the text by the unremitting use of the past tense.

The spatial arrangement of the objects in the case expressed this declining trajectory visually (figure 24.1). The eye was led downward from the "old" objects of quillwork, placed in the top center, to a lower row of works in beadwork on cloth, and then farther down to the despised Niagara Falls "whimsies," located close to the visual vanishing point at the bottom right edge of the side wall of the case. Specifically the plastic realization of the display articulated the theory of degenerationism, an application of cultural evolutionism to the study of material culture that became popular in American anthropological studies around 1900 (Holmes 1890; Goldwater 1967: 20–21; Hinsley 1981: 103–4).

Figure 24.1 "Iroquois Woman" case (detail), installed in the 1960s at the old Museum of the American Indian, New York, photographed in 1992. Photograph by Catherine Berlo

The particular fiction presented here is easily deconstructed by art-historical analysis. The two small quilled pouches that act as both the benchmark of authenticity and the starting point of the alleged decline do not, in fact, exemplify precontact object types, but are themselves "acculturated" objects. They adopt the forms of eighteenth- and early-nineteenth-century Euro-American pocketbooks and were very possibly made for trade. The beaded objects, so rigidly arranged in descending chronological sequence, were in fact all produced during the same period and represent contemporaneous styles of workmanship employed by different Iroquoian-speaking peoples in New York State and Canada (Phillips 1990). Although these objects were not well documented when they entered museum collections for reasons that will be discussed below, the comparative lack of subsequent research is striking evidence of the way in which the doctrines of cultural evolutionism have controlled and channeled empirical investigation.

The dismissive phrase "strictly commercial" in the Heye case label is significant, implying the acceptance by earlier generations of ethnologists of the "fine art" mystique of their time and its standard dichotomy between the sacred and the secular, and its hierarchy of fine and applied arts (Phillips 1989; Phillips and Steiner 1998). The comment also constitutes a willful refusal to represent hard economic realities, that the widespread reliance on craft production in the Northeast resulted both from economic marginalization and from the determination of Aboriginal people to resist Canadian and American government policies designed to transform them from nomadic hunters into settled agriculturalists (Hoxie 1984; Miller 1989: 189–207). Native Americans persisted in patterns of production and seasonal trading because they were continuous with their earlier lifestyles. As we saw in the last chapter, government officials regularly found this reliance on art commodity production a cause for complaint, but also had to concede that it could provide a good income.

A remarkable petition written during the 1890s by a group of Quebec Abenaki attests to Aboriginal peoples' awareness of their conditions of economic production and colonial domination (figure 24.2). The petition asks the proprietors of resort hotels in the White Mountains of New Hampshire "not to let any but Indians or those married to Indian women" sell on their premises, "the ladies and gentlemen, American Tourists, being similarly earnestly prayed to patronize

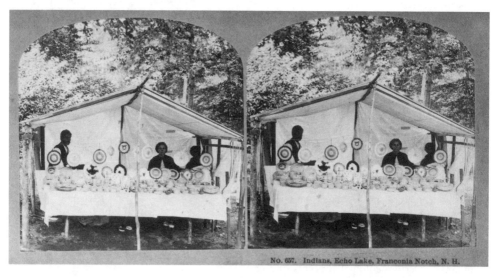

NO. 657.   Indians, Echo Lake, Franconia Notch, N. H.

Figure 24.2 Stereoscopic card showing an Abenaki souvenir art stand in the White Mountains of New Hampshire, second half of the nineteenth century. Robert Dennis Collection, Photography Collection, Miriam and Ira D. Wallach Division of Art, Prints and Photographs, the New York Public Library, Astor, Lenox and Tilden Foundations, NYPG91-F19

the Indians only, in their own and proper Basket Trade." The Abenaki plead their case on the basis of a historical argument that succinctly recapitulates the pattern of development common throughout the Northeast:

> That the primitive occupation of the Indians, for the support of their families, "Hunting and Fishing," has now gone by, because the French Canadians, owing to their number and having themselves taken that occupation, have got such a control in it that the poor Indians have had to GIVE IT UP and look for some other means for their livelihood;
>
> That the next way the Indians had to get their living, which was the "Tanning and making of Moccasins," has also gone by, again because the French Canadians STOLE the trade....
>
> That the only means they now have to honestly earn their livelihood is the "Making of Baskets," but this trade, as the former ones

pertaining to Indians, is now being STOLEN AGAIN by the French Canadians, who have already GRABBED it through the carelessness of some Indians who have taught them for the sake of a little pay.

If this continues, the Abenaki warn:

> "Indian Goods"... will unavoidably lose their GENUINENESS; and the ladies and gentlemen in buying those French Canadian INFERIOR QUALITY baskets – counterfeit goods – will be thereby deceived; and all will be for the harm of the Indians, the Aboriginals of the country.[5]

The Abenakis employ a language of authenticity ("GENUINENESS") and appropriation ("STOLEN AGAIN") that is instantly recognizable in the debates of the present day. They also equate cultural identity with a specific form of material production ("their own and

Figure 24.3 Stanislaus Francis, a Maliseet from Passamaquoddy, probably photographed at Tadoussac, ca. 1915. Notman Photographic Archives, McCord Museum of Canadian History, Montreal 8079-View

proper Basket Trade") in terms that would have been familiar to an ethnologist of the day. This should not be surprising; Native people had been learning to speak this language – like English or French – with its encoded concepts of copyright, cultural ownership, and commerce since the earliest days of contact (figure 24.3). As we saw in the last chapter, trade in specialized artisanal productions for which particular Native nations were famed long predated European contact.

The Abenaki petitioners understood that they could appeal to the hotel owners' understanding of the location of value in authenticity – in the "genuineness" of the objects sold on their premises. But the document also evinces the Abenakis' awareness of a further subtext to which they could appeal, the approval with which the white population of the day regarded Indian handicraft production as direct evidence of "industrial" competency and progress toward assimilation.[6] In this context a quite different significance was often assigned to objects like those in the Heye Iroquois beadwork display. One of the "lowliest" and most despised examples in the case, a large pincushion lavishly beaded with a flower-basket motif, is, for example, typologically very similar to beadwork singled out for special praise in a founding work of cultural evolutionist discourse, Lewis Henry Morgan's *The League of the Iroquois* of 1851 (figures 24.4 and 24.5).

Figure 24.5 "'Ya-wa-o-da-qua' or Pincushion," published by Lewis Henry Morgan in 1852. Photograph: Library, the Academy of Natural Sciences, Philadelphia

Morgan's work had helped to establish the tradition by which the signs of cultural identity, progress, and decay could be discerned in the study of material objects (Tooker 1994: 9–15). Although Morgan lamented the passing of older forms of Iroquois clothing and material production, the stronger voice in his text praised the successful absorption of Euro–North American technologies, styles, and iconographic motifs by Iroquois women as admirable evidence of the civilizability of the whole tribe – a promise of their successful modernization and assimilation:

> In the fabrics of the modern Iroquois there is much to inspire confidence in their teachableness in the useful arts. When their minds are unfolded by education, and their attention is attracted by habit to agricultural pursuits... this gifted race will be reclaimed, and raised, eventually, to citizenship among ourselves. (1962[1851]: 392)

As an early museum collector, Morgan had acquired examples of the "modern" acculturated styles together with older pieces in order to document not the decline but the progress of the Iroquois.[7] The Heye museum's Iroquois beadwork case, though inscribing a variant of cultural evolutionism, thus assigns meanings to the objects directly opposed to those of

Figure 24.4 Pincushion, Iroquois, cloth, beads, stuffing material. Canadian Museum of Civilization, Ottawa III-I-1748

later nineteenth- and early-twentieth-century liberal reformers – who were also confirmed cultural evolutionists. Cultural evolutionism was neither a fixed nor a homogeneous discourse. A series of diachronic shifts within the discourse resulted in contradictory readings of the significance of material objects. What had been regarded as crude and pagan became celebrated as authentic and admirable; what had been read as progressive became identified as degenerative. This development is directly related to the formalization of primitivist discourse in the early twentieth century, primarily among avant-garde artists, social reformers, and many anthropologists. Their championship of the primitive as a locus of value lost in the course of Western industrialization and urbanization is permeated with a tragic irony, for it threatened the futures of the peoples whose pasts it celebrated.

Ethnological Collectors, or How I Spent My Summer Vacation

The tension around tourist art can be illuminated by examining in greater detail the collecting practices of major museums. These practices are well documented in the correspondence files of museum archives. From these files I single out several texts that illustrate the activities and attitudes of the four kinds of collectors I have identified: the professional ethnologist, the rare art collector, the Native agent, and the tourist. These collectors speak from different social, economic, and political positions, although their planes of activity regularly intersect. The texts to be discussed have a broad relevance because the process of collection formation in the large North American museums followed a remarkably standardized pattern – and resulted, in consequence, in similar collection profiles.[8]

Professional ethnologists and their graduate students played the dominant role in collecting, providing the large conceptual framework into which objects were inserted. An efficient old boys' network directed the work they carried out; by means of this network the major metropolitan and university museums organized themselves into informal consortia that commissioned summer collecting trips "to the field" (the season being determined by both climate and the academic year). Field workers departed with "shopping lists" of desired

object types, and on their return the summer's haul was often divvied up according to the "needs" of several museums.

Museum collectors spread out over the continent in ever widening circles. As their letters show, their goal was to fill in the boxes of a kind of imagined chart of object types – a cross between a map and a periodic table – in which all functional categories would be represented for all tribal groups. These charts sorted the objects into representational domains of inclusion and exclusion; they universalized Western categories, such as "Transportation," "Hunting," "Toys and Games," "Religion," and "Art," that were not necessarily recognized by the peoples being studied (figure 24.6). The exclusions were as significant as the inclusions: "History" was normally a separate division within the museum dedicated to Euro-American objects, and there was no slot for "Industrial Production."

The project of ethnological collecting rested on the assumption that ethnicity and material culture were isomorphically related. This belief in the perfect coincidence of art and cultural style was also held by the art historians of the day (Belting 1987: 19; Phillips 1991a). Material objects have had undeniable pride of place in ethnological museum displays even though these institutions also carried out serious research in other areas, such as language, oral tradition, and music. The primary goal of all this activity was the physical installation of the object chart in the public halls of the museum. As Edward Sapir put it in 1912, describing his projected ethnological displays for the National Museum of Canada, the aim was to assemble "as representative collections as we can make of all the tribes of the Dominion."[9] The problem, of course, was that collections that excluded the interchangeable, mass-produced commodities that by 1912 were being used by North Americans could represent only imagined, not actual, lifestyles.

Frank Speck, the most active of the ethnologist-collectors working in the Northeast during the first half of this century, was employed by Sapir to accomplish this end. A letter written by Speck to Sapir in 1912 from northern Quebec captures the spirit of the era:

Now as to Ethnology (material culture). The Lake St. John supplementary collection was

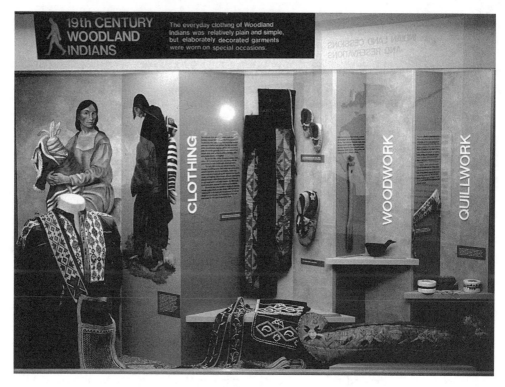

Figure 24.6 Case from the Woodlands Indian installation in the Public Museum of Grand Rapids, Michigan, taken down in 1994

shipped & reported on before we sailed. I hope it arrived safely, & that you will like it. There are still some gaps that need filling. On the coast here I have secured representative lots from 2 slightly different posts, Seven Island & Moisie river, the latter sort of mixed Naskapi & Montagnais band.[10]

The passage is well stocked with all the key signifiers. The parenthetical insertion of "material culture" after "Ethnology" indicates an assumed equation of object types and ethnicity, while the stress on the "representative" nature of what has been collected from different communities carries the related implication that separate bands (economic and political forms of organization) can be expected to produce visually distinct objects. The phrase "filling gaps" is a constant refrain in the documents, pointing clearly to the idealized taxonomic chart of culture that lay behind the ethnologist-collectors' project, with available slots waiting for the insertion of imagined

objects – objects which, if they did not exist "in the field" would have to be (re)invented.[11]

Speck's borrowing of the term "lots" from the language of commerce in referring to his collections is equally significant. In economic terms, the acquisition of objects from Native communities by museums – as well as by private collectors – was a transformative process. The things made by Indians became commodities to be exchanged in a market, and the ethnologist became a buyer – one who had to negotiate with competing buyers as well as with sellers. Most of the archival documentation, in fact, concerns negotiations over price, revealing the role played by the museum as a brokerage house. As Speck noted with reference to a collection from Abenaki Indians in the Adirondacks of New York, "I may say that all of these Indians, through contact with tourists, sports etc. have an exaggerated idea of the basic value of their heirlooms and hold to them for fancy prices which I had to pay."[12]

Native Agents as Collectors: Inscription and Resistance

The processes of "filling gaps" and of commoditization are described in some of the most fascinating documents in the museum archives. These detail the method by which the Western notions of commodity and money exchange were communicated to Aboriginal people. Professional museum collectors made regular use of well-placed or knowledgeable Native people as independent agents to collect for museums, as well as to make or commission models where original materials were not available.[13] Indeed we are only now recognizing how large a percentage of the extant ethnological material was collected directly by Native people rather than by the ethnologists who are listed as collectors.[14] Exchanges of letters between Aboriginal agents and museum administrators show ethnologists tutoring their Native associates in Western systems of object valuation. Speck's accounts of his collaboration with a Penobscot chief, Gabe Paul, show him busily inscribing the concepts of "collecting," the "type," and the "complete" in the Native consciousness:

> [Gabe] Paul has been my right hand man and I think will make a good collector and helper for Eastern Algonkian work. He is now amassing a Penobscot collection which it is his intention to make complete right through, including bark wigwams, full size, of several types. I have encouraged and instructed him as much as possible hoping that it will benefit the work.[15]

The documents strikingly illustrate the difference between Native and non-Native object/value systems as articulated by Native people in the course of their negotiations with non-Native buyers. Under colonial regimes these conflicts were nearly always resolved in favor of Western value systems. The acts of articulation constitute a form of resistance that needs to be acknowledged, however, for they lead to the highly effective reassertion of Aboriginal concepts of cultural property and replication made in recent years.

An exchange of letters during 1912 between Edward Sapir and another Chief Paul – James Paul, a Maliseet from New Brunswick – is particularly revealing of these problems. It begins with the commissioning of a birchbark canoe for the ethnographic museum in St. Petersburg, Russia. In each of his letters to Chief Paul, Sapir repeated the same instructions, hammering home the fundamental equation of age/premodernity/authenticity/value: "There are to be no nails or other white man's materials used in the canoe, but... it is to be made exactly of the style that the Indians used long ago before they knew anything about white man's ways."[16] When we consider that regular contacts between the Maliseet and the French began in the seventeenth century and that, by 1911, they had been trading with white men for more than two hundred years, the full burden of Sapir's instructions becomes clear. What he was really asking of Chief Paul was his collusion in the creation of one of the fictions of premodernity typical of the Museum Age – the reinvention of an object that they both could only imagine.[17]

Soon after he had carried out this commission, Chief Paul wrote to ask about a possible "gap" in the collection: "Have you any Indian carved paddles in your Museum?" Sapir cautiously asked in reply, "Are such Indian carved paddles as you speak of old fashioned Indian work or have they been made only in late days in order to sell to white people?" Chief Paul's answer evidences so fully the negotiations of value and the process of commoditization that it is worth citing in full:

> I am sending you two paddles. I don't think you have the Maliseet paddles and those I am sending, one of them is very old, but the other is not so old. You will take notice on one, there is some carving on it, that was done by some old Indian that had died long while ago. The oldest looking one is probably a hundred years old. I got them from a friend from Fredericton. He had them in his house for some time and never was used. I had to go to work and make him two new ones in place of the old ones that I got. On account I wanted them because they were so old. New paddles are worth $3.00 a pair. I am charg[ing] the half of what the new ones are worth so there will be no hard feelings between you and I. I think they are worth that to you on account they are so old but carved paddles it would be far much nicer what I make myself then what you see on that old one. I know you wouldn't feel like paying $10.00 a pair, but if you see them after all fixed up, you would say that they couldn't be bought for $25.00.[18]

Chief Paul uses the word "old" no less than eight times in these lines to reassure the ethnologist in Ottawa that his message had been received. A Native system of aesthetics, use, and value, however, also is articulated in the text, resisting the white man's insistence on the old and obsolete. Chief Paul asserts the value of the new and of the replica by assigning a money value that his white correspondent will understand as extravagant. He urges the proposition that a new paddle could be *more* beautiful than an old one, although his words remain at the level of suggestion, overwhelmed by the dominant culture's obsession with the old (figures 24.7a and 24.7b). Some further implications of this confrontation of value systems will be discussed below.

Figure 24.7a, b Two of four canoe paddles (details) commissioned by Frank Hazen from Maliseet carvers, ca. 1880. Figure 24.7a displays traditional double-curve motifs, while 24.7b displays an innovative pictorial vignette of a sporting camp scene, which would have been appreciated by touristic collectors but generally rejected by turn-of-the-century ethnological collectors. The New Brunswick Museum, St. John 59.66

The Rare Art Collector: Rarity versus Commodity

The valuing of age as a primary criterion of authenticity extended, of course, well beyond the ethnographic museum into many areas of museum practice. Players in the early-twentieth-century museum game were keenly aware of the subtle but important distinctions between the ethnologist's and the private collector's location of value in the old. George Heye, for example, fitted perfectly the mold of Alsop's rare art collector: the composition of his collections reflects his privileging of rarity and age, and his rigid association of the authentically Indian with the premodern.

Heye exercised autocratic control over his museum, and although he commissioned and funded important research and collecting expeditions, he bought from his hired ethnographers only the objects that fitted his tastes. "Heye is particularly mercenary these days," commented Speck in 1912, "desiring only the 'oldest,' 'used,' and 'rare' specimens, & 'not a cent for ethnology.' I myself have a little bunch of stuff rejected by Heye, including some good things which I was disappointed he did not want."[19] Speck here seems almost to articulate an oppositionality between his project and Heye's – "& not a cent for ethnology" – despite the clear coincidence of their agendas on most occasions. The point of difference is clarified by a further remark. "The mentioned articles are not all *old* and *antique* like Heye wants," he wrote, "but they are all typical of today."[20] Uninterested in representations of the twentieth-century life of Aboriginal people, Heye wanted only that which came from a "purer" past.

Though equally committed to the representation of the premodern, the ethnologist also was guided by his desire to complete his representative sets by including examples of the mundane and contemporary when they fitted slots in the taxonomy. He was not interested in uniqueness per se and actively sought out multiples to illustrate typologies of objects. He regularly commissioned replicas where used items were not available, or models when full-size objects could not be transported or stored. His main interest in market value was to keep it down so that his acquisition budget would stretch as far as possible.

To the private collector, by contrast, rarity and uniqueness were desiderata that could be separated from criteria of age and use, although the three were closely interconnected. A vivid example of the operation of these aspects of value in the acquisition of Native American objects is contained in a narrative written by the nineteenth-century Canadian author and journalist John Richardson. Richardson describes a pleasure trip he took in the eastern Great Lakes during the autumn of 1848 in the company of several other men to witness the annual distribution of treaty gifts at Sarnia and Walpole Island, Ontario. Richardson's narrative of the little expedition provides an extraordinarily full account of the individual acts of consumption that had characterized the curiosity trade for nearly two hundred years. On the lookout for "picturesque" Indians, he and his companions ignored those who "bore too many of the characteristics of semi-civilization, to render them either classical or interesting" (1849: 23). They approached

a small party of Pottowattamies who, in their war paint, stern rigidity of feature, and general demeanor, exhibited a most marked contrast to their deteriorated countrymen. This party was more immediately the object of attention with us, who were desirous of obtaining some reminiscences of our encounter with them. (1849: 23)

From an "old chief" one of the party, Captain Rooke, bought

a splendid war club, dark as ebony, and so polished from age, that it had evidently been one of the faithful and cherished companions of his youthful days, and sadly tempted must have been its owner, by the sight of the seductive silver dollar which had thus induced him to part with his treasure, for not the vestige even of a smile of satisfaction crossed his features, when the exchange had been affected. (1849: 23) (figure 24.8)

Richardson himself, the "first in the field," came away with a lead-inlaid stone pipe with a long stem carved in the form of a snake. He induced its owner to ornament it with ribbon and eagle feathers from his headdress and then completed the kit by buying a small beaded tobacco pouch. Richardson boasts of the good price he had paid for all this, which,

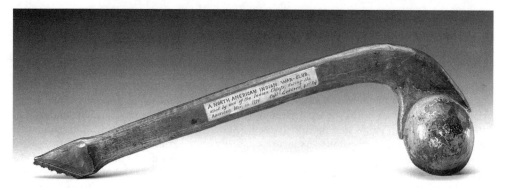

Figure 24.8 War clubs, Iroquois type, collected by Captain Goddard during the American Revolution. Ex-Wisbech Museum, Cambridge Museum of Archaeology and Anthropology, 49.212

"according to a jeweler's" estimate, could not have exceeded one tenth of its value." A third member of the party, a Mr. West, did even better, however, getting an even "more elegant pouch" for half the money Richardson had paid. "He had wisely tried his training powers, not upon an old file, but upon a youth, who, fascinated by the sight of the quarter of a dollar offered to him, could not resist the temptation, but nibbling at, and finally swallowing the bait, dispossessed himself of a perfect *bijou* in its way" (1849: 23). The men wrapped up the session by buying some mats and a bow and arrows. These purchases, Richardson concludes, "were rendered chiefly valuable, from the fact of their having belonged to men who regarded them as being, like themselves, relics of an original and fast departing race" (1849: 23).

Thus far, Richardson's text is breathtaking in its transparency. The privileging of rarity, of the patina of use, and of sheer age that are so fundamental to the Western tradition of collecting are clearly articulated, as are the attached significations of these objects as "relics of an original and fast departing race." Richardson's lack of hesitation in publicly proclaiming the exploitative and opportunistic nature of these acts of appropriation and consumption is striking. He glories in the detailing of transactions in which articles of ritual and functional use were commoditized, and in the shrewd bargaining of his companions. Richardson's self-congratulatory attribution to the Indians themselves of their alleged acceptance of the myth of the vanishing Indian is the ultimate appropriative strategy, and one

that also would characterize ethnological collectors as the Museum Age unfolded.[21] The Western recontextualization of Aboriginal objects in the curiosity cabinet, however, remains the dominant paradigm in this mid-nineteenth-century account, as indicated by such denotations as the "elegant" pouch that is "a perfect *bijou* in its way."

The frankness of Richardson's narrative might seem unaccountable in view of his own quarter-Indian ancestry and his youthful authorship of a romantic Indian epic novel. There was, of course, a text behind the text that proclaimed the necessity and inevitability of assimilating eastern Indians to white ways – to Christianity, to farming, and to the money economy. The ease with which the Indians are tricked is, to Richardson, evidence of their childlike status and, by implication, their need of the protective custody of the white man. By 1848 these views had gained wide acceptance among the colonial settlers of Upper Canada, although they were veiled in a lingering nostalgia for the old free men of the forest.

The passage which follows Richardson's account of the bargaining suggests this underlying text as well as his own repressed emotions of guilt and discomfort. He recounts how, at the moment of departure, he had tried to buy a mat from the same "stiff old warrior" who had earlier sold the fine club to his companion. Offering only a quarter for the mat, Richardson was turned down:

The look he gave me was eloquent, half with scorn, half with disappointment, but he uttered not a word – merely folding up his mat again, and walking, seemingly unconcerned, away. Shortly afterwards, as the steamer moved from the spot, we saw him seated on the bank, in an isolated position, moveless as a piece of statuary, and with his classically costumed upper form, strongly defined against the sky. The shaved and plastered crown – the long and solitary eagle's feather stuck on the top – the red painted face... the slight, very slight curvature of the shoulder, over which a sort of plaid mantle had been carelessly thrown – all contributed to form a *tout ensemble* that there, in its rudest state, sat the impersonation of man in the true and unshackled dignity of his nature. (1849: 23–24)

The paralyzing double bind is clearly stated. When Indians resist the commodification of their culture they retain respect and nobility but doom themselves, as cultural beings, to die. When they succumb, however, they reveal their weakness and are rejected as "deteriorated people" without cultural value. The figure of the "old Pottowattamie" is the ghost at the feast, silently reappearing throughout the account. Richardson continues to worry the image, examining the chagrin and mild guilt he feels as he imagines the man "perhaps mourning over the folly which had induced him to part, and for a mere trifle, with his favorite war-club" (1849: 24).

Richardson's narrative is constructed to end with an anecdote about war clubs which signals the new realities of the mid-nineteenth century. Mr. West, the successful purchaser of the elegant pouch, remaining discontented at not also having purchased a war club, persuades the group to visit the house of a prosperous Walpole Island Indian named George Rapp who had a side line as a trader. Rousing him from his sleep, they ask him

if he had any war clubs to dispose of. He said he had, and brought two to the large blazing log fire. Both of these, (of different shapes) he said, he had some trouble in fashioning; but they were clumsy, awkward looking things, and had an air of newness, which did not at all meet our ideas, *cognoscenti* as we had suddenly become in the particular article of war clubs. Indeed, compared with that purchased by Captain Rooke, from the old Pottowattamie, they were as a Norman dray horse to an English blood. Mr. West, who had a desire to obtain one, was discouraged by the comparison; but as Captain Eberts still remained a candidate for one of those "crackers of human skulls," Rapp was told to bring it to the steamer in the morning, at day light. In this he did not fail, when our friend was legitimately installed in the possession of a club. ... May he live a thousand years to enjoy it as a reminiscence of the very pleasant trip. (1849: 25) (figure 24.9)

This anecdote parallels Chief Paul's offer of the paddle to Edward Sapir, but it is narrated from the rare art collector's point of view. He sees the contemporary club as plebeian, while the old club belongs to an elite class of thoroughbred objects because of its very irreplaceability. The privileging of past over present meant that the Indian could never really win, even if he followed the government's script and engaged in commodity production. Only when the old and authentic were completely unavailable did the rare art collector accept the newer replica, but by this

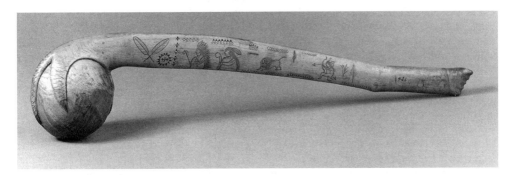

Figure 24.9 War club, Anishnabek, mid-nineteenth century, probably made for sale. Oronhyatekha Collection, Toronto, HD5828

very act he merged with the touristic collector. Richardson's heavy irony signaled his discomfort with his companion's compromise; his narrative denied to the new club essential meaning by naming it a mere "reminiscence" – a souvenir – of what once had been.

The Tourist: Collecting as Consumption

Multiple replication of the object – supply – is the essential precondition for a successful commodity trade, but this same condition empties the object of value for the rare art collector. In this sense the collector's interest runs counter not only to that of the Aboriginal producer but also to that of the tourist-collector. Mohawk women at Kahnawake today remember with pleasure and pride the great quantities of beaded souvenir objects that had to be prepared for a successful selling stint at Saratoga, or at the annual summer agricultural fairs in Ontario and Quebec. Keenly aware that a plentiful stock is an indispensable prerequisite for attracting buyers, they continue the traditional production of beaded horseshoes and pincushions – arts made throughout this century – for sale at the summer powwow recently founded at Kahnawake.[22]

Both the Niagara Falls buyer of beaded pincushions and the Anglo-Canadian gentleman in search of war clubs were motivated by a common need. Their purchases were displayed as trophies of imperial possession in the gentleman's den and as signs of a sentimental brush with an exotic and noble past in the "cozy corner" of a lady's parlor.[23] Viewed within the domestic spaces of the home, these trophies represented, in microcosm, the same drama of the displacement of the primitive by the modern as the more schematic and comprehensive public displays of the museum. Both public and private exhibits constituted ritual acts of consumption and display that naturalized immigrants and the descendants of immigrants as "native" North Americans.

As museum accession books show, the large majority of the beaded pincushions and souvenir clubs that are now in public collections came neither from the ethnologist-collector nor from the rare art collector, but were donated by a host of ordinary private individuals. Earlier in this century some of the more "serious" museums refused such

donations and even deaccessioned examples of tourist art. But with the passage of time many of these common domestic objects, having acquired their own patina of age, found their way onto museum storage shelves but, because they lacked histories of "authentic" Indian use, not into public exhibitions.[24]

The internal structure of the museum system, its subdivision into separate museums or discrete departments dealing with ethnology, history, folk art, fine art, and so on, has prevented the recognition of other kinds of authenticity inscribed in these objects (Phillips 1993). Tourist art did come with histories of use, although not ones that fitted conventional museum subject categories. The inattention to the testimony these objects offer is, in its way, as significant a silence as the rejection of the objects themselves. The written inscriptions on many examples of tourist art and the anecdotes of purchase recorded in museum accession books are hallmarks of "authentic" social history. They illuminate the histories of interaction between Native and non-Native, the intercultural story that the ethnologist's paradigm of race and exclusive ethnicity could not easily narrate, and in which the fine art curator, imbued with a disdain for popular art, was uninterested.

Postcards from the Field: The Ethnologist as Tourist

The four kinds of collectors that have been described are ideal types. On many occasions, as we have seen, the different players exchanged roles, swapped lines, or sang in chorus. Even the museum ethnologist, like the rare art collector, merged with the tourist-collector at times, straying across the professional lines that he himself had drawn. Speck carefully instructs the National Museum of Canada staff to forward his wife Florence's purchases of baskets and dolls, packed in with the ethnological specimens, to their summer home in Massachusetts. Chief Paul writes to Sapir asking his shoe size so that he can send him a pair of beaded moccasins as a Christmas present. And all the ethnologists collected Indian postcards and stereoscopic cards while in the field.

The postcard is a quintessentially touristic consumable, interchangeable with a beaded souvenir as a marker of touristic experience.

Many of the images on postcards sold in Native communities were perfect analogues for the ethnologists' reconstructed representations of the past, showing Native Americans dressed in "traditional" dress, archetypally posed in canoes or looking out across an empty landscape. The numerous examples of the ethnologists' use of these postcards as reasonable facsimiles of the historical past are even more striking evidence of the coincident gazes of scientist and tourist. In at least one case Speck used a postcard to illustrate a major ethnographic publication[25] (figure 24.10). If the condition of tourism is an integral aspect of modernity, then the ethnologist was a fully modern man.

So, too, of course, was his subject, the Indian. The successful commoditization of Indian arts and crafts and its capturing of transcultural motifs and forms accomplished a transition from the sophisticated systems of specialized craft production and exchange that had existed well before the arrival of Europeans to the new economic realities of the capitalist cash economy. This transition required versatility above all else. The full range of activities in which Native collectors typically engaged is clearly stated on the letterhead used by P. J. Atkins, a Six Nations Iroquois collector-agent, in his correspondence with the National Museum of Canada: "Dealer in Groceries and Provisions, Cured Meats; Contracts taken for Supplying Indians for Camps; Factories and all lines of work. Also for Concerts, Entertainment, Fall Fairs., etc., etc."[26] (figure 24.11). The mention of "Entertainment" and "Fall Fairs" is a clear indicator of involvement in the souvenir trade, for beadwork, baskets, and other items were regularly sold to spectators and visitors on these occasions. Similarly, Speck's own hand-picked Penobscot collecting agent, Chief Gabe Paul, was a seller of souvenir art. While on a month's visit to Speck in Philadelphia in 1912, Speck reported to Sapir that Paul "is in great confusion now clearing out his moccasin and basket stock to return home. He has been here three weeks pushing his business to pay expenses, souvenir goods."[27]

One final text is not a postcard but a letter from the field, written to Speck in 1942 by a student reporting on her reconnaissance trip to the Akwesasne (St. Regis) Mohawk reserve in northern New York State, which had been renowned as the major producer of ash splint baskets in the region since the nineteenth century.[28] The text is a paradigmatic statement of the salvage anthropology of the day, and it provides the ethnologist's gloss of the "Iroquois Women" text panels with which I began:

Figure 24.10 A postcard depicting the Indian John Snow, issued in 1912, with Frank Speck's note enquiring if he could use it to illustrate his ethnographic study, *Penobscot Man* (1940). Speck Papers, American Philosophical Society, Philadelphia

The four days I was there were just about enough to show me what a job it would be to work the place over right. (By the way, am I mistaken in thinking that the Mohawks as a whole and the St. Regis band in particular haven't been very thoroughly covered ethnographically?) Yet, from another point of view, they are so thoroughly acculturated – even prosperously so – that one would have to scratch under the surface pretty deep in some cases to get anything.

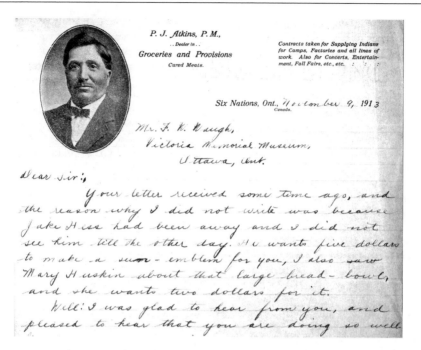

Figure 24.11 Letter from P. J. Atkins of the Six Nations reserve to Frederick Waugh, ethnographer at the National Museum of Canada, on Atkins's business letterhead. Waugh Papers, Archives, Canadian Ethnology Service, Canadian Museum of Civilization, Ottawa

This letter shows once again the ethnologist's commitment to freezing the representational moment in the past (Fabian 1983), for the notion that a community could be "covered" implicitly denies any interest in diachronic representation or any interest in "acculturation" itself.[29] The specific implications of this approach for the museum object are made clear in a subsequent paragraph:

> You wanted to know about basketry. Some of the women still make baskets, although not nearly so many as before this war plant boom. Their materials are supplied to them by a trading company, which takes the finished baskets and sells them to the tourist trade on the reservation and outside.... So I didn't get you a basket because none of the old plain splint ones are obtainable. These commercial ones are highly colored and made in the usual varied styles of present-day baskets in stores everywhere.[30]

The student takes for granted that the "impure" incorporation of imported materials, the commoditized (the "commercial"), the touristic, and the "highly colored" do not belong in the museum.

The lack of a slot for tourist art in the grand museum schema is intimately connected to the intercultural nature of the objects themselves. The problem with Indian tourist art was that it looked too "white." The same features that accounted for their appeal to consumers and their successful entry into the commodity system of Victorian North America prevented the objects from fitting comfortably into the categories of otherness. Tourist wares were threatening because they blurred the boundaries; they rendered the other unrecognizable. In symbolic terms we can interpret colonial museum representations as simple narratives of geographical displacement of the other by European colonization. If museums had assigned positive value to intercultural objects – as evidence of the ability of Aboriginal people to adapt, to survive, and even to thrive without assimilating – they would have subverted major subtexts of colonialism in two critical ways. They would have disrupted the rarity value produced by the evolutionist credo of the disappearing Indian, and they would have denied the escapist fantasy of refuge from industrialism that was structured by the dialectics of primitivist discourse.

Denial and Desire in the Museum

Such explanations do not completely satisfy, however, in the face of the sheer strength of the avoidance exhibited by many ethnologists of the modernity that was everywhere as they went about their work in Native communities. Igor Kopytoff's analysis of the process of commoditization is helpful in understanding the definitiveness of this rejection. In his model commoditization occurs along a spectrum with the singularized (rare) object at one end and its opposite, the replicatable commodity, at the other. In complex societies, he writes:

> Publicly recognized commoditization operates side by side with innumerable schemes of valuation and singularization devised by individuals, social categories, and groups, and these schemes stand in unresolvable conflict with public commoditization as well as with one another. (1986: 79–80)

The "yearning for singularization" that Kopytoff sees as characteristic of complex societies is immediately recognizable as the driving force behind the rare art collector and the ethnologist-collector. The rare art collector's desire for singularization is connected to aristocratic traditions of collecting, however, while the museum ethnologist values singularity as a cognitive tool. These contrasting motivations for valuing singularization are also related to the competing concepts of elitist "Kultur" and democratized Boasian "culture," both of which, as Dominguez (1992) has argued, are Western impositions on the conceptual schemes of many non-Western peoples.

The museum system empowered the rare art collector as patron and the professional ethnologist as gatekeeper. As a result, the singularized was privileged over the commodity in museum representation. The contrasting logic of "publicly recognized commoditization" is identifiable in the collecting activities of the Native agent-producer and the tourist consumer. These other collectors also have influenced the current shape of the museum collection, subverting its ideal purity through their donations of popular art and their offerings of the replica and the new.

Stewart (1984) and Vaessen (1989) have further analyzed the sources of the "yearning for singularization" – which Stewart terms "longing" – as products of the same processes of industrialized modernity that fostered extreme forms of commoditization. According to Stewart, as noted in chapter 3 of my book, the individual's alienation from his or her personal past creates needs that the souvenir and habits of private collecting attempt to satisfy. Vaessen, analogously, identifies the loss of ties to communal pasts produced by the dislocations of the industrial age as an important causal factor in the development of nineteenth-century museums. These institutions, he argues, compensated for loss on a public scale through their reconstructions of continuous, linear, and integrated historical narratives. Both of these theories suggest the nature of the desire that lay behind the emphasis on the premodern in museum displays about Indians. The flight of the rare art collector and the ethnologist from the commoditization and dislocation occurring in Western societies led them to make of the museum a shrine to the premodern. The pleasure produced by these acts of museological representation in non-Native viewers was in inverse proportion to the pain of denial they engendered in Native viewers. The avoidance of the commoditized is a sign of the silence about Native people's contemporary existences, of the lifestyles that had been imposed on them by force and then ingeniously negotiated under unavoidable conditions of colonial domination (figure 24.12).

Souvenir art is the product of a careful, anthropological study of the material culture and aesthetics of the Western other by Native artists and craftspeople. As I have noted, however, Aboriginal people regularly used within their own communities the same styles of beadwork and many of the same types of commodities that were made for sale. In many ways these souvenir and trade wares seem to be the most authentic representations of the courageous, innovative, and creative adaptation that Woodlands Aboriginal peoples made during one of the darkest periods in their history. In denying this modernity through their exhibitions, museums operated in apparent contradiction of official government assimilationist policies toward Native Americans. The arbitrary boundaries of time and space that museums established sliced

Figure 24.12 Postcard issued by the E. C. Kroppe Company of Milwaukee, Wisconsin, early twentieth century, with the caption: "Indian squaw watching the passing tourists". Private collection

through the unity of everyone's lived experience, Native and non-Native. The silence surrounding souvenir art is thus the expression of a tension between nostalgic primitivist desires deeply inscribed in the popular imagination (Price 1989; Torgovnik 1990) and the official acts of the state. Under colonial regimes this tension was unresolvable. Such a view of the museum helps to explain why it has been a major site of political confrontation as we emerge into the postcolonial era. This explanation also suggests that ethnographic museums have acted as arenas for complex negotiations of social constructions rather than – as has been argued – relatively straightforward instruments for the policing and education of the general public (Bennett 1990).

The signs that the colonial era of the museum is drawing to a close are many. As Aboriginal people become increasingly active in the area of museum representation, other perspectives on the histories of commodity production in their communities are being articulated in which experiences of modernity and the contemporary are privileged in relation to representations of a more remote past. One of the most active Iroquois museums is the Woodlands Indian

Museum on the Six Nations Reserve in Brantford, Ontario. Its exhibition *Fluffs and Feathers* examined images of Indians in popular culture and included tourist art of all kinds, Native and non-Native.[31] At the newly opened Institute of American Indian Arts Museum in Santa Fe in 1992, Iroquois curator Richard W. Hill prominently featured tourist-associated objects such as a Haida argillite model totem pole and a late-nineteenth-century Iroquois beaded Glengarry cap in the historical displays that introduced the installation of contemporary Native American art. In discussing the adoption by earlier Native artists of "inauthentic" Euro–American styles of floral decoration in their beadwork, he notes: "Even if there were a cross-cultural influence, the Great Lakes Indians believed that this style best represented their world view at that time" (1992: 23).[32] More recently, in *Creation's Journey*, an exhibition of historic traditions of Native art at the New York venue of the National Museum of the American Indian, Hill chose to foreground commoditized arts from the Northeast by placing them prominently in the introductory rooms. In a text panel entitled "Trapped in the Past" (the continuation of which is cited at the opening of this chapter), he wrote:

Scholars often debate the authenticity of Indian art when it shows European influences. New materials are looked on as signs of acculturation and are considered a creative blending of two traditions. Such works may have been the only way in which the skill of quillwork and the use of Native designs were able to continue. If Native art is denied any opportunity to change, it becomes a prisoner of its own past.

The ending of the silence about souvenir art in both Native and non-Native museums is an augury of the end of the colonial discourse of the museum because it deconstructs the dialectical rendering of the primitive as premodern, static, and dead in opposition to the Western as modern, dynamic, and living. The acceptance of souvenir arts on their own terms means valuing them not for the residue they may be seen to contain of older and more "authentic" traditions, but as objects that produce a new reality by successfully negotiating the challenge of the new and different. Museums have long validated the objects of the West for their innovative qualities and for their ability to be both old and new at the same time. In the postcolonial museum, the objects of others will be prized for the same qualities.

NOTES

1   This issue has been explored by Spencer R. Crew and James E. Sims with regard to museums of American history. As research in social history developed, they note, museum professionals discovered that "the holdings within their institutions created major stumbling blocks. Many times their collections did not contain the objects they needed" (1991: 164–65). Although, as Hooper-Greenhill argues, "the radical potential of material culture, of concrete objects, of real things, of primary sources, is the endless possibility of rereading," it is important to acknowledge that historical patterns of collecting that excluded certain kinds of objects also shape the potential for new representations in museums (1992: 215).

2   For rare art collecting, see Alsop 1982; for discussions of "natural history" as a dominant paradigm of late-nineteenth-century scientific knowledge, see Ginzburg 1980 and, with particular reference to the museum, Jordanova 1989.

3   Heye continued to control the activities of his museum until his death in 1957. In stark contrast, the new National Museum of the American Indian is directed and managed by Native American professionals. See Phillips 1995 (an earlier version of this chapter) for a more detailed discussion of the transition from the Heye Foundation to the National Museum of the American Indian.

4   As Jonaitis (1991) has shown in relation to Boas's early-twentieth-century representation of Northwest Coast women, the plastic arrangement of a museum display can convey messages that directly contradict the written anthropological texts of its own author. At the American Museum of Natural History, New York, as at the Heye Foundation, a Western story of patriarchy and gender roles is narrated through representations of the "other" (Clifford 1986). Although there were important female ethnologists such as Frances Densmore working among Woodlands peoples, patriarchal discourse dominated ethnological museum representation in the early twentieth century. Because most ethnological collectors were men, I use the masculine pronoun in referring to members of the group.

5   A copy of the printed petition is found in the Frank Speck papers at the American Philosophical Society, Philadelphia. It is dated "at the INDIAN CAMPS, INTERVALE, County of Carroll, N.H., 189–," and signed with the printed names of members of the Abenaki community. The possibility that a sympathetic non-Native helped to draft it and to suggest the language that is used does not diminish but rather reinforces its value as a historical documentation of concepts of property and appropriation.

6   The special flavor of this document is owed to an irony of which the white ethnologists of the period – and possibly the Abenaki themselves – were unaware. As Brasser (1975) and others have convincingly argued, specific techniques of splint basketry used by northeastern Aboriginal peoples during the nineteenth and twentieth

centuries (and grafted on to highly accomplished precontact basket weaving techniques) were probably not indigenous but were introduced by colonial settlers, probably Scandinavian or German, in the early contact period. The thoroughness with which Aboriginal groups in the Northeast mastered and elaborated splint basketry, together with their economic need, led to their establishing a near monopoly over basket making in the region. Unaware at the time that splint baskets participated in the despised realm of the acculturated, ethnologists enthusiastically collected and displayed them in museums.

7   See Tooker 1994, esp. pp. 60–84, for a full account of Morgan's ethnographic collecting. The terms of his mandate were spelled out in the New York State Regents report for 1849. He undertook "to bring together a full exhibition of the manufactures of the Indian tribes still remaining within our State, and thus to show, as it were, their transition condition, in the union of their ancient and rude constructions, with the improvements received through the whites" (quoted in Tooker 1994: 52).

8   See Cole 1985, Jonaitis 1988, and Penney 1992 for important studies exploring these standard patterns of collection formation on the Northwest Coast and in the Great Lakes and Plains.

9   Sapir to Mrs. James H. Peck, president of the Canadian Guild of Handicrafts, Ottawa, September 11, 1911, Edward Sapir correspondence, Archives of the Canadian Ethnology Service, Canadian Museum of Civilization (hereafter CANES Archives, CMC).

10 Dated "Seven Islands, St. Lawrence, June 26, 1912," Sapir correspondence, CANES Archives, CMC.

11 See Graburn 1996: 5–13 for a discussion of the links between commercial and scientific collecting in the case of the Alaska Commercial Company. Because such agents served both private and scientific clients, they collected some objects for which there were no scientific "slots," aiding in the creation of a historical legacy that would eventually challenge existing schema.

12 Speck to Sapir, n.d. [1912], Sapir correspondence, CANES Archives, CMC.

13 Proximity to Native communities, ease and availability of competent Aboriginal assistants, academic teaching loads, and liking for the comforts of home are all probable reasons for the fact that North American ethnologists made shorter and more frequent visits to the field than colleagues working in other parts of the world. An unexamined consequence of this pattern is, however, their more superficial immersion in community life and a less rigorous use of methods of participant observation as well as a greater reliance on Native collector-agents.

14 A number of recent projects have begun to raise the consciousness of contemporary museum audiences about the roles played by Native collector-agents. See Berlo and Phillips 1992 for a discussion of two recent exhibitions, the American Museum of Natural History's *Chiefly Feasts*, and the Brooklyn Museum's *Objects of Myth and Memory*, that highlighted this interaction. See also Jacknis 1991.

15 Speck to Sapir, Annisquam, Gloucester, Mass., n.d. [1912], Sapir correspondence, CANES Archives, CMC. See also H.N.W. 1937.

16 Sapir to James Paul, November 31, 1911, Sapir Correspondence, CANES Archives, CMC.

17 Examples abound of this kind of commissioning. Among the most extraordinary were Speck's "replicas" of archaic fire drills and tobacco containers, now in the American Museum of Natural History, New York, commissioned from the Huron-Wendat at Lorette-Wendake during his trip in 1908. At the beginning of the twentieth century, the material conditions of life in this community, located adjacent to Quebec City for two hundred years, were nearly indistinguishable from those of their French-Canadian neighbors. The objects Speck placed in the museum bear no resemblance to any documented Huron artifacts.

18 Headed "St. Mary's Reservation, December 26, 1911," Sapir correspondence, CANES Archives, CMC.

19 Speck to Sapir, Philadelphia, January 15, 1912, CANES Archives, CMC.

20 Speck to Sapir, Philadelphia, February 14, 1912, Sapir correspondence, CANES Archives, CMC. He was referring to Penobscot, Abenaki, and Huron objects.

21 Morgan's collecting of Iroquois objects for the New York State Museum is contemporary with this text. The contrast between rare art collectors and ethnologists discussed in relation to the activities of Heye and Speck more than half a century later is, however, already present between Richardson and Morgan, for the latter enthusiastically commissioned examples of contemporary beadwork and clothing.

22 Personal communications, Presida Stacey and Penny LeClaire, Kahnawake, Quebec, January 28, 1992.

23 See Gordon 1988: 6–8 and Lee 1991 on the display of Indian tourist art in the home around 1900 and the connection of the vogue for Indian art to the American Arts and Crafts movement.

24 The largest single private collection of northeastern tourist art, assembled by Mrs. June Bedford over the past few decades, was recently bought by the Royal Ontario Museum, Toronto. Mrs. Bedford bought many pieces inexpensively at flea markets and antique shops in Britain to which they had been sold by private owners whose antecedents had originally acquired them as souvenirs (Canada House Cultural Centre Gallery 1985).

25 The postcard is an illustration for Speck's *Penobscot Man*. It bears the printed caption "John Snow, Penobscot Tribe, Old Town," together with Speck's handwritten suggestion for the figure caption printed in the book: "Penobscot man with moose skin coat." Speck papers, American Philosophical Society, Philadelphia (572.97/Sp3).

26 An example of this letterhead is found in the Frederick Waugh correspondence, CANES Archives, CMC.

27 Speck to Sapir, Philadelphia, December 16, 1912, Sapir correspondence, CANES Archives, CMC.

28 In a series of feature articles on the "Reservation Indians of New York State," published in the *Illustrated Buffalo Express* circa January 1895, Harriet Converse notes that at St. Regis "the basket industry and supply is greater than that of all the other reservations combined, giving employment to nearly all the women and children." Scrapbook on Indians (unprovenanced), D72–23, containing newspaper clippings dated from 1882 to 1895, Buffalo and Erie County Historical Society, Buffalo, New York.

29 The strong interest in acculturation studies that at this time was developing in American anthropology was dissociated from museum collecting. The object record remained fixed by the earlier generation's efforts.

30 Letter to Speck signed "Mary," September 14, 1942, Speck papers, American Philosophical Society, Philadelphia.

31 See Doxtator 1988. The exhibition was revived and prepared for a North American tour in 1992–93 by the Woodlands Indian Museum in collaboration with the Royal Ontario Museum, Toronto.

32 In his work as an artist Hill has also contributed to the critique of the representation of souvenir arts. See Phillips 1998.

REFERENCES

Alpers, Svetlana 1983 *The Art of Describing: Dutch Art in the Seventeenth Century.* Chicago: University of Chicago Press.

Alsop, Joseph 1982 *The Rare Art Traditions: The History of Art Collecting and Its Linked Phenomena.* New York: Harper and Row.

Belting, Hans 1987 *The End of the History of Art?* Trans. Christopher S. Wood. Chicago: University of Chicago Press.

Bennett, Tony 1990 "The Political Rationality of the Museum," *Continuum: An Australian Journal of the Media* 4 (1).

Berlo, Janet Catherine, and Ruth B. Phillips 1992 "'Vitalizing the Things of the Past': Museum Representations of Native North American Art in the 1990s," *Museum Anthropology* 16(1): 29–43.

Brasser, Ted J. 1975 *A Basketful of Indian Culture Change.* Mercury Series, Canadian Ethnology Service Paper, no. 22. Ottawa: National Museums of Canada.

Canada House Cultural Centre Gallery 1985 *Mohawk Micmac Maliseet... And Other Indian Souvenir Art from Victorian Canada.* London.

Clifford, James 1986 "On Ethnographic Allegory." In *Writing Culture: The Politics and Poetics of Ethnography,* ed. James Clifford and George E. Marcus. Berkeley: University of California Press.

Cole, Douglas 1985 *Captured Heritage: The Scramble for Northwest Coast Artifacts.* Seattle: University of Washington Press.

Crew, Spencer R., and James E. Sims 1991 "Locating Authenticity: Fragments of a Dialogue." In *Exhibiting Cultures: The Poetics and Politics of Museum Display,* ed. Ivan Karp and Steven D. Lavine. Washington, D.C.: Smithsonian Institution Press.

Dominguez, Virginia 1992 "Invoking Culture: The Messy Side of 'Cultural Politics.' " *The South Atlantic Quarterly* 91 (1): 19–42.

Doxtator, Deborah 1988 *Fluffs and Feathers: An Exhibit on the Symbols of Indianness, A Resource Guide.* Brantford, Ont.: Woodland Cultural Centre.

Ginzburg, Carlo 1980 "Morelli, Freud and Sherlock Holmes: Clues and the Scientific Method." *The History Workshop* 9: 5–36.

Goldwater, Robert 1967 *Primitivism in Modern Art.* Rev. ed. New York: Vintage Books.

Gordon, Beverly 1988 "Collecting Indian Art: The Historical Context." In *American Indian Art: The Collecting Experience,* by Beverly Gordon and Melanie Herzog. Madison, Wisc.: Elvehjem Museum of Art, University of Wisconsin.

Graburn, Nelson H.H. 1996 Introduction to *Catalogue Raisonné of the Alaska Commercial Company Collection,* by Nelson H. H. Graburn, Molly Lee, and Jean-Loup Rousselot. University of California Publications in Anthropology, vol. 21. Berkeley: University of California Press.

Hill, Richard W. 1992 *Creativity Is Our Tradition.* Santa Fe, N.M.: Institute of American Indian Arts.

Hinsley, Curtis M., Jr. 1981 *Savages and Scientists: The Smithsonian Institution and the Development of American Anthropology: 1846–1910.* Washington, D.C.: Smithsonian Institution Press.

Holmes, W.H. 1890 "On the Evolution of Ornament – An American Lesson." *American Anthropologist* 3: 137–46.

Hooper-Greenhill, Eilean 1992 *Museums and the Shaping of Knowledge.* New York: Routledge.

Hoxie, Frederick E. 1984 *A Final Promise: The Campaign to Assimilate the Indians, 1880–1920.* Cambridge: Cambridge University Press.

Jonaitis, Aldona 1988 *From the Land of the Totem Poles: The Northwest Coast Indian Art Collection at the American Museum of Natural History.* Seattle: University of Washington Press.

—— 1991 "Representations of Women in Native American Museum Exhibitions: A Kwakiutl Example." *European Review of Native American Studies* 5 (2): 29–33.

Jordanova, Ludmilla 1989 "Objects of Knowledge: A Historical Perspective on Museums." In Vergo 1989.

Karp, Ivan, and Steven D. Lavine, eds. 1991 *Exhibiting Cultures: The Poetics and Politics of Museum Display.* Washington, D.C.: Smithsonian Institution Press.

Kopytoff, Igor 1986 "The Cultural Biography of Things: Commoditization as Process." In *The Social Life of Things: Commodities in Cultural Perspective,* ed. Arjun Appadurai. Cambridge: Cambridge University Press.

Lee, Molly 1991 "Appropriating the Primitive: Turn-of-the-Century Collection and Display of Native Alaskan Art." *Arctic Anthropology* 28 (1): 6–15.

Miller, J. R. 1989 *Skyscrapers Hide the Heavens: A History of Indian-White Relations in Canada.* Toronto: University of Toronto Press.

Morgan, Lewis Henry 1962 *League of the Ho-de-no-sau-nee or Iroquois.* 1851. Reprint, New York: Corinth Books.

Penney, David W. 1992 *Art of the American Indian Frontier: The Chandler-Pohrt Collection.* Seattle: University of Washington Press; Detroit: Detroit Institute of Arts.

Phillips, Ruth B. 1989 "What is 'Huron' Art?: Native American Art and the New Art History." *The Canadian Journal of Native Studies* 9 (2): 161–86.

—— 1990 "Great Lakes Textiles: Meaning and Value in Women's Art." In *On the Border: Native American Weaving Traditions of*

the Great Lakes and Plains, ed. David Woo-
ley. Moorehead, Minn.: Plains Art Museum.
—— 1991 "Glimpses of Eden: Iconographic
Themes in Huron Pictorial Tourist Art."
European Review of Native American Studies 5 (2): 19–28.
—— 1991 "Comment: 'Catching Symbolism':
Studying Style and Meaning in Native
American Art." Arctic Anthropology 28
(1): 92–100.
—— 1993 " 'Messages from the Past': Oral
Traditions and Contemporary Woodlands
Art." In In the Shadow of the Sun: Contemporary Indian and Inuit Art from Canada,
Mercury Series no. 124. Ottawa: Canadian
Museum of Civilization.
—— 1995 "Why Not Tourist Art? Significant
Silences in Native American Museum Representation." In After Colonialism: Imperial
Histories and Post-colonial Displacements,
ed. Gyan Prakash. Princeton: Princeton Uni-
versity Press.
—— 1998 Trading Identities: The Souvenir in
Native North American Art from the
Northeast, 1700–1900. Seattle: University
of Washington Press.
Phillips Ruth B., and Christopher B. Steiner
1998 Introduction to Phillips and Steiner
1998a.
Phillips, Ruth B., and Christopher B. Steiner,
eds. 1998a Unpacking Culture: Arts and
Goods in Colonial and Postcolonial Worlds.
Berkeley and Los Angeles: University of
California Press.

Price, Sally 1989 Primitive Art in Civilized
Places. Chicago: University of Chicago
Press.
Richardson, John 1849 "A Journey from
Walpole Island to Port Sarnia." Literary
Garland 7 (1): 17–26.
Stewart, Susan 1984 On Longing: Narratives
of the Miniature, the Gigantic, the Souvenir,
and the Collection. Baltimore: Johns
Hopkins University Press.
Stocking, George W., Jr., ed. 1985 Objects and
Others: Essays on Museums and Material
Culture. Madison, Wisc.: University of
Wisconsin Press.
Sturtevant, William C. 1969 "Does Anthropol-
ogy Need Museums?" Proceedings of the
Biological Society 82: 619–50.
Tooker, Elizabeth 1994 Louis H. Morgan on
Iroquois Material Culture. Tucson: Univer-
sity of Arizona Press.
Torgovnik, Marianna 1990 Gone Primitive:
Savage Intellects, Modern Lives. Chicago:
University of Chicago Press.
Vaessen, Jan 1989 "Opening and Closing: On
the Dialectics of the Museum." In Gener-
ators of Culture: The Museum as a Stage,
ed. Rob van Zoest/d'Arts. Amsterdam: AHA
Books.
Vergo, Peter, ed. 1989 The New Museology.
London: Reaktion Books.

25

The Art of the Trade
On the Creation of Value and Authenticity in the African Art Market

Christopher B. Steiner

Early in the spring of 1985, amidst the economic flamboyance of the 1980s and a dizzying trail of skyrocketing prices in the international art scene, there appeared in a French magazine a full-page advertisement for Jean-François Gobbi's Galerie d'Art. A dramatic black-and-white photograph depicts Monsieur Gobbi, dressed in a dark suit and sporting an oversized cigar, surrounded by some of his masterworks of European art. The text below the photograph reads as follows:

> The world's largest museums and collectors await your valuable paintings.... The problem, however, is that you don't know where they are – these museums and collectors who are ready to pay good money for your works of art. Jean-François Gobbi, *he* knows where they are: they are all his clients. Today, the demand for masterpieces is so great that museums and collectors don't even discuss price.... Now if you think you will some day come in contact with a big museum or an important collector willing to pay top dollar for your masterpiece, don't call Jean-François Gobbi. Otherwise dial 266–50–80. (*Galerie des Arts* no. 227, 1985: inside front cover)

In the art world, as in the world of all big business, the success of the middleman depends upon the separation of buyers from sellers. Social, legal, and bureaucratic barriers are erected at every level of the economic system to maintain the distance between the primary suppliers of art and their ultimate consumers. "The producers and consumers of the art," Bennetta Jules-Rosette has written with regard to the African tourist art industry, "live in quite different cultural worlds that achieve a rapprochement only through the immediacy of the artistic exchange" (1984:8). Art dealers earn their livelihoods as go-betweens – moving objects and artifacts across institutional obstacles which often they themselves have constructed in order to restrict direct contact or trade.

The market for African art and artifacts is characterized by precisely this sort of network of relations, in which a host of both African and non-African middlemen forge temporary links in a transnational chain of supply and demand. Art objects and cultural artifacts enter the market in two ways. Either they are bought from village inhabitants who are motivated by financial or personal reasons to sell family heirlooms and ritual paraphernalia, or

From George E. Marcus and Fred R. Myers (eds.), *The Traffic in Culture: Refiguring Art and Anthropology* (Berkeley: University of California Press, 1995), pp. 151–165. Reprinted by permission of the University of California Press.

they are purchased from artists who produce directly for the export trade. Both used and made-for-sale materials are collected by professional African traders who travel through rural communities in search of whatever they believe can be resold (cf. Ravenhill 1980a). Most of the suppliers have little or no idea where these objects are destined, why they are sought after, and for what price they will ultimately be bought.

After being collected in villages or workshops, objects are moved from town to town until they are eventually sold to a dealer who has direct contact with European or American clients. These dealers, most of whom are Hausa, Mande, or Wolof, are based in Abidjan, the chief economic port of Côte d'Ivoire, as well as in the larger towns of Man, Korhogo, Bouaké, and Yamoussoukro. Because their primary network of relations extend outward – i.e., into the world of Western buyers rather than inward into the world of local village suppliers – urban dealers are dependent upon village-level traders for their supply of goods. They themselves never buy art directly in villages (figure 25.1).

Through their interactions with Western buyers, dealers have partial understanding of the world into which African art objects are being moved. Their experience enables them to discern certain criteria underlying Western definitions of authenticity. They know, through trial and error, which items are easiest to sell, and they can predict which objects will fetch the highest market price. Using this refractured knowledge of Western taste, traders manipulate objects in order to meet perceived demand. In this essay, I will illustrate three ways in which African art objects are manipulated by African traders: the presentation of objects, the description of objects, and the alteration of objects. My remarks are based on eighteen months of field research from 1987 to 1991 conducted among African art traders in rural and urban Côte d'Ivoire.

Presentation of Objects

The presentation of an art object for sale is not something that is carried out in a haphazard manner. Careful preparations are made before an object is shown to a prospective buyer. The

Figure 25.1 African art trader with Senufo mask, Korhogo, Côte d'Ivoire, June 1991. Photograph by Christopher B. Steiner

context in which an object is placed and the circumstances surrounding its putative discovery weigh heavily in the buyer's assessment of quality, value, and authenticity. Presentation is always a key element in the success of a sale. If an object is uncovered by the buyer in what is thought to be its original or "natural" setting it is presumed to be closer to the context of its creation or use and therefore less likely to be inauthentic or fake.

The very process and act of discovery generally confirms the collector's sense of good taste. There is a long-standing tradition in travel writing that involves an author's arduous exploration for genuine cultural objects – the more difficult the search the more authentic the find. In his 1914 memoir, *The Sport of Collecting*, Sir Martin Conway recounts his search for ancient Egyptian artifacts: "I had spent two or three evenings in the *dark* native houses of Luxor, finding nothing but the ordinary poor rubbish that came to the surface everywhere in Egypt. At last I was taken...into the an *inner* room within the compound of a *specially secluded* house, and there, to my astonishment, they showed me a few quite extraordinary treasures" (1914:77, emphasis added). More recently, in a travelogue narration of a voyage to Côte d'Ivoire in the 1970s, an African art collector described his visit to the northern town of Korhogo in the following words: "While my travel companions were all taking naps, I *ventured* into the *obscurity* of a hut, which was *lost* somewhere in the heart of a labyrinth of identical alleys, where I saw a magnificent Senufo hunter's tunic covered with talismans: fetish horns, leather pouches, feline teeth, and small bones" (Lehuard 1977:28, emphasis added). And, in a subsequent article describing his travels through Burkina Faso, the same author provides his readers with the following piece of advice: "For those who collect antiques, but cannot afford the cost, or do not possess the training, to '*hunt*' for objects in the bush, it is always possible to *excavate* through the stock of the urban traders who are set up alongside the Hotel Ran in Ouagadougou. Although there is a preponderance of modern sculptures here, it is sometimes possible to *ferret out* a rare gem" (1979:19, emphasis added).

The manipulation of context through the calculated emplacement of objects is a wide-spread practice among art dealers around the world. One of the classic tricks of the French antique market, for example, was to plant reproduction furniture in old homes. In the autobiography of André Mailfert (1968), a cabinetmaker who produced reproduction antique furniture in Orléans from 1908 to 1930, the author unveils the so-called *coup du meuble "planqué."* A dresser was made to fit the specifications of a dealer who knew he could sell such a piece to a client who was soon scheduled to arrive from abroad. Once completed, the dresser was taken to the home of an elderly woman who lived on the outskirts of Paris. A wall in the front hall was thoroughly cleaned, the dresser was placed in front of it, and, with the help of an air compressor, dust was sprayed on the wall so as to leave a noticeable mark around the edge of where the dresser now stood. The dresser was scratched in appropriate places, the drawers were filled with odds and ends taken from the woman's closet, an accumulation of decades of floor wax was quickly applied to the brass rim of the dresser legs, and a yellowed envelope which dated from thirty years earlier was casually tucked under the marble top to support a corner which had been made to warp. The customer was told that an old woman needed to sell an antique dresser in order to pay her taxes. He was taken to the woman's home whereupon, after scrupulous inspection and words of encouragement from his dealer *expert*, the client bought the dresser for 12,000 francs. For the use of her home the woman received 1,000 francs, the cabinetmaker was paid for the price of the reproduction dresser, and the dealer kept the rest. "There is of course a question of conscience," Mailfert concludes, "but it's all so amusing that even the most virtuous among us could hardly resist such a wicked temptation" (1968:57).

In Côte d'Ivoire, as in France before World War I, one of the key factors in the presentation of an art object is to create an illusion of discovery. Because of the barriers, which I noted earlier, that separate art consumers from art suppliers, the Western buyer almost never has the opportunity to uncover an object by chance or recognize its potential value *before* it enters the market or *before* it becomes a commodity. Yet, part of the collector's quest, I would argue, is to discover what has previously gone unremarked. As one European art critic put it, "the charm [of an art object] is bound up with the accident of its discovery" (Rheims 1961:212). From the perspective of the Western collector, African traders are perceived as mere suppliers of raw materials. It is the gifted connoisseur, not the African middleman, who first "sees" the aesthetic quality of a piece and thereby "transforms" a neglected artifact into an object of art (cf. Price 1989).

African art dealers are acutely aware of the discovery element in Western taste. Depending on the circumstance, traders will sometimes feign ignorance or pretend not to know much about the goods they sell in order to let the buyers believe that they are getting something the true value or significance of which the seller does not recognize. In fact, the principal art market in Abidjan, known as the Plateau marketplace, is constructed in such a fashion as to facilitate this illusion of discovery. The front of the marketplace consists of a series of adjoining stalls, with layered shelves on which are displayed quantities of identical items. These objects are marketed largely as contemporary souvenirs made for the tourist trade (figure 25.2). In the back of the marketplace, which can only be accessed through a series of dark and narrow paths, there are a number of large wooden trunks in which some of the traders store their goods (figure 25.3). Many of the objects kept in the back of the marketplace are identical to those displayed in the front. The difference, however, is that they are *presented* to the buyer as unique and rare items.

Drawing on the dramaturgical idiom in the sociology of Erving Goffman, Dean MacCannell has noted the interplay between front and back regions in the construction of authenticity. "Just having a back region," writes MacCannell, "generates the belief that there is something more than meets the eye; even where no secrets are actually kept, back regions are still the places where it is popularly believed the secrets are" (1976:93). "Entry into this space," he concludes further on in the text, "allows adults to recapture virginal sensations of discovery" (1976:99). By permitting the buyer to penetrate the back region of the marketplace, the African art trader thus underscores the value and authenticity of the object he is showing.

Figure 25.2 African art trader at his stall in the front of the Plateau marketplace, Abidjan, Côte d'Ivoire, November 1988. Photograph by Christopher B. Steiner

Figure 25.3 African art trader with wooden storage trunk in the back section of the Plateau market-place, Abidjan, Côte d'Ivoire, May 1988. Photograph by Christopher B. Steiner

Like their counterparts in the French antique market, African traders also plant objects in remote and ingenious settings. An elderly Malian art trader recounted an instance in which he tried to sell a mask to an American buyer. The buyer carefully examined the mask but refused to purchase it, telling the trader that he doubted it was very "old" or "real." Several months later the buyer returned to Abidjan. The trader planted the very same mask (which had not yet been sold) in a village located not far from the urban capital. The buyer was brought to the village and taken with great circumstance into the house where the mask had been placed. The object was examined, as best it could, in the dim light of the house. This time the customer bought the piece and, in the trader's words, was delighted with his "find."

Description of Objects

Verbal cues affect judgment of authenticity and success of sale in ways similar to object emplacement. That is to say, what we are told about a work of art conditions what we see. In Europe, for example, the title of a painting is sometimes changed to fit the current taste of the market. In the 1950s, when macabre themes in art were apparently more difficult to sell than lighthearted and amusing works, the title of van Gogh's painting described in earlier references as *The Cemetery* was changed in an auction catalog to the more cheerful *Church under Snow* (Rheims 1961:209).

In Africa, traders communicate through verbal means two types of information about the objects they sell. On the one hand, traders convey to Western collectors and dealers specific information relating to an object's market history (i.e., when it was collected, how it was acquired, where it originates from, and so on). To foreign tourists, on the other hand, traders provide general information regarding an object's cultural meaning and traditional use. Both types of information are constructed to satisfy perceived Western taste and are intended to increase the likelihood of sale. In the language of mediation studies, one might say that the trader's description of an object is phrased at the level of metacommunication or "communication about communication." The sender's messages, to borrow Bateson's phrase, are "tailored to fit" according to his ideas about the receiver, and they include instructions on how the receiver should interpret their content (1951:210).

African art objects in the West are sometimes sold with a documented "pedigree" which consists of a list of previous owners. A quick glimpse at auction prices would indicate that a mask once owned by a Picasso or Rockefeller is worth far more money than an identical mask from the collection of an unknown patron (cf. Price 1989). Before an object leaves the African continent, however, its true pedigree is carefully hidden from prospective buyers. African traders are well aware that the Western collector is concerned with neither the identity of the artist nor a history of local ownership and exchange. Indeed, an object is generally worth far more if it is perceived by the buyer to have been created by a long departed and unknown artist and to have come directly out of a remote village community.

As a result of the economic structure of the market most European and American pur-

chasers of African art are not the first Westerners to have seen a particular object. Since art objects do not have a fixed monetary worth, traders often test an object's value by bargaining with different potential clients. In some instances, pieces are even tested in the markets of Europe and America before they are returned to Africa and sold to local expatriate collectors. In an attempt to hide the true channels of trade through which art objects are moved, traders will always tell their clients that they are the first Westerner to have an opportunity to buy a given piece. Even though most traders who have direct contact with Westerners are not the ones collecting art at the village level, they will always indicate that they themselves have just arrived from purchasing objects in a village. The mystique of "direct" contact thereby elevates the value and authenticity of the piece.

Malam Yaaro, a Hausa dealer specializing in the art of Ghana, recently shipped to New York City twenty-six Asante stools (figure 25.4). Upon arrival, an African colleague asked Yaaro to select six stools from the lot in order to show them to one of his clients.

Figure 25.4 Shipment of African art destined for New York City, Treichville quarter, Abidjan, Côte d'Ivoire, June 1991. Photograph by Christopher B. Steiner

After the six stools were picked out, Yaaro contacted one of his regular clients, a New York gallery owner, who purchased all twenty of the remaining stools. A few days later, the trader who had taken the six stools returned with the merchandise, informing Yaaro that his client did not want to buy the stools. Yaaro immediately contacted the gallery owner who had bought the original lot and told him that a smaller shipment of six very fine stools had just been sent to New York by an old Dioula woman. The true itinerary of the objects was kept hidden from the prospective buyer for several reasons. First, the seller did not want to anger a regular client by revealing that six of the finest stools had been removed from the original lot. Second, the seller did not want the buyer to know that the six stools had already been rejected by another Western buyer. And third, the seller wanted to create the illusion that the goods had been freshly brought from Africa and had not yet even been seen by other Western eyes. In fact, by saying that an old woman had transported the objects, he was further communicating to the buyer that not even another African art trader had yet seen the stools.

While collectors are interested in learning the path of objects from village to market, tourists in Africa are concerned with learning the traditional meaning and function of African art. Traders provide tourists not only with objects to take back home, but also with the knowledge of what the objects mean in their traditional contexts (cf. Spooner 1986:198). Indeed, it could be argued that for many tourists, their experience in the marketplace would not be complete unless the traders told them something "interesting" about the objects they wanted to buy. Jonathan Culler's remarks about tourist *sites* could easily be applied to an analysis of tourist *arts*. "To be fully satisfying," he writes, "the site needs to be certified as authentic. It must have markers of authenticity attached to it. Without those markers, it could not be experienced as authentic. . . . The paradox, the dilemma of authenticity, is that to be experienced as authentic it must be marked as authentic, but when it is marked as authentic it is mediated, a sign of itself, and hence not authentic in the sense of unspoiled" (1981:137). Traders are caught in the webs of this "paradox of authenticity." On the one

hand, by offering authenticity markers, traders satisfy tourist demand for "ethnographic" knowledge. Yet, on the other hand, their role as middlemen and economic intermediaries denies the tourist direct access to the "genuine" cultural encounters which they seek to achieve.

Most of the descriptions that traders use to embellish the objects they sell are derived from marketplace lore – stories that are passed from one trader to another, or that are simply overheard in the banter of marketplace discourse. Many of the stories that are circulated among traders have nothing to do with "traditional" object interpretation or usage – they are simply anecdotes invented to entertain prospective buyers. Among the common items sold in the art market are small wooden masks – palm-size replicas of larger forms. Most of these masks are carved in the style of the Dan of western Côte d'Ivoire; however, miniature masks carved in the styles of several other ethnic groups have also cropped up in recent years. In their original context, miniature masks were integrated into a system of belief in which they functioned as spiritual guides and personal protectors (Fischer and Himmelheber 1984:107). In the market, however, they are known as "passport" masks. Asan Diop, a Wolof trader in one of the art marketplaces of Abidjan, explains the function of "passport" masks to a captive audience of European tourists: "Before the whiteman brought paper and pen to Africa, these small masks were the only form of identification that we Africans could carry with us. Each person owned a carving of himself and each tribe had its own kind of masks. This is the only way people could cross the frontier between tribal groups." The tourists were all amused by the trader's story, and one asked rhetorically, "But where did they put the rubber stamp?" Collapsing the conventional categories of tradition and bureaucracy, the trader's explanation of the mask is phrased in terms which tourists easily can assimilate. It mocks the true meaning of the masks, reaffirms the tourist's sense of technical and cultural superiority, and provides an entertaining tale with which to return home.

Alteration of Objects

Together with presentation and description, traders satisfy Western demand through the material alteration of objects. These activities include the removal of parts, restoration of fractures and erosions, and artificial transformation of surface material and patina. The simplest kind of material alteration consists of removing an object from its mount. Objects from local private collections and galleries are sometimes put back on the market in the hands of African traders. Gallery owners who are having trouble selling certain pieces may choose to liquidate a portion of their stock by consigning objects to an African trader. The moment the trader receives the art he removes and discards any base on which the dealer may have mounted the object. I questioned a trader as to why he should remove the mount from a piece that was so unbalanced it could not otherwise stand. He told me that his clients would never buy something from him which had been mounted. The presence of the base, it could be argued, indicated that the object had already been "discovered" by another collector and that its "purity" had somehow been compromised by Western contact. Its removal reaffirmed the dominant image of traders collecting art directly from village sources.

To satisfy Western demand for strong evidence of age and ritual use, traders replicate the shiny, worn patina which results from years of object handling. They reproduce surface accumulation of smoke, soil, and dust. And they imitate the encrustation of blood, feathers, and kola nuts which results from repeated sacrificial offerings. Because it is inexpensive and easy, traders tend to spew chewed kola nuts on a wide variety of objects. The process is undertaken on pieces that might normally receive such a treatment, such as wooden face masks, but the principle is also extended to objects that would never receive kola sacrifice – such as wooden hair combs.

During the early eighteenth century in Paris, French collectors of Oriental art were offended by the nakedness of certain Chinese porcelain figures. In hopes of fetching higher prices, Parisian dealers responded to their clients' prudishness by dressing up the figures in French clothes (Rheims 1961:167). In a parallel (but inverted) case, African art traders involved directly with European buyers have remarked that their clients are more likely to buy *naked* Baule statues than those whose waist has been covered by a carved wooden loincloth. Collectors prefer to buy Baule statues that have no loincloth or those with loin protectors made of actual fabric which is affixed to the surface of the wooden sculpture. These type of Baule figures are thought by collectors to predate those that have loincloths carved into the sculptural form itself. Traders have responded to this preference among collectors by systematically removing, with the use of a chisel or knife, the wooden loincloths which cover certain Baule figures. The unstained wood which is left as a result of this process is restained with an appropriate dye, and an old piece of fabric is tied around the figure's waist to cover the damage. I have witnessed some collectors, who are now aware of this practice, peeking under a statue's loincloth to see if its nakedness is genuine or spurious.

Finally, a poignant example of object alteration can be found in one of the recent trends in the Ivoirian art market, namely in the sale of so-called "colonial" statues. Wooden carvings of colonial figures (representing either Europeans or Africans in Western attire) are found in societies throughout West Africa (Lips 1937). Though bearing elements of European design (clothing, posture, and various accoutrements) these statues were not originally conceived for the market but for indigenous use. Among the Baule, according to research conducted by Philip Ravenhill, statues in fashionable dress were used in the same manner as other wooden statues to represent a person's "spirit mate" in the other world. "A Baule statue in modern garb," he writes, "is neither a replica of a European nor the expression of a wish for a European other-world lover, but rather a desire that the 'Baule' other-world lover exhibit signs of success or status that characterize a White-oriented or -dominated world" (1980b:10).

During the colonial period, modern polychrome statues, such as Baule spirit mates clothed in European dress, were not generally sold in the African art market. A Wolof trader, who has been selling African art in central Côte d'Ivoire for over forty years, recounts the following:

My father began as an art dealer in Senegal in 1940. In 1945 we moved to Côte d'Ivoire and set ourselves up in the town of Bouaké. At the time, colonial [*colon*] statues had no value whatsoever in the art market. In the region of

Bouaké, where there were many such carvings, we called them 'painted wood' and would give them as gifts to customers who purchased large quantities of other merchandise.... But some clients even refused to take them for free. (quoted in Werewere-Liking 1987:15)

During the late 1950s, toward the end of French colonial rule in Côte d'Ivoire, foreign administrators, civil servants, soldiers, and other colonial expatriates began commissioning portraits of themselves – as souvenirs to take back home. This gave rise to a whole new genre of "tourist" art which grew out of an indigenous tradition of representing Africans in Western attitudes or attire.

The colonial style of carving has reached new heights of popularity during the past several years. Following a series of well-publicized auctions held recently in London and Paris – where colonial figures sold for significantly more money than they ever had before – the value of colonial statues in Côte d'Ivoire has been inflated dramatically and the production of replicas has swelled. In addition, Werewere-Liking's publication of *Statues colons* in 1987, a photographic guide to "colonial" figures that was widely distributed in Abidjan bookstores and hotel shops, has further increased the demand for such carvings by European expatriates and tourists alike.

Although the tradition of "colonial" figures dates to the advent of European exploration in Africa, most of the pieces on the market today were recently manufactured for the export trade. Traders have noticed, however, that buyers like to believe that the statues were made during the colonial era. When "colonial" carvings are purchased from workshop artists, they are always painted in lustrous enamel colors (figure 25.5). Traders have found, however, that brightly painted objects do not sell as well as faded, older-looking ones – that is, buyers enjoy the fact that the paint has eroded naturally through time. Thus, when a trader purchases a colonial figure from a workshop, he will invariably remove a layer of paint with sandpaper (figure 25.6). The object will then be stained with potassium permanganate or similar dye. This treatment of the object produces a darkened surface, with flaked paint, which can often be marketed as antique. The process of artificial aging underscores the separation of art suppliers from art

Figure 25.5 Guinean workshop artist with "colonial" figures, Port de Carena, Abidjan, Côte d'Ivoire, June 1988. Photograph by Christopher B. Steiner

Figure 25.6 African art trader sanding down the paint from newly arrived "colonial" statues, Abidjan, Côte d'Ivoire, June 1988. Photograph by Christopher B. Steiner

traders. Most of the artists producing colonial statues for the market have no idea that their works are being transformed by traders, and furthermore, I believe, they would not really understand why such a transformation would add value to the piece.

Conclusion

African art traders are links in a long chain of distribution over which they control neither the supply nor the demand. They can neither create a stock of objects necessary to satisfy the market to which they cater, nor can they create a market for the objects they have in stock. The two principal components of a market system – supply and demand – are controlled by forces external to the trader's world. Supply is dependent on the availability of objects from village sources and on the skills and production potential of contemporary artists. Demand is largely set by Western publications, museum exhibitions, auction records, and the tourist industry.

Like the *bricolage* of Lévi-Strauss's famous mythmaker, the African art trader constructs a product from raw materials and conceptual tools which are limited and predetermined by elements outside his immediate control. The best the trader can do is manipulate the perception of the objects he has with him in order to meet what he believes are the tastes and demands of the Western buyer. The "art of the trade," in this sense, does not involve the manufacturing of any product, but consists rather in the symbolic structuring and engineering of what is already at hand.

Although I respect and espouse E. P. Thompson's (1966) assertion (*contra* Althusser) that historical subjects are as much determining as determined in shaping the(ir) world through lived experience, I also believe that the intentionality of historical life is not without limitations. That is to say, culture must be understood as something that offers not only a range of possibilities but also something which presents a limit on the possible (cf. Ulin 1984:148–153). Thus, although African art traders fashion and market images of Africa and African art, these images are constrained by the buyer's a priori assumptions about what is being bought – that is, the images are constructed to *satisfy* demand rather than to *create* demand.

Separated by oceans of geographic distance and worlds of cultural differences, African traders and Western consumers are brought together in a fleeting moment of economic exchange. From this brief transaction, buyers and sellers leave with vastly different impres-

sions of their encounter. The buyers, on the one hand, depart with the artifacts of seemingly remote and distant cultures that will become integrated into a world of meaning and value comprehensible only through Western eyes. The sellers, on the other hand, walk away with renewed impressions of Western tastes and desires that will become part of their store of knowledge of how tourists and collectors perceive Africa and its art.

NOTE

All translations from the French in this article are by the author.

REFERENCES

Bateson, Gregory 1951 "Conventions of Communication: Where Validity Depends upon Belief." In Jurgen Reusch and Gregory Bateson, eds., *Communication: The Social Matrix of Psychiatry*, pp. 212–227. New York: W. W. Norton.

Conway, Sir Martin 1914 *The Sport of Collecting*. London: Fisher Unwin.

Culler, Jonathan 1981 "Semiotics of Tourism." *American Journal of Semiotics* 1(1–2): 127–140.

Fischer, Eberhard, and Hans Himmelheber 1984 *The Arts of the Dan in West Africa*. Zurich: Museum Rietberg.

Jules-Rosette, Bennetta 1984 *The Messages of Tourist Art: An African Semiotic System in Comparative Perspectives*. New York: Plenum Press.

Lehuard, Raoul 1977 "Un voyage en Côte d'Ivoire." *Arts d'Afrique Noire* 23:26–33.
—— 1979 "Un voyage en Haute-Volta." *Arts d'Afrique Noire* 31:11–19.

Lips, Julius E. 1937 *The Savage Hits Back*. Reissued 1966. New Hyde Park, N.Y.: University Books.

MacCannell, Dean 1976 *The Tourist: A New Theory of the Leisure Class*. New York: Schocken Books.

Mailfert, André 1968 *Au pays des antiquaires: confidences d'un "maquilleur" professionnel*. Paris: Flammarion.

Price, Sally 1989 *Primitive Art in Civilized Places*. Chicago: University of Chicago Press.

Ravenhill, Philip L. 1980a "Art." Ivory Coast Supplement to the *Financial Times* (London), Dec. 9, 19.

—— 1980b *Baule Statuary Art: Meaning and Modernization*. Working Papers in the Traditional Arts, vol. 5. Philadelphia: Institute for the Study of Human Issues.

Rheims, Maurice 1961 *The Strange Life of Objects*. New York: Atheneum.

Spooner, Brian 1986 "Weavers and Dealers: The Authenticity of an Oriental Carpet." In Arjun Appadurai, ed., *The Social Life of Things: Commodities in Cultural Perspec-tive*, pp. 195–235. Cambridge: Cambridge University Press.

Steiner, Christopher B. 1994 *African Art in Transit*. Cambridge: Cambridge University Press.

Thompson, E. P. 1966 *The Making of the English Working Class*. New York: Vintage Books.

Ulin, Robert C. 1984 *Understanding Cultures: Perspectives in Anthropology and Social Theory*. Austin: University of Texas Press.

Werewere-Liking 1987 *Statues colons*. Paris: Les Nouvelles Editions Africaines.

Part VI

Contemporary Artists

Introduction

The work of contemporary artists and their frequent engagement with anthropology has taken the anthropology of art in challenging and interesting new directions. The texts in this part concentrate primarily on the work being done in new contemporary media or formats by artists often described as non-Western or indigenous. Yet the most meticulous efforts to preserve past forms also qualify as contemporary – in the temporal and conceptual sense – once the expectation that contemporary art fit into a particularly Western notion of artistic progression is overcome. In that regard, most of the essays in this volume were written by anthropologists concerned with contemporary artists working in a range of traditions, forms, and media. As these artists engage with Western art institutions – through such avenues as training, exhibition or sale – their perspectives and reception highlight the contextualized nature of the Western art establishment. Internal critiques of the Western art system have long been a concern of artists and art critics and this has increasingly become a topic of interest for anthropologists (see Marcus 1995 for a critique of work by a number of contemporary American artists, and Herzfeld 1990 and 2004 on the interpretation of religious icons and the role of artisans respectively). Indeed anthropologists who address the reception of indigenous art by the Western art world (see the essays in Part II of this volume) are by default providing an anthropological critique of Western art. By speaking for themselves, however, artists who are working outside or across the Western system have the potential to challenge not only the way in which their work is received, but how that very system functions by providing examples of other, very different, systems of knowledge and representation.

The works discussed in this part are produced by those who, at least on some levels, create art by intention. The essay by Myers is particularly relevant in this regard as it addresses the work of contemporary Aboriginal Australian painters who produce works in non-indigenous media that now circulate in the realm of contemporary fine art – even as the paintings simultaneously hold dense indigenous meanings and perform particular ritual functions within the producing communities. The intersections between these paintings – representing interpretations of ancestral Dreamings and often produced by multiple participants – and the work of the

academically trained painter Gordon Bennett, raise many issues regarding the problematic classification of contemporary art based on education, ethnicity, technique,
media, or other equally fluid criteria. Bennett's critique of the stereotypes of Aboriginal Australian culture emerges from the conflict between racist imagery and his
discovery of his own Aboriginal identity (see Morphy 1995 for an interpretation of
Bennett's work in relation to that of other Aboriginal Australian artists).

The contradictions inherent in colonialism lie at the center of the work by
contemporary Maori artists as examined by Nicholas Thomas (and addressed at
greater length in Thomas 1999). Their art expresses colonial tensions explicitly and
intentionally by the juxtaposition of European and Maori themes in particular forms
and media that serve symbolic functions – pairing a European and Maori sail for
example. These combinations highlight the fact that the art forms, like the artists
who produce them, are derived from the fusion of traditions and techniques that, on
some levels, are the inheritance of all contemporary artists. A similar expression of
multiple forms and identities emerges in the essay by Charlotte Townsend-Gault in
its survey of contemporary First Nations art in Canada. It examines the dynamics
through which the first exhibition that was both "exclusively native and contemporary" was held at the National Gallery (see McMaster 1999 for a contrasting
approach). She explores the different forms of knowledge expressed in the work of
contemporary First Nations artists and the personal, political, and cultural circumstances that inform their art (similar themes are addressed with particular attention
to Native Northwest Coast American art in Townsend-Gault 1997). The final essay
by the artist and art historian Jolene Rickard draws together many of the themes
from this volume. A particular artwork that she produced – involving imagery of
relatives selling beaded souvenirs in the format of a contemporary photo montage –
highlights the broad continuum within which she works and the growing range of
contemporary indigenous art. Her essay provides a personal and cultural interpretation of the work in the context of her Tuscarora identity and the traditional and
political circumstances that are a challenge to cultural survival (see Doxtater 1995
for another perspective on "tradition" in contemporary Native North American art).

The close relationship between art and anthropology has evolved in new directions with the notion of artists as ethnographers (explored by Foster 1995 and
Schneider 1996). In the international art world where the artistic cutting edge is
increasingly concerned with the representation of difference, artists often position
themselves as outsiders in their own culture through their association with other
cultures (for additional perspectives on the relationship between anthropology and
contemporary art see Coles 2000; Küchler 2000; Schneider and Wright 2005). If
done in collaboration, such visual or artistic methodologies can, as with ethnographic film, play an important role, since expressive representations are natural
formats for the dissemination of anthropological research on cultural practices that
are themselves artistic or expressive forms in the communities where they are
produced. If heeded, the increasingly present voices of indigenous artists will ensure
that the interpretative process is a dialogue.

A particular challenge and opportunity for the anthropological study of contemporary art systems lies in the interpretation of the work and social systems of artists
(expatriates, for example) whose lives and works engage with more than one
cultural context. The social systems through which these artists circulate reveal
much about the process of cross-cultural communication and analysis of their art

demonstrates how cross-cultural meanings are encoded in new formats. They may use the "language" of contemporary international art – video, installation, or performance, for example – to express a range of indigenous themes. Great potential also lies in the analysis of the changing conventions and forms of indigenous systems of representation as artists trained in multiple systems circulate through different art worlds and thus can provide interpretations based upon their knowledge and experience with each. Such systemic analysis can illuminate the distinct processes through which members of different cultural systems transmit visual knowledge through education, attribute meaning, respond emotionally to form and ritual, and create a balance between preservation and innovation. If we appreciate the cohesiveness and characteristics through which greater or lesser degrees of adaptation may occur, these indigenous systems may then inform rather than serve the system of Western art and its changing conventions of collection, display, and interpretation.

REFERENCES

Coles, Alex, 2000 An Ethnographer in the Field: James Clifford Interview. In *Site-Specificity: The Ethnographic Turn*. Alex Coles, ed. London: Black Dog Press.

Doxtater, Deborah, 1995 Basket, Bead and Quill, and the Making of "Traditional" Art. In *Basket, Bead and Quill*. Exhibition Catalogue. Thunder Bay Art Gallery, Thunder Bay, Ontario.

Foster, Hal, 1995 The Artist as Ethnographer? In *The Traffic in Culture: Refiguring Art and Anthropology*, George Marcus and Fred Myers, eds. Berkeley: University of California Press.

Herzfeld, Michael, 1990 Icons and Identity: Religious Orthodoxy and Social Practice in Rural Crete. *Anthropological Quarterly* 63(3):109–121.

Herzfeld, Michael 2004 *The Body Impolitic: Artisans and Artifice in the Global Hierarchy of Value*. Chicago: University of Chicago Press.

Küchler, Susanne 2000 The Art of Ethnography: The Case of Sophie Calle. In *Site-Specificity: The Ethnographic Turn*. Alex Coles, ed. London: Black Dog Press.

Marcus, George, 1995 The Power of Contemporary Work in an American Art Tradition to Illuminate Its Own Power Relations. In *The Traffic in Culture: Refiguring Art and Anthropology*. George Marcus and Fred Myers, eds. Berkeley: University of California Press.

McMaster, Gerald, 1999 Towards an Aboriginal Art History. In *Native American Art in the Twentieth Century*. W. Jackson Rushing, ed. London: Routledge.

Morphy, Howard, 1995 Aboriginal Art in a Global Context. In *Worlds Apart: Modernity Through the Prism of the Local*. Daniel Miller, ed. Pp. 211–239. London: Routledge.

Schneider, Arnd, 1996 Uneasy Relationships: Contemporary Artists and Anthropology. *Journal of Material Culture* 1(2):183–210.

Schneider, Arnd and Christopher Wright, 2005 *Contemporary Art and Anthropology*. Oxford: Berg.

Thomas, Nicholas, 1999 *Possessions: Indigenous Art/Colonial Culture*. London: Thames and Hudson.

Townsend-Gault, Charlotte 1997 Art, Argument and Anger on the Northwest Coast. In *Contesting Art: Art, Politics and Identity in the Modern World*. Jeremy MacClancy, ed. Pp. 131–163. Oxford: Berg.

26

A Second Reflection
Presence and Opposition in
Contemporary Maori Art

Nicholas Thomas

Contradiction and Context

In an important essay on Maori art, Michael Jackson interpreted one of the classic forms of carving in terms informed by the Lévi-Straussian thesis that tensions and contradictions in social life 'tend towards their resolution' in myth and art (1972: 35). He suggested that *pare,* the elaborate lintels which generally combined human figures, the lizard-like *manaia,* and the double spirals that make Maori carving instantly recognizable, displayed a threefold structure. This form expressed a logic by which opposed or differentiated elements could be synthesized or unified through a third term. The upraised arms of the human figures, which in some cases seem to strain against a superior plane, themselves suggested the well-known myth of genesis in which the male sky (Rangi) was locked in embrace with the female earth (Papa), stifling their six sons, until one, Tane, succeeded in pushing them apart, opening up the world of light and creating the precondition both for his own subsequent exploits and for human life in general (Jackson 1972: 47–48) (figure 26.1).[1] The artefact would seem not only to recapitulate

the myth, but to augment and particularize its meanings in the patently liminal space of a house's threshold.

From the perspective of a poststructural anthropology, the strength of both Lévi-Strauss's original formulation and Jackson's application of it might lie not so much in the seductive analysis of oppositions and their resolution, but in the dynamism signalled by the point that the workings of myths and art forms 'tend towards' the resolution of contradictions. This is not to say that the contradictions *are* resolved; Jackson noted that the relationships he sought to identify were not static but 'dynamic and emotionally powerful, the results of continuous stresses to which man as a social person is put, of the intellectual contradictions which all human life creates' (1972: 72). The stresses here posited are, as for Lévi-Strauss, universal, and it might be objected that the tensions and contradictions that frequently preoccupy artists arise from cultural and historical particulars, rather than from predicaments of life or sociality as such. For a people such as the Maori experiencing colonization, dynamism does not derive so much from 'continuous' stresses as from radical changes,

From *Journal of the Royal Anthropological Institute* 1 (1995), pp. 23–46. Reprinted by permission of Blackwell Publishing. The arguments in this essay (written in 1993, and not altered here) were developed further in a number of later puplications, especially in *Possessions: Indigenous Art/Colonial Culture* (Thames and Hudson, 1999), which also discussed Robert Jahnke's subsequent work.

Figure 26.1 Examples of *pare* (lintels). From Augustus Hamilton, *Maori Art: Aspects of the Art Workmanship of the Maori Race in New Zealand*, Dunedin, New Zealand Institute, 1896. Courtesy National Library of Australia

impositions and innovations: land is expropriated, new exchange relations emerge, new forms of violence are confronted, and messianic resistance emerges. Lévi-Strauss claimed that the artist's 'genius consists in uniting internal and external knowledge, a "being" and a "becoming" ' (1962: 25), and this is suggestive for colonial circumstances. The process linking becoming and being can be understood as one of explication, as a production of explicit oppositions out of implicit tensions; what has been revealed can be reflected upon and transformed. Art may therefore be understood not merely to mediate or ameliorate problematic relations that already exist, but as an effort that presents and produces what is problematic.

This essay deals not with traditional Maori carving but with the recent work of one Maori artist which appears at least superficially to belong more to an internationalized contemporary style than a Polynesian tradition. Robert Jahnke's art is concerned above all with contradictions in colonial relationships, but apparently entails no dynamic of synthesis or resolution. The assemblages I discuss in detail below can be seen, rather, to insist that an opposition possesses an irreducibly contradictory character; complementarity creates no reassuring sense of balance or coherence, but an unsettling condition of tension. This condition appears permanent rather than temporary, and necessary rather than contingent, yet its formulation in these terms does not so much reinforce a deadening sense of inevitability, as empower a subversive and transformative historical imagination.

If an analysis privileges innovative action in historical contexts, it will be less concerned with transformations of structure than with practices that displace (or seek to displace) one account of structure by making another explicit. This is to move beyond rather than within a structural paradigm. 'Historical contexts' are not, of course, natural locations that require only a scholar's specification, but are both at issue in, and the products of, contentions concerning places, traditions and identities. Peoples in many times and places have made competing claims to land and to knowledge, and it would be ethnocentric to suppose that only modernity enables people to negotiate such issues reflexively; but these contentions have nevertheless acquired a novel intensity in the tentatively 'postcolonial' nations of Australia and Aotearoa New Zealand. In these societies made up of indigenous minorities, white settlers and non-white immigrants, issues concerning the definition and value of the different cultures each group is seen to possess can only arise constantly. There can only be tensions between ideas of culture and identity that privilege heritage and origin, and those that privilege new combinations and relocations; and the commemoration of historical events can only raise questions about how different groups are centred or marginalized within national narratives. Although the indigenous-settler relationship has not obviously entered a 'postcolonial' phase, the exhaustive debate around terms such as 'identity' makes colonial relationships and the identities they enabled on both sides

visible and susceptible to reformulation, to a novel degree. Contemporary art, in these settler-colonial societies as elsewhere, is frequently concerned in some sense with cultural politics; specifically because the issues are often handled reflexively. An anthropology of this kind of art might focus its attention upon the process of explicating or critically reaccentuating meanings, rather than upon their originary structuring.

'High Art' and National Imaginings

Anthropologists might be suspicious of the bias towards elite culture which an anthropology of contemporary art might have, as opposed to the studies of ritual arts or self-decoration that would seem to possess more collective salience in traditional milieux. Current work in the anthropology of material culture and cultural studies is certainly oriented away from 'high art' and towards popular media and apparently mundane artefacts such as domestic appliances, interior decorations and so on (Ang 1985; Miller 1987). Anthropology should certainly deal with cultural phenomena in their range and diversity, but it is important to recall that 'high art' frequently has a particular importance at a national level (as does the novel; cf. Anderson 1983: 32–7). This can be both at the time of its initial production, and through subsequent phases of display, which may involve heavily-promoted exhibitions, and the mass circulation of engraved reproductions (in the past) and posters and postcards (in the present).

While examples might be drawn from European paintings dealing with crucial national events such as the victory at Waterloo (Colley 1992: 364–7),[2] or from the representations of landscape traditions in terms that appeal to conservative notions of Englishness (cf. Barrell 1991), the significance of art in colonies of white settlement such as Australia and New Zealand is more immediately relevant to the present discussion. Bernard Smith has shown that landscape painting played a key role in fostering sentimental attachments to the antipodean environment on the part of a white population that was in the process of defining the land as its own (1985: ix, ch. 9, *passim*). While evocations of a wilderness giving way to pasture and ordered cultivation appear to be representational in the most straightforward sense, Forge's comment on the unimportance of representation in Abelam art might be relevant to these entirely different works: 'The meaning is not that a painting or carving is a picture or representation *of* anything in the natural or spirit world, rather it is *about* the relationships between things' (1973: 189). Settler paintings are also 'about' the relations between things: they do not represent the land or terrain itself, in any uncomplicated sense, but rather posit and seek to naturalize a sense of belonging, not least by presenting operations of cultivation and domestication which had long been constitutive of property rights, law, and civility in European thought. Here, surely, the artist is 'between being and becoming', not merely mediating a historical context, but contributing in a crucial way to the 'texting' of that context, by anticipating or making explicit something that might as yet have been inchoate, and that in any case required revelation and rediscovery for successive generations of settlers. What was being accomplished in the early days of settlement is currently being challenged if not undone, as indigenous rights in Australia are renegotiated through the land rights process, especially in the wake of the High Court's Mabo decision, which overturned the colonial doctrine of *terra nullius* by recognizing native title. Revisionist exhibitions may now subvert the intentions and effects of the settler landscapes by making the issue of literal and aesthetic appropriation explicit, and thus in turn contribute to a different definition of nationhood, in which dispossession is acknowledged as something that needs redress.

In Aotearoa New Zealand, art works and exhibitions are peculiarly important to the imagining of the nation's history and the future that should follow from it, for the same and somewhat more specific reasons. Like Australia and Canada, New Zealand is a former British colony of settlement, but the question of the ramifications of colonial history and their implications for New Zealanders' self-perceptions have been addressed in a more consistent and concerted way than in either of the other two countries, in part perhaps because the country lacks other major differences of culture and ethnicity comparable to those arising from francophone Quebec or the sheer extent

of non-British and non-European migration to Australia. New Zealand is importantly different also because the Maori were and are relatively homogeneous, in comparison with the indigenous populations of many settler colonies; the fact that there is one Maori language, and a sufficient degree of cultural commonality, means that 'Maori culture' can be understood as a totality that can be juxtaposed with that of Pakeha – immigrant whites being referred to, significantly, by a Maori term of nebulous origins and connotations (King 1991; Sharp 1990: 64–9).

An aim to redefine Aotearoa New Zealand as a 'bicultural' nation became increasingly intelligible over the 1980s, as the debate about 'race relations' in the country focused upon the meanings and significance of the 1840 Treaty of Waitangi (see Orange 1987). The Treaty, which effected an ambiguous cession of sovereignty on the part of Maori in return for rights and guarantees that were subsequently violated (plainly in some cases and arguably in others), acquired new centrality through the work of the Waitangi Tribunal in particular. The Tribunal was established in 1975 to hear Maori grievances against the Crown that related to the Treaty. It initially had only limited advisory powers, but became steadily more consequential from the mid-1980s, after it acquired the capacity to bind the government to implement decisions concerning the restitution of resources to Maori, and as its jurisdiction was radically expanded to make admissible retrospective claims over the whole period since 1840 (Sharp 1990: 74–81). Given that this highly-publicized, wide-ranging and open-ended legal process has proved such a crucial instrument for the redistribution of resources, in areas such as education as well as more obviously in relation to land and extractable resources, it is not surprising that Maori do not generally dismiss the Treaty – that is now, symptomatically, also referred to as Te Tiriti – as a tactic of dispossession, but insist rather that it possesses continuing salience and must be honoured.

The foundation of the whole process in a dyadic contract has reinforced the sense that what is at issue is a relationship between settlers and indigenous people that is irreducibly binary: even though the relation of various tribes to the Treaty was of course highly differentiated (and not all signed), the fact of a contract retrospectively constitutes two parties, as two parties are indeed arguably constituted, in a rivalrous and contradictory relationship, by the process of settler colonization itself. This is to say that the relationship would seem not only binary, but also ambiguously asymmetrical. On the one hand, to describe people as *tangata whenua*, as indigenous, is to accord them a unique status, even though it is not obvious what if any distinctive entitlements should follow from this;[3] on the other hand, the one-sided character of expropriation and discrimination gives the settler population a different kind of precedence. The debate has thus made the Treaty 'the founding text of Maori and Pakeha relations in New Zealand' (During 1992: 344), and enabled a particular understanding of the relationship as a violated covenant, a dishonoured partnership that may potentially be re-created and implemented afresh.

Maori Art, Traditional and Contemporary

Artists such as Robert Jahnke, whom I discuss in detail below, have contributed directly to this historical reimagining, but art has a prior importance in public culture in Aotearoa New Zealand, which might be attributed partly to the conspicuous and distinctive character of indigenous carving. Canoe prows, storage boxes, ancestral figures carved into house posts, and other components of meeting-houses, food storehouses, gateways and similar structures were frequently considered striking and emblematic by Europeans, even at times when Maori people and their cultures were, in other respects, most harshly denigrated. Maori motifs have frequently been appropriated to nationalist iconography and decorative purposes, across a bewildering range of commercial, official and high artistic products; the national airline, for instance, uses the distinctive *koru* motif (a line terminating in a bulb) on aeroplanes and as a logo in general. Here I am not concerned to trace the history of these borrowings and appropriations, but suggest rather that the longstanding representation of national distinctiveness through indigenous design created the preconditions for debates in which Maori art was peculiarly prominent and politicized.

The 'Te Maori' exhibition, which toured the United States from 1984 to 1986 and subsequently Aotearoa in 1986–87, marked crucial changes in the status of Maori culture within New Zealand. The exhibition consisted mainly of sculpture in wood, bone and nephrite, and emphasized classic and where possible precontact pieces to the exclusion of later neotraditional forms. While this selectivity raised a variety of questions, the pieces chosen were indeed remarkable, and the apparent primitivism no doubt helped ensure the success of the show, which was enthusiastically received in New York in particular. This external affirmation of Maori culture was widely publicized within New Zealand, and secured an extraordinary attendance within the country of over 750,000, or around 25 per cent. of the entire population. The effect of the exhibition arose not merely from the pieces themselves, or from their mode of display, but also from the dawn ritual openings of the show in each venue, and an emphasis in publications, educational material and commentaries by Maori guides upon the *tapu* (sacred) character of the work, which demanded continuing regard to protocol, and recognition that the gallery became a *marae*, a ceremonial meeting ground, for the duration of the exhibition (*Auckland Star*, 26 June 1987). The point was not that it was regarded as the *marae* of any particular tribe, but unambiguously as a Maori space, which others were privileged to visit; the exhibition as a whole thus appeared to be under indigenous control (even if there were many Maori misgivings behind the scenes). The moment was fortuitous: a political and cultural indigenous renaissance was under way but awaiting consolidation, and 'Te Maori' seemed not only to proclaim Maori tradition, but insist that it be upheld by the nation: it 'fuelled the expectation that these values and forms will be recognized and accepted by the rest of society. That is one of the important challenges *Te Maori* has set for Pakeha New Zealanders' (Kernot 1987: 7; see also Mead 1986).

The exhibition provoked debate around a range of issues, most of which need not be entered into here. The point of particular relevance is that the projection of a distinctly authentic corpus marginalized experimental nineteenth- and early twentieth-century work, including figurative painting, Maori carving on imported objects such as guns, pipes and articles of furniture, and artefacts that incorporated iron or wool in place of traditional materials. This effacement of postcontact dynamism, problematic enough in itself, was moreover accompanied by a complete exclusion of contemporary Maori art, and even a follow-up exhibition, 'Taonga Maori', included only three contemporary pieces out of 163, and these were clearly selected for their perpetuation of traditional forms. Anger on the part of contemporary artists was expressed particularly in Selwyn Muru's *Te Maaoorii*, a parodic sculpture marked by the tattoos of urban Maori youth and other signs of acculturation (figure 26.2). A metal oil tap in lieu of the figure's penis referred critically to the exhibition's sponsorship by the Mobil company, which was at the same time polluting particular Maori fishing grounds and the New Zealand environment in general; and the long vowels of the piece's title presumably made mockery of Pakeha efforts to emulate correct Maori pronunciation, and the well-intentioned but limited cross-cultural genuflexion that that signified (cf. Panoho 1991: 12–13). In retrospect, however, few would condemn the exhibition categorically: whatever limitations it (and 'Te Maori') possessed, their powerful traditionalism clearly helped create a climate of wider understanding and receptivity, in which other initiatives might be welcomed and funded: 'Kohia Ko Takaka Anake', a big overview of contemporary Maori art, was, for instance, staged by the National Art Gallery over 1990–91, and there have been many commissions for Maori artists from public bodies and corporations anxious to exhibit cultural sensitivity. A climate of marginalization has been replaced by one in which dealers and curators are taking great interest in Maori art. Some artists are now doing relatively well commercially, but there is also a good deal of suspicion about the selective and shallow interest that characterizes the 'bandwagon'.

In this context, contemporary Maori art has been predisposed to a critical reflexivity akin to, but more specifically motivated than, whatever reflexivity might be taken to characterize postmodern art in general. Many Maori artists draw upon and affirm traditional art forms through continuities of media, style or motif, yet adopt a critical attitude to the re-

Figure 26.2 Selwyn Muru, *Te Maaoorii*, ca. 1985, wood and metal. Collection of the artist

strictive curatorial practices that privilege such works and deny or marginalize the continuing dynamism of indigenous art. Even contemporary material that seems largely decorative and devoid of political reference makes a statement simply by precluding the primitivist predisposition to equate Maori art with archaic pieces, and indigenous creativity *per se* with the past. Given that settler colonialism is, in a simple and brutal sense, predicated on a denial of indigenous people's coevalness, this assertion of presence is fundamentally important. Much work is, however, more overtly directed against a political quietism on the part of viewers, who might 'appreciate' fine craft or painting from the past or the present, while neglecting the history of dispossession and continuing discrimination against living Maori. Emily Karaka, for instance, has conveyed, with extraordinary power, the pain that dispossession and racism have produced. Her work not only represents suffering in images of dismemberment and crucifixion, but moreover indexes it, through a directness of technique, and often through a tortuously dense application of oil paint, which suggests the immediate transcription of personal and collective anguish. Her painting, like the more subtly political work of Robert Jahnke, can be taken to define, or rather insist upon, its context; it is not merely defined by, or expressive of one.

In its relation to the past, much contemporary Maori art further questions museological practice and viewers' expectations. The traditionalist aesthetic of exhibitions such as 'Te Maori' values archaic work in proportion to its independence from external ('Western') cultural influences and contemporary work in so far as it resists borrowing and imitates traditional material.[4] The past is thus a source of techniques, forms, styles, motifs and generalized cultural principles such as *tapu* – but not of events. Narrative is not wholly excluded, but it is cosmogenic myth rather than more recent genealogy and history that is appropriately illustrated. Contemporary artists resist this dehistoricizing aesthetic, which is untrue to the narrative element in traditional and neotraditional art (see Neich 1993), and refer extensively to colonial relations in terms that frequently unite mythological references and recent developments (and thus preclude the reduction of the former to depoliticized folklore).

Selwyn Muru's major painting, *Papatuanuku* (figure 26.3), which has been prominently displayed in the National Art Gallery,[5] reproduces, across a stark, abstract field suggesting a spiritual landscape, a poem by Hone Tuwhare that described the 1975 Maori land rights march on Parliament as a caress of the earth mother (Papatuanuku) on the part of the marchers: 'We are massaging the ricked wracked back of the LAND with our sore but ever loving feet. Hell she loves it. The land turns over in great delight. WE LOVE HER.'[6] The invocation of the mythic person here effects a leap across epochs and contexts that empowers a transformation of the present; but the poem's almost indefinable combination of wit and seriousness is equally crucial to the painting's effect. Such ebullience in the face of discrimination is often characteristic of Maori practice,[7] yet alien to the frozen sanctity of a Maori artefact, given the unavoidable humourlessness of any appropriately respectful curatorial practice. If traditional art has acquired a burden and the power of permanent spirituality, contemporary art has inherited the task of producing innovation, paradigmatically through the marking of meanings which cannot be fixed, which empower through serious play.

The commemoration of post-contact and other recent events in contemporary art is also widely attested to by work concerned with nineteenth- and early twentieth-century millenarian movements (further discussed below). Reference to such narratives should not be seen as a mark of innovation or 'Western' influence in contemporary art, but rather as a recovery of the kind of historical significance that ancestral sculptures originally possessed. These were not generalized expressions of tribal and ethnic identity, but biographical and legendary mnemonics, that commemorated the accomplishments of particular warriors, chiefs and priests, and were elements of the architectural environments within which genealogical narratives concerning those figures were normally recounted. Without stretching the parallel, this typifies the way in which the adoption of 'Western' style or technique may be consistent with, rather than corrosive of, continuities between traditional culture and contemporary arts.

Much debate among artists and curators in Aotearoa has concerned precisely this issue – the relation between 'traditional' and 'Western' influences and aesthetics that are as clearly juxtaposed in critical discussion as they would seem integrated or combined in art works

Figure 26.3 Selwyn Muru, *Papatuanuku* (1990), oil on three canvases. Te Papa Tongarewa/National Art Gallery, Wellington

themselves (see, for example, Panoho 1991). The singular binarism of historical imaginings founded in the Treaty thus appears to function not only as a point of reference for artists, but also as a macrocosm for a Maori art negotiating the tension between indigenous and Pakeha traditions. Although this may not be precisely what Lévi-Strauss meant by 'uniting internal and external knowledge', that nexus is precisely where the asymmetries of colonial exchange might be recognized and renegotiated. I turn now to consider an artist whose work is especially distinctive for being animated by the space of colonial difference and by reflection upon it.

Robert Jahnke's *Mana Whenua*

What matters for the dialectician is having the winds of
world history in his sails. Thinking for him means: to set
sail. It is the way they are set that matters.

(Walter Benjamin, *Passagen-Werk*; quoted in Taussig 1987: 369)

Robert Jahnke (b. 1951) is a Maori sculptor and art teacher who trained at the Elam School in Auckland and in experimental film at the California Institute for the Arts; he subsequently worked variously in book illustration, film, carving and design before focusing on wooden and metal assemblages, and taught at college and polytechnic before moving to Maori Studies at Massey University in 1991. His father was German-Samoan and his mother Maori-Irish, but he was brought up in primarily Maori milieux. His work is distinctive for being informed both by training in western institutions and by a deep knowledge of Maori art, and most particularly of colonial history and cross-cultural exchange in New Zealand.

His first solo exhibition, in 1990, recast forms from meeting-house architecture in mixed-media assemblages, and focused upon the commemoration of late nineteenth- and early twentieth-century Maori prophets such as Te Kooti, Te Whiti and Rua Kenana (see figure 26.4). The choice of these figures and the associated histories is of particular interest, because many warriors and chiefs were of equal or greater importance in the resistance to European encroachment. The millenarian movements, however, were marked, as Pacific 'cargo cults' have frequently been, by experimental departures from tradition and appropriations of elements of colonial social organization and iconography which appeared esoteric and threatening from the viewpoint of the colonizers. Jahnke sees the prophets as having struggled to create independence in a period when Maori were disillusioned and oppressed by discriminatory government, and by educational policies that robbed them of 'the ability to transcribe or interpret traditional metaphor' (quoted in Sloan 1993). Rua and others responded by drawing upon European motifs that were more immediately accessible to their people, yet susceptible to redefinition. The triangles, missionary crosses and emblems from playing-cards that marked Te Kooti's flag and the gates and houses of Rua's New Jerusalem acquired politicized and mystical associations beyond the comprehension and control of the missionaries and colonists who had initially made these motifs available. The triangle, for instance, can figure as the sacred mountain of Maungapohatu, where Rua had his visions and subsequently established his separatist, reformist community; it can stand for peace or, once inverted to resemble a sergeant's stripes, war. What is crucial in these operations is the apparently arbitrary character of associations and inversions: the innovative iconography is not a derivative code, specified in advance by a colonial culture, but a set of resonances that are unpredictable and empowering.

The project of contemporary indigenous art, sometimes dismissed for its borrowings from western styles and for its *apparent* lack of grounding in indigenous tradition, can be seen to recapitulate the prophets' apparent hybridity, and it is therefore not surprising that artists might now privilege those moments of singular experimentation in Maori history.[8] Conspicuous among the symbols of Pakeha authority were flags, and one of Rua's most enduringly contentious acts was his use of a huge Union Jack upon which was inscribed in Maori, 'One law for both peoples: Maungapohatu'; this was seized by police as evidence of sedition, and described as late as 1957 by a New Zealand newspaper as bearing an 'insolent' inscription (Binney et al. 1979: 99). What the 'insolence' of Rua's project consisted in, presumably, was resistance to both segregation and assimilation: both autonomy and equality were demanded, and both cultural distinctiveness and modernity pursued. This is precisely the stance of much contemporary art in the face of the cultural legislation implied by 'Te Maori', but there is also a more important and particular connexion between Jahnke's recent work and such prophetic appropriations, in that the artist has been especially concerned with the subversive elaboration of meanings which are suggested by, though not conventionally attached to, the appropriated forms.

This is apparent, especially, in *Mana Whenua*, a work initially shown in 'Mana Tiriti: protest and partnership', an exhibition that marked the sesquicentenary of the Treaty of Waitangi, and which therefore directly addressed the debates referred to earlier (see Young 1991). It was then entitled *Nga Ata o te Whenua*, 'The Shadow of the Land', in reference to a famous statement by the chief Nopera Panakareao, that the effect of the Treaty was that the shadow of the land passed to the Queen, while the substance remained with the Maori. A year later, as alienation by Europeans proceeded apace, the disillusioned chief changed his mind and inverted the proposition. Jahnke's subsequent work, which I discuss below, literalizes the metaphor through a play of shadow and substance. The word *ata*, employed also in more recent work examining exchange objects-cum-icons of power such as the axe, may mean variously reflection, shadow, dawn light, and image, has become a kind of signature. *Mana Whenua* does not work with light in the same way as the works discussed below, but is similarly energized by the dynamics of opposition and inversion.

The interpretation which follows is neither simply a distillation of public responses to the work, nor a re-presentation of the artist's own exegesis. Although my discussion has been stimulated by and elaborated on the basis of discussions with the artist, and has drawn

Figure 26.4 Robert Jahnke, *Te Ata o nga Poropiti* (1989), wood, paint, stainless steel solder, metal. Waikato Museum of Art and History. Photograph by David Cook

upon the comments of reviewers and other individual viewers, the aim is speculatively to reconstruct the reaction of a New Zealand audience conscious of its own historical context and the debates about biculturalism, as the audience likely to see the work in the Museum of New Zealand/Te Papa Tongarewa can hardly avoid being. While responses to *Mana Whenua* are of course diverse, depending upon knowledge and political prejudices as well as other factors, and while Maori and Pakeha responses will possess different emphases, I suggest that much of what follows must bear upon or be implicit within the audience's experience of the work. Although therefore informed by public and private sources, the interpretation cannot readily be tested or validated, because it attempts to make explicit what the art does, which is largely nonverbal and implicit. This essay is therefore not so

much about textual 'meanings' that might be implicit in *Mana Whenua,* as about the work's non-textual efficacy.

The forms juxtaposed are those of a European sail and a Maori or Polynesian one (see figure 26.5). It is significant that while the indigenous sail is in fact an inverted triangle, and thus existed as such prior to colonial contact, the encounter renders it as the opposite of the European form: one stands as the negation of the other, and a process of reciprocal definition and stereotypy is inaugurated, which can be taken to be constitutive of the cultural dynamics of colonial if not also postcolonial relationships (cf. During 1992: 350). Each assemblage is inscribed ethnically through a series of numerals: on one side, the Maori words for numbers; on the other, roman numerals that mark the 'Western' origins of the form (figure 26.6). Something at once rather

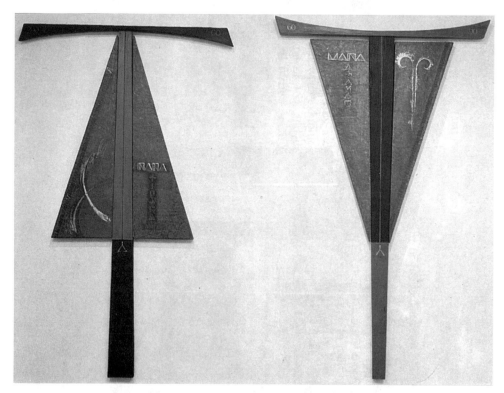

Figure 26.5 Robert Jahnke, *Mana Whenua* (1990), wood, lead, paint. This was photographed as it was exhibited in the Museum of New Zealand, with the 'Pakeha' sail on the left. As is made clear in the text, the artist's intention was that the 'Maori' sail was to be on the left. Te Papa Tongarewa/National Art Gallery, Wellington. Photograph: Museum of New Zealand, Te Papa Tongarewa, Wellington, New Zealand, transparency no. B42295 (CT)

Figure 26.6 Mana Whenua, detail of 'Pakeha' sail

more general and more specific than this appears to be important, however, if the artist's own statements are taken into account: what is connoted is not just Europe or its 'civilization', but the particular tradition of Roman and 'Western' law, which was especially relevant, of course, to the original exhibition, focused as it was upon the implications of the Treaty/te Tiriti for contemporary justice.

Apart from the sesquicentenary context, viewers would perhaps be more inclined to take the forms to refer more broadly to indigenous and European 'culture', and other features of the sails reinforce these identifications: one carries a motif based on the Maori *koru*, which contrasts with the other's elementary arcs. These crescents allude to a process of waxing and waning which is referred to in the catalogue of the *Mana Tiriti* exhibition: presence and absence, shadow and substance, possession and dispossession are not permanently established conditions but indeterminate and cyclical: 'Inversion of form, the waxing and waning of structures, refer to the usurpation of mana and land' (Young 1991: 30). As the truth of Maori ownership was clear prior to the Treaty, the fact of European dominance, which has since been conspicuous, may in the future diminish or be eclipsed. What is projected is not a definite prospect of progress, but an enduring state of contingency, in which any effect or political accomplishment may potentially be reversed. This is at once a historical work that imagines past relations in particular moral terms, and an effort to foreshadow a history, to create substance out of shadow.

This reading, which emphasizes the instability of relationships, is more or less what the exhibition catalogue encouraged, and is consistent with reviewers' responses (e.g. Dale 1990); but it is compelled in a more intricate and implicit way by the fact that the mere parity of Polynesian and Western forms, established and insisted upon through the forceful symmetry of this work, is challenging. In ethnographic museums, there are two more conventional ways of relating indigenous artefacts to their European counterparts which would be more familiar to Jahnke's audience. This work contradicts both equally. A now dated but hardly extinct understanding would place the indigenous and Western objects in an evolutionary relationship: the Polynesian canoe, however remarkable, is the product of a stone age technology and hence the precursor of more advanced craft;[9] one is linked to the other through a serial relationship rather than through simultaneous identification and contrast. In *Mana Whenua* neither form is prior to the other, either in the sense of being archaic, or in that of being original; correspondingly, neither is privileged as a successor, nor denigrated as a copy. However, the indigenous sail is accorded a degree of precedence, both by any viewer accustomed to reading European scripts from left to right, and by one aware of the opposition within formal greeting ceremonies within meetinghouses: *tangata whenua* or people of the land occupy the left of the house, while *manuhiri* or visitors are on the right.

It is however important, albeit in a wholly negative sense, that the gendered symbolism of left and right in Maori cosmology figures not at all in the work: while, in traditional terms, the left side is supposedly female, in-

auspicious, weak, and *noa*, the right is male, vigorous, strong, and *tapu* (Elsdon Best, quoted in Jackson 1972: 51–2).[10] It might appear striking that a work so preoccupied with opposition should exclude precisely the oppositions most deeply pervasive in Maori culture, such as those between male and female, senior and junior, raw and cooked, life and death, and so on (see, for example, Hanson and Hanson 1983; Sahlins 1985); but this is not at all surprising, given that these contrasts are all hierarchically valued and sometimes also transformatively related (in the case of life and death or raw and cooked). Against these relations, Jahnke's work would insist upon parity as opposed to asymmetry, and upon the permanence of opposition as opposed to the possibility of assimilation or transmutation.

The assemblage thus resists any hierarchizing differentiation of indigenous and European forms, although the upraised element of the top crosspiece in the Maori sail and the overall trend of its V are enabling and uplifting, in contrast to the downturning T and oppressive weight of the Pakeha form. The work also challenges a less overtly hierarchical mode of differentiation that is now probably more common in museums, and which is aesthetic rather than evolutionist. The archaism, beauty and rarity of a nephrite adze or feather cloak places the thing in an entirely different realm to its European equivalent; it is not and perhaps never has been a commodity, and is thus in a radically different space, even to a fine western garment or piece of jewellery. Of course, there are good reasons for treating rare indigenous artefacts – objects that were always *tapu* – carefully and respectfully, but the curatorial project has a sterilizing and segregationist aspect, that subtracts not only from the proximity of things, but also from the lives attested to in their decay. In some of his earlier assemblages about the prophets, Jahnke used recycled wood; though the use of old timber resonates with many artists' experiments with demolition materials and *objets trouvés*, it is here a kind of affirmation of the deterioration and loss that is necessary to a life cycle and a genealogy, and a protest against the clinical stabilization of heritage that the restoration of carvings and meeting houses entails. This is in the background in *Mana Whenua*;[11] but the insistent simultaneity of the two cultural forms interrupts any encroachment of the museum-cum-cultural mausoleum. For a Pakeha viewer, the Other can only be here and now, not in an antecedent or distant realm. What may be still more important is the fact that there is no perspectival space in this work, from which a self can gaze upon an other (in contrast, say, with any portrait, and particularly one of a Maori or Pacific Islander). However viewers identify themselves, they are compelled to conjure with both the fact of co-presence, and a relationship of mutual definition that cannot be eluded or wished away.

Mana Whenua is pervaded not only by opposition, but by tension, because the equivalences which are asserted conflict at once with the absolute difference between shadow and substance, and the circumstances of the world beyond the work. Despite the range and significance of Maori gains, the continuing dominance of Pakeha and continuing oppression of Maori are incontestable, most particularly because the latter have been injured disproportionately by the economic slide of the last decade, and are hardly likely to be the first beneficiaries of the recovery that is notionally now under way. Against the persistence of profound inequality, Jahnke disrupts the binarism of the work by inscribing on both sides certain motifs and words, such as 'Mana o te whenua' ('*mana* of the land')[12] and the esoteric squares and crosses reminiscent of Te Kooti's and Rua's signs. While the dates and numbers are marked on both sails, there is no Pakeha statement or slogan that is comparably imprinted on both (figure 26.7).

The overpowering but disrupted parallelism at once effects a critique of more conventional ways of seeing and curating cross-cultural relations, and gives material form to a basic paradox. One implication is that there is a fundamental and permanent difference between Maori and Pakeha, but this difference is explicit and visible specifically because the two are, in underlying respects, the same. Sail and mast are locked into a common relation and carry dates and numbers that are identical, inverted or otherwise linked. There is an affirmation of shared humanity that is surely politically rather than sentimentally motivated. The equivalence of Pakeha and Maori, as signatories to the Treaty, and equally committed partners in its development and implementation, is understood, as noted earlier, to be pivotal to progress towards a genuinely bicultural society.

Like Rua's flag, *Mana Whenua* disrupts a law of dominance by taking the principle of equality before that law too literally; it elaborates and pushes the principle to an absolute condition of formal pairing. Both the flag and the assemblage effect a kind of ironic displacement, which is enabled particularly by the official suppression of the flag, and the gap between *Mana Whenua* and the actualities of the Maori-Pakeha relations that the work seems to represent. These resistances of the world to the work expose ironies internal to colonial law – as a code ostensibly governed by principles of equality is shown to organize and disguise discrimination – and, on the basis of that explication, potentially produce a transformation of the law's effect. What began merely as an empty affirmation of Justice and Equality is given new substance, and its letter insisted upon, by those whom it was designed to disenfranchise. Whatever the actual effect of Jahnke's work upon its diverse viewers, the point might be that this process would match and reinforce the transformation of the Treaty/ te Tiriti itself, which now has binding effects that could surely never have been anticipated by the colonists who drafted and translated it in bad faith. One structure thus supplants another, as a shadow is given weight and the weight of a shadow insisted upon. The historical ironies here are acute, yet their presentation in this work is restrained and serious, as is consistent with its mood of unsettled anticipation rather than either revolutionary optimism or embittered pessimism.

A Second Reflection

In a similar way, Jahnke's more recent show, 'Te Ata Tuarua: the Second Reflection', is deeply if not explicitly political. Most of these installations consisted again of pairs; the crucial form was not a sail but a Doric column, which could be seen to have been extracted from Western culture in much the same way that the West appropriated artefacts and curiosities from indigenous peoples (see figures 26.8 and 26.9). Just as Oceanic sculptures and African masks were stripped of their

Figure 26.7 Mana Whenua, detail of 'Pakeha' sail

localized meanings and functions as they were relocated in private collections and museums, Jahnke's columns, in most cases, are deprived of architectural use; they do not support an edifice, but are framed within one. In both this operation and the colonial collecting that it ironically recapitulates, however, appropriation does not so much obliterate meaning as

make it highly allusive and elusive. Just as a mask could become an emblem for a fantasized and generalized 'primitive mentality', or for the mysteries of fetishism, so the column comes to signify European culture as such, from its imagined Greek beginnings to its late colonial extensions, so often expressed in neoclassical state architecture. The singular aptness of the isolated column arises from the fact that it suggests both imperial triumph (in the case of monuments such as Nelson's Column) and classical ruins. In European thought since Volney, antiquities were crucial markers of the cyclical character of history: Greek and Roman civility and power might be emulated, but the fragments of their former grandeur could only forcefully remind the viewer of the transience of particular civilizations and empires (a sentiment expressed particularly starkly in Shelley's 'Ozymandias'). The translator accompanying a French voyage even suggested in 1800 that New Zealand might one day produce her Montesquieus, Lockes and antiquarians who would travel 'to contemplate the ruins of *ancient* London and Paris' (quoted in Smith 1985: 150). These references may not have been present to Jahnke's intentions, but they certainly resonate with them.

For the artist himself, the connotation of the whole structure of colonialist law and regulation is most significant: with respect to the work 'Impediment', in which the columns did in fact frame an entry, he said 'You are invited to enter this foreign realm only to be confronted by an impediment... Such is life that illusion often substitutes for reality, the invitation to participate in this democratic society which has been founded on the edifying principles of classical heritage, is often a facade ... many entrances that invite and entice are often culturally exclusive.'[13] The Roman numerals, like those on the Pakeha sail in *Mana Whenua*, are thus to be taken less as a sign of Western civilization in general, and more as an emblem of an ambiguous political and legal heritage. The ambiguity is reinforced by the similarity between the column and a ship's cannon, an instrument of Enlightenment voyaging that was used as well as displayed in the course of early contacts in New Zealand.

Typically the column in one of the paired works is a solid wooden form and in the other a mirror or a void. The half marked as Maori by the words for numbers or other inscriptions was usually solid, which could be taken to reflect either a categorical pre-eminence that *tangata whenua* should possess, or echo an easy imputation common in some public discussion of New Zealand identities that Maori culture has a depth, spirituality and substance which Pakeha modernity lacks.

Although the works may well have been read in this way by some viewers, such an understanding is undermined, once again, by the operation of reversibility. The artist told me that he felt that these assemblages worked best in the Dowse Museum (at Lower Hutt near the capital, Wellington), where the lighting tended to reverse the qualities of the positive and the negative sides: 'if you play light on it, the three-dimensional form becomes vacant, or the shadow becomes meaningless... it has no shape, whereas if you play on the negative form it becomes positive, because it creates a shape' (interview, March 1993). Here again, the assertion that alternation is everywhere possible can only be politically charged.

These works have the look of international contemporary art, and indeed reflect art school training and 'Western' techniques, as they are also produced within and for a commercialized art world. Jahnke's work can, however, be seen to conform with certain features of classical Maori art, however sharply it differs from it on the surface. One of the most striking features of the sails of *Mana Whenua* is their weight and solidity; the idea of a lead and hardwood sail is not a joke, but a transposition of form across media, comparable directly to the replication of forms such as hand clubs in wood, bone and nephrite, and generally to the transposition of motifs between carving, painting and facial tattooing. These transformations suggest that what is important is not representation but the different values and potentialities the media possess: a nephrite piece, for example, will possess heirloom as well as functional status, and bear a genealogy and history. A European painting, and more especially something such as a flimsy snapshot, seems indisputably less substantial than the thing or person it represents; it consists merely of paint, pencil, emulsion or whatever, on canvas or paper. In the case of the sail, it is the canvas or pandanus that is insubstantial: the artwork is not a thinner copy, but a kind of prototype that has a permanence which no particular utilitarian expression can possess. The weight of *Mana Whenua* also lends it an iconic status; it has the capacity to define and produce relations and specifically irresolutions. It is a productive work, a work that produces presence, rather than a representational work that merely depicts existing

Figure 26.8 Exhibition view, 'Te Ata Tuarua/The Second Reflection' (1992). Courtesy Fox Gallery, Auckland

opposition or conditions in the world that are already visible. Like the transposition of forms across media of varying quality and substance, the orientation towards presentation rather than representation was fundamental in nineteenth-century Maori art: the sculpted ancestral figures in meeting-houses and the

architecture of those houses themselves created embodiments rather than depictions. The relation of ancestors to living descendants, to members of families and tribes, was not imaged, but more immediately produced.[14]

The overall logic of disrupted symmetry in *Mana Whenua* and the binary works of Te Ata

Figure 26.9 Robert Jahnke, *Te Iho I* (1992), wood, lead, acrylic, from the exhibition 'Te Ata Tuarua/ The Second Reflection'. Courtesy Fox Gallery, Auckland

Tuarua, moreover, parallel the *kowhaiwhai* painting of meeting-house rafters, which typically consist of arc and *koru* forms in white lines, filled in with black and red (figure 26.10). Allan Hanson has drawn attention to the elaborate bilateral symmetry characteristic of these patterns, which is however broken through interstitial additions, direct transposition in place of inversion, and a variety of other devices that are in most cases plainly deliberate. This formal language of broken bilateral symmetry is also attested to in facial tattoos and woodcarving, and in Hanson's view reflects a Maori construction of the world, in which 'the fundamental quality of reality is ambivalent tension – between identity and difference, attraction and repulsion, union and separation' (1983a: 215). In fact,

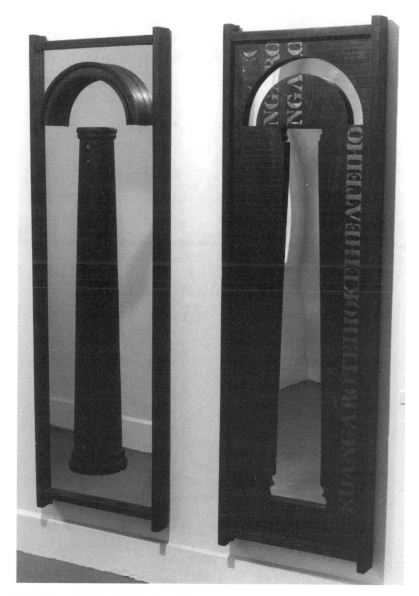

Figure 26.10 Robert Jahnke, *Te Iho II* (1992), wood, copper, acrylic, from the exhibition 'Te Ata Tuarua/The Second Reflection'. Courtesy Fox Gallery, Auckland

disrupted symmetry is common in Oceanic art, and is conspicuous, for instance, in canoe prows and dance paddles from the Trobriands and other parts of New Guinea, in Asmat and Sepik shields, and in the Marquesan clubs known as *'u'u*. It is significant that all these art forms are associated with warfare or competitive performances, or contexts in which a group sought to disorient or awe those who were enemies or visitors. This was certainly true of Maori meeting-houses, which were elaborated over the nineteenth century, a period of great conflict and instability, particularly in order to hold meetings with Europeans and other Maori relating to warfare, land acquisition and related matters. Even if the principle of ambivalent tension, and the disorienting effect of broken symmetry, are not peculiar to Maori culture, the continuities with Jahnke's work and with other contemporary Maori art are resonant: people of the land or place use a disorienting play of parity to awe their visitors, allies or opponents. While I have foregrounded the politics of both *Mana Whenua* and Te Ata Tuarua, other readings, emphasizing the forms of traditional culture, might also be advanced, and are encouraged by the titles of some of the works in the more recent exhibition, that refer to cosmogenesis. The importance of light, in particular, is perhaps more readily interpreted by New Zealanders with even a casual acquaintance with Maori mythology as a recapitulation of the oppositions between darkness and light that structure Maori cosmology and figure in the initial struggle of Tane to separate Rangi and Papa.

Jahnke's assemblages are pervaded with associations that can be pursued in a variety of directions, but their oppositions are not played out and transformed in a hermetic domain of mental or intellectual structure. The inversions and potential inversions of form, shadow, substance and hierarchy are not moves in a detached aesthetic game, but follow from a recognition of the locations from which the works can be viewed, and this is perhaps the most crucial of their several 'second reflections', or moments of further framing and implied contextualization. Those looking at 'Te Ata Tuarua' and *Mana Whenua* are caught up in relations that cannot prefigure the works' reciprocal and symmetrical forms; this disruption is made most explicit in *Impediment*, which was located in some venues at the entrance to the exhibition and in others at an end-point. Whether as entrance or terminus, it was intended, according to Jahnke, to tie 'the show together', to provide a 'commentary' on the whole (interview, March 1993). There was thus, on top of the juxtaposition of complementary forms, a further juxtaposition between the neatness of logical relations and the fact of an obstacle, something that was simply an impediment in general, rather than a negotiable impediment to a specific act or project. The sheer solidity and texture of the materials that were worked with such virtuosity, the absolute substance of beaten lead and copper, were in a way reassuring, as were the works' abstract regularities. But the larger spectre of the impediment, together with the succession of disruptions of symmetry that revealed themselves upon closer inspection, made these works, at the same time, profoundly unsettling. Jahnke's work simultaneously produces real parities that do not exist, and connects those equivalences with hierarchical relations which they do not match.

I have placed great emphasis upon the binary character of these works. This, and their attitude to contradiction, is in a way consistent with Michael Jackson's argument concerning the trinary structure of traditional *pare* carvings. He claimed that the presence of a third figure or term within the structures of those lintels mirrored a logic of synthesis within Maori culture and art, through which tensions and oppositions in social life were overcome. Since my suggestion is that Jahnke's work does not image a resolution – rather it posits a contradiction in terms that resist synthesis – it should not feature any third term and indeed appears not to do so. Unless, of course, the viewer and the audience stand as the third term; in which case all the energy and uncertainty, the historical burden, the risk and the promises of parity, slip out of a space that can possibly be described in an essay of this kind, and are bequeathed to those who constitute this work's audience.

NOTES

1   Jackson offers this speculatively, but it has been more recently stated unambiguously that *pare* carving 'symbolises the separation of Ranginui and Papatuanuku' (*Taonga Maori* 1989: 18, caption to figure 14). The presence of three anthropomorphic figures rather than one, together with the fact that some *pare* figures are clearly female, suggests that this is rather improbable.

2   The example Colley discusses is Sir David Wilkie's *Chelsea pensioners reading the gazette of the Battle of Waterloo* (1822), which thousands queued to see when it was first exhibited at the Royal Academy.

3   In this context it might be noted that a few Maori radicals enthusiastically supported Rabuka's 1987 coup in Fiji, which appeared permanently to privilege the

indigenous 'owners of the land' by disenfranchizing the descendants of immigrant Indians.

4   The point that what is recognized as traditional frequently entails a complex synthesis of pre- and postcontact influences is well established and need not concern us here (but, for an important demonstration in the New Zealand case, see Neich 1983).

5   In early 1993 it was in a large room with only two other works of comparable scale: Colin McCahon's *Second gate series* (1962) and Rosalie Gascoigne's *Pale landscape* (1977). This is significant as a summation of postwar New Zealand art, because McCahon is pre-eminent, and stands almost mythically for a distinctively antipodean and masculine yet poetic and reflective intellect; while the other two works would be said to represent the contributions of women and Maori to the national culture.

6   Tuwhare is a prominent Maori poet whose work often refers to contemporary politics, and has often been drawn upon in painting by Ralph Hotere and others; see his collection (1992).

7   Or rather, of course, that of oppressed people in the face of authority virtually everywhere. Notable Maori manifestations are important, though, in the main male characters in the widely discussed novels, *The bone people* (Hulme 1983) and *Once were warriors* (Duff 1990).

8   One exhibition, 'Te Mihaia Hou' (see Tyler 1991) was specifically concerned with Rua Kenana; the prophets have also been important in the work of the senior artist, Paratene Matchett, an important influence upon Jahnke; see Panoho (1987).

9   One anonymous referee pointed out that Polynesian double (if not single-hulled Maori) canoes were in fact highly sophisticated, and that the evolutionary comparison would therefore be false. My concern is not so much with the justifiability or otherwise of these claims on technical grounds, but the point that evolutionary comparison has been available, as a frame through which a variety of indigenous artefacts can be seen. In the early twentieth century an exhibition of 'naval architecture' at Sydney's Technological Museum (antecedent

to the present Powerhouse Museum) in fact incorporated a Niuean canoe among other 'primitive' vessels in an evolutionist display culminating in models of modern battleships (Stephen 1993: 15).

10 It is no longer generally accepted that Maori culture devalued women in terms of this kind, though the particular nature of notions of gender and their associations with *tapu* and *noa* continues to be debated (Hanson 1983*b*; Valeri 1985).

11 However, the process of waxing and waning that is directly alluded to also refers to the life cycle; as the missionary Thomas Kendall wrote, imposing his own idiom onto Maori thought, 'The Moon is man's time keeper and presides over his bones' (letter to Thomas Hassall, 1823, quoted in Binney 1968: 134).

12 In fact, the words on the Pakeha sail are 'Nana o te whenua'. While the word *mana* would primarily be associated with influence, prestige, power, and sanctity, and these meanings appropriately caption the work as a whole, another sense emerges from the comparison between the two sails: *mana* with a long first vowel like *nana* is a third person possessive pronoun; the former suggests future possession and the latter past. Future possession on the Maori sail implies 'the ideal for a return of lost taonga [treasured possessions] including land' (letter from the artist, 26 October 1993). In Maori conceptions of time, the future can be situated behind one, as one is faced by one's ancestors and the past. The slippage between the antithetical constructions in the bicultural or postcolonial time of the present suggests a meeting of past and future and a restoration of formerly inalienable possessions. I am grateful to Robert Jahnke for elucidation of the significance of these texts.

13 The artist, quoted in a Fox Gallery press release, February 1993.

14 This is a speculative proposition that is not easy to substantiate, particularly because the non-verbal character of the potency referred to makes direct or conclusive documentation unlikely, but possibly also beside the point (cf. O'Hanlon 1992: 588–9); Neich (1983: 264)

suggests that there was an overall trend in the 'attitude to [the] form and meaning' of Ngai Tarawhai carving from 'embodiment' in the early to mid-nineteenth century to a 'strong interest in referential denotation' in the early twentieth, but does not elaborate upon the notion of 'embodiment'.

REFERENCES

Anderson, B. 1983. *Imagined communities*. London: Verso.

Ang, I. 1985. *Watching Dallas*. London: Methuen.

Barrell, J. 1991. Constable's plenty. *Lond. Rev. Books* 13 (15), 15–16.

Binney, J. 1968. *The legacy of guilt: a life of Thomas Kendall*. Auckland: Oxford University Press.

——, G. Chaplin & C. Wallace 1979. *Mihaia: the prophet Rua Kenana and his community at Maungapohatu*. Wellington: Oxford University Press.

Colley, L. 1992. *Britons: forging the nation, 1707–1837*. New Haven, CT: Yale University Press.

Dale, R. 1990. Powerful images in Jahnke's art [review]. *N.Z. Herald*, July 19, 1990, sect 2, p. 2.

Duff, A. 1990. *Once were warriors*. Wellington: Tandem Press.

During, S. 1992. Postcolonialism and globalization. *Meanjin* 51, 339–53.

Forge, A. 1973. Style and meaning in Sepik art. In *Primitive art and society* (ed.) A. Forge. London: Oxford University Press.

Hanson, F.A. 1983*a*. Art and the Maori construction of reality. In *Art and artists of Oceania* (eds.) S. Mead and B. Kernot. Palmerston North: Dunmore Press.

—— 1983*b*. Female pollution in Polynesia? *J. Polynes. Soc.* 91, 335–81.

Hanson, F. A. and L. Hanson 1983. *Counterpoint in Maori culture*. London: Routledge.

Hulme, K. 1983. *The bone people*. London: Hodder & Stoughton.

Jackson, M. 1972. Aspects of symbolism and composition in Maori art. *Bijdr. Taal-, Land-, Volkenk.* 128, 33–80.

Kernot, B. 1987. Te Maori te hokinga mai: some reflections. *AGMANZ J.* 18, (2), 3–7.

King, M. (ed.). 1991. *Being Pakeha: the search for identity in New Zealand*. Auckland: Penguin.

Lévi-Strauss, C. 1962. *The savage mind*. London: Weidenfeld & Nicolson.

Mead, H.M. 1986. *Magnificent Te Maori*. Auckland: Heinemann.

Miller, D. 1987. *Material culture and mass consumption*. Oxford: Blackwell.

Neich, R. 1983. The veil of orthodoxy: Rotorua Ngai Tarawhai woodcarving in a changing context. In *Art and artists of Oceania* (eds) S. Mead and B. Kernot. Palmerston North: Dunmore Press.

—— 1993. *Painted histories: early Maori figurative painting*. Auckland: University Press.

O'Hanlon, M. 1992. Unstable images and second skins: artefacts, exegesis and assessments in the New Guinea Highlands. *Man* (N.S.) 27, 587–608.

Orange, C. 1987. *The Treaty of Waitangi*. Wellington: Allen & Unwin.

Panoho, R. 1987. Paratene Matchitt: the principle of change in Maori art. *Art N.Z.* 45, 63–7.

—— 1991. *Whatu aho rua: a weaving together of traditional and contemporary taonga*. Adelaide, Wanganui: Tandanya National Aboriginal Cultural Centre and the Serjeant Gallery.

Sahlins, M. 1985. Hierarchy and humanity in Polynesia. In *Transformations of Polynesian culture* (ed.) A. Hooper and J. Huntsman. Auckland: Polynesian Society.

Sharp, A. 1990. *Justice and the Maori*. Auckland: Oxford University Press.

Sloan, D. 1993. Cultures blended in symbolic art. *Evening Standard* (Palmerston North, New Zealand), March 6, 1993: 4.

Smith, B. 1985. *European vision and the south Pacific* (2nd edn.). New Haven: Yale University Press.

Stephen, A. 1993. Introduction. In *Pirating the Pacific* (ed.) A. Stephen. Sydney: Powerhouse Publishing.

Taonga Maori 1989. *Taonga Maori: treasures of the New Zealand Maori people*. Sydney: Australian Museum.

Taussig, M. 1987. *Shamanism, colonialism, and the wild man: a study in terror and healing*. Chicago: University of Chicago Press.

Tuwhare, H. 1992. *Deep river talk*. Auckland: Godwit Press.

Tyler, L. 1991. *Te mihaia hou: Maungapohatu and the prophet Rua Kenana*. Hamilton: Waikato Museum of Art and History/Te Whare Taonga o Waikato.

Valeri, V. 1985. Review of Hanson and Hanson, *Counterpoint in Maori culture*. *Am. Ethnol.* 12, 170–2.

Young, R. (ed.) 1991. *Mana tiriti: the art of protest and partnership*. Wellington: Daphne Brassel Associates.

27

Representing Culture
The Production of Discourse(s)
for Aboriginal Acrylic Paintings

Fred Myers

> To see something as art requires something the eye cannot descry – an atmosphere
> of artistic theory, a knowledge of the history of art: an artworld.
>
> Arthur Danto, "The Artworld"

My point in this article is to show that the production, circulation, and consumption of Aboriginal acrylic paintings constitutes an important dimension of self-production of Aboriginal people and of the processes of "representing culture" significant in what Appadurai and Breckinridge (1988:1) have described as the "global cultural ecumene" of the contemporary world. The task is to understand how these paintings have come to represent "Aboriginal culture" through a variety of practices and discourses: This is a hybrid process of cultural production, bringing together the Aboriginal painters, art critics, and ethnographers, in addition to curators, collectors and dealers: in short, an "artworld" (Becker 1982). I am particularly concerned with the attempts by critics to situate these art forms in cosmopolitan art circles. Such a situation places anthropologists in an unfamiliar relationship to their stock in trade – knowledge rooted in local constructions.

It seems to me, drawing upon my own experience, that anthropologists have been largely concerned to defend their own interpretations or to make them intelligible within the shadow of what they take to be the prevailing, culturally hegemonic notions of "art." In so doing, we have tended to reify our own culture's concepts into a more stable form than they actually have, and we fail to consider empirically (and critically) the processes in which we (and the art critics) are engaged as ethnographically important processes of cultural representation. This is ironic, I think, because the point of the struggle is almost entirely a question of how to represent others. Thus, if these antagonistic encounters (and I must admit to being a willing participant) about the imposition of Western art historical concepts often seem to be only so much turf warfare, they can also be conceived of as themselves forms of the social and cultural practices of representation. In reconceptualizing the relationship between art criticism and anthropology in this way, it may be possible to articulate more cogently the processes through which difference can be rendered intelligible.

From *Cultural Anthropology* 6 (1) (1991), pp. 26–62. Berkeley: University of California Press, 1991. Reprinted by the permission of the American Anthropological Association and the author. This version of the text has been abridged with the assistance of the author.

To be sure, such ethnocentrism persists, despite the interventions of anthropologists and art critics. However, the discourse of art critics (and art historians) is not a univocal one, and cases like those discussed by Price (1989) represent what is now only a portion of the Western discourse of art. This discourse is as unsettled and multiple as our own. What I want to trace out here is the "engagement" (is it a military metaphor or a romantic one?) between anthropological and indigenous accountings of Australian Aboriginal acrylic paintings and those of art critics. In part, the choice of subject is accidental, owing much to my personal circumstances and history.

Indigenous Discourse as Cultural Production

Before turning to the critical response(s) to the exhibition *Dreamings: the Aboriginal Art of Australia*, held at the Asia Society Galleries in New York in 1988, as constructive and deconstructive activities involved in defining the significance of Aboriginal painting, I want to discuss the accountings provided most directly by the Aboriginal producers (see figure 27.1). I am concerned with the disjunction between ethnographic/local accountings and those issuing from venues of cultural production at a greater distance.

The evaluation of Aboriginal practices is not a simple interpretation of "some facts" existing out there. In these constructive activities, rather, one discerns the properties of intertextuality or of what Bakhtin called the "dialogical" – in which one "word" is addressed to, assumes, or is aware of other interpretations. Before the appearance of reviews of Aboriginal art, for example, I was brought in most often as a translator and was asked to explain what these paintings "mean" to the Aborigines, as the way in which viewers might learn how to look at them, how to interpret their significance. This practice always tacitly assumed other readings, usually "ethnocentric" ones, that needed to be countered, but I rarely considered these worthy of analytic or ethnographic attention.

Anthropologists have tried – extending our role as translators – to stretch ourselves into a function usually allocated to critics: that is, to tell people what they should see in the paintings. This may be simply a promulgation of Aboriginal statements, but it does constitute a position – as authority, if you will – within the

Figure 27.1 Uta Uta Jangala and the painting of Yumari at Papunya, N.T., Australia, July 1981

definition of meaning. This is where we have been challenged by others with a different understanding of what there is to know about a surface, with different questions to engage, and often with a more developed and critical vocabulary for discussing visual phenomena and their production. Moreover, the evaluation of Aboriginal image production is not based on a static Western notion of "art" – since the tradition of cultural criticism in which art practices are themselves embedded has been questioning precisely what this category is and should be.

Be this as it may, "Aboriginal art" could not exist without Aboriginal culture(s), Aboriginal persons and traditions of body painting, sandpainting, and so on. We begin, therefore, with the practices through which Aboriginal producers assign significance to their productions. Nancy Munn's study of Walbiri Iconography (1973) and Howard Morphy's Too Many Meanings (1977) are well known for articulating the processes of producing and exchanging images in ritual in Central Australia and Arnhem Land respectively. Even though the acrylic images are not themselves produced for local consumption, these processes and co-ordinate social and cosmic identities represent the first level of organization and the basis for most Aboriginal evaluations of the objects. Nonetheless, most commentators gain access to these meanings not in the experience of daily life, but through some textualization.

My textualization of Pintupi practice

Let me begin with my understanding of Pintupi explanations and practices. What the Pintupi painters continually stress is (1) that their paintings are "stories" (*turiku*), representations of the events in the mythological past of the Dreaming, and (2) that they are "true" (*mularrpa*), that they are not made up. Like all the other Central and Western Desert people who do acrylics, the Pintupi have a rich ceremonial and ritual life in which songs, myths, and elaborate, complex body decorations as well as constructed objects are combined in performances that re-enact the somewhat mysterious events known as "the Dreaming" (*tjukurrpa*) which gave their world its form and order. The significance of

the paintings in their own eyes is bound up with their ideas about the relationship between this world and the Dreaming. All paintings represent stories from one of many cycles that concern traveling, mythical ancestral beings (Dreamings), and Pintupi country is laced by the paths of their travels. The value of the Dreaming lies in the fact that the world as it now exists is conceived to be the results of the actions of these beings. Persons, customs, geographical features are all said to have originated in the Dreaming, or as Pintupi people regularly say, *tjukurrtjanu, mularrarringu* ("from the Dreaming, it became real"). Access to knowledge of these events, to tell the stories, and the rights to re-enact the events and reproduce the designs and objects in ceremony are restricted, and transmitted through a variety of kinship links. Instruction in the most important details of esoteric knowledge takes place in ceremonies in which men (and women in their own ritual activities) re-enact the stories of the Dreaming, constructing ritual objects and decorating the actors in designs said to be "from the Dreaming." These designs, often forbidden for men or women to see if produced by the opposite sex, are in some ways iconic representations of the event and the landscape that records it, but they are also said to come from the Dreaming (indexically) and to have been "revealed" (*yutinu*).

Finally, like the rituals of which they are considered to be part – the story-song-design complexes are "owned" by various groups of persons, and the rights to "show" them are in the hands of the owners of the place, especially those whose own "spirits" come from that Dreaming. The particular formulations of ownership vary throughout Aboriginal Australia, but the overall features of these relations of image production are fairly consistent at least in Central Australia. Thus, Pintupi continue to think of their commercial paintings as related to and derived from their ceremonial designs and rock paintings, associated with important myths, and therefore possessing value other than that merely established in the marketplace.

I want to point out that no single significance is entailed by the account above. What is critical to recognize, I believe, is that the display of ritual knowledge is both a revelation of something "from the Dreaming" and one's rights to a place, but it is also a performance of a central component of the identities of those who produce the display. Nonetheless, the further movements of these objects through the world suggest that instead of regarding this discourse for image production as intrinsically the meaning of the paintings, we should consider how this (or other) discourses are drawn on by painters in accounts of their acrylic images.

Other textualizations

Aboriginal people increasingly have the opportunity to deploy their meanings directly, and their versions circulate fairly widely now in the press and in exhibition catalogues (where they are partly mediated by interpretive accounts of "the Dreaming" like mine above). I will make my point from these self-presentations.

Consider, for example, how one woman painter – in New York for the first time and on stage at the Asia Society for a symposium in which Aboriginal paintings are being discussed (22 October 1988) – defined her production. Dolly Granites spoke in Warlpiri; her words were translated into English by the anthropologist Françoise Dussart. "Dolly," Dussart reported,

> says that she holds the Dreaming from her father. She holds the Dreaming from her father's father, and she holds many Dreamings in her country. She also holds the Dreaming from her mother. She holds the Dreaming from her father's father and from her father's mother.

This was what an Aboriginal painter thought needed to be explained. No background or interpretive framework was offered beforehand. Indeed, the anthropologists and art adviser present on stage felt obliged to provide such a context in their comments.

An article in the *Sydney Morning Herald* (Kent 1987), on the occasion of a show at the Hogarth Gallery there, reports how Aboriginal painters in the Napperby Station community (northwest of Alice Springs) see their painting. "This dreaming," a painter named Cassidy says,

> is about the place where I was born...This waterhole and this emu track are part of my Dreaming. It takes me two weeks to make. *One day my painting will make Napperby number one....*I show the young fellas what

we Aboriginal people can do for ourselves. (Kent 1987:48; emphasis added)

Like Dolly, Cassidy's comments combine a reference to the Aboriginal worldview which is usually said to be embodied in the paintings – the Dreaming, as described above – with themes that are commonly part of Aboriginal thinking: usually the right to portray the designs of one's dreaming (that is, the ancestral/mythological being whose spirit animated one).

A good ethnographer might press further into what it could mean for Napperby to be "number one." At some level the quotation must generally be held to signify increasing self-esteem through external recognition – a form of self-production that is precisely what, one might argue, Aboriginal people typically accomplish in their traditional practices of "owning," producing and exchanging representations of the Dreaming (see Myers 1986, 1989). Most painters continue to think of their commercial paintings as related to and derived from their ceremonial designs and rock paintings, associated with important myths, and therefore possessing value other than that merely established in the marketplace.

The newspaper article, however, gave more prominence to another set of themes articulated by other Aboriginal painters in the Napperby community – about money, respect, self-esteem, and dignity. As Rita Nungala, a woman painter, put it:

> We have no grog here, on this station, because we don't want fights. We make that decision ourselves. We do have this painting, though and it gives us something to do. It is good that the youngsters see that, that they work and they get paid. (Rita Nungala in Kent 1987: 48)

The painters made it clear that while money is a principal reason for painting, they regard the canvases as more than mere commodities [...]

Constructions similar to those delineated briefly above are commonly offered in public presentations by painters. What these examples make clear is that these interpretations, those of the natives and others, are all accountings – constructions – each presuming a set of taken-for-granted givens which they also reproduce. The painters *presume* their own cultural discourses: they expect that those who see the paintings will recognize in them the assertion/demonstration of the ontological link between the painter, his/her Dreaming, the design, and the place represented. They also (tend to) presume the function these links will have. When Dolly Granites was at the Metropolitan Museum in New York, upon finding out that the Degas paintings were not "from the Dreaming," she classified them as "rubbish" (of no significance).

Clearly, the available meanings to Aborigines for this activity are many. To summarize briefly, they include painting as a source of income, painting as a source of cultural respect, painting as a meaningful activity defined by its relationship to indigenous values (in the context of "self-determination"), and also painting as an assertion of personal/sociopolitical identity expressed in rights to place.

Construction: Aboriginal Culture as Art

In this section, I want to explore how the representations of the acrylic paintings offered by whites, while basing themselves on remarks such as those I have described, have primarily constructed a permissible Aboriginal culture, that is, a representation that meets the approval of the dominant white society's notions of "common humanity." The reasons for this are complex and not possible to consider here, but let me start with the initial framing devices. Most of the constructions of acrylic paintings interpret them within the rubric of "art." This occurs at two levels: (1) the assertion/demonstration that they have "art," value it, and that the tradition is very old (implying that they are able to preserve things of value) and that therefore their culture is vital and worthy of respect; and (2) that this "art" contributes something important – something different or challenging – to the world of art. It will be clear that much of the "construction" of Aboriginal activities as art draws heavily on a variety of themes in modernist discourse, ranging from visual invention to human creativity and the loss of spirituality with development. These constructions, then, can be seen as a kind of cultural production.

The presentation of the objects at the *Dreamings* exhibition itself drew partly on such "humanistic" representations. According to the publicity circulated, the exhibition of these varied objects shows

> the extraordinary vitality of Aboriginal art. It is the oldest continuous art tradition in the world, and is flourishing with new energy and creativity in contemporary media. The works in the exhibition represent the "Dreamings," the spiritual foundation of Aboriginal life.

There are many significations in this theme, but one bears immediate tracing. The scientifically reported 30,000-year history of visual culture on the Australian continent has considerable salience for contemporary urban Aboriginal people, who treat this history in much the same way that the French conceive of their prehistoric cave paintings. The appearance of "art" in the Australian archaeological record precedes that of the Ice Age in Europe, for example, of Lascaux, so often regarded popularly as the first evidence of civilization. This representation offers an image of cultivated Aboriginal ancestors while Europe still lacked aesthetic vision. Moreover, in stressing that this tradition of visual culture is continuous, the museum publicity can attest to the survival, renewal ("flourishing"), and contemporary creative potential ("extraordinary vitality," "creative energy") of Aboriginal culture. The roots of this potential lie in the Dreamings, identified as the "spiritual foundation of Aboriginal life."

The spiritual is political

> Ordinary Australians, who may have had trouble dealing with the poverty, customs, and appearance of Aborigines, have finally been able to respect their artform. For Westerners, beautiful artifacts are the accepted currency of cultural accomplishment. (Pekarik 1988:52)

This construction is a step toward the synecdochic representation of Aboriginal culture itself by one form of its practice. Indeed, the significance or place of Aboriginal "art" in the representation of Aboriginal culture and identity owes much to motivations that are political, in the hope of improving the condition of Aboriginal people in Australia by gaining appreciation of their achievements.

The themes of Jane Cazdow's (1987a) article in the 1987 *Australian Weekend Magazine*, reporting on the art boom, are illustrative of the stories in which the paintings are embedded. She emphasizes three themes: (1) the financial and morale benefits to Aboriginal communities, (2) the controversy about the loss of "authentic" Aboriginal art as "the number of Aboriginals raised in traditional tribal societies is dwindling" (p. 15), according to one collector, and (3) the significance of the art's success for black-white relations.

Cazdow (1987a:15) reports that the (then) Minister for Aboriginal Affairs, C. Holding, believes that the boom in Aboriginal art is important in gaining respect for Aboriginal culture, "in creating bridges of understanding between Aboriginal and white Australia" (an important goal of the Department of Aboriginal Affairs' cultural policies). According to Holding,

> Many Australians have been taught that Aboriginal people have no traditions, no culture.... When they come to understand the depth of tradition and skill that's involved in this area, it's a very significant factor in changing attitudes. (Cazdow 1987a:15)

The capacity of the success of these paintings to signify for black-white relations depends largely on art's standing for the generically (good) human.

Many writers have drawn on explicit Aboriginal constructions about the political significance of their representation of places. The Australian fiction writer Thomas Keneally certainly drew on such statements and a wealth of anthropological material for his *New York Times* piece to place the paintings in a meaningful context for viewers. Keneally asked rhetorically what these men and women were "praising" in their work. This is something "we are entitled to ask . . . " he says. The answer he offers – that "Every stretch of land belongs to someone," that this is not art for art's sake (1988:52) – frames this work in the politics of Australia, the concern with land rights and the development of a movement of return to traditional homelands, and the need for money.

Visual invention

I like the way they move the paint around
(John Weber, personal communication)

Another important story, more recognizably "modernist," has been that they are "good"

art, describable in the conventions of contemporary Western visual aesthetics. Art critic Kay Larson, in *New York Magazine*, wrote

> Modernism has allowed us to comprehend the Aboriginal point of view... Aboriginal art at its best is as powerful as any abstract painting I can think of. I kept remembering Jackson Pollock, who also spread the emotional weight of thought and action throughout the empty spaces of his canvas. (Larson, 1988)

Others, like John Weber, the Soho gallery dealer, also thought it was "good art" (Sutton 1988; Wallach 1989; but see Michaels 1988).

But, as the art critic Nicolas Baume (1989:112) notes, the Aboriginal paintings do not simply repeat the familiar for Larson. They assert their differences, their challenge to contemporary norms.

Roberta Smith (1988) builds a different story, deriving from features of this same discourse. In her review in the *New York Times*, Smith judges that the exhibition "can unsettle one's usual habits of viewing," presenting a "constantly shifting ratio of alien and familiar aspects, undermining the efficacy of designating any art outside the mainstream." But the judgment is that "This is not work that overwhelms you with its visual power or with its rage for power; it all seems *familiar* and *manageable*" (emphasis added). Smith recognizes that the paintings are based on narratives and motifs handed down through generations, but for her,

> The more you read, the better things look, but they never look good enough. The accompanying material also suggests that these same motifs are more convincing in their original states. (Smith, 1988)

Thus, Smith is open to the possibility of this art but falls back to formalist conventions, in weighing the enduring problem of "context" in relation to "art."

While critics disagree, the important point is their assimilation of these forms to a historically and culturally specific discourse that focuses on creative invention and the way a painting, essentially self-designating, organizes color and other values on a two-dimensional surface. In some sense, the conventions of modernism suggest that the visual demonstrations of art can stand alone but that artifacts need contexts.

"Artistry" and human creativity

Some critics have focused on whether these works challenge Western conventions of the artist as individual producer either by their communal production, a feature stressed in several accounts (Cazdow 1987a; Michaels 1988), or notions of artistic specialty by virtue of the fact that "Traditionally, all people in the Aboriginal community are artists" (Stretton 1987: 32; see also Isaacs 1987).

With his usual acerbic eye, Eric Michaels caught this ideologically transparent combination of romantic and modernist conceit in a newspaper account (Cazdow 1987b) of the journey of the curators of the Asia Society exhibition to the Aboriginal community of Yuendumu:

These clever sorts managed to discover a whole tribe of Picassos in the desert, presumably a mysterious result of spontaneous cultural combustion. We're told of the curator's astonishment at finding more painters per capita of population than in Manhattan's Soho! (Michaels 1988: 62)

Spirituality and modernity

Other evaluations suggest that the acrylics offer a glimpse of the spiritual wholeness lost, variously, to "Western art," to "Western man," or to "modernity." Robert Hughes's (1988) glowing review of the Asia Society exhibition in Time draws precisely on this opposition:

Tribal art is never free and does not want to be. The ancestors do not give one drop of goanna spit for "creativity." It is not a world, to put it mildly, that has much in common with a contemporary American's – or even a white Australian's. But it raises painful questions about the irreversible drainage from our own culture of spirituality, awe, and connection to nature. (Hughes 1988:80)

In Hughes's estimation, and he is himself an Australian expatriate in New York, their "otherness" occupies a world without much in common with ours; the artistic values of individual creativity and freedom are not relevant. But this otherness is itself meaningful for us. Another line of evaluation asks if they can be viewed as a conceptual return to our lost ("primitive") selves, as suggested in Amei Wallach's subtitle:

"Aboriginal art as a kind of cosmic road map to the primeval" (Wallach 1989). Many of the visitors to the Asia Society certainly embraced this sort of New Age spiritualism.

Creativity as cultural renewal

Within the context of Australia more specifically, the significance of artistic activity among Aboriginal people is often embedded in a slightly different narrative of self-realization through aesthetic production – although still formulating potentially universalist meanings. Addressing conceptions of Aboriginal culture as inevitably on the course of assimilation, Westernization, or corruption, many observers ask whether these paintings are not evidence of cultural renewal, creativity, resistance, and survival (Isaacs 1987; Myers 1989; Sutton 1988; Warlukurlangu Artists 1987), whether they should be seen as an assertion of indigenous meanings rather than as homogenization.

Writing about an exhibition at the Blaxland Gallery in Sydney, for example, Jennifer Isaacs (1987) embraces more the pluralism compatible with postmodern art theory, in emphasizing that the admixture of European materials and venues for Western Desert visual culture (i.e., canvas, acrylics, and exhibitions instead of bodies, ochres, and ceremonies) is not a loss of authenticity or cultural subordination (which means a product that is not an expression of inner spirit). The hybridization, she argues, represents an explosion of creativity even breaking the bounds of the wrongheaded (to her mind) restraints for cultural "purity" urged by some advisers in the use of traditional ochre colors only. Such policies – which she characterizes as "bureaucratic" – are reminiscent, in her construction, of earlier policies for Aborigines that advocated separate development and postulated an unchanging Aboriginal culture.

The rhetoric of Isaacs's article is of "cultural explosion" as creativity and strength in opposition to "purity" as restraint, governmental, and bureaucratic. Isaacs's construction also must be seen as an interpretation that implicitly counters commonly held views of "the Aboriginal" as tradition bound, incapable of change and innovation (as Strehlow [1947] emphasized), unable to enter into the 20th century, doomed to extinction.

The representation of Aboriginal paintings appears to be defined in relation to the political discourse of "nationalism," on the one hand, and the spiritual and aesthetic ones of "modernism," on the other. Moreover, as we shall see, these concerns are often themselves related.

Contexts

Aborigine as sign

These discourses that develop around Aboriginal acrylic painting intersect some of the recent theorizing about "national imaginaries" (Anderson 1983), especially because of the Australian concern to create a national identity in which, increasingly, Aboriginal people or culture have figured. Reflecting on the significance of "Aborigines" and "Asians" in Australia, Annette Hamilton (1990) has tried to specify the process historically: she suggests that a concern with "Others" emerges most clearly at the same time as the sense of national identity is most threatened by emergent trends of internationalization and new forms of internal cleavage. Hamilton's analysis maintains that recent developments in Australia manifest not a rejection but an appropriation of – an identification with – certain features of the "Aborigine" as image. The significance of the "Aboriginal" as a sign is established by its placement in these historical contexts, with Aboriginality participating in multiple circuits of meaning.

If Aborigines were no longer themselves a threat to national development, as Native Americans were in a vital period in the formulation of their image in the American national identity, the "Aboriginal problem" was a central concern for the Labour Government that took office in 1972 and was addressed through welfare subsidies and policies promoting "Aboriginal self-determination" and "multiculturalism" (see Beckett 1985, 1988). "Self-determination" is the principal discourse underwriting cultural policies, anticipating that local control and autonomy will have beneficent effects on people's confidence, self-esteem, and success in acting on the world. The support of and recognition for Aboriginal art, for example, was seen by most of its promoters at this time as a way to promote appreciation for the accomplishments of Abo-

riginal culture. Such appreciation, it was believed, would not only provide a basis for self-esteem for a long disenfranchised racial minority, but would also support recognition for the value of Aboriginal culture in a context of increasing struggle with interests opposed to Aboriginal land rights, a struggle evidenced in the mounting campaigns by the mining companies in Western Australia.

There was an important combination of interests here involved in promoting appreciation for Aboriginal "artistry" and "spirituality." Many white Australian artists who opposed the dominant, rationalistic, and materialistic white culture were attracted to Aboriginality as an indigenous, local form expressive of their opposition. Elkin's (1977) *Aboriginal Men of High Degree* was republished, for example, and its representation of Aboriginal mysticism met with considerable popular enthusiasm among those who also attempted to establish Australia's regional identification with Southeast Asia in opposition to the cultural domination of Europe/America. Another intersection between the identities of a "spiritual" and "natural" Aboriginality (that was seen as "respecting" the land) and oppositional Australian culture was forged in the environmental movement – opposed to uranium mining in Arnhem Land, hydroelectric development in Tasmania. These economic developments were derogated by some as serving primarily the interest of foreign national economic exploiters, by others as expressive of the continued devastation of environmental relations by a mechanico-rationalistic culture, and so on.

Through such significations, the mysterious interior of Australia, a place long resistant to the purposes of (white) man in Australian lore, comes to stand for Australian identity as a spiritual/Aboriginal center on which to define an identity opposition to foreign, industrial control. Various meanings of Aboriginality are constituted in such processes of political incorporation. Hamilton's account is illuminating in showing that such significations draw on images of Aborigines constructed in earlier historical experience (see Hamilton 1990) – especially the dichotomizing ambivalent respect for the "wild bush black" and contempt for the "detribalized fringe campers," "mission blacks," and "half-castes." The "wildness" of the bush Aboriginal – an image focused on the bush, nature, mystic power and "tribalism" – while it "held a threat to the normal functioning of station life..." – "also marked Aborigines as somehow able to transcend everything which European civilization (itself a fragile flower on the frontier) was able to offer" (Hamilton 1990:18). Recent constructions draw on these previous images, manifesting a particular form of desire, according to Hamilton:

> the wish to move into the mystic space and spiritual power which has been retained from the earlier construction of "good" Aboriginality, and to somehow "become" the good Aborigine. (Hamilton 1990:18)

With an emphasis on "self-determination" through land rights and ultimately an ideology of "self-realization" in culture, these were bases for the inclusion of Aboriginal themes in the creation of a specifically Australian identity. Finally, the "difference" of Aborigines later allowed them to be figured as a symbol of exoticism and wildness (Morton 1988) to be sought out and consumed in a growing tourist industry, attempting to market the "true heart" of Australia.

Aboriginal painting

Modernist art narratives need not imply that Aboriginal paintings are simply the equivalents of Western forms. Critical discourse, modernist or not, is not so simpleminded. The question is whether this placement of the acrylics "into the existing structures of popular art theory" (Weber 1989) is appropriate or whether, as the New York dealer John Weber holds, "A new vision demands a new system of critical thought" (Weber 1989).

Most writers on the art recognize it to be decoratively pleasing and fitting comfortably enough within the visual expectations of the Western tastes for kinds of formalism of the '60s and '70s and busy surfaced acrylic work of the '80s. Thus, it not only suits the development of national identity, but it fits without discomfort on corporate walls and in the pre-existing collections filled with such works.

John Weber – who is known for supporting conceptual and minimal art and exhibits the work of site-specific artists like Richard Long

and political artists like Hans Haacke – is the first significant gallery owner in New York to take on the work, and he attempts to place the work's entry into the art market as demanding a rupture in critical constructions, as something more than 1970s formalism. He talks of the need for "an art dialogue sympathetic to the intent of this work...to engender a deeper understanding and appreciation of what the viewer sees and subsequently feels and thinks" (Weber 1989). If a new set of art critical theory is necessary to elucidate this new art, Weber's discussion suggests it should engage four central features, (1) the vitality and compositional complexity of the paintings, (2) their site-specific quality, (3) their political message, and (4) their narrative subject matter.

Weber's comments are also revealing of the accommodations it takes for these paintings to enter into the "fine art" market. Referring to the appearance of fly-by-night dealers and galleries and inflated prices, he argues that the current "commercial onslaught" in the marketing of the acrylic paintings threatens the continued existence of the movement. This is another institutional problem, in that, "as Australia has not previously generated an art movement of international significance, the art power structure is at a loss to deal professionally with the fast emerging Aboriginal scene" (Weber 1989). Only one commercial gallery – Gabrielle Pizzi's, which has exclusive rights to Papunya Tula Artists – has what he considers to be a "well thought out program of group and one person shows of this work" (Weber 1989).

There are more narratives for the paintings, but I want to turn my attention now to what are essentially responses to these initial constructions.

Disjunction as Discursive Incongruity

While anthropologists and Aboriginal painters have been inclined to emphasize the continuities between the paintings and indigenous Aboriginal traditions, emphasizing their authenticity as expressions of a particular worldview, these very terms – and their meanings – are among those most hotly contested in art critical circles. This discursive incongruity is a point that Eric Michaels, and others embracing a postmodern position, grasped immediately (and enthusiastically):

> traditionalism and authenticity are now completely false judgments to assign to contemporary Aboriginal painting practices. The situation I worked in at Yuendumu demonstrated unequivocally that the Warlpiri painting I saw, even if it accepts the label "traditional" as a marketing strategy, in fact arises out of conditions of historical struggle and expresses the contradictions of its production.... To make any other claims is to cheat this work of its position in the modernist tradition as well as to misappropriate it and misunderstand its context. (Michaels, 1988:62)

From here, it seems possible to go on to discuss the practices of cultural appropriation by the West, the impact of the West's "gaze" in defining the "other." Indeed, there has been much critical writing that has explored and deplored such "representational practices."

Deconstruction

The "appreciation" of Aboriginal acrylic paintings and their placement comfortably in the art world are problematic for critical-pluralist postmodernism like that embodied in James Clifford's (1988a) criticism of the much publicized 1984 exhibition at the Museum of Modern Art that was called "Primitivism in 20th Century Art: Affinity of the Tribal and the Modern." Clifford (1988a) and others (e.g., Moore and Muecke 1984) argue that the sort of humanism deployed in such representations makes the culturally different too familiar, when it should challenge the universality and natural status of Western categories. Clifford writes, "we need exhibitions that question the boundaries of art and the art world, an influx of truly indigestible 'outside' artifacts..." (1988a:213). From this position, the acrylic paintings – as they are inserted in the art scene and gathered for exhibitions as "fine art" – are seen as confirming the power of the formerly colonial masters to determine what matters.

The postmodern critique of "humanism," one which points out the loose ends (i.e., deconstructing) in attempts to make "them" look more like "us," locates a weakness that is common in projects of "imagining" differ-

ence and one with which anthropologists are familiar (see Marcus and Fischer 1986). Is it any wonder, therefore, that some anthropologists who have been engaged in the construction of Aboriginal culture have been surprised by the ferocity of the critique of our rhetoric (see Fry and Willis 1989; Michaels 1988; von Sturmer 1989; Sutton 1988)?

The generic critique of the "humanistic" does not compromise the full range of deconstruction's attack. In more specific and limited ways, the construction of the paintings as "art" has been undermined variously by "revealing" the essentially "economic motivation" of Aboriginal painting and/or the contrast between the supposed spirituality of the art and the destruction of its civilization by white settlement. Faced with other popular representations of Aboriginal people as drunks, as lazy, and/or as a morally dispirited remnant, many are critical of hopeful/poetic/romantic representations of Aboriginal cultural and spiritual renewal such as that offered by Isaacs (see above).

The Loss of the "Other"

Peter Schjeldahl's (1988) review in 7 Days finds the acrylic paintings to be not "other" enough, too accessible, and thereby essentially representative of the domination and destruction of Aborigines by whites. He contrasts a visit he once made to Alice Springs – remembering the challenge that an Aboriginal presence (although brief and insubstantial) offered to his sense of the universal and real – with the show, attacking the basic constructions of art as somehow redeeming of Aboriginal subordination: "the paintings are seen as a means to build independent wealth and self-esteem for a people gravely lacking both." Sadly, he writes, "In problem-solving terms the idea is impeccable. But the paintings are no good." The domination is unfortunate, he says, and it is probably praiseworthy to attempt to show good benefits for Aboriginal people, but this liberal solution will not wash: the paintings exhibit the final domination of Western categories. Indeed, their very recognition of his realities (manifest in the materials and the straight lines of the canvas) appears to undermine their ability to challenge them. So, "Don't go looking for that power of strangeness at the Asia Society."

Once upon a time, the mere interest in things Aboriginal in a metropolitan center like New York would have been seen as a triumph over ethnocentrism. Yet Australian critics Fry and Willis (1989: 159) criticize the emphasis on representing Aboriginal culture as the "spectacular primitive" because it diminishes "Aboriginals to a silenced and exoticized spectacle." They decry as "ethnocide" the manufacture of "Aboriginal culture" in the process through which "experts" who "trade in the knowledge of 'the other'" make their own careers (1989:159–160). And, if anthropologists once railed against art critics for the imposition of Western aesthetic categories on objects produced in other cultural contexts, some critics (Rankin-Reid 1989) attack anthropologists and curators for their emphasis on the "ethnographic," for focusing on the narrative and "mythological" content of the acrylic paintings – as a primitivizing device that precludes appreciation of the "patently visual accomplishments of the work." In the artists' home communities or traveling with the painters in New York, these positions seem terribly distant. They are artworld battles.

How is one to compare Schjeldahl's criticism with the self-esteem expressed in comments made to me by Michael Nelson, the Warlpiri painter, when he visited New York for the Asia Society show? The latter believes people are really interested in his work and the work of other "traditional" people. "They want to see paintings from the Centre," he said, contrasting this with the lack of white interest in the work of urban Aboriginal artists. This contrast makes sense to him in his own culture's terms in which religious knowledge is the basis for recognition:

Urban Aboriginal people *ngurrpaya nyinanyi* ("unknowing/without knowledge – they sit down"). I feel sorry for them. We're lucky. We still have our Law (religious traditions), everything.

Andrew Pekarik's reading of the relative popularity of the acrylic paintings (in comparison to the work of urban Aboriginal artists) follows this implicit contrast in another way, suggesting that the popularity of work like Nelson's owes much to a certain preservation of the cultural boundaries of the audience:

What people like is a safe way to incorporate an element of Aboriginality. They won't be as interested in what the urban [Aboriginal] artists do. There is too much pain. People don't like "accusatory art." They want something they can feel more positive about, they can feel good about. They see buying the paintings as helping to preserve these existing cultures. …This "traditional" Aboriginal art allows Australians to feel good about themselves. (Pekarik, personal communication)

That is, the "traditional" acrylics are not understood by audiences as challenging them where they live, so to speak, drawing the audience's accountability into the frame of the exchange. To follow Hamilton's (1990) terms, the acrylics of "traditional" people represent the "good" Aborigine – a spirituality, respect for land, and so on of people at a distance (see Fabian 1983) rather than people who are seen as contemporaries competing for the same lifespace – which viewers or buyers can incorporate. In a sense, this incorporation of "difference" is possible by virtue of the very self-contained and cultural confidence of artists like Michael Nelson and Dolly Granites, men and women who still remain relatively secure in their own cultural traditions.

Despite *their* assurance, however, Aboriginal people's expectations that knowledge of their culture's foundation in the Dreaming will result in recognition of their rights are not entirely fulfilled. The answer to such a question rests not so much on the qualities of the object, or even in the structural relations between cultural groups, but in the capacity to make one or another set of meanings prevail or even visible.

Critical Practice: "Origins" and Destinations

Fry and Willis maintain a suspicious and deconstructive stance toward an emphasis they see on Aboriginal painters as "all traditional people who have little experiences of cities" (1989:159–160). They find the same emphasis on the theme of the "spectacular primitive" at the display of artists and their work from all over the world, *Magiciens de la Terre*, where Warlpiri men from Yuendumu built a ground painting in Paris in spring 1989. However, while Schjeldahl is disappointed and angered at the domination of the authentic in the new medium and its recontextualization, they take an opposing position with respect to that theme:

> The marketing of contemporary Aboriginal art can be seen as a form of soft neo-colonialism, through which Aboriginal people are incorporated into commodity production (with the attendant reorganization of social relations). One result is that traditional beliefs and practices have to be reconfigured according to the relative success or failure of the commodity. There is thus no continuity of tradition, no 40,000-year-old culture, no "time before time." There are only objects produced by a range of fragmented cultures with varying connections to tradition and economic necessity, posed against the homogenized readings of these objects according to the meaning systems of the culture of dominance. (Fry and Willis 1989: 116)

At issue is the question of what one sees in these cultural productions, and Fry and Willis are concerned principally with the claim of the new art's "continuity" with (and renewal) of Aboriginal culture. Drawing on a "poststructuralist" approach which is highly critical of presumed essences and continuities, for Fry and Willis,

> in Australia, the romantic recovery of the past as a pre-colonial life is impossible... The return to the old culture is therefore really a new culture built upon the signs of the past... [Fry and Willis 1989: 160]

For these critics, displays of art as indigenous culture cannot be the basis for Aboriginal self-identity, being oriented largely "for the gaze of the colonizer and on terms and conditions set by the dominant culture" (Fry and Willis 1989:160). Rather than providing forms for the development of Aboriginal self-determination, "in the appropriation of Aboriginal culture, careers in 'white' society are being made." In this social field, moreover, the career advancement of these white experts depends upon the reproduction of "the primitive." Far from being a token of authenticity,

> In this process, "Aboriginal culture" is something manufactured within the parameters of the professional norms of the careerists; it becomes a culture from which Aboriginal

people are excluded either literally or by having to assume subject positions made available only by "the oppressor." (Fry and Willis 1989:159)

Not surprisingly, therefore, Fry and Willis claim that they have no authority to speak on behalf of what Aboriginal people mean. This position has the appearance of being politically more satisfactory in the avoidance of submitting "their" meanings to "our" categories, yet to hold such a position is still to assume one knows the impact of colonial practices on these subjects. For all the perspicacity, here are the outsiders who know more than the participants, outsiders whose representational practices directly thwart the representations of Aboriginal painters.

As we saw in the Schjeldahl and Smith reviews, Fry and Willis are not alone in showing little interest in finding out what the Aboriginal people are doing, saying, or understanding in these events which are addressed partly to us. They presume, following Eric Michaels (1988) for instance, that "looking" – as in attending a Warlpiri ceremony – is the privilege of domination. This is not necessarily or simply so in Aboriginal cultures where the revelation of forms to the sight of the uninitiated is a gift that carries responsibilities. In showing their paintings, Aboriginal people may require that to have seen something is to be responsible for understanding it.

Nonetheless, such criticism's point is that the terms and conditions for the display of indigenous culture are always set by the dominant culture and that the exchange will be massively unequal. Is this, as Fry and Willis claim, "ethnocide" – a cultural erasure accomplished by "obliging them to transform themselves to the point of total identification, if possible, with the model proposed to or upon them" (Clastres 1974, in Fry and Willis 1989:116)? What do such discourses mean for Aborigines? It appears that Aborigines have to establish themselves within or against these defining terms – or do they?

Controversy

My concern in this article is not so much to resolve the controversy about the acrylic paintings – to go beyond it in some way – but rather to present and understand it ethnographically as a form of cultural production.

Andrew Pekarik, the Director of the Asia Society Galleries during the show and a specialist in Asian art, sees the show as a success because of the controversy, but not just because any publicity is good. He explained this to a small group of collectors convened by the New Museum of Contemporary Art in February 1990, which I later asked him to articulate.

> This is a good thing. One of the worst things would be is [sic] if people said, "Yes, that's cute." If there is no controversy, that means nobody is thinking about it.

What Pekarik said about the controversy offers a curator's more concrete appreciation of education. He offered that

> The real significance of the acrylic movement is its ability to be a point of cultural communication. There hasn't been a language in terms of which these two sides [i.e., white and Aboriginal] could communicate. They are so far apart that they can't help but misunderstand each other. And in these misunderstandings, the Aboriginal side has had the worst of it. These paintings are the first occasion for cross-cultural communication. For Aborigines they represent a way of dealing with the majority world. For outsiders, they represent a way of trying to hear what the other side is saying, because it is in a language that is not threatening...
>
> Roy Wagner says that cargo cults are a kind of New Guinea anthropology, their way of understanding what they are seeing on the outside. That's what is taking place in the paintings. Outsiders have to make an effort to try to understand. Obviously, [given the controversy and disagreements] they are working on it. (Andrew Pekarik, personal communication)

Pekarik's analysis reflects an art world insider's understanding of its processes – processes in which artists, gallery dealers, museums, collectors, and critics are a kind of network, "all in it together." They produce meaning for objects and construct their place(s) in an overarching theory. The production of culture is a social process: the ideal-typical career course is for an artist to become taken up by a gallery, who shows his/her work and gets it placed with select collectors, gradually encouraging

and establishing recognition of its sensibilities and gaining a reputation for it with reviews. After a series of exhibitions, the next step would usually be placement with collectors and then with museums. In the case of the Asia Society show, evidently, the initial establishing exhibition was a more official recognition or certification of the objects' worth than that of a dealer's gallery. The reviews of a show in New York were significant in drawing attention to the work, here and in Australia, in legitimating it: "putting it on the map." Despite this flurry of attention, potential dealers for the acrylics in the United States realize that more shows are necessary to demonstrate the stability of the art as an object of interest. This is where the artworld network functions again: dealers need museums to show the paintings regularly in order to remind people such art is there.

Art worlds "make art," as Becker (1982) showed, and while one can view this cynically (as artists and dealers have been prone to do recently) or institutionally (as Becker did), it is also clear that the processes of "making art" require the establishing of a sensibility, a way of appreciating different forms of cultural activity. This is what the critic Clement Greenberg did for abstract art – focusing on "universal" aesthetic principles as an attempt to sustain modern art within a tradition, as not representing a radical break from the "Western tradition" – and what Lucy Lippard did for conceptual art (see Crane 1987). As an artist friend told me, "We all need a good scholar to write about our work: art and words, that's what you need." And art criticism – with its constant anticipation of the next movement, style, or fashion – partly is in the business of producing such styles and differences. Although criticized itself for such promotional/self-promotional celebration of certain trends and movements to the exclusion of the actual diversity of art (Alloway 1984), art criticism plays a significant role in this process of producing "difference" and rendering it intelligible.

From an outsider's vantage point, here is where the ambivalence and energetic responses of the art world seem to lie. Art critics produce their stories and sensibilities as part of larger, ideological concerns about art and the world – chiefly, it would appear, against the threat of "mass culture," "kitsch," "the market," and "commodification." Yet the work of critics is deeply embedded in a capitalist marketplace, fueled by novelty and "difference" to offer buyers. In this sense, and this is the chief irony with which many artists contend, the art world (despite its claims to the opposite) may itself reflect – rather than transcend – the placelessness of late capitalism (Jameson 1984; Lash and Urry 1987). Thus, within the art world, artists and critics struggle with the recognition that new differences – the regional, the local, the challenging – are too easily drawn within the common, "international culture" that subverts the initial differences and incongruities:

> The way [global culture] works now is by diversifying. It has to work by making regional differences active, making them recognisable but not really disturbing. It has to keep the structures in play and change the details. So regionality is really absolutely essential news for global capital at the moment, absolutely essential. (artist Terry Smith, quoted in Nairne et al. 1987:212)

Conclusion

It is clear that the "acrylic movement" may not only compete with modern art on its own level, but can just as easily defeat it in those same terms. This apparent victory for Aboriginal art may, however, turn out to be pyrrhic. If our pseudo-humility before Aboriginal art is based on its confirmation of our own aesthetic values and spiritual aspirations, it will simply be subsumed by the reactive processes of cross-cultural projection. Instead of confining our understanding to the illusory tradition created by visual association, we might seek out the unseen differences. Interpretations that reduce art to a literal content and a structural grammar only tame it, make it comfortable.

What Aboriginal acrylics may offer, unlike most recent art, is precisely their potential to make us nervous. (Baume 1989: 120)

Anthropology has been long concerned with the problem of interpreting or translating between the indigenous concepts and practices of other cultural orders and those of our own society. But we are not alone in our engagement in such interpretive activity. The easy

authority of our interpretations has been questioned in frequently cited works. The best known of these, surely, is that of Clifford (1988a, 1988b), representing the general pluralist positions delineated by the band of cultural theory known as "postmodernism."

A significant domain in which the question of such interpretation has regularly been of interest is that of "art." This is a concept about which most scholars are now self-conscious. "Art" is long recognized to be a cultural domain in the West, one not necessarily shared or similar in all societies, and one which has been convincingly historicized (R. Williams 1977). This is a problem on which anthropologists have fought the "good fight." Indeed, a good deal of self-satisfied writing by anthropologists has focused on this problem, criticizing the imposition of Western categories on the practices of other peoples.

These categorizations of "art," "creativity," or "humanity" matter in more than merely academic ways insofar as they can imply differing representations of cultures. To say that Aborigines do not have "art," however qualified by insisting that the category is a distinctively historical one in the west, without hierarchical and evaluative significance, can easily be read as "racism." Any anthropologist with the experience of trying to explain this issue to nonspecialists should recognize the practical problem.

Anthropological translations may founder as much in their transparencies with respect to cultural boundaries as their opacities. In an important sense, what Aboriginal producers say about their work – their own discourse for its interpretation – draws primarily on an indigenous tradition of accounting, and it is this discourse (frequently) that anthropologists have sought to present as the authentic meaning. But as one must learn from the appearance of the acrylic paintings in New York and elsewhere, this knowledge of the Aboriginal culture, persons, and traditions of image making – knowledge of what Aboriginal painters say about their work – does not necessarily recognize the potential and significance of these forms to engage interest from those concerned with visual images in our own culture.

One asks, therefore, whether the engagement with art criticism as a competing practice of   interpretation   offers   anything   for anthropological understanding? Art theory's concern with the boundaries between art and nonart, both as a modernist evaluative process (i.e., is it art?) or as a postmodernist critically problematized/oppositional practice (i.e., what does it mean to define such boundaries?) is a critical part of the processes through which Aboriginal people are producing themselves in the contemporary world. Thus, the reception of the paintings raises the broader question of the capacity of indigenous people to objectify their meanings into the discourses for their reception.

Can there genuinely be dialogue between their conventions and those of the art world? The examples I have presented suggest that Aborigines are triangulated by a series of discourses – which might represent positive benevolence, political support, sympathy, or renewed racism in which Aborigines are central but usually absent. Aboriginal accounts enter more explicitly into that Derridean world in which all signification exists in a context of other representations, in which there is no transcendental signified outside of representation. Are Aboriginal actors able to make their practices have just the meanings they claim?

To review briefly, I have delineated differences with three sets of critics.

1   There is Roberta Smith, who says we must hold these paintings up to standards of our own culture since they circulate in it now. In those terms, she says, "Too bad, they represent second rate neo-Expressionism." She rejects the paintings in terms of the art world.

2   Another set of critics, exemplified by Peter Schjeldahl, want the lost romance, and reject these paintings in terms of the West's nostalgia for some other that the Aboriginal paintings cannot represent by virtue of their "contamination" by Western forms.

3   The third set, Fry and Willis, treat the paintings in terms of commodity circulation and the inevitable corruption it entails. They reject the paintings, supposedly from an Aboriginal perspective.

Such criticisms are part of the discursive practices that define "high art." The fact of the debates, the very fact of them, is what has validated the acrylic paintings as objects worthy of broader consideration. This is exactly what John Weber desires in his plea for a "new art critical theory." He is, after all, a dealer and what he does is find paintings and transform them into "art" by selling them. The acrylic paintings not only have a meaning, they are being made to have a meaning about the nature of human creative activity, and made into saleable "fine art."

Those discourses fail to explain the meaning at the Aboriginal level. At best, the Aborigines are considered to be co-opted; at worst, they are not considered at all. It should be clear that my association with the painters makes it difficult to accept at face value criticisms of the acrylic movement which derogate the local focus on the "continuity" and "authenticity" themes as a "constructed primordialism" – to borrow a term from Arjun Appadurai (1990). Most Pintupi and Warlpiri painters have not constructed primordial identities, "origins," principally in opposition to wholly external "others," as in various nationalisms – not, that is, as an ethnic discourse of "Aboriginality."

Aboriginal people's primordialisms are constructed, of course, but they are frequently constructed and sustained in relation to processes different from colonial ones. They are constructed in complex systems of similarity and difference – "totemisms" if you will – in which larger collective identities are only temporary objectifications, shared identities produced for the moment (see Myers 1986; Sansom 1980). "Country" as most Aborigines would call the places represented in acrylic paintings, the token of the painter's identities, represent the basis for objectifications of shared identity through time.

A critical art theory struggles with the local message because of its own preoccupation with the global processes that suffocate it, threatening to make all the world the same, all processes and forms substitutable for each other. It is just such a fear of "cultural homogenization" at work – the incorporation of Aboriginal products into European fine art – that underlies much of the art critical writing. Such one-way narratives deny any "indigenization," despite the fact that the potential of such "indigenization" is what is ultimately of interest in Aboriginal paintings. The identities that many acrylic painters produce on their canvases are not uprooted or deterritorialized; this is their very claim.

The situation of Fourth World people should not be so loosely compared with other post-colonial circumstances that currently inform cultural theory. Pintupi – or Warlpiri or Anmatjira – claims that the paintings are "from the Dreaming" or that they are expressive of an ontology in which human beings gain their identity from associations with place do express a historical struggle, but initially at least they have done so in their own right, not simply in recognition of a colonizing threat from outside. To see these claims – their identities – as "our" product (as from colonialism) is to colonize doubly by denying them their own histories.

If art theory fails to grasp what the activity means to the painters, their critical responses so far only skirt the question of its appeal. I want to conclude by considering what this appeal might be and what it suggests about the contribution Aboriginal acrylics might be making as "art." The appeal of the paintings is not, I suggest, as ineffable as the best critics suggest.

Ironically, the paintings have significance in art theory and for the buyer because of their local meanings for Aboriginal people, the association they represent for buyers between an artist and a place. As forms acceptable to the art world, Aboriginal acrylics offer a powerful link to particular locations in a world which is said – according to most postmodern theorists – to have "no sense of place" (see Meyrowitz 1985). What the acrylics represent to their makers resists this sort of commodification: all places are not the same. Painters can only produce images from their own local area, all conceived of as different.

In Warlpiri artist Michael Nelson's explication of the meaning of the paintings, one traces the "original meanings" in the emergence of something that is new: an "Aboriginality" that is also becoming defined in opposition to "Europeans":

White people don't really fully appreciate these dreamings that we paint. These dreamings are part of this country that we all live in. Europeans don't understand this sacred ground and the law that constrains our interaction with it. We've been trying to explain it to them, to explain what it means to us. For the sake of all Australians, we try to show them that this is our land. We try to show them our dreamings which are part of this country that we all live in. But white people don't even recognize our ownership of it. We paint all these pictures and they still can't understand. They want them as souvenirs to hang on their walls but they don't realise that these paintings represent the country, all of this vast land.

In other countries, they're all right; the land belongs to them, it's their country. We belong to this country; that's why we keep saying that we want our land back. (Michael Nelson at the Sydney Biennale 1986, quoted in Nairne et al. 1987: 221)

Michael Nelson continues to deploy here the same principal discourses that an anthropologist is most likely to encounter. His statement reminds us that these discourses are not some intrinsic bottom line but that they take shape in the context of contemporary politics in Australia: but their goal, their intent, is not displaced.

I do not mean to say that the "place-meaning" of acrylic paintings is the totality of their signification or that the signification of this meaning is the same for all consumers. Given the regular association of purchasing the paintings with travel to the area in which they are produced and located, for instance, I suspect some particular thrill accompanies knowing the place that is represented in such utterly "other" (i.e., unfamiliar) graphic signs which hold a different meaning for "others." For Westerners, this both valorizes the travel – to a place that is genuinely different – and the painting as a sign of that difference.

Moreover, what is at stake in a "sense of place" in Australia is different from what it is for consumers from overseas. In Australia, for some, the places of Aboriginal people are places before history, a place in the Outback often coded as more primeval – a frontier in which Australians are fascinated to know that some real "stone age" hunting and gathering people still live (see Myers 1988). This primordial spirituality at the heart of Australia, especially at Ayers Rock but also (in a way) in each painting, provides links with tourism and travel away from the solid domesticity of suburban homes and rational order of "white science" (see Fiske, Hodge, and Turner [1987: 119–130] for a discussion of these themes).

The Aboriginal and the Outback are, increasingly, the source of Australia's self-marketing for the international tourist industry, the "difference" they have to offer. These constitute an important dialectical dimension of emerging formulations of Australian national identity: something essential outside and before the nation that lies also at its heart, central to its identity, these significations give Aboriginal representations of place a particular value. The paintings represent this mystery, in a way, by being the token of what the place/country is prior to or outside its appropriation into the uses and purposes of white society. Australians, therefore, can obtain such tokens and display them as representations of some part of themselves on their wall.

Their appeal is the sense of their rootedness in the world – although this "rootedness," the sense of place – is what appears to some of the critics to be undermined by the apparent cosmopolitanism of the painters and the circulation of their products. It is not that Western art critics understand the specific information or details of the Dreaming-places that are usually the subject of the paintings, but rather that the fact of these relations fulfills a real or nostalgic sense of the loss of attachment to place. The specific understanding of a story is not so important as that it signifies so rich, complex and unself-conscious a sense of connection.

It is not accidental that this sense is what informs postmodernism so strongly. There is a great irony of historical accident in this: the paintings make their way into the art market by virtue of their strong formal similarity to abstract expressionism, a movement defined by its detachment from specificity and location! Postmodernism looks to the margins of a dominant culture and minority voices not only for a critique of oppression, but also out of a genuine concern to reroot high culture to sources of the sensory and the intellectual delight in everyday life. This is what can be found in the descriptions of the "creative process" in Aboriginal communities – a sense of the "cottage industry" with painters sitting out in the sun, making images without the European's requisite sturm and drang.

Postscript. Because I would develop a more dialectical conception of knowledge, I seek to question both the increasingly popular identifications of ethnographic knowledge as merely domination of our objects but also the defensive reaction, by many anthropologists, to the revelation of our project's placement within history. Recognition of the social and cultural place of interpretive projects – positioning ethnography, reflexively, within its own frame of consideration – is an essential step for contemporary anthropology to gain insight into the multiple circuits in which the representation of culture operates. In writing this article, my hope is to help place anthropological practices of interpretation more adequately – more ethnographically – within our (limited) perspectives as acting subjects and within the larger historical perspectives which define us.

REFERENCES

Alloway, Lawrence, 1984 *Network: Art and the Complex Present.* Ann Arbor, Mich.: UMI Research Press.

Anderson, B. 1983 *Imagined Communities.* London: Verso Press.

Appadurai, A. 1990 Disjuncture and Difference in the Global Cultural Economy. *Public Culture* 2(2):1–24.

Appadurai, A., and C. Breckinridge 1988 Why Public Culture? *Public Culture* 1(1):5–9.

Baume, Nicholas 1989 The Interpretation of Dreamings: The Australian Aboriginal Acrylic Movement. *Art and Text* 33:110–120.

Becker, Howard 1982 *Art Worlds.* Berkeley: University of California Press.

Beckett, J. 1985 Colonialism in a Welfare State: The Case of the Australian Aborigines. In *The Future of Former Foragers.* C. Schrire and R. Gordon, eds. Pp. 7–24. Cambridge: Cultural Survival.

—— 1988 Aboriginality, Citizenship and Nation State. *Social Analysis* 24(special issue: Aborigines and the State in Australia):3–18.

Cazdow, J. 1987a The Art Boom of Dreamtime. *The Australian Weekend Magazine,* 14–15 March:1–2.

—— 1987b The Art of Desert Dreaming. *The Australian Weekend Magazine,* 8–9 August:6.

Clastres, Pierre 1974 *Society Against the State.* New York: Urizen Books.

Clifford, James 1988a Histories of the Tribal and the Modern. In *The Predicament of Culture.* Pp. 189–214. Cambridge: Harvard University Press.

Clifford, James 1988b On Ethnographic Authority. In *The Predicament of Culture*. Pp. 21–54. Cambridge: Harvard University Press.

Crane, Diana 1987 *The Transformation of the Avant-Garde*. Chicago: University of Chicago Press.

Danto, Arthur 1964 The Artworld. *Journal of Philosophy* 61:571–584.

Elkin, A. P. 1977 [1945] *Aboriginal Men of High Degree*. St. Lucia, Queensland: University of Queensland Press.

Fabian, Johannes 1983 *Time and the Other*. New York: Columbia University Press.

Fiske, J., B. Hodge, and G. Turner 1987 *Myths of Oz: Reading Australian Popular Culture*. Boston: Allen & Unwin.

Fry, T., and A. Willis 1989 Aboriginal Art: Symptom or Success? *Art in America* 77 (July):109–117, 159–160, 163.

Hamilton, Annette 1990 Fear and Desire: Aborigines, Asians and the National Imaginary. *Australian Cultural History* (July).

Hughes, R. 1988 Evoking the Spirit Ancestors. *Time*, 31 October:79–80.

Isaacs, J. 1987 Waiting for the Mob from Balgo. *Australian and International Art Monthly*, June:20–22.

Jameson, F. 1984 Postmodernism: or, the Cultural Logic of Late Capital. *New Left Review* 146:53–93.

Keneally, T. 1988 Dreamscapes: Acrylics Lend New Life to an Ancient Art of Australian Desert. *New York Times Sunday Magazine*, vol. 138, 13 November:52.

Kent, S. 1987 A Burst of Colour in the Western Desert. *Sydney Morning Herald*, 11 July:48.

Larson, K. 1988 Their Brilliant Careers. *New York Magazine*, 4 October:148–150.

Lash, S., and J. Urry 1987 *The End of Organized Capitalism*. Madison: University of Wisconsin Press.

Marcus, G., and M. Fischer 1986 *Anthropology as Cultural Critique*. Chicago: University of Chicago Press.

Meyrowitz, J. 1985 *No Sense of Place: The Impact of Electronic Media on Social Behavior*. New York: Oxford University Press.

Michaels, E. 1988 Bad Aboriginal Art. *Art and Text* 28:59–73.

Moore, C., and S. Muecke 1984 Racism, Aborigines and Film. *Australian Journal of Cultural Studies* 2:36–53.

Morphy, H. 1977 Too Many Meanings, Ph.D. dissertation, Department of Prehistory and Anthropology, Australian National University, Canberra.

Morton, John 1988 Black and White Totemism: Conservation, Animal Symbolism and Human Identification in Aboriginal and Non-Aboriginal Australia. Unpublished MS.

Munn, N. 1973 *Walbiri Iconography*. Ithaca, N.Y.: Cornell University Press.

Myers, F. 1986 *Pintupi Country, Pintupi Self: Sentiment, Place, and Politics among Western Desert Aborigines*. Washington, D.C. and Canberra: Smithsonian Institution Press and Aboriginal Studies Press.

—— 1988 Locating Ethnographic Practice: Romance, Reality and Politics in the Outback. *American Ethnologist* 15:609–624.

—— 1989 Truth, Beauty and Pintupi Painting. *Visual Anthropology* 2:163–195.

Nairne, S., Geoff Dunlop, and John Wyver 1987 *State of the Art*. London: Chatto and Windus.

Pekarik, A. 1988 Journeys in the Dreamtime. *World Archaeology*. Nov.–Dec.:46–52.

Price, Sally 1989 *Primitive Art in Civilized Places*. Chicago: University of Chicago Press.

Rankin-Reid, J. 1989 Colonial Foreplay. *Artscribe International*, Sept.–Oct.:12–13.

Sansom, B. 1980 *The Camp at Wallaby Cross*. Canberra: Australian Institute of Aboriginal Studies.

Schjeldahl, P. 1988 Patronizing Primitives. *7 Days*, November 16:13–15.

Smith, R. 1988 From Alien to Familiar. *The New York Times*, 16 December:C32.

Strehlow, T. G. H. 1947 *Aranda Traditions*. Melbourne: Melbourne University Press.

Stretton, R. 1987 Aboriginal Art on the Move. *The Weekend Australian*, 5–6 September:32.

Sturmer, J. von 1989 Aborigines, Representation, Necrophilia. *Art and Text* 32:127–139.

Sutton, P., ed. 1988 *Dreamings: The Art of Aboriginal Australia*. New York: George Braziller/Asia Society Galleries.

Wallach, A. 1989 Beautiful Dreamings. *Ms.*, March:60–64.

Weber, J. 1989 Papunya Tula: Contemporary Paintings from Australia's Western Desert. In *Papunya Tula*, catalogue for show at John Weber Gallery, 25 May–17 June 1989.

Williams, Raymond 1977 *Marxism and Literature*. Oxford: Oxford University Press.

28

Aesthetics and Iconography
An Artist's Approach

Gordon Bennett

The best thing that can be done is to shoot all the blacks and manure the ground with their carcasses.

William Cox, Landowner, 1824.[1]

It is now obvious that something has to be done with the Aborigines. There cannot be one law for them and another law for the rest of Australia.

B. L. Farnik, 1992.[2]

The above two statements, quoted from Australian newspapers 168 years apart, may seem like a strange way to introduce an essay on aesthetics and iconography but, given the strong social, political and spiritual aspects of a 'classical' Aboriginal aesthetic,[3] and as I proceed with my approach to the subject, I believe that their relevance will be revealed.

First and foremost aesthetics is a rubric term with no simple universally accepted definition.[4] One dictionary gives the term's linguistic root as from the Greek: aisthetikós – perceptible by the senses, from aisthesthai to perceive.[5] Therefore it may be understood from the outset that aesthetics embodies the notion of perception; to thoroughly grasp or comprehend; to recognise a thing through the senses especially the sense of sight. Now this may seem such an obvious thing to point out, but to me it begs the question of how do we 'recognise' what we perceive?

Recognition seems to suggest having already seen a thing, it implies previous knowledge of the thing being observed, or at least an already given knowledge from which to base one's observation. Knowledge is something we gain during our lifetime. It allows us to understand the world of experience. However, knowledge is learnt experience and to be learnt it needs a vehicle for its transmission and indeed for its very structure. This vehicle is of course language.

Language is something we are all very familiar with, in fact at times it is a faculty that is so taken for granted that it seems an entirely natural phenomenon intimately and directly related to the world in which we live. In fact it becomes all too easy to make the safe and simple assumption that language is a natural inventory of the world of experience.[6] However it is not, it is never natural, as anyone who can remember the childhood experience of learning the alphabet, spelling and the structure of sentences can attest.

As a child I remember wondering when receiving demerits for the incorrect spelling of a word that I had spelt phonetically; why that spelling rather than this one? Why this sound

From *Aratjara, Art of the First Australians* (Cologne: DuMont Buchverlag, 1993), pp. 85–91.

rather than that? It was the threat of more demerits, and in the long run of physical punishment, that discouraged pressing the point too far. And so it is that as children we become socialised into a particular societal structure; a network of relationships to, and ideas about, the world that is constructed by language. Indeed, language may be seen as the cement that binds and maintains the social organisation of a particular society or cultural group.

Language defines the invisible boundaries or limits to the understanding of the world of experience. It does not constitute a natural inventory of the world, but rather language is a system of conventional and arbitrary sounds and symbols that represent the subjective human perception of it. Thus a word does not represent an object in itself, it represents the image of the object reflected in the human mind.[7] In establishing this point of a conceptual gap or 'space' between language as a representational signifying sign system, and the world of objects and sensation this system signifies or refers to, it is possible now to reintroduce the subject of aesthetics and, by extension, iconography.

Howard Morphy, in his article *From Dull to Brilliant: The Aesthetics of Spiritual Power Among the Yolngu*, Chapter 17,[8] begins by establishing some broad definitions of what aesthetics is about; they are as follows:

'Aesthetics is concerned with how something appeals to the senses, in the case of paintings with the visual effect they have on the person looking at them. An aesthetic response concerns sensations or feelings that are evoked or caused in the viewer looking at a painting – a positive emotional response, one that can be associated with feelings of pleasure, but which is not necessarily interpreted to be pleasure. An aesthetic effect may be additional to some other kind of property of an object; for example its communicating functions or practical properties. The aesthetic effect may be complementary to some other kind of property of an object or necessary to its fulfilling some other function. For example, an object may be aesthetically pleasing in order to draw a person's attention to it so that some other function may be fulfilled or message communicated. An aesthetic effect may arise out of the way some other purpose of the object is achieved; for example, through the perfect functional utility

of a chair, the simplicity of an idea or the elegance of a solution to a problem.'

These broad definitions are familiar enough to those schooled in the art practice and traditions of what may be termed a Western art perspective. Also within this perspective other notions of aesthetics exist defined by the equally broad classification of beauty. For instance we may learn to experience a sunrise or sunset as beautiful, or the play of light across water. The experience and perception of nature is often expressed as beautiful; but all of these definitions have something in common and that is that they are all manifestations of learnt experience. We learn to 'recognise' beauty when we see it. Of course there is room for disagreement within this culturally conditioned grid of classification. We may wish to argue our definition of what is beautiful over another's but ultimately it remains caught up in the system of representation that is language and thus reflects the experiential world of our particular society or language community.[9]

A person may wish to communicate a sense of nature's perceived beauty through art. As I am a painter I will restrict myself to the art of painting in particular. In order to represent a certain notion of the beauty of nature on canvas a painter uses paint in a particular way: The paint is organised into areas of colour,

Figure 28.1 Gordon Bennett: detail of *The Nine Ricochets (Fall Down Black Fella, Jump Up White Fella)*, 1990, oil and acrylic on canvas board. Private collection

areas of light to dark tones, areas of varying shapes and size in order to create a painting that is a reflection of the artist's perception of the landscape. In fact the artist draws on a set of conventional visual signs and devices to represent an essentially subjective human perception of the world. The image produced does not represent the world itself but represents the image of the world reflected in and organised by the human mind. Thus a visual sign or 'icon' may be understood as separated from the world of things by the same conceptual space as language.

The system of visual signs that constitute the iconography of a Western art tradition of representation can therefore be determined as functioning in a similar way to a language in its structuring of a visual world view. Implicit in the term 'world view', it should be noted, is the notion of ideology. Ideology, when understood as a body of ideas about the world that reflects the beliefs and interests of a cultural group or society, is reflected, maintained and reinforced by visual representation. Representation is in fact a powerful social instrument for the creation and maintenance of the world in which we live.[10] This applies equally to Australian Aboriginal societies as it does to any Western society, indeed it applies to all societies.

My sense of aesthetics is that which was nurtured and developed within the structure of a eurocentric world view. I was socialised into a Euro-Australian system of representation which included an art school education. However, my approach to aesthetics is to seek to extend my concepts of it and by extension to expand my concepts of representation.

There came a time in my life, in my sense of self and identity as an Australian, when I became aware of my Aboriginal heritage. This may seem of no consequence to the subject at hand, but when the weight of European representation of Aboriginal people as the quintessential primitive 'other' is realised, and perhaps understood as a certain level of abstraction involving a discourse of self and other with which we become familiar in our books and our classrooms but which we rarely feel on our pulses;[11] then it may be seen that such an awareness was problematic for my sense of identity. The conceptual gap between self and other collapsed and I was thrown into turmoil.

Figure 28.2 Gordon Bennett and Eugene Carchesio: *Daddy's Little Girl*, 1989, watercolour on paper. Queensland Art Gallery, Brisbane

Michel Foucault talked of a concept of 'critical community' where something 'intolerable' is found in a system of identification. It is characterised as a refusal to participate in this system of recognition and thus 'problematises' identity and makes of 'subjectivity' an open and endless question, at once individual and collective.[12]

In Australia the dominant system of identification begins with the 'discovery' of the continent by Captain James Cook. It continues with the 'exploration' and 'pioneer settlement' of a seemingly empty land. Today the 'pioneer spirit' and a 'rugged outback image'[13] are still evoked as the identity all Australians share, even though the majority of Australians live in cities in one of the most urbanised countries in the world. I do not share this identity as I once did. My approach to the iconography that sustains it is deconstructive: This is not to deny the personal hardships of those European individuals who have been romanticised, indeed mythologised as heroes of Australian history but to expose other histories, other versions of settlement, of exploration and exploitation, and other systems of identification. I wish to reinstate a sense of Aboriginal people within the culturally dominant system of representation as human beings, rather than as a visual sign that signifies the 'primitive', the 'noble savage' or some other European construct associated with black skin.

Foucault maintained that a 'resistance' to a certain identity has an analytic role, related to a truth: it exposes what a particular strategy of 'power' is. It discloses something unseen and unacceptable in a form of identification, and exposes it to risk.[14] He thought that the historical construction of identity and the passion for identification should be a central issue.[15]

In 1835, the Reverend William Yates is quoted as referring to Aborigines as: '[...] nothing better than dogs, and [...] it was no more harm to shoot them than it would be to shoot a dog when he barked at you.'[16] Within the eurocentric system of representation and identification of the Reverend Yates, and others of the period, Aborigines were positioned as nothing more than dogs. Thus it was justifiable to shoot us as we were not seen as human beings. It followed then that Aborigines had no culture, did not own the land but merely foraged as did the animals. These are all value judgements that were manifestations of the system of representation of the period, as embodied through language and iconographical sign systems.

When James Cook first set eyes on Australian shores he already had a notion of the 'primitive'; it was just a matter of 'recognition' to position Aborigines as such in his mind. Cook also has his notions of culture and of landscape as property; it was only a matter of 'recognition' to see that Aborigines had neither: And so it was that Australia was declared 'terra nullius' or empty land and became the 'property' of the English Crown.

Aboriginal cultures are among the world's most ancient and impressive cultures; incorporating a subtle, complex and rich way of life. Aboriginal cave art predates the famous cave paintings of bulls, horses and deer at Lascaux in the French Dordogne by nearly 20,000 years. Evidence suggests that Aborigines developed religious beliefs and burial practices more than ten thousand years before similar ideas began to emerge along the Nile and in the Tigris-Euphrates delta.[17] This, of course, points

to a long tradition of cultural and self representation through language and through art in the form of ceremonial dance and painting.

Aboriginal iconography is also a system of signs that represents not the world of things but again the image of the world reflected in the human mind. This system of signs cements the social organisation of Aboriginal societal structures as solidly as any European language, visual or otherwise. Therefore, given that the linguistic root of aesthetics is that which is perceptible by the senses, I would contend that the mental act of representation may be understood as an act of creative perception; and that is where the embodiment of a culture's aesthetic is located. In other words, the aesthetics of a culture are located not externally in an 'art' object, or in narrow definitions of aesthetics standards, but internally in the conceptual space between signifier and signified. As Foucault indicates – 'We should not have to refer the creative activity of someone to the kind of relation he has to himself, but

Figure 28.3 Gordon Bennett: *Self-portrait* (*Gone Primitive*), 1992, black and white photograph, plastic wrapped book, sticky tape and white cord. Courtesy Bellas Art Gallery, Brisbane

should rather relate the kind of relation he has to himself to a creative activity.'[18] In this relation a sense of 'beauty' could count as an important ethical category in how we as human beings might live. This would involve a type of critical 'passion' that would be non-racist, or anti-racist, in the particular sense that identity would not be the source of self-assertion and exclusion but the target of a questioning through which people might start to depart from the historical limits of their identifications.[19] This is not to say that identity will be lost but to say that it may be transformed, expanded to transcend narrow cultural and national boundaries of identification to encompass a sense of identity as more properly and correctly human.

This then is my approach to aesthetics at its most extreme, but within narrower definitions I locate my aesthetic approach within the more conventional notions of Western aesthetic, and iconographical traditions. My approach is however deconstructive in its orientation. I use strategies of quotation and appropriation to produce what I have called 'history' paintings. I draw on the iconographical paradigm of

Figure 28.4 Gordon Bennett: *Australian Icon (Notes on Perception N1)*, 1989, oil and acrylic on paper

Australian, and by extension European, art in a way that constitutes a kind of ethnographic investigation of a Euro-Australian system of representation in general, but which has focussed on the representation of Aboriginal people in particular.

I foreground the use of perspective as fundamental to an eurocentric world view. As the foundation of a system of representation, perspective produces an illusion of depth on an essentially flat two dimensional surface by the use of invisible lines that converge to a vanishing point. The vanishing point may also be understood as the point from which these lines extend outward past the picture plane to include the viewer in the pictorial space; positioned as observer of a self-contained harmonious whole.

'Perspective has been called a systematic abstraction from the structure of [...] psycho-physiological space.'[20] In its positioning of the viewer and in relation to the horizon, line perspective may be seen as symbolic of a certain kind of power structure relating to a particular European world view. The viewer is placed in a position of centrality to an ordered array of phenomena which is rendered completely visible in a compressed symbolic configuration; particular inflections of knowledge are indexed allowing comparison, distinction, contrast and variation to be instantly legible.[21] It is an ideological fabrication, a powerful format of representation fixing relationships by which individuals represent themselves in their world of objects, their signifying universe, both a mirror of the world and a mirror of the self.[22] Aborigines caught in this system of representation remain 'frozen' as objects within the mapped territory of a European perceptual grid.

It has been said of Aboriginal art of the Western Desert that it produces a finite design by subtraction – even quotation – from a potentially infinite grid of connected places/'Dreamings'/ people, in which real spatial relationships are literally rectified and represented.[23] My approach to quotation within the European tradition is to select images from Euro-Australian art history, that have accumulated certain meaning over time, placing them in new relationships to other images. The images I select exist between the pages of art books and history books. Their unifying factor is the dot screen of their photomechanical reproduction and their iconographical relationships as points of reference on the Western cultural perceptual grid. By recontextualising images subtracted from this grid of Euro-Australian 'self' representation I attempt to show the constructed nature of history and of identification as arbitrary, not fixed or natural but open to new possibilities of meaning and of identification.

In a sense then, this strategy can be understood as Aboriginal in firstly its subtraction, quotation from a potentially infinite grid of points or 'sites' of identification; and secondly in its exposure of the fact that images, as iconographical sites of reference, can have different meanings in different contexts. It has been established elsewhere that Western Desert artists employ a basic set of iconographical symbols such as curved and straight lines, concentric circles and dots which all have multiple meanings depending upon their context.[24]

My use of dots in some works, apart from their aesthetic potential, is in one aspect a reference to the unifying dot matrix of photographic reproduction and in another sense it is Aboriginal referential in the dot's relationship to the unifying space between cultural sites of identification in a landscape that is not experienced as separate from the individual, but as an artifact of intellect. In traditional Aboriginal thought there is no nature without culture, just as there is no contrast either of a domesticated landscape with wilderness or of an interior scene with an expansive 'outside' beyond four walls.[25] This notion led me to conceive of the eurocentric perceptual grid, with its sites of iconographical signification, as a kind of landscape of the mind – a psycho-topographical map where sites, located in memory, represent the subjective human identification with the perceptual world.

By recontextualising images or fragments of images in particular relationships I hope to create a certain turbulence in the complacent sense of identification with popular history. I desire to create a kind of chaos of identification where new possibilities for signification in representation can arise. This is an extended concept of art and of aesthetics in the sense of Foucault's notion of the kind of relation we have to ourselves as being a creative activity as put forward earlier. Furthermore, in this way, new relationships to others may be forged by the insights gained from the understanding and perception of 'nuance' that exists between any hard-and-fast definitions of identification.

Thus I have returned to the approach to aesthetics that interests me most of all, which may be termed life as art. In this art the aesthetic locus lies in the creative perception of nuance in the world that lies in between predetermined categories of thought and historically constructed identities. It is the art of a beautiful life or the ancient notion of a noble existence. An art of being or of making oneself free, in the sense of questioning the ways our own history defines us.[26]

My approach to iconography can best be expressed as an allegorical approach where images as sites of historical meaning are fragmented and recontextualised to form new relationships and possibilities for the generation of nuance. The conceptual gap between

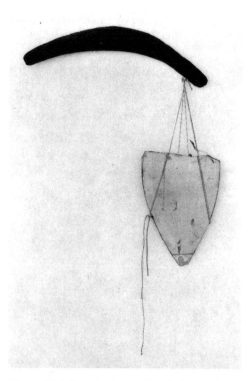

Figure 28.5 Joseph Beuys: *Untitled (Bumerang mit Spiegel)*, 1982, Australian boomerang, broken piece of mirror, string. Estate of Joseph Beuys

signifier and signified becomes most apparent in allegory and the real aesthetic enjoyment lies in the experience of interpretation, in the nuance of possible meanings.

In conclusion then, these approaches could be dismissed as utopian, and I would agree that they are utopian in focus but only in the literal sense of the word as 'no place', for if utopia were to come into existence it would be a stagnant and sterile environment, and that is never desirable. The path to 'no place' is one of attitude, a sensitivity to nuance and the possibilities of evolution toward a kind of ecological awareness in thought, and therefore in action. However, it is the path that is the key and not any final destination.

Perhaps this sense of attitude could be expressed in a less ideological way by referring to a work which, at the time of writing, is still in the early stages of development. It is to be constructed around a text that perhaps sums up my approach to aesthetics and iconography quite simply. The text is as follows:

I am trying to paint the one painting that will change the world, before which even the most narrow minded and rabid racists will fall to their knees in profound awareness and spiritual openness thus recognising their own stupidity, at once transcending it to become [...] Of course this is in itself stupid and I am a fool, but I think to myself, what have I got to lose by trying?

The unexamined Life is not worth living.
Socrates

NOTES

1   B. Elder, *Blood on the Wattle. Massacres and Maltreatment of Australian Aborigines Since 1788*, n.p./Australia 1988, p. 42.

2   Letter to the editor, *The Courier Mail*, a Brisbane based Queensland newspaper, February 7, 1992.

3   See Cat. Exh. *Dreamings: The Art of Aboriginal Australia*, ed. P. Sutton, Ringwood 1988, p. 8.

4   See H. Morphy, 'From Dull to Brilliant: The Aesthetics of Spiritual Power Among the Yolngu', in: *Man*, vol. 24 (no. 1)/ 1989, pp. 21–22 [p. 302 in this volume].

5   See *Collins English Dictionary,* ed. H. Collins, Glasgow 1991.

6   See D. Preziosi, *Rethinking Art History: Meditations on a Coy Science*, New Haven and London 1989, p. 97.

7   Ibid., p. 98.

8   H. Morphy, 1989, pp. 21–22 [p. 302 in this volume].

9   See D. Preziosi, 1989, p. 97.

10 Ibid., p. 49.

11 See M. Torgovnick, *Gone Primitive: Savage Intellects, Modern Lives*, Chicago and London 1990, p. 14.

12 See J. Rajchman, *Truth and Eros: Foucault, Lacan and the Question of Ethics*, New York and London 1991, p. 102.

13 Stanthorpe Art Gallery Society Incorporated in a pamphlet advertising the Stanthorpe Heritage Arts Festival held in February 1992. The major sponsor is the Heritage Building Society which is a Southern Queensland Finance and Investment company. Stanthorpe is a medium to large township situated close to the New South Wales/Queensland border. It is a major agricultural centre of the region.

14 See J. Rajchman, 1991, p. 102.

15 Ibid., p. 108.

16 B. Elder, 1988, p. 9.

17 Ibid., p. 199.

18 J. Rajchman, 1991, p. 98.

19 Ibid., p. 108.

20 See W.J.T. Mitchell, 'The Pictorial Turn', in: *Art Forum*, vol. 30 (No. 3)/1992, p. 91: in referring to the 1924 essay 'Perspective as Symbolic Form', by Erwin Panofsky.

21 See D. Preziosi, 1989, p. 66.

22 Ibid., p. 68.

23 See Cat. Exh. *Dreamings*, 1988, p. 84.

24 Ibid., p. 91.

25 Ibid., p. 18.

26 See John Rajchman, 1991, p. 109.

29

Kinds of Knowing

Charlotte Townsend-Gault

[Introduction, 2005]

An essay written for the catalogue of an exhibition – *Land, Spirit, Power: First Nations at the National Gallery of Canada* – needs to be set in its historical moment. 1992: the Columbus quincentenary was being widely de-celebrated in Native North America. In Canada, the "previously existing aboriginal rights" that had been recognised in the 1982 Constitution as existing prior to the foundation of Canada in 1867, were being asserted with increasing confidence. Native "art", contentious as the term remains, was proliferating and diversifying, being collected and commoditised. And its double history in a nation both colonised and colonising was becoming apparent. Indigenous cultural production had long been foregrounded as a spectacle for all to see, the focus of positivist and ocularcentric attention, to be collected, classified or confiscated by the fascinated and the fearful. It maintained another historic role as disguise, indigenous knowledge as impenetrable mystery, knowledge withheld, to be protected, and always political by virtue of its protection. It is, to co-opt Carl Beam's title for the first work by a native artist to be purchased by the National Gallery in 1986, at the tip of what should be understood disturbingly as *The North American Iceberg*.

The moment had arrived for the National Gallery to respond. It was also responding, by doing something different, to controversial recent exhibitions such as *Primitivism in 20th Century Art: Affinity of the Tribal and the Modern* (1984) and *Les Magiciens de la Terre* (1989). By being exclusively native *and* contemporary, it was "a symbolic first", as the senior Chipewayan artist Alex Janvier insisted. Furthermore it would have been unthinkable in the National Gallery in Washington, as Truman Lowe and James Luna pointed out. The three curators Robert Houle, Saulteaux artist, Diana Nemiroff, curator of contemporary art at the National Gallery, and the writer, anthropologist and art historian, could not but position the exhibition at the confluence of discrepant regimes of value. Houle asserted uncompromisingly in his essay for the catalogue that contemporary native art is part of *The Spiritual Legacy of the Ancient Ones* (1992). The history of the division of responsibility between the Canadian Museum of Civilization and the National Gallery of Art that reproduced Canada's version of the art/ethnology divide was set out in Nemiroff's essay.

Partly in response to what we were being told by artists on our journeys around North America, partly in the name of the autonomy of art on which the Gallery's operation is

From Diana Nemiroff, Robert Houle, and Charlotte Townsend-Gault, *Land, Spirit, Power: First Nations at the National Gallery of Canada* (Ottawa: National Gallery of Canada, 1992), pp. 76–101. Reprinted by permission of the National Gallery of Canada.

predicated, partly as an act of social justice, we made choices as though there were no significant distinctions between work made for community use or that made to be displayed and sold in an art gallery, or between traditional procedures and those learned at art school, while eliding the historical differences between the geographical and cultural regions of the continent. Also ignored was the contradiction in the hospitality of the National Gallery – federal institution – to the fierce critique of the federal government's handling of the recent Oka crisis in the film of Alanis Obomsawin in its smouldering incomplete version.

Without the kind of legitimizing that historical pieces might have conferred, the point was not to represent them as social texts, even though the works in the exhibition articulated many of the nervy debates that were going on elsewhere, within anthropology for example: rights over cultural knowledge, ethnic difference, reception ethics. That they were new, politically disruptive, transgressive of the orthodoxies, compelled avant-garde attention. But righteousness on all sides, and the social economy of the market ended that. At the time responses varied: *Land, Spirit, Power* was a symbolic triumph, another barrier breached, validation through acceptance by the highest art authority in the land. Alternatively, it was a spectacular co-optation and act of insincerity on all sides, native cultures forfeiting their claim to difference, and the institution compromising its grounds for judgement. The jury is still out.

Original

Does the very disparate art in *Land, Spirit, Power* have anything in common? Or, to phrase a vexed question another way, is there anything "different" about First Nations art now that it has found its place in the field of contemporary art?

You do not have to be an anthropologist to answer that the difference is cultural, nor an art expert to realise that cultural difference is also the reason why aboriginal art has been out of the field for so long. But you do have to be an artist of native ancestry to make the kinds of daring and inventive transformations of knowledge specific to given cultures that are evident in the exhibition. As someone who has

some knowledge of both anthropology and art, I see these transformations as so many ways of maintaining and recovering control of culturally specific knowledge – of the language, mythology, history, the rules and their every nuance – which are fully comprehensible only to those who live them, a way of knowing that is both exhilarating and profoundly challenging to the outside observer.

Evidence of this way of knowing can be found in much of the art made over the last decade by artists of native ancestry across North America. It may form the substance of the work, it may be the source of its critical intent, it may be both. Although *Land, Spirit, Power* does not attempt to represent fully the diversity of North American native cultural expression, the works in the exhibition are representative of the search for ways to translate, transform, re-invent, protect, and sometimes obscure the knowledge that is integral to these cultures. An important manifestation of this different way of knowing appears in the artists' working through of their spiritual relationship to land, to show that "land" and "spirit" are not really separate terms. Yet theirs is not some diffuse and generalised spirituality, but is very specific and locally rooted. Their explorations are done in ways that position the artists within the [troubled] discourse of postmodern art [or, as many would prefer, assert the viability of alternate modernisms]. In articulating their ideas, verbal as well as visual (which have shaped this essay), they illumine important aspects of the discourse, not by reproducing prevailing definitions, but by constructing them rather differently. They also position them within the much broader reach for cultural and political power currently being made by native groups across North America.

The power contained in knowing was unequivocally stated by Ovide Mercredi, the National Chief of the Assembly of First Nations, who put knowledge – knowledge of First Nations' distinctiveness, their difference – foremost on his agenda at a 1992 conference of Canadian First Ministers. In demanding acknowledgment of a difference that the colonial relationship had failed to recognise, Mercredi was establishing a position from which to counteract the ignorance and prejudice that has resulted.

This is an idea that takes many forms, and it has a history. A passage from the Two Row

Wampum Treaty of the Six Nations, which was ratified by *Gus-wen-tah*, a mid-sixteenth century wampum belt (figure 29.1), reads:

These two rows will symbolize two paths or two vessels, travelling down the same rivers together. One, a birch bark canoe, will be for the Indian people, their laws, their customs and their ways. The other, a ship, will be for the white people and their laws, their customs and ways. We shall each travel the river together, side by side, but in our own boat. Neither of us will try to steer the other's boat.[1]

The passage underlines a concept fundamental to understanding cultural racism, a form of racism that cannot even be identified when the fact of cultural difference is denied. "The ways in which minorities are stereotyped, marginalised and allowed to succeed only where they pay the price of disowning their origins, is much more to do with rejection on the basis of (mis)perceived culture than biology," according to cultural analyst Tariq Modood.[2] It may seem paradoxical that egalitarians have to emphasise what they would like to overlook, since difference can be so divisive.

Within this discussion, the contributions of artists have a special importance. James Lavadour has said: "Art has a use as a force vital to society – in this way it is recovering its aboriginal function...Art shouldn't be an homogenising force worldwide, but be generative and illuminative in specific ways."[3] In Canada, particularly today, cultural knowledge is being used by First Nations representatives, both politicians and artists, to resist misperceptions

and reshape their own social world[4] (a situation with contemporary parallels among marginalised communities in other parts of the world, such as Chile[5]).

To appreciate what it is that the artists contribute to the taking of cultural power, it must be pointed out that the knowledge which First Nations people hold about themselves and their cultures has been obscured for too long by another kind of knowledge constructed about Indians by others. There is a place where aboriginal knowledge is used to contest this historical misconstruction and misrepresentation. It is a place where the first is lived, researched, re-invented, and the latter critiqued, deconstructed, exposed. Where, however, even if it is recognised that there are irreconcilable differences between the two, one cannot be jettisoned in favour of the other. It is the space in which artists, involved themselves, usually with some irony, in the latter, seek to reclaim the former. A space where the cultural knowledge that governed the making and use of medicine bundles, of masks, of parfleches and talking sticks, and the history that has purloined and labelled and enclosed them in museum vitrines, are both locked into a present politics of representation. Artists are among the many who are implicated in the discourse wherein the politics is engaged.

One of the more agreed-upon defining characteristics of postmodernism is its querying of reference, of how one thing can confidently be thought to stand for something else, of how signs signify, of the ways in which works of art refer. One of the tenets of that discourse

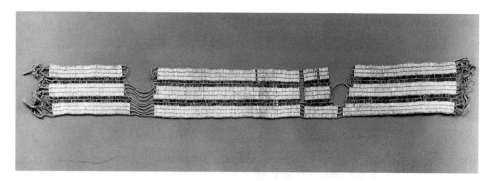

Figure 29.1 Gus-wen-tah – Two-Row Wampum Belt. The earliest known written reference to Gus-wen-tah was in the Treaty of Fort Albany, September 1664, with the Dutch. There were copies made in the 1700s. Woodland Cultural Centre, Brantford, Ontario

derives from social philosopher Jean Baudrillard's view that mass representation has perverted reality, producing a simulacrum of the real [so that the "real" is no longer real].[6] The perversion has furthermore infected the discourse of art, which cannot depend on reliable systems of representation; nor, therefore, can it subvert them – essentially what the inventions of modernism depended on. Indeed, Carl Beam, Jane Ash Poitras, and Jaune Quick-to-See Smith are among the many native artists whose work has been about exactly this, as they juxtapose signs of diverse origin, as if to enquire whether the technique can point up new meanings.

[The potentially disruptive practice of native artists, and its fascinated reception, can be taken to be one of] the disjunctures of contemporary culture [as represented by Jean Francois Lyotard, Fredric Jameson and Donna Haraway amongst others. Yet native art suffers, along with these social theorists, if it is thereby seen as prone] to the idealist notion that there can be, should be, or ever has been, a perfect mesh between form and meaning, between signifier and signified. Cultural theorist Linda Hutcheon, who has written on postmodernism, specifically in its manifestations in Canadian culture, states: "There is nothing natural about the 'real' and there never was – even before the existence of mass media."[7] This caution is doubly necessary in the age of the New Age, with its blandishments based on the idea of an Eden of perfect congruence, and the persistent belief that there is some necessary connection between aboriginal culture and a more natural way of knowing. Another form of idealism is at work in the notion that what is required is simply a peeling away of the distortions created by the lamentable history of misrepresentation to reveal a true, or historically pure, reality. This has been one of the staples of the definition of "primitive" upon which rights to superior power for the "civilised" were erected.[8] It meets the non-native observer's need to believe in the possibility of an earthly paradise, to romance the *other* and the *other's* meaning, to identify something "Indian" and "authentic." A swift corrective is offered in native museum director and lawyer Dick West's brisk: "I was born in a TV not a tipi."[9]

How First Nations artists choose to represent themselves, and how they contest the representations of others in a world of cultural disjuncture, fall centrally into what it is that the postmodern queries. There may be little agreement on how to define it, and too much generalising social metaphysics, but what is useful is the querying of signification, because we need to ask to what extent "meaning" depends on cultural difference. In my observation, aboriginal discourse does not seem to be lost in a morass of freely floating signifiers; rather, it appears to be able to replace this condition with one of a determined responsibility. It is as though First Nations artists, having access to what the French sociologist Pierre Bourdieu has called "symbolic capital"[10] – their cultural knowledge – have determined to invest it for the benefit of quite distinct audiences. They are in a position to take advantage of the permissions opened up by certain aspects of the postmodern discourse, and then to stop. To stop, that is, before they reach the paradoxes of the deconstructive process eating its own tail, the contortions of Western rationality trying to critique itself, or the point at which, as Jimmie Durham puts it, postmodernism, with its indiscriminate attention to everything and nothing, becomes "just another lock-out."[11] Given a set of circumstances, historical and political, these artists are making a space for themselves; challenging the colonial discourse, they undermine the authority of the signs that constitute its knowledge, and reassert the authority of the signs of their own rightful knowledge.

The situation is far too complex for their task to be a matter of the simple recovery of some "ancient" knowledge, with which these representations can have perfect congruence (figure 29.2). They reclaim, not some absolute knowledge, but their right to work with these now synthetic knowledges in a shared "reality," where such work is a way of "really dealing with a lot of the pain and suffering involved in not being able to really act in your reality, or in your landscape,"[12] as Carl Beam refers to his own struggle with the "real" and the "represented." In the same way, Faye HeavyShield depends on an understanding of arrowheads for the Blood, Teresa Marshall on the cosmological significance of the turtle for the Micmac, and Truman Lowe on the spirituality of wood for the Winnebago, while in Kay WalkingStick's series *Chief Joseph*, the power

Figure 29.2 City Hall, Prince Rupert, British Columbia. Partial view showing Northwest Coast motif by unknown Tsimshian artist. Built in 1938 by architect Max Downing as a federal building, this became City Hall in 1964. The meaning of representation, here in the Tsimshian designs, can be, literally, transformed as different kinds of knowledge work together. Lynne M. Hill, Department of Economic Development and Tourism, City of Prince Rupert, British Columbia

of the bow is drawn upon repeatedly to pay tribute to a great chief. Such substances, objects, events, hold meaning for people inasmuch as they represent and encapsulate a system of beliefs, an ideology. They are the symbolic capital, amassed in both the past *and* the present. The artists are responsible for the synthesizing and are not victimised by it; they are able to hold some sets of signification in question while asserting others. The stripped willow withes in many of Lowe's sculptures reference the waterways where the artist paddles his canoe to recover another way of moving through, that is, of *knowing*, the land. Lowe says: "I am interested in finding that point in time when 'history' stops and 'myth' begins. It is the time when a family's history leaves the page or the tribal record and becomes legendary. That realm approaches art. Then you begin to assemble images from somewhere in the deep recesses of your memory or that of an ancestor's mind."[13] Robert Davidson and Dorothy Grant transmit some of the "meaning" of the Haida ceremonial blanket, worn at potlatches and naming ceremonies, into a non-ceremonial context. *Seven Ravens* was "danced" (before it was framed for its own protection), and its story remains in-

separable from the appliquéd forms, even in an art gallery.

The specificity of pieces like these evades the diffuse mystifications of a universal artistic shamanism based on the psychic unity of humanity, which was the premise around which the exhibition *Magiciens de la Terre*,[14] held in Paris in 1989, was organised. Such exhibitions tend to weaken the very aboriginal identity that they are, with all good intention, attempting to strengthen and celebrate. Specific meanings contest the open season on all systems of signification, and the patronising permissiveness of postmodern pluralism, which has replaced, in turn, a patronising primitivising born out of romanticism and guilt.

This is not at all to imply that there is a genre of contemporary art that can be labelled "Indian," or even aboriginal. Such a notion has served a trivialising purpose in past history, as tokens of "Indianness," for example, have been seen as the authenticating factor; has had an economic use, in making works marketable to non-native audiences as curiosities or worse; and even a culturally destructive one, in delimiting the bounds of the authentic.[15] Yet it is not in "Indianness" that the difference lies. Rather, it lies in the fact that the histories, conflicts, and subjugations of aboriginal peoples, which cannot be generalised across North America, are as integral to the work of native artists as their work is integral to their participation in a community with aims far beyond that of art world accreditation. Acceptance from the latter, by authorising, gives one kind of power to the work, but it is far from being the only power it commands. These are not commentaries on socio-political issues that can be "read off" in any simple way, nor can they be best understood as art-with-a-message. These artists are making interventions into some of the most daunting ethical and epistemological issues of our shared time and space, including whether our ideas of that time and space are in fact commensurate and therefore can be shared.[16]

Knowing Difference: "It Was Made for Its Own Sake"

The history of the construction of knowledge of and about indigenous peoples is the history of the exercise of power. The duplicity and complicity involved in the colonial relationship has resulted in a situation of "dependency, coercion and domination," historian Bruce Trigger's dismal trilogy of the effects of colonialism.[17] Those who intruded upon, surveyed, and settled North America wielded intellectual, personal, administrative, and military powers that they seldom doubted were superior to, and more enduring than, the powers of those upon whom they imposed.

It is, however, not possible to generalise about a continent, nor is it simply a matter of tracing the history of the exercise of *force majeure*. The intruders were not "Europeans," but Basque whalers, West Country English fishermen, Dutch traders, and French missionaries whose "different natures and purposes"[18] meant that they established different relationships with the inhabitants. Generalised indictments against Europeans miss this point. Furthermore, in stressing the persistence of separate and distinct forms of knowledge and of constructing reality of inhabitants and settlers, it should not be forgotten that a symbiotic relationship between the two has existed now for five hundred years. It might also be observed that, in human affairs, "there is a case for coexistence effectively depending on mutual misunderstanding," a statement that in no way judges the quality of that coexistence.[19]

Many aboriginal groups at first welcomed the visitors, having things to teach, as well as to trade with them, and situations of mutual dependency developed out of commercial relationships and military alliances. Nevertheless, there are generalisations about the European societies from which "settlers" have emanated since the sixteenth century that help to account for the history of difference that persists to the present. The Canadian historian J. R. Miller explains that these societies "were highly stratified and their governments were coercive in nature. In all the Western European states there was a well-established hierarchy of nobles, gentry, burghers, and common people. Though those of higher rank could have obligations to the less fortunate, individualism was more deeply ingrained among them than it was among the peoples of North America ... European countries were not just structured societies and authoritarian polities; they were also acquisitive economies."[20]

Carl Beam has synopsized this as "Man shall have dominion over the beasts and all the little fishes, and the clams, the lobsters, water and trees; everything was made for man's usage." In contrast, he says:

> The Indian viewpoint is that it was made for its own sake; man has to live in accordance with that structure. One system believes that you are a part of everything, and one says that you are *on top* of everything, and everything is there for your use – everything else is *lower.* The hierarchy is already set up. You are it, man! The world is yours! You just have to go out there and harvest everything! The sheep and cows and all the good wine, the cigarettes, the real estate – all the prime waterfront footage – it's all yours. The trees and water – if you want to dump all your chemicals in there you can just go ahead. Who else would lay claim to all of that, other than man, anyway?[21]

In fact, the earliest accounts show Europeans grappling not with difference but with similitude. Most of those who wrote about the so-called New World, the historians and theologians, were searching for ways to incorporate their "discoveries" into their own existing conceptual frameworks. The reports, diaries, logs, and letters were intended for a readership somewhere else. As Anthony Pagden, the historian of those who thought they had discovered America, reminds us, "the distance between the kind of explanatory accounts of Indian behaviour current in the sixteenth century and those which had come into use in the eighteenth must be measured in terms of historical changes which had little or nothing to do with the presence of the real world of America."[22] It is anachronistic to judge them by current standards of "objective" accuracy. According to historian and philosopher Michel Foucault, it was not until the early seventeenth century that attempts were made to classify and describe difference and discontinuity.[23] However, the experimental scientific methods of the eighteenth century were crucial to the development of the discipline of anthropology, which, systematically and for the first time, did attempt to deal with Pagden's "real world of America."

The results were, and are, complex and morally ambiguous. Some part of the anthropological project has undoubtedly contributed to the construction of "Indianness," a concept which rivals that of "Orientalism" as an artifact of Eurocentrism. Anthropology, until very recently, has been part of an all-white history of the *other*. At times the whole enterprise has been seen as nothing more than a scapegoat for all the errors of colonial discourse.[24] But anthropology can be defended: its practitioners have always known both that there were things it could not know, and that there were things accessible to its researches worth finding out. Among the more notable recording projects in North America was the publication, started in 1852 by the Smithsonian Institution, and continued by the Bureau of American Ethnology, of a long series of anthropological texts, many of them verbatim transcripts. Certain volumes preserve important parts of Haida oral literature, notably the words of John Sky and Walter McGregor, as collected by Swanton.[25] Others constitute a record of Tsimshian and [Kwakwaka'wakw] mythology, much of the latter collected under the direction of Franz Boas by George Hunt, his native informant. Boas's record of the fishing grounds of [Kwakwaka'wakw] *numayms* has been used to confirm contemporary rights. This was not "salvage anthropology,"[26] as it has been dismissively termed, but [an attempt, at] preservation, followed in some cases by a synthesizing that made the world of the native more accessible

than it had been to the immigrant population. For example, it was an anthropologist, Diamond Jenness, who observed, in 1930 when such a perception would have been a revelation to his readers, that, for the Indian, "all objects have life, and life is synonymous with power, which may be directed for the Indians' good or ill. Just as man's power comes from his soul, or his intelligence, so does the power of the animal, tree, and stone. Therefore the Indians should treat with the respect befitting [it] a thing that has a soul and an image not unlike his own."[27]

Similarly, Ruth Benedict, the American anthropologist, was one of the first to promote the non-Eurocentric and non-hierarchical idea that a culture could only be understood in its own terms, and not through comparison, favourable or unfavourable, with any other. Ironically, *Patterns of Culture*, her very influential book published in 1934, did in fact allow for, even encourage, exactly this, giving contemporary North American society grounds to compare itself unfavourably with the cultures discussed, among them the Kwagiulth.

However, as historian Robert Berkhofer points out in *The White Man's Indian*, while shaking ethnocentric assumptions of centuries, Benedict did not question "the basic moral and intellectual assumption of the idea of culture itself"[28] – a concept which has only been queried in the last decades. Since the publication of *Patterns of Culture*, the focus in anthropology has shifted from a search for functioning systems, social control mechanisms, and static ideological maps to the study of non-order and of the dynamic parts of society – the indeterminate and marginal – with an appreciation of the essentially compromised position of the "objective" outside observer. It is only very recently that an anthropologist has been able to point out that, "what are opposed in conflict ... are not the same societies at different stages of development, but different societies facing each other at the same Time."[29]

In fact, anthropology has a particularly self-conscious contribution to make to the discourse on discourse, having been implicated in, and having collected, discourse itself for decades. Anthropologists, responsible for some of the best informed and most subtle interpretations of culture extant, are having to concede that, along with other intellectual schemas such as cultural theory and textual criticism, even a self-reflexive anthropology must perforce use one form of knowledge to approach and frame another. What persists is the attempt to focus on what differentiates one society from another, its specificity.

This stance differs markedly from the one based on a non-specific, diffuse, and generalised understanding that has sufficed for many modernists interested in alien cultures, and that is apparent in the records of twentieth century art. Artist Henry Moore voiced a widespread view when he wrote in 1941 that, "to understand and appreciate [primitive art], it is more important to look at it than to learn the history of primitive peoples, their religion and social customs...all that is really needed is response to the carvings themselves, which have a constant life of their own, independent of whenever and however they came to be made."[30] The exhibition *"Primitivism" in 20th Century Art: Affinities between the Tribal and the Modern* at the Museum of Modern Art in New York in 1984 has come to be seen as the classic exercise of this approach (figure 29.3).

Ron Hamilton, the Nuu-chah-nulth poet, scholar, and artist, has a clear position on this:

> Lately the rule is, "Don't interpret!"
> It's all art now.
> But that's an interpretation,
> Not ours.[31]

What the First Nations are up against is thus not only such romantic but hopeless representations as the paintings of Paul Kane or George Catlin, or the photographs of Edward Curtis, or, on the West Coast, Emily Carr's now canonical rendering of the native/nature relationship, but the legacy of a misrepresented history, and of representations that have successively conceived of culture as organism, as language, and as text, and which have all been prey to intellectual fashions. Marcia Crosby, Haida/Tsimshian scholar, expressed this predicament in a widely-consulted article "The Construction of the Imaginary Indian."[32] All habitually treat natives "more like props than like actors."[33]

Making History: "This Is Not New Jersey"

> Some are being made by history
> Some are "making" history.
> (Ron Hamilton)

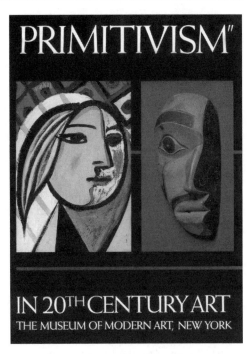

Figure 29.3 Jacket cover of *"Primitivism" in 20th Century Art*, showing a detail of *Girl Before a Mirror* by Pablo Picasso, Museum of Modern Art, New York, and *Mask Kwakiutl*, Museum für Völkerkunde, Berlin. The Museum of Modern Art, New York

How then is history to be re-told, the misrepresentations re-presented, the knowledge restored? In the work and words of the artists in this exhibition, representative of many others, certain recurrent themes and shared strategies emerge: the recovery of history, and with it the contesting of stereotypes and the restoration and reinvention of tradition; the identification of a space from which to be heard, by various audiences; a stress on local knowledge to make specific what has been generalised, to make actual what has been essentialised. And, perhaps most importantly, what emerges is the understanding that there is more than one kind of knowing: that there exists knowledge that can be shared, knowledge that may be intimated, and knowledge that should be withheld, to control translatability, in respect for the final untranslatability of the essence of cultural difference.

It is no longer possible, if it ever was, to account for the construction of the colonisers' knowledge within its own terms. As discussed above, the ideology upon which such a way of knowing was dependent has been exposed. The way in which that knowledge, like its objects, was acquired and exploited has come under too much critical scrutiny. Its history now is the history of its revising. Mounting what could be termed an "ethnocritique" by aboriginal peoples, the interrogation of their own misrepresentation in the inscription of history has been the driving force in the politics of representation. It is a politics that is played out in courtrooms and hearings, in classrooms and offices, as well as in museums and art galleries.

A telling example of rewriting is provided in the realisation by the Dunne-za/Cree that it was the hunting skills of their ancestors that kept the early traders alive. Chief Gerry Attachie, of the Doig River band, has talked about learning from a diary kept by Frank Beatton, who ran the Hudson's Bay Company post at Peace River in the late 1800s (where Beaver Indians had earlier made peace with Cree Indians): "In the late 1800s our people were hunting for them... that's how they survived. But... you don't read it in the paper... when I was reading the diary to our elders, I took them back, way back, and then, they remembered, when our people were hunting for early traders."[35] This kind of indebtedness is being put back into the histories, as part of a long tale of accommodation and intermarriage which counteracts the negative characterisations that suited the colonisers' purposes. This kind of retelling is providing material for a new generation of native artists.

While there were (and are) significant differences between the historical forces at work in the formation of Canada and the United States, there was an unfortunate similarity: it was referred to in the United States as Manifest Destiny, the misapprehension that a continent was there for the taking.

Jimmie Durham expresses it thus:

The Master Narrative of the United States proclaims that there were no Indians here, just wilderness. Then that the Indians were savages in need of the United States. Then that the Indians all died, unfortunately. Then, that the Indians still alive are (a) basically happy with the situation and (b) not the "real" Indians. Then, most importantly, that that is the complete story.[36]

Carl Beam puts several sides of the story under erasure as he deconstructs the systematisation of Western concepts of the natural world.[37] A work like *Plexiglas Landscape* (figure 29.4) conveys rather literally the shadowy hard-to-define relationships, the difficulty of establishing connections between conceptions of reality and their representations.

Over a long career, Alex Janvier has melded an indigenous narrative tradition, and the ancient double-curve motif, with linear pictorial conventions from both Western and Oriental art in order to tell the catastrophic story of cultural conflict.

Jane Ash Poitras elides her knowledge of early twentieth century European art with her knowledge of the educational system which came from the same place (figure 29.5). Her exposure is constructed of fragments of photographs, writing, newspaper articles, news

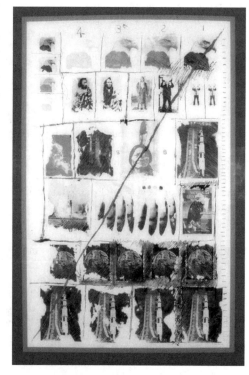

Figure 29.4 Carl Beam (b. 1943): *Plexiglas Landscape*, 1980, acrylic, photocopy transfer on plexiglas. Government of Ontario Art Collection. Thomas Moore Photography, Toronto

Figure 29.5 Jane Ash Poitras (b. 1951): *Family Blackboard*, 1989, mixed media. The Heard Museum, Phoenix, Arizona

headlines, and passages of paint knowingly applied.

In both Canada and the United States new ways of doing post-contact history are being developed – there is a move away from narratives of great battles and prominent figures such as chiefs, generals, and administrators, to social and community histories in a context of ethno-history. The ever greater intervention into this process by First Nations people, including artists, is evident in the growing number of publications devoted to native oratory, poetry, life histories, reminiscences, knowledge of the land and animals, plant use, medicines, and spiritual beliefs. It is increasingly clear that a proper attention to myth, story, and cosmol-

ogy gives the lie to a static, a-historical past, and shows that pre-Columbus North America was no more proof than the rest of the world against internal migration, contact, conflict, trade, domination, and subjugation. Origin myths may run counter to the archaeological record, but tradition and invented tradition have their own validity in terms of the construction of an identity for a people.[38]

Many artists are doing their own socio-historical research into their own families and cultures. This may take the form of learning or improving a language; of becoming a student under ritual experts; of compiling meticulously documented family albums, like George Littlechild (figure 29.6); of offering a re-

Figure 29.6 George Littlechild (b. 1958): *The Maternal Ancestry of George Littlechild*, 1992. Two pages from one of his family photograph albums, showing photos and text. Collection of the artist. Courtesy George Littlechild, Vancouver

interpretation of the ethnographies, as Colleen Cutschall has done in her series of paintings *Voice in the Blood* (figure 29.7); of monitoring the incursions made by mining and logging companies into land that belongs to aboriginal peoples, as does Lawrence Paul Yuxweluptun (figure 29.8). It may take the form of observing the daily life of the reservation – its economic, religious and interpersonal pressures – of which the work of James Luna is compelling evidence. It may replicate the social setting of a way of life now displaced, as Sak Kunuk has done in *Qaggiq* (figure 29.9); or capture the present with a movie camera as contemporary

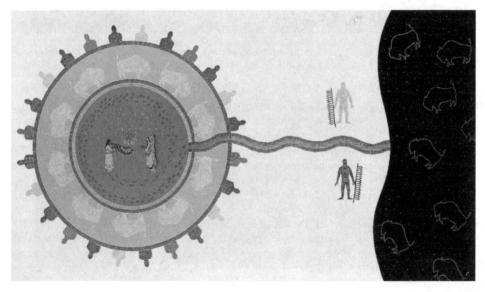

Figure 29.7 Colleen Cutschall (b. 1951): *She Is Walking in a Sacred Manner*, 1990, acrylic on canvas. Collection of Indian and Northern Affairs Visual Art Bank. Ken Fraser. Courtesy Colleen Cutschall, Brandon, Manitoba

Figure 29.8 Lawrence Paul Yuxweluptun (b. 1957): *The Protector*, 1990, acrylic on canvas. Collection of the artist

conflicts unfold, as Alanis Obomsawin did at Restigouche (figure 29.10) or Oka. All this material, and the processes of accumulating it, is inextricable from the artworks produced.

For the need to collect and preserve in order to establish cultural identity is a conscious intention, neither natural nor innocent, as anthropologist Richard Handler has observed with reference to the formation of Quebec's *patrimoine*.[39] For the First Nations, it feeds into their wider cultural project, the reintegration of disparate areas of life, and the reinstatement of many forms of aboriginal wisdom. As the Cree artist, curator, and writer Gerald McMaster says: "The more I look back at the traditions of my people the more I see that they didn't specialise."[40] And as Canadian Mohawk and director of the Institute of American Indian Art in Santa Fe, Rick Hill, extrapolates: "The interconnectedness of all Indian art is its perimeter of defence."[41]

Another form of historical imposition, that of alien names and boundaries on a map, is

uncovered in a work that Edgar Heap of Birds has installed in a number of places, including New York, Minneapolis, and Vancouver. Roadside signs reveal, by reinstating them, the names that were there first, names to which surveyors and cartographers were oblivious. They also reveal the imposed ownership. The work recalls Durham's poem "This Is Not New Jersey":

... You made the wrong turn.
This is not New Jersey and this is not the new world.
You need to get your bearings straight.
We live here and u are scaring the fish.
See, we don't call this place New Mongolia, or New Jersey.[42]

Reclaiming meaning involves, among other strategies, struggling with stereotypes – one-dimensional prototypes projected by European mythologising. Mohawk curator and historian Deborah Doxtator writes, "Non-Indian images of Indians are either at one extreme of the 'ranking' spectrum or the other – either Indians are depicted as 'savages' below Euro-Canadian 'civilization' or as 'noble savages' who are more moral, faster, stronger, kinder than any Euro-Canadian. Rarely have Indians been treated by Canadian society as equals."[43] Heap of Birds identifies some stereotypes, and they are not trivial ones, in *Telling Many Magpies, Telling Black Wolf, Telling Hachivi* (figure 29.11). Gerald McMaster's paintings set up both cowboys and Indians as fall guys in the narrative of the Wild West (figure 29.12). Richard Ray Whitman's photographic series *Street Chiefs* presents real people, in knowing opposition to the generic Indian whose costume rather than identity constitutes the classic stereotype (figure 29.13). Shelley Niro's photographs establish her own stereotypical Mohawk women: they are, unmistakably, having fun, not least at the expense of the stereotypes (figure 29.14). Such counter-stereotypes parallel the native community's efforts to oppose and gain control over the representations of "Indianness" and "Eskimoness" used by tourist boards to represent the quintessence of the Canadian and American "experience."[44]

It is, evidently, necessary to mount a defence in a world where modes of representation can themselves be the tools of predators. The view that appropriation in the arts is a

Figure 29.9 Zacharias Kunuk (b. 1957): Production still from *Qaggiq* (*Gathering Place*), 1989 (cat. 29). Zacharias Kunuk. Courtesy Igloolik Isuma Productions Inc, Igloolik, Northwest Territories

Figure 29.10 Alanis Obomsawin (b. 1932): Still from *Incident at Restigouche*, 1984 (cat. 43). *Le journal L'Aviron*, Campbellton, New Brunswick. Courtesy National Film Board of Canada

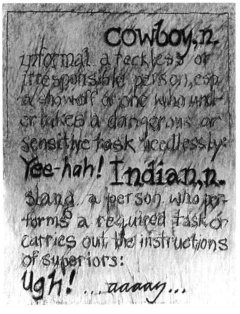

Figure 29.12 Gerald McMaster (b. 1953): *cowboy,n., Yee-hah! Indian,n., Ugh!*, 1990, acrylic on matt board. Collection of the artist. Larry Ostrom, Christie Lake Studios. Courtesy Ufundi Gallery, Ottawa

Figure 29.11 Hachivi Edgar Heap of Birds (b. 1954):*Telling Many Magpies,Telling Black Wolf, Telling Hachivi*, 1989, screenprint. Walker Art Center, Minneapolis, Walker Special Purchase Fund, 1990

form of predation is expressed by film-maker Loretta Todd:

> The valorisation of peripheral cultures is frequently undertaken through acts of cultural appropriation. In an extension of the concept of property and colonial conquest, the artists do not value or respect cultural difference, but instead seek to own difference, and with this ownership to increase their own worth. They become image barons, story conquistadors, and merchants of the exotic.[45]

Artistic appropriation has even raised questions within the native arts community. Rick Hill reported that Hopi people objected to students at the Institute of American Indian Art at Santa Fe attaching eagle feathers to their paintings. However, when appealed to, the elders approved of this reflection of sacred-

ness and saw that it was not really a challenge to the sacred things themselves. Nor were they against contemporary art.

Indeed, Domingo Cisneros skirts the issue of appropriation altogether by offering a cosmology of his own devising. He draws out a kind of power from his materials and their positioning which pays tribute to the animist philosophy of the northern culture where he, Tepehuane from Mexico, has lived for so long. In doing so, he puts signs up about his awareness of the dangers of cultural trespass.

As Teresa Marshall has written, the settler culture has "built distorted images and interpretations of Indians and Indianness that have, over the past five hundred years, supported the view of native culture as being primitive, artefactual, and collectable."[46] Her statement points to the dubious role of museums as ideological strong-boxes for the "collectable," in relation to the First Nations' struggle for control of their own history. Established museums everywhere are being challenged on their capacity to fossilise the past, to perpetuate the dubious opposition between modernity and

Figure 29.13 Richard Ray Whitman (b. 1949): *Street Chief No. 1*, 1986, silver gelatine print. Collection of the artist. Richard Ray Whitman, Norman, Oklahoma

tradition. Rather than calling for the abolition of the museum as an institution, an important part of the new move towards ethno-history has been the proliferation of local and tribal museums where displays and interpretations are directed towards specific audiences. Such museums use strategies that they share with artists and others involved in the politics of representation being played out in contemporary aboriginal culture. Among those in use at two West Coast museums, the Kwagiulth Museum and Cultural Centre at Cape Mudge and the U'mista Cultural Centre at Alert Bay, are: a deliberate redressing of the imbalances in the official telling of local history, to show that, more often, there are many histories, not necessarily linear; a disregard for, or subversion of the art/artefact or art/culture distinction as being an artificial imposition; and an intention to reach the audience to whom the things in the museum belong that surpasses any need for national or international status.[47] Most of this is summed up in comments made by Chief

Figure 29.14 Shelley Niro (b. 1954): *I Enjoy Being a Mohawk Girl*, 1991, hand-tinted photograph. Mark Marsters. Courtesy Ufundi Gallery, Ottawa

Harry Assu of Cape Mudge, in his autobiography, about the museum's role in the "reappropriation" of potlatch treasures: "It has all worked out pretty well. All our stuff that was brought back from Ottawa is in glass cases in the museum according to the family that owns them. That's what the masks and other things mean to us: family ownership. We are proud of that! It tells our family rights to the people."[48]

Localizing Strategies: "I Am Going to Speak to You"

Stand on the back of the Turtle, our mother, and look at the land and wonder what it would have been like if Columbus would have been successful in his pursuit of India and avoided the eastern shore of this continent. Wipe your Indian hands on your Levi jeans, get into your Toyota pick-up. Throw in a tape of Mozart or Led Zeppelin or ceremonial Sioux songs; then throw your head back and laugh – you are a survivor of a colonized people.[49]

Now, nearly a decade since those words were written to celebrate survival in the midst of a jumble of signs of diverse origins, their precise meanings apparently evaporated in Baudrillardian flux, it appears that, along with survival, a reliance has developed on localizing strategies, cultural specifics. Out of a meaningless pluralism, new meanings are being synthesised and controlled. Fears of continental homogenisation are thus being arrested by an insistence on differential response and different ways of constructing reality. [But it is too soon to tell whether the apparent re-arrangement of boundaries between local and global, between high and popular cultures, is not yet another mirage caused by desire for the cultural other.]

The master narratives of European-based cultures are thus currently being displaced in favour of local ones: Tlingit oratory, the teachings of the Ojibwa *midewiwin*, the revelations of the sweat lodge. Heap of Birds relates that he drove Lightning Woman, his grandmother, in his four-wheel-drive to look for hard weed – the plant with the straight, strong stem which was used to pin bison meat over the drying racks. In the text of the work *Hard Weed* (1991) he interprets the importance of this "modern herbal resource" as being that it has always "tested the knowledge, reverence and creativity of both tribe and individual."

Another way of knowing, locally, is expressed by James Luna: "I'm not interested in saving the world through my art. My first interest is working with Indian people to save themselves. The 'Rez' is the most comfortable thing

for me to make art about. I'm not a historian or a social scientist. I'm an artist and I stay close to the things I deal with every day."[50] In his installation, *Wee Wish* (figure 29.15), Luna sets out the implements used to make a traditional Luiseño dish from crushed and cooked acorns. Alongside are the implements of a modern home, food processor, vacuum cleaner, etc. A placard reads: "The Choice Is Yours" – but clearly it is not. A videotape, narrated by Adela Kolb, recounts the making of the dish, and would include the songs that her elders sang while cracking the acorns – if she knew them. This theme, of irreconcilable difference and cultural loss, could be universalised, but Luna chooses to deal with the power that resides in the objects he knows under a tight local focus.

The sweep of the bare basalt hills outside the window of James Lavadour's studio, in what used to be a church on the Umatilla reserve, is replicated in the sweep of his arm. It is the gesture that produces his paintings. He calls these gestures "events of nature." They implicate the artist with the land, not the landscape. Of the city Lavadour says, "the city is like a monster that sucks the clouds out of the sky and drinks the river. Coyote gets swallowed by the monster and chewed away inside. I went into the city. I love my work. I think it has power. There was no power, no light, in those empty rooms in the city."[51] Another implication with an "event of nature" is Lavadour's involvement with the return of the salmon to some local rivers, the result of cooperative management policies of the Riparian Zone Enhancement Project on which he works. He is passionate about his painting and about fishstocks, talking about them in the same breath and seeing both as part of the effort to restore a culture. "We've had our apocalypse – now we are going to refresh, psychologically, the whole society."[52]

If the revision of history is integral to taking control, then so is the positioning of the reviser, the claiming of the voice, and the locating of an audience.

> We are struggling to find our voice,
> The right tone, the right pitch,
> The right speed, the right code,
> The right thoughts, the right words
>
> (Ron Hamilton)[53]

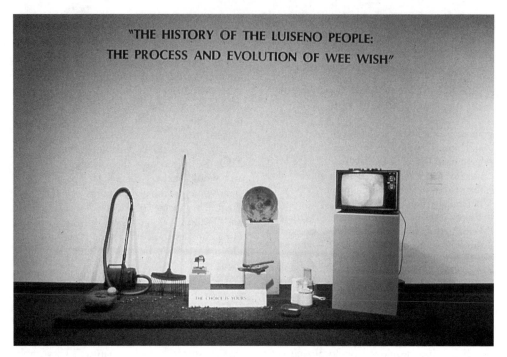

"THE HISTORY OF THE LUISENO PEOPLE:
THE PROCESS AND EVOLUTION OF WEE WISH"

Figure 29.15 James Luna (b. 1950): *The History of the Luiseño People: The Process and Evolution of Wee Wish*, 1991, installation view in the Boehm Gallery at Palomar College, San Diego. Found objects, monitor, videotape by Adela Kolb, titled *Making Wee Wish*. Collection of the artist. Courtesy James Luna, Valley Center, California

The artist Kay Miller expresses the search in another way: "I go to the edges of different cultures, all my life, and scout. But who do I report to?"[54]

And in what tone? Last autumn, in the lobby of the Holiday Inn in Ottawa, Jimmie Durham was talking about his position and the need for a Cherokee-centric view of the world. Behind him, as he talked, was a Thanksgiving display incorporating an electric toaster *circa* 1951, an iron of similar vintage, and some Mackintosh apples that were not aging well – references to a history starting solely with European immigration. Durham said: "I have decided not to be funny any more."[55]

Central to the de-colonisation project is the revival of tradition – the perceived need to perpetuate Tlingit oratory, for example, or to give expression to the relationship of the Haida individual's sense of self with the natural world. There is, however, a fine line between promoting a culture beyond its bounds and making a travesty of it, what social philosopher Homi K. Bhabha would call mimicry

– all the colonial discourse is capable of.[56] Robert Davidson is clearly one artist for whom tradition is an opportunity rather than a constraint. His collaboration with Dorothy Grant, his wife, who executes his designs in fabric, perpetuates a Haida tradition of co-operation between the roles of men and women. Grant speaks of the button blanket as a stage in the evolution of the woven ceremonial garment, from which a form such as that taken in *Seven Ravens* has evolved – in its turn, within a historical Haida context of experiments with materials and recombinant forms. For Grant and Davidson, positioning their work within a tradition is not a form of silent protest,[57] but a form of intervention.

An often-noted contradiction between pride in ethnicity and the wish to prove that one can do without it, is resolved in the realisation that, in the postmodern discourse, it is not possible to be detached from the way in which any representation is arrived at, and that includes the audience. Deconstruction of a history does not deliver the deconstructor to a privileged position from which to make comment proof against deconstruction. Infinite regress is an epistemological conundrum. The critique of forms of authority must involve a critique of one's own.

A solution, postmodern in its self-reflexivity, is offered in a piece of Tlingit metaoratory:

A person will often say
"I am going to speak to you."
Public speaking
is like a man walking up along a river
with a gaff hook.
He lets his gaff hook drift
over a salmon swimming at the edge of the river.
When he hooks on it, the salmon way over there
becomes one with him.
This is the way oratory is.
Even speech delivered at a distance
becomes one with someone.[58]

At a time of historical revisionism and the recovering of the collectivity, it has been asked whether, in discovering an individual voice, the artist forfeits the capacity to speak for the whole. Rick Hill asks whether the legitimacy of Indian art is its relationship to community; if so, does its success depend upon the closeness of that relationship? It has been pointed out by artist and theorist Jean Fisher[59] and art historian Carol Podedworny[60] that the individual stance is an alien mode of address in aboriginal society, and this is a commonly held view among non-native commentators. Anthropologist Marjorie Halpin offers a corrective:

being Native is not, as in the western culture of imaging, a matter of appearances, stereotypes, and props. It is a way of being, and a matter of shared values: respect for the family, the old, and the land. Paradoxically, perhaps, being Native is also being highly individualized – personal differences are permitted to flourish in these communities, and personal space is respected by others, to a degree unrecognized by the outsider culture.[61]

The idea that aboriginal society is communitarian at the expense of individualism does not recognise the possibilities within a discourse in which First Nations artists are able, through their specific, local, individual voices, to take control over the inscription of their own forms of knowledge – pure, impure, or synthetic as they may be. Lawrence Paul Yux-

weluptun gives as his reasons: "You can file documents and hide them away, but my paintings are too big to hide away."[62]

Yuxweluptun's taunt is echoed in Heap of Birds's statement on finding a place:

At this time the manifestation of our battle has changed. The white man shall always project himself into our lives using information that is provided by learning institutions and the electronic and print media. Through these experiences the non-Indian will decide to accept or reject that the Native Americans are a unique and separate people with the mandate to maintain and strengthen indigenous rights and beliefs. Therefore we find that the survival of our people is based upon our use of expressive forms of modern communication. The insurgent messages within these forms must serve as our present day combative tactics.[63]

In 1991, Rebecca Belmore used the technology of a two-metre-wide megaphone, with thirteen First Nations voices, to develop a mode of address aimed at the ultimate audience – the earth (figure 29.16). In her own address she said:

My heart is beating like a small drum, and I hope that you mother earth can feel it. Someday I will speak to you in my language. I have watched my grandmother live very close to you, my mother the same. I have watched my grandmother show respect for all that you have given her... Although I went away and left a certain kind of closeness to you, I have gone in a kind of circle. I think I am coming back to understanding where I come from.[64]

These artists choose to participate in the art discourse where they have made a space for themselves. Yet here too it is common to hear the caution expressed by performance artist Margo Kane: "We have to beware of the tyranny of any one discourse shaping us and what we do."[65] It should be obvious that First Nations artists do not, and do not have to, speak with one voice. Nor do they have to address one audience. There are clearly several audiences among the native community. As Hill puts it, "the need for art is the need for cultural therapy, therapy through satire, with artists the true Indian satirists."[66] This reintroduces the question of multiple audiences, a notion for which modernism had little use and which

Figure 29.16 Rebecca Belmore (b. 1960): *Ayum-ee-aawach Oomama-mowan: Speaking to Their Mother*, 27 July 1991, Banff, Alberta. Patricia Deadman, Woodstock, Ontario

postmodernism can reduce to a flabby polyvocality. Carl Beam has suggested a radical redefinition: "If we get past the idea of landscape, and of environment – environment for whom? For the humans? animals? fish? If someone could just bare their soul, and allow themselves to think in those terms, all kinds of discourse might be valuable."[67]

Evidently Beam's engagement with the Western avant-grade is hardly uncritical. But then the Western avant-garde is critical of itself. Speaking of the apparently terminal inward-turning etiolation of its enterprise, social art historian T. J. Clark identified as an opposing tendency "a search for another place in the social order. Art wants to address someone, it wants something precise and extended to do; it wants resistance, it needs criteria; it will take risks in order to find them, including the risk of its own dissolution."[68] The point is that railing against the hegemony of the avant-garde, or its attenuation, or its institutionalisation, does

not need to be an end in itself for First Nations artists. It could be argued that they have precisely the criteria for which Clark calls. Yet the avant-garde is only one of the places where they belong, its audience only one of their audiences, which should make these artists proof against the probable waning in the current fashion for marginality. Durham has suggested the art audience is only concerned "if our art is about our plight."[69] But there are others out there.

The Limits of Translation: "I Refuse to Tell It"

Long ago her mother had to sing this song and so she had to grind along with it. The corn people have a song too. It is very good. I refuse to tell it.[70]

Many of the works in *Land, Spirit, Power* could be thought of as forms of translation, reaching across cultures on many different levels. They also show that this is a complex and subtle operation, and not a relatively simple matter of translation from language A to language B. It is more a matter of transforming knowledge – ontological mysteries and body language, historical representations and storytelling – in ways that are controlled by those who hold it. Knowledge is willingly being shared, but a point is reached where translation stops. This point should mark the beginning of a more broadly encompassing, necessarily humbling, appreciation of the knowledge of other cultures – of cultural difference.

Although, like Davidson and Grant, Dempsey Bob carves for his own people, he also works for a non-native audience of connoisseurs and the fascinated. One does not have to know much to know that the suave elegance of his carvings conceals as much as it reveals – essentially un-knowable to a non-Tlingit audience. Narratives recalling how the spirits were originally revealed to the clan are essential to these works, but cannot travel into a collector's home with a carving. Nor can the concept of *at.óo'w*, which is fundamental to Tlingit social structure, oral literature, and ceremonial life. *At.óo'w* cannot readily be translated into English, yet it remains the spiritual, social, and rhetorical anchor for oratory, carving, and much else[71] (figure 29.17). The limit is set not for the sake of mystification, nor as a hostile withholding for the sake of individual or group power, but it *is* set to protect a cultural power.

During an interview that Durham gave at the time of his show at Exit Art in New York, curator Jeanette Ingberman addressed the issue of translation and comprehension:

Figure 29.17 Dempsey Bob (b. 1948): Ceremonial opening of *Dempsey Bob: Tahitan-Tlingit – Carver of the Wolf Clan*, Grace Gallery, Vancouver, 24 November 1989, showing Stan Bevan wearing *Wolf-Human Forehead Mask*. Harold Demetzer, Terrace, British Columbia

Ingberman: Can you tell me what the words mean?

Durham: No. (laughs) I'll tell you, but I don't want to be answering that question to everyone that asks.

Ingberman: Obviously a lot of people who come in to see the show won't know the meaning of the Cherokee words.

Durham: And I don't want them to know.

Ingberman: That doesn't matter to you?

Durham: What I want them to know is that they can't know that. That's what I want them to know. Here's a guy having his heart cut out with an obsidian knife and he's saying something in Cherokee and I don't want people that come into the gallery to know what he's saying... The first text is the real things, turquoise, words, gold, emeralds, obsidian and flint, the second text is the Cherokee counterpoint, and the third text is the fact that you don't know what the Cherokee means.[72]

Similarly, few of the people who read the words *tsitsitas* and *vehoe* on Heap of Birds's Spectacolor Light billboard above Times Square could have understood that the words are Cheyenne for "ourselves," and for "spider" – the Cheyenne term for the whiteman, weaving his treacherous webs. Silence can be taken for capitulation. Their naming and their withholding reassert the words as a source of power.

In the end, cultural difference is expressed not by attempting to find common ground, common words, common symbols across cultures. It is finally dignified by protecting all sides from zealous over-simplification, by acknowledging a final untranslatability of certain concepts and subtleties from one culture to another. Despite the immense generosity, the ethical injunction to share, and the holistic, animist philosophies that are essential to aboriginal societies across North America, self-definitions rooted in cultural distinctiveness must retain their untranslatable difference. The works in this exhibition contribute to, but also significantly adjust, by expanding, the discourse. We can know many things, whoever "we" may be. But we can never know everything.

NOTES

1 Quoted in David Neel, "Life on the 18th Hole," *BC Studies*, 89 (spring 1991: "A Special Issue – In Celebration of Our Survival"), p. 138.

2 Tariq Modood, "Beyond the melting-pot," *Times Literary Supplement*, 4634 (24 Jan. 1992), p. 27.

3 James Lavadour, speaking at the symposium that accompanied the opening of the exhibition *Shared Visions: Native American Painters and Sculptors in the Twentieth Century.* The Heard Museum, Phoenix, Arizona, May 1991.

4 An interpretation of this type is elaborated by James A. McDonald in "Poles, Potlatching, and Public Affairs: The Use of Aboriginal Culture in Development," *Culture.* X:2 (1990), pp. 103–20.

5 Nelly Richard, ["The Rhetoric of the Body' Margins and Institutions: Art in Chile since 1973." *Art and Text* (1986) 21: 64–73]. That there is a parallel with the situation for artists in Chile is suggested in her description of "the double and contradictory need to make the language of art explore its own autonomy and specific laws, and on the other to think in tactical terms about the social and historical context within which it has to operate," p. 90.

6 Jean Baudrillard's ideas on simulacra appear most fully in *Simulations*, trans. by Paul Foss, Paul Patton, and Phillip Beitchman (New York: Semiotext[e]. 1983), and in "The precession of simulacra," in *Art after Modernism: Rethinking Representation*, ed. by Brian Wallis (New York: New Museum of Contemporary Art, 1984).

7 Linda Hutcheon, *The Politics of Postmodernism* (London and New York: Routledge, 1989), p. 33.

8 Adam Kuper, *The Invention of Primitive Society: Transformations of an Illusion* (London: Routledge, 1988); and Susan Hiller, ed., *The Myth of Primitivism: Perspectives on Art* (London and New York: Routledge, 1991).

9 From conversations with the author in the past year.

10 The term "symbolic capital" has been developed by Pierre Bourdieu to refer to the repository of shared knowledge in which the members of a particular society have a heavy, but not necessarily equal, investment. Symbolic capital exists in close relationship with cultural capital, "the energy of social dynamics," and

economic capital. See *Outline of a Theory of Practice*, trans. by Richard Nice (Cambridge: Cambridge University Press, 1988, first English edition 1977), p. 183.

11 Jimmie Durham, "A Central Margin," in *The Decade Show*, ed. by Nilda Paraza, et al. (New York: Museum of Contemporary Hispanic Art, et al., 1990), p. 168.

12 Carl Beam, *The Columbus Project, Phase 1* (Peterborough: Artspace and The Art Gallery of Peterborough, 1989), p. 8.

13 *Truman Lowe: Streams* (La Crosse: University of Wisconsin–La Crosse, University Art Gallery, 1991), p. 20.

14 *Magiciens de la Terre* was held in Paris, France, at the Centre Georges Pompidou and the Grande Halle, La Villette, from 18 May to 14 August 1989.

15 The Indian Arts and Crafts Act of 1990, designed ostensibly to protect the interests of native craftspeople in the United States, by establishing limiting definitions of who is an "Indian" perpetuates the historical tendency to remove the "Indian problem" by reducing the number of Indians.

16 Deborah Doxtator, "Reconnecting the Past: An Indian Idea of History," in *Revisions* (Banff, Alberta: Walter Phillips Gallery, in press); and Johannes Fabian, *Time and the Other: How Anthropology Makes Its Object* (New York: Columbia University Press, 1983).

17 Bruce Trigger, "The Historian's Indian," in *Out of the Background: Readings on Canadian Native History*, ed. by Robin Fisher and Kenneth Coates (Toronto: Copp, Clark Pitman, 1988), p. 37.

18 J. R. Miller, *Skyscrapers Hide the Heavens: A History of Indian–White Relations in Canada* (Toronto: University of Toronto Press, 1989), p. 14.

19 Mark Hobart, "Who Do You Think You Are? The Authorised Balinese," in *Localizing Strategies*, ed. by Richard Fardon (Edinburgh: Scottish Academic Press, 1990), p. 307.

20 Miller, pp. 14–15.

21 Beam, p. 3. Homi K. Bhabha, whose theorising about colonial discourse has helped to account for the role of the *other* in Euro-American thought, would concur with Beam's analysis. See, for example, his article "The Other Question: Difference, Discrimination and the Discourse of Colonialism," in *Out There: Marginalization and Contemporary Cultures*, ed. by Russell Ferguson et al. (New York: New Museum of Contemporary Art, Cambridge, Mass., and MIT Press, 1990).

22 Anthony Pagden, *The Fall of Natural Man: The American Indian and the origins of comparative ethnology* (Cambridge: Cambridge University Press, 1982), p. 5.

23 Michel Foucault, *The Order of Things: An Archaeology of the Human Sciences* (New York: Random House, 1973), originally published as *Les mots et les choses* (Paris: Éditions Gallimard, 1966). Foucault summarises his concern in this book as being with "a history of resemblance: on what conditions was Classical thought able to reflect relations of similarity or equivalence between things, relations that would provide a foundation and a justification for their words, their classifications, their systems of exchange? What historical *a priori* provided the starting point from which it was possible to define the great checkerboard of distinct identities established against the confused, undefined, faceless, and, as it were, indifferent background of difference?" (p. xxiv).

24 Part of the problem is that views that have long been discredited in academic anthropology may remain in general circulation. For instance, the opposition between "tradition" and "modernity," which often turns up as the equation of "old" with "authentic," is, as Canadian anthropologist Valda Blundell has pointed out, "little more than a reformulation of the stage progressions of evolutionism." From "Speaking the Art of Canada's Native People," *The Journal of Australian and Canadian Studies*, VII:1 (2) (1989), p. 28.

25 Robert Bringhurst, the poet who is a scholar of the Haida language, has helped to introduce Sky, McGregor, and others to a wider audience in "That Also Is You: Some Classics of Canadian Native Literature," *Canadian Literature*, 124/25 (Spring/Summer 1990: "Native Writers and Canadian Literature"). Writing of the processes whereby written records were made of a great oral literature, he

observes: "It required the coincidence of poets and storytellers – some better and some worse – with anthropologists – some interested but incompetent, some competent but impatient, and a few who were patient, well trained and very lucky." (p. 37).

26   James Clifford, "On Ethnographic Allegory," in *Writing Culture: The Poetic and Politics of Ethnography* (Berkeley: University of California Press, 1986), p. 112–13. Clifford uses the term "salvage anthropology" to refer to the perception of anthropology as a perpetual rescue mission to societies on the verge of collapse.

27   Diamond Jenness, "The Indian's Interpretation of Man and Nature," in *Sweet Promises: A Reader on Indian–White Relations in Canada*, ed. by J. R. Miller (Toronto: University of Toronto Press, 1991), p. 443.

28   Robert F. Berkhofer, Jr., *The White Man's Indian: Images of the American Indian from Columbus to the Present* (New York: Random House, 1979), p. 66.

29   Fabian, p. 155.

30   Henry Moore, "On Sculpture and Primitive Art," in *Modern Artists on Art*, ed. by Robert L. Herbert (Englewood Cliffs: Prentice Hall, 1964), p. 149.

31   Ron Hamilton, "Box of Darkness," in *BC Studies*, p. 62–64.

32   [Crosby has subsequently further complicated the role and position of the aboriginal woman in "Haidas, Human Beings and Other Myths" in *Bill Reid and Beyond: Expanding on Modern Native Art*. 2004. Karen Duffek and Charlotte Townsend-Gault. Vancouver: Douglas & McIntyre.]

33   Trigger, p. 25.

34   Hamilton, "Our Story Not History," in *BC Studies*, p. 87.

35   Quoted in Robin Ridington, "Discourse, Culture, Law," in *Canadian Literature*, pp. 286–87.

36   Durham, "A Central Margin," p. 166.

37   Jacques Derrida's device of placing certain terms *sous rature* (under erasure) serves to hold them in question while simultaneously depending on at least some aspect of their "meaning".

38   Eric Hobsbawm and Terence Ranger, eds., *The Invention of Tradition* (Cambridge: Cambridge University Press, 1983).

39   Richard Handler, "On Having a Culture: Nationalism and the Preservation of Quebec's *Patrimoine*," in *Objects and Others: Essays on Museums and Material Culture*, ed. by George W. Stocking (Madison: University of Wisconsin Press, 1985).

40, 41   Conversations.

42   Jimmie Durham, *Columbus Day* (Minneapolis: West End Press, 1983), p. 60.

43   Deborah Doxtator, *Fluffs and Feathers* (Brantford: Woodland Cultural Centre, 1988), p. 68.

44   Valda Blundell, "The Tourist and the Native," in *A Different Drummer: Readings in Anthropology with a Canadian Perspective*, ed. by Bruce Cox, Jacques Chevalier, and Valda Blundell (Ottawa: Carleton University Anthropology Caucus, 1989).

45   Loretta Todd, "Notes on Appropriation," *Parallelogramme*, XVI:1 (Summer 1990), p. 30.

46   Teresa Marshall, artist's statement (as Teresa MacPhee) in *Mother, May I? An installation by Teresa MacPhee* (Halifax: The Art Gallery, Mount Saint Vincent University, 1991), n. p.

47   James Clifford, "Four Northwest Coast Museums," in *Exhibiting Cultures*, ed. by Ivan Karp (Chicago: University of Chicago Press, 1991). My argument builds on his observations about these two museums.

48   Harry Assu, with Joy Inglis, *Assu of Cape Mudge: Recollections of a Coastal Indian Chief* (Vancouver: University of British Columbia Press, 1989), p. 106.

49   George Longfish and Joan Randall, *Contemporary Native American Art* (Stillwater, Oklahoma: Gardiner Art Gallery, Oklahoma State University, 1983), n. p.

50   James Luna, in *ACA BA/MS* (Washington, D.C.: Washington Project for the Arts, 1990), n. p.

51, 52   Conversations.

53   Hamilton, "Our Voice – Our Struggle," in *BC Studies*, p. 7.

54, 55   Conversations.

56   Homi K. Bhabha, "Of Mimicry and Man: The Ambivalence of Colonial Discourse," *October* (Spring 1984).

57   Jean Fisher, "The Health of the People is the Highest Law," in *Revisions*.

58   A. P. Johnson, "Sitka, Speeches for Various Occasions," in *Haa Tuwunaagu Yis, for Healing Our Spirit: Tlingit Oratory,* ed. by Nora Marks Dauenhauer and Richard Dauenhauer (Juneau: Sealaska Heritage Foundation, 1987), p. 157.

59   Fisher.

60   Carol Podedworny, "First Nations Art and the Canadian Mainstream," *C Magazine,* 31 (Fall 1991), pp. 23–32.

61   Marjorie Halpin, *Our Chiefs and Elders: Photographs by David Neel, Kwagiutl: Museum of Anthropology Note 29* (Vancouver: University of British Columbia, 1990), p. 6.

62   Conversations.

63   Hachivi Edgar Heap of Birds, "Sharp Rocks," in *Blasted Allegories: An Anthology of Writings by Contemporary Artists,* ed. by Brian Wallis (New York: New Museum of Contemporary Art, 1985), p. 172.

64   Rebecca Belmore's performance art piece *Ayum·ee-aawach Oomama-mowan* took place in a meadow in the mountains near Banff, Alberta, in 1991.

65, 66   Conversations.

67   Beam, p. 7.

68   T. J. Clark, "More on the Differences between Comrade Greenberg and Ourselves," in *Modernism and Modernity,* ed. by Benjamin Buchloh, Serge Guilbaut, and David Solkin (Halifax: The Press of the Nova Scotia College of Art and Design, 1983), p. 168.

69   Conversations.

70   From Frank Boas, *Keresan Texts: Publications of the American Ethnological Society,* 8 (1928), as quoted in *Shaking the Pumpkin: Traditional Poetry of the Indian North Americas,* ed. by Jerome Rothenberg (New York: Doubleday, 1972), p. 403.

71   The concept of *at.óo'w* is discussed at length in *Haa Shuka: Our Ancestors – Tlingit Oral Narratives,* by Nora Marks Dauenhauer and Richard Dauenhauer (Juneau: Sealaska Heritage Foundation, 1987). This book, with its companion volume, *Haa Tuwunaagu Yis, for Healing Our Spirit: Tlingit Oratory,* are anthologies of the oratory, given in Tlingit and English, with glossary and commentary.

72   Jimmie Durham, in conversation with Jeanette Ingberman, in *Jimmie Durham: The Bishop's Moose and the Pinkerton Men,* by Jeanette Ingberman, et al. (New York: Exit Art, 1989), p. 31.

REFERENCES

Crosby, Marcia. 1991. "The Construction of the Imaginary Indian", in *Vancouver Anthology: The Institutional Politics of Art.* Vancouver: Talon Books.

Jameson, Fredric. 1991. *Postmodernism or, The Cultural Logic of Late Capitalism.* Durham, NC: Duke University Press.

Lyotard, Jean Francois. 1984 (first published in Paris 1979). *The Postmodern Condition: A Report on Knowledge.* Trans. Geoff Bennington and Brian Massumi. Minneapolis: Minnesota University Press.

30

Cew Ete Haw I Tih
The Bird That Carries Language Back to Another

Jolene Rickard

According to us, the Ska ru re (Tuscarora), it was a woman called Mature Flowers, or Mature Earth, who first tumbled through the sky world to this world. Her fall was broken by the united backs of waterfowl, and she was gently eased onto the back of a great turtle. On this tiny earth, she began at once to walk about, throwing dirt, causing it to grow. Mature Flowers, the first mother, brought with her the seeds of our life – corn, beans, squash, and tobacco – and so it continues...

Did all my grandmothers walk through time to be forgotten in their sleep? They send us reminders, tell us no. A quiet celebration of the initial planting of life is still stitched, woven, shaped, scraped, brushed, danced, and echoed in song into our memory. Our cultural clues expose both the net of colonization and the on-going fight/celebration of resistance.

A familiar sight: three Indian women sitting in a booth selling what they have made (figure 30.1). This particular bark-and-nail booth was on the grounds of "Indian Village" at the New York State Fair, near the territories of the Onondaga people. It's probably still there, but the women who once sat there are long gone, and new ones keep coming.

One such woman was my great-grandma, Florence Nellie Jones Chew, at the left of this photograph. The shadow of a beaded jitterbug has fallen on her cheek. The middle woman is my cousin, Louise Falling Husk Henry – Turtle Clanmother. The woman shadowed at the right is Mina Brayley. All three from Ska ru re.

The photograph of these three women was taken sometime during late summer in the 1940s, but before 1947, because that's when my great-grandma Flossie passed away. The collage was done in 1992. The first thought that came to my mother's mind when I asked her about Grandma Flossie was her unconditional generosity. Mother remembers large bins of four or five different types of apples, pears, potatoes, beans, squash in her root cellar. Anybody who came to her home was offered as much as they wanted from the bins. Flossie would always say, "Go ahead, take as much as you need." Since her husband, Willy Chew, was chief of the White Bear Clan and held the enrollment book, people were always dropping by. My great-grandma clung to the belief that it was the duty of the chiefs of the Ska ru re Nation to share whatever they had, thereby setting an example of humility. The people to whom she offered felt comfortable enough to take what they could use. They probably needed it. Times were pretty tough on the reservation before, during, and after the

From Lucy Lippard (ed.), *Partial Recall* (New York: New Press, 1992), pp. 105–111. Reprinted by permission of the New Press.

Figure 30.1 Jolene Rickard: Photomontage, 1992. Courtesy Jolene Rickard

Depression. There was no government relief and my people did not amass great monetary fortunes out of the oppression of other people and resources.

Truth was, the Ska ru re had been subjected to a process of cultural reconstruction since our migration from the land of the floating pine (North Carolina) in the mid-1700s. As early as 1585 the Ska ru re had sporadic contacts with the British, escalating to a full-blown war by 1711. A century of constant pressure from the British and their Indian allies finally forced us to migrate for our survival. The Ska ru re were formally adopted by the Iroquois as the Sixth Nation of the Confederacy by 1723. It was my great-grandma Flossie's grandmother who walked from North Carolina to where we live today, near the "thundering waters" of Niagara Falls. The Seneca people gave us a gift of one square mile and we worked and purchased the rest of our land.

Initially we survived as growers. The year after my great-grandma Flossie was born in 1891, the U.S. Census Office filed a report on Ska ru re. Its tone indicated obvious surprise at the productivity of our orchards, gardens, and grain fields. The shock at our ability to survive might well have been based on the knowledge of what we had been through. Such refusal to recognize indigenous peoples' ingenuity for survival is just another tactic in the colonizing process. By not recognizing our continuity as a separate and self-governing people, the U.S. government felt no need to observe their own laws and treaties.

A culturally mutual "sizing up" took place as early as the fur-trade days. The colonial gaze has never really ceased, and time has proven that it is never unintentionally directed. The darkest examples of this constant observation include the work of anthropologists, the policies of the Bureau of Indian Affairs, and the FBI's COINTELPRO activities against any Indian movement for human rights. Outwardly more innocent exchanges took place in the booths of the New York State Fair, Indian Markets, trading posts, and in Hollywood's promotions, from Tonto and the Lone Ranger to Kevin Costner and *Dances with Wolves*. And in the ever-present photographer.

Remember, indigenous people come from an oral tradition. The written word has only had real impact in the past two centuries. The relationship between the oral tradition and the mnemonic objects that serve it – the wampum belt, the condolence cane, the sacred tobacco, the rattles – continues to this day. In my community there is a relationship between all the objects that we create and the words that surround us. The words are here to teach and guide us through life; the objects are here to serve the memory and meaning of the word. The practice of looking at things to remember is our way. In the past it served the truth. Whose "truth" do we observe when we look at photographs?

The bark booths at the New York State Fair have become for me a classic projection of Indian people's place in this economy. Everyone knows that Indian handicrafts are harmless. But what is really negotiated in this trade of money for what we create? The people from Ska ru re and most other Indian nations developed specific items for this exchange. The dangling "jitterbug" pins made from odd beads, like the elaborately beaded pillows, birds, and pin cushions, are really messengers. What we create, tourist item or not, serves as a reminder of our spiritual, economic, and cultural survival. The strongest remaining symbols amongst the Ska ru re are the beadwork and the white corn.

The beadwork embodies a continued visual connection to the "power of the good mind." When this world was created, the grandsons of Mature Flowers walked the earth and created all the things that would help us to live and to destroy life. Night and day, the four-legged and the winged, the medicines and berries, both helpful and harmful – all of these things are held in balance by "the power of the good mind," revered in the time spent putting millions of tiny drops of glass onto hides or fabric. Ska ru re beadwork not only brings the knowledge from the past to our young ones, but at a critical point in our adaptation to relocation, it actually put food in our mouths.

Beads have historically been a catalyst for trade. Shells, the first form of beads, demonstrated an extensive trade network between the Americas well before contact. In the post-contact period, the beads became glass and were much sought-after by my people. They shaped our trade relationship with the Europeans in ways that remind me of multinational corporations removing people from the land today, destroying their subsistence, stealing their resources, leaving them with no option but that of wage labor. Trading beads – like "trading" inappropriate technology and unwanted borders to "developing" governments – was part of this exploitation. Land rights were traded away for glass beads and other European material culture. "Trade" is the wrong word in this context. Force, coercion, manipulation describe more clearly what has happened.

But with these beads my grandmothers made souvenirs to sell and served our beliefs as well. This strategy must be acknowledged as part of the beadwork. Did they know the beads would carry not only physical representations of our understanding of all the living things on this earth, but also a message, a measure of time to adjust to the changes that whirl through our existence? It takes time to put thousands of tiny beads on cloth; it teaches you the patience to observe, the ability to see things as a whole or a multitude of parts. It is important to see how things are connected and what gives them life.

In the early 1800s, the American public's imagination was focused on the sublime qualities of the falling waters at Niagara. The Ska ru re sold many a beaded piece to tourists flocking to stand near this force of nature. We made the objects specifically for this trade and they have been identified by antique dealers as "whimsies." When I polled the beadworkers and others in my community, no one referred to the beadwork in this way. Who has the right to name this art? Only the Ska ru re.

These beaded pieces were closely linked to the visitor's experiences at the falls. By the mid-1800s, Niagara Falls was surrounded by tourist traps, hucksters, and amusements. An "Indian" souvenir was part of the trip. The beadwork meant economic and cultural survival for the Ska ru re. For the tourist, it was a connection to the mysterious force buried in the carnival atmosphere around the falls. Today a piece like the one represented in my photo-collage would be sold for around $125.

As I look at this image of my great-grandma Flossie and her friends in the Indian Village at the New York State Fair, I chuckle at those silly bark booths and marvel at her willingness to continue this kind of inevitably lopsided cultural exchange. The money put down on the table is merely a token. What is really being purchased is a momentary release from the crimes of the past.

My great-grandma was truly generous.

I, on the other hand, am less generous about how we are represented. I am less willing to let this photo stand as it is. Without an accompanying text, it suggests a passive acceptance of great-grandma's role as "Indian selling exotica to the curious." For this reason, I hesitated to use this photograph, to risk reinforcing another stereotype. Yet I wanted to deal with what Ska ru re create and why it is significant. So in the photo-collage, I changed the scale relationship between my great-grandma and the beadwork she created, to avoid the possibility of further misrepresentation and to focus the observer on the beadwork, which is much more important than generally thought.

Jitterbugs are the little dangling stick figures at the top of the booth. They are made from odd buttons, scrapped jewelry, mixed beads, and wire. The little twisted figures sold for twenty-five cents in the past and were made mainly by young fingers. They were where you started to learn about beadwork. They had little safety pins on their tops. As children, we wore them around for decoration, sometimes five or ten at a time. Those wiry little bodies had personality. In my imagination they weren't children, but jitterbug people.

The bird, flowers, and cherries to feed the birds were a common theme for beadworkers at Ska ru re. A long time before we migrated, the Maker of All Things had given us a special bird to be cared for by the young. As the story goes, we became lax, and the bird went away, and the time of our greatest struggles began. The bird is still with us, but it isn't. The people put the bird into the beads to help remember its message. Maybe that's why we hang onto our beadwork. My own affection for beads is like that of a potmaker for clay. Beads shaped my world, from the frivolous dangling jitterbugs to the intensely bead-laden sculptures.

Surrounded by a culture that seeks to smother our own, the beadwork is an island of memory in the fog. The face of my great-grandma next to the face of this beadwork is the face of our survival. Both have given me life, and that is how they are connected. It was not enough for me to bring a photograph from the past and give it words. I felt the need to put myself in the image. But isn't that what all artists do? In joining the beaded bird with berries and my great-grandma Flossie, I show how the berries feed the birds, the beads feed me and all the Ska ru re who walk the path of the "good mind." Cultures that adapt survive.

But to adapt does not mean that we must mimic the younger brother – the Euro-American. Cloaking ourselves in "Western" values has only meant trouble. This is why I make photographs. For us, the mask form is the face of protection, and photographs become the beads that cover my mask. They act as a thin veil between myself and the constant pressure to follow the path of destruction.

I consciously avoid slipping into the narrow language of response to the colonizers, who press up against us so hard. But I refuse to let them block my vision. My images reflect the Indian agenda. I am careful to remember that I have to pay just as much attention to the corn as I do to the chemical bath the sun sets in every day. The technology of photography is a dilemma I balance against the impact my work has on our threatened existence. I put my thoughts into the visual arts because they are meant to be felt, communicated. Writing and speaking are different acts, and they just don't do it for me. We survived by watching, listening, and experiencing life. A photograph is not going to give that firsthand experience, but it may haunt your memory into seeking life.

I recall the words of my father's brother, my uncle William: "Indians are the canaries of humankind. When we go, it's too late." On Turtle Island, known as North America, we make up less than five-tenths of one percent of the total population, with or without BIA species-enrollment numbers.[1]

My work is another bead on the cloth, visually linking our worldview to our experience. It is on our experience that I focus my eye, looking at the bits and pieces of our daily life while sorting through what belongs to us and what we picked up along the way. These images are not radically chic. I am just one Tuscarora woman who has identified the "center" as anywhere indigenous people continue to live, knowing that we have the oldest continuously surviving cultures in the world. That has

to mean something. Every day I explore that meaning from the inside looking out.

NOTE

The artists whose work appeared in the Land, Spirit, Power exhibition were: Carl Beam, Rebecca Belmore, Dempsey Bob, Domingo Cisneros, Robert Davidson, Jimmie Durham, Dorothy Grant, Hachivi Edgar Heap of Birds, Faye Heavy Shield, Alex Janvier, Zacarias Kunuk, James Lavadour, Truman Lowe, James Luna, Teresa Marshall, Alanis Obomsawin, Kay Walkingstick, and Lawrence Paul Yuxweluptun.

1 Government-controlled tribal enrollment is a touchy issue in indigenous communities because it is imposed on our own ways of identifying each other. According to the old way, you inherited your nationhood and clan identity from your mother. In marriage, women stayed with their families and men moved into the women's families. The women were mostly in charge and possession of the material goods. Today some indigenous nations struggle to maintain control of who belongs with us, but the cataloguing of each indigenous birth by the U.S. government validates people who no longer understand the values which have sustained us since the beginning of time. At the same time it negates some who fall between the genealogical birthrights but do follow the path of the old ones, which is the path to the future. So the U.S. government continues to instigate our disappearance. For now, I fight with the barrel of my camera's lens.

REFERENCES

Interviews with Shirley Chew, Ska ru re Nation (1992); Lena Rickard, Ska ru re Nation (1991); Lucy Schubsta, Ska ru re Nation (1987). *The Tuscarora Legacy of J.N.B. Hewitt (J.N.B. Hewitt Wa? ekkirihwaye? O Ska ru re?)*, vol. 1 (Ottawa: Canadian Ethnographic Series 108, Canadian Museum of Civilization, National Museums of Canada, 1987).

Index

Numbers in bold indicate illustrations

Abelam (New Guinea)
  aesthetics, 119, 283
  analysis of art, 37
  art objects, 110–13, 114–15, 119
  ceremonies: initiation, 111–13, 118, 121;
      long-yam, 110, 115, 118; magico-
      religious aspects, 112, 113, 115, 117,
      118; peace, 113
  character, 114
  communication, 339
  concept of change, 110, 119–20
  connections with other villages, 113, 117,
      118
  engraving, 110, 114–15
  exchange, 110, 111, 112, 117
  hospitality, 113
  masks, 114
  materials and techniques, 114–17, 119,
      120–1
  netted string bags, 110–12
    indicator of male status, 111
    made by women, 110–11
  painting, 111–12, 113, 114–16, 118–21
  pottery, 110, 114
  sorcery, 114, 119
  status of artist, 113, 114, 116–18, 120,
      339
  tambaram cult, 110, 111–12, 115–16,
      120
  wood carving, 110, 112, 114, 115, 117–18,
      119–20
Abenaki (New York State), 449

economic conditions, 434–5
souvenirs, 434–5, 438: authenticity, 435–6;
    souvenir stand, **434**
Abinilekio of Otta (Yoruba tailor), 256–8, 265
Abipone (Paraguay)
  tattooing of women, 62, 64
Aboriginal Australian art see Australian
    Aboriginal art
Achebe, Chinua, 160–1
acrylic paintings see Australian Aboriginal art
Adam, Leonhard
  on Northwest Coast and Chinese art, 57
  on split images, 72
aesthetics
  and anthropology, 239–40, 281–98
  and beauty, 296
  change, 388
  and commerce (Africa), 209
  as creative perception, 518
  definitions, 13–14, 219, 239, 302–3
  independent of art, 282, 516
  and language, 387–8
  and the Primitive, 10, 14–15, 22, 91, 119,
      135, 137, 156, 159, 160–1, 176–8,
      223, 239–40, 242
  properties, 302
  responses to, 303, 319: and ancestral power,
      303
  unclouded by language, 208
  universal experience, 217
  vitality, 195, 206
  Yolngu, 302–17

affinities between Primitive and Western art,
    135, 147–154, **155, 157**, 164–5, 179,
    220, 222
  abstraction, 151
  conceptualism, 151
  "partially connected," 230
  see also commonality in art
African art and artifacts, 37, 75, 159, 164,
    209–34, 424
  and Absolute Spirit, 224, 226
  aesthetics and commerce, 209
  alteration of, 460–1
  anthropomorphism and anthropocentrism,
    136
  appeal to avant garde, 213
  art of belief, 74–5, 77
  art criticism, 242
  art v. anthropology, 211
  artifacts as masterpieces, 159–60, 165
  artifacts reclassified as art, 211–12, 213,
    215–17, 222
  and audience, 213–14
  authenticity, 455–8, 460
  cicatrization, 217, 252
  Classical, 136
  classified by Westerners, 209–10, 217
  communication, 74–7
  curiosity rooms, 210
  on display in museums, 158–60, 209, 211,
    212, 214, 220
  Earth Deity (Nigeria), **161**
  exhibition at 291 Gallery (1914), 212, **213**
  exorcism, 135–6
  and Expressionist *angst*, 135, 136
  influence on avant garde, 213
  influence or not on Picasso, 126, 129, 179
  magical, 154–5, 225
  masks, 209, 214, 455, **455**, 460
  metaphor, 226
  in Metropolitan Museum, 209
  painting, 217
  poured blood or wine, 127
  Pygmy traps, 226
  sculpture, 136, 214
  sculptures, 210–14, 217
  in situ, 209, 214
  textiles, 217
  trading, 454–64: Western buyers, 464
  traps, 226–32, **227, 229**
  utilitarian objects, 211, 212
  Western influence on, 76
"African Negro Art" exhibition (MOMA
    1935), 14

Ahauuta reclaimed by Zuni, 161, 165–6
Ahomey (Africa), 159, 215
Ajilete (Nigeria), 242
Akamba (East Africa) carving, 415, 416, **416**
Alado of Odo-Awaiye (Yoruba carver), 258
Alaga of Odo-Owa (Yoruba carver), 247,
    250–1, 252, 253, **253**, 258, 260, 263
Alaska
  carvings, 335
  inside of chief's house, **157**
  mask culture, 68
American aborgines *see* Native North
    Americans; Northwest Coast art
American Indian art in museums, 20–1
American Museum of Natural History, 159,
    215–16
  African Hall, **212**
Amur (Siberia) art, 57, 355
Andean culture *see* pre-Columbian, art;
    pre-Columbian, metallurgy
Aniakor, Chike C., 160
animal face designs
  Chilkat, 52–3
  Haida, **41**, 42, **42**, 45–7, **45–50**, 47–50
  Kwakiutl, 42–3, **43**, 49–51, **51**
  Nass River Indian, 43–4, **44**
  Northwest Coast, 40–54, **41–53**, 60, 67
  style, 40–1
  Tlingit, **41**, 42, **42**, 47, 48–9, **48**, 50, 53–4, **54**
  Tsimshian, 45, **45**, 46–7, **46**, 48
animism, 136, 533, 540
anthropology
  and aesthetics, 156, 233, 239–40, 281–98
  v. art criticism, 508–9
  v. art museums, 211
  categorization of Primitive art, 15–17, 156,
    165, 176, 211
  definition of art, 11–13, 140–1
  neglect of art, 11, 22
  purpose of, 508
Aotearoa/New Zealand *see* Maori art
Arapaho Indians
  pictorial designs, 331, 336–7
archaeology
  interpretations, 5
  and technology, 270, 275, 278
Archaic art, 132, 141–2, 143, 155
  African, 155
  Chinese, 199, 200
art
  v. anthropology, 176, 413–14
  and artifacts, 1, 7, 127, 176–7, 188–234,
    275, 278, 521: as complete or

incomplete, 224; and intention, 210, **210**; *see also* African art and artifacts; Euro-American bias
and capitalism, 1–2, 23
and change, 91, 110
of children, 25
as communication, 79–85, 105, 339
"concept" art, 219, 222
and consciousness, 81, 85–7, 91
and cross-cultural communication, 470–1
and culture, 1, 2, 105, 110, 385
dead shark as, 219, **220**
definitions, 91, 219, 323
denial of agency of artists, 19–20
"for its own sake," 525
form and function, 16, 25, 87–9, 91, 126–7
form and meaning, 323
and identification, 74–5
individual and traditional, 2–3, 165
influence on national identity, 474–6
"institutional" theory of, 220, 233–4
interdisciplinary discourse, 17–20, 25, 180
"interpretive" theory, 220, 222–3
and meaning, 187, 191, 387
as metaphor, 81, 84
and national identity, 474–6
natural objects as, 217
reflection of society, 109
ritual, 105, 110
as social texts, 521
sociological analysis, 220
technique and process, 17, 19, 24, 415, 419–20
tyres as, 210, **210**
and the unconscious, 81–2, 83
use of found objects, 105, 118, 136–7
and values, 110
art criticism
African, 242
v. anthropology, 508–9
Australian Aboriginal art, 503
criteria, 282, 503
ethnocentrism of, 136, 178
globalization, 508–10
rejection of acrylic painting, 509
role in commercialization of art, 507–8
Yoruba, 139–40, 242–67, 324
"Art from Another World" exhibition (Rotterdam), 179
art galleries *see* museums
art museums, 211, 432

and anthropology, 3–5, 6, 23, 24, 129–30, 136, 211
categories, 20–1, 156
display of objects, 159, 163, 186–208, 214–15
divorced from context, 340, 346
"imagined ecumene," 187
see also categories; collecting
art objects, 281
biography, 187
copying, 410, 419–20, 426
creation of value, 456
forgery, 410, 426
trading, 409–11, 413, 454–64: buyer's sense of discovery, 456–8; Côte d'Ivoire, 455; effect on innovation, 422; presentation, 455–8
"Art of this Land" (Canada), 25
art/ethnography divide, 520
and culture contact, 158
museums, 431
and specimens, 3–5, 6, 23, 24, 129–30, 136, 156, 159, 190, 191
Asante exhibition, 163, 182
Ashton, Leigh, 200
Assu, Chief Harry (Cape Mudge), 534–5
Atkins, P. J. (Iroquois), 445, 446
Attachie, Chief Gerry (Doig River band), 528
Australian Aboriginal art, 3, 5, 24, 324, 496, 499
acrylic paintings, 495–511: and abstract expressionism, 511; authenticity, 503–4; as cultural communication, 503–4; rejected by art critics, 509; and "sense of place," 510–11; trade, 503
Arunta, 24
categorized, 159
Central Australia, 331
commercialization, 418, 504, 506
contemporary, 19, 402
critical analysis, 503–4
domination by Western categories, 504
Dreaming, 402
"Dreamings: the Art of Australia" exhibition, 496, 499
encoding meaning, 324, 402
ethical and legal problems, 179
v. Euro-American conventions, 501, 504–5
iconography, 516
interpretation of, 496–7, 506
loss of the "other," 504–5
v. Modernism, 500, 508

Australian Aboriginal art (*cont'd*)
  Pintupi, 497
  as primeval, 501, 509
  quotation in, 517–18
  representation, 326, 336
  as representation of Dreaming, 497–8
  spirituality in, 501–2
  tourist art, 503
  traditional v. commercial, 497, 499
  urban artists, 505
  Uta Uta Jangala (Papanya), **496**
  visual categories, 326–37
  Walbiri visual designs, 326, 327, 328,
    330–5
  Western influence on, 21
  works in non-indigenous media, 469
  Yirrkala visual designs, 326, 327, 328,
    335–6
  Yolngu paintings, 16–17, 37, 229–30, **229**,
    326
Australian Aborigines
  Arunta photographed, 158
  "bush blacks," 502–3
  cultural identity, 502, 506, 518
  Dreaming as basis of culture, 499, 505
  land rights, 475, 502–3
  as "primitive," 515–16
  Westernization, 501
Australian identity Euro-Australian, 515,
    517–18
Avakofe, Pae, 101
avant garde
  appeal of Africa, 213
  in Chinese art, 2
  hegemony of, 538

Baker, Josephine, and *art nègre*, 154,
    155, 165
Bako of Iperu (Yoruba carver), 256, 257
Balinese painting and carving, 87–90, **88**
Bamileke (Africa), 159
Bandele of Osi-Ilorin (Yoruba carver), 250,
    251, 252, 254, 258, 262–3, 267
bark cloth of Tikopia, 92, 95
bark paintings
  by Mununggurtt, **312**
  trapped shark, 229
  Yirrkala, 326, 327, 328, 335–6
baskets
  Basket Folk (Africa), 223–4
  and basketwork, 449
  see also Yekuana
Bateson, Gregory, evaluation of work, 36

battle shields *see* Wahgi (Western Highlands,
    PNG)
beadwork
  Iroquois, 433, 436, 444
  Ska ru re (Tuscarora), 544–8
Beam, Carl (First Nations artist), 523, 525,
    528, 538
  Plexiglas Landscape, 528, **528**
beauty, 514
  and aesthetics, 296
  and ethics, 517
Belmore, Rebecca (First Nations artist), 537
Benin (Africa) bronzes, 212–13
Bennett, Gordon (Australian Aboriginal artist)
  aesthetics and iconography, 513–19
  Australian Icon (Notes on Perception N1),
    517
  Daddy's Little Girl, **515**
  identity, 515
  Self Portrait, Gone Primitive, **516**
  *The Nine Ricochets (Fall Down Black Fella,
    Jump Up White Fella)*, **514**
Beuys, Joseph (German conceptual artist)
  Untitled (Bumerang mit Spiegel, **518**
Binyon, Laurence, 194, 200, 205–6
black color appeals to Westerners, 5, 154, **155**,
    165
Boas, Franz, evaluation of work, 35–6
body painting
  Caduveo, 61
  Northwest Coast, 61
  Tikopia, 92
Brancusi, Constantin, *Sleeping Muse*, 215,
    216
Brayley, Mina, 544
Breckenridge, Carol
  classification of Chinese objects, 204
  "imagined ecumene," 187
British Museum, 190
  cataloguing, 192, 205
  Chinese art, 191, 192, 194, 195, 202
  displays, 187
Bush Negroes *see* Maroon (Suriname) people
Bushell, Stephen Wooton (cataloguer), 194,
    206

Caduveo (Guaicuru) art
  compared with Maori, 62, 64–5, 67
  compared with Northwest Coast, 60–2
  face painting, 59–60, **59**, 61, **61**, 62, 64–5
  sculpture, 62
  social positioning, 69
  tattooing, 64

Calder, Alexander, *The Arches*, **215**
Canada *see* First Nations (Canada)
Carroll, Father Kevin, 252, 258, 267–8
carving
    Alaskan, 335
    British Columbia, 39, **40**
    Maliseet Indians, 439–40
    and tattooing, 62, **63**, 65, **65**, **66**, 72
    trays, 43, **44**
    Yoruba, 250–1, 253–7, **253**, 266
    see also wood carving
Castron, Juan (basket-weaver), **382**
Castron, Pedrito (basket-weaver), **383**
cataloguing, 189
    at British Museum, 192, 205
    of Eumorfopoulos collection, 199
    Gramsci inventory, 186
    The Great Bronze Age of China, 199
    at Victoria and Albert Museum, 204
categories, 3–5, **4**, 7, 23
    anthropological, 15–17, 156, 165, 340
    art and artifacts, 1, 7, 127, 176–7, 188–208,
        224, 437
    Australian Aboriginal art, 159
    Chinese art, 126, 189, 191, 195
    diachronic v. synchronic, 190
    Far Eastern, 193
    functional v. decorative, 67, 189–90
    in museums, 20–1, 156, 186
    taxonomy, 190
    at Victoria and Albert Museum, 193
    see also art, and artifacts; visual categories
Center for African Art (Manhattan)
        exhibitions, 158–60, 220
ceramics
    of China, 193–4, 195, 196–9
    tomb, 195
ceremonies
    carved baton (Kwakiutl), 348
    ceremonial baskets (Yekuana), 377–8
    circumcision (Yolngu), 307, **307**, 308,
        308
    exchange (Wahgi), 394
    and gender divisions, 112, 120
    initiation, 111–13, 118, 121, 214
    kava (Samoa), 158
    long-yam (Abelam), 110, 115, 118
    magico-religious (Abelam), 112, 113, 115,
        117, 118
    peace (Abelam), 113
    regalia (Kwakiutl), 356
    ritual objects (Kwakiutl), 346–7, 348,
        349, 351

winter (Kwakiutl), 340–4, 350
    see also rituals and ritual objects
change
    as concept, 110, 119–20
    in culture, 420–1
Chew, Florence Nellie, 544–8
Chew, Willie (chief of White Bear clan),
        544
Chilkat/Chilkoot art, 52, **52**, 363
China, art of, 17
    Admonitions of the Court Instructress
        (painter Gu Kaizhi), 192
    as antiquities, 191
    archaeoloatry (worship of antiquity),
        199–200
    bronzes, 199, 200
    Buddhist sculpture, 199, 200
    categorized by West, 126, 189, 191, 194,
        195, 200, 204, 205–6
    categorized as "primitive," 126
    ceramics, 193–4, 195, 196–9, 200: Kangxi,
        195
    Chinese people unimaginative, 189, 193
    collecting and looting, 192–3, 195–9, 207:
        "Boxer indemnity," 199
    as displayed in Britain, 186–95
    domestic, 189
    exhaustion of tradition, 195
    fetishization of, 195, 196
    Gramsci inventory, 186
    imported to Britain, 188, 191–3, 195
    ink painting, 23
    jade carving, 200
    literati v. professional, 23
    mask culture, 68
    otherness, 188–9, 195
    owned by Britain, 186–208
    owned by USA, 200, 204
    oxymoron, 189
    painting, 192, 194, 200
    Qian-long emperor, 195
    Qing, 195, 196, 200
    resemblance to Northwest Coast, 56–9, **58**,
        67, 70–1
    Royal Academy of Art exhibition (1935),
        193, 194, 198
    social positioning through, 69
    Summer Palace, 197
    Tang-Song, 205
    thrones, 186, **188**, 196, **197**, **201**, 202,
        202, 207
    vase, 194
    Wen Fong (cataloguer), 199

cicatrization
  Africa, 217, 252
  Maroon, 168, 172
  Yoruba, 252
Cisneros, Domingo (First Nations artists), 533
classifications, 3–5, **4**, 7, 23
coffin lid painting
  Yirrkala, **312**, 315
  Yolngu, 229–30, **229**
collecting, 158, 160–4, 170–3, 181, 437–49
  bargaining, 170–1, 442–3
  Canadian First Nations art, 520–1
  Chinese art, 192–3, 195–9, 207
  Chinese and Japanese painting, 192–3
  and culture contact, 158, 160–4
  ethics, 179, 182
  ethnological, 437–8
  Europeans acquisitive, 525
  and looting, 192–3, 195–9, 207
  natural pastime, 187
  possessive individualism, 187
  rare art, 441–4, 447
  revival of interest from 1950s, 461–3
  see also Fourth World art; museum art;
    tourist art
commercialization, 160, 170–3, 179, 415,
  421–7
  Fourth World art, 419
  traffic in culture, 180
  value creation process, 19–20
commonality in art, 56–9, 135, 175, 177, 521,
  541
  and hierarchy, 69
  see also affinities between Primitive and
    Western art
communication
  in African art and artifacts, 74–7
  non-linguistic, 334
  through art, 79–85, 105, 339
  see also language; visual categories
Côte d'Ivoire, 454–64
  art traders, **457, 458**
  colonial figures, **462, 463**
Courtauld Institute, 199
Cree craft, 423, 426
  see also McMaster, Gerald (Cree artist)
crest art
  Kwakiutl, 55, 344, 346, 355
  Tlingit, 366
Cubism
  Analytic, 137
  and Primitive art, 133, 135, 137, 140, 149,
    195

culture, 1, 5
  and aesthetics, 156, 191
  and anthropology, 159
  "arts of acculturation," 414–15
  change, 420–1
  cultural racism, 522
  definitions, 190, 245, 275–6
  high and low, 208, 211
  ownership, 179, 182, 484, 521, 531, 534–5
  perceptions as cultural phenomena, 282,
    283
  primitive v. Western, 245–6, 248–9, 525
  social life of things, 187
  see also material culture
Curzon, George (Marquis), 203
Cutschall, Colleen (First Nations artist),
  529–30
  She is Walking in a Sacred Manner, **530**
  Voice in the Blood, 530

Dan (Africa) art, 131
dance costumes, 136, **354**
David, Sir Percival
  collector of Chinese ceramics, 196, 198,
    199, 207
  Percival David Foundation of Chinese Art
    (University of London), 199, 200, 202
Davidson, Robert & Dorothy Grant (Haida
  artists), 536, 539
Dempsey Bob (Tahitan-Tlingit carver), 539,
  539
Dickie, George, on aesthetics, 220
Dinka (Sudan), 285–6, 287, 290–1, 292, 293,
  296
Dogon (Mali), 24, 159
Doxtator, Deborah (Mohawk), 531
dualisms, 67
  depicted in Tlingit masks, 363–6, 370
  in Maori art, **62**, 64–7, **66**
  see also split images
Duchamp, Marcel, and artifacts, 229, 233
Duga of Meko (Yoruba carver), 256, 263
Durham, Jimmie (First Nations poet and
  artist), 523, 528, 531, 536, 539–40

Easter Island sculptures, 135, 144
Egyptian art, 131, 142–3
engraving by Abelam, 110, 114–15
Eskimo carving, 335
  Inuit, 21
Etoumbi (Africa) carved masks, 135
Eumorfopoulos, George
  catalogue of collection, 199

collection sold to British government, 199
founder of Oriental Ceramic Society, 196,
    198, **198**, 207
Euro-American bias in art, 1–3, 7, 12, 24,
    126–30, 132, 154–6, 179–80, 189–90,
    194, 211, 240, 242
  modified, 178–9, 181
  perspective, 517
  see also collecting; Western art
evolutionism, 3–6, 17, 23–4, 37
exchange
  Abelam, 9–10, 110, 111, 112, 117
  recontextualization of objects in Pacific
      Islands, 388
  Ska ru re (Tuscarora), 546
  Tikopia, 100, 102
  Wahgi, 394
Expressionist angst and African sculpture, 135

face designs see animal face designs; human
    face designs
face painting, 8–9, **59**
  Caduveo, 59–61, **59**, 61, **61**, 62, 64–5
Fagg, William, evaluation of work, 37
Falling Husk Henry, Louise, 544
Fang (Cameroon), 212
Far Eastern art as category, 193
Fatumaru, Pa, 101
fetishes, 138, 152, 156
  in Iowa, **214**
  Songye, 138
fine arts v. mechanical arts, 189, 192
First Nations (Canada)
  affected by colonization, 524–5
  animist philosophy, 533, 540
  art exhibition (1927), 14
  "Art of this Land" exhibition, 25
  artists, 523–43
  British Columbia, 39, **40**
  commodification of art, 520–1, 524
  contact history, 525–6, 528
  cultural knowledge, 521–2
  cultural racism, 522
  diversity of art, 521
  Gus-wen-tah belt, 522, **522**
  historical objects, 522
  history and myth, 524
  interpreted by Euro-Americans, 526–7
  kinds of knowing, 520–43
  Kwagiulth Museum and Cultural Center
      (Cape Mudge), 534
  "Land, Spirit, Power" exhibition (National
      Gallery of Canada), 520

limits of translation, 538–40
misappropriation of art, 531, 533–4
misrepresentations of past, 522, 527, 529
post-contact history, 529
and postmodern discourse, 522–3, 536–8
potlatch objects, 534–5
publications of oral art, 526, 529
real and represented, 523
reconstructing the past, 529–37
sacred objects, 533
sculpture, 524
shamanism, 524
spiritual relationship to land, 521
symbolism, 523–4
synthetic knowledges and a shared reality,
    523
Two Row Wampum Treaty of the Six
    Nations, 522
U'mista Cultural Center (Alert Bay), 534
see also Tsimshian (Northwest Coast) art
Firth, Raymond, evaluation of work, 36, 109
folk art see tourist art
Fon (Africa)
  fetishes, 138
  god of war, 159
Forge, A., evaluation of work, 37
form and function, 16, 25, 87–9, 91, 126–7
form, style and meaning, 323–5
Fourth World art, 412–30, 510
  commercialization, 419
  definition, 412
  process of change, 414–22
Fourth World societies, 427–8, 430
Franks, Sir Augustus, 191, 192, 204
Freer, Charles Lang, 195, 206
Freudian theory, 81, 82, 83

Gabe, Paul (chief of Penobscot Indians), 439
Gauguin, Paul, definition of "primitive" and
    "savage," 130–1
gender divisions
  appreciation of Chinese art, 189
  Archaic Africa, 155
  in basket making (Yekuana), 375–7
  and ceremonies, 112, 120
  in collecting, 189
  feminine art, 38, 62
  and headrests, 95, 107
  Maroon (Suriname) people, 168, 169, 171,
      173–4, **174**
  masculine art, 38, 62
  men's society masks, 214
  netted string bags, 110–11

gender divisions (*cont'd*)
  Northwest Coast, 38
  "otherness" of female (Chinese art), 188–9
  tattooing, 62
Giles, Lionel, 206
Gobbi, Jean-Francois (collector), 454
gold as symbol, 274
gourd bowls (Anauk), **295**
Granites, Dolly (Australian Aboriginal artist),
  498, 505
Grant, Dorothy (Haida artist), 536, 539
Gray, Basil, 198–9, 208
Great Britain
  as colonial power, 187, 193–208
  Great Exhibition (1851), 192, 196
  Indian collection, 193, 203
Gu Kaizhi, *Admonitions of the Court
  Instructress*, 192
Guaicuru art *see* Caduveo (Guaicuru) art
Gumana, Yangarinny (Australian Aboriginal
  artist), **305**

Haida, 41, **41**, **42**, 45, **45**, 46, **46**, 47, 48, 49,
  50, 70, 524
  oral literature, 526
  relationship to natural world, 536
  "Seven Ravens" blanket and dance, 524,
  536
Hamilton, Ron (Nuu-chah-nulth poet), 527,
  535
Hansford, S. Howard, 199–200, 208
headrests of Tikopia, 94–106, **96–100**
Heap of Birds, Hachivi Edgar (First Nations
  artist), 531, 537
  Hard Weed, 535
  Spectacolor Light, 540
  *Telling Many Magpies, Telling Black Wolf,
  Telling Hachivi*, 531, **533**
HeavyShield, Faye (First Nations artist), 523
Heye, George, 432–3, 441, 449
  see also National Museum of the American
  Indian
Hill, Rick (Canadian Mohawk), 531, 533,
  537
Hirst, Damien
  dead shark, 219, **220**, 229: comparison with
  Yolngu painting, 229–30
  sheep's head, 231
history
  approach to art, 126
  and concept of change, 110
  discovery of Primitive Art, 154
  of First Nations contact, 525

historians' assumptions about Modernism,
  129
  of museums, 190–1
  and myth, 524
  narrative art history, 190
Hobson, Robert Lockhart, 191–2, 198, 204,
  206
Honey, William Bowyer, 193, 198, 204, 206
Horn, Judith
  "concept" artist, *High Noon*, 230, **230**
Houle, Robert (Salteaux artist), 520
human face designs
  Caduveo, 59–65, **59**, **60**, **61**, 67
  Haida, 47, **48**
  Kwakiutl, 40, **41**
  Northwest Coast, 24, 39–40, **40–2**, 47, **48**,
  61–2
  Tlingit, 39, **40**
Hunt, Calvin (carver), 163
Hunt, George (Tsimshian informant), 526

Iban textiles, 24
iconography, 518–19
  Australian Aboriginal art, 516
"Igbo Arts: Community and Cosmos"
  exhibition (Center for African Art), 160
Igogo-Ekiti (Nigeria), 242
Indian Arts and Crafts Act (USA 1990), 541
Indian collections, 205
  Buddhas, 335
  Indian Museum, 193, 203
informants, 225–6, 346
  Tsimshian, 526
  unwilling, 171, 173, 402
  Wahgi, 391, 393, 394, 395, 404
initiation ceremonies *see* ceremonies
ink painting, Chinese, 23
interpretations, 37, 87–90, 91, 171–3, 194,
  214, 219–20, 402–3, 526–7
Inuit art
  carving, 21
  Western influence on, 21
Iperu-Remon (Nigeria), 24
Irian Jaya *see* West Papua
Iroquois (New York State)
  beadwork, 433, 436
  "Iroquois Women" display, 432–3, **433**, 445
  pincushions, **436**
  war clubs, 441, 442–3, **442**, **443**

Jahnke, Robert (Maori artist), 474, 476,
  478–91
  influenced by prophets, 480

Mana Whenua, 480, 482–8, **482**, **483**, **486**, 491

Te Ata nga Poropiti, **481**

"Te Ata Tuarua: the Second Reflection" exhibition (1992), 485, 488–9, **488**

Te Iho I, **489**

Te Iho II, **490**

Janvier, Alex (Chipewayan artist), 520, 528

Japanese art, 192, 203, 204

Jogomi of Ajilete (Yoruba critic), 258, 261

Johnson, Samuel (Yoruba critic), 259

Kaipei Ka (Wahgi shield painter), 396, 397, 398–400

Kalabu (Abelam artist), 120

Kane, Margo (First Nations artist), 537

Kaprow, Alan, *Yard*, 210, **210**

Karaka, Emily (Maori sculptor), 478

kava bowl of Tikopia, 103

kava ceremony of Samoa, 158

Keekete (Maroon carver), 170

Kenana, Rua (Maori prophet), 480

knowing
    kinds of, 520–40
    knowledge and levels of mind, 80–3
    natural way, 523
    synthetic knowledge, 523
    see also First Nations (Canada)

Kolb, Adela, *Making Wee Wish*, 535, 536

Kopytoff, Igor, 447

Kula (New Guinea), 10, 24

Kunuk, Zacharias/Sak (First Nations film-maker) *Qaggiq*, 530, **532**

Kwakiutl (British Columbia), 39–40, **41**, 42, **43**, 49–50, **51**, 55, 61, 163
    ancestors, 341, 342, 344
    animals: in art, 345–6; classified, 345, 351; Fabulous Beasts, 346; and humans, 343, 344, 345–6, 354, 356; man-animals, 346; men eat, 354; sea animals, 346
    anthropomorphic art, 345
    art objects, 340
    baxus (secular/summer) season, 340, 341–2, 344–5, 346, 352–3
    cannibals, 351, 354: animals as, 347, 348, 350, 351, 354; *Dzonokwa* as, 348; *hamatsa* as, 347, 350; spirits as, 343, 353–4, 355
    ceremonies, 340–5: carved baton, 348; regalia, 356; ritual objects, 346–7, 348, **349**, 351

chiefs, 341, 342, 345

commerce, 340–1

crest art, 55, 344, 346, 355

dance costumes, **354**

dances and songs, 342, 343, 344, 347, 348

dualisms, 340–5

Dzonokwa as wealth-givers, 348

European contact, 340

Fabulous Beasts, 346

female societies, 343

hamatsa as secret society, 343, 348, 350, **350**

he'ilq (healers) as shakers of rattles, 347, **349**

masks, 152, **153**, 346–52, **527**: in *baxus* v. in *tsetsequa*, 351; cannibal raven, 347, **347**, 348; crooked/curved beak, 346, 347, **347**, 351–2, **352**, **353**; *Dzonokwa*, 348; eagle, 351–2, **352**; Grisly/Grizzly bear, **348**, **354**; land animals, **348**, **352**, **354**; mythological ancestors, 347; Nulmul (Fool Dancer), 347, **347**, 350; raven, **348**; wolf, **354**

meaning and function, 346–7

meaning and representation, 345

myths: of ancestors and the supernatural, 341–2; of animals, 346; origin, 341

numayam (cognatic descent groups), 341–2, 345, 346: ancestors, 341, 356; chiefs, 341; house front, 42, **43**, 350, 351; origins of, 341, 342; potlatch seats, 341, 356; totem pole, 350

organizational principles, 340

ownership of decorations, 341

potlatches, 339–41, 342, 344, 345, 346, 348, 355: and marriages, 356

repurchase of bride, 342

ritual objects, 346–7, 348, **349**, 351

secret societies, 341–4, 356: initiation into during *tsetsequa*, 342–4, 346, 348, **350**

shamanism, 344, 346, 350: and animals, 346

Sisiutl serpent motif, 348

social organization, 340–5

spirits, 341, 342–3, 348: and ancestors, 342; eat humans, 343, 353–4, 355

spiritual protectors, 342

structural patterning, 339–55

and the supernatural, 342–3, 344

taming of hunger, 356

Kwakiutl (British Columbia), (cont'd)
    tsetsequa (sacred/winter season), 247, 340,
        341–4, 345, 347–52: awe and
        buffoonery, 355; madness and disorder,
        350, 352; social groups, 341; winter
        ceremonial, 340–4, 350
Kwayep (Bamileke carver), 159

Labintan of Otta (Yoruba carver), 257–8, 265
"Land, Spirit, Power" exhibition (National
        Gallery of Canada), 520, 538–9
Lander, Richard, 259
language
    African, 217
    and art, 78–80, 83, 105, 119, 127, 135, 136,
        139–40, 145, 211, 216–17, 339, 374,
        387
    Chinese art, 25, 205, 206
    and decoding/evaluation art, 75, 176, 387–8
    definition, 513–14
    disservice to art, 387
    linguistic model for meaning questioned,
        387–8
    Maroon, 170–1
    Mohawk art, 25
    pejorative origins, 132, 143
    and performance, 26
    seeing images linguistically, 387–8
    and time, 158
    see also art criticism
Lasi, Pu Kafika, 107
Lavadour, James (First Nations artist), 522,
        535
Les Magiciens de la terre exhibition (Paris
        1989), 179, 520, 524, 541
Lévi-Strauss, Claude
    art as communication, 339
    evaluation of work, 36
    on term "Primitive," 132
Littlechild, George (First Nations artist), 529
    The Maternal Ancestry of George
        Littlechild, 530
Loehr, Max, 199, 208
Lowe, Truman (First Nations artist), 520, 523,
        524
Lozi (Zambia) needle case, 216–17
Luna, James (First Nations artist), 520, 530,
        535
    Wee Wish, 535, 536
Lwalwa (Africa) masks, 135

Maasai (East Africa), 298, 299
McGregor, Walter (Haida elder), 526

McMaster, Gerald (Cree artist), 531
    cowboy,n., Yee-hah! Indian,n., Ugh!, 533
Makonde (Tanzania) carving, 415, 424, 425
Malangans (New Ireland), 19
Maliseet Indians
    carving, 439–40: canoe paddles, 439–40
    souvenir stand, 435
Mandari see Nilotes
Maori art, 472–7
    as basis of cultural identity, 475–6
    compared with Caduveo, 62, 64–5, 67
    compared with Northwest Coast, 67–8
    contemporary v. traditional, 478, 480
    exhibitions, 476–7: "Kohia Ko Takaka
        Anake" (1990–1), 477; "Mana Tiriti"
        (1990), 480, 483; sponsored by Mobil,
        166; "Taonga Maori" (1988), 477; "Te
        Ata Tuarua: The Second Reflection"
        (1992), 485, 488–9, 491; "Te Maori"
        (1984–7), 163, 476, 478, 480
    influence of colonization, 470, 472, 474–5
    Mana Whenua, 482, 483, 486
    millenarian influence on, 478, 480
    mythological basis, 472
    Papatuanuku, 479
    pare carved lintels, 473
    and politics, 163
    split imaging, 62, 64–7, 66
    tattooing, 62, 62, 63, 64
    Te Ata o nga Poropiti, 481
    Te Ibo I, 489
    Te Ibo II, 490
    Te Maaoorii, 477
    tiki, 64, 64
    Treaty of Waitangi (1840), 475–6
    wood carving, 65, 66, 68, 473, 477, 481,
        482
Margaret Mead Hall of Pacific Peoples, 156,
        157, 158, 159
Maroon (Suriname) people
    art, 126, 127, 168–83
    art v. anthropology, 176
    calabash carving by women, 168, 169
    cicatrization, 168, 172
    commercialization, 170–3
    condescension of Euro-Americans, 170–1,
        172, 402
    designs not symbols, 171–5
    exhibitions, 173–6, 178
    history of, 167–9
    independence from the Netherlands, 167
    innovations, 169
    Keekete (carver), 170

languages, 167, 170–2, 181
meanings imposed, 171, 173, 402
misleading descriptions, 169–70
ritual objects, 168, 171
Seketima (carver), 170
subgroups, 167
textile art of women, 168, 169, 173–4, **174**
wood carving by men, 168, 169, 171
Marshall (MacPhee), Teresa (First Nations
    artist), 523, 533
Mashudi of Meko, 251, 258, 260, 265
masks, 67–71
Abelam, 114
African, 136, 214, 455, 460
Alaskan, 68
Chinese, 67–8
Dogon, 160
Dzonokwa, 348
eagle, 351–2, **352**
Etoumbi, 135
Fang, 137
Ibibio, 148
in initiation ceremonies, 214
Kiwarani, 160
Kwakiutl, 152, **153**, 346–52, **347, 348,**
    351–2, **352, 353, 354, 527**
Lwalwa, 135
Maroon, 168
men's society, 214
Northwest Coast, 67–8
Oceanic, 131
in performance, 209
Senufo, **455**
as shamanic article, 358–9
Tlingit, 358–72, **359–62**
Tusyan, 134, 135
in Western context, 136
wolf-human (Tahitan-Tlingit), 539
see also animal face designs; human face
    designs
material culture, 10, 16, 75, 274–6, 323,
    437–8
considered inferior to art, 190
and meaning, 387
in Victoria and Albert Museum, 193
mats of pandanus from Tikopia, 92
Maymuru, Narritjin (Yolngu artist), **309**
meaning
and art, 187, 191, 339
encoded in Australian Aboriginal art, 324
and form, 323–5
and function, 346–7
graphicalization of, 387–404

linguistic models for, 387–8
and material culture, 387
through language, 339
Meko Gelede cult, 243
Melanesians
Anga eel-trap, 231–2
art more Romantic than African, 136
Highland New Guinea art, 324
Imunu use of found objects, 136–7
Kula (New Guinea), 10, 24
Malangans (New Ireland), 19
Maring shields, 403
New Hebrides fern sculpture, 135
see also Abelam; Wahgi
men *see* gender divisions
Mendi shield designs, 404
Mendiate, Ana, *Untitled*, **213, 214**
Mercredi, Ovide (National Chief of the
    Assembly of First Nations), 521
Mesoamerican art, 131, 142
Metropolitan Museum's African objects, 209
Miller, Kay (First Nations artist), 536
Modernism
awareness of world art, 136, 145
discovers Primitive art, 147–66
ethnocentrism of, 136
influence of, 4–5, 8, 10–11, 23, 129–31
interpretation of tribal art, 131, 136, 137,
    138, 142, 154–6, 178
not found in Third World, 163
recognition of masterpieces, 159–60, 165
signifiers and signified, 136
see also Picasso, Pablo
modernity, 388, 403
effect on battle shield designs, 388
Mohawk art and language, 25
monsters in art, 136–7
Morgan, Lewis Henry, 436
Mormon technology, 271–2
Motuata, Pa, 102
Mununggurr, Ma:w'
    Djapu Clan Shark Painting, **312**
Murngin *see* Yolngu
Muru, Selwyn (Maori artist), 477, 478, 479
    Papatuanuku, **479**
Musée de l'Homme (Paris), 160
Museum of Aboriginal Art (Utrecht), 179
Museum Age, 432, 439, 442
Museum of Modern Art (MOMA),
    125, 144
beautification of exhibits, 163
see also "Primitivism in 20th Century Art"
    exhibition (MOMA 1984)

museums
  history of, 191
  local and tribal, 534
  see also anthropology; art museums;
    museum art
music, 19–20
  American negro, 165
  defined in anthropology, 159

Nabokov, Vladimir
  on human behavior, 181–2
Namatjira, Albert (Australian Aboriginal
    artist), 417
  The Ancient Ghost Gum of Temple bar, **417**
Nass River Indian bracelet, 43, **44**
National Museum of the American Indian
    (Smithsonian), 20–1, 23, 163, 432–3,
    448–9
National Museum of Women in the Arts
    (Washington), 182
Native North Americans, 431–2, 435
  as collectors for museums, 439–40
Navajo
  communicating life values, 339
  sand paintings, 335, 336
Ndembu (Northern Rhodesia/Zimbabwe)
    figurine, 328, 330
Nelson, Michael (Australian Aboriginal artist),
    505–10
New Guinea art *see* Abelam
  Highland, 324, 387–406
New Hebrides (Vanuatu) fern sculpture, 135
Ngurruwutthun, Dula (Australian Aboriginal
    art), *Yirritja Moiety Painting*, **310**
Nilotes (Sudan), 240, 281–99
  aesthetics, 281, 284–98
  Agar Dinka: cattle post, **290**; dancing, **292**;
    hut-wall painting, **292**
  Anauk gourd bowl, **295**
  Apak Atuot, forked branch shrine, 291, **291**
  Atuot, 286, 291
  beauty, 295–6: *dheeng*, 296
  body decoration, 290, 291, 296
  cattle, 283–98, **285**
  deity as pied, 297–8
  Dinka, 285–6, 287, **287**, 290–1, **290**, 293,
    296: boy carving, **293**; song, 296
  Mandari, 286, 290
  Nuer, 286, 291: mud toys, **293**
  Pokot, 284: mud toys, 294, **294**
Niro, Shelley (First Nations photographer),
    531
  I Enjoy Being a Mohawk Girl, **534**

North American art
  Western influence on, 20–1
Northwest Coast art, 39–55, 324, 336, 339
  at IBM Gallery, 163
  compared with Amur, 57
  compared with Caduveo, 60–2, 67–8
  compared with Chinese, 56–9, **58**, 67–8,
    70–1
  compared with Maori, 67–8
  decorative preferred to realist, 40
  formal style (female), 38
  geometric design, 54, 67
  mask culture, 68
  potlatches, 339–40
  serene and carnival, 355
  social positioning, 54, 64
  split imaging, 58, 60–1, 65–7
  symbolic style (male), 38
  wood carving, 68
  see also First Nations (Canada)
Nukutapu, Pa, 101
Nulmul (Kwakiutl) mask, 347, **347**, 350

Obomsawin, Alanis (First Nations film-
    maker), *Incident at Restigouche*, 531,
    532
Oceanic art
  compared with African, 136
  and Gauguin, 131
  recontextualization of objects, 388
  Romantic, 136
  see also Melanesians; Polynesians
Ogidi of Igogo-Eketi (Yoruba carver), 258,
    261
Ogundeji of Iseyin (Yoruba), 260–1, 263
Ojibwa *midewiwin*, 535
Olodoye of Ijero-Eketi (Yoruba), 259
Onamosun of Iperu (Yoruba carver), 252, 254,
    256, **257**, 258–9
oratory
  Tlingit, 535, 536, 537
  Wahgi, 393
oriental antiquities defined, 192
  see also China, art of
Oriental Ceramic Society, 196–7, 202, 207
  exhibitions, 198
Osage Indians, totems, 333–4
otherness
  in Chinese art, 188–9, 195
  of female, 189
  loss of (Australian Aborigines), 504–5
  of primitive/First World art, 523
  of tribal art, 139, 177, 224

Otusoga of Odo-Nopa, 358
Owoeye of Efon-Alaiye (Yoruba carver), 250, 254

Pacific Peoples *see* Melanesians; Polynesians
painting
    Abelam, 111–12, 113, 114–16, 118–21
    acrylic *see* Australian Aboriginal art
    Admonitions of the Court Instructress (painter Gu Kaizhi), 192
    at top of art hierarchy, 189, 192
    Balinese, 87–90, **88**
    coffin lid, 229–30, **229**, **312**, 315
    see also bark paintings; body painting; face painting; tattooing
Panapa, Pa, 99, 100–1, 102, 107–8
Paul, James (chief of Maliseet Indians), 439–40, 444–5
Picasso, Pablo
    "broomstick" sculpture, 137, 145–6
    collage and *assemblage*, 137–8
    Girl before a Mirror, 152, **153**, **527**
    "Iberian" style, 137, 138, 143
    Les Demoiselles d'Avignon, 129, 135, 137, 138–9, 144, 145, 147, 148, 179, 220–1
    Minotaur, 137
    and pre-Columbian art, 131, 142
    on Primitive sculpture, 132, 133–4, 141
    resemblance to African masks, 129, 135, 179
    responses to tribal art, 126, 129, 134, 135–6, 137–9, 142, 143, 144–5, 148, 149, 150, 156
    on "simplicity," 143
Piro (Peru), Sangama "reading," 402
Pitt Rivers, A. H., classification, 3–4, **4**, 7
Pitt Rivers Museum, 3, 5, 190
Plains Indians and the supernatural, 342
Poitras, Jane Ash (First Nations artist), 523, 528–9
    Family Blackboard, 529
Polynesians *see* Easter Island; Maori; Tikopia
postcards, 445, **445**, 448
    see also tourist art
postmodernism
    in Canadian culture, 523
    defining reference, 522
    everything and nothing, 523
Pot People (Africa), 223–4
potlatches, 339–41, 342, 344, 345, 346, 348, 355
    hierarch of seating, 341, 356, 365

pottery
    Abelam, 110, 114
    Chinese, 194
    face designs on, 24
    Pot People in Africa, 223–4
pre-Columbian
    art, 131, 141, 151–2
    metallurgy, 272–3
Primitive art, 1–8, 131, 140, 414
    affected by colonization, 525–6
    art nègre, 131, 134, 141, 154–5, 165
    as artifacts, 7
    compared with tribal art, 131, 139–40
    curating and curated cultures, 180
    definitions, 125–6, 131, 132–3, 141, 143
    detached from context, 136
    and discovery of culture, 156
    fakes, 178
    and Gauguin, 131, 133
    interaction with Western, 20–1, 37–8, 129, 131, 133–47
    mimicked by West, **155**, 213
    not contemporary, 156
    skill and training, 26
    symbolic and thaumaturgic role, 136
    trading, 413
    in Western mythology, 130, 133
    see also African art and artifacts; Fourth World art; Primitivism; tribal art
"Primitivism in 20th Century Art" exhibition (MOMA 1984), 125–6, 129–46, 147–66, **162**, 175, 182, 211, 527
Primitivism
    admiration of the "savage," 130, 135
    and arts of primitive peoples, 130
    definitions, 13, 129, 130, 132
    nineteenth century, 130
    in Primitive art, 141, 246
    twentieth century, 130, 147–9, 220–1, 222, 437
    see also Modernism; Primitive art
Purdon Clarke, Caspar, 193, 205
Pygmies, African, 226

Quick-to-See Smith, Jaune (First Nations artist), 523

Rackham, Bernard, 193
ranking *see* social positioning
representation *see* visual categories
Richardson, John (journalist), 441–5
Rickard, Jolene (Ska ru re photographer), 544–8, **545**

rituals and ritual objects, 22, 67, 105, 110,
     168, 171, 214
  in hunting, 225–6, 232
  Kwakiutl, 346–7, 348, **349**, 351
  Yolngu, 307–8, 314, 318–19
Royal Academy of Art (Burlington House)
  exhibition of Chinese art, 193, 194, 198

Salawu of Otta (Yoruba carver),
     257–8, 265
Samoan kava ceremony, 158
Sangama of Piro "reads," 402
Sapir, Edward, 439, 443
School of Oriental and African Studies, 199,
     208
sculpture
  African, 136, 164, 214
  Benin, 151
  "broomstick," 137, 145
  Caduveo, 62
  distortion in, 137, 145–6, 149
  Easter Island, 135, 144
  fern sculpture of New Hebrides/Vanuatu,
     135
  First Nations, 524
  Ife, 151
  influence on Picasso, 132, 133–4, 138–9
  Nyamwezi, 137
  string, 220, **221**
  Yoruba, 243–64
  see also masks; wood carving
Seketima (Maroon carver), 170
Senufo (Africa) mask, **455**
Sepik (PNG) ancestor figures, 424
shamans
  art sacred, 355
  ascribed power, 365
  costumes, 355
  First Nations, 524
  Kwakiutl, 344, 346, 350
  Northwest Coast Indians, 355
  ritual objects, 346, 359: see also masks
  roles, 358
  Tlingit, 346, 355, 358, 359, 362, 365,
     366–7
silver as symbol, 274
Ska ru re (Tuscarora)
  art and artifacts, 545–8
  attempts to destroy, 545–8
  cultural reconstruction, 546
  exchange, 546
  Maker of All Things, 547
  migration, 546

oral tradition, 546
origin myth, 544, 546
Sky, John (Haida elder), 526
Sloane, Sir Hans, bequest to British Museum,
     191
Smith, Jaune see Quick-to-See Smith, Jaune
     (First Nations artist)
Snow, John, **445**
social positioning, 1–2, 23, 105
  Caduveo, 69
  China, 69
  Maori, 64
  Northwest Coast, 53
  Tikopia, 104–6
Songye fetishes, 138
sorcery
  Abelam, 114, 119
  exorcism: Africa, 135–6; Tlingit, 364, 370,
     371
  Wahgi, 389
South Kensington Museum
  Chinese art, 194–5, 205
  ornamental art, 192–3
  renamed Victoria and Albert Museum,
     190
  see also Victoria and Albert Museum
souvenirs see tourist art
Speck, Frank (ethnological collector), 437–9,
     441, 444–5, 449
split images
  face, 43–55, 56–71, **70**
  Melanesian, 72
  two bodies, 72
  "whirl of animals," 72
Strange, E. F. (cataloguer), 205
string and nets
  Abelam netted bags, 110–12
  sculpture, 220, **221**
  Tikopia, 92, 94
  Yirrkala, 336
  Zande hunting net, 215–16, 220, **221**,
     222–4
Sumba (Indonesia), 276
Sura, Ida Bagus Djati, 87, **88**
Suriname see Maroon (Suriname) people
Surrealists, 105, 138
  as amateur ethnologists, 130
  liking for found objects, 136
  prefer Oceanic to African art, 136
  and Primitive art, 195
symbolism, 9, 54, 67, 105, 137
  battle shield designs (Wahgi), 391, 393
  First Nations, 523–4

of gold, 274
of silver, 274
symbolic capital, 540–1
Tikopia, 94, 106

taboo
  in art, 355
  in tambaram cult, 112, 113
  touching father's head, 101
tambaram cult *see* Abelam (New Guinea)
tattooing, 67
  of Abipone women, 62
  Caduveo, 64
  and carving, 62, **63**, 65, **65**, 66, **66**, 72
  Haida, 46, **47**
  Maori, **62**, **63**, 64, 67–8, 72
  Northwest Coast, 61
  South America, 62
  Tikopia, 92
Taumako (Ariki), 101
technology
  and archaeology, 270, 275, 278
  battle shields (Wahgi), 388
  component activities, 271
  definition, 276
  Mormon, 271–2
  and style, 270–9
  as symbolic systems, 276–7
textiles
  African, 217
  Andean, 278
  bark cloth of Tikopia, 92, 95
  of Iban, 24
  Maroon, 168, 169, 173–4, **174**
  Sumba, 276
Tikopia, 91–108
  bark-cloth, 92, 95
  body painting, 92
  decorations, 93, 94, 107
  functional, 92, 94, 106, 107
  headrests, 94–105, **96–100**
  kava bowl, 103
  lack of plastic art, 92
  male and female, 95, 107
  music, poetry and dance, 92, 94
  pandanus mats, 92
  social positioning, 104–6
  string figures, 92, 94
  symbolism, 94, 106
  tattooing, 92
  value connections, 94
  wood carving, 93–5, **93**, 94–102, **96–100**,
    106: *see also* headrests

Tlingit (Alaska)
  art, 39, **40–2**, 41, 47, 48–49, **48**, 50, **52**,
    358–72, **539**
  cosmic levels, 363
  crest art, 366
  eight as significant number, 361
  giftgiving, 366
  grave houses, 359, 366
  masks, 358–72, **359–62**: angry spirit
    with bear's ears, 362, 363, 371;
    dualisms depicted, 363–6, 370;
    hawk spirit, 360; kingfisher spirit,
    360; mouth forms, **359–62**, 363,
    371; old woman, 360; painted lines,
    371; power of, 361–5; shaman,
    359, 362, 364–5, 366–71;
    significance of tongues, 361, 370,
    371; spirit, 361; spirit with devilfish,
    361
  metamorphoses, 370
  oratory, 535, 536, 537
  potlatch seat, 365
  sacred and profane in social order, 365
  shamans, 346, 355; appearance, 366;
    ascribed power, 365; burial, 366;
    exorcism of witches, 364, 370, 371;
    healing, 364; masks, 359, 362, 364–5,
    366–71; payment, 366; in profane and
    sacred order, 365–6; rituals and ritual
    objects, 352, 359, 364–5, 371–2;
    sacred and profane, 365; spirit helpers
    (*yek*), 358–9 (ghosts, 359, 361);
    transformations, 366, 370, 371
  social positioning, 365–6
  see also Chilkat/Chilkoot art
Todd, Loretta (First Nations film-maker),
    533
totems
  Kwakiutl, 350
  Osage Indians, 333–4
  poles, 41–2, **41**, 68, 419
  Walbiri, 329, 331, 333, 334
tourist art, 25, 402, 409, 413–16, 421–7, 437,
    447, 449, 524, 531, 546–7
  Akamba, 415, **416**
  Australian Aboriginal, 503
  collecting, 444–6, 448, 451
  ethnicity, 425, 427
  grotesqueness, 425
  Maliseet, **435**
  Maroon, 173
  production methods, 423, 426
  see also postcards

trading
    of art objects, 409–11
    of Australian Aboriginal acrylic paintings,
        503
    of Primitive art, 413
traps and trap-makers, 126, 226–32
    Anga eel-trap, 231–2
    arrow (Central Africa), 227, **227**, 230, 231
    from Guyana, 228, **228**, 231, **231**
    giraffe, 227, **227**
    hippopotamus, 228, **229**
    materials and models, 226–8
    and metaphor, 227–9, 231, 232
    painting of trapped shark on coffin lid
        (Yolngu), 229–30, **229**
    rat (Vanuatu), 227–8, **228**
    spring hook fishing trap (Guyana), 231, **231**
tribal art
    affinity with modern art, 135, 147–54
    animism aspects, 136
    anonymity, 176–7, 179
    complexity, 138
    and Cubism, 133
    discourse, 169–80
    innovations, 169, 179
    otherness, 139, 177, 224
    politics, 161, 163
    as problem solving, 135, 144
    satire, 160
    "tribal" as descriptor, 164
    use of natural materials, 163, 166, 217
    viewing, 161, 163
    Western perceptions, 133, 139–40, 158,
        164, 171–7
    see also African art and artifacts; Oceanic
        art; Primitive art; Primitivism
Trobriand islanders, 158
Tsimshian (Northwest Coast)
    art, 45, 45, 46–7, **46**, **48**, 524
    mythology, 526
tumbaga, 273–4
Tuscarora see Ska ru re
Tutuola, Amos (Yoruba novelist), 250, 253,
        259, 261
    quotation from *Palm-Wine Drunkard*, 253
Tuwhare, Hone (Maori poet), 478

United States of America
    and Chinese art, 206
    hegemony in culture, 204
    see also Euro-American bias in art
Universities China Committee, 199

Van Gogh, Vincent, reverence for "primitive"
        and "savage," 130
Vanuatu see New Hebrides (Vanuatu)
Victoria and Albert Museum
    displays of Chinese art, 186–201
    Primary Gallery of Far Eastern Art, 200,
        201, 202
    T. T. Tsui Gallery, 208
    "the nation's attic," 190
    see also China, art of
visual categories, 326–37
    continuous meaning ranges, 327–30, 332,
        335, 336
    core-adjunct construction, 333, 334, 337
    discontinuous meaning ranges, 327, 330,
        331, 332, 335, 336

Wahgi (Western Highlands, PNG)
    battle shields: disappear, 394, 395, 404;
        recontextualization, 388, 401–2;
        reinvented, 389–90, 395–400 (all-
        metal, 395; dangerous to user, 400;
        decorators, 396, 397, 398; materials
        used, 395; motifs, 395–8, **396**,
        398–400, 402)
    battle shields designs: with cassowary
        plumes, **390**, 391; changes in, 388;
        effect of modernity, 388; geometric,
        391, **392**; graphical significance, 393,
        404; material, 391, 395; materials used,
        389, 391; military technology, 388;
        motifs, 391; ochre and charcoal, 391;
        punctuate, 403; related to body parts,
        391; revealing of owner, 393;
        traditional, 388–94; underlying
        symbolism, 391, 393
    dance decorations, 393
    dream interpretation, 393, 397
    early contact, 389
    exchange ceremonies, 394
    geography, 389
    informants, 391, 393, 394, 395, 404
    Kaipei Ka (shield painter), 396, 397,
        398–400
    kinship, 389, 403
    men/warriors and birds, 391
    moral issues, 393, 397, 401, 403
    oratory and song, 393
    social organization, 389
    source clans, 389
    structural contradiction, 389
    tribal solidarity, 389, 403, 404

warfare (*opo*): causes of, 389; compared
    with fighting (*nganmal*), 390;
    controlled, 390; dress, 389, 403; with
    guns, 399–401; resurgence of fighting
    (1980s), 395; ritual before, 389, 393
weaponry: axes, 390, 395, **396**; bows and
    arrows, 390, 395, 397, 403; effects of
    modernity, 388, 394–7; grenades, 400;
    guns, 399–401, 403; restraint on using
    modern, 401; spears, 390, 403
witchcraft, 389
Walbiri (Northern Territory, Australia), 276
    communication, 339
    composite visual designs, 329, 331–3, 335
    core adjunct construction, 333
    cosmology, 334
    totem designs, 329, 331, 333, 334, 335, 337
    visual designs in sand drawings, 326, 327,
        332, 336
Waley, Arthur (linguist and cataloguer), 194,
        200, 205
WalkingStick, Kay (First Nations artist), 523–4
    Chief Joseph, 523–4
Ward, John Quincy Adams, *The Freedman*,
    215
Warnambi, Welwi (Australian Aboriginal
        artist)
    Dhuwa Moiety Wild-Honey Painting, **309**
Watson, William (China expert), 199, 202
Wen Fong (cataloguer), 199, 208
West Papua *sabalhe* boards, 402
Western art
    criticisms of realism, 131
    exists for its own sake, 212
    influence of African, 213
    medieval saints, 335
    mimics "Primitive," 213
    needs Primitive, 413
    pseudo artifacts, 213
    tyres as, 210, **210**
    visual categories, 328, 330, 335
    see also Euro-American bias; Primitivism
"whirl of animals" theme (Euroasia), 72
Whitfield, Roderick, 202
Whitman, Richard Ray (First Nations
        photographer), 531
    Street Chiefs, 531, **534**
Wiha (Haida Indian), 49
Windsor, Jackie
    Bound Square, 220, **221**, 222
witches *see* sorcery
women *see* gender divisions

wood carving, **65**, **66**, 67, 72
    Abelam, 110, 112, 114, 115, 117–18,
        119–20
    African, 211
    Akamba, 415, **416**
    Balinese, 89
    Bamileke, 159
    by Alaga, **253**, **255**
    by Owoeye, **254**
    Chokwe, **155**
    headdress of Egugun cult, **266**
    headdress of the Gelede cult, **256**, **266**
    Image (Onamosun), **257**
    Iroquois war clubs, **442**, **443**
    Maliseet canoe paddles, **440**
    Maori, **65**, **66**, 68, **473**, **477**, **481**, **482**
    Maroon, 168
    Tikopia, 93–5, **93**, 94–102, **96–100**, 106
    on tree trunks, 67
    twin (Bako), **257**
    verandah post (Alaga), **225**
    Wum wooden bowl, 217
    see also carving; masks
Woodlands Indians, 432, 438, 447–8
    installation, **438**
Wum (Cameroon), 217

Yekuana (South America)
    baskets, 323, 374–86: bichromatic plaited,
        378–83; ceremonial, 377–8 cover
        baskets (*wayatabudi*), 379, **379**;
        cycle of, 380–4; designs, 374, 378, 379,
        380; firefan (*wariwari*), 375–6, **376**;
        made by men, 375–7; made by women
        (*wuwa*), 375; *manade*, 376; and
        marriage, 380–4, 386; materials,
        379; materials used, 375–6, 377,
        380; men's carrying baskets (*cetu*,
        377, **378**; *dakisi*, 377; *duma*, 377;
        mahidi for game, 377, **377**; *tudi*,
        377, **377**); *mudoi* (fish creel), 377;
        painted, 380, **381**, **383**; poetics of
        weaving, 484–5; quality of weaving,
        484–5; round trays for food
        preparation (*waja tingkuihato*), 376,
        382; serving trays (*waja*), 379, 380,
        381, **383**; techniques of making,
        375–6, 377, 378, 379, 380, **381**,
        385–6; telescoping (*kungwa*), 379–80;
        trade items, 380; women's carrying
        baskets (*wuwa*), 375; yuca press
        (*intgkui*), 376

Yekuana (South America) (*cont'd*)
 Garden Festival, 377–8
 mesoma (stuff), 374: insipid or alien
  object, 374
 shamans, 380
 skills and status, 374–5, 380, 385
 tidi'uma (collective artifacts), 374:
  handmade, 374; magical power, 374;
  metaphysical dialogue, 374;
  significance of creation, 374–5;
  symbolic elements, 374, 375
Yetts, Walter Perceval, 199, 207, 208
Yirrkala (Northern Territory, Australia)
 Long-Necked Freshwater Tortoise
  (Yangarinny Gumana), **305**
 string figures, 336
 visual designs on bark paintings,
  326, 327, 328, 335–6
Yolngu (Northern Territory, Australia)
 aesthetics, 302–17
 ancestral power, 303, 308, 311, 317
 artists and kinship, 303
 artists' technical skill, 303
 burial ceremonies, 314–16
 circumcision ceremony, 307, **307**, 308, **308**,
  313–14
 paintings, 16–17, 229–30, **229**, 304–17:
  ancestral designs, 305, 310; *bir'yun*
  (brilliance), 308–9, 311, 313,
  316–17, 318, 319; blood, 310–11;
  body, 307–8, 313–14; clan designs,
  308, 310; coffin, 315; colors, 318;
  cross-hatching, 306–9, 316; mythology
  in, 304–6; process, 307, 311; as
  representation of beauty, 304–17; ritual
  significance, 307–8, 314; shark design,
  229–30, 311, 312, **312**, 315–17;
  tortoise design, **305**; wild-honey
  designs, **309**, **310**
 rituals, 318–19
 songs, 313
Yoruba (West Africa), 37, 75–6, 127

aesthetics, 239–40, 247–8: art criticism,
  139–40: criteria, 247–65, 324;
  influenced by commercial transactions,
  243, 247, 267; influenced by utility,
  248–9; opinions, 246–7;
  oral skills, 243, 267; sculpture, 243,
  245, 246, 247–8, 250; vocabulary,
  244–5
carving, 250–1, 253–7, **253**, 266
cicatrization, 252
"civilized," 245
color preference, 265
concepts of beauty, 240
craftsmanship, 244, 245
headdresses, 256, 266
language, 267
metallurgy, 267
Motinu and the Monkeys (fable), 249
sculpture, 243, 245, 246, 247–8:
  abstraction, 250; angularity, 262;
  carving, 250–1, 253–7, 266;
  composition, 258–9; delicacy, 259–60;
  "emotional proportion," 255–8;
  ephebism, 264–5; luminosity, 252–5;
  mimesis, 249–50; positioning, 258;
  protrusions, 261–2; roundness, 260–1,
  262; skill, 264; straightness, 262–3;
  symmetry, 263–4; visibility, 250–2
Yuendumu settlement (Central Australia) *see*
  Walbiri
Yuxweluptun, Lawrence Paul (First Nations
  artist), 530, 537
 sketch for *The Protector*, 531

Zande (Zaire) hunting net, 215–16, 220, **221**,
  222–4
Ze (chanter), 225–6
Zuni (New Mexico)
 modern Shalako ceremony, 164
 sacred representation of war god, 161,
  165–6
 time dimension of war god, 16